THE GUINNESS OLYMPICS FACT BOOK

THE GUINNESS OLYMPICS FACT BOOK

Stan Greenberg

GUINNESS PUBLISHING

Editor: Charles Richards
Text design and layout: Steve Leaning
Cover design: Ad Vantage Studios
Picture editor: Alex Goldberg

Published in Great Britain by Guinness Publishing Ltd,
33 London Road, Enfield, Middlesex

Typeset in Baskerville/Helvetica by
Ace Filmsetting Ltd, Frome, Somerset
Printed and bound in Great Britain by
The Bath Press, Bath, Avon

'Guinness' is a registered trademark of
Guinness Publishing Ltd

British Library Cataloguing in Publication Data
Greenberg, Stan *1931*
   The Guinness Olympics fact book
   1. Olympic games, history
   I. Title II. Greenberg, Stan *1931-. Guinness book of
   Olympics facts and feats*
   796.4809

ISBN 0-85112-956-0

CONTENTS

Acknowledgements 6

Official Abbreviations 7

Conversion Tables 8

The Ancient Games 9

The Modern Games 11

1896 12
1900 13
1904 14
1906 16
1908 17
1912 20
1920 23
1924 Winter 25
1924 Summer 26
1928 Winter 28
1928 Summer 30
1932 Winter 32
1932 Summer 34
1936 Winter 37
1936 Summer 38
1948 Winter 41
1948 Summer 42
1952 Winter 45
1952 Summer 46
1956 Winter 50
1956 Summer 50
1960 Winter 54
1960 Summer 55
1964 Winter 57
1964 Summer 59
1968 Winter 60
1968 Summer 62
1972 Winter 64
1972 Summer 67
1976 Winter 70
1976 Summer 72
1980 Winter 75
1980 Summer 77
1984 Winter 81
1984 Summer 83
1988 Winter 86
1988 Summer 90

1992 Winter 93
1992 Summer 94
1994 Winter 94
1996 Summer 94
1998 Winter 94
2000 Summer 94

Olympics Fact File 95
Celebrations of the Games – Summary 95
Official Openings 96
The Olympic Oath 96
The Olympic Flame 98
Presidents of the IOC 98
Mascots 98
Participating Countries 100
Olympic Medals Table (Nations) 1896–1988 103
Olympics Superlatives 104
Olympic Sports Doubles 106

The Summer Olympic Sports 107
Archery 107
Badminton 110
Baseball 110
Basketball 110
Boxing 112
Canoeing 120
Cycling 124
Equestrian 130
Fencing 135
Gymnastics 140
Handball 148
Hockey (Field) 149
Judo 151
Modern Pentathlon 153
Rowing 156
Shooting 161
Soccer 168
Swimming 171
Table Tennis 185
Tennis (Lawn) 186
Track & Field (Athletics) 187
Volleyball 207
Weightlifting 208
Wrestling 211
Yachting 220

Discontinued Sports 223

The Winter Olympic Sports 225
Alpine Skiing 225
Bobsledding 229
Figure Skating 230
Ice Hockey 233
Nordic Skiing 234
Speed Skating 241
Tobogganing (Lugeing) 245

Demonstration Sports 247

Index 248

ACKNOWLEDGEMENTS

I am much indebted to the original research of Olympic historians Erich Kamper (AUT) and Volker Kluge (formerly GDR). Other important work has been done by Bill Mallon (USA) and Ian Buchanan (GBR). My main sources, in alphabetical order:

The Associated Press and Grolier – *Pursuit of Excellence: The Olympic Story* (1979)

Sándor Barcs (HUN) – *The Modern Olympics Story* (1964)

Pat Besford (GBR) – *Encyclopaedia of Swimming* (1976)

John Durant (USA) – *Highlights of the Olympics* (1961)

Erich Kamper – *Enzyklopadie der Olympischen Spiele* (1972), *Lexikon der Olympischen Winter Spiele* (1964), and *Lexikon der 14,000 Olympioniken* (1983)

Lord Killanin (IRL) and John Rodda (GBR) – *The Olympic Games* (1976)

Volker Kluge – *Die Olympischen Spiele von 1896 bis 1980* (1981)

Bill Mallon and Ian Buchanan – *Quest for Gold* (1984)

Bill Mallon – *The Olympic Record Book* (1988)

Peter Matthews (GBR) – *Track and Field Athletics; The Records* (1986)

Norris and Ross McWhirter (GBR) – *The Guinness Book of Olympic Records* (1980)

David Wallechinsky (USA) – *The Complete Book of the Olympics* (1988)

Melvyn Watman (GBR) – *The Encyclopaedia of Track and Field Athletics* (1981)

Other experts and organisations whose publications and personal help have been invaluable include:

Richard Ayling, Howard Bass, Harry Carpenter, Jim Coote, Peter Diamond (USA), Maurice Golesworthy, John Goodbody, Mark Heller, Richard Hymans, Peter Johnson, Ferenc Mézo (HUN), Ron Pickering, Jack Rollin, Bob Sparks, Stuart Storey, Dave Terry, Lance Tingay, Martin Tyler, David Vine, Alan Weeks, Dorian Williams and Don Wood.

The Association of Track and Field Statisticians (ATFS) and its members, British Olympic Association, International Amateur Athletic Federation (IAAF), International Olympic Committee (IOC), International Weightlifting Federation, National Ski Federation of Great Britain, National Union of Track Statisticians (NUTS) and its members, *New York Times*, *Sports Illustrated*, *The Times*, *Track & Field News* and many national and international sports bodies.

I would particularly like to thank Keith Greenberg for his advice and help with my word processor, and Carole Greenberg for her good humour and understanding. Where contradictions have been found in different sources, I have invariably used Kamper or Kluge as the final arbiter.

Stan Greenberg
London 1991

ILLUSTRATIONS

Allsport: pp 10, 12, 17, 21, 25, 35, 39, 43, 52, 56, 63, 76, 78, 80, 82, 84, 87, 88, 91, 92, 99, 107, 111, 126, 131, 138, 146, 149, 165, 168, 170, 185, 188, 190, 191, 225, 226, 231, 233, 236, 239

AP: pp 66, 124, 151, 235, 241, 243

Author: p 40

W Baxter: p 215
Mary Evans: p 33
GSL: pp 29, 37, 97 (top)
Hulton Picture Company: pp 9, 11, 14, 18, 19, 22, 27, 31, 32, 41, 45, 47, 48, 49, 55, 57, 59, 61, 67, 69, 71, 73, 74, 79, 97 (bottom), 105, 113, 136, 150, 154, 174, 179, 207, 212

George Konig: p 65
ED Lacey: pp 114, 155
London & Wideworld: p 53
Popperfoto: pp 23, 51, 58, 85
Dave Terry: pp 157, 189
UPI: p 62
World Sports: p 140

All colour illustrations courtesy of *Allsport*.

Front cover Janet Evans (USA), Jesse Owens (USA), Alberto Tomba (ITA)

OFFICIAL ABBREVIATIONS

AFG	Afghanistan	GBR	Great Britain	NGU	Papua New Guinea
AHO	Netherlands Antilles	GDR	German Democratic Republic	NIG	Niger
ALB	Albania	GEQ	Equatorial Guinea	NOR	Norway
ALG	Algeria	GER	Germany	NZL	New Zealand
AND	Andorra	GHA	Ghana (formerly Gold Coast)	OMA	Oman
ANG	Angola	GRE	Greece	PAK	Pakistan
ANT	Antigua	GRN	Grenada	PAN	Panama
ARG	Argentina	GUA	Guatemala	PAR	Paraguay
ARU	Aruba	GUI	Guinea	PER	Peru
ASA	American Samoa	GUM	Guam	PHI	Philippines
AUS	Australia	GUY	Guyana (formerly British Guiana)	POL	Poland
AUT	Austria	HAI	Haiti	POR	Portugal
BAH	Bahamas	HKG	Hong Kong	PRK	Dem People's Republic of Korea
BAN	Bangladesh	HOL	Netherlands	PUR	Puerto Rico
BAR	Barbados	HON	Honduras	QAT	Qatar
BEL	Belgium	HUN	Hungary	ROM	Romania
BEN	Benin	INA	Indonesia	RWA	Rwanda
BER	Bermuda	IND	India	SAF	South Africa
BHU	Bhutan	IRL	Ireland	SAM	Western Samoa
BIR	Burma	IRN	Iran	SAR	Saar
BIZ	Belize (formerly British Honduras)	IRQ	Iraq	SEN	Senegal
BOH	Bohemia	ISL	Iceland	SEY	Seychelles
BOL	Bolivia	ISR	Israel	SIN	Singapore
BOT	Botswana	ISV	Virgin Islands	SLE	Sierra Leone
BRA	Brazil	ITA	Italy	SMR	San Marino
BRN	Bahrain	IVB	British Virgin Islands	SOL	Solomon Islands
BRU	Brunei	JAM	Jamaica	SOM	Somalia
BUL	Bulgaria	JOR	Jordan	SRI	Sri Lanka (formerly Ceylon)
BUR	Burkina Faso (formerly Upper Volta)	JPN	Japan	SUD	Sudan
CAF	Central African Republic	KEN	Kenya	SUI	Switzerland
CAN	Canada	KOR	Korea	SUR	Surinam
CAY	Cayman Islands	KSA	Saudi Arabia	SWE	Sweden
CGO	Congo	KUW	Kuwait	SWZ	Swaziland
CHA	Chad	LAO	Laos	SYR	Syria
CHI	Chile	LAT	Latvia	TAN	Tanzania
CHN	China	LBA	Libya	TCH	Czechoslovakia
CIV	Ivory Coast	LBR	Liberia	THA	Thailand
CMR	Cameroon	LES	Lesotho	TOG	Togo
COK	Cook Islands	LIB	Lebanon	TON	Tonga
COL	Colombia	LIE	Liechtenstein	TPE	Taipei (formerly Formosa/Taiwan)
CRC	Costa Rica	LIT	Lithuania	TRI	Trinidad & Tobago
CUB	Cuba	LUX	Luxembourg	TUN	Tunisia
CYP	Cyprus	MAD	Madagascar	TUR	Turkey
DEN	Denmark	MAL	Malaysia	UAE	United Arab Emirates
DJI	Djibouti	MAR	Morocco	UGA	Uganda
DOM	Dominican Republic	MAW	Malawi	URS	Soviet Union
ECU	Ecuador	MDV	Maldives	URU	Uruguay
EGY	Egypt	MEX	Mexico	USA	United States
ESA	El Salvador	MGL	Mongolia	VAN	Vanuatu
ESP	Spain	MLI	Mali	VEN	Venezuela
EST	Estonia	MLT	Malta	VIE	Vietnam
ETH	Ethiopia	MON	Monaco	VIN	St Vincent
FIJ	Fiji	MOZ	Mozambique	YAR	Yemen Arab Republic
FIN	Finland	MRI	Mauritius	YMD	Yemen Democratic Republic
FRA	France	MTN	Mauretania	YUG	Yugoslavia
FRG	Federal Republic of Germany	NCA	Nicaragua	ZAI	Zaire
GAB	Gabon	NEP	Nepal	ZAM	Zambia (formerly Northern Rhodesia)
GAM	Gambia	NGR	Nigeria	ZIM	Zimbabwe (formerly Rhodesia)

CONVERSION TABLES

TRACK AND FIELD

1.55 metres	5ft 1in	5.75	18ft 10½in	22.00	72ft 2¼in		
1.60	5ft 3in	5.80	19ft 0¼in	22.50	73ft 10in		
1.65	5ft 5in	6.00	19ft 8¼in	23.00	75ft 5½in		
1.70	5ft 7in	6.25	20ft 6¼in	40.00	131ft 3in		
1.75	5ft 8¾in	6.50	21ft 4in	42.00	137ft 9in		
1.80	5ft 10¾in	6.75	22ft 1¾in	44.00	144ft 4in		
1.85	6ft 0¾in	7.00	22ft 11¾in	46.00	150ft 11in		
1.90	6ft 2¾in	7.25	23ft 9½in	48.00	157ft 6in		
1.95	6ft 4¾in	7.50	24ft 7¼in	50.00	164ft 0in		
2.00	6ft 6¾in	7.75	25ft 5¼in	52.00	170ft 7in		
2.05	6ft 8¾in	8.00	26ft 3in	54.00	177ft 2in		
2.10	6ft 10¾in	8.25	27ft 0¾in	56.00	183ft 9in		
2.15	7ft 0½in	8.50	27ft 10¾in	58.00	190ft 3in		
2.20	7ft 2½in	8.75	28ft 8½in	60.00	196ft 10in		
2.25	7ft 4½in	9.00	29ft 6½in	62.00	203ft 5in		
2.30	7ft 6½in	12.50	41ft 0¼in	64.00	210ft 0in		
2.35	7ft 8½in	13.00	42ft 8in	66.00	216ft 6in		
2.40	7ft 10½in	13.50	44ft 3½in	68.00	223ft 1in		
2.45	8ft 0½in	14.00	45ft 11¼in	70.00	229ft 8in		
3.00	9ft 10in	14.50	47ft 7in	72.00	236ft 3in		
3.20	10ft 6in	15.00	49ft 2½in	74.00	242ft 9in		
3.40	11ft 1¾in	15.50	50ft 10¼in	76.00	249ft 4in		
3.60	11ft 9¾in	16.00	52ft 6in	78.00	255ft 11in		
3.80	12ft 5½in	16.50	54ft 1¾in	80.00	262ft 5in		
4.00	13ft 1½in	17.00	55ft 9¼in	82.00	269ft 0in		
4.20	13ft 9¼in	17.50	57ft 5in	84.00	275ft 7in		
4.40	14ft 5¼in	18.00	59ft 0¾in	86.00	282ft 2in		
4.60	15ft 1in	18.50	60ft 8½in	88.00	288ft 8in		
4.80	15ft 9in	19.00	62ft 4in	90.00	295ft 3in		
5.00	16ft 4¾in	19.50	63ft 11¾in	92.00	301ft 10in		
5.20	17ft 0¾in	20.00	65ft 7½in	94.00	308ft 5in		
5.40	17ft 8½in	20.50	67ft 3¼in	96.00	314ft 11in		
5.50	18ft 0½in	21.00	68ft 10¾in	98.00	321ft 6in		
5.60	18ft 4½in	21.50	70ft 6½in	100.00	328ft 1in		

WEIGHTLIFTING

kg	lb
100kg	220¼lb
125	275½
150	330½
175	385¾
200	440¾
225	496
250	551
275	606¼
300	661¼
325	716½
350	771½
375	826½
400	881¾
425	936¾
450	992
475	1047
500	1102¼
525	1157¼
550	1212¼
575	1267½
600	1322¾

THE ANCIENT GAMES

The Olympic Games evolved from legendary conflicts among the Greek gods and the religious ceremonies held in their honour. Historical evidence dates the Games from about 900 BC, but there is good reason to believe that a similar festival existed four centuries previously. Indeed the modern word 'athlete' derives from Aethlius, King of Elis.

The area in which Olympia lies is in the plain of Elis, on the banks of the River Alpheus, and it was Iphitus, a successor of King Aethlius, who was instrumental in reviving the then faltering Olympic concept in the late 9th century BC. He also arranged a truce between the continually warring states of the region, which recognised the neutrality and sanctity of Olympia and lasted for the duration of the Games. The first firm record dates from 776 BC and the Games were numbered at four-yearly intervals from then.

At that time there was only one event, the *stade* race, and the winner, the first recorded Olympic champion, was Coroibis of Elis. The stade was 192.27m long, reputedly 60 times the length of Heracles' foot. After thirteen Olympiads, in 724 BC, a race of two stade, the *diaulus*, was also contested, and in the following celebration the 24-stadia *dolichus*, about 4.5km in length, was instituted. In 708 BC came the *pentathlon*, consisting of running, jumping (with the aid of hand-held weights), throwing the discus and javelin, and wrestling. Chariot racing, running in armour and boxing were also eventually included and were joined in 648 BC by the *pankration*, a brutal mix of boxing and wrestling. Numerous variants of these sports appeared over the years, as did activities of a less sporting nature such as contests for trumpeters.

Initially competitors wore simple shorts-like garments, but from about 720 BC they

Above and overleaf *Rather romanticised images of athletics in Ancient Greece. Note the runners wear helmets and carry shields, but are unclothed.*

competed naked. Until 692 BC the Games only lasted for a single day, but this was then increased to two days and in 632 BC to a total of five days, of which the middle three were for actual competitions.

For the next six centuries the fame of Olympia spread throughout the known world, and many famous people visited the Games. Victors in those early days only won a crown of wild olive leaves, but they were often richly rewarded by the home states and some became very wealthy. Crowd figures were not published, but archaeologists have estimated that the stadium at Olympia could hold over 20 000 spectators.

For reasons not fully understood today, women and slaves were strictly forbidden, under pain of death, even to attend the Games. An exception does appear to have been made for high-ranking priestesses of the most important gods, and in fact it was possible for a woman to gain an Olympic prize, since in the chariot race the chaplet of olive leaves was awarded to the owner of the horses and not the driver. One of the first women

to win an Olympic title in this way was Belistike of Macedonia in 268 BC, as owner of the champion two-horse chariot.

It is recorded that some women did disguise themselves and defy the ban on spectating, but they were thrown over a cliff to their deaths on discovery. There is a story, perhaps apocryphal, that Pherenice of Rhodes acted as a second to watch her son Pisidores win his event and in her excitement she gave herself away. But when it was realised that not only her son but also her father and brothers had all been Olympic champions, she was pardoned.

Possibly the most famous champion of early times was Leonidas of Rhodes, who won the three 'track' events on four consecutive occasions from 164–152 BC, making a total of 12 victories which has not been surpassed since. The first recorded triple gold medallist at one Games was Phanas of Pellene in 512 BC, while the Spartan runner Chionis won the stade in three successive Games from 664–656 BC. Other outstanding champions included Theagenes of Thassos, who won

eight titles at boxing, wrestling and pankration from 468–456 BC, and Milon of Croton who won six wrestling titles from 536–516 BC.

The very success of the Games ultimately led to its downfall. The importance of winning at Olympia, and the reflected glory it bestowed on the winner's birthplace, led cities to hire professionals and bribe judges. With the dawn of the Christian Era, the religious and physical backgrounds of the Games were attacked. An irreversible decline set in under Roman influence, so much so that in AD 67 a drunken Emperor Nero was crowned victor of the chariot race despite the fact that there were no other entrants (who could blame them?) and Nero did not even finish the course. In AD 393, the Roman Emperor Theodosius I issued a decree in Milan which prohibited the Games, and within a few generations the ravages of foreign invaders, earthquakes and flooding had virtually obliterated the site of Olympia, and the world forgot the glory that once had been.

THE MODERN GAMES

There had been a resurgence of interest in Ancient Greece in the 17th and 18th centuries and references to the Olympic Games in the poems of Pindar and other Greek poets were noted. In Britain, the Cotswold Olympic Games were inaugurated in 1636 and in 1850 the Much Wenlock Olympic Society was founded by Dr William Penny Brookes. At the end of the 18th century, in Germany, the famed founder of modern gymnastics, Johann Guts Muths, had suggested the revival of the Olympic ideal. Some 50 years later, in 1852, his fellow-countryman

Ernst Curtius, who had done archaeological work at Olympia (started by the French in 1829), reiterated the idea in a lecture he gave in Berlin. In Greece itself, in 1859, Major Evangelis Zappas organised a Pan-Hellenic sports festival which attracted a great deal of public support and was revived at intervals over the next 30 years.

But the true founder of the modern Olympic Games is commonly acknowledged to be the Frenchman Pierre de Fredi, Baron de Coubertin. In 1889, a French government commission to study physical culture

methods led him to meet with Dr Brookes of Much Wenlock and at the end of his travels he formed his concept of a revived Games, which he first propounded publicly in a lecture at the Sorbonne, Paris, on 25 November 1892. The enthusiastic reception accorded to him there gave him an impetus, as did his meeting with representatives of the top American universities in the following year.

In June 1984 he convened an international conference, also at the Sorbonne, at which 12 countries were represented and

The IOC in 1896. Seated, left to right: Baron de Coubertin (FRA), Demetrius Vikelas (GRE) and A de Boutovsky (URS). Standing: Dr W Gebhardt (GER), Jiri Guth-Jarkovsky (TCH), Francois Kemeny (HUN) and General Victor Balck (SWE).

another 21 sent messages of support. The outcome was a resolution on 23 June calling for sports competitions along the lines of the Ancient Games to be held every fourth year. The International Olympic Committee (IOC) was inaugurated under the presidency of Demetrius Vikelas of Greece, with de Coubertin as secretary-general. The Frenchman had hoped to herald the new century by staging the first Games in Paris in 1900, but the delegates were impatient. Budapest in Hungary was strongly mooted at first, but at the instigation of Vikelas, Athens was finally selected and the date set as 1896.

1896

1st OLYMPIC GAMES
Athens, Greece
6–15 April
(25 March–3 April by the Julian Calendar)

Attended by representatives of 13 countries, comprising 311 competitors.

Although the Greek government were apparently not consulted, and were anyway beset with internal financial and political problems, the Greek public were very enthusiastic. However, it was not until Crown Prince Constantine set up a committee and began organising and collecting funds that the project became feasible and the prospect of Budapest getting the honour by default faded. The turning point came with the generosity of a Greek businessman, Georges Averoff (formerly Avykeris), who actually lived in Alexandria, Egypt. He offered to pay for the reconstruction of the Panathenean Stadium in Athens at a cost of 920 000 drachma (about £36 500 at the

There was tremendous excitement amongst the home crowd when Spyridon Louis, here in Greek national costume, won the 1896 marathon.

1896 exchange rate). The stadium had first been built in 330 BC by the orator Lycurgus, a disciple of Plato. It was rebuilt 500 years later by Herodes Atticus but had gradually disintegrated and was covered up until 1870 when King George of Greece arranged for its excavation by the German, Ziller. The new track measured 333.33m and had very sharp turns; the competitors ran in a clockwise direction.

The opening of the Games

coincided with the 75th anniversary of the declaration of Greek independence from Turkish rule. Over 40 000 spectators in the stadium, plus thousands more on the surrounding hills, saw King George I formally open the proceedings. The great bulk (230) of the competitors were from Greece itself. Many athletes entered privately, including holiday-makers, and the British contingent included two employees of the Embassy in Athens. Another member of the British team was an Irishman, John Boland, who happened to be on holiday in Greece at the time and entered the tennis events. He won the singles and, partnering a German, also won the pairs. Another nice contemporary touch was provided by the French sprinter who insisted on wearing his gloves as he was running before royalty.

Not for the last time a gymnast, Hermann Weingärtner (GER), was the most successful competitor, with three first places, two seconds and a third. Frenchman Paul Masson won three cycling events but perhaps the most outstanding achievement was that of Carl Schuhmann of Germany who not only won three gymnastic events but also won the wrestling title. Another competitor to gain medals in two sports was gymnast Fritz Hofmann (GER) whose total of five placings included a silver medal in the 100 metres. In shooting, John and Sumner Paine (USA) became the first brothers to win Olympic gold medals, in military pistol and free pistol respectively. Their father had successfully defended yachting's America's Cup some years before.

The first competition of the modern Olympic Games was heat one of the 100m, and it was won in 12.5sec by the American Francis Lane of Princeton University, who thus carved a niche in history for himself. The first gold medallist of modern times was James Brendan Connolly (USA) in the hop, step and jump (now known as the triple jump). In fact the American team, composed exclusively of college students, dominated events in the stadium, despite arriving only the day before the start of the competitions after travelling by ship to France and then by train to Greece. Victors actually

received a silver medal and a crown of olive leaves; runners-up were given bronze medals and a crown of laurel; no award was made for third place.

Two new sporting events were introduced at these Games: the discus throw and the marathon. Both were based on Greek antiquity and the hosts were eager to win them but the former was taken by Robert Garrett (USA). He had inadvertently practised with an implement much larger and heavier than the one which was actually used at Athens. The marathon had been proposed by a Frenchman, Michel Bréal, to commemorate the legendary run of a Greek courier, possibly Pheidippides, with the news of a Greek victory over the Persians in 490 BC. He is supposed to have run from the site of the battle and, after crying out 'Rejoice! We conquer', collapsed and died. To the great delight of the hosts the race was won by a Greek shepherd, Spyridon 'Spyros' Louis, who was escorted into the stadium by Crown Prince Constantine and Prince George.

The oldest gold medallist, at 36yr 102 days, was Georgios Orphanidis (GRE) in the free rifle contest, while the youngest was swimmer Alfred Hajós (HUN), who won the 100m and 1200m freestyle events aged 18yr 70 days. One member of the Greek bronze medal team in gymnastics was, according to some reports, under 11 years of age but doubts exist about the veracity of this.

In view of the modern saturation coverage of the Olympics by the media, it is interesting to note that the British press gave little space to reports from Athens, despite an earlier complaint in *The Times* about the lack of knowledge of the event in the country and Britain's inadequate representation. Nevertheless the Games had

been a tremendous success and certainly Greece looked forward to the next celebration, which they also expected to host.

1896 MEDALS

Country	G	S	B
United States	11	7	1
Greece	10	19	18
Germany	7	5	2
France	5	4	2
Great Britain	3	3	1
Hungary	2	1	3
Austria	2	–	3
Australia	2	–	–
Denmark	1	2	4
Switzerland	1	2	–

1900

IInd OLYMPIC GAMES
Paris, France
20 May–28 October

Attended by representatives of 22 countries, comprising 1330 competitors, of which 12 were women.

Despite strong Greek pressure for the exclusive rights to organise future Games, Baron de Coubertin won agreement to hold the 1900 Games in Paris; but he made a serious mistake in making it part of the Universal Exposition also being held there. In the event, the Games became merely a sideshow to the fair. Numerous internal rivalries within French sport left many events without experienced officials or adequate venues, with the track and field events being held on uneven turf at Croix-Catelan in the Bois de Boulogne, where it was reported that the jumpers had to dig their own pits. Many of the competitors, especially the Americans, had never run on a grass track before.

Generally there were few spectators, and even these were nearly reduced in number when the 1896 discus champion despatched the implement into the

The United States Olympic team of 1900. Included are Tewksbury (back row, far left), Kraenzlein (fifth left), Baxter (second right), Ewry (second row, fourth left) and Garrett (fourth right).

crowd on all three throws. Cricket, croquet and golf made their appearance and amid the general confusion many competitors, even medal winners, were not aware until much later that they had been competing at the Olympic Games.

France, the host country, had a record-sized team numbering 884, the largest ever entered for the Games. The Americans were still represented by colleges and clubs, and the decision to have competition on Sunday upset many of those whose colleges were Church-controlled. Thus the long jump world record holder Myer Prinstein, a Jew but under the aegis of the University of Syracuse, a strong Methodist institution, gained a silver medal with his Saturday qualifying round jump (such performances then counted for medals) but had to withdraw from the

Sunday final. The eventual winner, Alvin Kraenzlein (USA) set a record of four individual gold medals, a feat never surpassed in track and field at one Games.

Also much in evidence, at the start of his fabulous Olympic career, was America's Ray Ewry, the standing jump expert, with three gold medals here. Behind him in the standing jumps was his fellow countryman Irving Baxter, who had already won the regular high jump and the pole vault and reputedly became the first athlete of North American Indian ancestry to win at the Olympic Games. In a similar vein, Norman Pritchard of India, later to become a successful actor in Hollywood silent films, won the first medals by an Asian sportsman with two silvers in the 200m flat and hurdles races.

Women were allowed to com-

pete for the first time, but only in golf and tennis and the first female Olympic champion in history was Britain's Charlotte Cooper, a Wimbledon champion, who won the tennis singles title on 9 July. Another unique record was set in the coxed pairs rowing final, in which a small French boy was drafted in at the last moment to cox the winning Dutch crew. His name was never recorded and he disappeared without trace afterwards, but he was no more than 10 years old and possibly as young as 7, in either case the youngest ever Olympic gold medallist. The oldest gold medallist in 1900 at 53yr 55 days was the French-born Comte Hermann de Pourtales (SUI) in the 1–2 ton class yachting.

Press coverage was barely apparent with many of the events not mentioned at all, and for years afterwards there was much confusion as to the names and nationalities of even the medallists. Thus it was that the first Olympic medals won by Canada, a gold and bronze gained by George Orton, were not 'discovered' for some years, as Orton had been entered by his American university and was billed as an American. Even more recently it has been found that the winner of the marathon, Michel Théato (FRA), was actually a Luxembourgeois – in this case the medal tables have not been altered.

1900 MEDALS

Country	G	S	B
France	27	39	33
United States	19	15	15
Great Britain	17	7	12
Switzerland	6	3	1
Belgium	5	5	4
Germany	3	2	2
Australia	2	–	4
Denmark	2	3	2
Italy	2	2	–
Netherlands	1	1	4
Hungary	1	2	2
Cuba	1	1	–
Canada	1	–	1
Sweden	1	–	1
Austria	–	3	3
Norway	–	2	3
Czechoslovakia	–	1	2
India	–	2	–

1904

IIIrd OLYMPIC GAMES
St Louis, USA
1 July–23 November

Attended by representatives of 13 countries, comprising 625 competitors, of which 8 were women.

These Games had seemed likely to go to Britain, and then to Philadelphia, though de Coubertin favoured New York. The IOC finally designated Chicago, but at the request of President Theodore Roosevelt, also president of the US Olympic Committee, the venue was changed to St Louis to coincide with the World's Fair being held there to celebrate the centenary of the Louisiana Purchase. Thus again the Games became merely a sideshow.

With the venue being in the centre of the North American continent, the problems of distance and travel meant that there were few overseas entrants. Indeed, even de Coubertin did not attend. Thus 85 per cent of the competitors were from the host country and not surprisingly they won 84 per cent of the medals. In fact the Games were a virtual college and club tournament with the New York AC beating the Chicago Athletic Association for the track and field team title (a points table was actually published). In swimming it was also noted that New York beat Germany and Hungary overall.

In such circumstances, the Games degenerated into something of a farce – the cycling events, which had no foreign entrants at all and included a number of professional riders, were initially refused official Olympic status. However, recent scholarship suggests that they should be included in medal tables and results. Thus the unique achievement of Marcus Hurley in winning four cycling events should now be given due credit. Gymnast Anton Heida (USA) won 5 golds and 1 silver to be the most successful competitor at these Games.

Under the rather loose controls imposed on most sports, some strange things happened. In the 400m track race no heats were held and all 13 entrants ran in the final. Rowing events were held over a 1½-mile course which entailed making a turn. The swimming events were held over Imperial distances, while the athletics track (in the grounds of Washington University, St Louis) measured one-third of a mile in circumference and had a 220-yard straight, which was quite an innovation for the visiting Europeans.

In the track and field programme only two events went to non-Americans. The 56lb (25.4kg) weight throw went to the French-Canadian policeman Étienne Desmarteau, who unfortunately died the following year of typhoid; a park was named after him in his home city of Montreal. The 10-event all-round competition, a forerunner of the decathlon, was won by one of only two British entries, Thomas Kiely, who like the silver medallist in the 2500m steeplechase, John Daly, was an Irishman. The unfortunate Myer Prinstein redressed his grievance of four years previously by taking the long jump title as well as winning the hop, step and jump. He was also fifth in both the 60m and 400m finals. The ever liberal Prinstein was representing the Greater New York Irish AA.

The 200m final, uniquely held on a straight, was won by Archie Hahn, with all three of his opponents being given a yard handicap under the rules then governing false starts. Joseph Stadler won a silver medal in the standing high jump and George Poage bronzes in the 200m and 400m hurdles races, as they became the first black men to win medals in the Olympics. Despite the lack of foreign opposition, the standard in many sports was very high and the triple victories of Archie Hahn, Harry Hillman, James Lightbody, Ray Ewry and swimmer Charles Daniels were outstanding. Daniels, in winning the 220yd, 440yd and mile freestyle events was the prototype of the American swimmers who were to dominate Olympic freestyle swimming for many years.

There was a scandal in the marathon when the first man out of the stadium, Fred Lorz (USA), was also the first man back, looking remarkably fresh. It later transpired that he had received a lift in a car after suffering cramp, and when the car itself broke down near the stadium he resumed running – as a joke, he claimed. He was banned for life (but was competing again after only a year) and the title awarded to the British-born American Thomas Hicks, who had finished in a daze due to being administered strychnine by his handlers as a stimulant – a practice then common and allowable. In ninth place was Lentauw (SAF), a Zulu who was in St Louis as part of a World's Fair exhibit and the first black African distance runner to compete in the Olympics.

The youngest gold medallist, at 19yr 167 days, was shot-putter Ralph Rose (USA), while the oldest was the Reverend Galen Spencer (USA), an archer aged 64yr 2 days. Another American archer, Samuel Duvall, won a silver medal aged 68yr 194 days – the oldest American medallist ever. The oldest female champion was archer Lida Howell (USA) aged 45yr 25 days, while yet another American, Frank Kungler, won a silver in wrestling, a bronze in tug-of-war and two bronzes in weight-lifting to become the only Olympian to win medals at three different sports at a single Games.

1904 MEDALS

Country	G	S	B
United States	81	85	78
Germany	4	4	5
Canada	4	1	–
Cuba	4	–	–
Austria	2	1	1
Hungary	2	1	1
Great Britain	1	1	–
Greece	1	–	1
Switzerland	1	–	1
France	–	1	–

A final insult to the Games were the Anthropology Days during which competitions were held, parodying the regular Olympic events, for aboriginal peoples such as American Indians, African pygmies, Patagonians, Ainus from Japan and the like. Finally in November, with the Association Football competition won by a Canadian college ahead of two American teams, the IIIrd Olympic Games came to an end. Many in Europe wondered if the fledgling movement would recover.

1906

THE INTERIM or INTERCALATED GAMES
Athens, Greece
22 April–2 May

Attended by representatives of 20 countries, comprising 884 competitors, of which 7 were women.

After two debacles something was needed to revive the flagging Olympic movement and de Coubertin, with some misgivings, agreed a series of four-yearly meetings, interspersed with the main Games, to be held in Athens. Although these had the blessing of the IOC, it was decided that the Interim Games would not be numbered in sequence. In the event only this meeting of the projected series was ever held. Again the Greeks showed their enthusiasm and large crowds, missing for the past 10 years, were in evidence. The marble stadium in Athens was full to capacity, and enthusiasm often helped to overcome organisational mishaps.

The 20 countries included the first 'official' American team, selected and sent by the US Olympic Committee, so ending the practice of colleges, clubs

Right Bill Sherring (CAN) is escorted over the last few strides of the 1906 marathon by Prince George of Greece.

and private individuals entering. Also present was the first ever team from Finland, with the doyen of the famous Järvinen family, Werner, gaining his country's first ever Olympic gold medal. The programme of track and field events was altered by a reduction in the number of sprint and hurdles races and the addition of the javelin throw and pentathlon.

There were some excellent performances, especially by some of the 1904 champions such as the perennial Ray Ewry and the New York policeman Martin Sheridan. Another American, with the apt name of Paul Pilgrim, had only been added to the team at the last moment after he had privately raised the money for the fare. He had won a gold medal in 1904 as a member of the New York AC relay team, but in Athens surprisingly won the 400m and 800m titles, a double not to be equalled until 1976.

The new pentathlon event, consisting of a 192m run, standing long jump, discus and javelin throws and Greco-Roman wrestling, was won by Hjalmar Mellander of Sweden. In third place was his countryman Erik Lemming who also gained bronze medals in the shot and tug-of-war as well as winning the first of three Olympic javelin titles. There was a real surprise in the 1500m walk, which was also the scene of a number of purely chauvinistic decisions by the various national judges. The American distance runner George Bonhag had disappointed in the 1500m and 5-mile runs, and had entered the walk, an entirely new event to him, in a last effort to win a medal. Owing mainly to the

excessive number of disqualifications, which saw all the favourites ruled out, Bonhag won the gold. With all three previous Olympic marathons having been won by the host country, the Greeks were hopeful of continuing the tradition, but despite half the entrants coming from Greece the event was won by William Sherring of Canada by a massive margin of nearly 7 minutes.

The oldest gold medallist was Maurice Lecoq (FRA), aged 52yr 31 days when he won the rapid fire pistol event. The youngest was the coxswain of the Italian fours crew, Giorgio Cesana, aged 14yr 12 days.

Despite the soft cinder track in the stadium, poor facilities for the swimmers in the sea at Phaleron and complaints about food and judging decisions, these Interim Games put the whole Olympic concept back on a path towards de Coubertin's ideal.

1906 MEDALS

Country	G	S	B
France	15	9	16
United States	12	6	5
Greece	8	13	13
Great Britain	8	11	6
Italy	7	6	3
Switzerland	5	4	2
Germany	4	6	4
Norway	4	1	–
Austria	3	3	2
Sweden	2	5	7
Hungary	2	5	3
Belgium	2	2	3
Denmark	2	2	1
Finland	2	–	1
Canada	1	1	–
Netherlands	–	1	2
Australia	–	–	3
Czechoslovakia	–	–	2
South Africa	–	–	1

1908

IVth OLYMPIC GAMES
London, Great Britain
27 April–31 October

Attended by representatives of 22 countries, comprising 2056 competitors, of which 36 were women.

Originally awarded to Rome, the IVth Games were reallocated to London when the Italian authorities informed the IOC during the Interim Games that they would have to withdraw because of financial problems; London formally accepted on 19 November 1906. They were the most successful held so far and set the pattern for future Games. Drawing on the expertise of many

British sporting governing bodies – such as the Amateur Swimming Association, founded in 1869, and the Amateur Athletic Association, founded in 1880 – the organising committee under Lord Desborough went to work.

A 68 000 capacity stadium was built in West London, for a reported cost of £40 000. (The stated 'capacity' was apparently well exceeded on a number of occasions.) It contained an athletics track of three laps to the mile, inside a 660yd banked concrete cycle track. On the grass infield stood a giant (330ft × 50ft/*100m × 15.24m*) pool for the swimming events. Rowing was on the Thames at Henley, tennis was held at the All-England Club, Wimbledon, yachting at Ryde, Isle of Wight, and

the new sport of motorboating was on Southampton Water. The main competitions took place in July, although the overall programme lasted from April to October. There were 21 sports in all, including four ice skating events. There was also a demonstration sport, bicycle polo, in which Ireland beat Germany 3–1.

Entries were only by nations, as opposed to individuals, and this tended to underscore the element of nationalism which undoubtedly caused some of the disputes that marred this first truly international sporting occasion. The problems started during the formal opening of the Games by King Edward VII at the White City Stadium on 13 July, with Sweden and the United States upset that their

flags had been inadvertently missed from those flying round the stadium. Then Ralph Rose, the American flag bearer, and eventual winner of the shot, refused to dip the Stars and Stripes to King Edward in the march past. The Finnish team would not march behind the flag of Czarist Russia and came in without any banner. Later things got worse as complaints came from all sides, but especially from US officials. They complained about 'fixed' heats, illegal coaching, rule breaking and British chauvinism. The weather was also rather foul, even by British standards, and badly affected the cycling and tennis in particular.

All the rancour came to a head in the final of the 400m, in which three of the four finalists

Mel Sheppard (USA) wins the 1908 1500m from Harold Wilson (GBR) at the White City. Sheppard also won gold in the 800m and medley relay.

Dorando Pietri (ITA) is helped over the line by officials at the end of the 1908 marathon.

were Americans. They were accused of impeding the sole British runner, Lieutenant Wyndham Halswelle, and a re-run was ordered for the next day with the winner of the disputed race, Carpenter, being disqualified. The other Americans refused to appear and Halswelle gained the gold medal with the only walkover in Games history. One of the runners involved was John Taylor who, as a member of the winning medley relay team, became the first black man to win an Olympic gold medal.

A more imaginative resolution to a problem came in the 110m hurdles. The favourite, Forrest Smithson, an American student of theology, protested against the official decision to run the final on a Sunday and then proceeded to break the world record, running 15.0sec, carrying a bible in his left hand.

The bitterness reached such a level that it was thought necessary to produce a booklet entitled *Replies to Criticism of the Olympic Games*; which, owing to its rather pompous tone, did little to alleviate the situation. One result of all this was that future control of competitions should be in the hands of the various international governing bodies of the sports and not left solely to the host country.

The previous year, the IOC had decided that medals should be awarded for the first three places in all events. There were many excellent performances throughout the Games, despite all the problems, not least by the ubiquitous Ray Ewry, now 33 years old. He won his record-breaking ninth and tenth gold medals in the standing jumps, while John Flanagan (one of the so-called Irish-American 'Whales') won his third hammer

title. Middle-distance runner Mel Sheppard (USA) was a triple gold medallist, as was British swimmer Henry Taylor. Charles Daniels (USA) won the 100m freestyle to add to his three titles from the last two Games and set a record of four individual event swimming gold medals that has not yet been beaten. The Hungarian swimmer Zoltán Halmay increased his total medal haul to nine since 1900, a total unsurpassed in the sport until 1972.

The introduction of skating events gave Russia the opportunity to win its first Olympic title, courtesy of Nikolai Panin (actually Kolomenkin) who four years later was a member of the fourth-placed revolver shooting team. Another Olympic first came in the London shooting programme when Oscar and Alfred Swahn of Sweden became the first father and son

1908 MEDALS

Country	G	S	B
Great Britain	56	50	39
United States	23	12	12
Sweden	8	6	11
France	5	5	9
Germany	3	5	5
Hungary	3	4	2
Canada	3	3	10
Norway	2	3	3
Italy	2	2	–
Belgium	1	5	2
Australia*	1	2	1
Russia	1	2	–
Finland	1	1	3
South Africa	1	1	–
Greece	–	3	1
Denmark	–	2	3
Czechoslovakia	–	–	2
Netherlands	–	–	2
Austria	–	–	1
New Zealand*	–	–	1

*Australia and New Zealand combined as Australasia

to win gold medals.

Undoubtedly the most famous event in the IVth Games was the marathon. Originally the distance was to be about 25 miles, but when the start was moved to Windsor Castle it became an exact 26 miles. Then at the request of Princess Mary it was moved again to start beneath the windows of the royal nursery in the Castle grounds, making a final distance of 26 miles 385yd (42.195m). This arbitrarily arrived-at distance was later (1924) accepted worldwide as the standard marathon length.

The race itself was run in intensely hot and humid conditions, quite the opposite of most of the preceding weather, and was watched by an estimated 250 000 people. The little Italian Dorando Pietri reached the stadium first in a state of near collapse, and fell five times on the last part-lap of the track. Over-zealous officials, reputedly including the famous author Sir Arthur Conan Doyle, helped him over the finish line, thus leading to his disqualification. On behalf of the second finisher, Johnny Hayes, the

Americans lodged a protest which was upheld and the Italian was disqualified. The wave of public sympathy found expression in the gift of Queen Alexandra to Pietri of a special gold cup.

Great Britain won the greatest number of medals overall, but the United States, as always, was well in front in the centrepiece of the Games, the track and field events. Two sportsmen, fencer Ivan Osiier (DEN) and yachtsman Magnus Konow (NOR), though unplaced in their events, began Olympic careers which continued until the next Games in London in 1948, setting a record-breaking span for Olympic competition of 40 years. The oldest gold medallist at these Games was Oscar Swahn (SWE), aged 60yr 265 days, in the Running Deer shooting event. Britain's Colonel Joshua Millner, winner of the 1000yd Free Rifle, was also well over 60 years of age. The youngest winner was William Foster (GBR), six days past his 18th birthday, in the 4 × 200m swimming relay. The oldest female gold medallist was tennis player Dorothea Chambers (GBR), aged 29yr 316 days.

1912

Vth OLYMPIC GAMES
Stockholm, Sweden
5 May–22 July

Attended by representatives of 28 countries, comprising 2546 competitors, of which 55 were women.

Stockholm finally attained the honour that Sweden had wanted from the very beginning, and Torben Grut designed and built a 31 000 capacity stadium, with a 383m track laid out under the direction of Charles Perry, the Englishman responsible for the

1896 and 1908 tracks. Baron de Coubertin had insisted that the number of sports be cut, and now with only 14 there were high standards of performance and sportsmanship with few arguments or protests. Boxing was not held, the last time that it was left out of the Olympic programme. One of the rare complaints at these Games, which were opened officially by King Gustav V, was from the Finns, again about competing under the Russian flag. Indeed the triple gold medallist Kolehmainen stated that he almost wished he had not won rather than see the hated flag raised for his victories.

Various innovations included the first use of electrical timing equipment for the running events. Baron de Coubertin had asked for a new event to be introduced, the modern pentathlon, which consisted of five disciplines in different sports. It was dominated by the Swedes but in fifth place was one Lieutenant George S Patton (USA), later to become a controversial Second World War general. As previously, the American team lived on the liner that had brought them across the Atlantic, ironically named *Finland* – for this was the Games in which the first of the 'Flying Finns', Hannes Kolehmainen, made his appearance, winning the 5000m, 10 000m and 12 000m cross-country. Thus began a domination which lasted into the 1940s.

Kolehmainen's race with Jean Bouin of France in the 5000m was one of the most enthralling races ever seen with the Finn winning by a stride in 14:36.6, improving the world record by a margin of 24.6sec. Other track stars were Ted Meredith (USA), gold medallist in the 800m in a new world record, and Ralph Craig (USA) who took both sprints. Under current rules

Craig would not have won as he was responsible for three of the seven false starts to the race. He reappeared at the Games, as a yachtsman, 36 years later in London when he was given the honour of carrying the US team flag.

In the swimming pool the first of the great Hawaiian competitors, Duke Kahanamoku, won the 100m freestyle. The son of Hawaiian royalty, he received his first name as a mark of respect for the Duke of Edinburgh, Queen Victoria's second son, who was visiting the islands at the time of his birth. He competed in three more Games before becoming a film star.

There was only one cycling event, but it was unique in that it was the longest road race ever held in the Games. It was won by Rudolph Lewis (SAF), who took the 320km event in just short of 10¾ hours. A great impetus was given to the game

of soccer at these Olympics, with 25 000 spectators present to see Great Britain beat Denmark 4–2 in the final. Gymnastics, which like wrestling was held outdoors, also gained new status.

In wrestling itself, problems were caused by the extreme length of some of the bouts. In the light-heavyweight final the judges called a halt after the bout had gone on for nine hours and gave both wrestlers silver medals, with no gold awarded. Even this was surpassed in the middleweight category where the tussle for the silver medal between Asikainen (FIN) and Klein, an Estonian representing Russia, went on for 11hr 40min, a record for the sport. Klein finally triumphed.

The first known twins to win Olympic gold medals were the Carlberg brothers, Vilhelm (3) and Eric (2), in shooting, while an even rarer sibling combina-

tion came in the 6m class yachting when the French winner *Mac Miche* was crewed by the three Thubé brothers.

However, the star of the Games was undoubtedly Jim Thorpe. Of Irish, French, but mainly American Indian ancestry, Thorpe won both the newly-constituted athletic pentathlon and decathlon events with consummate ease, and was fifth in the individual high jump and seventh in the long jump. Presenting him with his medals, King Gustav V called him 'the greatest athlete in the world'. Thorpe reportedly replied, 'Thanks, King!' Six months later a sportswriter for the *Worcester Telegram* in Massachusetts, Roy Johnson, reported that Thorpe had played minor baseball for money. Owing to the violent amateur/professional dichotomy of the time, perhaps reinforced by American anti-Indian prejudice, Thorpe's medals

The Swedish gold medal gymnastics team in 1912 on, by modern standards, rather bizarre equipment in the Stockholm stadium.

'The greatest athlete in the world', Jim Thorpe (USA), won the athletics pentathlon and the decathlon at Stockholm in 1912.

1912 MEDALS

Country	G	S	B
United States[1]	25	19	18
Sweden	24	24	16
Great Britain	10	15	16
Finland	9	8	9
France	7	4	3
Germany	5	13	7
Norway	4	1	5
Hungary	3	2	3
Canada	3	2	2
Italy	3	1	2
South Africa	3	1	–
Australia[2]	2	2	2
Belgium	2	1	3
Denmark	1	6	4
Greece	1	–	1
New Zealand[3]	1	–	1
Switzerland	1	–	–
Russia	–	2	3
Austria	–	2	2
Netherlands	–	–	3

[1]*Adjusted by reinstatement of Jim Thorpe in 1982*
[2]*Australia and New Zealand combined as Australasia*

were taken back and his performances removed from Olympic annals. It seems almost certain that he was ignorant of the amateur laws of the time, and the amount involved was very small.

Twenty years after his death in 1953 the American Athletic Union reinstated him as an amateur, but the IOC stubbornly refused all entreaties on his behalf. It had been suggested that his cause was not helped by the fact that the President of the IOC from 1952 to 1972 was Avery Brundage, a team-mate of Thorpe's in 1912 who had placed fifth (or sixth, depending on your view) in the pentathlon. To their credit the runners-up to Thorpe, Hugo Wieslander (SWE) and Ferdinand Bie (NOR), initially refused to accept the gold medals when they were sent them, although their names were inscribed in Olympic annals as winners of the events. Finally, in October 1982 Thorpe, the man who had been voted in 1950 as the greatest athlete of the first half-century, was pardoned by the IOC and the medals were presented to his family.

The oldest gold medallist at these Games was the ubiquitous Oscar Swahn (SWE), by now aged 64yr 258 days, while teammate diver Greta Johansson was the youngest, aged 17yr 186 days. Only 40 days older was Isabella Moore (GBR) in the winning freestyle swimming relay team; she became Britain's youngest ever female gold medallist. The youngest male champion was fencer Nedo Nadi (ITA), aged 18yr 30 days.

At the Stockholm Games the Olympic movement finally 'came of age' and the marvellous efforts of the organising committee under Sigfrid Edstrom, later deservedly President of the IOC, must take much of the credit. The only unfortunate incident at the Games was the collapse and death of Francisco Lazzaro (POR) during the marathon – ironically it was the first Games that his country had attended. Another 'new' country was Japan, and the Games were beginning to achieve the worldwide support originally envisaged for them.

Britain's Albert Hill won both 800m and 1500m at Antwerp in 1920, a double not achieved again for 44 years.

1920

VIIth OLYMPIC GAMES
Antwerp, Belgium
20 April–12 September

Attended by representatives of 29 countries, comprising 2692 competitors, of which 64 were women.

When the venue of the VIth Games, due in 1916, came to be discussed in Stockholm, three cities were put forward as candidates: Budapest, Alexandria and Berlin. It is said that the last was chosen in an attempt to avert the war that was then threatening Europe. With the outbreak of hostilities in 1914, hopes of holding the Games virtually disappeared, although the Germans still made preparations for them, believing that the war would not last very long. In 1920, although Antwerp was sorely affected by the human tragedy and economic ruin of the conflict, the organizing committee under Count Henri de Baillet-Latour, later President of the IOC, overcame all difficulties to put the Games on.

The recent enemies – Germany, Austria, Hungary and Turkey – were not invited but still a record number of countries and competitors attended. Debutants included New Zealand as a separate entity (previously it had been part of an Australasian team), Argentina and Brazil. The Games were opened by King Albert, and the concept of the Olympic oath was introduced. It was taken here by Victor Boin, who had competed in two previous Games, winning medals at water polo; in Antwerp he gained another at fencing. Another newcomer at these Games was the newly devised Olympic flag. It had been designed by Baron de Coubertin in 1913, based on a design depicted on an ancient Greek artefact, and consisted of five interlaced rings coloured (from left to right) blue, yellow, black, green and red. The rings were meant to symbolise the friendship of mankind, with the colours representing all nations, as every national flag contains at least one of these colours.

Unfortunately the 400m running track at the new 30 000-seat stadium was very poor (Charles Perry, the famous groundsman, had not been able to do much with it) and it was badly affected by the persistent rain. Due to the weather and the economic aftermath of the recent conflict, crowds generally were small. The competitors were housed in school buildings, which caused something of a revolt among the US team – though they were even more incensed by the intolerable conditions experienced aboard the old freighter which had brought them to Belgium.

For the first time Finland competed under its own flag, having gained independence in 1917, and they celebrated the occasion by halting the US track and field juggernaut, winning as many athletics gold medals as the Americans. The star of 1912, Hannes Kolehmainen, made a surprise return to win the marathon but his mantle had been taken over by another outstanding Finnish runner, Paavo

Nurmi. Although he lost his very first Olympic final, over 5000m to the gassed French war veteran Joseph Guillemot, he was at the start of a brilliant career in which he won a record 12 Olympic medals – nine of them gold – and set 29 world records of one type or another. Also outstanding was 31-year-old Albert Hill of Great Britain who, having fought throughout the war, here gained the 800m/1500m double, a feat not repeated for 44 years. Hill also gained a silver medal in the 3000m team race. Second in the 1500m was Philip Baker (GBR) who later in life, as Philip Noel-Baker MP, was the recipient of the 1959 Nobel Peace Prize – a unique achievement for an Olympian.

Charley Paddock retained the 100m sprint title for the United States, delighting the spectators with his spectacular jump finish. A Second World War marine corps hero, he posthumously had a ship named after him. The most successful competitors were Willis Lee (USA) who won five golds, one silver and one bronze, and his teammate Lloyd Spooner who won four golds, one silver and two

1920 MEDALS

Country	G	S	B
United States	41	27	28
Sweden	19	20	25
Great Britain	15	15	13
Finland	15	10	9
Belgium	14	11	11
Norway	13	9	9
Italy	13	5	5
France	9	19	13
Netherlands	4	2	5
Denmark	3	9	1
South Africa	3	4	3
Canada	3	3	3
Switzerland	2	2	7
Estonia	1	2	–
Brazil	1	1	1
Australia	–	2	1
Japan	–	2	–
Spain	–	2	–
Greece	–	1	–
Luxembourg	–	1	–
Czechoslovakia	–	–	2
New Zealand	–	–	1

bronzes; both were shooting competitors. The shooting events also produced the first gold medal won by a South American country, when Guilherme Paraense (BRA) took the rapid-fire pistol title. Another shooter, the phenomenal Oscar Swahn (SWE) became the oldest ever Olympic medallist, with a silver at the age of 72yr 280 days. Another outstanding competitor was fencer Nedo Nadi (ITA) who won two individual and three team golds. His younger brother Aldo added another three to the family total.

Returning to Olympic competition for the first time since 1906, when he had won two golds and a silver, archer Hubert van Innis (BEL) won four golds and two silvers and was the oldest champion at these Games, aged 54yr 187 days. The youngest gold medallist was tiny (1.43m) diver Aileen Riggin (USA) at 14yr 119 days. Indeed she was the youngest Olympic champion ever to that date, but almost lost the honour to Sweden's Nils Skoglund, who finished a very close second in the men's plain high-diving when 3 months younger. Riggin won a diving silver four years later and, more unusually, a bronze in the 100m backstroke. The oldest female champion was Winifred McNair (GBR) in tennis, aged 43yr 15 days.

Swimming was dominated by two Americans who captured three gold medals each. Ethelda Bleibtrey, who had suffered from polio as a child, won all events open to her in world record times. The year before, she had been arrested in America and charged, under local decency laws, with swimming 'nude' at a public beach – all she had done was to remove her stockings. Norman Ross won the individual 400m and 1500m freestyle, was part of the win-

ning relay team and also figured in an unusual incident when he was disqualified in the 100m final for impeding an Australian swimmer. The race had been won by Duke Kahanamoku in world record time. The re-swim was also won by the Hawaiian but in a slower time. Another incident, of a more serious nature, occurred in the soccer final when Czechoslovakia were disqualified for leaving the field after 40 minutes' play in protest at decisions by the British referee. Belgium were leading 2–0 at that point.

Daniel Carroll completed a unique double in the rugby final when he won a second gold medal as part of the US team. He had played for the victorious Australian team of 1908 but had emigrated in the meantime. The tennis events were the stage for one of the greatest players in the game, Suzanne Lenglen (FRA), eventually six times winner of the Wimbledon title. The winner of the single sculls and, teamed with his cousin, the double sculls was the American John Kelly, who earlier in the year had been refused entry to the Henley Regatta in England on the grounds that as a bricklayer he had an unfair advantage over 'gentlemen'. Ironically, after he had become a millionaire, his son John Jr won at Henley in 1947, and his daughter Grace, the film actress, became Princess of Monaco. Coincidentally, these were the first Games at which Monaco participated.

Two winter sports were also held, ice hockey and figure skat-

ing, attracting 73 men and 12 women from 10 countries. The latter witnessed the first gold medals won by a husband and wife, the pairs champions being Walter Jakobsson of Finland and his German-born wife Ludowika. On the subject of matrimonial bliss, it may be that the first Olympic 'marriage' was that of American diver Alice Lord and high jump champion Dick Landon soon after they returned home, while it was revealed after the competitions that the women's skating champion, Magda Mauroy-Julin (SWE), was three months pregnant.

1924

Ist WINTER GAMES
Chamonix/Mont Blanc
25 January–4 February

Attended by representatives of 16 countries, comprising 294 competitors, of which 13 were women.

After skating and ice hockey events were held in 1908 and 1920 as part of the Summer Games, it was finally decided to hold a separate Winter festival. Although initially opposed by the Scandinavian countries, who felt that Winter Olympics would detract from their own Nordic Games, an 'International Winter Sports Week' was held at Chamonix, France. In 1926 it was accorded the title of Winter Games retrospectively. The French Under-Secretary for Physical Education, Gaston Vidal, formally opened the proceedings and the oath was taken by all the flag bearers, France's being a skier, Camille Mandrillon. Seventeen countries marched in the opening ceremony, but of these Estonia did not have any competitors in the actual competitions.

The first ever official Winter Olympic gold medallist was

Charles Jewtraw (USA) who won the 500m speed skating on 26 January, which also made it the earliest gold medal ever won in an Olympic year. It was the only speed skating medal won by a competitor from outside Finland and Norway. Clas Thunberg (FIN) won three golds, one silver and a bronze (tied) to dominate the sport. In skiing only the Nordic variety was held, as Alpine skiing was still in its infancy. Norway's Thorleif Haug won three gold medals and was also originally awarded the bronze in the special jumping event, but 50 years later a Norwegian sports historian, Jacob Vaage, discovered that the points had been added incorrectly and that the fourth-placed jumper Anders Haugen, a Norwegian-born American, had beaten Haug. In place of her deceased father, Haug's daughter presented the bronze medal to the 86-year-old Haugen in 1974.

Canada retained its title from 1920 in ice hockey, scoring 110 goals and conceding only 3 in five matches. At figure skating Gillis Grafström (SWE) gained the second of his three gold medals. He was later to gain even more fame as coach of Sonja Henie (NOR) who was an 11-year-old competitor in Chamonix, finishing eighth and last in the women's skating. Aside from her Olympic successes she was to earn an estimated $47.5 million from her film and ice show activities, making her the richest ever female Olympian. The inaugural 4-man bobsleigh contest was won by the Swiss, the first of a record four titles they have won in this discipline. Curling and a military patrol were held as demonstration events.

The oldest champion was speed skater Julius Skutnabb (FIN) aged 34yr 229 days, and the youngest was Heinrich

1924 MEDALS *Winter*

Country	G	S	B
Norway	4	7	6
Finland	4	3	3
Austria	2	1	–
United States	1	2	1
Switzerland	1	–	1
Canada	1	–	–
Sweden	1	–	–
Great Britain	–	1	2
Belgium	–	–	1
France	–	–	1

Schläppi, in Switzerland's 4-man bob, aged 18yr 279 days. The oldest medallist was ice hockey player Irving Small (USA) at 42yr 194 days. Of particular note were the silver medals won by Walter and Ludowika Jakobsson (FIN) in the pairs skating – he was just short of his 42nd birthday and she was well past her 39th. Two days before the closing ceremony, a meeting established the International Ski Federation (FIS).

1924

VIIIth OLYMPIC GAMES
Paris, France
4 May–27 July

Attended by representatives of 44 countries, comprising 3092 competitors, of which 136 were women.

Originally scheduled for Amsterdam, the Games were transferred to Paris at de Coubertin's request, in the hope that the bad image acquired in 1900 could be eradicated. The IOC had taken steps to impose its authority on the staging of the Olympics so that never again could a host country add events as it wished. The Colombes stadium, with a 500m track built in 1909, was enlarged to hold 60 000 spectators. An Olympic village had been proposed but the idea was not carried through, although in the end competitors were

housed in huts scattered around the main site.

Four of the five 'enemy' countries in the war returned among the record number of nations accepting invitations, but Germany was still not present due to her particularly frosty relations with France. Also among the newcomers were Ireland, competing separately from Britain for the first time, Romania and Poland. Polish sportsmen had competed previously but always in the teams of other countries. The Games were formally opened by the President of France, Gaston Doumergue, and were attended by well over 600 000 spectators in total. However, the chauvinism of the French supporters was outrageous at times. The weather was good, in fact too good – for the 10 000m cross-country event it was reported to be over 40°C and over half of the starters did not finish.

Despite the fact that, for the first time, all sports were being organised by their international governing bodies, and the instigation of Juries of Appeal, there were still many complaints of unfair decisions, notably in boxing. But the newly instituted Olympic motto, *Citius, Altius, Fortius* (faster, higher, stronger), originally composed by Father Henri Didon in 1895, was taken to heart and numerous records were set, sometimes unexpectedly. The long jump was won by William DeHart Hubbard (USA) with a leap of 7.44m. Another American, Robert LeGendre, had been left out of that event but entered for the athletic pentathlon, in which he broke the world long jump record with 7.76m on the way to winning a bronze medal. Incidentally, Hubbard was the first black athlete to win a gold medal in an individual, as opposed to a team, event.

The track events were dominated by the resurgent Finns with their outstanding stars Paavo Nurmi and Ville Ritola. Nurmi won what was then a record five gold medals, and America-based Ritola four golds and two silvers. The remarkable Nurmi won the 1500m and 5000m titles within 100 minutes on the same day – a unique performance. His other victories came in the 3000m team race and the 10000m cross-country team and individual events. It was this latter event that was run in the record high temperatures, with only 15 of the 38 starters finishing as Nurmi beat Ritola by well over a minute. The statue of Nurmi which stands outside Helsinki stadium was sculpted in 1925 to commemorate his Paris triumphs. Two Britons scored upset wins as Harold Abrahams became the first European to win an Olympic sprint title and Eric Liddell set a world record in taking the 400m crown. Abrahams, coached by Sam Mussabini who had also trained Reggie Walker to victory in 1908, later recollected that there were no victory ceremonies and that he received his gold medal in the post some time later. Third in that 100m final was New Zealand's Arthur Porritt, who later became Governor-General of his country.

A unique double was achieved by Harold Osborn (USA) who won the decathlon title and the high jump. In the latter event, Osborn's habit of pressing the bar back against the uprights with his hand as he jumped, using the Western Roll technique, led to a change in the event's rules. The rules in another event resulted in a strange set of circumstances when the third finisher in the 400m hurdles was credited with a new Olympic record (also bettering the world mark). This happened because the winner, Frank Morgan Taylor (USA), had knocked down a hurdle, while the second finisher, Charles Brookins (USA), had been disqualified for leaving his lane. Thus the eventual silver medallist, third finisher Erik Vilén (FIN), claimed the record. In fourth place was Georges André (FRA), a silver medallist in the 1908 high jump, who had taken the oath at the opening ceremony.

Harold Osborn, high jump and decathlon winner in 1924, later married Ethel Catherwood, the 1928 women's high jump champion.

In the pool Johnny Weissmuller (USA) won three golds in freestyle swimming and a bronze at water polo. After more medals four years later, he turned to films and in the 1930s he became the most famous screen 'Tarzan' of them all. His teammate in Paris, Gertrude Ederle, who in 1919 at the age of 12yr 298 days had become the youngest person ever to set a world record, here won a gold in the relay and two years later became the first woman to swim the English Channel. Incidentally, this Games was the first to use lane dividers in the pool.

Another American to gain fame elsewhere was rower Benjamin Spock, number 7 in the winning eight, who later gained renown as a best-selling writer and paediatrician. France came into her own in the fencing and cycling events. In the former Roger Ducret won three golds and one silver, while in the latter Armand Blanchonnet won the 188km road race by a near-record margin of over nine minutes. A pointer to the future came in the soccer final which was won by Uruguay, the first South American country to compete in Olympic football.

Now aged 45, Alfred Swahn (SWE) won his ninth shooting medal in four Games. His father, the incredible Oscar, had been picked for the team, but at 76 was too ill to compete. However, he and Alfred won a family total of six golds, four silvers and five bronzes. The American shooter Carl Osburn gained another silver to raise his individual total since 1912 to 11, comprising five gold medals, four silver and two bronze. Tennis made its last appearance for 64 years, but had an all-star entry with all titles being won by Wimbledon champions. One of them, Norris Williams, who partnered Hazel Wightman in the mixed

doubles, had been a survivor of the *Titanic* disaster in 1912. Rugby also disappeared from the Games, leaving the United States as the reigning Olympic champions.

The oldest gold medallist at Paris was Allen Whitty, a member of the British team in the Running Deer shooting event. A major in the Worcestershire Regiment who was awarded the DSO in 1916, he became Britain's oldest ever Olympic champion, aged 58yr 78 days. The youngest winner at Paris was featherweight boxer Jackie Fields (USA) at 16yr 162 days. The youngest female winner was 400m freestyle champion Martha Norelius (USA) at 16yr 177 days, while the oldest female gold medallist was Hazel Wightman (USA) in tennis, aged 37yr 213 days. The United States won the major share of the medals at Paris, but a record number of 30 countries shared in the total.

1924 MEDALS *Summer*

Country	G	S	B
United States	45	27	27
Finland	14	13	10
France	13	14	10
Great Britain	9	13	12
Italy	8	3	5
Switzerland	7	8	10
Norway	5	2	3
Sweden	4	13	12
Netherlands	4	1	5
Belgium	3	7	3
Australia	3	1	2
Denmark	2	5	2
Hungary	2	3	4
Yugoslavia	2	–	–
Czechoslovakia	1	4	5
Argentina	1	3	2
Estonia	1	1	4
South Africa	1	1	1
Luxembourg	1	1	–
Greece	1	–	–
Uruguay	1	–	–
Austria	–	3	1
Canada	–	3	1
Ireland	–	1	1
Poland	–	1	1
Haiti	–	–	1
Japan	–	–	1
New Zealand	–	–	1
Portugal	–	–	1
Romania	–	–	1

1928

IInd WINTER GAMES
St Moritz, Switzerland
11–19 February

Attended by representatives of 25 countries, comprising 495 competitors, of which 27 were women

The decision that the same country should host both Summer and Winter editions of the Games had to be abandoned in 1928, although the principle was still thought to be a sound one. These Winter Games were officially declared open by the President of Switzerland, Edmund Schulthess, and the oath was taken by Hans Eidenbenz, a skier. Japan, Holland, Romania and Mexico were making their Winter debuts. Unseasonal weather threatened the programme – on one day the temperature varied by over 20°C from morning to afternoon. One of the speed skating events had to be cancelled and the bobsleigh had only two runs instead of four.

The cancellation of the 10 000m skating event by the Norwegian referee caused bad feeling among the American team as at that point Irving Jaffee (USA) was surprisingly leading and seemed likely to retain that lead. Despite vigorous protests by all nationalities, no medals were awarded. Perhaps the unfortunate circumstances at Lake Placid four years later (see p. 33) provided Jaffee with a form of rough justice. In the other speed skating events, Clas Thunberg (FIN) added two more golds to his 1924 haul to amass a total of five gold, one silver and one bronze, a record for the sport. There was a unique occurrence in the 500m in which two men tied for first place and three men for third, with no silver medal awarded.

All-time skating great Sonja Henie won three consecutive Olympic titles from 1928 to 1936. Her achievements included 10 world titles before she went to Hollywood and made a series of highly popular movies.

Another uncommon happening was in the skeleton toboggan race conducted on the famous Cresta Run, where brothers Jennison and John Heaton (USA) gained the gold and silver respectively.

The bobsleigh, composed of 5-man teams for the first and only time, also went to the United States. Their driver, William Fiske, was aged only 16yr 260 days, and is still the youngest ever male gold medallist in the Winter Games. Also in the team was the oldest gold medallist at these Games, Nion Tucker, aged 42yr 182 days. The youngest was Sonja Henie (NOR), taking the first of her three titles aged 15yr 316 days. She was the 'star' of the Games with her interpretation of 'The Dying Swan', which began a whole new era for figure skating. By contrast, pairs skating witnessed the last appearance of 1920 champions Ludowika and Walter Jakobsson (FIN) who took fifth place, their ages totalling 89 years. The men's skating event gave Gillis Grafström (SWE) his third consecutive gold medal, an achievement unmatched to the present day.

In ski-jumping, the defending champion Jacob Tullin-Thams (NOR) was nearly killed, crashing at the end of a 73m jump on a hill designed for jumps of considerably less. A true Olympian, he reappeared in 1936 to gain a silver medal

1928 MEDALS Winter

Country	G	S	B
Norway	6	4	5
United States	2	2	2
Sweden	2	2	1
Finland	2	1	1
Canada	1	–	–
France	1	–	–
Austria	–	3	1
Belgium	–	–	1
Czechoslovakia	–	–	1
Germany	–	–	1
Great Britain	–	–	1
Switzerland	–	–	1

at yachting. Johan Gröttums-braaten (NOR) won the 18km race and the Nordic Combination title to match Clas Thunberg's two wins. As was fast becoming a habit, the Canadians easily won the ice hockey tournament, scoring a total of 38 goals without reply. The only demonstration event was a military patrol contest.

1928

IXth OLYMPIC GAMES
Amsterdam, Netherlands
17 May-12 August

Attended by representatives of 46 countries, comprising 3014 competitors, of which 209 were women.

After unsuccessfully applying for the Games of 1916, 1920 and 1924, the Dutch were finally rewarded, and a new 40 000 capacity stadium was built on reclaimed land in Amsterdam. The 400m running track was encircled by a cycling track, and the size was made the standard for future Games. The design of the stadium won the architect, Jan Wils, an Olympic prize in the architecture competition. One innovation was the erection of a large results board; others included the release of pigeons at the Opening Ceremony – to symbolise peace – and the burning of an Olympic flame throughout the period of competitions. The formal opening was by HRH Prince Hendrik, the consort of Queen Wilhelmina who was on a state visit to Norway, although the Queen herself did hand out medals at the end of the Games. The record number of countries included Rhodesia and Panama for the first time. Germany made its return to the Olympics in great strength.

After much argument in

world sporting circles, and in the face of opposition from Baron de Coubertin himself, women were allowed to compete in track and field, albeit in only five events. World records were set in all five, although there were such harrowing scenes of distress in the 800m that it was then omitted from the programme until 1964! In winning that 800m, Lina Radke won the first ever Olympic track and field gold medal for Germany. Her teammate Anni Holdmann became the first woman to win an Olympic track race by finishing first in Heat 1 of the 100m on 30 July. Another first in the sport was a gold medal for Japan by Mikio Oda in the triple jump.

The Finns again dominated the athletics, although the fabulous Nurmi won only one gold and two silvers. Looking far older than his 31 years, due to his increasing baldness, the dour Finn offered some light relief when he competed in the steeplechase. Unused to the event, he had problems with most of the barriers and, in his heat, ignominiously fell into the water jump. A Frenchman, Lucien Duquesne, stopped and courteously helped him to his feet. An obviously grateful Nurmi's renowned inscrutability cracked and he proceeded to 'shepherd' the French runner for the rest of the race, even inviting him to break the tape first. This Duquesne, to his eternal credit, declined to do. Despite running his fifth distance race in seven days, Nurmi won the silver medal (behind a teammate) in the final. It was later reported that the great Finn had damaged his famous stopwatch in the fall.

The unheralded Canadian youngster Percy Williams took both sprints. With Lord Burghley becoming the first member of the British House of

The shock winner of the 100m and 200m at the 1928 Games, Percy Williams of Canada.

Lords to win an Olympic athletics title, and Douglas Lowe (GBR) successfully defending his 800m title, the Americans had a lean time. A pointer for the future was the victory in the marathon of Mohammed El Ouafi, representing France, but an Algerian and the pathfinder for future great African distance runners. The US team was under the control of the President of the US Olympic Committee, Major-General Douglas MacArthur, later in command of the victorious Americans in the Pacific theatre of the Second World War.

In the swimming pool another threat to United States dominance came in the form of the Japanese. In Amsterdam they won their first ever swimming medals, giving an indication of things to come.

American honour was saved by Johnny Weissmuller in the 100m freestyle and relay. Dorothy Poynton (USA) won a silver medal in springboard diving just 24 days past her 13th birthday, one of the youngest medallists ever. She won gold medals at the next two Games. There was an unfortunate mix-up in the result of the men's high diving when Farid Simaika of Egypt was initially awarded the gold on the basis of his greater points score. The result was later reversed and the title given to Ulise 'Pete' Desjardins (USA) as more first place decisions had been made in his favour by the judges. Canadian-born Desjardins had been the first Olympic diver to be awarded a score of 10, in the 1924 springboard event.

Another Egyptian, Ibrahim

Moustafa, won the light-heavyweight wrestling title to become the first non-European to take a Greco-Roman event. Not for the first nor the last time, boxing was beset with protests about the standard of officiating. In yachting, Crown Prince Olav, later King Olav V of Norway, gained the first Olympic victory by a member of a royal house when he was a crew member of the 6m yacht *Norna*. (His son, now King Harald, also competed in Olympic yachting, from 1964 to 1972, but not with his father's success.) In the soccer tournament, Uruguay retained the title beating their South American rivals Argentina in the final. In front of 50 000 people, India won the first of their six consecutive hockey gold medals, retaining the title until 1960. Their

Elizabeth Robinson (879) wins the Amsterdam 100m for the United States from the Canadians Fanny Rosenfeld (677) and Ethel Smith (678). The Canadians won gold in the relay.

goalkeeper, Richard Allen, did not concede a single goal in the tournament.

A teammate of the Crown Prince in the *Norna*, Johann Anker, was the oldest gold medallist in Amsterdam, aged 57yr 44 days, while the youngest, also waterborne, was the Swiss pairs cox Hans Bourquin, aged 14. The youngest female champion was Elizabeth Robinson (USA) who won the 100m sprint aged 16yr 343 days, while the oldest woman to win a gold medal was Virginie Hériot (FRA) in the 8m yachting aged 38yr 15 days. The youngest medallist was America's Dorothy Poynton (USA).

1928 MEDALS *Summer*

Country	G	S	B
United States	22	18	16
Germany	10	7	14
Finland	8	8	9
Sweden	7	6	12
Italy	7	5	7
Switzerland	7	4	4
France	6	10	5
Netherlands	6	9	4
Hungary	4	5	–
Canada	4	4	7
Great Britain	3	10	7
Argentina	3	3	1
Denmark	3	1	2
Czechoslovakia	2	5	2
Japan	2	2	1
Estonia	2	1	2
Egypt	2	1	1
Austria	2	–	1
Australia	1	2	1
Norway	1	2	1
Poland	1	1	3
Yugoslavia	1	1	3
South Africa	1	–	2
India	1	–	–
Ireland	1	–	–
New Zealand	1	–	–
Spain	1	–	–
Uruguay	1	–	–
Belgium	–	1	2
Chile	–	1	–
Haiti	–	1	–
Philippines	–	–	1
Portugal *	–	–	1

1932

IIIrd WINTER GAMES
Lake Placid, USA
4–15 February

Attended by representatives of 17 countries, comprising 306 competitors, of which 32 were women.

Snow had to be brought over to the United States from Canada by lorries for some of the venues at Lake Placid, and a thaw caused the 4-man bob event to be held after the official closing ceremony on 13 February. The Games were opened by the Governor of New York State, Franklin D Roosevelt, who became President of the United States the following year. Incidentally, Eleanor, his redoubtable wife, took a ride down the bob course. The oath was taken by Jack Shea, who won the 500m speed skating gold later in the day. An Olympic first was achieved by the British contingent when their flag was carried by a woman, skater Mollie Phillips. Innovatively, figure skating was held indoors and drew large crowds, and three speed skating events for women were given demonstration status – 28 years later such events were on the programme proper. Demonstrations were also given of curling and dog sled racing, the latter won by Emile St Goddard of Canada.

Not surprisingly the Scandinavians swept the Nordic skiing, but an upset occurred in the speed skating where the Americans and Canadians dominated.

It is arguable whether this was as much to do with the abilities of the North Americans as with the change of rules that the organising committee had invoked. Instead of the more usual European system of competition taking place in pairs with the fastest times deciding the medal places, American rules were in force, under which mass start races were held, similar to track running, with heats and finals. Lack of familiarity with the tactics employed, often quite physical, put the Europeans at a distinct disadvantage. Indeed Finland's four-time gold medallist Clas Thunberg did

not even bother to appear at Lake Placid. The Canadians won the ice hockey title for the fourth consecutive time, but only on goal average after three periods of overtime against the United States in the final game.

In figure skating the peerless Sonja Henie (NOR) easily retained her title, but triple champion Gillis Grafström (SWE), now 38, was the victim of an unfortunate accident. During the compulsory figures he collided with a badly positioned movie camera and fell, suffering a mild concussion. This may well have cost him an unprecedented fourth title. The

The Canadian ice hockey team won their fourth consecutive title at Lake Placid. They are seen here (in white) playing the United States in the final, which was decided on goal average.

oldest ever Winter Games skater was Joseph Savage (USA), aged 52yr 144 days, in the pairs skating. The winners of that title, Pierre and Andrée Brunet (FRA), became the only pair to win both as an unmarried and married couple. In so doing, Andrée was the oldest female gold medal winner in Lake Placid, aged 30yr 149 days. In the women's individual event, Cecilia Colledge was Britain's youngest ever Olympic competitor at any sport, at 11yr 73 days. She was probably the youngest ever competitor in the Winter Olympic Games.

History of a different kind was made by Eddie Eagan (USA) in the 4-man bob as a late and virtually untried draftee. As part of the winning team he became the only man to win gold medals in both Summer and Winter celebrations – he was a 1920 boxing champion. The 2-man bob was won by brothers Curtis and Hubert Stevens (USA), and a third brother, Paul, won a silver medal in the 4-man event. The oldest gold medallist at Lake Placid was Eagan's bob teammate Jay O'Brien, aged 48yr 359 days, while Sonja Henie was again the youngest, now aged 19yr 308 days. The youngest male champion was ski-jumper Birger Ruud (NOR) at the start of his superb career, aged 20yr 173 days. O'Brien is still the oldest person to have won a Winter Olympics gold medal.

1932 MEDALS *Winter*

Country	G	S	B
United States	6	4	2
Norway	3	4	3
Sweden	1	2	–
Canada	1	1	5
Finland	1	1	1
Austria	1	1	–
France	1	–	–
Switzerland	–	1	–
Germany	–	–	2
Hungary	–	–	1

1932

Xth OLYMPIC GAMES
Los Angeles, USA
30 July–14 August

Attended by representatives of 37 countries, comprising 1408 competitors, of which 127 were women.

As early as 1920 the US delegation to the IOC, led by William May Garland, had applied for either the 1924 or 1928 Games to be held in Los Angeles. Despite trepidation felt over the memory of the 1904 'farce' at St Louis, in 1923 Los Angeles was awarded the 1932 Games. Against further worries of distance and cost of travel were set the advantages of favourable weather and competitive conditions. The announcement by the organising committee that they would subsidise transportation, housing and feeding costs helped greatly at a time of Depression, and did much to offset the critics.

One source of income was a new three-cent postage stamp which depicted a runner, for which the model was the anchorman of the 1924 gold medal relay team, Alfred Leconey. The concept of an Olympic 'village' came to fruition with the construction of 550 specially designed small houses for male competitors in the Baldwin Hills area. It was strictly guarded by cowboys who 'rode the fences' around the perimeter. Female competitors were put up separately in the Chapman Park Hotel on Wilshire Boulevard, and the strict rule banning women from the village barred the Finnish team's lady cook. However, despite the strictures of Prohibition, the French team were allowed to bring in wine for their own consumption. After journeys which had lasted up to two weeks, the foreigners found excellent weather and facilities awaiting them.

The main stadium was the Los Angeles Coliseum which had opened in 1923, two years after construction had begun. In 1930 it had been enlarged to hold 101 000 seated spectators, and the track had a new crushed-peat running surface. There was also the 10 000-seat Swimming Stadium, the State Armory where fencing took place, the Olympic Auditorium seating 10 000 to watch boxing, wrestling and weightlifting events, and a specially built wooden track was erected in the world-famous Pasadena Rose Bowl for the cycling. Long Beach harbour was the venue for yachting and Long Beach Marine Stadium hosted the rowing. The Los Angeles Museum of History, Science and Art was the home for the fine art competitions.

The Games were formally opened by the Vice-President of the United States, Charles Curtis, on behalf of President Hoover who was in the middle of an electioneering tour. The oath on behalf of the competitors was taken by an American fencer, Lieutenant George Calnan of the US Navy, who died the following April when the dirigible airship *Akron* crashed into the Pacific Ocean. Although the numbers of teams and total competitors were lower than at Amsterdam, there were two countries making their Olympic debuts, Columbia and China, both with sole representatives, neither of whom achieved any success. However, another small team, Ireland with only eight men, finished well up the medals table with two golds.

At these Games, new ideas included the use of photo-finish equipment – the Kirby Two-Eyed Camera – for track races.

Although it could accurately provide times to one-hundredth of a second, it was only used to decide close finishes and only a few of the times recorded have ever come to light. Another innovation was the three-tiered victory stand, with medal-awarding ceremonies involving the raising of national flags taking place at the end of each day's events. In boxing, the system of having the referee in the ring with the boxers was introduced into the Games for the first time, although it did not settle all arguments in that sport. Remarkably there was only one knockout – a technical knockout (TKO) in the preliminaries of the heavyweight division – throughout the whole boxing programme.

As with all such international gatherings there were some unfortunate incidents, but in the main they were of minor importance. Prior to the arrival of the teams there was a major 'scandal' with the banning of the great Finnish runner, Paavo Nurmi, on charges of professionalism – he was accused of accepting unduly large expenses on a German tour. Despite vigorous protests on his behalf, the Finnish Federation finally accepted the ruling although he had already been selected for the marathon and, indeed, arrived with the team in Los Angeles. It seems not unreasonable to suggest that he would have finished a remarkable career with another gold medal. The Finns were also involved in another incident once the Games were under way when the runners in the 3000m steeplechase ran an extra lap due to a miscalculation by the lap counter. Happily the error did not appear to have altered the final medal placings.

Another minor irritant was the American habit of announcing all the field event results only in Imperial units of measurement, much to the annoyance and bafflement of the foreign competitors and spectators. But there were two more serious occurrences, one on the track and one in the swimming pool. The first came in the 5000m when the eventual winner, Lauri Lehtinen (FIN),

Mildred Didrikson (far right), seen here winning the 80m hurdles in 1932, later gained greater fame as champion golfer 'Babe' Zaharias.

deliberately blocked the American Ralph Hill twice in the final stages of the race, a not-uncommon practice in Europe but one which drew loud booing from the partisan crowd. They were quickly quietened by the announcer Bill Henry, whose words, 'Remember, please, these people are our guests', have entered Olympic lore. The second incident was of a much more serious nature when the Brazilian water polo team, after losing 7–3 to Germany, lost their tempers and insulted the referee. They were disqualified from the tournament.

On the brighter side was the performance of the outstanding individual of the Games, the American Mildred 'Babe' Didrikson (since her death, her family has insisted that the surname should be spelt with an 'e', not an 'o'). Much to her annoyance she was allowed to enter only three events, but she set Olympic records in each of them, winning the javelin and

1932 MEDALS Summer

Country	G	S	B
United States	41	32	30
Italy	12	12	12
France	10	6	4
Sweden	9	5	9
Japan	7	7	4
Hungary	6	4	5
Finland	5	8	12
Germany	4	12	5
Great Britain	4	7	5
Australia	3	1	1
Argentina	3	1	–
Canada	2	5	8
Netherlands	2	5	–
Poland	2	1	4
South Africa	2	–	3
Ireland	2	–	–
Czechoslovakia	1	2	1
Austria	1	1	3
India	1	–	–
Denmark	–	3	3
Mexico	–	2	–
Latvia	–	1	–
New Zealand	–	1	–
Switzerland	–	1	–
Philippines	–	–	3
Spain	–	–	1
Uruguay	–	–	1

80m hurdles and gaining a silver in the high jump. She is thus the only athlete to win medals at running, jumping and throwing. In the high jump there was a strange judgement made, for although Didrikson cleared the same height as her teammate Jean Shiley, and then tied in a jump-off, the judges decided that her 'Western Roll' style of jump had been performed illegally with her head preceding her body over the bar, and illogically they placed her second. She later became the world's greatest female golfer under her married name of Zaharias.

Another unusual thing occurred in the 400m hurdles where Irishman Bob Tisdall, who reportedly spent most of the preceding days in bed recuperating from a long and tiring journey, won the gold medal in a time superior to the world record. However, because he knocked down the last hurdle, the world record was given to the runner-up Glenn Hardin (USA). Uniquely, the first four finishers were all gold medallists in the event – Tisdall (1932), Hardin (1936), Taylor (1924) and Burghley (1928).

In the 200m final Ralph Metcalfe was inadvertently made to start about 1½m before the correct place, thus almost certainly costing him a silver medal. As Americans had placed 1–2–3 Metcalfe, later a US Congressman, declined the offered re-run. The Indian hockey team, while not looking quite so invincible as previously, set a record-breaking score by defeating the United States 24–1, with Roop Singh scoring 12 goals. Similarly, in the water polo competition Hungary beat Japan with a record score of 18–0. Nevertheless, the Japanese were particularly noteworthy in swimming, highlighted by their superb 4 × 200m team breaking the world record

by a remarkable 37.8sec.

The oldest gold medallist at Los Angeles was dressage champion Xavier Lesage (FRA), aged 46yr 290 days, while the youngest was 1500m freestyle champion Kusuo Kitamura (JPN), aged 14yr 309 days. The youngest female champion was Claire Dennis (AUS) who won the 200m breaststroke aged 16yr 117 days. The oldest female winner was Lillian Copeland (USA) in the discus, aged 27yr 251 days. The youngest medallist was diver Katharine Rawls (USA), just 58 days past her 14th birthday.

As demonstration sports the hosts, perhaps not surprisingly, provided American football and lacrosse. During the closing ceremony the President of the IOC, Count Henri de Baillet-Latour, presented Olympic Merit Awards for Alpinism to Franz and Toni Schmid (GER) for the first climb of the north face of the Matterhorn. Despite all the economic and organisational misgivings, the Xth Games were a great success, attended by a total of 1.25 million spectators, and realised a profit of about $1 million.

One last innovation at these Games was the use of two sentences, attributed to Baron de Coubertin but actually based on words used by the Bishop of Central Pennsylvania, Ethelbert Talbot, in a sermon at St Paul's Cathedral, London, on 19 July 1908. Displayed on the scoreboard at every opening ceremony since, the words are: 'The most important thing in the Olympic Games is not to win but to take part, just as the most important thing in life is not the triumph but the struggle. The essential thing is not to have conquered but to have fought well.'

1936

IVth WINTER GAMES
Garmisch-Partenkirchen,
Germany
6–16 February

*Attended by representatives of 28
countries, comprising 755
competitors, of which 80 were
women.*

It is not always remembered
that when the Winter and Summer Games of 1936 were
awarded to Germany, five years

previously, Adolf Hitler was virtually unknown to the rest of the
world. However, by the year of
the Games the question of how
the German Olympic Committee would react to the demands
of their National Socialist government was a major issue.
There had been much heated
discussion around the world as
to the advisability of attending
these Games – and the Summer
celebration – at all, given the
racialist policies of Hitler's government.

In spite of this a record entry

*Norway's Birger Ruud successfully
defended his ski-jump title in 1936,
as well as performing creditably in
the Alpine combination.*

for the Winter Games included
teams from Bulgaria, Turkey,
Australia, Spain and Liechtenstein for the first time. The
Games were declared open by
Chancellor Adolf Hitler, and
Wilhelm Bogner, a skier, took
the oath on behalf of the competitors. By the end of the
competitions, over 500 000 paying spectators had watched the

1936 MEDALS *Winter*

Country	G	S	B
Norway	7	5	3
Germany	3	3	–
Sweden	2	2	3
Finland	1	2	3
Austria	1	1	2
Switzerland	1	2	–
Great Britain	1	1	1
United States	1	–	3
Canada	–	1	–
France	–	–	1
Hungary	–	–	1

six different sports. These now included Alpine skiing, although the only event was a combination one, for both men and women.

Birger Ruud (NOR) successfully defended his ski-jump title, and then caused a major surprise by winning the downhill segment of the men's Alpine combination. By dint of a 5.9sec margin of victory in the slalom segment, the title went to Franz Pfnür (GER) and Ruud fell back to fourth place. In the women's event there was a similar situation when the downhill race was won by 16-year-old Laila Schou Nilsen (NOR), who held five world speed skating records but had entered the skiing in the absence of such events for women. In the slalom Christl Cranz (GER), who was eventually to win a record 12 world skiing championships, won by the quite astounding margin of 11.3sec and took the overall gold medal, Nilsen gaining the bronze.

The top medal winner was speed skater Ivar Ballangrud (NOR) with three golds and a silver. Contrary to the Lake Placid conditions of four years earlier, the racers competed under European-style rules with pairs of skaters racing against the clock, and instead of four gold medals the Americans gained a solitary bronze. Sonja Henie (NOR) won her third consecutive figure skating title, to add to her ten world championships, and then went off to Hollywood, followed some time later by the 12th-placed British girl Gladys Jepson-Turner, who gained cinematic fame as Belita. The British caused a major upset by winning the ice hockey, albeit with a team that contained some Anglo-Canadians. In this competition appeared Rudi Ball, one of only two athletes of Jewish origin selected by Germany in 1936. Ball, a bronze medallist from 1932, was especially requested to return from his exile in France to compete, the hosts hoping to offset criticisms of their attitude to Jewish competitors by this act.

A most unusual double nearly came the way of Ernst Baier (GER), who won the pairs skating with Maxi Herber but only came second in the men's singles. It remains the highest such double placing ever. His pairs partner was the youngest gold medallist, aged 15yr 128 days, while sister and brother Ilse and Erik Pausin (AUT), the pairs silver medallists, were the youngest ever couple to gain a medal in the event, their ages totalling a mere 32yr 307 days. The oldest gold medallist was Carl Erhardt (GBR), one day past his 39th birthday in the ice hockey final. The demonstration events were German curling and the military patrol.

<table>
<tr><td>

1936

</td></tr>
</table>

XIth OLYMPIC GAMES
Berlin, Germany
1–16 August

Attended by representatives of 49 countries, comprising 4066 competitors, of which 328 were women.

Not surprisingly, political overtones overshadowed these Games, as abhorrence of Germany's policies under Hitler led many countries, not least the United States, to propose a boycott; but the President of the US Olympic Committee, Avery Brundage, was strongly in favour of participation and won the day. In Germany itself the notorious Heinrich Himmler was actually opposed to the Games being held, and it was Josef Goebbels who convinced Hitler that they would present tremendous propaganda opportunities. Political problems continued to plague the Games right up to the last moment when Spain withdrew owing to the outbreak of the Civil War there.

The original intention had been to enlarge the stadium that had been built for the aborted 1916 Games, but Hitler decreed that a brand new 100 000 capacity stadium be built. The architect was Werner March, whose father had designed the 1916 stadium. Other fine stadia and halls were erected, and for the competitors a magnificent 'village' of 150 buildings. Yachting events were held at Kiel on the north-west coast. At the instigation of Carl Diem, the main organiser, a torch relay was inaugurated to bring the sacred Olympic flame from the Temple of Zeus at Olympia – 3000 runners crossed seven countries in ten days. The Games were formally opened by Chancellor Hitler, as a specially commissioned 16½-ton bell was rung and thousands of pigeons set free. As the massive German contingent, 406 strong, entered the stadium, the giant airship *Hindenburg* flew overhead.

The German team, with full government backing, was probably the best prepared team ever in the Games. As a sop to foreign criticism it contained one athlete of Jewish origin, Helene Mayer, persuaded to return from America with the promise of full 'Aryan' classification. Ironically, she placed

Jesse Owens wins the 100m at Berlin ahead of teammate Metcalfe and black-shorted Osendarp of Holland.

second in the foil to the Hungarian Jewess Ilona Elek, with another Jewish fencer in third. An even greater irony was in evidence at the Opening Ceremony when the 1896 marathon victor, Spyridon Louis, attired in national dress, presented Hitler with an olive branch – signifying peace – from Olympia.

In the march-past of teams, a number of them gave the Nazi salute, but the United States and Great Britain, to their credit and the annoyance of the crowd, merely made the traditional 'eyes right'. The music for the ceremony was conducted by the famous composer Richard Strauss. An indication of the future came with the first ever use of television at the Games, with a closed-circuit system relayed to special halls by the Reich Rundfunkgesellschaft and watched by 150 000 people at 28 venues around Berlin. The

torch relay across Europe from Olympia, where the sacred flame, lit by 'priestesses' Koula Pratsika and Aleka Katseli, was handed to a Greek runner, Kondylis, ended with the last runner, athlete Fritz Schilgen, coming into the stadium to light the cauldron.

Very high standards were set at these Games, and at the forefront of the record breaking were the ten black members of the US track and field team. Anathema to the German propaganda machine, which dubbed them 'Black Auxiliaries', they won seven gold, three silver and three bronze medals – more than any national team, including their own white teammates. Outstanding among them was Jesse Owens with four gold medals, in the 100m, 200m, long jump and as a member of the 4 × 100m relay team. The runner-up in the 200m was

Mack Robinson, whose brother Jackie was the first black Major League baseball player. It should be noted that the attitude of the German government to Owens was not shared by the majority of the fans – he was in tremendous demand by autograph hunters.

Much has been written about Hitler refusing to meet and congratulate Owens and the other black gold medallists. In fairness it should be realised that after Hitler had made a point of personally greeting the German victors on the first day, he was rebuked for the practice by the President of the IOC, Henri de Baillet-Latour, who informed him that only IOC-designated people performed such duties in an Olympic stadium. After that, Hitler refrained from any further congratulatory meetings, although it is reported that he met all the

German medallists in private. Thus, if he did snub anybody, it would have been the only black winner on the first day, high jumper Corny Johnson.

Other track highlights included the superb sprinting of Helen Stephens (USA), the decathlon victory of teammate Glenn Morris, later to be another screen Tarzan, and the 1500m world record by Jack Lovelock (NZL). This last event is considered by many to have been the highlight of the Games. The Finns took all three medal places in the 10 000m as well as the first two in the 5000m and steeplechase, Volmari Iso-Hollo successfully defending his title in the latter. Outstanding in the pool were the Dutch women led by Hendrika Mastenbroek, who personally won three golds and a silver. The winner of the women's springboard diving, Marjorie

New Zealand's Jack Lovelock wins the 1936 1500m in world record time (3:47.8) from Glenn Cunningham (USA).

1936 MEDALS Summer

Country	G	S	B
Germany	33	26	30
United States	24	20	12
Hungary	10	1	5
Italy	8	9	5
Finland	7	6	6
France	7	6	6
Sweden	6	5	9
Japan	6	4	8
Netherlands	6	4	7
Great Britain	4	7	3
Austria	4	6	3
Czechoslovakia	3	5	–
Argentina	2	2	3
Estonia	2	2	3
Egypt	2	1	2
Switzerland	1	9	5
Canada	1	3	5
Norway	1	3	2
Turkey	1	–	1
India	1	–	–
New Zealand	1	–	–
Poland	–	3	3
Denmark	–	2	3
Latvia	–	1	1
Romania	–	1	–
South Africa	–	1	–
Yugoslavia	–	1	–
Mexico	–	–	3
Belgium	–	–	2
Australia	–	–	1
Philippines	–	–	1
Portugal	–	–	1

Gestring (USA), became the youngest ever female gold medallist and the youngest ever individual event champion, aged 13yr 267 days. The oldest gold medallist at Berlin was Friedrich Gerhard (GER) in the dressage team, aged 52yr 20 days. The youngest male champion was Adolph Kiefer (USA) who won the 100m backstroke aged 18yr 48 days, while the oldest female champion was fencer Ilona Elek (HUN) at 29yr 79 days.

Robert Charpentier (FRA) won three gold medals in cycling, while Toni Merkens (GER) won the 1000m sprint despite being fined, but not disqualified, for obstruction in the first race. In wrestling, Kristian Palusalu of Estonia matched the achievement of Ivar Johansson (SWE) in 1932 by winning titles in both freestyle and Greco-Roman. Interestingly, the list of gold medallists at Berlin includes the name *Nurmi* – not Paavo in this case but the name of the horse ridden by Ludwig Stubbendorf (GER) to his easy victory in the tough three-day event. Of the fourteen teams which started only four finished with sufficient scorers. These included Britain, whose final placer, Captain Richard Fanshawe, gained his team the bronze medal despite numerous penalty points incurred by having to chase his horse for 2½ miles before remounting.

In the single-handed Olympia class yachting, the bronze medal went to Peter Markham

Scott, son of the tragic Antarctic explorer and later himself a world-famous naturalist. Canoeing and basketball made their official debuts, with the inventor of the latter, Dr James Naismith, on hand to see the US team begin its remarkable sequence of victories. At the end of the Games a magnificent film, *Olympische Spiele* – Olympic Games – was produced by Leni Riefenstahl; although criticised as propaganda, it is still the best documentary record of an Olympic Games.

1948

Vth WINTER GAMES
St Moritz, Switzerland
30 January–8 February

Attended by representatives of 28 countries, comprising 713 competitors, of which 77 were women.

The Winter Games scheduled for 1940 were initially awarded to Sapporo, Japan, in 1936, but as a consequence of the Sino-Japanese conflict they were reallocated to St Moritz. Due to some disagreements the IOC transferred them again in June 1939 to Garmisch-Partenkirchen, Germany, at the same time deciding that the 1944 meeting should be held at Cortina d'Ampezzo, Italy. The Second World War then upset these plans and in 1946 a postal vote of IOC members relocated the 1948 Games in St Moritz, as neutral Switzerland had been virtually untouched by the war. Chile, Denmark, Iceland, Korea and Lebanon competed for the first time in the Winter Games; Germany and Japan were not invited, although strangely Italy was.

Dick Button literally leapt to the first of his two Olympic titles at St Moritz in 1948.

The oath was taken by ice hockey player Richard Torriani on behalf of the competitors, and Swiss President Enrico Celio formally declared the Games open. There were now six Alpine events which attracted larger fields than the Nordic disciplines. Poor weather affected some of the competitions, and there were a number of disputes.

The most medals were won by Henri Oreiller (FRA) with gold in the downhill (by a record margin of 4.1sec) and combination, and a bronze in the slalom. Alpine skier Gretchen Fraser (USA) gained the first skiing title ever won by a non-European. In Nordic skiing, the Swedes broke the Norwegian monopoly. They took the three medals and fifth place in the 18km, first two and fifth in the 50km, and won the 4 × 10km relay by a margin of nearly 9 minutes. They also won their first ever speed skating title when Ake Seyffarth took the 10km event. The athletic American figure skaters brought a new concept to figure skating as Dick Button gained an easy victory.

The ice hockey competition was the cause of a major row. Two American teams appeared in St Moritz. One represented the Amateur Hockey Association of the United States (AHA) and the other was picked by the US Olympic Committee. The AHA, while not affiliated to the USOC, was a member of the International Hockey Federation (IHF). This last was the governing body of most of the other teams at the Games, and threatened to withdraw all the other teams if the AHA team were not allowed to play. The USOC in turn threatened to withdraw its whole Olympic team if it did! Initially the IOC decided to bar both teams, but then agreed with the Swiss organisers and the IHF to allow the AHA team to compete. Strangely, however, the USOC team members marched in the opening ceremony. The AHA team eventually finished fourth, but a year later the AHA was disqualified for non-affiliation to the Olympic movement. The Canadians won the title once again, but only just. The title was decided on goal average, with the Czechs taking the silver. The Swiss in third place contained the man who had taken the oath, Richard 'Bibi' Torriani, thus adding another bronze medal to the one he had won 20 years earlier when he was just past his 16th birthday.

The US bobsleds were sabotaged prior to the competitions, but it did not prevent them from winning a gold and two bronzes. They have never won an Olympic bob event since! In the skeleton toboggan, which is held only when the Games are at St Moritz, on the Cresta Run, John Heaton (USA) won his second silver medal, 20 years after his first. The gold medal went to Nino Bibbia of Italy. Bibbia was a master of the Cresta Run and won many titles and championships over the next quarter of a century.

The great Norwegian ski jumper Birger Ruud, nearly 37 years old and a survivor of a wartime concentration camp, ended his Olympic career with a silver medal to add to his golds from 1932 and 1936. He and his brother Sigmund had made the event a family preserve since 1928. A third brother, Asbjörn, was also in the 1948 team.

A record 13 countries shared out the medals, and Italy and Belgium won their first ever Winter Games titles. There were two demonstration events: a military ski patrol and a winter pentathlon. This latter consisted of 10km cross-country skiing, pistol shooting, downhill skiing, fencing and horse riding. No medals were awarded, but in second place was Captain Willie Grut (SWE) of whom much more was to be heard six months later in London.

The oldest gold medallist was Francis Tyler of the US 4-man bob, aged 43yr 58 days, while the youngest was skater Dick Button, aged 18yr 202 days. The youngest female champion was skater Barbara-Ann Scott (CAN), aged 19yr 273 days, while the oldest female winner was Gretchen Fraser (USA) in the slalom, aged 28yr 360 days. The youngest medallist was skater Jeanette Altwegg (GBR) with a bronze, aged 17yr 151 days, while the oldest was bobsledder Max Houben (USA) at 49yr 38 days.

1948

XIVth OLYMPIC GAMES
London, Great Britain
29 July–14 August

Attended by representatives of 59 countries, comprising 4099 competitors, of which 385 were women.

In 1936 the XIIth Games were awarded to Tokyo, to take place from 24 August to 8 September 1940. When the Sino-Japanese war began in 1938, the Games were transferred to Helsinki only for the Soviet invasion of Finland to scupper those plans.

1948 MEDALS *Winter*

Country	G	S	B
Norway	4	3	3
Sweden	4	3	3
Switzerland	3	4	3
United States	3	4	2
France	2	1	2
Canada	2	–	1
Austria	1	3	4
Finland	1	3	2
Belgium	1	1	–
Italy	1	–	–
Czechoslovakia	–	1	1
Hungary	–	1	–
Great Britain	–	–	2

Arthur Wint wins the 1948 400m from Jamaican teammate Herb McKenley, with 800m champion Mal Whitfield in third place.

In June 1939, a very optimistic IOC awarded the XIIIth Games, for 1944, to London, over competing claims from Detroit, Lausanne and Rome. Then after the war, a postal vote of IOC members called by the President, Sigfrid Edström of Sweden, in 1946, awarded the XIVth Games to London for 1948. In the meantime, Baron de Coubertin had died, in 1937, and his heart was buried at Olympia in Greece.

Organised by the British Olympic Association, under the Presidency of Lord Burghley, the 1948 Olympics were an austerity Games – after six years of war Britain still had rationing of food and clothing. Housing was in very short supply due to wartime destruction, and competitors were housed at RAF and Army camps (for men) and colleges (for women). A temporary running track was laid at the 83 000 capacity Wembley Stadium, the home of British foot-

ball. Other existing buildings were adapted. Rowing was held at Henley, on the River Thames, and the yachting was at Torbay, Devon. The total expenditure amounted to no more than £600 000 and final accounts suggested that a profit of over £10 000 was made.

The Games were opened by King George VI. Not surprisingly, Germany and Japan were not invited, but a record 59 countries attended. These included the first entries by countries under Communist governments. Some of the hottest weather for years occurred on the opening days, but later it rained. Photo-finish equipment, as used on racecourses, was used for the track events, but only to decide places.

The undoubted star of the Games was Francina 'Fanny' Blankers-Koen (HOL), who won four gold medals, a record for a woman. By now 30 years of

age and a mother of two children, she had previously finished in sixth place in the 1936 high jump and in 1948 she held seven world records including those in the high and long jumps, neither of which she contested in London. The gap between her and the second girl in the 200m, 0.7sec, remains the largest margin of victory ever achieved in an Olympic sprint, by men or women. In the high jump Britain's Dorothy Tyler (née Odam) was second again, 12 years after taking the silver medal in Berlin. Both times she had cleared the same height as the winner.

Bob Mathias (USA) became the youngest ever male Olympic individual athletics champion when he won the decathlon aged 17yr 263 days. He retained

1948 MEDALS *Summer*

Country	G	S	B
United States	38	27	19
Sweden	16	11	17
France	10	6	13
Hungary	10	5	12
Italy	8	12	9
Finland	8	7	5
Turkey	6	4	2
Czechoslovakia	6	2	3
Switzerland	5	10	5
Denmark	5	7	8
Netherlands	5	2	9
Great Britain	3	14	6
Argentina	3	3	1
Australia	2	6	5
Belgium	2	2	3
Egypt	2	2	1
Mexico	2	1	2
South Africa	2	1	1
Norway	1	3	3
Jamaica	1	2	–
Austria	1	1	3
India	1	–	–
Peru	1	–	–
Yugoslavia	–	2	–
Canada	–	1	2
Portugal	–	1	1
Uruguay	–	1	1
Ceylon (now Sri Lanka)	–	1	–
Cuba	–	1	–
Spain	–	1	–
Trinidad	–	1	–
Korea	–	–	2
Panama	–	–	2
Brazil	–	–	1
Iran	–	–	1
Poland	–	–	1
Puerto Rico	–	–	1

the title in 1952, made a film of his life, and later was elected a US Congressman. Another athlete to catch the eye was Emil Zatopek (TCH), not so much by his easy win in the 10 000m but by his remarkable sprint over the last 300 metres as he just failed to win the 5000m. An American, Harrison Dillard, acknowledged as the world's best high hurdler, had fallen in the US trials and failed to make their team in his best event. In London he won his 'second-string' event, the 100m, and won another gold in the relay.

Two of the debuting countries made their marks early in the Games. Duncan White of Ceylon (now Sri Lanka) gained the only medal his country has ever

won with a silver in the 400m hurdles. Jamaica made an even bigger impact with a gold, two silvers and two other finalists in the 200, 400 and 800m. The marathon provided its usual drama when Etienne Gailly, a Belgian paratrooper, entered the stadium first but, exhausted, was passed by two runners before the tape.

An outstanding competitor in the modern pentathlon was Willie Grut of Sweden who won three disciplines of the five-sport event and placed fifth and eighth in the others to win by a large margin. He was the son of the designer of the 1912 Olympic stadium. South African boxer George Hunter not only won the light-heavyweight title but also the Val Barker Trophy as the best stylist in the whole competition. However, lack of experienced referees and judges resulted in much criticism of the boxing tournament. There were problems too at Herne Hill stadium where some of the cycling events finished in very poor light due to the lack of floodlighting.

There was an unfortunate turn of events in the equestrian competitions, where the team dressage contest was won by the Swedes. The following year, they were disqualified and their medals taken away when it was learned that one of their number, Gehnäll Persson, was not a commissioned officer as the rules then required. In fencing Ilona Elek (HUN) retained her 1936 title even though she was now over 41 years of age. Her sister Margit finished in sixth place. The 1932 champion, Ellen Müller-Preis (AUT) gained the bronze medal. An even more outstanding veteran was 40-year-old Heikki Savolainen, the famous Finnish gymnast, who in his fourth Olympics won his first gold medal, on the pommel horse.

The soccer gold medallists Sweden were involved in one of the strangest goals in the history of the sport in their semi-final against Denmark. The Swedish centre-forward Gunnar Nordahl, one of three brothers in the team, leapt into the Danish goalnet to avoid being offside during a Swedish attack. At the end of the move his inside-left headed the ball into the goal, where in the absence of the Danish keeper it was caught by Nordahl. Sweden went on to win the gold medal. Yachting witnessed the end of one long Olympic career when Ralph Craig, the 1912 double sprint champion, reappeared in the American yachting team. Although he carried the US flag in the opening ceremony he did not actually compete.

Torbay also saw the start of another exceptional career with the appearance of Durward Knowles, competing for Britain. He then competed in yachting events for the Bahamas in the next six Games and made it an eighth time in 1988. A rare happening at the yachting was the victory of father-son combination Paul and Hilary Smart (USA) in the Star class. At the Empire Pool, site of the swimming competitions, US competitors won 12 of the 15 events excluding water polo. One of the rare non-American champions was Greta Andersen (DEN) in the 100m freestyle; sixteen years later, she set a female record for swimming the English Channel. In diving, Vicki Draves (USA) won both titles, then a unique achievement.

The oldest gold medallist in London was the aforementioned Paul Smart in yachting, aged 56yr 212 days, and the youngest was Thelma Kalama (USA) in the swimming sprint relay for women, aged 17yr 135 days. Bob Mathias, the decathlon winner, was the youngest male champion, while the oldest female winner was fencer Ilona Elek (HUN), aged 41yr 77 days.

1952

VIth WINTER GAMES
Oslo, Norway
14–25 February

Attended by representatives of 22 countries, comprising 732 competitors, of which 109 were women.

These Games, held in Oslo, are the only Winter Olympics so far to be held in a Nordic country, even though Norway, Sweden and Finland between them have won 369 medals to date, including 123 golds. A feature of these

Games was the enormous crowds at all venues, including a record for any Olympic event at the ski jumping at Holmenkollen, estimated at 150 000. An innovation was the Olympic flame coming not from Olympia but from Morgedal in southern Norway, the home of Sondre Nordheim, the father of modern skiing. The last relay 'runner' who brought the flame into the Bislett Stadium was Eigil Nansen, the grandson of the renowned Polar explorer Fridtjof Nansen. The oath was taken by ski-jumper Torbjörn Falkanger. All entrants from Commonwealth countries wore black armbands as the opening day coincided with the funeral of Britain's King George VI. As King Haakon and the Crown Prince were in London for this, the Games were opened by

HRH Princess Ragnhild. Back in the Olympic fold were Germany and Japan, and for the first time in the Winter Games entries included Portugal and New Zealand.

Bad weather conditions necessitated the start of the women's giant slalom and the 2-man bob on the day before the opening ceremony. Of the three Alpine events, the giant slalom and downhill races were held some 120km from Oslo, at Norefjell. In the men's giant slalom Stein Eriksen (NOR) became the first ever winner of an Alpine skiing event to come from a Nordic country. This did not happen again until 1980.

The star of the Games was Hjalmar Andersen of the host country, winning three speed skating gold medals. The women's figure skating title

An historic moment: Stein Eriksen wins the giant slalom, the first Alpine event won by a Nordic skier.

went to Jeanette Altwegg for Britain's first skating gold medal since Madge Syers in 1908. Instead of turning professional, as did most of her predecessors and successors, she went to work at the famed village for orphan children, Pestalozzi in Switzerland. The men's title went to defending champion Dick Button (USA) with some of the most remarkable jumps ever seen in competition. Finishing sixth was Carlo Fassi (ITA), later to coach Olympic champions Peggy Fleming (USA), Dorothy Hamill (USA), John Curry (GBR) and Robin Cousins (GBR).

The basic running abilities required by cross-country skiers were highlighted in the Nordic skiing when the 18km gold medal was won by Hallgeir Brenden (NOR), who went on to win two national steeplechase titles; and in sixth place was his countryman Martin Stokken, who had finished fourth in the 10 000m track final in 1948. By competing again at Helsinki later in 1952, Stokken became one of the few men to compete in a Winter and Summer Games in the same year. For the first time there was a Nordic ski race for women, dominated by Finland with four of the first five places. Bandy, a distant relative of ice hockey, was played as a demonstration sport and won by Sweden.

1952 MEDALS *Winter*

Country	G	S	B
Norway	7	3	6
United States	4	6	1
Finland	3	4	2
Germany	3	2	2
Austria	2	4	2
Canada	1	–	1
Italy	1	–	1
Great Britain	1	–	–
Netherlands	–	3	–
Sweden	–	–	4
Switzerland	–	–	2
France	–	–	1
Hungary	–	–	1

The oldest gold medallist at Oslo was Franz Kemser in the German 4-man bob, aged 41yr 103 days; the youngest was slalom winner Andrea Mead-Lawrence (USA), aged 19yr 301 days. The youngest male winner was Robert Dickson (CAN) in ice hockey, aged 20yr 308 days, while the oldest female champion was Lydia Wideman (FIN) in the 10km cross-country, aged 31yr 282 days. The youngest medallist was skater Tenley Albright (USA) with a silver, aged 16yr 297 days. Albert Madörin (SUI) won a bronze in the 4-man bob, aged 46yr 342 days.

1952

XVth OLYMPIC GAMES
Helsinki, Finland
19 July–3 August

Attended by representatives of 69 countries, comprising 4925 competitors, of which 518 were women.

One of the greatest Olympian countries, Finland, finally hosted the Games. President Juho Paasikivi formally opened the Games in the smallest city ever to be the Olympic host, Helsinki having a population of only 367 000. There were two dramatic moments during the ceremony, first when a so-called 'Angel of Peace', an apparently mentally-deranged German girl in a flowing white robe, ran around part of the track. More appropriate to the occasion, though, was the moment when the last relay runner was due and the scoreboard indicated the first letter of his name. the stadium erupted to cheers as 55-year-old Paavo Nurmi, arguably the greatest distance runner the world has seen, ran a lap and lit the flame in the stadium. He

then passed the torch to 62-year-old Hannes Kolehmainen, who ascended the stadium tower by lift and lit another flame there.

After 40 years the Russians returned to the Olympics, now in the guise of the Soviet Union. Fears of a confrontation between them and the United States team proved unfounded as the competitors seemed to treat each other quite cordially, if somewhat coolly. Attending the Games for the first time were teams from the Bahamas, Gold Coast (now Ghana), Guatemala, Dutch Antilles, Hong Kong, Indonesia, Israel, Nigeria, Thailand, Vietnam and, for the only time ever, the Saar. Because mainland China had been invited, the Nationalist Chinese (Taiwan) had withdrawn. Although all the competitors marched together there were two Olympic villages; surprisingly, the IOC allowed the Soviet bloc to set up their own at Otaniemi, while everybody else was at Käpylä.

The athlete of these Games was the Czech runner Emil Zatopek who won an unprecedented triple of the 5000m, 10 000m and marathon. To crown his achievements, his wife Dana, born on the same day as Emil, also won a gold medal, in the javelin, within an hour of his 5000m victory. The outstanding female track athlete, though, was Australia's Marjorie Jackson, who set world records winning the 100m and 200m but dropped the baton when certain to win a third gold in the sprint relay. Incidentally, she retrieved the baton and finished in fifth place. In the winning American team was Barbara Jones who became the youngest ever track and field gold medallist, aged 15yr 123 days. However, the youngest gold medallist at Helsinki was French cox Bernard Malivoire

The legendary Paavo Nurmi brings the torch into the stadium in 1952, style as good as ever.

at 14yr 94 days in the pairs event.

Once again small nations did well, with Jamaican runners invincible over 400m and Josy Barthel causing the band some problems as they tried to find the anthem of his native Luxembourg when he scored an upset win in the 1500m. The 1948 100m sprint champion, Harrison Dillard (USA), was here back to his first love, winning the 110m hurdles and taking his fourth gold medal in the sprint relay. His teammate Horace Ashenfelter gained America's first win in a distance run since 1908 when he set an inaugural official world record for the 3000m steeplechase. The press had great fun with the fact that Ashenfelter, an FBI agent, was followed home by a Russian!

The Soviet Union's first ever Olympic gold medal was won by Nina Romashkova in the women's discus. Highly questionable disqualifications by blatantly biased judges marred the 10 000m track walk but did not stop the Swiss and Russian second and third place medallists literally running the last 30m to the line, outsprinting the judge who vainly tried to reach them to rule them out. The event was dropped from future Games. The winner of the high jump, Walt Davis (USA), was at 2.04m probably the tallest competitor ever to win an individual event at the Games.

In the swimming pool the Hungarians won four of the five events for women. Almost matching the Zatopeks were Éva Székely, who won the 200m breaststroke, and her husband Dezsö Gyarmati, a member of the victorious Hungarian water polo team four days later. Much media attention was gained by the 400m freestyle for men when the father of the winner, Jean Boiteux (FRA), jumped into the pool fully clothed to congratulate his son. In diving,

Chris Chataway (GBR) trips as Emil Zatopek (TCH) heads for victory over Alain Mimoun (FRA) and Herbert Schade (GER) in the 5000m. It was the Czech's second win of his fabulous triple.

the tiny (1.56m) Dr Sammy Lee, an American of Korean origin, became the first man to successfully defend a diving title, in this case the highboard. He later coached the next man to achieve this feat, Bob Webster in 1960 and 1964.

The gymnastics competitions were dominated by the Soviet teams, led by Viktor Chukarin, with four golds and two silvers, and his female counterpart Maria Gorokhovskaya, with two golds and five silvers. The Finnish veteran Dr Heikki Savolainen, who had taken the oath at the opening ceremony, gained a team bronze just two

The last leg of the Helsinki sprint relay and Marjorie Jackson of Australia fails to take the baton from Winsome Cripps.

1952 MEDALS *Summer*

Country	G	S	B
United States	40	19	17
Soviet Union	22	30	19
Hungary	16	10	16
Sweden	12	13	10
Italy	8	9	4
Czechoslovakia	7	3	3
France	6	6	6
Finland	6	3	13
Australia	6	2	3
Norway	3	2	–
Switzerland	2	6	6
South Africa	2	4	4
Jamaica	2	3	–
Belgium	2	2	–
Denmark	2	1	3
Turkey	2	–	1
Japan	1	6	2
Great Britain	1	2	8
Argentina	1	2	2
Poland	1	2	1
Canada	1	2	–
Yugoslavia	1	2	–
Romania	1	1	2
Brazil	1	–	2
New Zealand	1	–	2
India	1	–	1
Luxembourg	1	–	–
Germany	–	7	17
Netherlands	–	5	–
Iran	–	3	4
Chile	–	2	–
Austria	–	1	1
Lebanon	–	1	1
Ireland	–	1	–
Mexico	–	1	–
Spain	–	1	–
Korea	–	–	2
Trinidad	–	–	2
Uruguay	–	–	2
Bulgaria	–	–	1
Egypt	–	–	1
Portugal	–	–	1
Venezuela	–	–	1

months short of his 45th birthday. It was the fifth consecutive Games at which he had won a medal. Other veterans doing well included Ilona Elek (HUN), who added a silver to her two fencing golds at the age of 45yr 41 days, and André Jousseaume (FRA) with an individual bronze medal in the dressage two days after his 58th birthday and 20 years after his gold medal at Los Angeles. In all he finished in the first five positions in five Games.

Another great sportsman, Károly Takács (HUN), won the rapid-fire pistol for the second time. Before the war he had won the European title as a right-handed shooter, but in 1938 he had lost his right hand when a grenade he was holding exploded. He painstakingly taught himself to shoot with his left and won two Olympic titles. On a less uplifting note there was the disqualification of Ingemar Johansson (SWE) in the heavyweight boxing final for 'not trying'. His silver medal was withheld for 14 years. In 1959 he won the world professional title from the 1952 Olympic middleweight champion Floyd Patterson (USA).

The oldest gold medallist at these Games was Everard Endt

(USA) in the 6m yachting, aged 59yr 112 days. The youngest male and female champions were the aforementioned Bernard Malivoire and Barbara Jones. The oldest female winner was Sylvi Saimo (FIN) in the 500m kayak event, aged 37yr 260 days. At the end of the Games a record 43 countries had won medals in Helsinki, and it was announced that Avery Brundage (USA) had taken over the Presidency of the IOC from the retiring Sigfrid Edström.

1956

VIIth WINTER GAMES
Cortina d'Ampezzo, Italy
26 January–5 February

Attended by representatives of 32 countries, comprising 819 competitors, of which 132 were women.

Most of the money spent on these Games came from the Italian Soccer Pools, but despite excellent facilities there were still problems with the weather. Once again snow needed to be 'imported' for some venues. The President of Italy, Giovanni Gronchi, formally opened the Games. Giuliana Chenal-Minuzzo, who won the 1952 bronze medal in downhill skiing, became the first woman in Olympic history to pronounce the oath on behalf of all the competitors. The last runner in the torch relay, speed skater Guido Caroli, fell as he completed a circuit of the arena but happily the flame did not go out. The entry of the Soviet Union provided the first Russian competitors in Olympic 'Winter' events since 1908. These were the first Winter Games to be televised, which undoubtedly contributed to there being a smaller number of spectators than previously.

Most attention was gained by the Austrian plumber Toni Sailer who gained a 'grand slam' of all three Alpine titles – downhill, slalom and giant slalom – winning in treacherous conditions by outstanding margins of 3.5sec, 4.0sec and 6.2sec respectively. Second in the slalom was Asia's first Winter medallist, Chiharu Igaya (JPN), an American college student. He had to wait anxiously while the jury investigated an unsubstantiated claim by Sweden and the United States that he had missed a gate. Madeleine Berthod (SUI) won the women's downhill by a (still) record margin of 4.7sec.

The most medals won at Cortina were by Sixten Jernberg (SWE) with one gold, two silvers and a bronze in Nordic skiing. Hallgeir Brenden (NOR) successfully defended his 1952 title, the distance now reduced from 18km to 15km, the only man ever to do so at cross-country skiing. Using a new style, the Finns dominated the ski jumping; and the Norwegians, who had won 15 of the 18 medals available in the sport since 1924, failed to place in the first six. Though Germany competed as a single team, the jumping bronze, won by Harry Glass, is claimed by the GDR as its first Olympic medal.

The speed skating surface on Lake Misurina, at an altitude of 1755m, was considered to be the fastest ever and witnessed a wholesale attack on the record book. The winner of the 500m title, Yevgeniy Grishin (URS), had been a member of the Soviet cycling team in Helsinki. In figure skating, America's Hayes (gold) and David (bronze) Jenkins were the first brothers to win medals in the same skating event. Their teammate, women's champion Tenley Albright, had been a victim of polio as a child.

A member of the winning

1956 MEDALS *Winter*

Country	G	S	B
Soviet Union	7	3	6
Austria	4	3	4
Finland	3	3	1
Switzerland	3	2	1
Sweden	2	4	4
United States	2	3	2
Norway	2	1	1
Italy	1	2	–
Germany	1	–	1
Canada	–	1	2
Japan	–	1	–
Hungary	–	–	1
Poland	–	–	1

Italian 2-man bob, Giacomo Conti, at 47yr 216 days was the oldest gold medallist at Cortina. The youngest champion was Elisabeth Schwarz (AUT) in pairs skating, aged 19yr 260 days. The youngest male winner was Toni Sailer (AUT) in the giant slalom, aged 20yr 73 days, and the oldest female champion was Siiri Rantanen (FIN) in the cross-country relay, aged 31yr 49 days. The youngest medallist was skater Ingrid Wendl (AUT) with a bronze, aged 15yr 260 days.

The Soviet competitors won a total of 16 medals to head the unofficial medals table – a position they were rarely to lose in future Winter Games.

1956

XVIth OLYMPIC GAMES
Stockholm, Sweden,
10–17 June
Melbourne, Australia,
22 November–8 December

Stockholm was attended by representatives of 29 countries, comprising 158 competitors, of which 13 were women; Melbourne by representatives of 67 countries, comprising 3184 competitors, of which 371 were women.

In 1949 the IOC had decided on Melbourne as the Olympic venue by only one vote, and they were disquieted, to say the least, by first the apparent tardi-

The opening of the Equestrian Games at Stockholm in 1956, Pat Smythe with the British team in the foreground.

ness in finishing facilities, and second the inability of the Australians to hold the equestrian events. This was due to their stringent animal quarantine laws.

Thus for the first and only time, contrary to the Olympic Charter, a sport was detached from the main Games and held elsewhere, in Stockholm. Except for the cross-country section of the three-day event, the venue was the 1912 Olympic Stadium. The host country won three of the six titles, but there was strong criticism and accusations of chauvinism by the judges in the dressage competition. Furthermore, the aforementioned cross-country was thought to be too dangerous in the existing wet conditions.

The Games proper, the only celebration so far in the Southern Hemisphere, opened in Melbourne under a cloud of international ill-will, occasioned by the Soviet invasion of Hungary and the Franco-British military intervention in the Suez Canal dispute. The Netherlands, Spain and Switzerland withdrew because of the former, and Egypt and Lebanon because of the latter. This time mainland China withdrew because of the presence of Taiwan. Perhaps surprisingly, the Hungarians did compete, and with good effect. West and East Germany entered a combined team and continued to do so until after 1964.

In addition to Taiwan, Olympic debuts were made by teams from Ethiopia, Fiji, Kenya, Liberia, Uganda, Malaya and North Borneo (the latter two now combined as Malaysia).

Cambodia's appearance in the Stockholm events was its first Olympic participation. HRH The Duke of Edinburgh opened the Games at the Melbourne Cricket Ground, the main venue. The final torch-bearer was a 19-year-old Australian miler, Ron Clarke, destined to be one of the world's greatest runners.

The distance runs in Melbourne were dominated by the Soviet sailor Vladimir Kuts, with record-breaking victories at 5000m and 10000m. Ireland won its first gold medal since 1932 as Ronnie Delany took the 1500m with an exceptionally fast last 300m. In the sprints both Bobby-Joe Morrow (USA) and Betty Cuthbert (AUS) gained three gold medals, including the relays. Teamed with Cuthbert in the 4 × 100m

Al Oerter (USA) at the start of his marvellous Olympic career at Melbourne in 1956. He won this and the next three discus titles to set a unique record.

1956 MEDALS *Summer*

Country	G	S	B
Soviet Union	37	29	32
United States	32	25	17
Australia	13	8	14
Hungary	9	10	7
Italy	8	8	9
Sweden	8	5	6
Germany	6	13	7
Great Britain	6	7	11
Romania	5	3	5
Japan	4	10	5
France	4	4	6
Turkey	3	2	2
Finland	3	1	11
Iran	2	2	1
Canada	2	1	3
New Zealand	2	–	–
Poland	1	4	4
Czechoslovakia	1	4	1
Bulgaria	1	3	1
Denmark	1	2	1
Ireland	1	1	3
Norway	1	–	2
Mexico	1	–	1
Brazil	1	–	–
India	1	–	–
Yugoslavia	–	3	–
Chile	–	2	2
Belgium	–	2	–
Argentina	–	1	1
Korea	–	1	1
Iceland	–	1	–
Pakistan	–	1	–
South Africa	–	–	4
Austria	–	–	2
Bahamas	–	–	1
Greece	–	–	1
Switzerland	–	–	1
Uruguay	–	–	1

Australia's Murray Rose followed up his great performance in 1956 by winning the 1960 400m freestyle (above).

was Shirley de la Hunty (née Strickland), who ended her three-Games career with an unbeaten total of seven medals (three golds, one silver, three bronze). A photo-finish picture, which was not unearthed until many years after the event, indicates that she also finished third, not fourth, in the 200m in 1948. She made no official claim and the result remains as it was.

After placing second to Emil Zatopek in three Olympic races since 1948, Frenchman Alain Mimoun finally beat him into sixth place, by taking the marathon – the oldest man to do so at only a month short of his 36th birthday. The 50km walk was won by Norman Read, representing his adopted country,

New Zealand. As a former English junior mile walk champion, Read had watched the 1952 Games as a spectator (sitting next to the author).

Another English-born competitor, Murray Rose (AUS), was the first male swimmer to win two individual freestyle events since 1924. He also won a third gold medal in the relay. Pat McCormick (USA) achieved a unique 'double double' by retaining both her diving titles from Helsinki. Boxing too had its record-breaker when László Papp, doing his bit to raise Hungarian spirits, gained an unprecedented third gold medal.

It was no surprise when bad feelings erupted in the water polo semi-final between Hungary and the Soviet Union. By a nice touch of irony the referee was from the perennially neutral Sweden. With Hungary leading 4–0 he ended the game, as it had degenerated into a 'boxing match under water'. However, by beating Yugoslavia in the soccer final on the last day, 8 December, the Soviet

Union made history as winners of the latest gold medal ever won in an Olympic year.

John Kelly Jr, the son of the 1920 gold medallist, won a bronze in the single sculls as Vyacheslav Ivanov (URS) gained the first of his record three consecutive titles. At the shooting range, Gerald Ouellette (CAN) won the prone small-bore rifle competition with a world record 'maximum' of 600, only to have the record, but not the gold medal, disallowed because the range was found to be 1.5m short of the international distance of 50m.

The oldest gold medallist in the Summer Games was Henri St Cyr (SWE) in dressage, aged 54yr 93 days, while the youngest was Sandra Morgan (AUS) in the 4 × 100m freestyle relay, aged 14yr 183 days. The youngest male winner was Murray Rose (AUS), aged 17yr 332 days, while the oldest female champion was Hungarian gymnast Ágnes Keleti at 35yr 171 days. Although not even a medallist, Gunhild Larking, a beautiful

Swedish high jumper, undoubtedly had more photographs taken of her than any of the more successful competitors. A member of the combined Germany team, Wolfgang Behrendt, winner of the boxing bantamweight title, was the GDR's first Summer gold medallist.

At the closing ceremony for the first time the athletes entered *en masse*, signifying the friendship of the Games. The idea for this had come from an Australian-born Chinese boy, John Wing, in a letter to the chairman of the organising committee, the Hon WS Kent-Hughes.

A happy postscript to these Games occurred in Prague in March 1957 when the American hammer winner, Harold Connolly, married Olga Fikotova, the Czech Olympic discus champion. The best man at this 'Olympic' wedding was, appropriately, Emil Zatopek.

1960

VIIIth WINTER GAMES
Squaw Valley, USA
18–28 February

Attended by representatives of 30 countries, comprising 665 competitors, of which 144 were women.

When the IOC voted narrowly, 32–30, to give these Games to Squaw Valley, USA, instead of Innsbruck, virtually nothing existed at the site. Due to the efforts of Alexander Cushing, who owned most of the area, it became the first purpose-built Winter Games venue. Despite initial delays, everything was ready for the official opening, under the direction of Walt Disney. The formal opening was by Richard Nixon, then Vice-President of the United States. The last relay runner was Ken

Henry, the 500m speed skating champion of 1952, and the oath was taken by figure skater Carol Heiss, who went on to win the women's title.

There were a number of protests and problems. Bobsledding was dropped as the organisers would not accept the cost of building a run for what they considered would be a small entry. Artificial obstacles were built into the downhill runs to make them more difficult, and concern was expressed over the altitude (over 1900m) at which the Nordic skiing events were held. East and West Germany competed as one entity, with agreement reached whereby the popular theme from Beethoven's Ninth Symphony would be played for any victory ceremonies instead of their respective national anthems. A team from South Africa competed for the first and only time in the Winter Games as they were banned thereafter. The biathlon and speed skating for women made Olympic debuts, the biathlon being the successor to the military patrol which had been a demonstration event on four previous occasions.

The speed skating times in general were excellent, with Knut Johannesen (NOR) beating the 10000m world record by 46.0sec, the greatest margin achieved this century. Yevgeniy Grishin (URS) equalled his own world mark to become the first man to successfully defend the 500m title. Helga Haase (GER) became the first ever women's Olympic champion in speed skating when she won the 500m. In figure skating David Jenkins (USA) kept the men's title in the family – his brother Hayes had won in 1956 – and made the family even more Olympian by marrying Squaw Valley's women's champion Carol Heiss two months later.

1960 MEDALS *Winter*

Country	G	S	B
Soviet Union	7	5	9
Germany	4	3	1
United States	3	4	3
Norway	3	3	–
Sweden	3	2	2
Finland	2	3	3
Canada	2	1	1
Switzerland	2	–	–
Austria	1	2	3
France	1	–	2
Netherlands	–	1	1
Poland	–	1	1
Czechoslovakia	–	1	–
Italy	–	–	1

There was a first in the Nordic Combination when George Thoma, a German postman from the Black Forest who was often forced to deliver mail on skis in bad weather, achieved the first victory by a non-Scandinavian in the sport. The winner of the inaugural biathlon, Klas Lestander (SWE), was only 15th in the cross-country segment of the contest but scored a maximum possible 20 in the shooting. The Soviet Union's women dominated their 10000m race, taking the first four places, but lost the relay, a virtual certainty, when their first girl fell and broke a ski. A protest was made against the first Swedish girl, who was accused of deliberate fouling, but it was not upheld.

In Alpine skiing, metallic skis were used in the Games for the first time. The medals were more widespread than usual, with no skier winning more than one event and only Penny Pitou (USA) winning more than one medal, with two silvers. The outstanding competitor was Anne Heggtveit (CAN), who won the women's slalom by a margin of 3.3sec, only ever bettered by the 1936 combination winner, Christl Cranz (GER).

The oldest gold medallist was Veikko Hakulinen (FIN) in the Nordic relay, aged 35yr 52 days, and the youngest Heidi Biebl (GER), the downhill champion just three days past her 19th birthday. The youngest male champion was American ice hockey player Thomas Williams, aged 19yr 317 days. The oldest female gold medallist was Sonja Ruthström (SWE) in the Nordic relay, aged 29yr 94 days. The youngest medallist was skier Traudl Hecher (AUT) with a downhill bronze, aged 16yr 145 days.

1960

XVIIth OLYMPIC GAMES
Rome, Italy
5 August–11 September

Attended by representatives of 83 countries, comprising 5346 competitors, of which 610 were women.

Rome had just missed out in 1908, but over fifty years on, the Games finally went to the Eternal City, home of the Emperor Theodosius who had ended the Ancient Games 1567 years before. A number of old Roman sites were utilised as well as a brand-new 100 000 capacity stadium. The Baths of Caracalla housed the gymnastics and the Basilica di Massenzio held the wrestling competitions. The marathon began at the Capitol Hill and finished on the Appian Way, near the Arch of Constantine. It was the first time that an Olympic marathon had not started or finished in the main Olympic stadium. Yachting was held in the Bay of Naples under the shadow of Mount Vesuvius. The Games were opened by the President of Italy, Giovanni Gronchi, and the oath was taken by the 1948 discus champion Adolfo Consolini. Morocco, Tunisia, Sudan and San Marino made their debuts. Nationalist China protested, but competed, when they were told by the IOC to appear under the name of Taiwan and not China. These Games were the first to have worldwide television coverage.

The extreme heat undoubtedly caused upsets but did nothing to hinder the successes of the Australasians in the middle-distance running events. Peter Snell (NZL) won the 800m, Herb Elliott (AUS) won the 1500m by a record margin of 2.8sec in world record time, and Murray Halberg (NZL), handicapped by a withered arm, won the 5000m. An unknown runner, Abebe Bikila, won the marathon barefoot and signalled the entry of Ethiopia on to the world distance running scene. The team from Taiwan were cheered up somewhat when their decathlete Yang

Herb Elliott (AUS) wins the 1500m in 1960 by a remarkable margin (2.8sec) over the second runner and breaks his own world record, to crown a remarkable career.

1960 MEDALS *Summer*

Country	G	S	B
Soviet Union	43	29	31
United States	34	21	16
Italy	13	10	13
Germany	12	19	11
Australia	8	8	6
Turkey	7	2	–
Hungary	6	8	7
Japan	4	7	7
Poland	4	6	11
Czechoslovakia	3	2	3
Romania	3	1	6
Great Britain	2	6	12
Denmark	2	3	1
New Zealand	2	–	1
Bulgaria	1	3	3
Sweden	1	2	3
Finland	1	1	3
Austria	1	1	–
Yugoslavia	1	1	–
Pakistan	1	–	1
Ethiopia	1	–	–
Greece	1	–	–
Norway	1	–	–
Switzerland	–	3	3
France	–	2	3
Belgium	–	2	2
Iran	–	1	3
Netherlands	–	1	2
South Africa	–	1	2
Argentina	–	1	1
Egypt (UAR)	–	1	1
Canada	–	1	–
Ghana	–	1	–
India	–	1	–
Morocco	–	1	–
Portugal	–	1	–
Singapore	–	1	–
Taiwan (Taipei)	–	1	–
Brazil	–	–	2
Jamaica*	–	–	2
Barbados*	–	–	1
Iraq	–	–	1
Mexico	–	–	1
Spain	–	–	1
Venezuela	–	–	1

*Double-counted, part of West Indies team

Cassius Clay (later Muhammad Ali) wins the light-heavyweight boxing title at Rome. The silver medallist (right) is Zbigniew Pietrzykowski (POL) with bronze medals to Tony Madigan (AUS) and Giulio Saraudi (ITA).

Chuan-Kwang had a tremendous battle with Rafer Johnson (USA), a teammate at the University of Southern California, and only narrowly lost the gold medal. The stadium was captivated by sprinter Wilma Rudolph (USA), who won three gold medals – she was one of 19 children and had suffered from polio as a child. Sisters Irina and Tamara Press (URS) won the 80m hurdles and shot respectively, while their teammate Ludmila Shevtsova won the first 800m event for women since 1928.

In the swimming pool the only one of the fifteen events not won by either Australia or the United States went to Anita Lonsbrough (GBR). The outstanding swimmer was America's Christine von Saltza, a descendant of Prussian/Swedish nobility, with three golds and a silver. The standard was very high, with Olympic records broken in every event. An unfortunate incident occurred in the men's 100m freestyle, though, when Lance Larson (USA) was timed at 0.1sec faster than John Devitt (AUS) but was placed second to him despite slow-motion film indicating that the American was first. In future Games full electronic timing was used.

Only the second royal gold medal in Olympic history was won by Crown Prince Constantine (later King Constantine II of Greece) in the Dragon class yachting. It is reported that he still received the traditional winner's ducking, being pushed into the water by his mother, Queen Frederika. In the Flying Dutchman class Peder Lunde Jr (NOR) became the third generation of his family to win a medal, equalling his grandfather's gold of 1924 but going one better than his mother and father in 1952. Paul Elvström (DEN) won his fourth consecutive individual gold medal in dinghy sailing, the first sportsman from any sport to achieve this distinction. The canoeing, on Lake Albano, had a particularly distinguished spectator as the Pope apparently watched some of the competitions from his summer palace. In boxing the light-welterweight silver medallist Clement 'Ike' Quartey (GHA) was the first black African to win an Olympic medal.

The most medals won in Rome were the seven (4 gold, 2 silver, 1 bronze) gained by gymnast Boris Shakhlin (URS). Aladár Gerevich (HUN), at 50yr 178 days the oldest champion in Rome, won his sixth team sabre gold medal in as many Games – a feat unsurpassed by any other Olympic competitor. In the foil and épée events, Edoardo Mangiarotti (ITA) brought his total of fencing medals to a record 13 (6 gold, 5 silver, 2 bronze) in 5 Games (1936–60).

The light-heavyweight boxing title went to Cassius Clay (USA), who as Muhammad Ali amassed the greatest amount ever earned by a sportsman, $68 million. He became a professional after the Games. In soccer Yugoslavia won the gold medal after three consecutive runner-up placings. The first loss suffered by India in Olympic hockey since they entered the competition in 1928 occurred when Pakistan beat them 1–0 in the final.

The youngest gold medallist was Carolyn Wood (USA) in the freestyle relay, aged 14yr 260 days. The oldest female winner was discus champion Nina Ponomaryeva (URS) at 31yr 131 days. (She had achieved earlier fame, or notoriety, in 1956 when it was alleged that she stole hats from an Oxford Street store while on a trip to London for an international match, which was thereby cancelled.) The youngest male gold medallist in Rome was Klaus Zerta, cox to the German pairs, aged 14yr 283 days.

A tragic note was struck by the collapse and death of cyclist Knut Jensen (DEN), originally diagnosed as due to the excessive heat but later revealed as due to a drug overdose. By the end of the Games, a then record 44 countries had shared in the medals.

1964

IXth WINTER GAMES
Innsbruck, Austria
29 January–9 February
Attended by representatives of 36 countries, comprising 1093 competitors, of which 200 were women.

Awarded to Innsbruck in 1959, these Games were the most successful yet with over a million spectators attending a record 34 events, among which were lugeing and a second ski jump. However, weather again was a problem and snow had to be manhandled to some venues by the Austrian Army. During practice before the Games began there were two tragic deaths, of a British tobogganist and an Australian skier.

The official opening by the Austrian President, Dr Adolf Schärf, took place at the Bergisel ski jump in front of 60 000 people. The last relay runner, who lit the flame, was skier Joseph Rieder and the oath was taken by a bobsledder, Paul Aste. Mongolia and India competed for the first time, while Korea was split into North and South teams. South Africa was now banned from the Olympics. An innovation was the use of computers officially to aid judging as well as to provide electronic timing.

The Games were dominated by the Soviet Union and for the first and only time ever Switzerland failed to gain a single medal. Lydia Skoblikova (URS), a teacher from Siberia, won all four women's speed skating events to give her a total of six gold medals in two Games, a

Oleg Protopopov and his wife Ludmila Belousova of the Soviet Union winning the first of their pairs titles.

1964 MEDALS *Winter*

Country	G	S	B
Soviet Union	11	8	6
Austria	4	5	3
Norway	3	6	6
Finland	3	4	3
France	3	4	–
Sweden	3	3	1
Germany	3	2	3
United States	1	2	4
Canada	1	1	1
Netherlands	1	1	–
Great Britain	1	–	–
Italy	–	1	3
North Korea (PRK)	–	1	–
Czechoslovakia	–	–	1

record for the sport. The Soviet husband and wife skating pair, Ludmila Belousova and Oleg Protopopov, brought a new concept, classical ballet, to the sport. The silver medal went for the second consecutive occasion to Marika Kilius and Hansjürgen Bäumler (GER), but two years later they were disquali-fied owing to professional activities which came to light. The women's individual skating title went to Sjoukje Dijkstra; it was Holland's first ever Winter Games gold medal.

The first sisters to win gold medals at the same Games were Marielle and Christine Goitschel (FRA) who swapped first and second places in the Alpine slalom events. The re-introduced bobsleigh events were won, for the first time, by countries which did not possess bob runs of their own – the victory by Tony Nash and Robin Dixon (GBR) in the 2-man bob was also the first by a 'lowland' country and owed much to a replacement bolt supplied by an Italian adversary, Eugenio Monti. He was later awarded the Pierre de Coubertin Fair Play Trophy for this action. Klaudia Boyarskikh (URS) won three gold medals in Nordic skiing, while Sixten Jernberg (SWE) brought his total to a record nine medals in three Games. A demonstration of German cur-ling was also held.

The oldest gold medallist was Sixten Jernberg, winning his fourth gold medal two days after his 35th birthday. The youngest was Manfred Stengl (AUT), aged 17yr 310 days, in the 2-man luge, with Marielle Goitschel (FRA) in the giant slalom the youngest female winner, aged 18yr 128 days. The oldest female champion was Alevtina Koltschina (URS) in the Nordic relay, four days short of her 34th birthday. Scott Allen (USA) was the youngest medallist with his bronze in the men's figure skating just two days short of his 15th birthday, while the oldest was Eugenio Monti (ITA), aged 36yr 15 days.

Tony Nash and Robin Dixon give Britain its only gold medal ever in bobsledding at Innsbruck in 1964.

1964

XVIIIth OLYMPIC GAMES
Tokyo, Japan
10–24 October

Attended by representatives of 93 countries, comprising 5140 competitors, of which 683 were women.

Asia's first Games saw large crowds and a tremendous assault on the record books. Vast sums, estimated to be as much as $3 billion, were spent not only on stadia but also on transport facilities. Teams from 14 countries made their first appearance at the Games, but South Africa no longer received an invitation. Also missing were Indonesia and North Korea, whose athletes, having competed in the previous year's unsanctioned GANEFO Games (Games of the New Emergent Forces), were banned. Emperor Hirohito performed the formal opening, and the flame was brought into the stadium by a young runner who had been born near Hiroshima on the day that the atom bomb was dropped there in 1945. The Olympic flag was raised to the top of a flagpole which measured 15.21m, the distance reached in the triple jump by Mikio Oda in 1928 when he won Japan's first Olympic gold medal.

The growth of the Games was highlighted by distance runner Ron Clarke's remark after failing to gain the gold medal over 10000m. Having dropped all the known opposition he looked over his shoulder and saw 'an Ethiopian, a North African Arab and an American Indian'. This last, Billy Mills, a part-Sioux Indian Marine officer, was America's first ever winner at the distance. In the marathon, Bikila (ETH) – this time wearing shoes – became the first man to retain the title, and Peter Snell (NZL) achieved the rare 800/1500m double.

The winner of the 100m, Bob Hayes, ran a phenomenal last leg in the 4 × 100m relay to regain the title that the USA had

Bob Hayes (702) wins the 100m from Enrique Figuerola (80) and Harry Jerome (56) in the first eight-man Olympic sprint final.

lost in Rome for the first time in 40 years. There is a story told that one of the beaten teams decried the US team to the effect that all they had was Hayes. This was met by the now famous rejoinder, 'Man, that's all we needed.' Britain won its first ever gold in women's athletics when Mary Rand took the long jump – her room-mate Ann Packer added the 800m gold for good measure.

At the much-admired pool Australia and the United States won all the titles bar one. That was the women's 200m breaststroke, the event which had also prevented a clean sweep by the two swimming superpowers in Rome. Here it was won by Galina Prozumenshchikova (later Stepanova), the Soviet Union's first ever swimming gold medallist – she won a further two silver and two bronze at the next two Games. Don

1964 MEDALS *Summer*

Country	G	S	B
United States	36	26	28
Soviet Union	30	31	35
Japan	16	5	8
Germany	10	22	18
Italy	10	10	7
Hungary	10	7	5
Poland	7	6	10
Australia	6	2	10
Czechoslovakia	5	6	3
Great Britain	4	12	2
Bulgaria	3	5	2
Finland	3	–	2
New Zealand	3	–	2
Romania	2	4	6
Netherlands	2	4	4
Turkey	2	3	1
Sweden	2	2	4
Denmark	2	1	3
Yugoslavia	2	1	2
Belgium	2	–	1
France	1	8	6
Canada	1	2	1
Switzerland	1	2	1
Bahamas	1	–	–
Ethiopia	1	–	–
India	1	–	–
Korea	–	2	1
Trinidad	–	1	2
Tunisia	–	1	1
Argentina	–	1	–
Cuba	–	1	–
Pakistan	–	1	–
Philippines	–	1	–
Iran	–	–	2
Brazil	–	–	1
Ghana	–	–	1
Ireland	–	–	1
Kenya	–	–	1
Mexico	–	–	1
Nigeria	–	–	1
Uruguay	–	–	1

Schollander (USA) became the first swimmer to win four golds in a single Games, and close behind him came Sharon Stouder (USA) with three golds and a silver in the women's events. Australia's Dawn Fraser, just past her 27th birthday, won her third consecutive 100m title, a unique achievement in swimming, and added a relay silver to take her total haul to eight medals, a record for a female swimmer.

Another competitor to complete a unique triple was Soviet rower Vyacheslav Ivanov by winning the single sculls once again. An unusual thing occurred in the eights where the cox of the winning American crew, Robert Zimonyi, aged 46, had been cox of the third-placed Hungarian pairs in 1948. In water polo the Hungarian veteran Deszö Gyarmati won his third gold medal, his fifth medal in as many Games.

The most medals were won by gymnast Larissa Latynina (URS) with two golds, two silvers and two bronzes. Her teammate Boris Shakhlin brought his total of golds since 1956 to seven, of which a record six were in individual events. In weightlifting, Norbert Schemansky (USA) won a bronze to add to his previous gold, silver and bronze since 1948, giving him a record for his sport of four medals. Wrestler Imre Polyák (HUN) finally won gold in his fourth Games after an unprecedented three silvers.

There were two new sports, volleyball and judo, the latter having been included at the express wish of the host country. It was considered to be a Japanese monopoly and the whole country suffered a terrible shock when the Open class title went to the giant (1.98m) Dutchman Anton Geesink. Leading the United States basketball team to its sixth consecutive victory was Bill Bradley, later to become a member of the US Senate.

The oldest gold medallist in Tokyo was the Australian 5.5m yachtsman William Northam, aged 59yr 23 days, and the youngest was swimmer 'Pokey' Watson (USA), aged 14yr 96 days, in the freestyle relay. The oldest female winner was Katalin Juhász-Nagy (HUN), a member of the foil team, at 31yr 328 days, while the youngest male champion was swimmer Richard Roth (USA) in the 400m medley, 18 days past his 17th birthday.

1968

Xth WINTER GAMES
Grenoble, France
6–18 February

Attended by representatives of 37 countries, comprising 1293 competitors, of which 228 were women.

There were complaints that venues at Grenoble were very widespread, with some 40km distant, but the new 12 000-seat indoor ice stadium delighted everyone. For the first time sex tests for female competitors were held. The political split between East and West Germany was finally acknowledged and separate teams accepted. Morocco made its debut, and the official opening was performed by the President of France, Charles de Gaulle. The last relay runner was Alain Calmat, the 1964 skating silver medallist, and the oath taken by Leo Lacroix, a 1964 skiing silver medal winner.

The IOC attempted to control the exploitation of the Games by commercial interests by banning the use of trade names on competitors' equipment, but following the threat of a withdrawal by some leading skiers, who relied very heavily on ski company sponsorship, it was finally agreed that they need only remove the equipment before appearing in photographs or on television.

The undoubted star of these Games was Jean-Claude Killy (FRA), who emulated Toni Sailer's 1956 record by winning all three Alpine skiing events. However, in the last of the three, the slalom, Karl Schranz (AUT) claimed that in his second-round run he had been distracted by a policeman cutting across the course in front of him. He was allowed another run, which he accomplished in a

Great Austrian skiers Alfred Matt, Herbert Huber, Toni Sailer and Karl Schranz congratulate Jean-Claude Killy (FRA).

faster time to become the overall winner. Then it was decided that on his first attempt he had already missed a gate before the policeman incident, and his rerun was disqualified. (He was to be even more unlucky four years later.) The best of the women Alpinists was Canada's Nancy Greene with a gold in the giant slalom and a silver in the slalom. The latter was won by Marielle Goitschel (FRA) to keep the title in the family – her sister had won in 1964.

1968 MEDALS *Winter*

Country	G	S	B
Norway	6	6	2
Soviet Union	5	5	3
France	4	3	2
Italy	4	–	–
Austria	3	4	4
Netherlands	3	3	3
Sweden	3	2	3
Germany (FRG)	2	2	3
United States	1	5	1
Finland	1	2	2
GDR	1	2	2
Czechoslovakia	1	2	1
Canada	1	1	1
Switzerland	–	2	4
Romania	–	–	1

The most successful Nordic skier was Toini Gustafsson (SWE) with two gold medals and a silver in the women's events. By winning the 30km race, Franco Nones (ITA) became the first ever non-Scandinavian winner in Nordic skiing, and another shock to Scandinavian sensibilities occurred in the two jumps and the combination event, when they won only a single bronze from the nine medals available. Yet another upset came in the women's luge, where the GDR girls, in first, second and fourth places, were disqualified for illegally heating their sled runners.

The bob run at Alpe d'Huez, which was badly sited and considered to be very dangerous, was the scene of total triumph for the 'good sport' of Innsbruck four years previously, Eugenio Monti. The Italian, nine times a world champion bobsledder, won both Olympic gold medals. In the 2-man event the total times after four runs for Monti's bob and that of the Germans were equal. The tie was decided in the Italians' favour as they had the fastest single run. Aged 40yr 24 days, Monti was the oldest gold medallist at Grenoble.

The youngest champion was skater Peggy Fleming (USA), aged 19yr 198 days. The youngest male gold medallist was Wolfgang Schwarz, winning Austria's first skating title since 1936 aged 20yr 155 days. Ludmila and Oleg Protopopov (URS) retained their pairs title, with Ludmila the oldest female champion at 32yr 84 days. In 26th place in the men's figure skating was Jan Hoffmann, at 12yr 110 days the youngest ever male competitor in the Olympic Winter Games. Twelve years later he won the silver medal. The oldest female medallist was Nordic skier Alevtina Koltschina (URS) with a bronze 5 days past her 38th birthday.

For the only time to date no speed skater gained more than one victory. The women's 500m was reminiscent of the men's event of 1948 and 1964 as three women tied for the silver medal.

Making this occasion unique was the fact that all three of them were from the same country, the United States. Norway topped the medal table – but for the last time.

1968

XIXth OLYMPIC GAMES
Mexico City, Mexico
12–27 October

Attended by representatives of 112 countries, comprising 5530 competitors, of which 781 were women.

From 1963, when these Games were awarded to Mexico City, there was a gradually increasing furore about the effects of its altitude, 2240m above sea level, on competitors in events which required endurance. Some medical authorities even forecast

possible deaths. This extreme view was, thankfully, overly pessimistic, but many cases of severe exhaustion occurred. When Australian distance runner Ron Clarke developed serious heart problems in 1981, there was speculation that his condition had been aggravated by his efforts in Mexico City in 1968.

Certainly standards were low in events which required over three minutes of continuous effort. However, the same conditions contributed to some startling performances in the 'explosive' events. Outstanding was the 8.90m (29ft 2½in) long jump by Bob Beamon (USA) – a performance of 21st-century quality. At the time of writing, some 22 years later, the world records set in the long jump and 4 × 400m relay at Mexico City still stand.

The thin air was not the only

complaint raised prior to these Games. Some felt that the traditional 'mañana' attitude attributed to the Mexicans would result in incomplete facilities. In fact all were ready in good time. There was, however, a threat of a boycott by black African nations over the readmission of South Africa earlier in the year. After 40 countries had indicated that they would withhold their teams, the IOC reversed its decision and South Africa was barred again, permanently.

In August the Soviet Union and its allies invaded Czechoslovakia, and international tension mounted. A few weeks before the Games began, serious student riots erupted at the University of Mexico which were ruthlessly suppressed, with dozens killed and hundreds injured. In America there was a move to get black athletes to boycott the US team to protest the alleged bad treatment of black people in general in the United States. When this appeared to get little support, those behind the boycott implied that some type of demonstration would be held at the Games.

Despite all these problems, President Gustavo Diaz Ordaz declared the formal opening of the Games to a record number of teams and athletes. Enriqueta Basilio, a hurdler, became the first woman to light the Olympic flame in the stadium.

Due to the conditions, the distance running events were dominated by athletes who lived and trained at high altitude, such as the Kenyans and Ethiopians. Exceptional performances abounded in the sprints and jumps. Bob Beamon's great jump was actually beyond the limits of the measuring device in use at the pit, and a steel tape had to be used. In the triple jump the existing Olympic record was beaten by seven

Vera Cáslavská (TCH) in 1968 with four golds and two silvers, adding to her three golds and a silver from Tokyo.

men and the world mark improved on five occasions. The high jump winner, Dick Fosbury (USA), used the 'flop' style which he popularised and which was to revolutionise the event. Al Oerter (USA) won his record fourth consecutive discus title, and Wyomia Tyus (USA) was the first sprinter successfully to defend an Olympic 100m crown, other than Archie Hahn (USA) in the 1906 Intercalated Games.

The men's 100m final was unique up to that time in that all eight finalists were black. A more heralded expression of Black Power was the demonstration by the black American athletes Tommie Smith and John Carlos (USA) in the 200m victory ceremony when, having come first and third respectively, they raised black-gloved, clenched fists during the play-

Dick Fosbury opened a new, exciting chapter in high jump history using his revolutionary 'Fosbury Flop' technique at Mexico City.

ing of the American anthem. For this action they were suspended and expelled from the Olympic village. Some old-timers noted that their action was no more, nor less, insulting than that of the numerous medallists who had given the Nazi salute in 1936.

The marathon was won, for the third consecutive time, by an Ethiopian, but this time by Mamo Wolde after two-time champion Abebe Bikila withdrew at 17km. He had had his appendix removed only six weeks prior to the Games. Tragically, he was paralysed in a car accident the following year and died in 1973 at the age of 41.

The greatest individual medal hauls were achieved, as usual, by gymnasts. Although Mikhail Voronin (URS) won seven medals (two gold, four silver,

1968 MEDALS *Summer*

Country	G	S	B
United States	45	28	34
Soviet Union	29	32	30
Japan	11	7	7
Hungary	10	10	12
GDR	9	9	7
France	7	3	5
Czechoslovakia	7	2	4
Germany (FRG)	5	11	10
Australia	5	7	5
Great Britain	5	5	3
Poland	5	2	11
Romania	4	6	5
Italy	3	4	9
Kenya	3	4	2
Mexico	3	3	3
Yugoslavia	3	3	2
Netherlands	3	3	1
Bulgaria	2	4	3
Iran	2	1	2
Sweden	2	1	1
Turkey	2	–	–
Denmark	1	4	3
Canada	1	3	1
Finland	1	2	1
Ethiopia	1	1	–
Norway	1	1	–
New Zealand	1	–	2
Tunisia	1	–	1
Pakistan	1	–	–
Venezuela	1	–	–
Cuba	–	4	–
Austria	–	2	2
Switzerland	–	1	4
Mongolia	–	1	3
Brazil	–	1	2
Belgium	–	1	1
Korea	–	1	1
Uganda	–	1	1
Cameroon	–	1	–
Jamaica	–	1	–
Argentina	–	–	2
Greece	–	–	1
India	–	–	1
Taiwan (Taipei)	–	–	1

one bronze), the star of the sport was Vera Cáslavská (TCH) with four golds and two silvers. Her floor exercises routine, to the music of the 'Mexican Hat Dance', was immensely popular. Soon after her events were over, but still during the Games, she married her countryman Josef Odlozil, the 1964 1500m silver medallist. Incidentally, Voronin's wife Sinaida won a gold, a silver and two bronze medals in the Soviet women's gymnastics team.

The outstanding swimmers were Charles Hickcox (USA) with three golds and a silver, and Debbie Meyer (USA) who uniquely to that date won three individual events. Six other swimmers won two gold medals each, including an 18-year-old American named Mark Spitz. Mexico's first ever swimming gold medal was won by Felipe Muñoz in the 200m breaststroke. He was nicknamed 'Tibio', which means lukewarm in English. This was no reflection on his determination, but was the result of his father coming from a town named Aguascalientes ('hot waters') and his mother from Rio Frio ('cold river').

Although eliminated in the fencing, Janice Romary (USA) became the first woman to compete in six consecutive Games and because of this also became the first woman to carry the flag for the United States in a Games Opening Ceremony. The 5.5m class yachting, held at the resort city of Acapulco, produced the unique result of triple gold medal siblings as the Swedish brothers Ulf, Peter and Jörgen Sundelin crewed *Wasa IV* to an easy victory. Behind them, skippering the second placed Swiss boat *Toucan*, was Louis Noverraz, at 66yr 154 days the oldest medallist at these Games.

The oldest gold medallist was Josef Neckermann (FRG) in the dressage team, aged 56yr 141 days, while the youngest was Gunther Tiersch (GDR), cox of the winning eight, aged 14yr 172 days. The oldest female champion was Liselott Linsenhoff (FRG), also in the dressage team, aged 41yr 58 days, while the youngest female gold medallist was swimmer Susan Pedersen (USA) in the medley relay the day after her 15th birthday.

The oldest competitor at Mexico City was Roberto Soundy, a trapshooter from El Salvador aged 68yr 229 days, and the same country had the youngest male competitor in Ruben Guerrero, a medley relay swimmer aged 13yr 351 days. However, the youngest competitor of all was Liana Vicens of Puerto Rico, aged only 11yr 328 days, in the women's 100m breaststroke. The oldest woman was Britain's Lorna Johnstone, who was 13th in the dressage at 66yr 51 days.

For the first time since they had entered the hockey competition in 1928, India failed to reach the final. In soccer, won for a record third time by Hungary, the surprise bronze medallists were Japan. They were the first – and to date the only – Asian team to win a soccer medal, and the first non-European team to do so for 40 years.

1972

XIth WINTER GAMES
Sapporo, Japan
3–13 February

Attended by representatives of 35 countries, comprising 1232 competitors, of which 217 were women.

The Games finally came to Sapporo 32 years after they were first awarded to the city but cancelled due to World War II.

Gustavo Thoeni (ITA) won the giant slalom gold and a slalom silver at Sapporo, adding another silver in 1976.

It was the most populous city, with one million inhabitants, ever to host the Winter Games. Some $555 million was spent on facilities over a five-year period, not least for the enormous number of media personnel who outnumbered competitors by two to one.

Arguments between the IOC and sponsored skiers, which had caused problems in 1968, came to a head and resulted in Austria's star skier Karl Schranz being expelled. Although there was a list of 40 competitors apparently under threat of suspension, only he was banned. This led to an initial threat of withdrawal by the Austrian team, but at Schranz's urging this was averted. Another aspect of the amateur/professional debate was highlighted by Canada's refusal to compete at ice hockey due to the state-sponsored players from the Eastern bloc. Their call for 'open' Olympic ice hockey was ignored.

The Games were formally opened by Emperor Hirohito. The flame was delivered by Hideki Takada, a speed skater, and another, Keichi Suzuki, took the oath. Teams from Taiwan and the Philippines competed for the first time. First ever Winter gold medals were won by Poland (ski jumping), Spain (slalom) and the host country (ski jumping). In the latter event, on the 70m hill, Japan achieved a unique grand slam of all three medals. To win only the second Olympic gold medal won by his country, Spanish skier Francisco Fernandez-Ochoa beat the Italian cousins Gustavo and Rolando Thoeni. The women's slalom was won by Barbara Cochran (USA) by 0.02sec, the smallest margin

ever in an Olympic Alpine event. Her sister Marilyn and brother Bob were also in the US team.

Galina Kulakova (URS) won three gold medals in Nordic skiing and this total was matched in the speed skating by Ard Schenk of Holland. The Dutchman might have had more but

he fell in the 500m event and finished 34th out of 37 competitors. East Germany (GDR) returned to total domination of the luge competitions. The women's event was won by Anna-Maria Müller, one of the three girls who had been disqualified for heating their runners at the previous Games.

Galina Kulakova (URS) winning the 10km cross-country race in 1972. She won four gold, two silver and two bronze medals from 1968 to 1980.

Austria's Trixie Schuba took the women's figure skating title despite a comparatively poor (7th-placed) free skating segment – her compulsory figures were excellent and at the time the two segments scored on a 50–50 basis. Soon after the Games this method was changed in favour of free skating ability. An *affaire de coeur* involving Alexey Ulanov (URS), who with Irina Rodnina won the skating pairs, and Ludmila Smirnova, his teammate who placed second with her partner Andrey Suraikin, titillated the skating world. Later they married and competed internationally as partners, but never with the success they had attained with their original partners.

The oldest gold medallist was Jean Wicki (SUI) in the 4-man bob, aged 38yr 239 days. The youngest was Anne Henning (USA) who won the 500m speed skating title aged 16yr 157 days. The oldest female winner was Christina Baas-Kaiser (HOL) with her 3000m speed skating victory at 33yr 268 days, and the youngest male champion was Wojciech Fortuna (POL) who won the 90m ski jump aged 19yr 189 days. The youngest medallist was skater Manuela Gross (GDR), bronze in the pairs, aged 15yr 10 days. Medals were won by a record 17 countries, with 14 of them gaining gold.

1972 MEDALS *Winter*

Country	G	S	B
Soviet Union	8	5	3
GDR	4	3	7
Switzerland	4	3	3
Netherlands	4	3	2
United States	3	2	3
Germany (FRG)	3	1	1
Norway	2	5	5
Italy	2	2	1
Austria	1	2	2
Sweden	1	1	2
Japan	1	1	1
Czechoslovakia	1	–	2
Poland	1	–	–
Spain	1	–	–
Finland	–	4	1
France	–	1	2
Canada	–	1	–

1972

XXth OLYMPIC GAMES
Munich, Federal Republic of Germany
26 August–10 September

Attended by representatives of 122 countries, comprising 7156 competitors, of which 1070 were women.

Awarded the Games in 1966, Munich built a magnificent complex on the rubble of World War II bombing. Total costs were estimated at $650 million. Just prior to the opening day, the IOC expelled Rhodesia under intense pressure from black African nations.

A number of new electronic devices were used in the conduct of the Games, including a triangulation device to measure distances in the athletics throwing events. Archery and men's handball returned to the Olympic progamme and there were additions to other sports, making a total of 195 gold medals available – the Soviet Union took over a quarter of them.

These Games were the most widely covered in history with over 4000 representatives of the world's media on hand. When the German President Gustav Heinemann opened the Games in a colourful ceremony, there was a television audience estimated at an all-time live viewing record of 1000 million. The oath was taken by athlete Heidi

The memorial service for the massacred Israeli athletes at Munich, with the Olympic flag at half-mast.

Schüller, the first woman ever to do so. The record number of countries taking part included first-timers Albania, Dahomey, Lesotho, Malawi, Upper Volta, Somalia, Swaziland, Togo and North Korea (South Korea sent a separate team).

The first week was dominated by swimmer Mark Spitz (USA), who smashed all records for a single Games by winning seven gold medals – four individual and three relay – and there were world records in all of his events. With his medals from Mexico City he had a total of nine golds, one silver and a bronze. Just as dominant in the women's events was Shane Gould (AUS), who won three golds, a silver and a bronze, swimming in 12 races, itself a record for a female swimmer in the Games. The closest win in Olympic history came in the men's 400m medley relay when Gunnar Larsson (SWE) was given the decision over Tim McKee (USA) by two-thousandths of a second. This decision led to a change in the rules so that in future, times and place would be decided in hundredths.

Valeriy Borzov (URS) became the first European to win a men's sprint double on the track, and Ulrike Meyfarth (FRG) equalled the world high jump record to win the gold medal aged 16yr 123 days, becoming the youngest ever individual athletics event champion. Germany's triumph in hockey was the first time since 1920 that a team from outside the Indian sub-continent had won the title. However, the outstanding attraction of the first few days was gymnast Olga Korbut (URS), whose gamine qualities stole the show from her more illustrious colleague Ludmilla Tourischeva (who later married sprint champion Borzov). Virtually overnight, with blanket media coverage, Korbut became a 'superstar', although she only finished 7th in the all-round competition.

On the morning of 5 September all the euphoria evaporated when a band of eight Arab terrorists broke into the Israeli team headquarters at 31 Connollystrasse in the Olympic village. Two Israelis were killed immediately and nine others held hostage as German police and the world's press surrounded the area. After lengthy negotiations the terrorists and their hostages were allowed to go to the airport, where an abor-

tive rescue attempt resulted in the murder of all nine Israeli hostages and the death of some of their captors.

The following morning the Games were suspended for a memorial service in a packed stadium, but with the agreement of most of the parties involved, including the Israeli officials, competitions were resumed later in the day. The overall feeling seemed to be that the Games should go on, although a number of individuals, notably from Holland, Norway and the Philippines, decided to withdraw. The Israeli team returned home immediately.

The Games continued with the United States suffering an unusual number of misfortunes and reverses. Two prospective medallists had missed the 100m second-round heats due to a misreading by their coach of the starting time. Their world 1500m record holder Jim Ryun did not get seeded as his entry performance, a fast mile time, was mistakenly interpreted as a slow 1500m time. Then, to add to his misfortune, he fell in his heat and was eliminated. A pre-Games banning of the poles used by the American vaulters probably ended a 13-Games winning streak, and their gold and silver medallists in the 400m were banned from further competition for a 'Black Power' protest which meant that the Americans could not field a team in the 4 × 400m relay, for which they were the favourites. Since 1912, teams from the USA had always won a medal in this event.

In swimming, Rick DeMont was disqualified after winning the 400m freestyle after a dope test proved positive. If the US team officials had notified the IOC beforehand that he had to take a certain drug containing the prohibited substance to alle-

1972 MEDALS *Summer*

Country	G	S	B
Soviet Union	50	27	22
United States	33	31	30
GDR	20	23	23
Germany (FRG)	13	11	16
Japan	13	8	8
Australia	8	7	2
Poland	7	5	9
Hungary	6	13	16
Bulgaria	6	10	5
Italy	5	3	10
Sweden	4	6	6
Great Britain	4	5	9
Romania	3	6	7
Cuba	3	1	4
Finland	3	1	4
Netherlands	3	1	1
France	2	4	7
Czechoslovakia	2	4	2
Kenya	2	3	4
Yugoslavia	2	1	2
Norway	2	1	1
North Korea (PRK)	1	1	3
New Zealand	1	1	1
Uganda	1	1	–
Denmark	1	–	–
Switzerland	–	3	–
Canada	–	2	3
Iran	–	2	1
Belgium	–	2	–
Greece	–	2	–
Austria	–	1	2
Colombia	–	1	2
Argentina	–	1	–
Lebanon	–	1	–
Mexico	–	1	–
Mongolia	–	1	–
Pakistan	–	1	–
Korea	–	1	–
Tunisia	–	1	–
Turkey	–	1	–
Brazil	–	–	2
Ethiopia	–	–	2
Ghana	–	–	1
India	–	–	1
Jamaica	–	–	1
Niger Republic	–	–	1
Nigeria	–	–	1
Spain	–	–	1

viate an asthma condition, he would have retained his title. Then to cap it all, the American basketball team were controversially defeated by the Soviet Union – ending a remarkable run of 63 consecutive victories in the Games since 1936. Another incident, with a happier conclusion, occurred when the 800m champion Dave Wottle, in his excitement at the victory ceremony, forgot to remove his lucky cap during the American national anthem. He

The first of the great Kenyans – Kipchoge Keino. In Munich he won the steeplechase (above) and took the silver in the 1500m, to match his gold (1500m) and silver (5000m) from 1968.

was very embarrassed and proffered apologies to everyone who would listen.

On the track, Kipchoge Keino (KEN) added the 3000m steeplechase title to the 1500m he had won four years earlier. This made him the first runner since James Lightbody (USA) in 1904 to win Olympic titles at the two distances. Lasse Viren (FIN) won the 5000m/10 000m double, setting a world record in the latter despite falling over early in the race, and America's Frank Shorter won the marathon in the city of his birth.

Romanian discus thrower Lia Manoliu competed in her record sixth Games, taking ninth place with a performance superior to that which won her the gold medal in Mexico City. In the women's pentathlon, silver medallist Heide Rosendahl (FRG) theoretically held the Olympic and world records for the event for 1.12sec, the difference between her winning time in the last discipline, the 200m, and that of the eventual overall champion, Mary Peters (GBR).

By winning the five-sport modern pentathlon individual title, Hungary's András Balczó brought his total medals haul since 1960 to an event record of three gold and two silver. For the second consecutive Games the three medallists in skeet shooting all achieved the same score, the tie being broken by shooting another 25-bird round. The double cycling gold medallist from 1968, Daniel Morelon (FRA), added a third by retaining the sprint title, and Aleksandr Medved (URS) won his third Olympic wrestling title in a row (and his tenth world championship) with a disputed decision over the giant American Chris Taylor. Taylor, reportedly weighing 182kg or more, was the heaviest known man to have competed in the Olympic Games. Among serious doping disqualifications at these Games were those of Bakhaavaa Buidaa, who had won a wrestling silver medal for Mongolia, Jaime Huelamo (ESP), the bronze medallist in the cycling road race, and the Dutch four who had gained third place in the cycling team race.

The oldest gold medallist at Munich was Hans Günter Winkler (FRG), aged 46yr 49 days, in the show-jumping team, and the youngest Deena Deardurff (USA), aged 15yr 118 days, in the swimming medley relay. The oldest female champion was Liselott Linsenhoff (FRG) in the dressage at 45yr 13 days, and she was also the first woman to win an individual equestrian event. In that competition Britain's Lorna Johnstone set a record as the oldest ever female competitor in the Olympics when she reached the last 12 five days past her 70th birthday. A bronze medallist in this event was Maud Van Rosen (SWE), one of the oldest ever female medallists in Olympic history at 46yr 258 days. The youngest male gold medallist at Munich was Uwe Benter (FRG), cox of the winning fours, at 16yr 276 days, although it should be noted that the unfortunate Rick DeMont was 143 days younger.

The tallest competitor at the Games – and the tallest medallist ever in the Olympics – was Tom Burleson (USA), the 2.23m basketball player. One of the runners in the torch relay bringing the Olympic flame to Munich was Edgar Fried, a former general secretary of the Austrian Olympic Committee who had been in the original torch relay in 1936. He was the only one to be involved again in 1972, in his 78th year. At the end of the XXth Games a record 48 countries had won at least one medal.

Attended by representatives of 37 countries, comprising 1128 competitors, of which 228 were women.

These Games were originally awarded in 1970 to Denver, Colorado, but two years later a State referendum decided against providing the necessary finance. So in February 1973 Innsbruck became the first centre to be awarded the Winter Games for a second time. Most facilities were still available from 1964, and 'only' $44 million was required to refurbish and update.

The Games were opened by the President of Austria, Dr Rudolf Kirchschläger, and uniquely two Olympic flames were lit, by Christl Haas, the 1964 gold medal skier, and Josef Feistmantl, the 1964 gold medal luger. The oath was taken by Werner Delle-Karth, a bobsledder. A total of 1.5 million spectators watched the 37-event schedule, and there were also 600 million television viewers around the world. Unfortunately, an influenza outbreak affected some of the competi-

1976 MEDALS *Winter*

Country	G	S	B
Soviet Union	13	6	8
GDR	7	5	7
United States	3	3	4
Norway	3	3	1
Germany (FRG)	2	5	3
Finland	2	4	1
Austria	2	2	2
Switzerland	1	3	1
Netherlands	1	2	3
Italy	1	2	1
Canada	1	1	1
Great Britain	1	–	–
Czechoslovakia	–	1	–
Liechtenstein	–	–	2
Sweden	–	–	2
France	–	–	1

Austria's Franz Klammer won the 1976 downhill at an average speed well in excess of 100kph.

tors. Two of the smallest states in the world, Andorra and San Marino, made their Winter Games debuts.

The outstanding competitor was Rosi Mittermaier (FRG), who by winning the downhill and slalom races and taking second place in the giant slalom set up the best series of performances ever by a female Alpine skier. She failed by a mere 0.13sec, in the giant slalom, to match the male record of three golds held by Sailer and Killy. In taking the men's downhill on the Patscherkofel course, Austria's Franz Klammer achieved the then highest speed

recorded in an Olympic downhill race, 102.828kph.

In Nordic skiing Galina Kulakova (URS) was disqualified from third place in the 5000m event when a banned drug was found present in a nasal spray she was using to combat influenza, but she was allowed to compete in other events and won a gold and another bronze. Her teammate Raisa Smetanina won two golds and a silver to be the most successful Nordic skier. Particular attention, and some ridicule, was given to Bill Koch (USA), who used his newly developed 'skating' style of skiing. Rather

more attention, and less ridicule, came when he won a silver medal in the 30km race, the only Nordic skiing medal ever won by an American.

However, the greatest tally of medals at these Games was two gold and two bronze by Tatyana Averina (URS) in speed skating. Preventing a clean sweep of those titles by the Soviet women was Sheila Young (USA), who took the 500m title. Later in the year she won her second world cycling championship.

In figure skating the 'jilted' Irina Rodnina (URS) successfully defended her pairs skating title, but this time with a different partner, her new husband Aleksandr Zaitsev. The men's champion John Curry (GBR) brought balletic art to his event just as the Protopopovs had to the pairs in 1964 and 1968. His Italian-American coach Carlo Fassi became the first to train both individual champions at a single Games when Dorothy Hamill (USA) won the women's title. In the new ice dancing event Soviet couples were placed first, second and fourth. All five luge and bobsled events were won by the GDR.

The oldest gold medallist was Meinhard Nehmer (GDR) in the 2-man bob, aged 35yr 25 days, and the youngest was Canada's Kathy Kreiner who won the giant slalom aged 19yr 213 days. The youngest male gold medallist was Sergey Babinov (URS) in the champion ice hockey team, aged 20yr 218 days, while the oldest female champion was Galina Kulakova (see above) in the Nordic relay, aged 33yr 289 days. Toni Innauer (AUT) won a silver in ski jumping aged 17yr 320 days, while the oldest medallist was Marjatta Kajosmaa (FIN) with a Nordic relay silver 9 days after her 38th birthday. The oldest competitor at these Games was 46-year-old Carl Erik Eriksson (SWE) in the bob events, while the youngest was figure skater Yelena Voderzova (URS), still three months away from her 13th birthday.

1976

XXIst OLYMPIC GAMES
Montreal, Canada
17 July–1 August

Attended by representatives of 92 countries, comprising 6085 competitors, of which 1251 were women.

When the Games were initially awarded to Montreal, mainly

due to the efforts of Mayor Jean Drapeau, it was estimated that they would cost $310 million. Because of planning errors, strikes, slowdowns and, it has been suggested, widespread corruption, the final bill amounted to $1400 million – the stadium alone cost $485 million, and the projected 160m-high tower and suspended roof were never completed. After the Munich disaster, security arrangements involving 10 000 police and soldiers cost $100 million. Six months before the opening it seemed that the main facilities would not be finished in time, but by the official opening, pronounced by Queen Elizabeth II, all that was necessary was ready.

The expected record number of entries was well down due to a last-minute boycott by 20 Third World, mainly African, nations, protesting against the inclusion of New Zealand, whose rugby union team had visited South Africa. Also withdrawing was Taiwan because Canada refused to recognise them under the title of Republic of China, a situation which owed much, it was suggested, to Canada's grain-trading relations with mainland China. The withdrawals, mostly only two days prior to the start of competitions, caused some problems with seeding arrangements, and particularly affected the quality of boxing and some running events.

Efforts had been made by the IOC to prune the programme, and to this end the 50km walk, tandem cycling, slalom canoeing, the free rifle and three swimming events had been eliminated. However, with the addition of women's basketball and handball, four canoeing races and seven rowing events, of which six were for women, the total number of gold medals available was now 198 – three more than at Munich. The torch

1976 MEDALS *Summer*

Country	G	S	B
Soviet Union	49	41	35
GDR	40	25	25
United States	34	35	25
Germany (FRG)	10	12	17
Japan	9	6	10
Poland	7	6	13
Bulgaria	6	9	7
Cuba	6	4	3
Romania	4	9	14
Hungary	4	5	13
Finland	4	2	–
Sweden	4	1	–
Great Britain	3	5	5
Italy	2	7	4
France	2	3	4
Yugoslavia	2	3	3
Czechoslovakia	2	2	4
New Zealand	2	1	1
Korea	1	1	4
Switzerland	1	1	2
Jamaica	1	1	–
North Korea (PRK)	1	1	–
Norway	1	1	–
Denmark	1	–	2
Mexico	1	–	1
Trinidad	1	–	–
Canada	–	5	6
Belgium	–	3	3
Netherlands	2	3	–
Portugal	–	2	–
Spain	–	2	–
Australia	–	1	4
Iran	–	1	1
Mongolia	–	1	–
Venezuela	–	1	–
Brazil	–	–	2
Austria	–	–	1
Bermuda	–	–	1
Pakistan	–	–	1
Puerto Rico	–	–	1
Thailand	–	–	1

was brought into the stadium by two 15-year-olds, a girl and a boy: Sandra Henderson of English descent and Stéphane Préfontaine of French stock, each with a hand on the torch, signifying Canada's joint heritage. In true storybook fashion the pair were married some years later.

The star of Munich, gymnast Olga Korbut, competed at Montreal but she was overshadowed by a 14-year-old Romanian, Nadia Comaneci, who on the first day scored the first-ever maximum 10.00 marks achieved at the Olympics, and ended the Games with a total of seven such maximums, having

Nadia Comaneci on the asymmetrical bars at Montreal. She scored a maximum possible 10.00 on seven occasions, winning the overall title and Romania's first ever gold medals in Olympic gymnastics.

drawn a world record crowd for gymnastics of 18 000 to the finals of the women's events. Nelli Kim (URS) also scored two maximums. The men's individual champion, Nikolai Andrianov (URS), won the most medals at Montreal with four gold, two silver and a bronze. In the swimming pool, Kornelia Ender (GDR) and John Naber (USA) each won four golds and a silver, with Ender and her team-mates failing to win only two of the 13 women's swimming titles.

The American men did even better, losing only one of their 13 events when David Wilkie won Britain's first swimming gold since 1908. Ender later married her teammate, back-stroke specialist Roland Matthes, giving them a 'family' total of 8 gold, 6 silver and 2 bronze medals from three Games. In highboard diving the Austrian-born Italian Klaus Dibiasi, competing in his fourth Games, became the first diver to gain three consecutive gold medals. A member of the Hungarian water polo team which won their country's record sixth victory in the sport was István Szivós, whose father had been in the winning 1952 and 1956 teams.

In the main stadium Lasse

Viren, the latest 'Flying Finn', completed his 'double double' by successfully defending both his 5000m and 10000m titles. He attempted to emulate Zatopek's 1952 feat but could finish only fifth in the marathon. The Cuban Alberto Juantorena, nicknamed 'El Caballo' – The Horse – won a rare 400m/800m double (only America's Paul Pilgrim had previously achieved it, in the 1906 Interim Games). Irena Szewinska (POL), now aged 30, won the 400m in her fourth Games to equal the record total of seven medals in athletics. The winner of the men's javelin, with a new world record, was Miklós Németh (HUN), the son of the 1948 hammer winner. They remain the only father and son in track and field to win gold medals.

Three sets of brothers did very well in the Montreal rowing events. Frank and Alf Hansen (NOR) won the double sculls, while the Landvoigt twins, Jörg and Bernd (GDR), took the coxless pairs. Another set of GDR twins, Walter and Ullrich Diessner, were in the silver-medal coxed fours crew. Elsewhere the Flying Dutchman class yachting was won by another set of brothers, Jörg and Eckart Diesch (FRG).

In women's fencing, Elena Novikova-Belova (URS) won her record fourth gold medal in the team contest, while Hungary's Ildikó Sagi-Retjö set an all-medal record of seven, comprising two gold, three silver and two bronze collected at five Games. America's Margaret Murdock became the first woman to win a shooting medal, and was unlucky not to win the gold. Initially she was declared

Left David Wilkie of Great Britain catching John Hencken (USA) to win the 200m breaststroke title in a new world record time.

the winner of the small-bore rifle (three positions) event, but an error was discovered which gave her a tie with her teammate, Lanny Bassham. A closer examination of targets then relegated her down a place. Although placed only twelfth this time, show jumper Raimondo D'Inzeo (ITA) set an unprecedented record by competing in his eighth Games (1948–76). Alwin Schockemöhle (FRG) became only the third rider in the history of the Games to win the jumping title without any faults.

The new Olympic sport of women's basketball produced the tallest known woman ever to compete in the Games. She was Iuliana Semenova (URS), unofficially reported to be 2.18m tall and weighing 127kg. Her team won the title, and she is one of the tallest, including men, to win an Olympic gold medal.

In weightlifting, two Bulgarians and a Pole, all medallists, were later disqualified for failing dope tests, but a far greater scandal occurred in the modern pentathlon when one of the favourites, Boris Onischenko (URS), was discovered to have tampered with his épée in the fencing segment of the competition. His disqualification eliminated the Soviet team and the team gold medal went to Great Britain. The revenge basketball match between the USA and USSR never materialised as the Soviets were beaten by Yugoslavia in the semi-finals. Thus the United States regained the title, making their Olympic match record played 70, won 69.

The oldest gold medallist at Montreal was Harry Boldt (FRG) in the winning dressage team, aged 46yr 157 days. The youngest was gymnast Nadia Comaneci, who won her first gold medal aged 14yr 252 days.

The youngest male champion was Brian Goodell (USA), aged 17yr 109 days when he won the 1500m freestyle, while the oldest female gold medallist was Sinaida Tourchina (URS) in the winning handball team, aged 30yr 72 days. The youngest medallist was Canadian swimmer Robin Corsiglia in the medley relay, aged 13yr 341 days.

One of the youngest competitors ever in the Olympics was Spanish swimmer Antonia Real, aged 12yr 310 days. At these Games Canada gained the unhappy distinction of being the only host country of a Summer Olympics not to win a single gold medal.

1980

XIIth WINTER GAMES
Lake Placid, USA
13–24 February

Attended by representatives of 37 countries, comprising 1067 competitors, of which 234 were women.

Lake Placid had been applying for the Games unsuccessfully for 12 years when they were finally rewarded in 1974. Most of the facilities used in 1932 had to be rebuilt, and new ones constructed, so the budget for these Games was nearly 80 times the $1.1 million spent in 1932. Some complaints were voiced about the 'village', a building later to be used as a penal institution, but as a report noted, 'at least security would not be a problem'. Once the Games were under way the accommodation was found to be quite suitable and acceptable.

One pre-Games worry which did turn into a major problem was transport for the spectators and press. At times it was virtually impossible to reach and/or return from venues. The official

opening was undertaken by Walter Mondale, Vice-President of the United States. The last relay runner was Dr Charles Morgan Kerr, a psychiatrist, and the honour of taking the oath went, with outstanding foresight, to the American speed skater Eric Heiden. The People's Republic of China and Cyprus both made their debuts in the Winter Games.

It was Eric Heiden who subsequently stole all the headlines by gaining an unprecedented sweep of all five speed skating gold medals, all in Olympic record times. His sister Beth also won a bronze in the women's events. Her teammate Leah Poulos-Mueller won two silver medals but could not match her husband Peter's gold performance of 1976. In Nordic skiing Nikolay Simyatov (URS) won a unique three golds in one Games, while teammate Galina Kulakova raised her record total of medals over four Games to eight. Ulrich Wehling (GDR) won his third consecutive gold medal in the Nordic combination, while Aleksandr Tikhonov (URS) won a fourth consecutive gold in the biathlon relay.

The closest ever result in Olympic Nordic skiing came in the men's 15km cross-country event when Thomas Wassberg (SWE) beat Juha Mieto (Fin) by one-hundredth of a second. Eight years previously the unlucky Finn had lost a bronze medal by only six-hundredths. However, he did win a gold in the 1976 relay.

Slalom specialist Ingemar Stenmark (SWE) won both of his races to become the most successful male Alpine skier at these Games, but Hanni Wenzel from tiny Liechtenstein won

When the United States surprisingly beat the Soviet Union in the 1980 ice hockey tournament, the whole nation celebrated. The Americans then defeated Finland for the title.

both women's slaloms and the silver medal in the downhill. Her brother Andreas added a silver to put their country in sixth place on the unofficial medal table. Another sister, Petra, was also in the team of seven.

In winning the 90m ski jump, Jouko Törmänen (FIN) made the longest jump ever in Olympic competition to that date as he cleared 117m. In the 70m event there was an unfortunate incident when after nine competitors had taken their jumps the judges ruled that conditions were too dangerous. The start point was moved lower down, to reduce take-off speed, and the competition begun again.

Irina Rodnina (URS) equalled the record of three gold medals by a figure skater when she and her husband Aleksandr Zaitsev retained the pairs title. In successfully defending the men's singles for Great Britain, Robin Cousins won his country's only medal of these Games. The bobsledding was a virtual replay of the 1976 rivalry between the Swiss and East German teams. A member of the American 12th-placed 4-man bob was Willie Davenport, who had competed in the Summer Games from 1964 to 1976 and had won the 110m hurdles in 1968.

By far the most popular win was that of the United States ice hockey team over the Soviet Union (their first defeat since 1964) on the way to the final. The celebrations which followed were described on American television as the biggest since the end of World War II. In the final, the US then beat Finland.

The oldest gold medallist was Meinhard Nehmer (GDR) in the 4-man bob, aged 39yr 42 days, and the youngest was his teammate Karin Enke who won the 500m speed skating title aged 18yr 240 days. The youngest

male winner was Mike Ramsey of the victorious US ice hockey team, aged 19yr 83 days. the oldest female champion was Irina Rodnina, aged 30yr 159 days. Special mention must also be made of Marina Tcherkasova (URS), a silver medallist in pair skating only 93 days past her 15th birthday.

At the end of these Games only Great Britain, Sweden and the United States could claim to have been represented in all winter events of the Modern Olympics, including those of 1908 and 1920.

1980

XXIInd OLYMPIC GAMES
Moscow, USSR
19 July–1 August

Attended by representatives of 81 countries, comprising 5326 competitors, of which 1088 were women.

There had been only a little dissent when the IOC awarded these Games to Moscow in 1974. Tsarist Russia had competed in 1900 and from 1906 to 1912. Athletes from Lithuania, Estonia and Latvia, which had been provinces of Russia prior to 1918 and were taken over by the Soviet Union in 1940, had competed independently between 1920 and 1936. The Soviet Union had entered the Olympics in force in 1952 and was now the second highest medal-scorer of all time – a remarkable achievement. However, in December 1979 the Soviet Union invaded Afghanistan, and much of the non-Communist world, led by the United States, tried to impose a boycott on the Games – although not, it should be noted, on trade or other economic activity.

Not all such countries sup-

ported the boycott, although sports within them sometimes did. Because a number of countries which were unlikely to go to Moscow anyway for financial reasons found it politic to 'jump on the bandwagon', it is difficult to complete a list of boycotting nations. The most reliable estimate is 45–50, of which the most important in sporting terms were the United States, the Federal Republic of Germany, and Japan. When the Games were officially opened by Leonid Brezhnev, President of the USSR, there were eight first-time entries, not including Zimbabwe which had previously competed as Rhodesia.

Facilities in Moscow were excellent, not least the 103 000 capacity Lenin stadium, and large crowds attended most sports. It must be stated that although the Soviet spectators were in the main very knowledgeable, they left something to be desired in their treatment of foreign competitors, particularly those from other Eastern bloc countries. New competitions, such as women's hockey, two extra judo classes, one extra weightlifting class and various reintroduced events, brought the total of gold medals available to a record 203 (barring ties). The heroine of Montreal, Nadia Comaneci (ROM), returned but was no longer the force she had been, and for the first time for many years the star of gymnastics was a male, Aleksandr Dityatin (URS). His haul of eight medals was the greatest number ever won by a competitor at any sport at one Games. Furthermore, his maximum 10.00 in the horse vault was the first ever awarded to a male gymnast in the Olympics. His teammate, Nikolay Andrianov, brought his own total of medals to a male record of 15 overall, in three Games. This total has only ever been

1980 MEDALS *Winter*

Country	G	S	B
Soviet Union	10	6	6
GDR	9	7	7
United States	6	4	2
Austria	3	2	2
Sweden	3	–	1
Liechtenstein	2	2	–
Finland	1	5	3
Norway	1	3	6
Netherlands	1	2	1
Switzerland	1	1	3
Great Britain	1	–	–
Germany (FRG)	–	2	3
Italy	–	2	–
Canada	–	1	1
Hungary	–	1	–
Japan	–	1	–
Bulgaria	–	–	1
Czechoslovakia	–	–	1
France	–	–	1

Gymnast Alexandr Dityatin (URS) won a record eight medals, including gold on the rings, at the 1980 Games.

exceeded by Larissa Latynina, also a Soviet gymnast.

East African athletes dominated the distance runs, led by Miruts Yifter (ETH) with a 5000m/10 000m double. The 100m was the closest for 28 years with Britain's Allan Wells given the verdict over Silvio Leonard of Cuba. Two other Britons, Steve Ovett and Sebastian Coe, each won the 'wrong' event for which the other was favourite, taking the 800m and 1500m respectively. Waldemar Cierpinski (GDR) became only the second man successfully to defend the marathon title, although he was over a minute slower than in 1976.

In the triple jump Viktor Saneyev (URS) ended his remarkable career with a silver to add to his three gold medals

since 1968. By repeating her Montreal gold medals in the 200m and relay, Bärbel Wöckel (GDR) equalled the female track and field record of four. In that relay, Ludmila Maslakova of the silver medal Soviet team was running in her fourth consecutive relay final since 1968. Although winning only the pentathlon silver medal, Olga Rukavishnikova (URS) theoretically held the world record, albeit for only 0.4sec, as she finished first in the last discipline, the 800m. That gave her the shortest reign of any world record holder ever.

Once more the GDR girls dominated the swimming events, winning 26 of the available 35 medals. Highest medal scorers were Caren Metschuck with three golds and a silver and

Ines Diers with two golds, two silvers and a bronze. More unusually, their teammate Rica Reinisch won three gold medals all in world record times. The inaugural women's hockey competition resulted in Zimbabwe gaining a gold medal in its debut at the Games, while India was back to its former winning ways, taking a record eighth title in the men's competition. In the yachting events held at Tallinn, the former capital of Estonia, the Finn class dinghy event was won appropriately enough by a Finn, Esko Rechardt.

Vladimir Parfenovich (URS) was the first canoeist to win three gold medals at the same Games, and the Cuban heavyweight Teofilo Stevenson became the only boxer to win the same event in three Games –

Risen from the ashes, Sebastian Coe (GBR) wins the 1500m after losing his favourite event, the 800m. Second is Jürgen Straub (GDR), and third Steve Ovett (GBR), Coe's erstwhile conqueror.

Boycott or no, it seems unlikely that anyone would have stopped Ethiopia's Miruts Yifter winning the 5000m – here he passes Alexandr Fedotkin (URS) – or the 10000m at Moscow in 1980.

the great Hungarian László Papp had won his three golds at two different weights. In rowing, the Landvoigt twins, Jörg and Bernd (GDR), retained their coxless pairs title by beating the Soviet Pimenov twins, Yuriy and Nikolay. The other GDR twins, Ullrich and Walter Diessner, went one better than at Montreal and won gold medals in the coxed fours. Yet another pair of twins won titles in wrestling when Anatoly and Sergey Beloglasov (URS) won the 52kg and 57kg freestyle events respectively.

The oldest gold medallist at Moscow – or rather Tallin – was Valentin Mankin (URS) in the Star yachting, aged 41yr 346 days, while the youngest champion at the Games was swimmer Rica Reinsch (GDR), winning

1980 MEDALS *Summer*

Country	G	S	B
Soviet Union	80	69	46
GDR	47	37	42
Bulgaria	8	16	17
Cuba	8	7	5
Italy	8	3	4
Hungary	7	10	15
Romania	6	6	13
France	6	5	3
Great Britain	5	7	9
Poland	3	14	15
Sweden	3	3	6
Finland	3	1	4
Czechoslovakia	2	3	9
Yugoslavia	2	3	4
Australia	2	2	5
Denmark	2	1	2
Brazil	2	–	2
Ethiopia	2	–	2
Switzerland	2	–	–
Spain	1	3	2
Austria	1	2	1
Greece	1	–	2
Belgium	1	–	–
India	1	–	–
Zimbabwe	1	–	–
North Korea (PRK)	–	3	2
Mongolia	–	2	2
Tanzania	–	2	–
Mexico	–	1	3
Netherlands	–	1	2
Ireland	–	1	1
Uganda	–	1	–
Venezuela	–	1	–
Jamaica	–	–	3
Guyana	–	–	1
Lebanon	–	–	1

the first of her three golds aged 15yr 105 days. The oldest female winner was Vera Misevich (URS) at 36yr 112 days in the dressage team contest, while the youngest male gold medallist was the Hungarian backstroker Sándor Wladar, seven days past his 17th birthday. The youngest medallist was Zirvard Emirzyan (URS) with a silver in diving aged 14yr 52 days, while the youngest competitor of all was the Polish gymnast Anita Jokiel at 13yr 232 days. In the same competition was Myong Hui Choe of North Korea, the smallest competitor of all at 1.35m tall and weighing 25kg. At the other end of the scale were the Soviet basketball player Vladimir Tkachenko, standing 2.20m tall, and the Greco-Roman wrestler Roman Codrean (ROM), who weighed 170kg. Despite the unfillable losses and gaps caused by the boycott, the standard of performances was very high throughout the Games.

1984

XIVth WINTER GAMES
Sarajevo, Yugoslavia
8–19 February

Attended by representatives of 49 countries, comprising 1278 competitors, of which 276 were women.

This first Winter Games to be held in Eastern Europe had been awarded to Sarajevo in 1978. With a population of 500 000 it was the second-largest city to host the Winter celebration, and was previously famous only as the site of the assassination of Archduke Ferdinand on 28 June 1914 – an act which historians argue caused the First World War. There were a record 49 countries attending,

including debuts by the British Virgin Islands, Egypt, Costa Rica, Puerto Rico and perhaps the most unlikely, Senegal.

The Games were opened by Mika Spiljak, the President of the Socialist Federal Republic of Yugoslavia. After running up 94 steps in the Kosevo stadium, Sanda Dubravcic lit the Olympic flame. She later placed tenth in the women's figure skating. The oath was taken by skier Bojan Krizaj, later seventh in the slalom. The competitions had actually started the day before the official opening, with preliminary rounds of the ice hockey tournament.

Prior to the Games much had been made of the wolf mascot, Vucko, being depicted with its claws crossed – as though hoping for the best. In fact, although the weather caused some problems, the enthusiasm of the organisers and the local populace overcame most difficulties. Even the transport system worked. One of the few things that did cause hackles to rise was outside the control of the host city, namely the highly questionable, or at the least confusing, judging of the figure skating – a problem not unique to Sarajevo in recent years. One *cause célèbre* just prior to the Games was the banning, as professionals, of the two defending champions in the men's and women's slalom races, Ingemar Stenmark (SWE) and Hanni Wenzel (LIE). There was one new event in the programme, a 20km Nordic skiing race for women.

For the first time, the GDR won more gold medals than the Soviet Union, although not total medals. However, in the men's luge, in which they had won seven gold, two silver and four bronze medals in the last four Games, they took only a single bronze. The outstanding competitor, unusually, was a female

Nordic skier, Marja-Liisa Hämäläinen (FIN), who won all three individual events and a bronze in the relay.

Britain's Jayne Torvill and Christopher Dean gained the most media attention, with their superb ice dancing – their artistic interpretation of Ravel's *Bolero* was awarded an unprecedented nine perfect sixes, with another three for technical merit. The women's singles winner, Katarina Witt (GDR), was trained by Jutta Muller, who had not only coached her daughter Gabriele Seyfert to a silver in 1968 but had also been the driving force behind the 1980 champion Annet Poetsch. Coincidentally, Witt's brother Axel married Poetsch in 1984.

Alpine skiers from the United States made a major impact with three titles. Bill Johnson, hardly a retiring personality, proved he was as good as he had been saying he was to everyone who would listen. His Olympic downhill victory, the first by an American, was achieved at a record average speed of 104.532kph. His teammates, twins Phil and Steve Mahre, took the gold and silver medals in the slalom.

By winning the women's downhill race, Michaela Figini (SUI) became the youngest ever Alpine skiing gold medallist, aged 17yr 314 days, as well as being the youngest champion overall at Sarajevo. Unusually in Alpine skiing, only one skier, Perrine Pelen (FRA), won more than one medal. Few begrudged the silver gained by Jure Branko in the giant slalom, the first Winter Games medal ever by Yugoslavia. One unusual feature of these events was the participation of Sam Guss, not because he was an Australian but because he stood 2.08m tall, possibly the tallest ever Alpine skier.

In speed skating, Tomas Gustafsson (SWE) and Igor Malkov (URS) swapped medals over 5000m and 10 000m, in two of the closest races ever skated in the Games, unique over such distances. The Swede won the shorter race by 0.02sec and the Soviet won the longer by 0.05sec. The Soviet ice hockey team equalled Canada's record with a sixth gold medal. Just prior to the Games another ice

Gold and silver medallists in the 1984 slalom – the American twin skiers Phil and Steve Mahre.

hockey eligibility controversy had arisen with the decision that an amateur for Olympic purposes was someone who had not played in the National Hockey League of North America. One other bone of contention had been resolved before competitions began, when the revolutionary rocket-shaped Soviet bobs were barred. The 90m ski jump was won by a young Finn, Matti Nykänen, by a record margin of 18.5 points, but he was to make a far greater impression four years later.

The oldest gold medallist at Sarajevo was hockey player Vladislav Tretyak (URS), aged 31yr 300 days, while the youngest was Michaela Figini. The youngest male champion was speed skater Igor Malkov (URS), just 9 days past his 19th birthday, while the oldest female gold medallist was Marja-Liisa Hämäläinen, aged 28yr 161 days. The oldest competitor was Carl-Erik Eriksson (SWE) at 53yr 289 days, competing in his record sixth successive Olympic bobsleigh competition. The youngest was Babette Preussler (GDR) in pairs skating, aged 15yr 143 days. One of the victorious German pair in the luge, Hans Stanggassinger, had another distinction. He was reportedly the heaviest champion, weighing 111kg.

1984 MEDALS *Winter*

Country	G	S	B
GDR	9	9	6
Soviet Union	6	10	9
United States	4	4	–
Finland	4	3	6
Sweden	4	2	2
Norway	3	2	4
Switzerland	2	2	1
Canada	2	1	1
Germany (FRG)	2	1	1
Italy	2	–	–
Great Britain	1	–	–
Czechoslovakia	–	2	4
France	–	1	2
Japan	–	1	–
Yugoslavia	–	1	–
Liechtenstein	–	–	2
Austria	–	–	1

1984

XXIIIrd OLYMPIC GAMES
Los Angeles, USA
28 July–12 August

Attended by representatives of 140 countries, comprising 7078 competitors, of which 1620 were women.

The IOC awarded the Games to Los Angeles in 1978 only after protracted negotiations about the financial guarantees usually required from a host city. Various innovations to protect the city from a Montreal-like deficit were implemented, not least widespread sponsorship by private corporations. Television rights alone amounted to $287 million – one of the largest TV audiences in history, some 2500 million, watched the Games – of which the great bulk came from the ABC network for US rights. The programme was expanded to 221 events, including an extra 12 for women, while baseball and tennis were demonstration sports. The Memorial Coliseum, main site for the 1932 Games, was fully refurbished and had a seating capacity of 92 607. Many other venues, often famous in their own right, were utilised. There were complaints that some of these venues were too far-flung, but the overall good weather and the (at times overwhelming) enthusiasm of the American crowds offset most problems.

The one disaster suffered by these Games, and a major one, was the last-minute boycott by the Soviet Union, which announced its non-participation on the very day, 8 May 1984, that the Olympic flame arrived in the United States to begin a nationwide torch relay. Within a week or so most of the Soviet bloc had also pulled out – with the notable exception of Romania. Additionally, but not

surprisingly, Iran and Libya did not appear. However, of 159 invitations sent out, 140 countries accepted, beating the Munich record. Nevertheless, a number of sports were very seriously affected although standards were still generally high. In particular, canoeing, fencing, gymnastics, weightlifting, wrestling and women's athletics were diminished, both in numbers and quality.

The Games were formally opened by President Ronald Reagan, the first incumbent ever to do so. The final runner on the torch relay was Gina Hemphill, a granddaughter of that great Olympian Jesse Owens. Interestingly, she had also run the first leg on American soil, jointly with Jim Thorpe's grandson Bill. Some years after the Games she married Henry Tillman, who won the heavyweight boxing title at Los Angeles. In the stadium she handed over the torch to the 1960 Olympic decathlon champion Rafer Johnson, who lit the flame on top of the stadium peristyle by means of a 96-step hydraulic slip-stair. Apparently in rehearsals Johnson had developed a leg injury and 1976 champion Bruce Jenner, one of the Olympic flag's escorts, stood by in case he was needed to replace him. The oath was taken, somewhat stumblingly, by the 1976 400m hurdles champion Edwin Moses, who went on to win a second gold medal. There followed a three-hour Hollywood-style extravaganza featuring, among other things, marching bands and 85 pianos, which was produced by film producer David Wolper.

Smoke and traffic congestion did not materialise to anything like the degree predicted, although one unfortunate phenomenon was the orgy of American chauvinism displayed – especially by the media. Attendances at all

Valerie Brisco-Hooks (364) wins the 200m at Los Angeles, with Grace Jackson of Jamaica outside her in fifth place. The American had also won the 400m final.

Daley Thompson hurdling in the 1984 decathlon, which he won with a new world record score.

sports were quite remarkable, with a final total figure of 5.7 million and a highest single figure of 101 799, for the final of the soccer tournament (France beat Brazil 2–0) in the famed Rose Bowl at Pasadena. One particular feature of these Games was the tremendous outlay made on security – some 7000 personnel and ancillary equipment costing as much as $100 million.

The first gold medal of the Games was won by shooter Xu Haifeng, for China's first ever Olympic title. Aided enormously by the absence of Soviet and East German opposition, the United States gained the lion's share of the medals. Leading their gold rush was sprinter/ jumper Carl Lewis, who exactly equalled Jesse Owens's feat of 1936 with four gold medals in the 100m, 200m, long jump and sprint relay. Another athlete, Valerie Brisco-Hooks, and five swimmers, all won three golds each, but the most successful competitors were gymnasts Ecaterina Szabo (ROM), with four golds and a silver, and Li

Ning (CHN), with three golds, two silvers and a bronze.

The introduction of consolation finals, for non-qualifiers to the regular finals, led to the unusual situation of an Olympic record being set in the men's 400m freestyle 'B' final, faster than the gold medallist had attained. The judo Open champion Yasuhiro Yamashita (JPN) extended his career winning streak to 198 bouts, despite the handicap of a foot injury.

1984 MEDALS *Summer*

Country	G	S	B
United States	83	61	30
Romania	20	16	17
Germany (FRG)	17	19	23
China	15	8	9
Italy	14	6	12
Canada	10	18	16
Japan	10	8	14
New Zealand	8	1	2
Yugoslavia	7	4	7
Korea	6	6	7
Great Britain	5	11	21
France	5	7	16
Netherlands	5	2	6
Australia	4	8	12
Finland	4	2	6
Sweden	2	11	6
Mexico	2	3	1
Morocco	2	–	–
Brazil	1	5	2
Spain	1	2	2
Belgium	1	1	2
Austria	1	1	1
Kenya	1	–	2
Portugal	1	–	2
Pakistan	1	–	–
Switzerland	–	4	4
Denmark	–	3	3
Jamaica	–	1	2
Norway	–	1	2
Greece	–	1	1
Nigeria	–	1	1
Puerto Rico	–	1	1
Colombia	–	1	–
Egypt	–	1	–
Ireland	–	1	–
Ivory Coast	–	1	–
Peru	–	1	–
Syria	–	1	–
Thailand	–	1	–
Turkey	–	–	3
Venezuela	–	–	3
Algeria	–	–	2
Cameroon	–	–	1
Dominican Republic	–	–	1
Iceland	–	–	1
Taiwan (Taipei)	–	–	1
Zambia	–	–	1

A number of families were particularly successful. Twins Mark and David Schultz (USA) and Lou and Ed Banach (USA) all won wrestling medals; William Buchan (USA) and his son William Jr won yachting titles, but not together. British husband Gary (silver, 4 × 400m) and wife Kathy Cook (bronze, 400m and 4 × 100m) both won medals, while Al Joyner and his sister Jackie (USA) won gold and silver in the triple jump and heptathlon respectively. Brothers Carmine and Giuseppe Abbagnale (ITA) won the coxed pairs rowing event.

In the dressage event, 48-year-old Reiner Klimke (FRG) won two gold medals in his fourth Games over a 20-year period, equalling his countryman Hans-Günter Winkler's equestrian records of five golds and seven medals. One of the few negative things at Los Angeles was the disqualification for doping offences of 12 competitors from weightlifting, wrestling, volleyball and athletics. Probably the most well-known of these was Martti Vainio (FIN), who finished second in the 10 000m on the track but was subsequently stripped of his silver medal.

The oldest gold medallist at Los Angeles was William Buchan (USA) in the Star yachting, aged 49yr 91 days. The youngest was Romanian gymnast Simona Pauca in the team event, aged 14yr 317 days. She won the individual beam title four days later. The youngest male champion was Perica Bukic (YUG) in water polo, aged 17yr 264 days, while the oldest female gold medallist was Linda Thom (CAN), winning the women's pistol aged 40yr 253 days. Worthy of mention is the lady who finished third in that competition, Patricia Dench (AUS), in her 53rd year. At the other end of the scale was Belgian coxswain Philippe

Cuelenaere, the youngest competitor at Los Angeles, a month short of his 13th birthday.

At the end of the Games – after a closing extravaganza featuring one of the greatest fireworks displays ever seen – the organisers reported a profit of $215 million, prompting the suggestion that perhaps the pendulum had swung too far the other way since Montreal! The whole thing was a triumphant vindication of the leadership of Peter Ueberroth, President of the Los Angeles Olympic Organising Committee. Coincidentally, Ueberroth was born on the very day, 2 September 1937, that Baron de Coubertin died.

1988

XVth WINTER GAMES
Calgary, Canada
13–28 February

Attended by representatives of 57 countries, comprising 1428 competitors, of which 315 were women.

Having had three unsuccessful bids previously, Calgary was finally awarded these Games in 1981. Most of the venues were close together except for Mount Allan and Kenmore, some 90km away, where the Alpine and Nordic skiing took place. The programme was stretched to 16 days to include three weekends, particularly favourable for television coverage. ABC paid $309 million for the North American rights, over three times the sum received for the Sarajevo coverage. There were a number of new events: Nordic Combination for teams, Team Jumping, Alpine Combination, Super Giant Slaloms for men and women, and a 5000m speed skating event for women. In all

there were 46 events, as well as the demonstration sports of curling, short-track speed skating and freestyle skiing. Five teams made their Winter Games debuts: Fiji, Guam, Guatemala, Ireland and Jamaica.

The official opening was performed by the Governor-General of Canada, Jeanne Sauvé, on behalf of Queen Elizabeth II. The torch was brought into the stadium by a couple, speed skater Cathy Priestner and skier Ken Read, and then handed to a 12-year-old girl skater, Robyn Perry, who lit the flame. Set at the top of the 626ft (191m) Calgary Tower, the flame was easily the highest ever. The oath was taken by Pierre Harvey, a Nordic skier who had also represented Canada at cycling in the 1984 Olympics.

The facilities in the main were excellent, and expected local transport problems were few and far between. Accommodation was at a premium with so many teams and competitors present, and some officials were based in an establishment which had previously been a 'house of ill-repute'. However, one unforeseen occurrence caused real problems, namely a dramatic climatic change caused by the 'chinook' wind, which gave spring-like weather and strong winds which played havoc with the timetable. These conditions, which primarily affected the bob, luge and ski jumping events, had some unexpected results. The exposed ski jumps were very dangerous at times, and caused the Nordic combination event, comprising jumping and cross-country skiing, to be contested on a single day.

Winner of the women's slalom and giant slalom events at Calgary in 1988, Vreni Schneider of Switzerland in action.

Nevertheless, there were many excellent performances, although it must be noted that the 'star' of these Games was an unknown British ski jumper. Despite, or more likely because of, his being totally inept by world standards, Michael 'Eddie the Eagle' Edwards stole the media attention from the great and famous, to the amusement of many and the chagrin of some. Britain's first Olympic entrant ever in this sport, he finished last in both jumps, albeit with a British record of 71m, over 20m behind the rest of the competitors.

The most successful com-

petitors were Yvonne van Gennip (HOL), who won three speed skating titles, and Matti Nykänen (FIN), who won all three gold medals open to him. The Finn totally dominated his sport and leapt to 118.5m on the 90m hill, the greatest distance ever achieved in the Games. In Alpine skiing there was victory in both the slalom and giant slalom for Vreni Schneider (SUI) in the women's competition and Alberto Tomba (ITA) in the men's. The men's giant slalom saw a record entry, for an Alpine event, of 117.

Frank-Peter Rötsch (GDR) became the first man to win both individual biathlon races in a single Games, while the Soviet Union won the relay for the sixth consecutive time. The Soviet women hardly made an error in the Nordic skiing, taking seven of the nine individual medals on offer as well as the relay. Although not in that relay, 35-year-old Raisa Smetanina gained a silver and a bronze to raise her total from four Games to a record nine medals for the sport.

After the shocks of Sarajevo the East German lugers were back, winning all three golds, two silvers and a bronze. Steffi Walter (née Martin) was the first luger to retain an individual title, and led her teammates to a clean sweep. Incidentally, one of the British competitors in this sport was Nick Ovett, whose elder brother Steve won the 800m on the track in Moscow.

Left *A record eight medals were won by Karin Kania (née Enke) of the GDR from 1980 to 1988. At Lake Placid she and her teammates won nine of the twelve medals available, including all the gold and silver.*

The bobsleigh course was likened to sandpaper after the winds blew so much dirt on to it, and many of the top crews were upset. There was bitter rivalry between the Swiss and GDR 4-man crews, with officials of both teams checking the legality of each other's sleds. The coach of the Swiss team was 1980 gold medallist Erich Schärer, while the GDR coach was Horst Hörnlein, who had won gold in the 2-man luge in 1972. After the fourth and final run, the Swiss were triumphant by 0.07sec, the smallest margin ever in the event. The drama was heightened even further when the rather unlikely crew from Jamaica crashed badly, but happily no one was seriously hurt. Bogdan Musiol (GDR), with two silver medals, raised his total to a record equalling six. Placed 25th (of 41) in the 2-man bob was Prince Albert of Monaco, himself a member of the IOC, partnered by a croupier from the Principality's casino. The Prince's grandfather and uncle – both named Jack Kelly – have won Olympic rowing medals.

Katarina Witt (GDR) was the first individual skater since 1952 to retain a figure skating title, amid some criticism – not shared by the spectators – about her skimpy costumes. Third-placed Debi Thomas (USA) was the first black skater to win an Olympic skating medal. Speed skating was held indoors for the first time at the Olympics, in the superb $39 million Olympic Oval. It proved to be the fastest circuit in the world, with world records in seven of the nine events and as many as 29 skaters bettering the world mark in the men's 5000m. The East German Karin Kania (née Enke) added two silvers and a bronze for a record medal haul of eight overall since 1980. Monika Holzner (FRG), the

1972 1000m champion, competed in her fifth Games, a record number of appearances for a female Winter Olympics competitor.

The Soviet Union moved past Canada in ice hockey with its seventh title, while the host nation and the United States, who won in 1980, failed to gain a medal. A small consolation prize for Canada was that the most prolific goalscorer in the tournament, with seven, was their own Serge Boisvert. There was only one competitor in Calgary who failed a dope test, and he was a Polish ice hockey player.

The youngest gold medallist was Ekaterina Gordiyeva (URS) in the pairs skating, aged 16yr 264 days, while the oldest was Ekkehard Fasser (SUI) in the 4-man bob, aged 35yr 178 days. The youngest male champion was Ari Pekka Nikkola (FIN) in the 90m team ski jump at 18yr 284 days, and the oldest female gold medallist was Christa Rothenburger (GDR) who won the 1000m speed skating aged 28yr 84 days. Competitors' ages ranged from a 14-year-old North Korean girl skater to a 52-year-old bobsledder, Harvey Hook, from the US Virgin Islands.

1988 MEDALS *Winter*

Country	G	S	B
Soviet Union	11	9	9
GDR	9	10	6
Switzerland	5	5	5
Finland	4	1	2
Sweden	4	–	2
Austria	3	5	2
Netherlands	3	2	2
Germany (FRG)	2	4	2
United States	2	1	3
Italy	2	1	2
France	1	–	1
Norway	–	3	2
Canada	–	2	3
Yugoslavia	–	2	1
Czechoslovakia	–	1	2
Japan	–	–	1
Liechtenstein	–	–	1

1988

XXIVth OLYMPIC GAMES
Seoul, South Korea
17 September–2 October

Attended by representatives of 159 countries, comprising 8465 competitors of which 2186 were women.

The capital of Korea, Seoul, has one of the largest populations of any city on earth – an estimated 9 million. Nearly all facilities for the Games were *in situ* by the end of 1986 when the Asian Games were held there. Most major installations are part of the sports complex on the banks of the Han river, and include a 100 000-spectator stadium. Once again the programme was expanded, with the reintroduction of tennis (for the first time since 1924), the addition of table tennis, and the inclusion of a number of extra events which brought the total to a record 237. Baseball, taekwondo and women's judo were the demonstration sports.

American television companies offered incredible sums (up to $750 million) for the US rights, providing the major sports finals took place during the American prime-time viewing. That would have required that athletics finals be held between 9.00 and 11.00 am Korean time. This was opposed by the International Amateur Athletic Federation, and indeed by the IOC, although some compromise was finally agreed. The income from television sources was still immense, NBC acquiring the American rights alone for $300 million. There were an stimated 16 000 media personnel at these Games.

Prior to the Opening Ceremony the most tenacious problem was the claim of North Korea to host half the Games.

Against IOC rules, but with their blessing, some sports were offered to them, but they continued to be intransigent. They finally refused to attend and attempted to get the Eastern bloc to support them. However, only the hard-line Communist countries backed them and thus the only absentees were Albania, Cuba, Ethiopia, Madagascar, Nicaragua and the Seychelles. Against that there were a number of first-timers including American Samoa, Aruba, Burkina Faso (which had competed as Upper Volta in 1972), Cook Islands, Guam, the Maldives, St Vincent, Vanuatu and the Democratic Republic of Yemen. Also attending was Brunei, but only with an official, so that the officially claimed figure of 160 countries *participating* is not correct.

The Opening Ceremony began on the Han River and then transferred to the main stadium. The President of South Korea, Roh Tae-Woo, declared the Games open and the oath was taken by Hur Jae, a basketball player. One unusual feature of the ceremony was that as the Korean alphabet begins with the letter G, the traditional first team, Greece, was then followed by Gabon and Ghana. A more entertaining occurrence in that march-past was the inclusion in the Thailand contingent of the reigning Miss Universe, a beautiful Thai girl, which delighted the spectators.

Because the original 1920 Olympic flag had been fading away, a new one was presented to the IOC by the Seoul Organising Committee and was flown for the first time on 17 September 1988. The torch was carried for part of the distance on the track by 76-year-old Sohn Kee-Chung (better known as Kitei Son), the 1936 marathon champion – a Korean who had been forced to run for

Japan, the occupying power at the time. He passed it to the final runner, a female athlete, Lim Chun-Ae. The torch was raised to the top of the cauldron tower, and the flame was lit by three representatives of Science, Art and Sport. (Their names were Ching Sun-Man, Kim Won-Tuk and Sohn Mi-Chung.) It is feared that some of the pigeons

1988 MEDALS *Summer*

Country	G	S	B
Soviet Union	55	31	46
GDR	37	35	30
United States	36	31	27
Korea	12	10	11
Germany (FRG)	11	14	15
Hungary	11	6	6
Bulgaria	10	12	13
Romania	7	11	6
France	6	4	6
Italy	6	4	4
China	5	11	12
Great Britain	5	10	9
Kenya	5	2	2
Japan	4	3	7
Australia	3	6	5
Yugoslavia	3	4	5
Czechoslovakia	3	3	2
New Zealand	3	2	8
Canada	3	2	5
Poland	2	5	9
Norway	2	3	–
Netherlands	2	2	5
Denmark	2	1	1
Brazil	1	2	3
Finland	1	1	2
Spain	1	1	2
Turkey	1	1	–
Morocco	1	–	2
Austria	1	–	–
Portugal	1	–	–
Surinam	1	–	–
Sweden	–	4	7
Switzerland	–	2	2
Jamaica	–	2	–
Argentina	–	1	1
Chile	–	1	–
Costa Rica	–	1	–
Indonesia	–	1	–
Iran	–	1	–
Netherlands Antilles	–	1	–
Peru	–	1	–
Senegal	–	1	–
Virgin Islands	–	1	–
Belgium	–	–	2
Mexico	–	–	2
Colombia	–	–	1
Djibouti	–	–	1
Greece	–	–	1
Mongolia	–	–	1
Pakistan	–	–	1
Philippines	–	–	1
Thailand	–	–	1

Kitei Son, a Korean, won the 1936 marathon running for Japan. He carried the torch in 1988.

which had been released during part of the ceremony, and had perched on the cauldron, were caught in the rush of flame.

The athlete who gained most attention at these Games was undoubtedly the Canadian sprinter Ben Johnson, initially for the best of reasons and then for the worst. Having looked somewhat out of form in the preliminary rounds of the 100m, he blasted away in the final to destroy a talented field including arch-rival Carl Lewis, and record an almost unbelievable world record time of 9.79sec. Three days later it was revealed that he had failed a drug test, and he was disqualified, Lewis moving up to the gold medal with a more than respectable 9.92sec. Another nine competitors, from weightlifting (4), modern pentathlon (2), judo, wrestling and shooting were dis-

qualified for drug-related offences.

Although African men won everything on the track over 400m, the outstanding athlete at the Games was a woman, Florence Griffith-Joyner, who won three golds and a silver in the sprints and relays, running a total of 11 races. Her sister-in-law, Jackie Joyner-Kersee, won the heptathlon, as expected, and the long jump. Continuing the Olympic tradition of successful families, Viktor Bryzgin (4 × 100m) and his wife Olga Bryzgina (400m and 4 × 400m) both won gold medals. In rowing, Carmine and Giuseppe Abbagnale (ITA) retained their coxed pair title from 1984, and a third brother, Agostino, was a member of the winning quadruple sculls crew.

The most successful competitor in Seoul was Kristin Otto

Ben Johnson (CAN) wins the Seoul 100m in sensational time, prior to being disqualified for use of prohibited drugs.

(GDR), who not only won six gold medals (a record by any woman in any sport at any Games) but also became the first swimmer to win titles at three different strokes at the same Games. America's Matt Biondi, saddled before the Games with an impossible Mark Spitz-like scenario, nonetheless ended the Games with seven medals (five gold, one silver, one bronze). Vladimir Salnikov (URS) became the only swimmer to regain a title eight years after winning it for the first time. Greg Louganis (USA) gained the first 'double double' by a male diver when he successfully defended his two titles from Los Angeles, despite hitting his head on the board during a dive in the springboard preliminaries. Also in the pool Anthony Nesty of Surinam became the first black and the first South American to win a swimming gold medal by taking the 100m butterfly. Similarly Kenny Monday (USA) was the first black wrestler to win a gold medal.

A number of 'old-timers' reappeared on the Olympic scene. Fifty-two-year-old Reiner Klimke (FRG) won his sixth dressage gold medal, and his eighth medal in five Games over a 24-year period, all records for his sport. His horse *Ahlerich* also set a record. One of Klimke's compatriots in the winning team was Ann-Kathrin Linsenhoff, and remarkably her mother had been his teammate in the gold medal team of 1968. Britain's David Broome returned after three Games out as a 'professional', 28 years after he first competed.

The yachting events, held at Pusan, involved two of the greatest Olympians of all time. Quadruple gold medallist Paul Elvström (DEN), partnered by his daughter Trine, was competing in a record-equalling eighth Games over a 40-year span. This was matched by yachtsman Durward Knowles (BAH), a 1964 gold medallist, also in his eighth celebration over a similar span. By winning the silver medal in women's sprint cyling, East Germany's Christa Luding (née Rothenburger) became the first competitor in Olympic history to win medals at Summer and Winter celebrations in the same year. She had won a speed skating gold and silver at Calgary.

Because of a record number of entries in boxing, two rings were used simultaneously. Not surprisingly this caused some confusion. Also, not for the first time, the boxing competitions

witnessed some bizarre, often 'home-town' decisions, one of the most scandalous in Olympic boxing history occurring when Roy Jones (USA) was judged to have lost his light-middleweight bout against Park Si-Hun of Korea. Pointedly, the International Amateur Boxing Association awarded Jones the Val Barker Cup as the best stylist at the Games. There were other disputed decisions and some of the judges were suspended. One of the Korean boxers, Byun Jong-Il, refused to leave the ring after the decision went against him in his bantamweight bout, and remained there, a solitary figure, for over an hour.

The oldest gold medallist at Seoul was Reiner Klimke, aged 52yr 255 days. The youngest was a member of the victorious Soviet women's gymnastics team, Natalia Lachtchenova, five days past her 15th birthday. The oldest female champion was hockey player Elspeth Clement (AUS), aged 32yr 103 days, while the youngest male winner was Sergey Kharikov (URS) in the gymnastics team, aged 17yr 308 days. The oldest medallist at Seoul was shooter Ragnar Skanaker (SWE) with a silver in the free pistol, aged 54yr 102 days, while the youngest was Xiong Ni (CHN) with a silver in diving, aged 14yr 247 days. The oldest competitor was Durward Knowles in the Star class yachting, aged 70yr 331 days, while the youngest was swimmer Nadia Cruz of Angola, aged 13yr 73 days. The oldest female competitor was Kikuko Inoue (JPN) in the dressage, aged 63yr 297 days. The tallest gold medallist of all time competed in these Games, namely the Soviet basketballer Arvidas Sabonis, who was 2.23m (7ft 4in) tall.

Thus despite threats of boycotts, of North Korean terror and of student riots, the Games on the whole went very well. The

good humour, flexibility and courtesy of the hosts overcame most minor problems. Some time after the Games ended, it was reported that a record profit of $288 million had been made.

1992

XVIth WINTER GAMES
Albertville, France
8–23 February

In October 1986 the IOC awarded these Winter Games to Albertville, ahead of six other sites in six other countries. Events will be staged over a fairly wide area of Savoie. There will be nine additional events comprising freestyle mogul skiing for men and women, short-track speed skating for men and women (two events each) and three biathlon events for women. Another change affects figure skating, in which compulsory exercises have been eliminated. Speed skiing will be a demonstration sport at nearby Les Arcs.

The 1968 triple gold medallist Jean-Claude Killy is co-president of the Organising Committee for what will be the last of the Winter Games to be held in the same year as the Summer celebration. In future the Winter Games will be held on the even-numbered years between the editions of the Summer Games, so that the next celebration will be in 1994, and thence in 1998 etc. The remarkable political changes witnessed in 1990 mean that beginning with these Games there will be a unified German team once more. There is also the possibility of a unified Korean team.

1992

XXVth OLYMPIC GAMES
Barcelona, Spain
25 July–9 August

After intense 'politicking' the 1992 Summer Games were awarded to Barcelona in October 1986. The city, which is the birthplace of the current President of the IOC, Juan Antonio Samaranch, had first been promised the Games in 1924 but Baron de Coubertin changed his mind and opted for Paris. Barcelona was then suggested for the 1936 celebration, but by then the spectre of civil war meant that the IOC decided in favour of Berlin. The stadium intended for those Games, built in 1929 on Montjuic, has been completely refurbished, and will be the main venue. Most of the other venues are within the city limits, with only the soccer (preliminary games), rowing, canoeing and road cycling sites at any great distance. Television revenue has already set a record with NBC paying $401 million for the American rights.

As well as two new sports, baseball and badminton, being added to the official programme there are also a number of extra events. These include seven for women in judo, a women's 10km walk, two extra sailing competitions for women, and four canoe-slalom contests. The total number of medal events will be 257, an increase of 20 over Seoul. An outbreak of African equine plague in Spain originally cast considerable doubt as to whether the equestrian events could be held, but at time of writing it is thought to have been curtailed. There will be three demonstration sports: pelota Basque, taekwondo and roller hockey. An estimated 15 000 competitors and officials are expected for the Games and the IOC have been discussing the need for 'quotas' to limit the numbers in this and future Games. Recent research indicates that Spain's first Olympic champion Lucius Minicius, winner of the chariot race in AD 129, was born in Barcelona.

1994

XVIIth WINTER GAMES
Lillehammer, Norway
20 February–6 March

This will be the first time that the Winter Games are not held in the same year as the main Summer celebration. It was during the Olympic Games at Seoul in September 1988 that the IOC decided to award these Games to Lillehammer, a town of 22 000 people some 180km north of Oslo. Three other cities had made bids – Östersund (Sweden), Sofia (Bulgaria) and Anchorage (USA) – but the Norwegian town, which had lost out to Albertville in the 1992 vote, won the IOC's approval this time.

1996

XXVIth OLYMPIC GAMES
Atlanta, USA
20 July–4 August
(provisional)

As these Games will be the 100th anniversary of the birth of the Modern Olympics, Athens was thought to be the most likely venue, although there were excellent rival bids from Manchester, Toronto, Atlanta, Belgrade and Melbourne. The somewhat surprising decision, made in September 1990, was in favour of Atlanta. It was immediately suggested that many in the IOC were swayed by the financial support that the city will receive from American TV and other corporate sponsors. Whatever, the team from Atlanta undoubtedly made an excellent presentation. Most of the sports will be held within the periphery of the city, but yachting will be on the Georgia coast at Savannah. There may be a cutting back on the number of sports and events by the time these Games are held, and it has already been decided that demonstration sports will no longer be held as part of this and future celebrations.

1998

XVIIIth WINTER GAMES

Six cities have been officially listed as candidates to host these Games: Val d'Aosta (Italy), Jaca (Spain), Nagano (Japan), Östersund (Sweden), Salt Lake City (USA) and Sochi (USSR).

2000

XXVIIth OLYMPIC GAMES

China has already expressed interest in hosting these Games, and there has also been the suggestion of bids from Berlin, Manchester and Sydney.

OLYMPICS FACT FILE

CELEBRATIONS OF THE GAMES SUMMARY

SUMMER

	Year	Venue	Date	Nations	Women	Men	Total
I	1896	Athens, Greece	6–15 April[1]	13	–	311	311
II	1900	Paris, France	20 May–28 October	22	12	1318	1330
III	1904	St Louis, USA	1 July–23 November	13[2]	8	617	625
*	1906	Athens, Greece	22 April–2 May	20	7	877	884
IV	1908	London, England	27 April–31 October	22	36	2020	2056
V	1912	Stockholm, Sweden	5 May–22 July	28	55	2491	2546
VI	1916	Berlin, Germany	Not held due to war	–	–	–	–
VII	1920	Antwerp, Belgium	20 April–12 September	29	64	2628	2692
VIII	1924	Paris, France	4 May–27 July	44	136	2956	3092
IX	1928	Amsterdam, Netherlands	17 May–12 August	46	290	2724	3014
X	1932	Los Angeles, USA	30 July–14 August	37	127	1281	1408
XI	1936	Berlin, Germany	1–16 August	49	328	3738	4066
XII	1940	Tokyo, then Helsinki	Not held due to war	–	–	–	–
XIII	1944	London, England	Not held due to war	–	–	–	–
XIV	1948	London, England	29 July–14 August	59	385	3714	4099
XV	1952	Helsinki, Finland	19 July–3 August	69	518	4407	4925
XVI	1956	Melbourne, Australia[3]	22 Nov–8 December	67	371	2813	3184
XVII	1960	Rome, Italy	25 Aug–11 September	83	610	4736	5346
XVIII	1964	Tokyo, Japan	10–24 October	93	683	4457	5140
XIX	1968	Mexico City, Mexico	12–27 October	112	781	4749	5530
XX	1972	Munich, FRG	26 Aug–10 September	122	1070	6086	7156
XXI	1976	Montreal, Canada	17 July–1 August	92	1251	4834	6085
XXII	1980	Moscow, Soviet Union	19 July–3 August	81	1088	4238	5326
XXIII	1984	Los Angeles, USA	28 July–12 August	140	1620	5458	7078
XXIV	1988	Seoul, Korea	17 Sep–2 October	159	2186	6279	8465
XXV	1992	Barcelona, Spain	25 July–9 August	–	–	–	–
XXVI	1996	Atlanta, USA	20 July–4 August (prov)	–	–	–	–

*This celebration (to mark the tenth anniversary of the Modern Games) was officially intercalated but not numbered.
[1]Actually 25 March–3 April by the Julian Calendar then in force in Greece
[2]Including recently discovered French national
[3]The equestrian events were held in Stockholm, Sweden, 10–17 June, with 158 competitors (of which 13 women) from 29 countries

WINTER

	Year	Venue	Date	Nations	Women	Men	Total
I	1924	Chamonix, France	25 Jan–4 February	16	13	281	294
II	1928	St Moritz, Switzerland	11–19 February	25	27	468	495
III	1932	Lake Placid, USA	4–15 February	17	32	274	306
IV	1936	Garmisch-Partenkirchen, Germany	6–16 February	28	80	675	755
	1940	Sapporo, then St Moritz, then Garmisch-Partenkirchen	Not held due to war	–	–	–	–
	1944	Cortina d'Ampezzo, Italy	Not held due to war	–	–	–	–
V	1948	St Moritz, Switzerland	30 Jan–8 February	28	77	636	713
VI	1952	Oslo, Norway	14–25 February	30	109	623	732
VII	1956	Cortina d'Ampezzo, Italy	26 Jan–5 February	32	132	687	819
VIII	1960	Squaw Valley, USA	18–28 February	30	144	521	665
IX	1964	Innsbruck, Austria	29 Jan–9 February	36	200	986	1186
X	1968	Grenoble, France	6–18 February	37	212	1081	1293
XI	1972	Sapporo, Japan	3–13 February	35	217	1015	1232

	Year	Venue	Date	Nations	Women	Men	Total
XII	1976	Innsbruck, Austria	4–15 February	37	228	900	1128
XIII	1980	Lake Placid, USA	13–24 February	37	234	833	1067
XIV	1984	Sarajevo, Yugoslavia	8–19 February	49	276	1002	1278
XV	1988	Calgary, Canada	13–28 February	57	315	1113	1428
XVI	1992	Albertville, France	8–23 February	–	–	–	–
XVII	1994	Lillehammer, Norway	20 Feb–6 March	–	–	–	–

OFFICIAL OPENINGS

The Olympic Games traditionally are opened by a member of the reigning Royal Family or a representative of the national government of the host country.

SUMMER

1896	King George I
1900	–
1904	Mr David Francis
1906	King George I
1908	King Edward VII
1912	King Gustav V
1920	King Albert
1924	President Gaston Doumergue
1928	HRH Prince Hendrik
1932	Vice President Charles Curtis
1936	Chancellor Adolf Hitler
1948	King George VI
1952	President Juho Paasikivi
1956	HRH The Duke of Edinburgh
1960	President Giovanni Gronchi
1964	Emperor Hirohito
1968	President Gustavo Diaz Ordaz
1972	President Gustav Heinemann
1976	Queen Elizabeth II
1980	President Leonid Brezhnev
1984	President Ronald Reagan
1988	President Roh Tae-Woo

WINTER

1924	Under-Secretary Gaston Vidal
1928	President Edmund Schulthess
1932	Governor Franklin D Roosevelt
1936	Chancellor Adolf Hitler
1948	President Enrico Celio
1952	HRH Princess Ragnhild
1956	President Giovanni Gronchi
1960	Vice-President Richard Nixon
1964	President Adolf Schärf
1968	President Charles de Gaulle
1972	Emperor Hirohito
1976	President Rudolf Kirchschläger
1980	Vice-President Walter Mondale
1984	President Mika Spiljak
1988	Governor-General Jeanne Sauvé

THE OLYMPIC OATH

At the opening ceremony a representative of the host country, usually a veteran of previous Games, mounts the rostrum, holds a corner of his national flag and, with the flag bearers of all the other countries drawn up in a semi-circle, pronounces the oath:

'In the name of all competitors, I promise that we will take part in these Olympic Games, respecting and abiding by the rules which govern them, in the true spirit of sportsmanship, for the glory of sport and the honour of our teams.'

The following have taken the Olympic oath:

SUMMER

1920	Victor Boin	Fencer
1924	Georges André	Athlete
1928	Harry Denis	Footballer
1932	George Calnan	Fencer
1936	Rudolf Ismayr	Weightlifter
1948	Donald Finlay	Athlete
1952	Heikki Savolainen	Gymnast
1956	John Landy	Athlete
1960	Adolfo Consolini	Athlete
1964	Takashi Ono	Gymnast
1968	Pablo Garrido	Athlete
1972	Heidi Schüller	Athlete
1976	Pierre St Jean	Weightlifter
1980	Nikolay Andrianov	Gymnast
1984	Edwin Moses	Athlete
1988	Hur Jae	Basketballer

WINTER

1924	All flag bearers	
1928	Hans Eidenbenz	Skier
1932	Jack Shea	Speed skater
1936	Wilhelm Bogner	Skier
1948	Richard Torriani	Ice hockey player
1952	Torbjörn Falkanger	Ski jumper
1956	Giuliana Chenal-Minuzzo	Skier
1960	Carol Heiss	Figure skater
1964	Paul Aste	Bobsledder
1968	Leo Lacroix	Skier
1972	Keichi Suzuki	Speed skater
1976	Werner Delle-Barth	Bobsledder
1980	Eric Heiden	Speed skater
1984	Bojan Krizaj	Skier
1988	Pierre Harvey	Skier

The Norwegian and Swedish teams parading at the opening of the 1908 Games at the White City, London. Note the 100m swimming pool inside the track.

The 'priestesses' round the sacred altar at Olympia in 1976, prior to the flame being run to Athens on its way to the Winter Games at Innsbruck.

97

THE OLYMPIC FLAME

The Olympic flame was introduced to the modern Games at Amsterdam in 1928, and since then has always burned throughout the duration of a Games. It symbolises the endeavour for perfection and struggle for victory. The torch relay from Olympia to the Games venue was first staged in 1936, and first for the Winter Games in 1964. The torch first travelled by air when the Games were held in Melbourne in 1956.

The following have lit the Olympic Flame in the stadium:

1936	Fritz Schilgen
1948	John Mark
1952	Paavo Nurmi (Hannes Kolehmainen on tower)
1956	Ron Clarke
1960	Giancarlo Peris
1964	Yoshinori Sakai
1968	Enriqueta Basilio
1972	Günter Zahn
1976	Stéphane Préfontaine & Sandra Henderson
1980	Sergey Belov
1984	Rafer Johnson
1988	Chung Sun-Man, Kim Won-Tuk & Sohn Mi-Chung

PRESIDENTS OF THE IOC

1894–1896	Demetrius Vikelas (Greece)
1896–1925	Baron Pierre de Coubertin (France)
1925–1942	Henri de Baillet-Latour (Belgium)
1942–1952	Sigfrid Edström (Sweden)
1952–1972	Avery Brundage (USA)
1972–1980	Lord Killanin (Ireland)
1980–	Juan Antonio Samaranch (Spain)

MASCOTS

The various symbols and emblems used to publicise the Olympic Games over the years have generally been very successful, but it was only in 1968 that the first Olympic mascot made its appearance. For the Mexico City Games it was a Red Jaguar, selected because of its cultural and geographical associations. However, it was not given a name and was not marketed with any particular enthusiasm. Since then, however, the mascot has become an institution and in 1980 spread to the Winter Games.

	SUMMER		WINTER	
Year	Name	Animal	Name	Animal
1968	–	Jaguar		
1972	Waldi	Dachshund		
1976	Amik	Beaver		
1980	Misha	Bear	–	Raccoon
1984	Sam	Eagle	Vucko	Wolf
1988	Hodori	Tiger	Hidy & Howdy	Polar bears
1992	Cobi	Dog	–	Chamois

Right *The Korean tiger Hodori, advertising the XXIVth Games at Seoul in 1988, was the latest in a series of such mascots used to popularise the Games since 1968.*

PARTICIPATING COUNTRIES

Only five countries have never failed to be represented at celebrations of the Summer Games since 1896 (including those of 1906): Australia, France, Greece, Great Britain and Switzerland. Of these, only France and Great Britain have been present at all Winter Games as well. However, only Great Britain also competed in the skating and ice hockey events of 1908 and 1920, 'Winter' events attached to the Summer Games.

Country		Summer Games		Winter Games	
		Debut	Number attended	Debut	Number attended
AFG	Afghanistan	1936	9	–	–
AHO	Netherlands Antilles	1952	8	–	–
ALB	Albania	1972	1	–	–
ALG	Algeria	1964	6	–	–
AND	Andorra	1976	4	1976	4
ANG	Angola	1980	2	–	–
ANT	Antigua	1976	3	–	–
ARG	Argentina	1920	15	1908	11
ARU	Aruba	1988	1	–	–
ASA	American Samoa	1988	1	–	–
AUS	Australia[1]	1896	22	1936	11
AUT	Austria[2]	1896	21	1924	15
BAH	Bahamas	1952	9	–	–
BAN	Bangladesh	1984	2	–	–
BAR	Barbados	1968	5	–	–
BEL	Belgium	1900	20	1920	14
BEN	Benin	1980	3	–	–
BER	Bermuda	1936	11	–	–
BHU	Bhutan	1984	2	–	–
BIR	Burma	1948	10	–	–
BIZ	Belize (formerly British Honduras)	1968	5	–	–
BOL	Bolivia	1936	7	1956	4
BOT	Botswana	1980	3	–	–
BRA	Brazil	1920	15	–	–
BRN	Bahrain	1976	3	–	–
BRU	Brunei[3]	–	–	–	–
BUL	Bulgaria	1896	13	1936	12
BUR	Burkina Faso (formerly Upper Volta)	1972	2	–	–
CAF	Central African Republic	1968	3	–	-
CAN	Canada	1900	20	1920	16
CAY	Cayman Islands	1976	3	–	–
CGO	Congo	1964	5	–	–
CHA	Chad	1964	5	–	–
CHI	Chile	1896	16	1948	9
CHN	China	1932	6	1980	3
CIV	Ivory Coast	1964	6	–	–
CMR	Cameroon	1964	7	–	–
COK	Cook Islands	1988	1	–	–
COL	Colombia	1932	12	–	–
CRC	Costa Rica	1936	8	1984	2
CUB	Cuba	1900	13	–	–
CYP	Cyprus	1980	3	1980	3
DEN	Denmark	1896	21	1948	6
DJI	Djibouti	1984	2	–	–
DOM	Dominican Republic	1964	7	–	–
ECU	Ecuador	1924	7	–	–
EGY	Egypt[4]	1906	16	1984	1
ESA	El Salvador	1968	4	–	–
ESP	Spain	1900	16	1936	12
EST	Estonia[5]	1920	5	1928	2
ETH	Ethiopia	1956	6	–	–
FIJ	Fiji	1956	7	1988	1
FIN	Finland	1906	19	1920	16
FRA	France	1896	22	1920	16
FRG	Federal Republic of Germany (West)[6]	1896	18	1908	14

Country		Summer Games		Winter Games	
		Debut	Number attended	Debut	Number attended
GAB	Gabon	1972	3	–	–
GAM	Gambia	1984	2	–	–
GBR	Great Britain	1896	22	1908	17
GDR	German Democratic Republic (East)[7]	1968	5	1968	6
GEQ	Equatorial Guinea	1984	2	–	–
GHA	Ghana (formerly Gold Coast)	1952	7	–	–
GRE	Greece	1896	22	1936	11
GRN	Grenada	1984	2	–	–
GUA	Guatemala	1952	7	1988	1
GUI	Guinea	1968	4	–	–
GUM	Guam	1988	1	1988	1
GUY	Guyana (formerly British Guiana)	1948	10	–	–
HAI	Haiti	1900	9	–	–
HKG	Hong Kong	1952	9	–	–
HOL	Netherlands	1900	20	1928	13
HON	Honduras	1968	4	–	–
HUN	Hungary[2]	1896	20	1924	15
INA	Indonesia	1952	8	–	–
IND	India	1900	17	1964	3
IRL	Ireland[8]	1924	14	1988	1
IRN	Iran	1948	9	1956	5
IRQ	Iraq	1948	7	–	–
ISL	Iceland	1908	14	1948	10
ISR	Israel	1952	9	–	–
ISV	Virgin Islands	1968	5	1984	2
ITA	Italy	1900	20	1924	15
IVB	British Virgin Islands	1984	2	–	–
JAM	Jamaica[9]	1948	11	1988	1
JOR	Jordan	1980	3	–	–
JPN	Japan	1912	15	1928	13
KEN	Kenya	1956	7	–	–
KOR	Korea (South)[10]	1948	10	1928	10
KSA	Saudi Arabia	1976	3	–	–
KUW	Kuwait	1968	6	–	–
LAO	Laos	1980	2	–	–
LAT	Latvia[5]	1924	4	1924	3
LBA	Libya	1968	4	–	–
LBR	Liberia	1956	7	–	–
LES	Lesotho	1972	4	–	–
LIB	Lebanon	1948	10	1948	11
LIE	Liechtenstein	1936	10	1936	11
LIT	Lithuania[5]	1924	2	1928	1
LUX	Luxembourg	1912	16	1928	3
MAD	Madagascar	1964	5	–	–
MAL	Malaysia[11]	1956	8	–	–
MAR	Morocco	1960	7	1968	3
MAW	Malawi	1972	3	–	–
MDV	Maldives	1988	1	–	–
MEX	Mexico	1924	15	1928	3
MGL	Mongolia	1964	6	1964	6
MLI	Mali	1964	6	–	–
MLT	Malta	1928	9	–	–
MON	Monaco	1920	13	1984	2
MOZ	Mozambique	1980	3	–	–
MRI	Mauritius	1984	2	–	–
MTN	Mauretania	1984	2	–	–
NCA	Nicaragua	1968	5	–	–
NEP	Nepal	1964	6	–	–
NGR	Nigeria	1952	9	–	–
NGU	Papua-New Guinea	1976	3	–	–
NIG	Niger	1964	5	–	–
NOR	Norway	1900	20	1920	16
NZL	New Zealand[1]	1908	18	1952	8
OMA	Oman	1984	2	–	–
PAK	Pakistan	1948	10	–	–
PAN	Panama	1928	10	–	–
PAR	Paraguay	1968	5	–	–

Country		Summer Games		Winter Games	
		Debut	Number attended	Debut	Number attended
PER	Peru	1936	11	–	–
PHI	Philippines	1924	14	1972	2
POL	Poland	1924	14	1924	15
POR	Portugal	1912	17	1952	2
PRK	Dem People's Republic of Korea (North)[10]	1972	3	1964	5
PUR	Puerto Rico	1948	11	1984	2
QAT	Qatar	1984	2	–	–
ROM	Romania	1924	13	1928	13
RWA	Rwanda	1984	2	–	–
SAF	South Africa[12]	1904	13	1960	1
SAM	Western Samoa	1984	2	–	–
SAR	Saar[13]	1952	1	–	–
SEN	Senegal	1964	7	1984	1
SEY	Seychelles	1980	2	–	–
SIN	Singapore	1948	10	–	–
SLE	Sierra Leone	1968	4	–	–
SMR	San Marino	1960	6	1976	3
SOL	Solomon Islands	1984	2	–	–
SOM	Somalia	1972	3	–	–
SRI	Sri Lanka (formerly Ceylon)	1948	10	–	–
SUD	Sudan	1960	5	–	–
SUI	Switzerland	1896	22	1920	16
SUR	Surinam	1968	5	–	–
SWE	Sweden	1896	21	1908	17
SWZ	Swaziland	1972	3	–	–
SYR	Syria	1948	6	–	–
TAN	Tanzania	1964	6	–	–
TCH	Czechoslovakia[14]	1900	19	1920	16
THA	Thailand	1952	9	–	–
TOG	Togo	1972	3	–	–
TON	Tonga	1984	2	–	–
TPE	Taipei (formerly Formosa/Taiwan)	1956	7	1972	4
TRI	Trinidad & Tobago[9]	1948	11	–	–
TUN	Tunisia	1960	7	–	–
TUR	Turkey	1908	15	1936	9
UAE	United Arab Emirates	1984	2	–	–
UGA	Uganda	1956	8	–	–
URS	Soviet Union[15]	1952	9	1956	9
URU	Uruguay	1924	14	–	–
USA	United States	1896	21	1908	17
VAN	Vanuatu	1988	1	–	–
VEN	Venezuela	1948	11	–	–
VIE	Vietnam[16]	1952	8	–	–
VIN	St Vincent	1988	1	–	–
YAR	Yemen, Arab Republic (North)	1984	2	–	–
YMD	Yemen, Democratic Republic (South)	1988	1	–	–
YUG	Yugoslavia	1912	17	1924	13
ZAI	Zaire	1968	3	–	–
ZAM	Zambia (formerly Northern Rhodesia)	1964	6	–	–
ZIM	Zimbabwe (formerly Rhodesia)	1928	6	–	–

[1]Australia and New Zealand combined as Australasia 1908–1912
[2]Not invited in 1920
[3]In 1988 Brunei sent only an official
[4]As United Arab Republic 1960–1968
[5]Annexed by the Soviet Union in 1940
[6]Not invited 1920, 1924 and 1948; United German team except 1968–88
[7]Separate team 1968–1988; part of combined German team 1956–1964
[8]Part of Great Britain team until 1924
[9]Jamaica and Trinidad combined as Antilles in 1960
[10]Country partitioned in 1945, and separate regimes established in 1948
[11]Prior to 1964 consisted of Malaya and North Borneo who had competed separately in 1956; in 1964 also included Singapore
[12]Not invited since 1960
[13]Independent 1947–1957, then incorporated into Germany
[14]Czechoslovakia was represented by Bohemia up to 1912.
[15]As Czarist Russia 1900–1912
[16]From 1952 to 1972 only a South Vietnamese team competed

OLYMPIC MEDALS TABLE (NATIONS) 1896–1988

These totals include all first, second and third places, including those events no longer on the current (1992) schedule. The 1906 Games, which were officially staged by the International Olympic Committee (IOC), have also been included. However, medals won in the Art Competitions (1912–1948) have not been included. Medals won in 1896, 1900 and 1904 by mixed teams from two countries have been counted twice, for both countries.

Figures in brackets denote a country's position in the medals tables for both the Summer and Winter Games respectively.

	Country	Summer G	S	B	Total		Winter G	S	B	Total		Overall Total
1	United States	752	569	481	1802	(1)	42	46	35	123	(3)	1925
2	Soviet Union[1]	397	323	304	1024	(2)	79	57	59	195	(1)	1219
3	Germany (FRG)[2]	153	206	208	567	(4)	26	26	23	75	(8)	642
4	Great Britain	172	221	206	599	(3)	7	4	10	21	(15)	620
5	France	153	170	175	498	(5)	13	10	16	39	(12)	537
6	Sweden	132	142	167	441	(6)	36	25	31	92	(7)	533
7	East Germany (GDR)[3]	154	131	126	411	(7)	39	36	35	110	(=4)	521
8	Italy	147	121	123	391	(8)	14	10	9	33	(13)	424
9	Finland	97	75	110	282	(10)	33	43	34	110	(=4)	392
10	Hungary	125	112	137	374	(9)	–	2	4	6	(18)	380
11	Norway	41	33	33	107	(22)	54	60	54	168	(2)	275
12	Japan	87	75	82	244	(11)	1	4	2	7	(17)	251
13	Switzerland	41	63	58	162	(16)	23	25	25	73	(9)	235
14	Australia	71	67	87	225	(12)	–	–	–	–	–	225
15	Canada	39	62	73	174	(15)	14	12	18	44	(10)	218
16	Romania	55	64	82	201	(13)	–	–	1	1	(=22)	202
17	Netherlands	43	46	65	154	(17)	13	17	12	42	(11)	196
18	Poland	40	56	95	191	(14)	1	1	2	4	(=19)	195
19	Austria	19	27	33	79	(25)	28	38	32	98	(6)	177
20	Czechoslovakia[4]	45	48	48	142	(19)	2	8	13	23	(14)	165
21	Bulgaria	35	62	49	146	(18)	–	–	1	1	(=22)	147
22	Belgium	35	46	42	123	(21)	1	1	2	4	(=19)	127
23	Denmark	25	50	49	124	(20)	–	–	–	–	–	124
24	Greece	22	40	39	101	(23)	–	–	–	–	–	101
25	Yugoslavia	26	29	28	83	(24)	–	3	1	4	(=19)	87
26	Korea (South)	19	22	29	70	(26)	–	–	–	–	–	70
27	China	20	19	21	60	(27)	–	–	–	–	–	60
28	New Zealand	26	6	23	55	(28)	–	–	–	–	–	55
29	Cuba	22	19	12	53	(29)	–	–	–	–	–	53
30	South Africa[5]	16	15	20	51	(30)	–	–	–	–	–	51
31	Turkey	24	13	10	47	(31)	–	–	–	–	–	47
32	Argentina	13	19	14	46	(32)	–	–	–	–	–	46
33	Mexico	9	12	18	39	(33)	–	–	–	–	–	39
34	Brazil	7	9	21	37	(34)	–	–	–	–	–	37
35	Kenya	11	9	11	31	(35)	–	–	–	–	–	31
36	Iran	4	11	15	30	(36)	–	–	–	–	–	30
37	Spain	4	12	8	24	(37)	1	–	–	1	(=22)	25
38	Jamaica	4	10	8	22	(38)	–	–	–	–	–	22
39	Estonia	6	6	9	21	(39)	–	–	–	–	–	14
40	Egypt	6	6	6	18	(40)	–	–	–	–	–	18
41	India	8	3	3	14	(41)	–	–	–	–	–	14
=42	Ireland	4	4	5	13	(=42)	–	–	–	–	–	13
=42	North Korea (PRK)[6]	2	5	5	12	(44)	–	1	–	1	(=22)	13
=42	Portugal	2	4	7	13	(=42)	–	–	–	–	–	13
45	Mongolia	–	5	6	11	(45)	–	–	–	–	–	11
46	Ethiopia	5	1	4	10	(46)	–	–	–	–	–	10
=47	Pakistan	3	3	3	9	(=47)	–	–	–	–	–	9
=47	Liechtenstein	–	–	–	–	–	2	2	5	9	(16)	9
=47	Uruguay	2	1	6	9	(=47)	–	–	–	–	–	9
=50	Venezuela	1	2	5	8	(=49)	–	–	–	–	–	8
=50	Chile	–	6	2	8	(=49)	–	–	–	–	–	8
=52	Trinidad & Tobago	1	2	4	7	(=51)	–	–	–	–	–	7
=52	Philippines	–	1	6	7	(=51)	–	–	–	–	–	7

	Country	Summer						Winter				Overall
		G	S	B	Total			G	S	B	Total	Total
54	Morocco	3	1	2	6	(53)		–	–	–	–	6
=55	Uganda	1	3	1	5	(=54)		–	–	–	–	5
=55	Tunisia	1	2	2	5	(=54)		–	–	–	–	5
=55	Colombia	–	2	3	5	(=54)		–	–	–	–	5
=58	Lebanon	–	2	2	4	(=57)		–	–	–	–	4
=58	Nigeria	–	1	3	4	(=57)		–	–	–	–	4
=58	Puerto Rico	–	1	3	4	(=57)		–	–	–	–	4
=61	Peru	1	2	–	3	(=60)		–	–	–	–	3
=61	Latvia	–	2	1	3	(=60)		–	–	–	–	3
=61	Ghana	–	1	2	3	(=60)		–	–	–	–	3
=61	Taipei	–	1	2	3	(=60)		–	–	–	–	3
=61	Thailand	–	1	2	3	(=60)		–	–	–	–	3
=66	Luxembourg	1	1	–	2	(=65)		–	–	–	–	2
=66	Bahamas	1	–	1	2	(=65)		–	–	–	–	2
=66	Tanzania	–	2	–	2	(=65)		–	–	–	–	2
=66	Cameroon	–	1	1	2	(=65)		–	–	–	–	2
=66	Haiti	–	1	1	2	(=65)		–	–	–	–	2
=66	Iceland	–	1	1	2	(=65)		–	–	–	–	2
=66	Algeria	–	–	2	2	(=65)		–	–	–	–	2
=66	Panama	–	–	2	2	(=65)		–	–	–	–	2
=74	Surinam	1	–	–	1	(=73)		–	–	–	–	1
=74	Zimbabwe	1	–	–	1	(=73)		–	–	–	–	1
=74	Costa Rica	–	1	–	1	(=73)		–	–	–	–	1
=74	Indonesia	–	1	–	1	(=73)		–	–	–	–	1
=74	Ivory Coast	–	1	–	1	(=73)		–	–	–	–	1
=74	Netherlands Antilles	–	1	–	1	(=73)		–	–	–	–	1
=74	Senegal	–	1	–	1	(=73)		–	–	–	–	1
=74	Singapore	–	1	–	1	(=73)		–	–	–	–	1
=74	Sri Lanka	–	1	–	1	(=73)		–	–	–	–	1
=74	Syria	–	1	–	1	(=73)		–	–	–	–	1
=74	Virgin Islands	–	1	–	1	(=73)		–	–	–	–	1
=74	Barbados	–	–	1	1	(=73)		–	–	–	–	1
=74	Bermuda	–	–	1	1	(=73)		–	–	–	–	1
=74	Djibouti	–	–	1	1	(=73)		–	–	–	–	1
=74	Dominican Republic	–	–	1	1	(=73)		–	–	–	–	1
=74	Guyana	–	–	1	1	(=73)		–	–	–	–	1
=74	Iraq	–	–	1	1	(=73)		–	–	–	–	1
=74	Niger Republic	–	–	1	1	(=73)		–	–	–	–	1
=74	Zambia	–	–	1	1	(=73)		–	–	–	–	1

[1]Includes Czarist Russia
[2]Germany 1896–1964, West Germany 1968–1988
[3]1968–1988 only
[4]Includes Bohemia
[5]South Africa, up to 1960
[6]From 1964

OLYMPICS SUPERLATIVES

MOST GOLDS – SUMMER

Men – **10** Ray Ewry (USA), 1900–1908, Athletics
Women – **9** Larissa Latynina (URS), 1956–64, Gymnastics
Men, in one Games – **7** Mark Spitz (USA), 1972, Swimming
Women, in one Games – **4** by six women

MOST MEDALS – SUMMER

Men – **15** Nikolay Andrianov (URS), 1972–80, Gymnastics
Women – **18** Larissa Latynina (URS), 1956–64, Gymnastics
Men, in one Games – **8** Alexandr Dityatin (URS), 1980, Gymnastics
Women, in one Games – **7** Maria Gorokhovskaya (URS), 1952, Gymnastics

MOST GOLDS – WINTER

Men – **5** Clas Thunberg (FIN), 1924–1928, Speed Skating; Eric Heiden (USA), 1980, Speed Skating
Women – **6** Lydia Skoblikova (URS), 1960–1964, Speed Skating
Men, in one Games – **5** Eric Heiden (USA), 1980, Speed Skating
Women, in one Games - **4** Lydia Skoblikova (URS), 1964, Speed Skating

MOST MEDALS – WINTER

Men – **9** Sixten Jernberg (SWE), 1956–1964, Nordic Skiing
Women – **9** Raisa Smetanina (URS), 1976–1988, Nordic Skiing
Men, in one Games – **5** Clas Thunberg (FIN), 1924 Speed Skating; Roald Larsen (NOR), 1924, Speed Skating; Eric Heiden (USA), 1980, Speed Skating
Women, in one Games – **4** Lydia Skoblikova (URS), 1964, Speed Skating; Tatyana Averina (URS) 1976, Speed Skating; Karin Enke (GDR), 1984, Speed Skating; Marja-Liisa Hämäläinen (FIN), 1984, Nordic Skiing

MOST GAMES & LONGEST SPAN (SUMMER)

Men

8 Games – Raimondo d'Inzeo (ITA), 1948–76, Equestrianism
40 yr – Ivan Osiier (DEN), 1908–48, Fencing; Magnus Konow (NOR), 1908–48, Yachting; Durward Knowles (GBR/BAH), 1948–1988, Yachting; Paul Elvström (DEN), 1948–1988, Yachting

Women

7 Games – Kerstin Palm (SWE), 1964–1988, Fencing
24 yr – Ellen Müller-Preis (AUT), 1932–1956, Fencing; Kerstin Palm (SWE), 1964–1988, Fencing

Soviet gymnast Nikolay Andrianov, the most bemedalled man in Olympic history with a total of 15.

MOST GAMES & LONGEST SPAN (WINTER)

Men

6 Games – Colin Coates (AUS), 1968–1988, Speed Skating; Carl-Erik Eriksson (SWE), 1964–1984, Bobsledding
20 yr – John Heaton (USA), 1928–1948, Tobogganing; Max Houben (BEL), 1928–1948, Bobsledding; Richard Torriani (SUI), 1928–1948, Ice Hockey; Frank Stack (CAN), 1932–1952, Speed Skating; Stanislaw Marusarz (POL), 1932–1952, Nordic Skiing; James Bickford (USA), 1936–1956, Bobsledding; Sepp Bradl (AUT), 1936–1956, Ski Jumping; Carl-Erik Eriksson (SWE) 1964–1984, Bobsledding; Colin Coates (AUS), 1968–1988, Speed Skating

Women

5 Games – Monika Holzner-Pflug (FRG), 1972–1988, Speed Skating
16 yr – Monika Holzner-Pflug (FRG), 1972–1988, Speed Skating

AGE RECORDS – SUMMER

Oldest Male Gold – **64yr 258d** Oscar Swahn (SWE), 1912, Shooting

Oldest Female Gold – **53yr 275d** Queenie Newall (GBR), 1908, Archery

Oldest Male Medal – **72yr 279d** Oscar Swahn (SWE), 1920, Shooting

Oldest Female Medal – **53yr 275d** Queenie Newall (GBR), 1908, Archery

Youngest Male Gold – **7–10yr** Unknown French boy, 1900, Rowing

Youngest Female Gold – **13yr 267d** Marjorie Gestring (USA), 1936, Diving

Youngest Male Medallist – **7–10yr** Unknown French boy, 1900, Rowing

Youngest Female Medallist – **12yr 24d** Inge Sörensen (Den), 1936, Swimming

Oldest Competitor (Male) – **72yr 279d** Oscar Swahn (SWE), 1920, Shooting

Oldest Competitor (Female) – **70yr 5d** Lorna Johnstone (GBR), 1972, Equestrianism

Youngest Competitor (Male) – **7–10yr** Unknown boy (FRA), 1900, Rowing

Youngest Competitor (Female) – **11yr 328d** Liana Vicens (PUR), 1968, Swimming

AGE RECORDS – WINTER

Oldest Male Gold – **48yr 359d** Jay O'Brien (USA), 1932, Bobsledding

Oldest Female Gold – **35yr 276d** Ludowika Jakobsson (FIN), 1920, Figure Skating

Oldest Male Medal – **49yr** Max Houben (BEL), 1948, Bobsledding

Oldest Female Medal – **39yr 189d** Ludowika Jakobsson (FIN), 1924, Figure Skating

Youngest Male Gold – **16yr 260d** William Fiske (USA), 1928, Bobsledding

Youngest Female Gold – **15yr 128d** Maxi Herber (GER), 1936, Figure Skating

Youngest Male Medal – **14yr 363d** Scott Allen (USA), 1964, Figure Skating

Youngest Female Medal – **15yr 10d** Manuela Gross (GDR), 1972, Figure Skating

Oldest Competitor (Male) – **53yr 297d** James Coats (GBR), 1948, Tobogganing

Oldest Competitor (Female) – **43yr 209d** Ludowika Jakobsson (FIN), 1928, Figure Skating

Youngest Competitor (Male) – **12yr 110d** Jan Hoffmann (GDR), 1968, Figure Skating

Youngest Competitor (Female) – **11yr 73d** Cecilia Colledge (GBR), 1932, Figure Skating

OLYMPIC SPORTS DOUBLES

There have been a number of multi-talented sports people who have won Olympic medals in different sports. The only one to win gold medals in both Summer and Winter Games was Eddie Eagan (USA), who won the 1920 light-heavyweight boxing title and was a member of the 1932 winning 4-man bob. His closest rival has been Jacob Tullin Thams (NOR) who won the ski jump in 1924 and then took a silver in yachting in 1936. The most outstanding woman in this line of endeavour is Christa Rothenburger-Luding (GDR), who won a gold and a silver at speed skating at Calgary in 1988 and then came second in the sprint cycling at Seoul later the same year.

In the Summer Games, the earliest gold medallist at two sports was Carl Schuhmann (GER) with three gymnastic events and the wrestling in 1896. At the same games, Viggo Jensen (DEN) won a gold and a silver in weightlifting, a silver and a bronze at shooting, and was fourth in the rope climb. Morris Kirksey (USA) won gold medals in the 4 × 100m relay and as a member of the American rugby team in 1920, while Daniel Norling (SWE) won gymnastic golds in 1908 and 1912, and then an equestrian gold in 1920. John Derbyshire (GBR) and Paul Radmilovic (GBR) won golds at swimming and the allied sport of water polo in the early part of the century. Examples of women excelling in two summer Olympic sports

are rare, with the most outstanding probably being Roswitha Krause (GDR) who won a 1968 silver in the 4 × 100m freestyle and then won silver and bronze in the 1976 and 1980 handball tournaments.

One of the more unusual doubles was that of Fernand de Montigny (BEL), who won a gold, two silvers and two bronze medals in fencing in five Games (1906–1924), and another bronze on the hockey field in 1920. However, Frank Kungler (USA) has the unique distinction of winning medals at three sports at the same Games. In 1904 he won a silver at wrestling, a bronze at tug-of-war and two bronzes at weightlifting.

ARCHERY

The sport made its first appearance in the 1900 Games in Paris, with six events on the programme. Some Olympic historians consider that another, live pigeon shooting, was an official event, but the majority think not, and this book follows that opinion. The contests were held in Continental style, with each archer shooting a single arrow at a time in competition order, as against the British method of three arrows at each turn.

The eligibility of the 1904 archery competitions is also disputed by some, particularly as only American archers took part. However, the majority of historians and the author accept them as Olympic events. The competitors in the 1904 women's contests were among the first women to compete in the Olympics, only the tennis players in 1900 having a prior claim.

The competitions of 1908 were accorded a much higher status than before, although only three nations took part. The men's York Round was won by William Dod (GBR), while his remarkable sister Charlotte took the silver behind Queenie Newall in the women's event. Lottie Dod, then over 36 years old, was one of the greatest sportswomen of her, or any other, generation. She had won the Wimbledon tennis singles five times, the British Ladies

golf crown in 1904, and had represented England at hockey. She also excelled at skating and tobogganing. She and William were also the first brother and sister, in any sport, to win medals at the Oympic Games.

Archery was not included in the 1912 Games but, reflecting Belgium's great interest in the sport, there were ten events at Antwerp in 1920, all in the Belgian style of shooting. With only three countries present again, Hubert van Innis (BEL), now 54, brought his total medals to a record six gold and three silver.

The sport was then dropped from the Games until 1972, when events were standardised into contests over Double FITA Rounds for men and women. A FITA (*Federation Internationale de Tir a l'Arc**) Round

Gold medallists in the 1988 archery team competition – Chun In-Soo, Lee Han-Sup and Park Sung-Soo of Korea.

ARCHERY MEDALS *1900–1920*

	Gold	Silver	Bronze
1900	*Au cordon doré −50m*		
	Henri Herouin (FRA)	Hubert van Innis	Emile Fisseux
	Au cordon doré − 33m		
	Hubert van Innia (BEL)	Victor Thibaud (FRA)	Charles Petit (FRA)
	Au chapelet – 50m		
	Eugène Mougin (FRA)	Henri Helle (FRA)	Emile Mercier (FRA)
	Au chapelet – 33m		
	Hubert van Innis (BEL)	Victor Thibaud (FRA)	Charles Petit (FRA)
	Sur la perche à la herse		
	Emmanuel Foulon (FRA)	Serrurier (FRA)	Druart Jr (BEL)
	Sur la perche à la pyramide		
	Emile Grumiaux (FRA)	Louis Glineux	–
1904	**Men**		
	Double York Round		
	Phillip Bryant (USA)	Robert Williams (USA)	William Thompson (USA)
	Double American Round		
	Philip Bryant (USA)	Robert Williams (USA)	William Thompson (USA)
	Team Round		
	Potomac Archers (USA)	Cincinatti Archery Club (USA)	Boston AA (USA)
	Women		
	Double National Round		
	Lida Howell (USA)	Jessie Pollack (USA)	Emma Cooke (USA)
	Double Columbia Round		
	Lida Howell (USA)	Emma Cooke (USA)	Jessie Pollack (USA)
	Team Round		
	Cincinatti Archery Club (USA)	Potomac Archers (USA)	–
1908	**Men**		
	York Round		
	William Dod (GBR)	RB Brooks-King (GBR)	Henry Richardson (USA)
	Continental Style		
	EG Grisot (FRA)	Louis Vernet (FRA)	Gustave Cabaret (FRA)
	Women		
	National Round		
	Queenie Newall (GBR)	Charlotte Dod (GBR)	Hill-Lowe (GBR)
1920	*Fixed bird target – small birds – individual*		
	Edmond van Moer (BEL)	Louis van de Perck (BEL)	Joseph Hermans (BEL)
	Fixed bird target – small birds – team		
	Belgium	–	–
	Fixed bird target – large birds – individual		
	Edouard Cloetens (BEL)	Louis van de Perck (BEL)	Firmin Flamand (BEL)
	Fixed bird target – large birds – team		
	Belgium	–	–
	Moving bird target – 28m – individual		
	Hubert van Innis (BEL)	Léonce Quentin (FRA)	–
	Moving bird target – 28m – team		
	Netherlands	Belgium	France
	Moving bird target – 33m – individual		
	Hubert van Innis (BEL)	Julien Brulé (FRA)	–
	Moving bird target – 33m – team		
	Belgium	France	–
	Moving bird target – 50m – individual		
	Julien Brulé (FRA)	Hubert van Innis (BEL)	–
	Moving bird target – 50m – team		
	Belgium	France	–

ARCHERY MEDALS *1972–1988*

DOUBLE FITA ROUND (Maximum possible score 2880 points)

Men

1972	John Williams (USA) 2528 pts	Gunnar Jarvil (SWE) 2481 pts	Kyösti Laasonen (FIN) 2467 pts
1976	Darrell Pace (USA) 2571 pts	Hiroshi Michinaga (JPN) 2502 pts	Giancarlo Ferrari (ITA) 2495 pts
1980	Tomi Poikolainen (FIN) 2455 pts	Boris Isachenko (URS) 2452 pts	Aleksandr Gazov (URS) 2449 pts
1984	Darrell Pace (USA) 2616 pts	Richard McKinney (USA) 2564 pts	Hiroshi Yamamoto (JPN) 2563
1988	Jay Barrs (USA) 338 pts (2605)	Park Sung-Soo (KOR) 336 pts (2614)	Vladimir Yecheyev 335 pts (2600)

Women

1972	Doreen Wilber (USA) 2424 pts	Irena Szydlowska (POL) 2407 pts	Emma Gapchenko (URS) 2403 pts
1976	Luann Ryon (USA) 2499	Valentina Kovpan (URS) 2460 pts	Zebeniso Rustamova (URS) 2407 pts
1980	Keto Losaberidze (URS) 2491 pts	Batalya Butuzova (URS) 2477 pts	Päivi Meriluoto (FIN) 2449 pts
1984	Seo Hyang-Soon (KOR) 2568 pts	Li Lingjuan (CHN) 2559 pts	Kim Jin-Ho (KOR) 2555 pts
1988	Kim Soo-Nyung (KOR) 344 ptsd (2683*)	Wang Hee-Kyung (KOR) 332 pts (2612)	Yung Young-Sook (KOR) 327 pts (2603)

Team – Men

1988	Korea	United States	Great Britain

Team – Women

1988	Korea	Indonesia	United States

*Olympic record

ARCHERY MEDAL TOTALS

	MEN			WOMEN			
Country	G	S	B	G	S	B	Total
United States	7	5	4	5	3	3	27
France	6	10	6	–	–	–	22
Belgium	10	5	3	–	–	–	18
Korea	1	1	–	3	1	2	8
Soviet Union	–	1	2	1	2	2	8
Great Britain	1	1	1	1	1	1	6
Finland	1	–	1	–	–	1	3
Japan	–	1	1	–	–	–	2
Netherlands	1	–	–	–	–	–	1
China	–	–	–	–	1	–	1
Indonesia	–	–	–	–	1	–	1
Poland	–	–	–	–	1	–	1
Sweden	–	1	–	–	–	–	1
Italy	–	–	1	–	–	–	1
	27[1]	25	19[2]	10	10	9[3]	100

[1]*Only a gold medal awarded in two 1920 events*
[2]*No bronze medals in one 1900 and six 1920 events*
[3]*No bronze medal in 1904 team event*

consists of 144 arrows, comprising 36 each over distances of 90m, 70m, 50m and 30m for men and 70m, 60, 50m and 30m for women. From 1988 the medals were decided by the scores in a final round of 36 arrows. Also in 1988 team competitions were introduced.

The first paraplegic to compete in a normal Olympic event was Neroli Fairhall (NZL), who finished 35th, from her wheelchair, in the 1984 women's archery event.

The oldest gold medallist was the Rev Galen Spencer (USA) in the winning 1904 team, two days past his 64th birthday. The youngest champion was Seo Hyang-Soon (KOR), aged 17yr 34 days, winning the 1984 women's title. The youngest male winner was Park Sung-Soo (KOR) in the 1988 team, aged 18yr 135 days, while the oldest female champion was Queenie Newall (GBR) in 1908, aged 53yr 275 days.

The oldest ever medallist was Samuel Harding Duvall (USA), aged 68yr 194 days, winning a silver in the 1904 team contest, while the youngest was Denise Parker (USA) with a team bronze in 1988 aged 14yr 294 days. The youngest male medallist was Henry Richardson (USA) with a team bronze in 1904 aged 15yr 126 days. Hubert van Innis (BEL) won gold medals over a record span of 20 years (1900–20).

*International Archery Federation

BADMINTON

A new Olympic sport, introduced for the first time in 1992. It was a demonstration sport in 1972 when 25 competitors from 11 countries took part in a tournament of the highest quality, highlighted by the men's singles victory of Rudy Hartono of Indonesia.

BASEBALL

This is to be held as an official medal sport for the first time in 1992, when there will be an eight-nation tournament. There have been six occasions when American baseball has been demonstrated, plus an exhibition of Finnish baseball in 1952. In 1912 the USA team, containing many track and field medallists, beat Sweden 13–3. In 1936 a 'World Amateurs' team beat an American 'Olympic' team in front of 100 000 spectators in Berlin. In 1956 an American Services team beat an Australian team 11–5 before an estimated 114 000 people, a record crowd for any baseball game anywhere. At Tokyo in 1964 a United States team beat two Japanese teams, and in 1984 Japan won an eight-nation tournament. In 1988 the USA also won an eight-nation tournament, beating Japan in the final.

BASKETBALL

The game made its Olympic debut in 1936, although it was demonstrated in 1904 and the analogous Dutch game Korfball was demonstrated in 1928. The 1936 tournament was uniquely played outdoors, and one of the referees was Avery Brundage (USA), later to become President of the IOC, while the man who had devised the modern game, Dr James Naismith, was among those who presented the medals. The tournament was won by the United States, beginning a winning streak of seven titles and 63 victories.

That run began with a walkover against Spain – whose team had returned home to fight in the Spanish Civil War – and lasted until they were beaten 51–50 by the Soviet Union in the controversial 1972 final, the Americans claiming that too much overtime was played during which the Soviet Aleksandr Belov (who tragically died six years later) scored the winning basket. With one second to go, and the USA in the lead 50–49, the Soviet inbounds pass had been deflected and everyone thought the game was over. However, the Soviet team was given another inbounds chance, but did not score. Again the game seemed to be over. But Dr William Jones (GBR), Secretary-General of FIBA (*Federation Internationale de Basketball Amateur**), then stated that play was incorrectly restarted at one second and that there should have been three seconds allowed. The clock was reset to three seconds and the Soviet team scored. The US team protested vigorously and refused to accept the silver medals. Unbeaten again until another defeat by the Soviet Union in the 1988 semi-final, the overall Olympic win–loss record of US teams is now 84–2.

After various changes in qualifying conditions the IOC has since 1976 accepted 18 teams in basketball, so allowing FIBA to allocate 12 places to the men's competition and six to the women. The Palacia de los Deportes in Mexico City in 1968 had a record capacity for an Olympic basketball game of 22 370 seats.

Bob Kurland (1948–52), Bill Hougland (1952–56) and Burdette Haldorson (1956–60), all US players, are the only men to win two gold medals. Two men have won medals at four Games; Gennadiy Volnov (URS) with a gold, two silvers and a bronze (1960–72) and Sergey Belov (URS) with a gold and three bronzes (1968–80). At the latter Games in Moscow Belov brought the torch into the stadium and lit the Olympic flame.

A number of American players went on to starring careers in the professional game, including Bill Russell and KC Jones (1956), Oscar Robertson, Jerry Lucas and Jerry West (1960) and Michael Jordan and Patrick Ewing (1984). In April 1989 it was decided to allow professional players to compete in the Olympic tournaments.

The oldest gold medallist was Gennadiy Volnov (URS) in 1972, aged 32yr 286 days, while the youngest was Spencer Haywood (USA), aged 19yr 186 days, in 1968. Teofilo Cruz (PUR) competed at a record five Games (1960–76). The oldest medallist was Sergey Belov

*International Amateur Basketball Federation

Spain beat Brazil 118–110 in a basketball preliminary match in Seoul, Brazil's Oscar Schmidt scoring 55 points.

(URS) in 1980, aged 36yr 189 days, while the youngest medallist was Spencer Haywood.

The highest aggregate score in a game is 238 points when Brazil beat China 130–108 in 1988. In that same tournament Brazil also scored the highest ever by a team in Olympic contests when they beat Egypt 138–85. The biggest margin of victory is 100 points, Korea beating Iraq 120–20 and China defeating the same opponents 125–25, both in 1948. The highest score by an individual in a single game is 55 points by Oscar Schmidt (BRA) in a 1988 qualifying round encounter in which Spain beat Brazil 118–110. In his eight games in Seoul, Schmidt averaged a record 42.5 points.

In the women's game, Japan beat Canada 121–89 for an aggregate record of 210 points in 1976, while the highest total was 122 by the Soviet Union against Bulgaria (83) in 1980. The biggest margin was 66 points, the Soviet Union beating Italy 119–53 in 1980. Miyako Otsuka (JPN) scored a record 38 points against Canada in 1976.

Eight Soviet players have won two gold medals, all in 1976 and 1980. Two golds have also been attained by Teresa Edwards and Anne Donovan (both USA) in 1984 and 1988. The oldest female gold medallist was Nadyezda Sakharova (URS) in 1976, aged 31yr 169 days, while the youngest was Teresa Edwards (USA) in 1984, aged 20yr 19 days.

The tallest ever players in Olympic basketball, and the tallest ever medallists in any sport, were Tommy Burleson (USA), silver medallist in 1972, and Arvidas Sabonis (URS), gold in 1988, both at 2.23m/7ft 4in. The tallest female player, and the tallest Olympic female gold medallist ever, was Iuliana Semenova (URS) at 2.18m/7ft 1¾in in 1976 and 1980. She was also the heaviest female gold medallist ever at 129kg/284lb. Incidentally, during the first tournament in 1936 there was a move to ban all players taller than 1.90m/6ft 2¾in, but happily this was withdrawn.

BASKETBALL MEDALS

	Gold	Silver	Bronze
Men			
1936	United States	Canada	Mexico
1948	United States	France	Brazil
1952	United States	Soviet Union	Uruguay
1956	United States	Soviet Union	Uruguay
1960	United States	Soviet Union	Brazil
1964	United States	Soviet Union	Brazil
1968	United States	Yugoslavia	Soviet Union
1972	Soviet Union	United States	Cuba
1976	United States	Yugoslavia	Soviet Union
1980	Yugoslavia	Italy	Soviet Union
1984	United States	Spain	Yugoslavia
1988	Soviet Union	Yugoslavia	United States

1896–1932 Event not held

	Gold	Silver	Bronze
Women			
1976	Soviet Union	United States	Bulgaria
1980	Soviet Union	Bulgaria	Yugoslavia
1984	United States	Korea	China
1988	United States	Yugoslavia	Soviet Union

1896–1972 Event not held

BASKETBALL MEDAL TOTALS

	MEN			WOMEN			
Country	G	S	B	G	S	B	Total
United States	9	1	1	2	1	–	14
Soviet Union	2	4	3	2	–	1	12
Yugoslavia	1	3	1	–	1	1	7
Brazil	–	–	3	–	–	–	3
Bulgaria	–	–	–	–	1	1	2
Uruguay	–	–	2	–	–	–	2
Canada	–	1	–	–	–	–	1
France	–	1	–	–	–	–	1
Italy	–	1	–	–	–	–	1
Korea	–	–	–	–	1	–	1
Spain	–	1	–	–	–	–	1
China	–	–	–	–	–	1	1
Cuba	–	–	1	–	–	–	1
Mexico	–	–	1	–	–	–	1
	12	12	12	4	4	4	48

BOXING

Contests were included in the Ancient Games in 688 BC, when competitors wore leather straps on their hands. As the status of the Games deteriorated in Roman times, metal studs were added. Later still, boxers wore metal 'knuckledusters'. One of the earliest known champions was Onomastos of Smyrna and the last known champion before the Games were abolished was Varazdetes (or Varastades), the winner in AD 369, who later became King of Armenia. This type of boxing should not be confused with the pankration event, which was a brutal combination of boxing and wrestling in which virtually anything was permitted. It is recorded that Arrachion of Phigalia was awarded that title in 564 BC, as his opponent 'gave up' – although Arrachion himself was by then lying dead in the arena.

Boxing was included in the Modern Games in 1904, when the USA won all the titles. A pattern was set by the first heavyweight champion, Samuel Berger, when he turned professional after his victory. He was a member of the San Francisco Olympic Club which had also produced 'Gentleman Jim' Corbett who had won the world title in 1892. Over the years the weight limits for the various classes have changed, and new classes added. Bronze medals for losing semi-finalists were not awarded until 1952.

Two men have won three golds. László Papp (HUN), a southpaw, won the middle-weight division in 1948 and the light-middleweight class in 1952 and 1956, while Teofilo Stevenson (CUB) won the same class, heavyweight, from 1972 to 1980. In 1904 Oliver Kirk (USA) uniquely won two events at the same Games, but only fought one bout in each class. The first boxer successfully to defend a title was Harry Mallin (GBR) with the middleweight crown in 1920 and 1924. In those latter Games the standard of refereeing was highly suspect, not least because the European custom of seating the referees outside the ring was followed. Mallin was continually fouled by his French opponent in a preliminary bout, and ended the fight with teeth marks on his chest. Despite this, the outclassed Frenchman was declared the winner of the bout. An immediate appeal, backed by a threat of withdrawal of all 'English-speaking countries, was upheld.

A strange occurrence was the disqualification of Ingemar Johansson (SWE) in the 1952 heavyweight final and the withholding of his silver medal due to 'inactivity in the ring'. In 1959 he won the world professional title and 30 years after the Games, on his 50th birthday, he was finally presented with his medal. There have been many controversies in Olympic boxing, over the years, one bizarre example being in the 1908 middle-weight final when John Douglas (GBR) – later to captain England at cricket – defeated Reg 'Snowy' Baker (AUS). The Australian understandably complained that the referee had not been impartial – the official was Douglas's father!

The oldest gold medallist was Richard Gunn (GBR), the 1908 featherweight champion, aged 37 yr 254 days. The youngest was the American Jackie Fields (né Jacob Finkelstein) who won the 1924 featherweight crown aged 16 yr 162 days. Floyd Patterson (USA) won the 1952 middleweight title aged 17 yr 211 days, and four years later was the youngest ever world professional heavyweight champion. The first black African boxer to win a gold medal was Robert Wangila (KEN) in 1988. A number of brothers have won medals, but the only known father and son medallists are Jose Villanueva (PHI), bronze 1932 bantamweight, and Anthony

One of the stars of Olympic boxing, László Papp, a Hungarian railway clerk, with three gold medals from 1948 to 1956.

Teofilo Stevenson of Cuba (right) beating Duane Bobick (USA) on his way to the first of his record three consecutive heavyweight titles at Munich in 1972.

Villanueva (PHI), silver 1964 featherweight.

Olympic boxing champions who have won world professional titles include (alphabetically): Nino Benvenuti (ITA), Mark Breland (USA), Cassius Clay (later Muhammad Ali, USA), Jackie Fields (USA), George Foreman (USA), Joe Frazier (USA), Frankie Genaro (USA), Marvin Johnson (USA), Fidel LaBarba (USA), Ray Leonard (USA), Patrizio Oliva (ITA), Mate Parlov (YUG), Floyd Patterson (USA), Pascual Perez (ARG), Leo Randolph (USA), Willie Smith (SAF), Leon and Michael Spinks (USA), Mauricio Stecca (ITA), Meldrick Taylor (USA) and Pernell Whitaker (USA).

VAL BARKER CUP

1936	Louis Lauria (USA)	bronze	– flyweight
1948	George Hunter (SAF)	gold	– light-heavyweight
1952	Norvell Lee (USA)	gold	– light-heavyweight
1956	Dick McTaggart (GBR)	gold	– lightweight
1960	Giovanni Benvenuti (ITA)	gold	– welterweight
1964	Valeriy Popentschenko (URS)	gold	– middleweight
1968	Philip Waruinge (KEN)	bronze	– featherweight
1972	Teofilo Stevenson (CUB)	gold	– heavyweight
1976	Howard Davis (UA)	gold	– lightweight
1980	Patrizio Oliva (ITA)	gold	– light-welterweight
1984	Raul Gonzales (USA)	gold	– light-flyweight
1988	Roy Jones (USA)	silver	– light-middleweight

The Val Barker Cup is presented by the International Amateur Boxing Association (AIBA) – Val Barker was a former President of the organisation – to the competitor adjudged the best stylist at the Games. First awarded in 1936.

In the 1988 tournament, because of a record 441 entries, two rings were used simultaneously. There is still pressure to drop boxing from the Olympic programme, despite the introduction of new gloves, safer protective helmets and five rounds of two minutes.

BOXING MEDALS

	Gold	Silver	Bronze

Light-Flyweight
Weight up to 48kg/105.8lb

	Gold	Silver	Bronze
1968	Francisco Rodriguez (VEN)	Yong-ju Jee (KOR)	Harlan Marbley (USA)
			Hubert Skrzypczak (POL)
1972	György Gedo (HUN)	U Gil Kim (PRK)	Ralph Evans (GBR)
			Enrique Rodriguez (ESP)
1976	Jorge Hernandez (CUB)	Byong Uk Li (PRK)	Payao Pooltarat (THA)
			Orlando Maldonado (PUR)
1980	Shamil Sabirov (URS)	Hipolito Ramos (CUB)	Byong UK Li (PRK)
			Ismail Moustafov (BUL)
1984	Paul Gonzales (USA)	Salvatore Todisco (ITA)	Keith Mwila (ZAM)
			Jose Bolivar (VEN)
1988	Ivailo Hristov (BUL)	Michael Carbajal (USA)	Robert Isaszegi (HUN)
			Leopoldo Serantes (PHI)

1896–1964 Event not held

Flyweight
From 1948 the weight limit has been 51kg/112½lb. In 1904 it was 105lb/47.6kg. From 1920 to 1936 it was 112lb/50.8kg.

	Gold	Silver	Bronze
1904	George Finnegan (USA)	Miles Burke (USA)	–*
1920	Frank Di Gennara (USA)	Anders Petersen (DEN)	William Cuthbertson (GBR)
1924	Fidel LaBarba (USA)	James McKenzie (GBR)	Raymond Fee (USA)
1928	Antal Kocsis (HUN)	Armand Appel (FRA)	Carlo Cavagnoli (ITA)
1932	István Enekes (HUN)	Francisco Cabanas (MEX)	Louis Salica (USA)
1936	Willi Kaiser (GER)	Gavino Matta (ITA)	Louis Laurie (USA)
1948	Pascual Perez (ARG)	Spartaco Bandinelli (ITA)	Soo-Ann Han (KOR)
1952	Nathan Brooks (USA)	Edgar Basel (GER)	Anatoliy Bulakov (URS)
			William Toweel (SAF)
1956	Terence Spinks (GBR)	Mircea Dobrescu (ROM)	John Caldwell (IRL)
			René Libeer (FRA)
1960	Gyula Török (HUN)	Sergey Sivko (URS)	Kyoshi Tanabe (JPN)
			Abdelmoneim Elguindi (EGY)
1964	Fernando Atzori (ITA)	Artur Olech (POL)	Robert Carmody (USA)
			Stanislav Sorokin (URS)
1968	Ricardo Delgado (MEX)	Artur Olech (POL)	Servilio Oliveira (BRA)
			Leo Rwabwogo (UGA)
1972	Gheorghi Kostadinov (BUL)	Leo Rwabwogo (UGA)	Leszek Blazynski (POL)
			Douglas Rodriguez (CUB)
1976	Leo Randolph (USA)	Ramon Duvalon (CUB)	Leszek Blazynski (POL)
			David Torosyan (URS)
1980	Petar Lessov (BUL)	Viktor Miroshnichenko (URS)	Hugh Russel (IRL)
			Janos Varadi (HUN)
1984	Steve McCrory (USA)	Redzep Redzepovski (YUG)	Eyup Can (TUR)
			Ibrahim Bilali (KEN)
1988	Kim Kwang-Sun (KOR)	Andreas Tews (GDR)	Mario Gonzalez (MEX)
			Timofey Skriabin (URS)

1896–1900, 1906–1912 Event not held

*No third place.

Bantamweight
From 1948 the weight limit has been 54kg/119lb. In 1904 it was 115lb/52.16kg. In 1908 it was 116lb/52.62kg. From 1920 to 1936 118lb/53.52kg.

	Gold	Silver	Bronze
1904	Oliver Kirk (USA)	George Finnegan (USA)	–*
1908	Henry Thomas (GBR)	John Condon (GBR)	W Webb (GBR)
1920	Clarence Walker (SAF)	Christopher Graham (CAN)	James McKenzie (GBR)
1924	William Smith (SAF)	Salvadore Tripoli (USA)	Jean Ces (FRA)
1928	Vittorio Tamagnini (ITA)	John Daley (USA)	Harry Isaacs (SAF)
1932	Horace Gwynne (CAN)	Hans Ziglarski (GER)	José Villanueva (PHI)
1936	Ulderico Sergo (ITA)	Jack Wilson (USA)	Fidel Ortiz (MEX)
1948	Tibor Csik (HUN)	Giovanni Zuddas (ITA)	Juan Venegas (PUR)
1952	Pentti Hämäläinen (FIN)	John McNally (IRL)	Gennadiy Garbuzov (URS)
			Joon-Ho Kang (KOR)
1956	Wolfgang Behrendt (GER)	Soon-Chun Song (KOR)	Frederick Gilroy (IRL)
			Claudio Barrientos (CHI)
1960	Oleg Grigoryev (URS)	Primo Zamparini (ITA)	Brunoh Bendig (POL)
			Oliver Taylor (AUS)

	Gold	Silver	Bronze
1964	Takao Sakurai (JPN)	Shin Cho Chung (KOR)	Juan Fabila Mendoza (MEX)
			Washington Rodriguez (URU)
1968	Valeriy Sokolov (URS)	Eridadi Mukwanga (UGA)	Eiji Morioka (JPN)
			Kyou-Chull Chang (KOR)
1972	Orlando Martinez (CUB)	Alfonso Zamora (MEX)	George Turpin (GBR)
			Ricardo Carreras (USA)
1976	Yong Jo Gu (PRK)	Charles Mooney (USA)	Patrick Cowdell (GBR)
			Viktor Rybakov (URS)
1980	Juan Hernandez (CUB)	Bernardo Pinango (VEN)	Dumitru Cipere (ROM)
			Michael Anthony (GUY)
1984	Maurizio Stecca (ITA)	Hector Lopez (MEX)	Dale Walters (CAN)
			Pedro Nolasco (DOM)
1988	Kennedy McKinney (USA)	Alexandar Hristov (BUL)	Jorge Julio Rocha (COL)
			Phajol Moolsan (THA)

1896–1900, 1906, 1912 Event not held

No third place.

Featherweight
From 1952 the weight limit has been 57kg/126lb. In 1904 it was 125lb/56.70kg. From 1908 to 1936 it was 126lb/57.15kg. In 1948 it was 58kg.

1904	Oliver Kirk (USA)	Frank Haller (USA)	Fred Gilmore (USA)
1908	Richard Gunn (GBR)	CW Morris (GBR)	Hugh Roddin (GBr)
1920	Paul Fritsch (FRA)	Jean Gachet (FRA)	Edoardo Garzena (ITA)
1924	John Fields (USA)	Joseph Salas (USA)	Pedro Quartucci (ARG)
1928	Lambertus van Klaveren (HOL)	Victor Peralta (ARG)	Harold Devine (USA)
1932	Carmelo Robledo (ARG)	Josef Schleinkofer (GER)	Carl Carlsson (SWE)
1936	Oscar Casanovas (ARG)	Charles Catterall (SAF)	Josef Miner (GER)
1948	Ernesto Formenti (ITA)	Denis Shepherd (SAF)	Aleksey Antkiewicz (POL)
1952	Jan Zachara (TCH)	Sergio Caprari (ITA)	Joseph Ventaja (FRA)
			Leonard Leisching (SAF)
1956	Vladimir Safronov (URS)	Thomas Nicholls (GBR)	Henryk Niedzwiedzki (POL)
			Pentti Hämäläinen (FIN)
1960	Francesco Musso (ITA)	Jerzy Adamski (POL)	William Meyers (SAF)
			Jorma Limmonen (FIN)
1964	Stanislav Stepashkin (URS)	Antony Villaneuva (PHI)	Charles Brown (USA)
			Heinz Schultz (GER)
1968	Antonio Roldan (MEX)	Albert Robinson (USA)	Philip Waruinge (KEN)
			Ivan Michailov (BUL)
1972	Boris Kuznetsov (URS)	Philip Waruinge (KEN)	Clemente Rojas (COL)
			András Botos (HUN)
1976	Angel Herrera (CUB)	Richard Nowakowski (GDR)	Juan Paredes (MEX)
			Leszek Kosedowski (POL)
1980	Rudi Fink (GDR)	Adolfo Horta (CUB)	Viktor Rybakov (URS)
			Krzysztof Kosedowski (POL)
1984	Meldrick Taylor (USA)	Peter Konyegwachie (NGR)	Turgut Aykac (TUR)
			Omar Peraza (VEN)
1988	Giovanni Parisi (ITA)	Daniel Dumitrescu (ROM)	Lee Jae-Hyuk (KOR)
			Abdelhak Achik (MAR)

1896–1900, 1906, 1912 Event not held.

Lightweight
From 1952 the weight has been 60kg/132lb. In 1904 and from 1920 to 1936 it was 135lb/61.24kg. In 1908 it was 140lb/63.50kg. In 1948 it was 62kg/ 136½lb.

1904	Harry Spanger (USA)	James Eagan (USA)	Russell Van Horn (USA)
1908	Frederick Grace (GBR)	Frederick Spiller (GBR)	HH Johnson (GBR)
1920	Samuel Mosberg (USA)	Gotfred Johansen (DEN)	Clarence Newton (CAN)
1924	Hans Nielsen (DEN)	Alfredo Coppello (ARG)	Frederick Boylstein (USA)
1928	Carlo Orlandi (ITA)	Stephen Halaiko (USA)	Gunnar Berggren (SWE)
1932	Lawrence Stevens (SAF)	Thure Ahlqvist (SWE)	Nathan Bor (USA)
1936	Imre Harangi (HUN)	Nikolai Stepulov (EST)	Erik Agren (SWE)
1948	Gerald Dreyer (SAF)	Joseph Vissers (BEL)	Svend Wad (DEN)
1952	Aureliano Bolognesi (ITA)	Aleksey Antkiewicz (POL)	Gheorge Fiat (ROM)
			Erkki Pakkanen (FIN)
1956	Richard McTaggart (GBR)	Harry Kurschat (GER)	Anthony Byren (IRL)
			Anatoliy Lagetko (URS)
1960	Kazimierz Pazdzior (POL)	Sandro Lopopoli (ITA)	Richard McTaggart (GBR)
			Abel Laudonio (ARG)
1964	Józef Grudzien (POL)	Vellikton Barannikov (URS)	Ronald Harris (USA)
			James McCourt (IRL)

	Gold	Silver	Bronze
1968	Ronald Harris (USA)	Józef Grudzien (POL)	Calistrat Cutov (ROM) Zvonimir Vujin (YUG)
1972	Jan Szczepanksi (POL)	László Orban (HUN)	Samuel Mbugua (KEN) Alfonso Perez (COL)
1976	Howard Davis (USA)	Simion Cutov (ROM)	Ace Rusevski (YUG) Vasiliy Solomin (URS)
1980	Angel Herrera (CUB)	Viktor Demianenko (URS)	Kazimierz Adach (POL) Richard Nowakowski (GDR)
1984	Pernell Whitaker (USA)	Luis Ortiz (PUR)	Martin Ebanga (CMR) Chun Chi-Sung (KOR)
1988	Andreas Zülow (GDR)	George Cramne (SWE)	Nerguy Enkhbat (MGL) Romallis Ellis (USA)

1896–1900, 1906, 1912 Event not held

Light-Welterweight
Weight up to 63.5kg/140lb

	Gold	Silver	Bronze
1952	Charles Adkins (USA)	Viktor Mednov (URS)	Erkki Mallenius (FIN) Bruno Visintin (ITA)
1956	Vladimir Yengibarvan (URS)	Franco Nenci (ITA)	Henry Loubscher (SAF) Constantin Dumitrescu (ROM)
1960	Bohumil Nemecek (TCH)	Clement Quartey (GHA)	Quincy Daniels (USA) Marian Kasprzvk (POL)
1964	Jerzy Kulej (POL)	Yegeniy Frolov (URS)	Eddie Blay (GHA) Habib Galhia (TUN)
1968	Jerzv Kulej (POL)	Enrique Regueiferos (CUB)	Arto Nilsson (FIN) James Wallington (USA)
1972	Ray Seales (USA)	Anghel Anghelov (BUL)	Zvonimir Vujin (YUG) Issaka Daborg (NIG)
1976	Ray Leonard (USA)	Andres Aldama (CUB)	Vladimir Kolev (BUL) Kazimierz Szczerba (POL)
1980	Patrizio Oliva (ITA)	Serik Konakbayev (URS)	Jose Aguilar (CUB) Anthony Willis (GBR)
1984	Jerry Page (USA)	Dhawee Umponmana (THA)	Mircea Fuger (ROM) Mirko Puzovic (YUG)
1988	Vyacheslav Janovski (URS)	Grahame Cheney (AUS)	Lars Myrberg (SWE) Reiner Gies (FRG)

1896–1948 Event not held.

Welterweight
From 1948 the weight limit has been 67kg/148lb. In 1904 it was 14¾lb/65.27kg. From 1920 to 1936 it was 147lb/66.68kg.

	Gold	Silver	Bronze
1904	Albert Young (USA)	Harry Spanger (USA)	Joseph Lydon (USA) James Eagan (USA)
1920	Albert Schneider (CAN)	Alexander Ireland (GBR)	Frederick Colberg (USA)
1924	Jean Delarge (BEL)	Héctor Mendez (ARG)	Douglas Lewis (CAN)
1928	Edward Morgan (NZL)	Raul Landini (ARG)	Raymond Smillie (CAN)
1932	Edward Flynn (USA)	Erich Campe (GER)	Bruno Ahlberg (FIN)
1936	Sten Suvio (FIN)	Michael Murach (GER)	Gerhard Petersen (DEN)
1948	Julius Torma (TCH)	Horace Herring (USA)	Alessandro D'Ottavio (ITA)
1952	Zygmunt Chychla)POL)	Sergey Schtsherbakov (URS)	Victor Jörgensen (DEN) Günther Heidemann (GER)
1956	Nicholae Lince (ROM)	Frederick Tiedt (IRL)	Kevin Hogarth (AUS) Nicholas Gargano (GBR)
1960	Giovanni Benvenuti (ITA)	Yuriy Radonyak (URS)	Leszek Drogosz (POL) James Lloyd (GBR)
1964	Marian Kasprzyk (POL)	Ritschardas Tamulis (URS)	Pertti Perhonen (FIN) Silvano Bertini (ITA)
1968	Manfred Wolke (GDR)	Joseph Bessala (CMR)	Vladimir Musalinov (URS) Mario Guilloti (ARG)
1972	Emilio Correa (CUB)	Janos Kajdi (HUN)	Dick Murunga (KEN) Jesse Valdez (USA)
1976	Jochen Bachfeld (GDR)	Pedro Gamarro (VEN)	Reinhard Skricek (FRG) Victor Zilberman (ROM)
1980	Andrew Aldama (CUB)	John Mugabi (UGA)	Karl-Heinz Krüger (GDR) Kazimierz Szczerba (POL)
1984	Mark Breland (USA)	An Young-Su (KOR)	Joni Nyman (FIN) Luciano Bruno (ITA)
1988	Robert Wangila (KEN)	Laurent Boudouani (FRA)	Jan Dydak (POL) Kenneth Gould (USA)

1896–1900, 1906–1912 Event not held

	Gold	Silver	Bronze

Light-Middleweight
Weight up to 71kg/157lb.

1952	László Papp (HUN)	Theunis van Schalkwyk (SAF)	Boris Tishin (URS)
			Eladio Herrera (ARG)
1956	László Papp (HUN)	José Torres (USA)	John McCormack (GBR)
			Zbigniew Pietrzkowski (POL)
1960	Wilbert McClure (USA)	Carmelo Bossi (ITA)	Boris Lagutin (URS)
			William Fisher (GBR)
1964	Boris Lagutin (URS)	Josef Gonzales (FRA)	Nohim Maivegun (NGR)
			Jozef Grzesiak (POL)
1968	Boris Lagutin (URS)	Rolando Garbey (CUB)	John Baldwin (USA)
			Günther Meier (FRG)
1972	Dieter Kottysch (FRG)	Wieslaw Rudkowski (POL)	Alan Minter GBR)
			Peter Tiepold (GDR)
1976	Jerzy Rybicki (POL)	Tadija Kacar (YUG)	Roland Garbey (CUB)
			Viktor Savchenko (URS)
1980	Armando Martinez (CUB)	Aleksandr Koshkin (URS)	Jan Franck (TCH)
			Detlef Kastner (GDR)
1984	Frank Tate (USA)	Shawn O'Sullivan (CAN)	Manfred Zielonka (FRG)
			Christophe Tiozzo (FRA)
1988	Park Si-Hun (KOR)	Roy Jones (USA)	Richard Woodhall (GBR)
			Raymond Downey (CAN)

1896–1948 Event not held

Middleweight
From 1952 the weight limit has been 75kg/165lb. From 1904 to 1908 it was 158lb/71.68kg. From 1920 to 1936 it was 160lb/72.57kg. In 1948 it was 73kg/161lb.

1904	Charles Mayer (USA)	Benjamin Spradley (USA)	–*
1908	John Douglas (GBR)	Reginald Baker (AUS/NZL)	W Philo (GBR)
1920	Harry Mallin (GBR)	Georges Prud'homme (CAN)	Moe Herscovitch (CAN)
1924	Harry Mallin (GBR)	John Elliott (GBR)	Joseph Beecken (BEL)
1928	Piero Toscani (ITA)	Jan Hermanek (TCH)	Léonard Steyaert (BEL)
1932	Carmen Barth (USA)	Amado Azar (ARG)	Ernest Pierce (SAF)
1936	Jean Despeaux (FRA)	Henry Tiller (NOR)	Raúl Villareal (ARG)
1948	László Papp (HUN)	John Wright (GBR)	Ivano Fontana (ITA)
1952	Floyd Patterson (USA)	Vasile Tita (ROM)	Boris Nikolov (BUL)
			Stig Sjolin (SWE)
1956	Gennadiy Schatkov (URS)	Ramon Tapia (CHI)	Gilbert Chapron (FRA)
			Victor Zalazar (ARG)
1960	Edward Crook (USA)	Tadeusz Walasek (POL)	Ion Monea (ROM)
			Yevgeniy Feofanov (URS)
1964	Valeriy Popentschenko (URS)	Emil Schultz (GER)	Franco Valle (ITA)
			Tadeusz Walasek (POL)
1968	Christopher Finnegan (GBR)	Aleksey Kisselyov (URS)	Agustin Zaragoza (MEX)
			Alfred Jones (USA)
1972	Vyatcheslav Lemechev (URS)	Reima Virtanen (FIN)	Prince Amartey (GHA)
			Marvin Johnson (USA)
1976	Michael Spinks (USA)	Rufat Riskiev (URS)	Alec Nastac (ROM)
			Luis Martinez (CUB)
1980	Jose Gomez (CUB)	Viktor Savchenko (URS)	Jerzy Rybicki (POL)
			Valentin Silaghi (ROM)
1984	Shin Joon-Sup (KOR)	Virgil Hill (USA)	Mohamed Zaoui (ALG)
			Aristides Gonzales (PUR)
1988	Henry Maske (GDR)	Egerton Marcus (CAN)	Chris Sande (KEN)
			Hussain Shaw Syed (PAK)

1896–1900, 1906, 1912 Event not held

*No third place.

Light-Heavyweight
From 1952 the weight limit has been 81kg/178½lb. From 1920 to 1936 it was 175lb/79.38kg. In 1948 it was 80kg/186¼lb.

1920	Edward Eagan (USA)	Sverre Sörsdal (NOR)	H Franks (GBR)
1924	Harry Mitchell (GBR)	Thyge Petersen (DEN)	Sverre Sörsdal (NOR)
1928	Victor Avendano (ARG)	Ernst Pistulla (GER)	Karel Miljon (HOL)
1932	David Carstens (SAF)	Gino Rossi (ITA)	Peter Jörgensen (DEN)
1936	Roger Michelot (FRA)	Richard Vogt (GER)	Francisco Risiglione (ARG)
1948	George Hunter (SAF)	Donald Scott (GBR)	Maurio Cia (ARG)

	Gold	Silver	Bronze
1952	Norvel Lee (USA)	Antonio Pacenza (ARG)	Anotiliy Perov (URS)
			Harri Siljander (FIN)
1956	James Boyd (USA)	Gheorghe Negrea (ROM)	Carlos Lucas (CHI)
			Romualdas Murauskas (URS)
1960	Cassius Clay (USA)	Zbigniew Pietrzykowski (POL)	Anthony Madigan (AUS)
			Giulio Saraudi (ITA)
1964	Cosimo Pinto (ITA)	Aleksey Kisselyov (URS)	Aleksandr Nikolov (BUL)
			Zbigniew Pietrzykowski (POL)
1968	Dan Poznyak (URS)	Ion Monea (ROM)	Georgy Stankov (BUL)
			Stanislav Gragan (POL)
1972	Mate Parlov (YUG)	Gilberto Carrillo (CUB)	Isaac Ikhouria (NGR)
			Janusz Gortat (POL)
1976	Leon Spinks (USA)	Sixto Soria (CUB)	Costica Danifoiu (ROM)
			Janusz Gortat (POL)
1980	Slobodan Kacar (YUG)	Pavel Skrzecz (POL)	Herbert Bauch (GDR)
			Ricardo Rojas (CUB)
1984	Anton Josipovic (YUG)	Kevin Barry (NZL)	Mustapha Moussa (ALG)
			Evander Holyfield (USA)
1988	Andrew Maynard (USA)	Nourmagomed Chanavazov (URS)	Damir Skaro (YUG)
			Henryk Petrich (POL)

1896–1912 Event not held.

Heavyweight

From 1984 the weight limit has been 91kg/200½lb. From 1904 to 1908 it was over 158lb/71.67kg. From 1920 to 1936 it was over 175lb/79.38kg. In 1948 it was over 80kg/176¼lb. From 1952 to 1980 it was over 81kg/178½lb.

	Gold	Silver	Bronze
1904	Samuel Berger (USA)	Charles Mayer (USA)	William Michaels (USA)
1908	AL Oldham (GBR)	SCH Evans (GBR)	Frederick Parks (GBR)
1920	Ronald Rawson (GBR)	Sören Petersen (DEN)	Xavier Eluère (FRA)
1924	Otto von Porat (NOR)	Sören Petersen (DEN)	Alfredo Porzio (ARG)
1928	Arturo Rodriguez Jurado (ARG)	Nils Ramm (SWE)	Jacob Michaelsen (DEN)
1932	Santiago Lovell (ARG)	Luigi Rovati (ITA)	Frederick Feary (USA)
1936	Herbert Runge (GER)	Guillermo Lovell (ARG)	Erling Nilsen (NOR)
1948	Rafael Iglesias (ARG)	Gunnar Nilsson (SWE)	John Arthur (SAF)
1952	Hayes Edward Sanders (USA)	Ingemar Johansson* (SWE)	Andries Nieman (SAF)
			Ilkka Koski (FIN)
1956	Peter Rademacher (USA)	Lev Mukhin (URS)	Daniel Bekker (SAF)
			Giacomo Bozzano (ITA)
1960	Franco de Piccoli (ITA)	Daniel Bekker (SAF)	Josef Nemec (TCH)
			Günter Siegmund (GER)
1964	Joe Frazier (USA)	Hans Huber (GER)	Guiseppe Ros (ITA)
			Vadim Yemelyanov (URS)
1968	George Foreman (USA)	Ionas Tschepulis (URS)	Giorgio Bambini (ITA)
			Joaquin Rocha (MEX)
1972	Teofilo Stevenson (CUB)	Ion Alexe (ROM)	Peter Hussing (FRG)
			Hasse Thomsen (SWE)
1976	Teofilo Stevenson (CUB)	Mircea Simon (ROM)	Johnny Tate (USA)
			Clarence Hill (BER)
1980	Teofilo Stevenson (CUB)	Pyotr Zayev (URS)	Jurgen Fanghanel (GDR)
			Istvan Levai (HUN)
1984	Henry Tillman (USA)	Willie Dewitt (CAN)	Angelo Musone (ITA)
			Arnold Vanderlijde (HOL)
1988	Ray Mercer (USA)	Baik Hyun-Man (KOR)	Andrzej Golota (POL)
			Arnold Vanderlijde (HOL)

1896–1900, 1906, 1912 Event not held.

Silver medal originally not awarded; Johansson disqualified but reinstated in 1982.

Super-Heavyweight

From 1984 the class has been for those over 91kg/200½lb.

	Gold	Silver	Bronze
1984	Tyrell Biggs (USA)	Francesco Damiani (ITA)	Robert Wells (GBR)
			Salihu Azis (YUG)
1988	Lennox Lewis (CAN)	Riddick Bowe (USA)	Alexandr Mirochnitchenko (URS)
			Jasz Zarenkiewicz (POL)

1896–1980 Event not held.

BOXING MEDALS

Country	G	S	B	Total
United States	45	20	28	93
Soviet Union	14	19	18	51
Great Britain	12	10	20	42
Poland	8	9	25	42
Italy	14	12	13	39
Cuba	12	8	5	25
Argentina	7	7	9	23
Germany (FRG)	4	10	9	23
South Africa	6	4	9	19
Romania	1	8	10	19
Hungary	9	2	4	15
Canada	3	5	6	14
GDR	5	2	6	13
Korea	3	5	5	13
France	3	4	6	13
Finland	2	1	10	13
Bulgaria	3	2	6	11
Yugoslavia	3	2	6	11
Mexico	2	3	6	11
Denmark	1	5	5	11
Sweden	–	5	6	11
Kenya	1	1	5	7
Ireland	–	2	5	7
Czechoslovakia	3	1	2	6
Norway	1	2	2	5
Venezuela	1	2	2	5
Australia	–	2	3	5
North Korea (PRK)	1	2	1	4
Belgium	1	1	2	4
Netherlands	1	–	3	4
Uganda	–	3	1	4
Puerto Rico	–	1	3	4
Japan	1	–	2	3
Chile	–	1	2	3
Ghana	–	1	2	3
Nigeria	–	1	2	3
Philippines	–	1	2	3
Thailand	–	1	2	3
Colombia	–	–	3	3
New Zealand	1	1	–	2
Cameroon	–	1	1	2
Algeria	–	–	2	2
Turkey	–	–	2	2
Estonia	–	1	–	1
Bermuda	–	–	1	1
Brazil	–	–	1	1
Dominican Rep	–	–	1	1
Egypt	–	–	1	1
Guyana	–	–	1	1
Mongolia	–	–	1	1
Morocco	–	–	1	1
Niger	–	–	1	1
Pakistan	–	–	1	1
Tunisia	–	–	1	1
Uruguay	–	–	1	1
Zambia	–	–	1	1
	168	168	274[1]	610

[1]From 1952 both losing semi-finalists have been awarded a bronze medal.

CANOEING

Official canoeing competitions were first held in 1936, although kayak and Canadian events were demonstrated in 1924. Uniquely in 1972 at Munich four slalom events were held. The most successful competitor has been Gert Fredriksson (SWE) with six gold medals, one silver and one bronze from 1948–60, all in kayaks. The most medals won by a woman is three golds and a bronze by Ludmila Pinayeva (née Khvedosyuk) of the Soviet Union, from 1964–72. Two men, Vladimir Parfenovich in 1980 and Ian Ferguson (NZL) in 1984, have won three gold medals at one Games. The best by a woman at one Games is two golds and a silver, by Agneta Andersson (SWE) in 1984 and Birgit Schmidt (GDR) in 1988.

The highest speed achieved in the Games over the standard 1000m course is 20.16kph when the Hungarian K4 clocked 2min 58.54sec in a heat in 1988. In 1980 the Soviet K4 team achieved an average speed of 21.15kph over the first 250m in a heat of the event. The fastest by a female crew over the 500m course is 18.59kph when the East German K4 clocked 1min 36.84 sec in a heat in 1988. In the 1984 final the Romanian women's K4 achieved an average speed of 18.92 kph over first 250m.

The closest finish in an Olympic canoeing final occurred in the K2 1000m in 1952 when the timekeepers were unable to separate the first and second placed pairs. The closest finish in women's conoeing was in the K1 500m in 1988 when the winning margin was 0.12sec.

The oldest ever canoeing gold medallist was Gert Fredriksson (SWE) aged 40yr 292 days in the 1960 K2 over 1000m. The youngest was Bent Peder Rasch (DEN) in the 1952 C2 at 1000m, aged 18yr 58 days. The youngest female champion was Birgit Fischer (GDR), aged 18yr 158 days, in the 1980 K1, while the oldest was Sylvi Saimo (FIN) in

CANOEING MEDAL TOTALS

Country	MEN			WOMEN			Total
	G	S	B	G	S	B	
Soviet Union	21	11	7	8	2	3	52
Hungary	7	16	12	–	3	4	42
Germany (FRG)	6	8	8	2	6	2	32
GDR	8	5	8	6	2	1	30
Romania	8	8	8	1	1	3	29
Sweden	11	7	2	2	1	–	23
France	1	5	10	–	–	–	16
Canada	3	5	3	–	1	1	13
Austria	3	4	4	–	1	1	13
United States	4	2	3	–	1	1	11
Denmark	2	3	4	1	–	1	11
Czechoslovakia	6	3	1	–	–	–	10
Bulgaria	1	1	4	1	2	1	10
Finland	3	2	3	1	–	–	9
Netherlands	–	1	3	–	2	2	8
New Zealand	5	1	1	–	–	–	7
Poland	–	2	3	–	–	2	7
Yugoslavia	2	2	1	–	–	–	5
Australia	–	2	3	–	–	–	5
Norway	1	1	2	–	–	–	4
Spain	–	2	2	–	–	–	4
Italy	–	1	–	–	–	–	1
	92	92	92	22	22	22	342

the 1952 K1, aged 37yr 259 days. The youngest medallist was Francine Fox (USA), who won a silver medal in the K2 500m in 1964 aged 15yr 220 days. Incidentally, her partner was 20 years older.

Ivan Patzaichin (ROM) won gold medals over a 16-year period, 1968–84, in the Canadian events. When Philippe Renaud (FRA) won a bronze in the C2 500m in 1988 he was

the latest success of an Olympic family – his brother won a canoe bronze in 1984, their father gained a canoe silver in 1956, and a great-uncle won a cycling bronze in 1924.

CANOEING MEDALS– MEN

	Gold	Silver	Bronze
500 Metres Kayak Singles (K1)			
1976	Vasile Diba (ROM) 1:46.41	Zoltan Szytanity (HUN) 1:46.95	Rüdiger Helm (GDR) 1:48.30
1980	Vladimir Parfenovich (URS) 1:43.43	John Sumegi (AUS) 1:44.12	Vasile Diba (ROM) 1:44.90
1984	Ian Ferguson (NZL) 1:47.84	Lars-Erik Möberg (SWE) 1:48.18	Bernard Bregeon (FRA) 1:48.41
1988	Zsolt Gyulay (HUN) 1:44.82	Andreas Stähle (GDR) 1:46.38	Paul McDonald (NZL) 1:46.46

1896–1972 Event not held.

	Gold	Silver	Bronze
1000 Metres Kayak Singles (K1)			
1936	Gregor Hradetsky (AUT) 4:22.9	Helmut Cämmerer (GER) 4:25.6	Jacob Kraaier (HOL) 4:35.1
1948	Gert Fredriksson (SWE) 4:33.2	Johann Kobberup (DEN) 4:39.9	Henri Eberhardt (FRA) 4:41.4
1952	Gert Fredriksson (SWE) 4:07.9	Thorvald Strömberg (FIN) 4:09.7	Louis Gantois (FRA) 4:20.1
1956	Gert Fredriksson (SWE) 4:12.8	Igor Pissaryev (URS) 4:15.3	Lajos Kiss (HUN) 4:16.2
1960	Erik Hansen (DEN) 3:53.00	Imre Szöllösi (HUN) 3:54.02	Gert Fredriksson (SWE) 3:55.89
1964	Rolf Peterson (SWE) 3:57.13	Mihály Hesz (HUN) 3:57.28	Aurel Vernescu (ROM) 4:00.77
1968	Mihály Hesz (HUN) 4:02.63	Aleksandr Shaparenko (URS) 4:03.58	Erik Hansen (DEN) 4:04.39
1972	Aleksandr Shaparenko (URS) 3:48.06	Rolf Peterson (SWE) 3:48.35	Geza Csapo (HUN) 3:49.38
1976	Rüdiger Helm (GDR) 3:48.20	Geza Csapo (HUN) 3:448.84	Vasile Diba (ROM) 3:49.65
1980	Rüdiger Helm (GDR) 3:48.77	Alain Lebas (FRA) 3:50.20	Ion Birladeanu (ROM) 3:50.49
1984	Alan Thompson (NZL) 3:45.73	Milan Janic (YUG) 3:46.88	Greg Barton (USA) 3:47.38
1988	Greg Barton (USA) 3:55.27	Grant Davies (AUS) 3:55.28	Andre Wohllebe (GDR) 3:55.55

1896–1932 Event not held.

	Gold	Silver	Bronze
10 000 Metres Kayak Singles (K1)			
1936	Ernst Krebs (GER) 46:01.6	Fritz Landertinger (AUT) 46:14.7	Ernest Riedel (USA) 47:23.9
1948	Gert Fredriksson (SWE) 50:47.7	Kurt Wires (FIN) 51:18.2	Ejvind Skabo (NOR) 51:35.4
1952	Thorvald Stromberg (FIN) 47.22.8	Gert Fredriksson (SWE) 47:34.1	Michel Scheuer (GER) 47:54.5
1956	Gert Fredriksson (SWE) 47:43.4	Ferenc Hatlaczky (HUN) 47:53.3	Michel Scheuer (GER) 48:00.3

1896–1932, 1960–1988 Event not held.

	Gold	Silver	Bronze
500 Metres Kayak Pairs (K2)			
1976	GDR 1:35.87	Soviet Union 1:36.81	Romania 1:37.43
1980	Soviet Union 1:32.38	Spain 1:33.65	GDR 1:34.00
1984	New Zealand 1:34.21	Sweden 1:35.26	Canada 1:35.41
1988	New Zealand 1:33.98	Soviet Union 1:34.15	Hungary 1:34.32

	Gold	Silver	Bronze
1000 Metres Kayak Pairs (K2)			
1936	Austria 4:03.8	Germany 4:08.9	Netherlands 4:12.2
1948	Sweden 4:07.3	Denmark 4:07.5	Finland 4:08.7
1952	Finland 3:51.1	Sweden 3:51.1	Austria 3:51.4
1956	Germany 3:49.6	Soviet Union 3:51.4	Austria 3:55.8
1960	Sweden 3:34.7	Hungary 3:34.91	Poland 3:37.34
1964	Sweden 3:38.4	Netherlands 3:39.30	Germany 3:40.69
1968	Soviet Union 3:37.54	Hungary 3:38.44	Austria 3:40.71
1972	Soviet Union 3:31.23	Hungary 3:32.00	Poland 3:33.83
1976	Soviet Union 3:29.01	GDR 3:29.33	Hungary 3:30.56
1980	Soviet Union 3:26.72	Hungary 3:28.49	Spain 3:28.66
1984	Canada 3:24.22	France 3:25.97	Australia 3:26.80
1988	United States 3:32.42	New Zealand 3:32.71	Australia 3:33.76

1896–1932 Event not held.

	Gold	Silver	Bronze
10 000 Metres Kayak Pairs (K2)			
1936	Germany 41:45.0	Austria 42:05.4	Sweden 43:06.1
1948	Sweden 46.09.4	Norway 46:44.8	Finland 46:48.2
1952	Finland 44:21.3	Sweden 44:21.7	Hungary 44:26.6
1956	Hungary 43:37.0	Germany 43:40.6	Australia 43:43.2

1896–1932, 1960–1988 Event not held.

	Gold	Silver	Bronze

1000 Metres Kayak Fours (K4)

	Gold	Silver	Bronze
1964	Soviet Union 3:14.67	Germany 3:15.39	Romania 3:15.51
1968	Norway 3:14.38	Romania 3:14.81	Hungary 3:15.10
1972	Soviet Union 3:14.02	Romania 3:15.07	Norway 3:15.27
1976	Soviet Union 3:08.69	Spain 3:08.95	GDR 3:10.76
1980	GDR 3:13.76	Romania 3:15.35	Bulgaria 3:15.46
1984	New Zealand 3:02.28	Sweden 3:02.81	France 3:03.94
1988	Hungary 3:00.20	Soviet Union 3:01.40	GDR 3:02.37

1896–1960 Event not held.

500 Meters Canadian Singles (C1)

	Gold	Silver	Bronze
1976	Aleksandr Rogov (URS) 1:59.23	John Wood (CAN) 1:59.58	Matija Ljubek (YUG) 1:59.60
1980	Sergey Postrekhin (URS) 1:53.37	Lubomir Lubenov (BUL) 1:53.49	Olaf Heukrodt (GDR) 1:54.38
1984	Larry Cain (CAN) 1:57.01	Henning Jakobsen (DEN) 1:58.45	Costica Olaru (ROM) 1:59.86
1988	Olaf Heukrodt (GDR) 1:56.42	Mikhail Slivinskiy (URS) 1.57.26	Martin Marinov (BUL) 1:57.27

1896–1972 Event not held.

1000 Metres Canadian Singles (C1)

	Gold	Silver	Bronze
1936	Francis Arnyot (CAN) 5:32.1	Bohuslav Karlik (TCH) 5:36.9	Erich Koschik (GER) 5:39.0
1948	Josef Holoček (TCH) 5:42.0	Douglas Bennet (CAN) 5:53.3	Robert Boutigny (FRA) 5:55.9
1952	Josef Holoček (TCH) 4:56.3	János Parti (Hun) 5:03.6	Olavi Ojanpera (FIN) 5:08.5
1956	Leon Rotman (ROM) 5:05.3	István Hernek (HUN) 5:06.2	Gennadiy Bukharin (URS) 5:12.7
1960	János Parti (HUN) 4:33.93	Alexsandr Silayev (URS) 4:34.41	Leon Rotman (ROM) 4:35.87
1964	Jürgen Eschert (GER) 4:35.14	Andrei Igorov (ROM) 4:37.89	Yevgeny Penyayev (URS) 4:38.31
1968	Tibor Tatai (HUN) 4:36.14	Detlef Lewe (FRG) 4:38.31	Vitaly Galkov (URS) 4:40.42
1972	Ivan Patzaichin (ROM) 4:08.94	Tamas Wichmann (HUN) 4:12.42	Detlef Lewe (FRG) 4:13.36
1976	Matija Ljubek (YUG) 4:09.51	Vasiliy Urchenko (URS) 4:12.57	Tamas Wichmann (HUN) 4:14.11
1980	Lubomir Lubenov (BUL) 4:12.38	Sergey Postrekhin (URS) 4:13.53	Eckhard Leue (GDR) 4:15.02
1984	Ulrich Eicke (FRG) 4:06.32	Larry Cain (CAN) 4:08.67	Henning Jakobsen (DEN) 4:09.51
1988	Ivan Klementyev (URS) 4:12.78	Jörg Schmidt (GDR) 4:15.83	Nikolay Boukhalov (URS) 4:18.94

1896–1932 Event not held.

10 000 Metres Canadian Singles (C1)

	Gold	Silver	Bronze
1948	Frantisek Capek (TCH) 62:05.2	Frank Havens (USA) 62:40.4	Norman Lane (CAN) 64:35.3
1952	Frank Havens (USA) 57:41.1	Gabor Novak (HUN) 57:49.2	Alfred Jindra (TCH) 57:53.1
1956	Leon Rotman (ROM) 56:41.0	János Parti (HUN) 57:11.0	Gennadiy Bukharin (URS) 57:14.5

1896–1936, 1960–1988 Event not held.

500 Metres Canadian Pairs (C2)

	Gold	Silver	Bronze
1976	Soviet Union 1:45.81	Poland 1:47.77	Hungary 1:48.35
1980	Hungary 1:43.39	Romania 1:44.12	Bulgaria 1:44.83
1984	Yugoslavia 1:43.67	Romania 1:45.68	Spain 1:47.71
1988	Soviet Union 1:41.77	Poland 1:43.61	France 1:43.81

1000 Metres Canadian Pairs (C2)

	Gold	Silver	Bronze
1936	Czechoslovakia 4:50.1	Austria 4:53.8	Canada 4:56.7
1948	Czechoslovakia 5:07.1	United States 5:08.2	France 5:15.2
1952	Denmark 4:38.3	Czechoslovakia 4:42.9	Germany 4:48.3
1956	Romania 4:47.4	Soviet Union 4:48.6	Hungary 4:54.3
1960	Soviet Union 4:17.94	Italy 4:20.77	Hungary 4:20.89
1964	Soviet Union 4:04.64	France 4:06.52	Denmark 4:07.48
1968	Romania 4:07.18	Hungary 4:08.77	Soviet Union 4:11.30
1972	Soviet Union 3:52.60	Romania 3:52.63	Bulgaria 3:58.10
1976	Soviet Union 3:52.76	Romania 3:54.28	Hungary 3:55.66
1980	Romania 3:47.65	GDR 3:49.93	Soviet Union 3:51.28
1984	Romania 3:40.60	Yugoslavia 3:41.56	France 3:48.01
1988	Soviet Union 3:48.36	GDR 3:51.44	Poland 3:54.33

1896–1932 Event not held.

10 000 Metres Canadian Pairs (C2)

	Gold	Silver	Bronze
1936	Czechoslovakia 50:33.5	Canada 51:15.8	Austria 51:28.0
1948	United States 55:55.4	Czechoslovakia 57:38.5	France 58:00.8
1952	France 54:08.3	Canada 54:09.9	Germany 54:28.1
1956	Soviet Union 54:02.4	France 54:48.3	Hungary 55:15.6

1896–1932, 1960–1988 Event not held

Gold	Silver	Bronze

4 x 500 Metres Kayak Singles (K1) Relay

1960 Germany 7:39.43	Hungary 7:44.02	Denmark 7:46.09

1896–1956, 1964–1988 Event not held

10 000 Metres Folding Kayak Singles (K1)

1936 Gregor Hradetzky (AUT) 50:01.2	Henri Eberhardt (FRA) 50:04.2	Xaver Hörmann (GER) 50:06.5

1896–1932, 1948–1988 Event not held

10 000 Metres Folding Kayak Pairs (K2)

1936 Sweden 45:48.9	Germany 45:49.2	Netherlands 46:12.4

1896–1932, 1948–1988 Event not held

Slalom Racing
Only held in 1972

Kayak Singles (K1)

Siegbert Horn (GDR) 268.56	Norbert Sattler (AUT) 270.76	Harald Gimpel (GDR) 277.95

Canadian Singles (C1)

Reinhard Eiben (GDR) 315.84	Reinhold Kauder (FRG) 327.89	Jamie McEwan (USA) 335.95

Canadian Pairs (C2)

GDR 310.68	FRG 311.90	France 315.10

CANOEING MEDALS – WOMEN

Gold	Silver	Bronze

500 Metres Kayak Singles (K1)

1948 Karen Hoff (DEN) 2:31.9	Alide Van de Anker-Doedans (HOL) 3:32.8	Fritzi Schwingl (AUT) 2:32.9
1952 Sylvi Saimo (FIN) 2:18.4	Gertrude Liebhart (AUT) 2:18.8	Nina Savina (URS) 2:21.6
1956 Yelisaveta Dementyeva (URS) 2:18.9	Therese Zenz (GER) 2:19.6	Tove Söby (DEN) 2:22.3
1960 Antonina Seredina (URS) 2:08.08	Therese Zenz (GER) 2:08.22	Daniel Walkowiak (POL) 2:10.46
1964 Ludmila Khvedosyuk (URS) 2:12.87	Hilde Lauer (ROM) 2:15.35	Marcia Jones (USA) 2:15.68
1968 Ludmila Pinayeva (URS) 2:11.09	Renate Breuer (FRG) 2:12.71	Viorica Dumitru (ROM) 2:13.22
1972 Yulia Ryabchinskaya (URS) 2:03.17	Mieke Jaapies (HOL) 2:04.03	Anna Pfeffer (HUN) 2:05.50
1976 Carola Zirzow (GDR) 2:01.05	Tatyana Korshunova (URS) 2:03.07	Klara Rajnai (HUN) 2:05.01
1980 Birgit Fischer (GDR) 1:57.96	Vanya Gheva (BUL) 1:59.48	Antonina Melnikova (URS) 1:59.66
1984 Agneta Andersson (SWE) 1:58.72	Barbara Schuttpelz (FRG)	Annemiek Derckx (HOL) 2:00.11
1988 Vania Guecheva (BUL) 1:55.19	Birgit Schmidt (GDR) 1:55.31	Izabela Dylewska (POL) 1:57.38

500 Metres Kayak Pairs (K2)

1960 Soviet Union 1:54.76	Germany 1:56.66	Hungary 1:58.22
1964 Germany 1:56.95	United States 1:59.16	Romania 2:00.25
1968 FRG 1:56.44	Hungary 1:58.60	Soviet Union 1:58.61
1972 Soviet Union 1:53.50	GDR 1:54.30	Romania 1:55.01
1976 Soviet Union 1:51.15	Hungary 1:51.69	GDR 1:51.81
1980 GDR 1:43.88	Soviet Union 1:46.91	Hungary 1:47.95
1984 Sweden 1:45.25	Canada 1:47.13	FRG 1:47.32
1988 GDR 1:43.46	Bulgaria 1:44.06	Netherlands 1:46.00

1896–1956 Event not held

500 Metres Kayak Fours (K4)

1984 Romania 1:38.34	Sweden 1:38.87	Canada 1:39.40
1988 GDR 1:40.78	Hungary 1:41.88	Bulgaria 1:42.63

1896–1980 Event not held

Slalom Racing
(Only held in 1972)

Kayak Singles (K1)

Angelika Bahmann (GDR) 364.50	Gisela Grothaus (FRG) 398.15	Magdalena Wunderlich (FRG) 400.50

Patrick Sercu (BEL) winning the 1964 1000m time trial – one of the few Olympic cycling champions later to compete successfully as a professional.

CYCLING

The first Olympic cycling champion was Léon Flameng (FRA), winner of the 100km race in 1896, which was held on a 333.33m cement track and involved 300 circuits. Four men have won three gold medals: Paul Masson (FRA) in 1896, Francesco Verri (ITA) in 1906, Robert Charpentier (FRA) in 1936, and Daniel Morelon (FRA) in 1968 (2) and 1972. Of these only Morelon won a bronze as well. He also won a record seven world amateur titles. Although initially the 1904 cycling events were not considered official, recent thinking has 're-instated' them. Thus it should be noted that Marcus Hurley (USA) won a record four titles, and a bronze medal, at that Games. His teammate Burton Downing also set a record at St Louis with six medals, comprising two gold, three silver and one bronze.

The first pair of brothers to win a medal were the German Götze duo, Bruno and Max, with a tandem silver in 1906. The greatest family performance in Olympic cycling was by the Pettersson brothers of Sweden, Gösta, Sture, Erik and Tomas. The first three won a bronze in the 1964 team road race with Sven Hamrin, and then in 1968 won the silver with their younger brother.

One of the first modern sporting drug abuse cases occurred in the 1960 100km race when two Danish cyclists collapsed and one of them, Knut Jensen, died from what was originally thought to be sunstroke. It transpired that they had both taken overdoses of a blood-circulation stimulant. Two other extremes of sportsmanship have been highlighted in Games cycling. In 1936 Robert Charpentier beat his team-mate Guy Lapébie by 0.2sec at the end of the 100km, the latter 'inexplicably' slowing down just before the line. A photograph showed that Charpentier had pulled his rival back by his shirt. More credit-worthy was another Frenchman, Flameng, who, when far ahead of his only opposition, a Greek, in 1896, stopped when the man's cycle broke down and waited for it to be replaced. Flameng still won by six laps. After the 1984 Games it was admitted that many of the US cycling team had indulged in 'blood-boosting' procedures – not illegal at the time. Those Games had also witnessed numerous 'space-age' innovations, especially in the composition and construction of wheels.

Of the many excellent facilities that have been built for Olympic cycling programmes, one of the most remarkable sites was the magnificent Hachioji velodrome in Tokyo. Built at a cost of $840 000, it was used for only four days during the 1964

Games and within a year was demolished. Track cycling was held indoors for the first time in 1976.

The greatest speed ever achieved in Olympic cycling was in the altitude of Mexico City in 1968 when Daniel Morelon and Pierre Trentin (FRA) clocked 9.83 sec for the last 200m in the tandem race, an average of 73.24kph. The greatest speed by an individual rider was 68.76kph by Sergey Kopylov (URS) in Moscow, 1980, when he clocked 10.47 sec for the last 200m in the 1000m sprint. The longest race ever held in the Games, at any sport, was the 1912 cycling road race over a distance of 320km.

Few future top professionals competed at the Games successfully as amateurs, but of those who did the most notable was Patrick Sercu (BEL), who went on to win a record 86 professional six-day events. The two co-record holders in the Tour de France with five wins each, Eddy Merckx (BEL) and Jacques Anquetil (FRA), both finished twelfth in the Olympic race, in 1964 and 1952 respectively.

The youngest gold medallist was Franco Giorgetti (ITA) in the 1920 team pursuit, aged 17yr 304 days, while the oldest was Maurice Peeters (HOL), aged 38yr 99 days, in the 1920 1000m sprint. Winning a bronze four years later in the tandem, Peeters, at 42yr 83 days, was also the oldest ever medallist.

In 1984, the first race for women, a road race, was won by Connie Carpenter-Phinney (USA), whose husband Davis won a bronze in the 100km team event. She had competed in the 1972 Winter Games as a 14-year-old speed skater. Taking the 1984 bronze medal was Sandra Schumacher (FRG), aged 17yr 217 days.

CYCLING MEDALS - TOTALS

Country	MEN			WOMEN			Total
	G	S	B	G	S	B	
France	27	15	20	–	–	–	62
Italy	26	14	6	–	–	–	46
Great Britain	8	21	14	–	–	–	43
United States[1]	10	9	12	1	1	1	34
Germany (FRG)	6	11	12	–	1	1	31
Soviet Union	10	4	8	1	–	1	24
Netherlands	8	11	4	1	–	–	24
Belgium	6	6	9	–	–	–	21
Denmark	6	6	7	–	–	–	19
GDR	7	5	4	–	1	–	17
Australia	5	6	4	–	–	–	15
Sweden	3	2	8	–	–	–	13
South Africa	1	4	3	–	–	–	8
Poland	–	5	3	–	–	–	8
Czechoslovakia	2	2	2	–	–	–	6
Switzerland	1	3	2	–	–	–	6
Greece	1	3	1	–	–	–	5
Austria	1	–	2	–	–	–	3
Canada	–	2	1	–	–	–	3
Norway	1	–	1	–	–	–	2
Jamaica	–	–	1	–	–	–	1
Japan	–	–	1	–	–	–	1
Mexico	–	–	1	–	–	–	1
	129	129	126[2]	3	3	3	393

[1]Includes 7 events in 1904 formerly excluded.
[2]No bronzes in 1896 100km, 1972 road team trial and individual road race.

CYCLING MEDALS – MEN

	Gold	Silver	Bronze
1000 Metres Time-Trial			
1896[1]	Paul Masson (FRA) 24.0	Stamatios Nikolopoulos (GRE) 25.4	Adolf Schmal (AUT) 26.6
1906[1]	Francesco Verri (ITA) 22.8	Herbert Crowther (GBR) 22.8	Menjou (FRA) 23.2
1928	Willy Falck-Hansen (DEN) 1:14.4	Gerard Bösch van Drakestein (HOL) 1:15.2	Edgar Gray (AUS) 1:15.6
1932	Edgar Gray (AUS) 1:13.0	Jacobus van Egmond (HOL) 1:13.3	Charles Rampelberg (FRA) 1:13.4
1936	Arie van Vliet (HOL) 1:12.0	Pierre Georget (FRA) 1:12.8	Rudolf Karsch (GER) 1:13.2
1948	Jacques Dupont (FRA) 1:13.5	Pierre Nihant (BEL) 1:14.5	Thomas Godwin (GBR) 1:15.0
1952	Russell Mockridge (AUS) 1:11.1	Marino Morettini (ITA) 1:12.7	Raymond Robinson (SAF) 1:13.0
1956	Leandro Faggin (ITA) 1:09.8	Ladislav Foucek (TCH) 1:11.4	J Alfred Swift (SAF) 1:11.6
1960	Sante Gaiardoni (ITA) 1:07.27	Dieter Gieseler (GER) 1:08.75	Rotislav Vargashkin (URS) 1:08.86
1964	Patrick Sercu (BEL) 1:09.59	Giovanni Pettenella (ITA) 1:10.09	Pierre Trentin (FRA) 1:10.42
1968	Pierre Trentin (FRA) 1:03.91	Niels-Christian Fredborg (DEN) 1:04.61	Janusz Kierzkowski (POL) 1:04.63
1972	Niels-Christian Fredborg (DEN) 1:06.44	Daniel Clark (AUS) 1:06.87	Jürgen Schuetze (GDR) 1:07.02
1976	Klaus-Jürgen Grunke (GDR) 1:05.93	Michel Vaarten (BEL) 1:07.52	Niels-Christian Fredborg (DEN) 1:07.62
1980	Lothar Thoms (GDR) 1:02.955*	Aleksandr Pantilov (URS) 1:04.845	David Weller (JAM) 1:05.241
1984	Fredy Schmidtke (FRG) 1:06.10	Curtis Harnett (CAN) 1:06.44	Fabrice Colas (FRA) 1:06.65
1988	Alexandr Kiritchenko (URS) 1:04.499	Martin Vinnicombe (AUS) 1:04.784	Robert Lechner (FRG) 1:05.114

1908–1924 Event not held.

[1]Held over 333.33 metres. *Olympic record.

France's Daniel Morelon (left) tracks Klaas Balk (HOL) in a semi-final of the 1000m sprint in 1972. Morelon went on successfully to defend the title that he had won in Mexico City.

1000 Metres Sprint

	Gold	Silver	Bronze
1896[1]	Paul Masson (FRA) 4:56.0	Stamatios Nikolopoulos (GRE)	Léon Flemeng (FRA)
1900[1]	Georges Taillandier (FRA) 2:52.0	Fernand Sanz (FRA)	John Lake (USA)
1906	Francesco Verri (ITA) 1:42.2	HC Bouffler (GBR)	Eugène Debougnie (BEL)
1920	Maurice Peeters (HOL) 1:38.3	H Thomas Johnson (GBR)	Harry Ryan (GBR)
1924[3]	Lucien Michard (FRA) 12.8	Jacob Meijer (HOL)	Jean Cugnot (FRA)
1928	René Beaufrand (FRA) 13.2	Antoine Mazairac (HOL)	Willy Falck-Hansen (DEN)
1932	Jacobus van Egmond (HOL) 12.6	Louis Chaillot (FRA)	Bruno Pellizzari (ITA)
1936	Toni Merkens (GER) 11.8	Arie van Vliet (HOL)	Louis Chaillot (FRA)
1948	Mario Ghella (ITA) 12.0	Reginald Harris (GBR)	Axel Schandorff (DEN)
1952	Enzo Sacchi (ITA) 12.0	Lionel Cox (AUS)	Werner Potzernheim (GER)
1956	Michel Rousseau (FRA) 11.4	Guglielmo Pesenti (ITA)	Richard Ploog (AUS)
1960	Sante Gaiardoni (ITA) 11.1	Leo Sterckx (BEL)	Valentina Gasparella (ITA)
1964	Giovanni Pettenella (ITA) 13.69	Sergio Bianchetto (ITA)	Daniel Morelon (FRA)
1968	Daniel Morelon (FRA) 10.68	Giordano Turrini (ITA)	Pierre Trentin (FRA)
1972	Daniel Morelon (FRA) 11.25	John Nicholson (AUS)	Omarc Pchakadze (URS)
1976	Anton Tkac (TCH) 10.78	Daniel Morelon (FRA)	Hans-Jurgen Geschke (GDR)
1980	Lutz Hesslich (GDR) 11.40	Yave Cahard (FRA)	Sergey Kopylov (URS)
1984	Mark Gorski (USA) 10.49	Nelson Vails (USA)	Tsutomu Sakamoto (JPN)
1988	Lutz Hesslich (GDR)	Nikolay Kovche (URS)	Gary Neiwand (AUS)

1904, 1908[2]–1912 Event not held.

[1]*Held over 2000 metres. In 1900 Taillandier's last 200 was 13.0 sec.*
[2]*There was a 1000 metres sprint event in the 1908 Games, but it was declared void because the riders exceeded the time limit, in spite of repeated warnings.*
[3]*Since 1924 only times over the last 200 metres of the event have been recorded.*

	Gold	Silver	Bronze

4000 Metres Individual Pursuit
Note: Bronze medal times are set in a third place race, so can be faster than those set in the race for first and second place.

Year	Gold	Silver	Bronze
1964	Jiři Daler (TCH) 5:04.75	Giorgio Ursi (ITA) 5:05.96	Preben Isaksson (DEN) 5:01.90
1968	Daniel Rebillard (FRA) 4:41.71	Mogens Frey Jensen (DEN) 4:42.43	Xaver Kurmann (SUI) 4:39.42
1972	Knut Knudsen (NOR) 4:45.74	Xaver Kurmann (SUI) 4:51.96	Hans Lutz (FRG) 4:50.80
1976	Gregor Braun (GDR) 4:47.61	Herman Ponsteen (HOL) 4:49.72	Thomas Huschke (GDR) 4:52.71
1980	Robert Dill-Bundi (SUI) 4:35.66*	Alain Bondue (FRA) 4:42.96	Hans-Henrik Orsted (DEN) 4:36.54
1984	Steve Hegg (USA) 4:39.35	Rolf Golz (FRG) 4:43.82	Leonard Nitz (USA) 4:44.03
1988	Gintaoutas Umaras (URS) 4:32.00	Dean Woods (AUS) 4:35.00	Bernd Dittert (GDR) 4:34.17

1896–1960 Event not held.

Olympic record.

4000 Metres Team Pursuit
Note: Bronze medal times are set in a third place race, so can be faster than those set in the race for first and second place.

Year	Gold	Silver	Bronze
1908[1]	Great Britain 2:18.6	Germany 2:28.6	Canada 2:29.6
1920	Italy 5:20.0[2]	Great Britain n.t.a.	South Africa n.t.a.
1924	Italy 5:15.0	Poland n.t.a.	Belgium n.t.a.
1928	Italy 5:01.8	Netherlands 5:06.2	Great Britain n.t.a.
1932	Italy 4:53.0	France 4:55.7	Great Britain 4:56.0
1936	France 4:45.0	Italy 4:51.0	Great Britain 4:52.6
1948	France 4:57.8	Italy 4:36.7	Great Britain 4:55.8
1952	Italy 4:46.1	South Africa 4:53.6	Great Britain 4:51.5
1956	Italy 4:37.4	France 4:39.4	Great Britain 4:42.2
1960	Italy 4:30.90	Germany 4:35.78	Soviet Union 4:34.05
1964	Germany 4:35.67	Italy 4:35.74	Netherlands 4:38.99
1968	Denmark 4:22.44[3]	FRG 4:18.94	Italy 4:18.35
1972	FRG 4:22.14	GDR 4:25.25	Great Britain 4:23.78
1976	FRG 4:21.06	Soviet Union 4:27.15	Great Britain 4:22.41
1980	Soviet Union 4:15.70*	GDR 4:19.67	Czechoslovakia[4]
1984	Australia 4:25.99	United States 4:29.85	FRG 4:25.60
1988	Soviet Union 4:13.31*	GDR 4:14.09	Australia 4:16.02

1896–1906, 1912 Event not held.

[1]*Held over 1810.5 metres.*
[2]*Great Britain finished first but were relegated to second for alleged interference.*
[3]*Federal Republic of Germany finished first but were disqualified for illegal assistance. After the Games ended the International Cycling Federation awarded them the silver medal.*
[4]*Italy disqualified in third place race.*
Olympic record.

2000 Metres Tandem

Year	Gold	Silver	Bronze
1906	Great Britain 2:57.0	Germany 2:57.2	Germany n.t.a.
1908	France 3:07.8	Great Britain n.t.a.	Great Britain n.t.a.
1920	Great Britain 2:94.4	South Africa n.t.a.	Netherlands n.t.a.
1924[1]	France 12.6	Denmark	Netherlands
1928	Netherlands 11.8	Great Britain	Germany
1932	France 12.0	Great Britain	Denmark
1936	Germany 11.8	Netherlands	France
1948	Italy 11.3	Great Britain	France
1952	Australia 11.0	South Africa	Italy
1956	Australia 10.8	Czechoslovakia	Italy
1960	Italy 10.7	Germany	Soviet Union
1964	Italy 10.75	Soviet Union	Germany
1968	France 9.83	Netherlands	Belgium
1972	Soviet Union 10.52	GDR	Poland

1896–1904, 1912, 1976–1988 Event not held.

[1]*Since 1924 only times over last 200m have been recorded.*

Individual Points Race

Year	Gold	Silver	Bronze
1984	Roger Ilegems (BEL)	Uwe Messerschmidt (FRG)	Jose Youshimatz (MEX)
1988	Dan Frost (DEN)	Leo Peelen (HOL)	Marat Ganeyev (URS)

1896–1980 Event not held.

	Gold	Silver	Bronze

Team Road Race
(Consisting of the combined times of the best three – four 1912–20 – riders from each country in the individual race. In 1956 based on placings.)

	Gold	Silver	Bronze
1912	Sweden 44h 35:33.6	Great Britain 44h 44:39.2	United States 44h 47:55.5
1920	France 19h 16:43.2	Sweden 19h 23:10.0	Belgium 19h 28:44.4
1924	France 19h 30:14.0	Belgium 19h 46:55.4	Sweden 19h 59:41.6
1928	Denmark 15h 09:14.0	Great Britain 15h 14:49.0	Sweden 15h 27:49.0
1932	Italy 7h 27:15.2	Denmark 7h 38:50.2	Sweden 7h 39:12.6
1936	France 7h 39:16.2	Switzerland 7h 39:20.4	Belgium 7h 39:21.0
1948	Belgium 15h 58:17.4	Great Britain 16h 03:31.6	France 16h 08:19.4
1952	Belgium 15h 20:46.6	Italy 15h 33:27.3	France 15h 38:58.1
1956	France 22 points	Great Britain 23 points	Germany 27 points

Road Team Time-Trial
Over 100km except in 1964 (108.89km), 1968 (102km), 1980 (101km)

	Gold	Silver	Bronze
1960	Italy 2h 14:33.53	Germany 2h 16:56.31	Soviet Union 2h 18:41.67
1964	Netherlands 2h 26:31.19	Italy 2h 26:55.39	Sweden 2h 27:11.52
1968	Netherlands 2h 07:49.06	Sweden 2h 09:26.60	Italy 2h 10:18.74
1972	Soviet Union 2h 11:17.8	Poland 2h 11:47.5	*
1976	Soviet Union 2h 08:53.0	Poland 2h 09:13.0	Denmark 2h 12:20.0
1980	Soviet Union 2h 01:21.7	GDR 2h 02:53.2	Czechoslovakia 2h 02:53.9
1984	Italy 1h 58:28.0	Switzerland 2h 02:38.0	United States 2h 02:46.0
1988	GDR 1h 57:47.7	Poland 1h 57:54.2	Sweden 1h 59:47.3

1896–1908 Event not held.

Netherlands finished in third place but their bronze medal was withdrawn following a drug test.

Individual Road Race
	Gold	Silver	Bronze
1896	Aristidis Konstantinidis (GRE) 3H 22:31.0	August Goedrich (GER) 3h 42:18.0	F Battel (GBR) d.n.a.
1906	Fernand Vast (FRA) 2h 41:28.0	Maurice Bardonneau (FRA) 2h 41:28.4	Edmund Lugnet (FRA) 2h 41:28.6
1912	Rudolph Lewis (SAF) 10h 42:39.0	Frederick Grubb (GBR) 10h 51:24.2	Carl Schutte (USA) 10h 52:38.8
1920	Harry Stenqvist (SWE) 4h 40:01.8	Henry Kaltenbrun (SAF) 4h 41:26.6	Fernand Canteloube (FRA) 4h 42.54.4
1924	Armand Blanchonnet (FRA) 6h 20:48.0	Henry Hoevenaers (BEL) 6h 30:27.0	René Hamel (FRA) 6h 40:51.6
1928	Henry Hansen (DEN) 4h 47:18.0	Frank Southall (GBR) 4h 55:06.0	Gösta Carlsson (SWE) 5h 00:17.0
1932	Attilio Pavesi (ITA) 2h 28:05.6	Guglielmo Segato (ITA) 2h 29:21.4	Bernhard Britz (SWE) 2h 29:45.2
1936	Robert Charpentier (FRA) 2h 33:05.0	Guy Lapebie (FRA) 2h 33:05.2	Ernst Nievergeit (SUI) 2h 33:05.8
1948	Jose Bevaert (FRA) 5h 18:12.6	Gerardus Voorting (HOL) 5h 18:16.2	Lode Wouters (BEL) 5h 18:16.2
1952	Andre Nouvelle (BEL) 5h 06:03.4	Robert Grondelaers (BEL) 5h 06:51.2	Edi Ziegler (GER) 5h 07:47.5
1956	Ercole Baldini (ITA) 5h 21:17.0	Arnaud Gevre (FRA) 5h 23:16.0	Alan Jackson (GBR) 5h 23:16.0
1960	Viktor Kapitonov (URS) 4h 20:37.0	Livio Trape (ITA) 4h 20:37.0	Willy van den Berghen (BEL) 4h 20:57.0
1964	Mario Zanin (ITA) 4h 39:51.63	Kjell Rodian (DEN) 4h 39:51.65	Walter Godefroot (BEL) 4h 39:51.74
1968	Pierfranco Vianelli (ITA) 4h 41:25.24	Leif Mortensen (DEN) 4h 42:49.71	Gösta Pettersson (SWE) 4h 43:15.24
1972	Hennie Kuiper (HOL) 4h 14:37.0	Kevin Sefton (AUS) 4h 15:04.0	*
1976	Bernt Johansson (Swe) 4h 46:52.0	Giuseppe Martinelli (ITA) 4h 47:23.0	Mieczyslaw Nowicki (POL) 4h 47:23.0
1980	Sergey Sukhoruchenkov (URS) 4h 48:28.9	Czeslaw Lang (POL) 4h 51:26.9	Yuriy Barinov (URS) 4h 51:26.9
1984	Alexi Grewal (USA) 4h 59:57.0	Steve Bauer (CAN) 4h 59:57.0	Dag Otto Lauritzen (NOR) 5h 00:18.0
1988	Olaf Ludwig (GDR) 4h 32:22.0	Bernd Gröne (FRG) 4h 32:25.0	Christian Henn (FRG) 4h 32:46.0

1900–1904, 1908 Event not held.

This event has been held over the following distances: 1896 – 87km; 1906 – 84km; 1912 – 320 km; 1920 – 175km; 1924 – 188km; 1928 – 168km; 1932 and 1936 – 100km; 1948 – 194.63km; 1952 – 190.4km; 1956 – 187.73km; 1960 – 175.38km; 1968 – 196.2km; 1972 – 182.4km; 1976 – 175km; 1980 – 189km; 1984 – 190km; 1988 – 196.8km.
Jaime Huelamo (ESP) finished third but medal withdrawn following a drug test.

CYCLING MEDALS – WOMEN

	Gold	Silver	Bronze

Sprint
	Gold	Silver	Bronze
1988	Erika Saloumae (URS)	Christa Rothenburger-Luding (GDR)	Connie Young (USA)

1896–1984 Event not held

Individual Road Race
	Gold	Silver	Bronze
1984	Connie Carpenter-Phinney (USA) 2h 11:14.0	Rebecca Twigg (USA) 2h 11:14.0	Sandra Schumacher (FRG) 2h 11:14.0
1988	Monique Knol (HOL) 2h 00.52	Jutta Niehaus (FRG) close	Laima Zilporiteye (URS) close

1896–1980 Event not held.

Event held over 79.2km in 1984; 82km in 1988.

Previous page *The fabulous opening ceremony at the Seoul Olympic Games. The flame has been lit and the hydraulic lift descends to off-load the three representatives of Science, Art and Sport.*

Right *Diver par excellence, Greg Louganis completed his double 'double' by taking both titles in Seoul, despite a nasty accident in the springboard event.*

Above *Anthony Nesty of Surinam, in the 1988 100m butterfly, became the first Olympic gold medallist from his country and the first black swimmer to win an Olympic event.*

Left *Kristin Otto gave a 'last hurrah' for the East German swimming regime by winning a record six gold medals in Seoul, including – uniquely – three different stroke events.*

Above *Joe DeLoach (USA) wins the 200m in Seoul from defending champion Carl Lewis, with Robson da Silva (BRA) taking bronze from Linford Christie (GBR).*

Left *Kenyan John Ngugi wins the 1988 5000m with a commanding lead over Dieter Baumann (FRG), with the GDR's Hansjörg Kunze (in blue) just beating Domingos Castro (POR) for the bronze medal.*

Facing page *Florence Griffith-Joyner wins the first of her three gold medals at Seoul in 1988, in the 100m. She established new sprinting standards for women.*

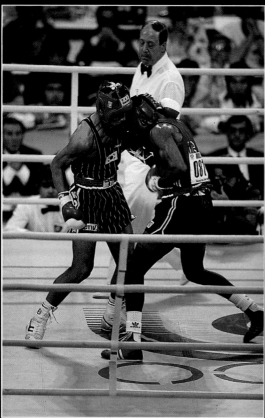

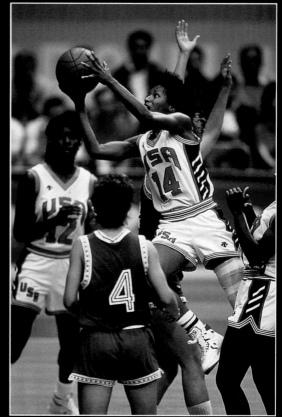

Left *The world's top tennis player, Steffi Graf (GER), caused no surprise by winning the 1988 Olympic singles, 64 years after Helen Wills won the previous Olympic tournament.*

Below *Imre Gedovari wins his sabre match to lead the Hungarians to a record 10th team title in 1988.*

Top left *Finn class yachting at the port of Pusan in 1988.*

Far left *Park Si-Hun (KOR) was given the verdict over Roy Jones in what is known as a 'home-town' decision, but the American was significantly awarded the Val Barker Trophy as the best boxer in Seoul.*

Right *Nino Saloukvadze of the Soviet Union wins the Sport Pistol gold in 1988. She also took silver in the Air Pistol event.*

Left *High-scoring Cynthia Cooper (14) leaps as the United States defeat Yugoslavia 77–70 in the 1988 women's basketball final.*

Above *Naim Suleymanoglu of Turkey, the 'Mighty Atom', set a new world mark in his class at Seoul, equalling the Olympic record of the next weight class.*

Above *New Zealand's Mark Todd on Charisma winning the first of their two individual gold medals, at Los Angeles in 1984.*

Left *Euphoria as Great Britain beat Australia 3–2 to reach the hockey final in Seoul. They went on to beat West Germany and take the gold medal after a gap of 68 years.*

Above *Christa Rothenburger-Luding (GDR) is the only woman to win Olympic medals in Summer and Winter Games in the same year. In 1988 she won gold and silver speed skating medals at Calgary and silver in the sprint cycling at Seoul. Her achievement will now stand for all time.*

Right *Britain's great middle-distance triumvirate: Sebastian Coe, Steve Cram and Steve Ovett contest the 1500m final in 1984. They dominated the athletics world for ten years.*

Above *Using 'space-age' technology for the wheels, Steve Hegg won the United States' first track cycling gold medal for 80 years when he took the individual pursuit title in 1984.*

Holland's Yvonne Van Gennip, seen here winning the 3000m gold, also took the 1500m and the inaugural 5000m title at Calgary in 1988. Her winning time in the 5000m would have gained her the bronze medal in the men's race at the previous Games, and the gold medal in 1976.

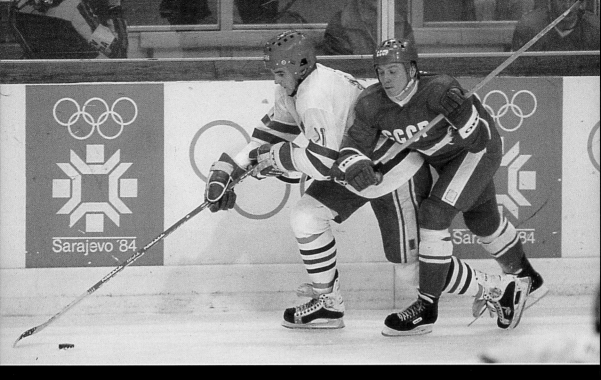

The Soviet Union regained their supremacy in Olympic ice hockey by beating Czechoslovakia 2–0 in the 1984 final. They had famously lost it to the Americans at Lake Placid four years earlier.

Below *One of the most exciting skaters to grace Olympic competition, Katarina Witt narrowly retained her title in 1988. Her famous coach Jutta Müller had also trained her predecessor, the 1980 Olympic champion Annet Pötsch.*

Above *The superb artistry of ice dancers Jayne Torvill and Christopher Dean was rewarded by the judges with unique points scores at Sarajevo in 1984 – their interpretation of 'Bolero' remains a classic. After the Games they turned professional.*

Right *Setting the seal on a great career, Ingemar Stenmark of Sweden won gold in the slalom and giant slalom at Lake Placid in 1980.*

Below *Michela Figini of Switzerland became the youngest ever skier to win an Olympic gold medal when she won the 1984 women's downhill race. Four years later she won a silver in the super giant slalom.*

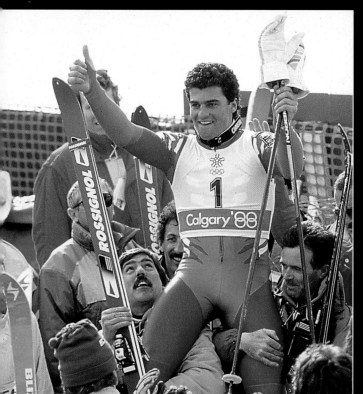

Above *Although born in Germany, Hanni Wenzel represented Liechtenstein at the Olympic Games, winning two golds and a silver in 1980. Her brother and sister were also in the team.*

Left *Wearing the appropriate number, Alberto Tomba won both the slalom and giant slalom at Calgary, Italy's only gold medals at those Games.*

Overleaf *Perhaps the greatest ski jumper of all time, Matti Nykänen, winner of three gold medals in 1988, adding to his gold and silver from 1984.*

DISCONTINUED EVENTS – MEN

	Gold	Silver	Bronze
440 yards Track (402.34m)			
1904	Marcus Hurley (USA) 31.8	Burton Downing (USA)	Edward Billingham (USA)
⅓ mile Track (536.45m)			
1904	Marcus Hurley (USA) 43.8	Burton Downing (USA)	Edward Billingham (USA)
660 yards Track (603.5m)			
1908	Victor Johnson (GBR) 51.2	Emile Demangel (FRA) *close*	Karl Neumer (GER) *1 length*
880 yards Track (804.67m)			
1904	Marcus Hurley (USA) 1:09.0	Edward Billingham (USA)	Burton Downing (USA)
1 mile Track (1609.34m)			
1904	Marcus Hurley (USA) 2:41.4	Burton Downing (USA)	Edward Billingham (USA)
2 miles Track (3218.6m)			
1904	Burton Downing (USA) 4:57.8	Oscar Goerke (USA)	Marcus Hurley (USA)
5000m Track			
1906	Francesco Verri (ITA) 8:35.0	Herbert Crowther (GBR)	Fernand Vast (FRA)
1908	Benjamin Jones (GBR) 8:36.2	Maurice Schilles (FRA)	Andre Auffray (FRA)
5 miles Track (8046.57m)			
1904	Charles Schlee (USA) 13:08.2	George Wiley (USA)	A Andrews (USA)
10 000m Track			
1896	Paul Masson (FRA) 17:54.2	Leon Flameng (FRA)	Adolf Schmal (AUT)
20 000m Track			
1906	William Pett (GBR) 29:00.0	Maurice Bardonneau (FRA) 29:30.0	Fernand Vast (FRA) 29:32.0
1908	Charles Kingsbury (GBR) 34:13.6	Benjamin Jones (GBR)	Joseph Werbrouck (BEL)
25 miles Track (40.225m)			
1904	Burton Downing (USA) 1h 10:55.4	A Andrews (USA)	George Wiley (USA)
50 000m Track			
1920	Henry George (BEL) 1h 16:43.2	Cyril Alden (GBR)*	Petrus Ikelaar (HOL)
1924	Jacobus Willems (HOL) 1:18:24	Cyril Alden (GBR)	Frederick Wyld (GBR)

Most eyewitnesses considered that Ikelaar finished second.

	Gold	Silver	Bronze
100km Track			
1896	Leon Flameng (FRA) 3h 08:19.2	G. Kolettis (GRE) 6 laps	–*
1908	Charles Bartlett (GBR) 2h 41:48.6	Charles Denny (GBR)	Octave Lapize (FRA)

Only two riders finished

	Gold	Silver	Bronze
12 hours Track			
1896	Adolf Schmal (AUT) 314.997km	F. Keeping (GBR) 314.664km	Georgios Paraskevopoulos (GRE) 313.330km

EQUESTRIAN

In the ancient Games, the first known event using horses was a chariot race in 680 BC, while horses with riders came into the Games in 648 BC. The first equestrian gold medallist of the modern Olympics was Aimé Haegeman (BEL) on *Benton II* in the 1900 show jumping. In 1956 the equestrian events were held at Stockholm, separate from the main Games in Melbourne due to the strict Australian quarantine laws.

The most gold medals by a rider is six (one individual and five team events) by Reiner Klimke (FRG) from 1964–1988. Klimke's eight medals overall, comprising the six golds and two bronzes, also constitutes a record for equestrianism, as does his feat of winning golds in five separate Games over a 24-year period. The two

EQUESTRIAN MEDAL TOTALS

Country	G	S	B	Total
Germany (FRG)	24	15	18	57
Sweden	17	8	14	39
France	11	12	9	32
United States	8	15	9	32
Italy	7	9	7	23
Great Britain	5	7	9	21
Switzerland	4	8	7	19
Soviet Union	6	5	4	15
Belgium	4	2	5	11
Netherlands	5	3	1	9
Mexico	2	1	4	7
Poland	1	3	2	6
Australia	2	1	2	5
Denmark	–	4	1	5
Canada	1	1	2	4
New Zealand	2	–	1	3
Portugal	–	–	3	3
Spain	1	1	–	2
Austria	1	–	1	2
Chile	–	2	–	2
Romania	–	1	1	2
Czechoslovakia	1	–	–	1
Japan	1	–	–	1
Argentina	–	1	–	1
Bulgaria	–	1	–	1
Norway	–	1	–	1
Hungary	–	–	1	1
	103[1]	101	101[2]	305

[1] Two golds in 1900 high jump.
[2] No bronze in 1932 Three-day team event.

medals won by Gustav-Adolf Boltenstern Jr (SWE) over a similar 24-year period (1932–1956) were not both gold.

The oldest gold medallist was Josef Neckermann (FRG) in the 1968 dressage team, aged 56yr 141 days. The oldest individual event winner was Ernst Lindner (SWE) in the 1924 dressage, aged 56yr 91 days. The youngest individual champion was Edmund Coffin (USA) in the 1976 three-day event, aged 21yr 77 days. However, Mary Tauskey (USA) won a gold medal in the three-day team event in 1976 aged 20 yr 235 days.

Raimondo d'Inzeo (ITA) competed in a record eight Games (1948–1976) winning a gold, two silver and three bronze medals. No Olympian has bettered that number of celebrations. A Bulgarian, Kroum Lekarski, competed in the three-day event for a record period of 36 years between 1924 and 1960, but only competed in four Games. The record competition span by a woman (28 years) was set by British-born Jessica Ransehousen (née Newberry) representing the United States in 1988. Of the six known competitors who have competed in two different equestrian disciplines, the most successful was Age Lundström (SWE) with a gold in the 1920 three-day event and another in the 1924 show jumping.

Women first competed in 1952 and Lis Hartel (DEN) won the first female medal that year with a silver in the dressage, which she repeated in 1956. Since 1984 equestrianism has been the only Olympic sport in which men and women compete against each other in individual events.

The only horse to be ridden to medals in three Games was

Absent in the Soviet dressage team, with a gold and two bronze under Sergey Filatov in 1960 and 1964, and a silver with Ivan Kalita in 1968.

The most successful father and son have been Hans von Blixen-Finecke senior and junior (SWE), with the former winning a dressage team gold and individual bronze in 1912, and the latter the three-day event individual and team golds 40 years later. Liselott Linsenhoff (FRG) won two dressage golds and a silver in 1968–72, and her daughter Ann-Kathrin won a gold in 1988.

In 1936 Germany completed the only six gold medal 'clean sweep' in Games equestrian history. In the 1912 and 1920 individual dressage Sweden took the first three places both times, a unique occurrence.

SHOW JUMPING

This was the first equestrian event to be included in the Games, along with high and long jumping contests, in 1900. From 1924 until 1968 teams comprised three members, all counting for the final score, which led to many teams not finishing. In 1932, for example, no team medals were awarded at all, and in 1948 only four of the 14 competing teams finished. Since 1972, though, teams have consisted of four riders, with the best three scoring.

The most gold medals won are five by Hans-Günter Winkler (FRG) from 1956–72. His total of seven medals, including a silver and bronze, is also a record for the discipline as is his feat of winning medals in six Games. Only Pierre Jonquères d'Oriola (FRA) has won the individual title twice. The first woman to win a medal was Pat Smythe (GBR) in the 1956 team event, while the first individual

medallist was Marion Coakes (GBR) in 1968.

The oldest gold medallist was Winkler in 1972, aged 46yr 49 days, while the oldest individual champion was Jonquères d'Oriola, aged 44 yr 266 days, in 1964. Bill Steinkraus (USA) won medals over a twenty-year period (1952–1972), a record matched by Winkler (1956–1976). The youngest gold medallist was Jim Day (CAN) in the 1968 team, aged 22yr 117 days.

The lowest score obtained by a winner is no faults by Frantisek Ventura (TCH) on *Eliot* in 1928, Jonquères d'Oriola (FRA) on *Ali Baba* in 1952, and Alwin Schockemöhle (FRG) on *Warwick Rex* in 1976. The most successful horse was Winkler's *Halla* with three golds in 1956 and 1960.

DRESSAGE
The most successful rider was Reiner Klimke (*see above*), but only Henri St Cyr (SWE) won the individual title twice. In all St Cyr won four golds and was denied a fifth only when his team was disqualified in 1948 after finishing first; one of its members, Gehnäll Persson, was not a fully commissioned officer – a requirement at that time. With the rules changed, Persson was in the 1952 and 1956 winning teams. This Swedish team of St Cyr, Persson and Gustav-Adolf Boltenstern Jr uniquely finished in first place three times in a row, and can claim to be the most successful combination in Olympic history.

The first woman to win a medal was Lis Hartel (see above). Amazingly she was a polio victim who had to be helped on and off her horse.

Three-Day Event, 1984. Mark Todd (centre) of New Zealand takes gold from Karen Stives (silver) and Virginia Holgate (bronze).

The first female gold medallist was Liselott Linsenhoff (FRG) in 1972. The silver medallist that year, Yelena Petushkova (URS), won gold in the team event and was for a time married to Valery Brumel, the 1964 Olympic high jump champion.

The oldest gold medallist was Josef Neckermann (see above), who was also the oldest medallist in 1972, aged 60yr 96 days. The oldest competitor in Olympic equestrian history was General Arthur von Pongracz (AUT), who began his Olympic career in 1924 aged 60 and finished it in 1936 – just missing a bronze medal – as one of the oldest ever Olympians, aged 72yr 49 days.

The oldest woman ever to compete in the Olympic Games, at any sport, was Lorna Johnstone (GBR) who finished twelfth in the 1972 dressage five days after her 70th birthday. The youngest rider to win a gold medal was Nicole Uphoff (FRG) in the 1988 team event, aged 22yr 244 days.

The most successful horse has been *Ahlerich*, ridden by Reiner Klimke (FRG) to three golds in 1984 and 1988. Remarkably Klimke won his last gold, in the 1988 team event, in a team including Ann-Kathrin Linsenhoff, the daughter of his gold-winning team partner of 20 years before.

THREE-DAY EVENT

It is worth noting that this three-part competition actually lasts four days, as the dressage segment occupies two days.

Charles Pahud de Mortanges (HOL) won the individual title twice, in 1928 and 1932, as did Mark Todd (NZL) in 1984 and 1988. However, the Dutchman also won a record total of four golds and a silver from 1924 to 1932. His Dutch team, including Gerard de Kruyff and Adolph van der Voort van Zijp, uniquely won two team titles with the same team members. The longest span of competition by a medal winner is 20 years by Mickey Plumb (USA) from 1964–1984.

The first female competitor was Helena Dupont (USA), 33rd in 1964, while the first female gold medallists were Mary Gordon-Watson and Bridget Parker (both GBR) in 1972. The first individual medals won by women were in 1984 by Karen Stives (USA) and Virginia Holgate (GBR).

The oldest gold medallist was Derek Allhusen (GBR), aged 54yr 286 days, in 1968, while the youngest was Mary Tauskey (USA) in 1976, aged 20yr 235 days. The oldest medallist was William Roycroft (AUS) with a bronze in 1976, aged 61yr 130 days, in the same team as his son Wayne.

The most successful horse was *Marcroix*, ridden by Charles Pahud de Mortanges (HOL) to three golds and a silver in 1928 and 1932. Both *Silver Piece*, ridden by Voort van Zijp (HOL) in 1924 and 1928, and *Charisma*, ridden by Mark Todd (NZL) in 1984 and 1988, also won three golds.

The 1936 cross-country course was so tough that only four teams out of 14 finished. One of the members of that fourth-placed team, Otomar Bures of Czechoslovakia, had over 18 000 penalty points against him at the finish, due to having taken over 2¾ hours to catch his horse after a fall. Britain's Captain Richard Fanshawe, with a similar problem, gained over 8000 penalty points but had the satisfaction of finishing with a team bronze. In 1920 the dressage was excluded, with two cross-country runs, at 20km and 50km, added to the jumping.

EQUESTRIAN MEDALS

Grand Prix (Jumping)

	Gold	Silver	Bronze
1900	Aime Haegeman (BEL) *Benton II*	Georges van de Poele (BEL) *Windsor Square*	M de Champsvin (FRA) *Terpsichore*
1912	Jean Cariou (FRA) 186pts *Mignon*	Rabod von Kröcher (GER) 186 *Dohna*	Emanuel de Blomaert de Sove (BEL) 185 *Clonmore*
1920	Tommaso Lequio (ITA) 2 faults *Trebecco*	Alessandro Valerio (ITA) 3 *Cento*	Gustaf Lewenhaupt (SWE) 4 *Mon Coeur*
1924	Alphonse Gemuseus (SUI) 6 faults	Tommaso Lequio (ITA) *Trebecco*	Adam Krolikiewicz (POL) 10 *Picador*
1928	Frantisek Ventura (TCH) no faults *Eliot*	Pierre Bertrand de Balanda (FRA) 2 *Papillon*	Charles Kuhn (SUI) 4 *Pepita*
1932	Takeichi Nishi (JPN) 8 pts *Uranus*	Harry Chamberlain (USA) 12 *Show Girl*	Clarence von Rosen Jr (SWE) 16 *Empire*
1936	Kurt Hasse (GER) 4 faults *Tora*	Henri Rang (ROM) 4 *Delius*	József von Platthy (HUN) 8 *Sellö*
1948	Humberto Mariles Cortés (MEX) 6.25 faults *Arete*	Rubén Uriza (MEX) 8 *Harvey*	Jean d'Orgeix (FRA) 8 *Sucre de Pomme*
1952	Pierre Jonquères d'Oriola (FRA) no faults *Ali Baba*	Oscar Cristi (CHI) 4 *Bambi*	Fritz Thiedemann (GER) 8 *Meteor*
1956	Hans Günter Winkler (GER) 4 faults *Halla*	Raimondo d'Inzeo (ITA) 8 *Merano*	Piero d'Inzeo (ITA) 11 *Uruguay*
1960	Raimondo d'Inzeo (ITA) 12 faults *Posillipo*	Piero d'Inzeo (ITA) 16 *The Rock*	David Broome (GBR) 23 *Sunslave*
1964	Pierre Jonquères d'Oriola (FRA) 9 faults *Lutteur*	Hermann Schridde (GER) 12.75 *Dozent*	Peter Robeson (GBR) 16 *Firecrest*
1968	William Steinkraus (USA) 4 faults *Snowbound*	Marian Coakes (GBR) 8 *Stroller*	David Broome (GBR) 12 *Mister Softee*
1972	Graziano Mancinelli (ITA) 8 faults *Ambassador*	Ann Moore (GBR) 8 *Psalm*	Neal Shapiro (USA) 8 *Sloopy*
1976	Alwin Schockemöhle (FRG) no faults *Warwick Rex*	Michael Vaillancourt (CAN) 12 *Branch County*	François Mathy (BEL) *Gai Luron*
1980	Jan Kowalczyk (POL) 8 faults *Artemor*	Nikolai Korolkov (URS) 9.50 *Espadron*	Joaquin Perez Heras (MEX) 12 *Alymony*
1984	Joe Fargis (USA) 4 faults *Touch of Class*	Conrad Homfeld (USA) 4 *Abdullah*	Heidi Robbiani (SUI) 8 *Jessica V*
1988	Pierre Durand (FRA) 1.25 faults *Jappeloup*	Greg Best (USA) 4 *Gem Twist*	Karsten Huck (FRG) 4 *Nepomuk 8*

1896, 1904–1908 Event not held.

	Gold	Silver	Bronze

Grand Prix (Jumping) Team

	Gold	Silver	Bronze
1912	Sweden 545pts	France 538	Germany 530
1920	Sweden 14 faults	Belgium 16.25	Italy 18.75
1924	Sweden 42.25 pts	Switzerland 50	Portugal 53
1928	Spain 4 faults	Poland 8	Sweden 10
1932[1]	–	–	–
1936	Germany 44 faults	Netherlands 51.5	Portugal 56
1948	Mexico 34.25 faults	Spain 56.50	Great Britain 67
1952	Great Britain 40.75 faults	Chile 45.75	United States 52.25
1956	Germany 40 faults	Italy 66	Great Britain 69
1960	Germany 46.50 faults	United States 66	Italy 80.50
1964	Germany 68.50 faults	France 77.75	Italy 88.50
1968	Canada 102.75 faults	France 110.50	FRG 117.25
1972	FRG 32 faults	United States 32.25	Italy 48
1976	France 40 faults	FRG 44	Belgium 63
1980	Soviet Union 16 faults	Poland 32	Mexico 39.25
1984	United States 12 faults	Great Britain 36.75	FRG 39.25
1988	FRG 17.25 faults	United States 20.50	France 27.50

1896–1908 Event not held.

[1]*There was a team competition but no nation had three riders complete the course.*

Grand Prix (Dressage)

	Gold	Silver	Bronze
1912	Carl Bonde (SWE) 15pts *Emperor*	Gustaf-Adolf Boltenstern Sr 21 *Neptun*	Hans von Blixen-Finecke (SWE) 32 *Maggie*
1920	Janne Lundblad (SWE) 27 237pts *Uno*	Bertil Sandström (SWE) 26 312 *Sabel*	Hans von Rosen (SWE) 15 125 *Running Sister*
1924	Ernst Linder (SWE) 276.4pts *Piccolo-mini*	Bertil Sandström (SWE) 275.8 *Sabel*	Xavier Lesage (FRA) 265.8 *Plumard*
1928	Carl von Langen (GER) 237.42pts *Draüfgänger*	Charles Marion (FRA) 231.00 *Linon*	Ragnar Olsson (SWE) 229.78 *Günstling*
1932	Xavier Lesage (FRA) 1031.25pts *Taine*	Charles Marion (FRA) 916.25 *Linon*	Hiram Tuttle (USA) 901.50 *Olympic*
1936	Heinz Pollay (GER) 1760pts *Kronos*	Friedrich Gerhard (GER) 1745.4 *Absinth*	Alois Podhajsky (AUT) 1721.5 *Nero*
1948	Hans Moser (SUI) 492.5pts *Hummer*	André Jousseaume (FRA) 480.0 *Harpagon*	Gustaf-Adolf Boltenstern Jr (SWE) 477.5 *Trumpf*
1952	Henri St Cyr (SWE) 561pts *Master Rufus*	Lis Hartel (DEN) 541.5 *Jubilee*	André Jousseaume (FRA) 541.0 *Harpagon*
1956	Henri St Cyr (SWE) 860pts *Juli*	Lis Hartel (DEN) 850 *Jubilee*	Liselott Linsenhoff (GER) 832 *Adular*
1960	Sergey Filatov (URS) 2144pts *Absent*	Gustav Fischer (SUI) 2087 *Wald*	Josef Neckermann (GER) 2082 *Asbach*
1964	Henri Chammartin (SUI) 1504 pts *Woermann*	Harry Boldt (GER) 1503 *Remus*	Sergey Filatov (URS) 1486 *Absent*
1968	Ivan Kizimov (URS) 1572pts *Ikhov*	Josef Neckermann (FRG) 1546 *Mariano*	Reiner Klimke (FRG) 1527 *Dux*
1972	Liselott Linsenhoff (FRG) 1229pts *Piaff*	Yelena Petuchkova (URS) 1185 *Pepel*	Josef Neckermann (FRG) 1177 *Venetia*
1976	Christine Stückelberger (SUI) 1486pts	Harry Boldt (FRG) 1435 *Woycek*	Reiner Klimke (FRG) 1395 *Mehmed*
1980	Elisabeth Theurer (AUT) 1370 pts *Mon Cherie*	Yuriy Kovshov (URS) 1300 *Igrok*	Viktor Ugryumov (URS) 1234 *Shkval*
1984	Reiner Klimke (FRG) 1504pts *Ahlerich*	Anne Grethe Jensen (DEN) 1442 *Marzog*	Otto Hofer (SUI) 1364 *Limandus*
1988	Nicole Uphoff (FRG) 1521pts *Rembrandt 24*	Margit Otto Crepin (FRA) 1462 *Corlandus*	Christine Stückelberger (SUI) 1417 *Gauguin De Lully*

1896–1908 Event not held.

Grand Prix (Dressage Team)

	Gold	Silver	Bronze
1928	Germany 669.72pts	Sweden 650.86	Netherlands 642.96
1932	France 2828.75pts	Sweden 2678	United States 2576.75
1936	Germany 5074pts	France 4846	Sweden 4660.5
1948[1]	France 1269pts	United States 1256	Portugal 1182
1952	Sweden 1597.5pts	Switzerland 1759	Germany 1501
1956	Sweden 2475pts	Germany 2346	Switzerland 2346
1964	Germany 2558pts	Switzerland 2526	Soviet Union 2311
1968	FRG 2699pts	Soviet Union 2657	Switzerland 2547
1972	Soviet Union 5095pts	FRG 5083	Sweden 4849
1976	FRG 5155pts	Switzerland 4684	United States 4670
1980	Soviet Union 4383pts	Bulgaria 3580	Romania 3346
1984	FRG 4955pts	Switzerland 4673	Sweden 4630
1988	FRG 4302pts	Switzerland 4164	Canada 3969

1896–1924, 1960 Event not held

[1]*Sweden were originally declared winners with 1366 pts but were subsequently disqualified one year later.*

Three-Day Event

	Gold	Silver	Bronze
1912	Axel Nordlander (SWE) 46.59pts *Lady Artist*	Friedrich von Rochow (GER) 46.42 *Idealist*	Jean Cariou (FRA) 46.32 *Cocotte*
1920	Helmer Mörner (SWE) 1775pts *Germania*	Age Lundström (SWE) 1738.75 *Yrsa*	Ettore Caffaratti (ITA) 1733.75 *Traditore*

	Gold	Silver	Bronze
1924	Adolph van der Voort van Zijp (HOL) 1976pts *Silver Piece*	Fröde Kirkebjerg (DEN) 1853.5 *Meteor*	Sloan Doak (USA) 1845.5 *Pathfinder*
1928	Charles Pahud de Mortanges (HOL) 1969.82pts *Marcroix*	Gerard de Kruyff (HOL) 1967.26 *Va-t-en*	Bruno Neumann (GER) 1944.42 *Ilja*
1932	Charles Pahud de Mortanges (HOL) 1813.83pts *Marcroix*	Earl Thomson (USA) 1811 *Jenny Camp*	Clarence von Rosen Jr (SWE) 1809−42 *Sunnyside Maid*
1936	Ludwig Stubbendorff (GER) 37.7 faults *Nurmi*	Earl Thomson (USA) 99.9 *Jenny Camp*	Hans Mathiesen Lunding (DEN) 102.2 *Jason*
1948	Bernard Chevallier (FRA) +4pts *Aiglonne*	Frank Henry (USA) −21 *Swing Low*	Robert Selfelt (SWE) −25 *Claque*
1952	Hans von Blixen-Finecke (SWE) 28.33 faults *Jubal*	Guy Lefrant (FRA) 54.50 *Verdun*	Wilhelf Büsing (GER) 55.50 *Hubertus*
1956	Petrus Kastenman (SWE) 66.53 faults *Illuster*	August Lütke-Westhues (GER) 84.87 *Trux von Kamax*	Frank Weldon (GBR) 85.48 *Kilbarry*
1960	Lawrence Morgan (AUS) +7.15pts *Salad Days*	Neale Lavis (AUS) −16.50 *Mirrabooka*	Anton Bühler (SUI) −51.21 *Gay Spark*
1964	Mauro Checcoli (ITA) 64.40pts *Surbean*	Carlos Moratorio (ARG) 56.40 *Chalan*	Fritz Ligges (GER) 49.20 *Donkosak*
1968	Jean-Jacques Guyon (FRA) 38.86pts *Pitou*	Derek Allhusen (GBR) 41.61 *Lochinvar*	Michael Page (USA) *Faster*
1972	Richard Meade (GBR) 57.73pts *Laurieston*	Alessa Argenton (ITA) 43.33 *Woodland*	Jan Jonsson (SWE) 39.67 *Sarajevo*
1976	Edmund Coffin (USA) 114.99pts *Bally-Cor*	Michael Plumb (USA) 125.85 *Better & Better*	Karl Schultz (FRG) 129.45 *Madrigal*
1980	Federico Roman (ITA) 108.60pts *Rossinan*	Aleksandr Blinov (URS) 120.80 *Galzun*	Yuriy Salnikov (URS) 151.60 *Pintset*
1984	Mark Todd (NZL) 51.60pts *Charisma*	Karen Stives (USA) 54.20 *Ben Arthur*	Virginia Holgate (GBR) 56.80 *Priceless*
1988	Mark Todd (NZL) 42.60pts *Charisma*	Ian Stark (GBR) 52.80 *Sir Wattie*	Virginia Leng (GBR) 62.00 *Master Craftsman*

1896–1908 Event not held

Three-Day Event Team

1912	Sweden 139.06pts	Germany 138.48	United States 137.33
1920	Sweden 5057.5pts	Italy 4735	Belgium 4560
1924	Netherlands 5297.5pts	Sweden 4743.5	Italy 4512.5
1928	Netherlands 5865.68pts	Norway 5395.68	Poland 5067.92
1932	United States 5038.08pts	Netherlands 4689.08	−¹
1936	Germany 676.75pts	Poland 991.70	Great Britain 9195.90
1948	United States 161.50pts	Sweden 165.00	Mexico 305.25
1952	Sweden 221.49pts	Germany 235.49	United States 587.16
1956	Great Britain 355.48pts	Germany 475.61	Canada 572.72
1960	Australia 128.18pts	Switzerland 386.02	France 515.71
1964	Italy 85.80pts	United States 65.86	Germany 56.73
1968	Great Britain 175.93pts	United States 245.87	Australia 331.26
1972	Great Britain 95.53pts	United States 10.81	FRG −18.00
1976	United States 441.00pts	FRG 584.60	Australia 599.54
1980	Soviet Union 457.00pts	Italy 656.20	Mexico 1172.85
1984	United States 186.00pts	Great Britain 189.20	FRG 234.00
1988	FRG 225.95pts	Great Britain 256.80	New Zealand 271.20

1896–1908 Event not held.

¹*No other teams finished.*

DISCONTINUED EVENTS

	Gold	Silver	Bronze
Equestrian High Jump			
1900	Dominique Gardères (FRA) 1.85m *Canela*	–	A Moreau (FRA) 1.70 *Ludlow*
	Gian Giorgio Trissino (ITA) 1.85m *Oreste*		
Equestrian Long Jump			
1900	Constant van Langhendonck (BEL) 6.10 *Extra Dry*	Gian Giorgio Trissino (ITA) *Oreste*	de Prunelle (FRA) 5.30 *Tolla*
Figure Riding			
(Only open to soldiers below the rank of NCO)			
1920	Bouckaert (BEL) 30.5pts	Fiel (FRA) 29.5	Finet (BEL) 29.0
	Teams		
	Belgium	France	Sweden

FENCING

This was one of the original sports held in 1896, when the first Olympic champion was Emile Gravelotte (FRA) in the foil. Until recently it was the only sport in which professionals had openly competed in the Games, as special events for fencing masters were held in 1896 and 1900. At the latter Games they even competed against other competitors, so that Albert Ayat (FRA) beat his pupil Ramón Fonst (CUB) in the épée. When Léon Pyrgos won the foil contest for fencing masters in 1896, he became the first Greek Olympic champion of modern times. A foil competition for women was introduced in 1924 and a team contest for them in 1960. Electronic scoring equipment was introduced for épée in 1936, and for foil in 1956. It will be used for the first time for the sabre in 1992.

Aladár Gerevich (HUN) won a record seven gold medals in the sabre between 1932 and 1960. The record for most medals is 13 by Edoardo Mangiarotti (ITA) in foil and épée from 1936–1960, comprising six golds, five silvers and two bronzes. His elder brother Dario won a gold and two silvers in 1948 and 1952. Nedo Nadi (ITA) won an unequalled five golds at one Games in 1920, and his younger brother Aldo added three more golds and a silver – a family record total for one Games.

The most individual event gold medals is three, achieved by Ramón Fonst (CUB) in 1900 and 1904 (two), and by Nedo Nadi (ITA) in 1912 and 1920 (two). The only man, in any sport, to win Olympic gold medals at six consecutive Games was Aladár Gerevich (see above); his medal winning span of 28 years is also a record. Brit-

ain's Bill Hoskyns also competed at six Games (1956–1976) but only won two silver medals. The equal longest span of competition by any Olympic competitor is 40 years by Ivan Osiier (DEN) who fenced from 1908 to 1948, during which time he won a silver medal in 1912 and became the oldest Olympic fencer in 1948, aged 59yr 240 days. His wife Ellen won a gold medal in 1924.

Four fencers have won individual medals in all three disciplines at one Games. Both Nedo Nadi and his brother Aldo won golds in each of the team events in 1920, while Roger Ducret (FRA) won foil and épée golds and a sabre silver in 1924. In the sparsely-supported 1904 events, American-born Albertson Van Zo Post (CUB) won a foil silver, and bronzes in the other two disciplines.

The oldest gold medallist was Aladár Gerevich (HUN) in 1960, aged 50yr 178 days, while the youngest was Ramón Fonst

(CUB), aged 16yr 289 days in 1900. The family of Gerevich has a unique position in Olympic fencing. Aladár himself won seven golds, a silver and two bronzes; his wife Erna Bogen won a bronze in 1932, his father-in-law Albert Bogen won a silver in 1912; and Aladár's son Pal won bronze medals in 1972 and 1980.

FOIL

Only Nedo Nadi (ITA) in 1912 and 1920, and Christian d'Oriola (FRA) in 1952 and 1956 have won two individual titles. In addition d'Oriola won two team golds and two silvers for a record six medals. The oldest gold medallist was Henri Jobier (FRA) who was over 44 years old in the winning 1924 team, while the youngest was Nedo Nadi (ITA) in 1912, aged 18yr 29 days. In the 15 Games from 1920 to 1984, France only once failed to gain a team competition medal.

ÉPÉE

Ramón Fonst (CUB) was the only double winner of the

FENCING MEDAL TOTALS

Country	MEN			WOMEN			Total
	G	S	B	G	S	B	
France	32	31	24	2	1	2	92
Italy	30	31	19	2	2	3	87
Hungary	26	11	19	5	6	5	72
Soviet Union	13	12	14	5	3	2	49
Germany (FRG)	6	9	3	5	4	3	30
United States	2	6	11	–	–	–	19
Poland	4	6	6	–	–	1	17
Belgium	5	3	5	–	–	–	13
Great Britain	–	6	–	1	3	–	10
Greece	3	3	2	–	–	–	8
Romania	1	–	2	–	2	3	8
Netherlands	–	1	7	–	–	–	8
Sweden	2	3	2	–	–	–	7
Austria	–	1	3	1	–	2	7
Cuba	5	1	–	–	–	–	6
Denmark	–	1	1	1	1	2	6
Switzerland	–	2	3	–	–	–	5
Bohemia (Czech)	–	–	2	–	–	–	2
China	–	–	–	1	–	–	1
GDR	–	1	–	–	–	–	1
Mexico	–	–	–	–	1	–	1
Argentina	–	–	1	–	–	–	1
Portugal	–	–	1	–	–	–	1
	129	128	125	23	23	23	451

individual title, but the most successful was Edoardo Mangiarotti (ITA) with five gold, one silver and two bronze medals (1936–1960). The oldest gold medallist was Fiorenzo Marini (ITA), aged 46yr 179 days, in the 1960 team, and the youngest was Ramón Fonst (see above).

SABRE

Jean Georgiadis (GRE), Jenö Fuchs (HUN), Rudolf Kárpáti (HUN), Viktor Krovopouskov (URS) and Jean François Lamour (FRA) have all won two individual titles. Gerevich won a record seven gold medals (only one individual) and was also the oldest gold medallist. The youngest was Mikhail Burtsev (URS), aged 20yr 36 days in the 1976 team event.

Hungarians have dominated the discipline to an unparalleled extent, winning eleven gold, six silver and eight bronze individual medals. They won the individual title at every Games from 1908 to 1964, except in 1920 when they were not invited. They have won the team title ten times, been second once and third on three occasions, winning 46 consecutive contests from 1924 to 1964. Their 1960 team included Gerevich, Kárpáti and Pál Kovács, who between them amassed a total of 19 gold medals. The winning Hungarian teams of 1948 and 1952 comprised the same members.

WOMEN'S FOIL

Only Ilona Elek (HUN) has won two individual titles, in 1936 and 1948, but Elena Novikova-Belova (URS) won a record four golds from 1968 to 1976. The record for most medals is seven by Ildikó Sagi-Retjö (formerly Ujlaki-Retjö) of Hungary in a record five Games (1960–1976). Surprisingly she had been born deaf.

Ellen Preis (AUT) at the start of her record 24 years of Olympic fencing, with the gold medal in 1932.

Ellen Müller-Preis (AUT) competed over a record 24-year period from 1932–1956. This was matched by Kerstin Palm (SWE) from 1964–1988, but the latter notched up a record seven Games – the most attended by any female Olympic competitor, in any sport. The period of 24 years is also a record span of competition for any female Olympian.

The oldest gold medallist was Elek, aged 41yr 77 days in 1948,

while the youngest was Helene Mayer (GER) in 1928, aged 17yr 225 days. Elek was also the oldest medallist, taking the silver in 1952 aged 45yr 71 days.

When Gillian Sheen (GBR) won her gold medal in 1956 there were hardly any members of the British press corps on hand as they considered that fencing was a 'minor' sport, and anyway she had not been expected to achieve anything of note!

FENCING MEDALS – INDIVIDUAL

	Gold	Silver	Bronze

Foil (Men)

Wins are assessed on both wins (2pts) *and* draws (1pt) so, as in 1928, the winner does not necessarily have most wins.

	Gold	Silver	Bronze
1896	Emile Gravelotte (FRA) 4 wins	Henri Callott (FRA) 3	Perikles Mavromichalis-Pierrakos (GRE) 2
1900	Emile Cost (FRA) 6 wins	Henri Masson (FRA) 5 (USA)	Jacques Boulenger (FRA) 4
1904	Ramón Fonst (CUB) 3 wins	Albertson Van Zo Post[1](USA)2	Charles Tatham[1](USA) 1
1906	Georges Dillon–Kavanagh (FRA) d.n.a.	Gustav Casmir (GER) d.n.a.	Pierre d'Hugues (FRA) d.n.a.
1912	Nedo Nadi (ITA) 7 wins	Pietro Speciale (ITA) 5	Richard Verderber (AUT) 4
1920	Nedo Nadi (ITA) 10 wins	Philippe Cattiau (FRA) 9	Roger Ducret (FRA) 9
1924	Roger Ducret (FRA) 6 wins	Philippe Cattiau (FRA) 5	Maurice van Damme (BEL) 4
1928	Lucien Gaudin (FRA) 9 wins	Erwin Casmir (GER) 9	Giulio Gaudini (ITA) 9
1932	Gustavo Marzi (ITA) 9 wins	Joseph Levis (USA) 6	Giulio Gaudini (ITA) 5
1936	Giulio Gaudini (ITA) 7 wins	Edouard Gardère (FRA) 6	Giorgio Bocchino (ITA) 4
1948	Jean Buhan (FRA) 7 wins	Christian d'Oriola (FRA) 5	Lajos Maszlay (HUN) 4
1952	Christian d'Oriola (FRA) 8 wins	Edoardo Mangiarotti (ITA) 6	Manlio di Rosa (ITA) 5
1956	Christian d'Oriola (FRA) 6 wins	Giancarlo Bergamini (ITA) 5	Antonio Spallino (ITA) 5
1960	Viktor Zhdanovich (URS) 7 wins	Yuriy Sissikin (URS) 4	Albert Axelrod (USA) 3
1964	Egon Franke (POL) 3 wins	Jean-Claude Magnan (FRA) 2	Daniel Revenu (FRA) 1
1968	Ion Drimba (ROM) 4 wins	Jenö Kamuti (HUN) 3	Daniel Revenu (FRA) 3
1972	Witold Woyda (POL) 5 wins	Jenö Kamuti (HUN) 4	Christian Nöel (FRA) 2
1976	Fabio Dal Zotto (ITA) 4 wins	Aleksandr Romankov (URS) 4	Bernard Talvard (FRA) 3
1980	Vladimir Smirnov (URS) 5 wins	Paskal Jolyot (FRA) 5	Aleksandr Romankov (URS) 5
1984	Mauro Numa (ITA)	Matthias Behr (FRG)	Stefano Cerioni (ITA)
1988	Stefano Cerioni (ITA)	Udo Wagner (GDR)	Alexandr Romankov (URS)

1908   Event not held.

[1]*Van Zo Post and Tatham were American citizens wrongly reported as competing for Cuba.*

Épée (Men)

	Gold	Silver	Bronze
1900	Ramon Fonst (CUB)	Louis Perree (FRA)	Léon Sée (FRA)
1904	Ramon Fonst (CUB) 3 wins	Charles Tatham (USA) 2	Albertson Van Zo Post (USA)[1]
1906	Georges de la Falaise (FRA) d.n.a.	Georges Dillon-Kavanagh (FRA) d.n.a.	Alexander van Blijenburgh (HOL) d.n.d.
1908	Gaston Alibert (FRA) 5 wins	Alexandre Lippmann (FRA) 4	Eugène Olivier (FRA) 4
1912	Paul Anspach (BEL) 6 wins	Ivan Osiier (DEN) 5	Philippe Le Hardy de Beaulieu (BEL) 4
1920	Armand Massard (FRA) 9 wins	Alexandre Lippmann (FRA) 7	Gustave Buchard (FRA) 6
1924	Charles Delporte (BEL) 8 wins	Roger Ducret (FRA) 7	Nils Hellsten (SWE) 7
1928	Lucien Gaudin (FRA) 8 wins	Georges Buchard (FRA) 7	George Calnan (USA) 6
1932	Giancarlo Cornaggia-Medici (ITA) 8 wins	Georges Buchard (FRA) 7	Carlo Agostini (ITA) 7
1936	Franco Riccardi (ITA) 5 wins	Saverio Ragno (ITA) 6	Giancarlo Cornaggia-Medici (ITA) 6
1948	Luigi Cantone (ITA) 7 wins	Oswald Zappelli (SUI) 5	Edoardo Mangiarotti (ITA) 5
1952	Edoardo Mangiarotti (ITA) 7 wins	Dario Mangiarotti (ITA) 6	Oswald Zappelli (SUI) 6
1956	Carlo Pavesi (ITA) 5 wins	Giuseppe Delfino (ITA) 5	Edoardo Mangiarotti (ITA) 5
1960	Giuseppe Delfino (ITA) 5 wins	Allan Jay (GBR) 5	Bruno Khabarov (URS) 4
1964	Grigoriy Kriss (URS) 2 wins	William Hoskyns (GBR) 2	Guram Kostava (URS) 1
1968	Gyozo Kulcsár (HUN) 4 wins	Grigoriy Kriss (URS) 4	Gianluigi Saccaro (ITA) 4
1972	Csaba Fenyvesi (HUN) 4 wins	Jacques la Degaillerie (FRA) 3	Gyözö Kulcsár (HUN) 3
1976	Alexander Pusch (FRG) 3 wins	Jürgen Hehn (FRG) 3	Gyözö Kulcsár (HUN) 3
1980	Johan Harmenberg (SWE) 4 wins	Ernö Kolczonay (HUN) 3	Philippe Riboud (FRA) 3
1984	Philippe Boisse (FRA)	Bjorne Vaggo (SWE)	Philippe Riboud (FRA)
1988	Arnd Schmitt (FRG)	Philippe Riboud (FRA)	Andrey Chouvalov (URS)

1896   Event not held.

[1]*Van Zo Post and Tatham were American citizens wrongly reported as competing for Cuba.*

Sabre (Men)

	Gold	Silver	Bronze
1896	Jean Georgiadis (GRE) 4 wins	Telemachos Karakalos (GRE) 3	Holger Nielsen (DEN) 2
1900	Georges de la Falaise (FRA) d.n.a.	Léon Thiébaut (FRA) d.n.a.	Siegfried Flesch (AUT) d.n.a.
1904	Manuel Diaz (CUB) 4 wins	William Grebe (USA) 3	Albertson Van Zo Post[1](USA) 2
1906	Jean Georgiadis (GRE) d.n.a.	Gustav Casmir (GER) d.n.a.	Federico Cesarano (ITA) d.n.a.
1908	Jeno Fuchs (HUN) 6 wins	Béla Zulavsky (HUN) 6	Vilem Goppold von Lobsdorf (BOH) 4
1912	Jeno Fuchs (HUN) 6 wins	Béla Békéssy HUN) 5	Ervin Mészaros (HUN) 5
1920	Nedo Nadi (ITA) 11 wins	Aldo Nadi (ITA) 9	Adrianus EW de Jong (HOL) 7
1924	Sándor Posta (HUN) 5 wins	Roger Ducret (FRA) 5	János Garai (HUN) 5
1928	Odön Tersztyanszky (HUN) 9 wins	Attila Petschauer (HUN) 9	Bino Bini (ITA) 8
1932	György Piller (HUN) 8 wins	Giulio Gaudini (ITA) 7	Endre Kabos (HUN) 5
1936	Endre Kabos (HUN) 7 wins	Gustavo Marzi (ITA) 6	Aladár Gerevich (HUN) 6
1948	Aladár Gerevich (HUN) 7 wins	Vincenzo Pinton (ITA) 5	Pál Kovács (HUN) 5
1952	Pál Kovács (HUN) 8 wins	Aladár Gerevich (HUN) 7	Tibor Berczelly (HUN) 5
1956	Rudolf Kárpáti (HUN) 6 wins	Jerzy Pawlowski (POL) 5	Lev Kuznyetsov (URS) 4

	Gold	Silver	Bronze
1960	Rudolf Kárpáti (HUN) 5 wins	Zoltán Horvath (HUN) 4	Wladimiro Calarese (ITA) 4
1964	Tibor Pézsa (HUN) 2 wins	Claude Arabo (FRA) 2	Umar Mavlikhanov (URS) 1
1968	Jerzy Pawlowski (POL) 4 wins	Mark Rakita (URS) 4	Tribor Pézsa (HUN) 3
1972	Viktor Sidiak (URS) 4 wins	Peter Maroth (HUN) 3	Vladimir Nazlimov (URS) 3
1976	Viktor Krovopouskov (URS) 5 wins	Vladimir Nazlimov (URS) 4	Viktor Sidiak (URS) 3
1980	Viktor Krovopouskov (URS) 5 wins	Mikhail Burtsev (URS) 4	Imre Gedovari (HUN) 3
1984	Jean François Lamour (FRA)	Marco Marin (ITA)	Peter Westbrook (USA)
1988	Jean François Lamour (FRA)	Janusz Olech (POL)	Giovanni Scalzo (ITA)

[1]Van Zo Post and Tatham were American citizens wrongly reported as competing for Cuba.

Women's Foil

1924	Ellen Osiier (DEN) 5 wins	Gladys Davis (GBR) 4	Grete Heckscher (DEN)] 3
1928	Helène Mayer (GER) 7 wins	Muriel Freeman (GBR) 6	Olga Oelkers (GER) 4
1932	Ellen Preis (AUT) 9 wins	Heather Guinness (GBR) 8	Ena Bogen (HUN) 7
1936	Ilona Elek (HUN) 6 wins	Helène Mayer (GER) 5	Ellen Preis (AUT) 5
1948	Ilona Elek (HUN) 6 wins	Karen Lachmann (DEN) 5	Ellen Müller-Preis (AUT) 5
1952	Irene Camber (ITA) 5 wins	Ilona Elek (HUN) 5	Karen Lachmann (DEN) 4
1956	Gillian Sheen (GBR) 6 wins	Olga Orban (ROM) 6	Renée Garilhe (FRA) 5
1960	Heidi Schmid (GER) 6 wins	Valentina Rastvorova (URS) 5	Maria Vicol (ROM) 4
1964	Ildikó Ujlaki-Reitó (HUn) 2 wins	Helga Mees (GER) 2	Antonella Ragno (ITA) 2
1968	Elena Novikova (URS) 4 wins	Pilar Roldan (MEX) 3	Ildikó Ujlaki-Rejtó (HUN) 3
1972	Antonella Ragno-Lonzi (ITA) 4 wins	Ildikó Bóbis (HUN) 3	Galina Gorokhova (URS) 3
1976	Ildikó Schwarczenberger (HUN) 4 wins	Maria Collino (ITA) 4	Elena Novikova-Belova (URS) 3
1980	Pascale Trinquet (FRA) 4 wins	Magda Maros (HUN) 3	Barbara Wysoczanska (POL) 3
1984	Jujie Luan (CHN)	Cornelia Hanisch (FRG)	Dorina Vaccaroni (ITA)
1988	Anja Fichtel (FRG)	Sabine Bau (FRG)	Zita Funkenhauser (FRG)

1896–1920 Event not held.

FENCING MEDALS – TEAM

Foil (Men)

	Gold	Silver	Bronze
1904	Cuba/USA	United States	–[1]
1920	Italy	France	United States
1924	France	Belgium	Hungary
1928	Italy	France	Argentina
1932	France	Italy	United States
1936	Italy	France	Germany
1948	France	Italy	Belgium
1952	France	Italy	Hungary
1956	Italy	France	Hungary
1960	Soviet Union	Italy	Germany
1964	Soviet Union	Poland	France
1968	France	Soviet Union	Poland
1972	Poland	Soviet Union	France
1976	FRG	Italy	France
1980	France	Soviet Union	Poland
1984	Italy	FRG	France
1988	Soviet Union	FRG	Hungary

1896–1900, 1906–1912 Event not held.

[1] No other teams entered.

Women's Foil

	Gold	Silver	Bronze
1960	Soviet Union	Hungary	Italy
1964	Hungary	Soviet Union	Germany
1968	Soviet Union	Hungary	Romania
1972	Soviet Union	Hungary	Romania
1976	Soviet Union	France	Hungary
1980	France	Soviet Union	Hungary
1984	FRG	Romania	France
1988	FRG	Italy	Hungary

1896–1956 Event not held

Left, facing page *Franco Riccardi of Italy (144) scores a hit against Ian Campbell-Gray (GBR) in the 1936 épée, winning the individual gold in his third Games, as well leading his team to victory.*

Épée (Men)

	Gold	Silver	Bronze
1906	France	Great Britain	Belgium
1908	France	Great Britain	Belgium
1912	Belgium	Great Britain	Nethlands
1920	Italy	Belgium	France
1924	France	Belgium	Italy
1928	Italy	France	Portugal
1932	France	Italy	United States
1936	Italy	Sweden	France
1948	France	Italy	Sweden
1952	Italy	Sweden	Switzerland
1956	Italy	Hungary	France
1960	Italy	Great Britain	Soviet Union
1964	Hungary	Italy	France
1968	Hungary	Soviet Union	Poland
1972	Hungary	Switzerland	Soviet Union
1976	Sweden	FRG	Switzerland
1980	France	Poland	Soviet Union
1984	FRG	France	Italy
1988	France	FRG	Soviet Union

1896–1904 Event not held.

Sabre (Men)

	Gold	Silver	Bronze
1906	Germany	Greece	Netherlands
1908	Hungary	Italy	Bohemia
1912	Hungary	Austria	Netherlands
1920	Italy	France	Netherlands
1924	Italy	Hungary	Netherlands
1928	Hungary	Italy	Poland
1932	Hungary	Italy	Poland
1936	Hungary	Italy	Germany
1948	Hungary	Italy	United States
1952	Hungary	Italy	France
1956	Hungary	Poland	Soviet Union
1960	Hungary	Poland	Italy
1964	Soviet Union	Italy	Poland
1968	Soviet Union	Italy	Hungary
1972	Italy	Soviet Union	Hungary
1976	Soviet Union	Italy	Romania
1980	Soviet Union	Italy	Hungary
1884	Italy	France	Romania
1988	Hungary	Soviet Union	Italy

1896–1904 Event not held.

DISCONTINUED EVENTS

Foil for Fencing Masters

1896	Léon Pyrgos (GRE)	M Perronnet (FRA)	–
1900	Lucien Mérignac (FRA)	Alphonse Kirchhoffer (FRA)	Jean-Baptiste Mimiague (FRA)

Épée for Fencing Masters

1900	Albert Ayat (FRA)	Emile Bougnol (FRA)	Henri Laurent (FRA)
1906	Cyrille Verbrugge (BEL)	Mario Gubiani (ITA)	Ioannis Raissis (GRE)

Épée for Amateurs and Fencing Masters

1900	Albert Ayat (FRA)	Ramón Fonst (CUB)	Léon Sée (FRA)

Sabre for Fencing Masters

1900	Antonio Conte (ITA)	Italo Santelli (ITA)	Milan Neralic (AUT)
1906	Cyrille Verbrugge (BEL)	Ioannis Raissis (GRE)	–

Three Cornered Sabre

1906	Gustav Casmir (GER)	George van Rossem (HOL)	Péter Tóth (HUN)

Single Sticks

1904	Albertson Van Zo Post[1] (USA)	William Grebe (USA)	William O'Connor (USA)

[1] Van Zo Post was an American citizen wrongly reported as competing for Cuba.

Soviet gymnast Boris Shakhlin, here on the pommel horse, won 4 golds, 2 silvers and a bronze at Rome in 1960.

GYMNASTICS

In artistic gymnastics there are eight interlinked events for men and six for women. A team competition comes first, comprising one compulsory and one optional exercise for each separate discipline. For men these are: floor exercises, pommel horse, rings, horse vault, parallel bars and horizontal bar. For women: floor exercises, asymmetrical bars, horse vault and balance beam. Each competitor is marked out of 10 for both the exercises at each discipline. The best total of five gymnasts per country decides the team medals.

The best 36 individuals then qualify for the individual all-round competition. They each complete a further optional exercise for each discipline, and are awarded new marks which are added to the average of their previous best total from the team competition. The best six in each discipline go forward to the individual final for that event. A new mark for a further optional exercise is added to the average of their previous marks from the team competition

With the exception of 1948, when scores were marked out of 20, points since 1936 are of some comparative value. In 1984 a modern rhythmic event for women was introduced.

The first gymnastics gold medal was won by the German team on the parallel bars event in 1896, and the first individual champion was Carl Schuhmann of that team in the vault. Due to the large number of disciplines, each with their own medals awarded, gymnasts are among the greatest collectors of Olympic medals. The most successful was Larissa Latynina (URS) who won a record 18 medals from 1956–1964, comprising nine golds (the most by any female Olympian), five silver and four bronze – unsurpassed in any sport.

The most individual gold medals is seven won by Vera Cáslavská (TCH) in 1964 and 1968. The male record for individual golds is six by Boris Shakhlin (URS) and Nikolay Andrianov (URS). The latter also holds the absolute Olympic record for most medals by a male competitor, in any sport, with a total of fifteen. In 1980 Aleksandr Dityatin (URS) became the only male gymnast to gain medals in all eight events open to him at one Games.

In recent years the sport has caught the imagination of the public due to a tremendous increase in media – especially television – coverage. In 1968 it was the attractive blonde Vera Cáslavska of Czechoslovakia who caught the public eye by defeating the Soviet women only two months after the invasion of her country. At Munich it was the elfin Olga Korbut (URS) who was the focus of all, even though she was outshone, technically, by her illustrious teammate Ludmila Tourischeva.

In 1976 the unsmiling Nadia Comaneci (ROM) deserved all the adulation as she scored the ultimate 10.00 on seven occasions, while the photogenic Nelli Kim (URS) attained that score twice. Aleksandr Dityatin stole the show from the girls in 1980, and also gained the first Olympic 10.00 by a man in the horse vault. At Los Angeles the television cameras made a superstar of Mary Lou Retton (USA) in the absence of the East Europeans.

The oldest gold medallist was Masao Takemoto (JPN), aged 40yr 344 days, in the 1960 team event. Only 24 days younger was Heikki Savolainen (FIN) in the 1948 team event, and in 1952 he in fact became the oldest medallist, with a bronze aged 44yr 297 days. He also competed in a record five Games over a record span of 24 years from 1928 to 1952.

The youngest champion was Nadia Comaneci (ROM) aged 14yr 252 days in 1976, while the oldest female champion was Agnes Keleti (HUN) in 1956, aged 35 yr 171 days. The youngest male to win a gold medal was Harald Eriksen (NOR) in 1906, aged 17yr 292 days. The youngest medallist was Dimitrios Loundras (GRE), who gained a bronze in the parallel bars team event of 1896, reputedly aged 10yr 215 days. However some doubt exists about his exact age.

Since 1984 male competitors must be a minimum of 16yr and females must be 15yr. Recent revelations suggest that some countries in the Eastern bloc faked the ages of their young female performers, making them older than in fact they were.

The closest margin of victory in the individual all-round contest was 0.025pts in 1984 when Koji Gushiken (JPN) beat Peter Vidmar (USA). The closest in the women's competition was in 1988 when Yelena Chouchounova (URS) beat Daniela Silivas (ROM) also by 0.025pts. On two occasions there has been a triple tie for a gold medal – both times in the pommel horse event, in 1948 and 1988. Since the Soviet Union entered Olympic competition in 1952 they have won the women's team title nine times. They were not present in 1984.

One of the most amazing competitors in Olympic history must be the American gymnast George Eyser, who won six medals, including three golds, in the 1904 Games. He was well over 30 years of age, but even more remarkably had a wooden leg. Despite this, he also competed in the all-round contest (the forerunner of the decathlon) in the track and field programme. In 1988 Vladimir Gogoladze (URS) performed a triple somersault in the team floor exercises – the first achieved in the Olympics. The largest crowd to watch an Olympic gymnastic event is 18 000 at the Montreal Forum in 1976 for the final of the women's individual apparatus contests. In the 1988 modern rhythmic competition, Marina Lobatch (URS) scored the maximum possible 60.00 pts.

GYMNASTICS MULTI-MEDAL WINNERS

		G	S	B
Larissa Latynina (URS)	1956–64	9	5	4
Sawao Kato (JPN)	1968–76	8	3	1
Nikolay Andrianov (URS)	1972–80	7	5	3
Boris Shakhlin (URS)	1956–64	7	4	2
Vera Cáslavská (TCH)	1960–68	7	4	0
Viktor Chukarin (URS)	1952–56	7	3	1

GYMNASTICS MEDAL TOTALS

	MEN			WOMEN			
Country	G	S	B	G	S	B	Total
Soviet Union	40	38	18	34	29	27	186
Japan	27	27	28	–	–	1	83
United States	21	15	19	1	3	5	64
Switzerland	15	19	13	–	–	–	47
Hungary	7	5	6	6	5	10	39
Romania	–	–	2	13	10	11	36
Czechoslovakia	3	7	9	9	6	1	35
GDR	3	3	9	3	10	7	35
Germany (FRG)	11	7	11	1	1	–	31
Italy	12	7	9	–	1	–	29
Finland	8	5	12	–	–	–	25
France	4	7	9	–	–	–	20
China	5	4	2	1	–	1	13
Yugoslavia	5	2	4	–	–	–	11
Sweden	5	2	–	1	1	1	10
Greece	3	2	4	–	–	–	9
Norway	2	2	1	–	–	–	5
Denmark	1	3	1	–	–	–	5
Bulgaria	1	–	2	–	1	1	5
Austria	2	1	–	–	–	–	3
Great Britain	–	1	1	–	–	1	3
Belgium	–	1	1	–	–	–	2
Poland	–	1	1	–	–	–	2
Canada	–	–	–	1	–	–	1
Netherlands	–	–	–	1	–	–	1
Korea	–	–	1	–	–	–	1
	175	159	163	71	67	66	701

GYMNASTICS MEDALS – MEN

	Gold	Silver	Bronze
Team			
1904	United States/Austria 374.43pts	United States 356.37	United States 349.69
1906	Norway 19.00pts	Denmark 18.00	Italy 16.71
1908	Sweden 438pts	Norway 425	Finland 405
1912	Italy 265.75pts	Hungary 227.25	Great Britain 184.50
1920	Italy 359.855pts	Belgium 346.745	France 340.100
1924	Italy 839.058pts	France 820.528	Switzerland 816.661
1928	Switzerland 1718.625pts	Czechoslovakia 1712.250	Yugoslavia 1648.750
1932	Italy 541.850pts	United States 522.275	Finland 509.995
1936	Germany 657.430pts	Switzerland 654.802	Finland 638.468
1948	Finland 1358.3pts	Switzerland 1356.7	Hungary 1330.35
1952	Soviet Union 575.4pts	Switzerland 567.5	Finland 564.2
1956	Soviet Union 568.25	Japan 566.40	Finland 555.95
1960	Japan 575.20pts	Soviet Union 572.70	Italy 559.05
1964	Japan 577.95pts	Soviet Union 575.45	Germany 565.10
1968	Japan 575.90pts	Soviet Union 571.10	GDR 557.15
1972	Japan 571.25pts	Soviet Union 564.05	GDR 559.70
1976	Japan 576.85pts	Soviet Union 576.45	GDR 654.65
1980	Soviet Union 589.60pts	GDR 581.15	Hungary 575.00
1984	United States 591.40pts	China 590.80	Japan 586.70
1988	Soviet Union 593.350pts	GDR 588.450	Japan 585.600

1896–1900 Event not held.

	Gold	Silver	Bronze
Individual Combined Exercises			
1900	Gustave Sandras (FRA) 302pts	Noël Bas (FRA) 295	Lucien Démanet (FRA) 293
1904	Julius Lennard (AUT) 69.80pts	Wilhelm Weber (GER) 69.10	Adolf Spinnler (SUI) 67.99
1906²	Pierre Paysse (FRA) 97pts	Alberto Braglia (ITA) 95	Georges Charmoille (FRA) 94
1906	Pierre Paysse (FRA) 116pts	Alberto Braglia (ITA) 115	Georges Charmoille (FRA) 113
1908	Alberto Braglia (ITA) 317.0pts	SW Tysal (GBR) 312.0	Louis Ségura (FRA) 297.0
1912	Alberto Braglia (ITA) 135.0pts	Louis Ségura (FRA) 132.5	Adolfo Tunesi (ITA) 131.5
1920	Giorgio Zampori (ITA) 88.35pts	Marco Torres (FRA) 87.62	Jean Gounot (FRA) 87.45
1924	Leon Stukelj (YUG) 110.340pts	Robert Pražák (TCH) 110.323	Bedrich Supcik (TCH) 106.930
1928	Georges Miez (SUI) 247.500pts	Herman Hänggi (SUI) 246.625	Leon Stukelj (YUG) 244.875
1932	Romeo Neri (ITA) 140.625pts	István Pelle (HUN) 134.925	Heikki Savolainen (FIN) 134.575
1936	Alfred Schwarzmann (GER) 113.100pts	Eugen Mack (SUI) 112.334	Konrad Frey (GER) 111.532
1948	Veikko Huhtanen (FIN) 229.7pts	Walter Lehmann (SUI) 229.0	Paavo Aaltonen (FIN) 228.8
1952	Viktor Chukarin (URS) 115.70pts	Grant Shaginyan (URS) 114.95	Josef Stalder (SUI) 114.75
1956	Viktor Chukarin (URS) 114.25prs	Takashi Ono (JPN) 114.20	Yuriy Titov (URS) 113.80
1960	Boris Shakhlin (URS) 115.95pts	Takashi Ono (JPN) 115.90	Yuriy Titov (URS) 115.60
1964	Yukio Endo (JPN) 115.95pts	Shuji Tsurumi (JPN) 115.40	–
		Viktor Lisitsky (URS) 115.40	
		Boris Shakhlin (URS) 115.40	
1968	Sawao Kato (JPN) 115.90pts	Mikhail Voronin (URS) 115.85	Akinori Nakayama (JPN) 115.65
1972	Sawao Kato (JNP) 114.650pts	Eizo Kenmotsu (JPN) 114.575	Akinori Nakayama (JPN) 114.325
1976	Nikolay Andrianov (URS) 116.650pts	Sawao Kato (JPN) 115.650	Mitsuo Tsukahara (JPN) 115.575
1980	Aleksandr Dityatin (URS) 118.650pts	Nikolay Andrianov (URS) 118.225	Stoyan Deltchev (BUL) 118.000
1984	Koji Gushiken (JPN) 118.700pts	Peter Vidmar (USA) 118.675	Li Ning (CHN) 118.575
1988	Vladimir Artemov (URS) 119.125pts	Valeriy Lyukhine (URS) 119.025	Dmitry Bilozertchev (URS) 118.975

1896 Event not held.
¹Lenhart was a member of the Philadelphia Club, USA, which won the team event.
²Two competitions in 1906, one of five events and one of six.

	Gold	Silver	Bronze
Floor Exercises			
1932	Istvan Pelle (HUN) 9.60	Georges Miez (SUI) 9.47	Mario Lertora (ITA) 9.23
1936	Georges Miez (SUI) 18.666	Josef Walter (SUI) 18.5	Konrad Frey (GER) 18.466
			Eugen Mack (SUI) 18.466
1948	Ferenc Pataki (HUN) 38.7	János Mogyorosi-Klencs (HUN) 38.4	Zdenek Ružička (TCH) 38.1
1952	William Thoresson (SWE) 19.25	Tadao Uesako (JPN) 19.15	–
		Jerzy Jokiel (POL) 19.15	
1956	Valentin Muratov (URS) 19.20	Nobuyuki Aihara (JPN) 19.10	–
		William Thoresson (SWE) 19.10	
1960	Nobuyuki Aihara (JPN) 19.450	Yuriy Titov (URS) 19.325	Franco Menichelli (ITA) 19.275
1964	Franco Menichelli (ITA) 19.45	Viktor Lisitsky (URS) 19.35	–
		Yukio Endo (JPN) 19.35	
1968	Sawao Kato (JPN) 19.475	Akinori Nakayama (JPN) 19.400	Takeshi Kato (JPN) 19.275
1972	Nikolay Andrianov (URS) 19.175	Akinori Nakayama (JPN) 19.125	Shigeru Kasamatsu (JPN) 19.025
1976	Nikolay Andrianov (URS) 19.450	Vladimir Marchenko (URS) 19.425	Peter Kormann (USA) 19.300

	Gold	Silver	Bronze
1980	Roland Brückner (GDR) 19.750	Nikolay Andrianov (URS) 19.725	Aleksandr Dityatin (URS) 19.700
1984	Li Ning (CHN) 19.925	Yun Lou (CHN) 19.775	Koji Sotomura (JPN) 19.700
			Philippe Vatuone (FRA) 19.700
1988	Sergey Kharikov (URS) 19.925	Vladimir Artemov (URS) 19.900	Lou Yun (CHN) 19.850
			Yukio Iketani (JPN) 19.850

Parallel Bars

1896	Alfred Flatow (GER) d.n.a.	Jules Zutter (SUI)	Hermann Weingartner (GER)
1904	George Eyser (USA) 44	Anton Heida (USA) 43	John Duha (USA) 40
1924	August Güttinger (SUI) 21.63	Robert Pražák (TCH) 21.61	Giorgio Zampori (ITA) 21.45
1928	Ladislav Vácha (TCH) 18.83	Josip Primožič (YUG) 18.50	Hermann Hänggi (SUI) 18.08
1932	Romeo Neri (ITA) 18.97	István Pelle (HUN) 18.60	Heikki Savolainen (FIN) 18.27
1936	Konrad Frey (GER) 19.067	Michael Reusch (SUI) 109.034	Alfred Schwarzmann (GER) 18.967
1948	Michael Reusch (SUI) 39.5	Veikkö Huhtanen (FIN) 39.3	Christian Kipfer (SUI) 39.1
			Josef Stalder (SUI) 39.1
1952	Hans Eugster (SUI) 19.65	Viktor Chukarin (URS) 19.60	Josef Stalder (SUI) 19.50
1956	Viktor Chukarin (URS) 19.20	Masami Kubota (JPN) 19.15	Takashi Ono (JPN) 19.10
			Masao Takemoto (JPN) 19.10
1960	Boris Shakhlin (URS)	Giovanni Carminucci (ITA) 19.375	Takashi Ono (JPN)19.350
1964	Yukio Endo (JPN) 19.675	Shuji Tsurumi (JPN) 19.450	Franco Menichelli (ITA) 19.350
1968	Akinori Nakayama (JPN) 19.475	Mikhail Voronin (URS) 19.425	Vladimir Klimenko (URS) 19.225
1972	Sawao Kato (JPN) 19.475	Shigeru Kasamatsu (JPN) 19.375	Eizo Kenmotsu (JPN) 19.25
1976	Sawao Kato (JPN) 19.675	Nikolay Andrianov (URS) 19.500	Mitsuo Tsukahara (JPN) 19.475
1980	Aleksandr Tkachev (URS) 19.775	Aleksandr Dityatin (URS) 19.750	Roland Brückner (GDR) 19.650
1984	Bart Conner (USA) 19.950	Nobuyuki Kajitani (JPN) 19.925	Mitchell Gaylord (USA) 19.850
1988	Vladimir Artemov (URS) 19.925	Valeriy Lyukhine (URS) 19.900	Sven Tippelt (GDR) 19.750

1900, 1906–1920 Event not held.

Pommel Horse

1896	Jules Zutter (SUI) d.n.a.	Hermann Weingartner (GER)	Gyula Kakas (HUN)
1904	Anton Heida (USA) 42	George Eyser (USA) 33	William Merz (USA) 29
1924	Josef Wilhelm (SUI) 21.23	Jean Gutweiniger (SUI) 21.13	Antoine Rebetez (SUI) 20.73
1928	Hermann Hänggi (SUI) 1975	Georges Miez (SUI) 19.25	Heikki Savolainen (FIN) 18.83
1932	Istvan Pelle (HUN) 19.07	Omero Bonoli (ITA) 18.87	Frank Haubold (USA) 18.57
1936	Konrad Frey (GER) 19.333	Eugen Mack (SUI) 19.167	Albert Bachmann (SUI) 19.067
1948	Paavo Aaltonen (FIN) 38.7	Luigi Zanetti (ITA) 38.3	Guido Figone (ITA) 38.2
	Veikkö Huhtanen (FIN) 38.7		
	Heikki Savolainen (FIN) 38.7		
1952	Viktor Chukarin (URS) 19.50	Yevgeniy Korolkov (URS) 19.40	–
		Grant Shaginyan (URS) 19.40	
1956	Boris Shakhlin (URS) 19.25	Takashi Ono (JPN) 19.20	Viktor Chukarin (URS) 19.10
1960	Eugen Ekman (FIN) 19.375	–	Shuji Tsurumi (JPN) 19.150
	Boris Shakhlin (URS) 19.375		
1964	Miroslav Cerar (YUG) 19.525	Shuji Tsurumi (JPN) 19.325	Yuriy Tsapenko (URS) 19.200
1968	Miroslav Cerar (YUG) 19.325	Olli Laiho (FIN) 19.225	Mikhail Voronin (URS) 19.200
1972	Viktor Klimenko (URS) 19.125	Sawao Kato (JPN) 19.00	Eizo Kenmotsu (JPN) 18.950
1976	Zoltan Magyar (HUN) 19.700	Eizo Kenmotsu (JPN) 19.575	Nikolay Andrianov (URS) 19.525
1980	Zoltan Magyar (HUN) 19.925	Aleksandr Dityatin (URS) 19.800	Michael Nikolay (GDR) 19.775
1984	Li Ning (CHN) 19.950	–	Timothy Daggett (USA) 19.825
	Peter Vidmar (USA) 19.950		
1988	Lubomir Gueraskov (URS) 19.950	–	–
	Zsolt Borkai (HUN) 19.950		
	Dmitry Bilozertchev (URS) 19.950		

1900, 1906–1920 Event not held.

Rings

1896	Ioannis Mitropoulos (GRE) d.n.a.	Hermann Weingartner (GER)	Petros Persakis (GRE)
1904	Herman Glass (USA) 45	William Merz (USA) 35	Emil Voight (USA) 32
1924	Franco Martino (ITA) 21.553	Robert Pražák (TCH) 21.483	Ladislav Vácha (TCH) 21.430
1928	Leon Skutelj (YUG) 19.25	Ladislav Vácha (TCH) 19.17	Emanuel Löffler (TCH) 18.83
1932	George Gulack (USA) 18.97	William Denton (USA) 18.60	Giovanni Lattuada (ITA) 18.50
1936	Alois Hudec (TCH) 19.433	Leon Škutelj (YUG) 18.867	Matthias Volz (GER) 18.667
1948	Karl Frei (SUI) 39.60	Michael Reusch (SUI) 39.10	Zdenek Ružička (TCH) 38.30
1952	Grant Shaginyan (URS) 19.75	Viktor Chukarin (URS) 19.55	Hans Eugster (SUI) 1940
			Dimitriy Leonkin (URS) 19.40
1956	Albert Azaryan (URS) 1935	Valentin Muratov (URS) 19.15	Masao Takemoto (JPN) 19.10
			Masami Kubota (JPN) 19.10
1960	Albert Azaryan (URS) 19.725	Boris Shakhlin (URS) 19.500	Velik Kapsazov (BUL) 19.425
			Takashi Ono (JPN) 19.425

	Gold	Silver	Bronze
1964	Takuji Hayata (JPN) 19.475	Franco Menichelli (ITA) 19.425	Boris Shakhlin (URS) 19.400
1968	Akinori Nakayama (JPN) 19.450	Mikhail Voronin (URS) 19.325	Sawao Kato (JPN) 19.225
1972	Akinori Nakayama (JPN) 19.350	Mikhail Voronin (URS) 19.275	Mitsuo Tsukahara (JPN)
1976	Nikolay Andrianov (URS) 19.650	Aleksandr Dityatin (URS) 19.550	Danut Grecu (ROM) 19.500
1980	Aleksandr Dityatin (URS) 19.875	Aleksandr Tkachev (URS) 19.725	Jiri Tabak (TCH) 19.600
1984	Koji Gushiken (JPN) 19.850	–	Mitchell Gaylord (USA) 19.825
	Li Ning (CHN) 19.850		
1988	Holger Behrendt (GDR) 19.925	–	Sven Tippelt (GDR) 19/875
	Dmitry Bilozertchev (URS) 19.925)		

1900, 1906–1920 Event not held.

Horizontal Bar

	Gold	Silver	Bronze
1896	Hermann Weingartner (GER) d.n.a.	Alfred Flatow (GER)	Petmesas (GRE)
1904	Anton Heida (USA) 40	–	George Eyser (USA) 39
	Edward Hennig (USA) 40		
1924	Leon Strukelj (YUG) 19.730	Jean Gutweniger (SUI) 19.236	André Higelin (FRA) 19.163
1928	Georges Miez (SUI) 19.17	Romeo Neri (ITA) 19.00	Eugen Mack (SUI) 18.92
1932	Dallas Bixler (USA) 18.33	Heikki Savolainen (FIN) 18.07	Einari Teräsvirta (FIN) 18.07[1]
1936	Aleksanteri Saarvala (FIN) 19.367	Konrad Frey (GER) 19.267	Alfred Schwarzmann (GER) 19.233
1948	Josef Stalder (SUI) 39.7	Walter Lehmann (SUI) 39.4	Veikkö Huhtanen (FIN) 39.2
1952	Jack Günthard (SUI) 19.55	Josef Stalder (SUI) 19.50	–
		Alfred Schwarzmann (GER) 19.50	
1956	Takashi Ono (JPN) 19.60	Yuriy Titov (URS) 19.40	Masao Takemoto (JPN) 19.30
1960	Takashi Ono (JPN) 19.60	Masao Takemoto (JPN) 19.525	Boris Shakhlin (URS) 19.475
1964	Boris Shakhlin (URS) 19.625	Yuriy Titov (URS) 19.55	Miroslav Cerar (YUG) 19.50
1968	Mikhail Voronin (URS) 19.550		Eizo Kenmotsu (JPN) 19.375
	Akinori Nakayama (JPN) 19.550		
1972	Mitsuo Tsukahara (JPN) 19.725	Sawao Kato (JPN) 19.525	Shigeru Kasamatsu (JPN) 19.450
1976	Mitsuo Tsukahara (JPN) 19.675	Eizo Kenmotsu (JPN) 19.500	Eberhard Gienger (FRG) 19.475
			Henry Boërio (FRA) 19.475
1980	Stoyan Deltchev (Bul) 19.825	Aleksandr Dityatin (URS) 19.750	Nikolay Andrianov (URS) 19.675
1984	Shinje Morisue (JPN) 20.00	Tong Fei (CHN) 19.955	Koji Gushiken (JPN) 19.950
1988	Vladimir Artemov (URS) 10.900	–	Holger Behrendt (GDR) 19.800
	Valeriy Lyukhine (URS) 19.900		Marius Germann (ROM) 19.800

1900, 1906–1920 Event not held.

[1] Teräsvirta conceded second place to Savolainen.

Horse Vault

	Gold	Silver	Bronze
1896	Carl Schuhmann (GER) d.n.a.	Jules Zutter (SUI)	–
1904	Anton Heida (USA) 36	–	William Merz (USA) 31
	George Eyser (USA) 36		
1924	Frank Kriz (USA) 9.98	Jan Koutny (TCH) 9.97	Bohumil Mořkovsky (TCH) 9.93
1928	Eugen Mack (SUI) 9.58	Emanuel Lóffler (TCH) 9.50	Stane Derganc (YUG) 9.46
1932	Savino Guglielmetti (ITA) 18.03	Alfred Jochim (GER) 17.77	Edward Carmichael (USA) 17.53
1936	Alfred Schwarzmann (GER) 19.200	Eugen Mack (SUI) 18.967	Matthias Volz (GER) 18.467
1948	Paavo Aaltonen (FIN) 39.10	Olavi Rove (FIN) 39.00	János Mogyorosi-Klencs (HUN) 38.50
			Ferenc Pataki (HUN) 38.50
			Leos Sotornik (TCH) 38.50
1952	Viktor Chukarin (URS) 19.20	Masao Takemoto (JPN) 19.15	Tadao Uesako (JPN) 19.10
			Takashi Ono (JPN) 19.10
1956	Helmuth Bantz (GER) 18.85	–	Yuriy Titov (URS) 18.75
	Valentin Muratov (URS) 18.85		
1960	Takashi Ono (JPN) 19.350	–	Vladimir Portnoi (URS) 19.225
	Boris Shakhlin (URS) 19.350		
1964	Haruhiro Yamashita (JPN) 19.600	Viktor Lisitsky (URS) 19.325	Hannu Rantakari (FIN) 19.300
1968	Mikhail Voronin (URS) 19.000	Yukio Endo (JPN) 18.950	Sergey Diomidov (URS) 18.925
1972	Klaus Koste (GDR) 18.850	Viktor Klimenko (URS) 18.825	Nikolay Andrianov (URS) 18.800
1976	Nikolay Andrianov (URS) 19.450	Mitsuo Tsukahara (JPN) 19.375	Hiroshi Kajiyama (JPN) 19.275
1980	Nikolay Andrianov (URS) 19.825	Aleksandr Dityatin (URS) 19.800	Roland Brückner (GDR) 19.775
1984	Lou Yun (CHN) 19.950	Li Ning (CHN) 19.825	–
		Koji Gushiken (JPN) 19.825	
		Mitchell Gaylord (USA) 19.825	
		Shinje Morisue (JPN) 19.825	
1988	Lou Yun (CHN) 19.875	Sylvio Kroll (GDR) 19.862	Park Jong-Hoon (KOR) 19.775

1900, 1906–1920 Event not held.

GYMNASTICS MEDALS – WOMEN

	Gold	Silver	Bronze
Team			
1928	Netherlands 316.75pts	Italy 289.00	Great Britain 258.25
1936	Germany 506.50pts	Czechoslovakia 503.60	Hungary 499.00
1948	Czechoslovakia 445.45pts	Hungary 440.55	United States 422.63
1952	Soviet Union 527.03pts	Hungary 520.96	Czechoslovakia 503.32
1956	Soviet Union 444.80pts	Hungary 443.50	Romania 438.20
1960	Soviet Union 382.320pts	Czechoslovakia 373.323	Romania 372.053
1964	Soviet Union 380.890pts	Czechoslovakia 379.989	Japan 377.889
1968	Soviet Union 382.85pts	Czechoslovakia 382.20	GDR 379.10
1972	Soviet Union 380.50pts	GDR 376.55	Hungary 368.25
1976	Soviet Union 390.35pts	Romania 387.15	GDR 385.10
1980	Soviet Union 394.90pts	Romania 393.50	GDR 392.55
1984	Romania 392.20pts	United States 391.20	China 388.60
1988	Soviet Union 395.475pts	Romania 394.125	GDR 390.875

1896–1924, 1932 Event not held.

	Individual Combined Exercises		
1952	Maria Gorokhovskaya (URS) 76.78	Nina Bocharova (URS) 75.94	Margit Korondi (HUN) 75.82
1956	Larissa Latynina (URS) 74.933	Agnes Keleti (HUN) 74.633	Sofia Muratova (URS) 74.466
1960	Larissa Latynina (URS) 77.031	Sofia Muratova (URS) 76.696	Polina Astakhova (URS) 76.164
1964	Vera Caslavska (TCH) 77.564	Larissa Latynina (URS) 76.998	Polina Astakhova (URS) 76.965
1968	Vera Caslavska (TCH) 78.25	Zinaida Voronina (URS) 76.85	Natalya Muchinskaya (URS) 76.75
1972	Ludmila Tourischeva (URS) 77.025	Karin Janz (GDR) 76.875	Tamara Lazakovitch (URS) 76.850
1976	Nadia Comaneci (ROM) 79.275	Nelli Kim (URS) 78.675	Ludmila Tourischeva (URS) 78.625
1980	Yelena Davydova (URS) 79.150	Maxi Gnauck (GDR) 79.075	–
		Nadia Comaneci (ROM) 79.075	
1984	Mary Lou Retton (USA) 79.175	Ecaterina Szabo (ROM) 79.125	Simona Pauca (ROM) 78.675
1988	Yelena Chouchounova (URS) 79.662	Daniela Silivas (ROM) 79.637	Svetlana Bogunskaya (URS) 79.40

	Asymmetrical Bars		
1952	Margit Korondi (HUN) 19.40	Maria Gorokhovskaya (URS) 19.26	Ágnes Keleti (HUN 19.16
1956	Agnes Keleti (HUN) 18.966	Larissa Latynina (URS) 18.833	Sofia Muratova (URS) 18.800
1960	Polina Astakhova (URS) 19.616	Larissa Latynina (URS) 19.416	Tamara Lyukhina (URS) 19.399
1964	Polina Astakhova (URS) 19.332	Katalin Makray (HUN) 19.216	Larissa Latynina (URS) 19.199
1968	Vera Caslavska (TCH) 19.650	Karin Janz (GDR) 19.500	Zinaida Voronina (URS) 19.425
1972	Karin Janz (GDR) 19.675	Olga Korbut (URS) 19.450	
		Erika Zuchold (GDR) 19.450	
1976	Nadia Comaneci (ROM) 20.00	Teodora Ungureanu (ROM) 19.800	Marta Egervari (HUN) 19.775
1980	Maxi Gnauck (GDR) 19.875	Emila Eberle (ROM) 19.850	Steffi Kräker (GDR) 19.775
			Melita Rühn (ROM) 19.775
			Maria Filatova (URS) 19.775
1984	Ma Yanhong (CHN) 19.950	–	Mary Lou Retton (USA) 19.800
	Julianne McNamara (USA) 19.950		
1988	Daniela Silivas (ROM) 20.00	Dagmar Kersten (GDR) 19.987	Yelena Chouchounova (URS) 19.962

1896–1948 Event not held.

	Balance Beam		
1952	Nina Bocharova (URS) 19.22	Maria Gorokhovskaya (URS) 19.13	Margit Korondi (HUN) 19.02
1956	Agnes Keleti (HUN) 18.80	Eva Bosáková (TCH) 18.63	–
		Tamara Manina (URS) 18.63	
1960	Eva Bosakova (TCH) 19.283	Larissa Latynina (URS) 19.233	Sofia Muratova (URS) 19.232
1964	Vera Caslavska (TCH) 19.449	Tamara Manina (URS) 19.399	Larissa Latynina (URS) 19.382
1968	Natalya Kuchinskaya (URS) 19.650	Vera Caslavska (TCH) 19.575	Larissa Petrik (URS) 19.250
1972	Olga Korbut (URS) 19.575	Tamara Lazakovitch (URS) 19.375	Karin Janz (GDR) 18.975
1976	Nadia Comaneci (ROM) 19.950	Olga Korbut (URS) 19.725	Teodora Ungureanu (ROM) 19.700
1980	Nadia Comaneci (ROM) 19.800	Yelena Davydova (URS) 19.750	Natalya Shaposhnikova (URS) 19.725
1984	Simona Pauca (ROM) 19.800	–	Kathy Johnson (USA) 19.650
	Ecaterina Szabo (ROM) 19.800		
1988	Daniela Silivas (ROM) 19.924	Yelena Chouchounova (URS) 19.875	Gabriela Potorac (ROM) 19.837
			Phoebe Mills (USA) 19.837

1896–1948 Event not held.

	Floor Exercises		
1952	Agnes Keleti (HUN) 19.36	Maria Gorokhovskaya (URS) 19.20	Margit Korondi (HUN) 19.00
1956	Larissa Latynina (URS) 18.733	–	Elena Leustean (ROM) 18.70
	Agnes Keleti (HUN) 18.733		
1960	Larissa Latynina (URS) 19.583	Polina Astakhova (URS) 19.532	Tamara Lyukhina (URS) 19.449

The delightful Ludmila Tourischeva (URS), individual champion in 1972. She later married her teammate, the double sprint champion from the same year, Valeriy Borzov.

	Gold	Silver	Bronze
1964	Larissa Latynina (URS) 19.599	Polina Astakhova (URS) 19.500	Anikó Jánosi (HUN) 19.300
1968	Larissa Petrik (URS) 19.675	–	Natalya Kuchinskaya (URS) 19.650
	Vera Caslavska (TCH) 19.675		
1972	Olga Korbut (URS) 19.575	Ludmila Tourischeva (URS) 19.550	Tamara Lazakovitch (URS) 19.450
1976	Nelli Kim (URS) 19.850	Ludmila Tourischeva (URS) 19.825	Nadia Comaneci (ROM) 19.750
1980	Nelli Kim (URS) 19.875	–	Natalya Shaposhnikova (URS) 19.825
	Nadia Comaneci (ROM) 19.875		Maxi Gnauck (GDR) 19.825
1984	Ecaterina Szabo (ROM) 19.975	Julianne McNamara (USA) 19.950	Mary Lou Retton (USA) 19.775
1988	Daniela Silivas (ROM) 19.937	Svetlana Bogunskaya (URS) 19.887	Diana Doudeva (BUL) 19.850

1896–1948 Event not held

Horse Vault

1952	Yekaterina Kalinchuk (URS) 19.20	Maria Gorokhovskaya (URS) 19.19	Galina Minaitscheva (URS) 19.16
1956	Larissa Latynina (URS) 18.833	Tamara Manina (URS) 18.800	Ann-Sofi Colling (SWE) 18.733
			Olga Tass (HUN) 18.733
1960	Margarita Nikolayeva (URS) 19.316	Sofia Muratova (URS) 19.049	Larissa Latynina (URS) 19.016
1964	Vera Caslavska (TCH) 19.483	Larissa Latynina (URS) 19.283	–
		Birgit Radochla (GER) 19.283	
1968	Vera Caslavska (TCH) 19.775	Erika Zuchold (GDR) 19.625	Zinaida Voronina (URS) 19.500
1972	Karin Janz (GDR) 19.525	Erika Zuchold (GDR) 19.275	Ludmila Tourischeva (URS) 19.250
1976	Nelli Kim (URS) 19.800	Ludmila Tourischeva (URS) 19.650	–
		Carola Dombeck (GDR) 19.650	
1980	Natalya Shaposhnikova (URS) 19.725	Steffi Kräker (GDR) 19.675	Melita Rühn (ROM) 19.650
1984	Ecaterina Szabo (ROM) 19.875	Mary Lou Retton (USA) 19.850	Lavinia Agache (ROM) 19.750
1988	Svetlana Bogunskaya (URS) 19.905	Gabriela Potorac (ROM) 19.830	Daniela Silivas (ROM) 19.818

1896–1948 Event not held.

Modern Rhythmic

1984	Lori Fung (CAN) 57.950	Doina Staiculescu (ROM) 57.900	Regina Weber (FRG) 57.700
1988	Marina Lobatch (URS) 60.00	Adriana Dounavska (BUL) 59.950	Alexandra Timochenko (URS) 59.875

1896–1980 Event not held.

DISCONTINUED EVENTS

Parallel Bars (Men's Teams)

1896	Germany	Greece	Greece

Horizontal Bars (Men's Teams)

1896	Germany[1]		

[1]Walk-over.

Rope Climbing (Men)

1896	Nicolaos Andriakopoulos (GRE) 23.4sec	Thomas Xenakis (GRE)	Fritz Hofmann (GER)
1904	George Eyser (USA) 7.0sec	Charles Krause (USA) 7.8	Emil Voigt (USA) 9.8
1906	Georgios Aliprantis (GRE) 11.4sec	Béla Erödy (HUN) 13.8	Konstantinos Kozantis (GRE) 13.8
1924	Bedrich Supcik (TCH) 7.2sec	Albert Séguin (FRA)	August Güttinger (SUI) 7.8
			Ladislav Vácha (TCH) 7.8
1932	Raymond Bass (USA) 6.7sec	William Galbraith (USA) 6.8	Thomas Connelly (USA) 7.0

Club Swinging (Men)

1904	Edward Hennig (USA) 13pts	Emil Voigt (USA) 9	Ralph Wilson (USA) 5
1932	George Roth (USA) 8.97pts	Philip Erenberg (USA) 8.90	William Kuhlmeier (USA) 8.63

Tumbling (Men)

1932	Rowland Wolfe (USA) 18.90pts	Edward Gross (USA) 18.67	William Herrmann (USA) 19.37

Nine Event Competition (Men)

1904	Adolf Spinnler (SUI) 43.49pts	Julius Lenhart (AUT) 43.00	Wilhelm Weber (GER) 41.60

Triathlon (Men)

(Comprised 100 yards, long jump and shot put)

1904	Max Emmerich (USA) 35.70pts	John Grieb (USA) 34.00	William Merz (USA) 33.90

Four Event Competition (Men)

1904	Anton Heida (USA) 161 pts	George Eyser (USA) 152	William Merz (USA) 135

	Gold	Silver	Bronze
Sidehorse Vault (Men)			
1924	Albert Séguin (FRA) 10.00pts	Jean Gounot (FRA) 9.93	–
		François Gangloff (FRA) 9.93	
Swedish System (Men's Teams)			
1912	Sweden 937.46pts	Denmark 808.84	Norway 857.21
1920	Sweden 1364pts	Denmark 1325	Belgium 1094
Free System (Men's Teams)			
1912	Norway 114.25pts	Finland 109.25	Denmark 106.25
1920	Denmark	Norway	–[1]

[1]Only two teams competed.

	Gold	Silver	Bronze
Portable Apparatus (Women's Teams)			
1952	Sweden 74.20pts	Soviet Union 73.00	Hungary 71.60
1956	Hungary 75.20pts	Sweden 74.20	Poland 74.00
			Soviet Uniuon 74.00

HANDBALL

The sport was introduced in 1936 – appropriately, since it was a German invention – and was played as an outdoor 11-a-side game. When reintroduced in 1972 it was as an indoor seven-a-side competition. Six members of the Soviet women's team won gold medals in 1976 and 1980: Lubov Odinkova, Zinaida Tourchina, Tatyana Kochergina, Ludmila Poradnik, Aldona Nenenene and Larissa Karlova. Tourchina and Karlova also won a bronze in 1988. Four Romanian players have won medals in three Games, but none of them was gold.

The oldest gold medallist was Yuriy Klimov (URS), aged 36yr 6 days in 1976, while the oldest female to win gold was Ludmila Poradnik (URS) in 1980, aged 34yr 200 days. Zinaida Tourchina (URS) won a bronze medal in 1988 aged 42yr 126 days. The youngest gold medallist was Larissa Karlova (URS), aged 17yr 356 days in 1976, while the youngest male winner was Günther Ortmann (GER), aged 19 yr 257 days, in 1936. Willy Hufschmid (SUI) won a bronze medal in 1936 aged 17yr 310 days.

The greatest margin of victory was 34 when Yugoslavia beat Kuwait 44–10 in 1980. The comparable margin among the women was 30 when Yugoslavia beat Congo 39–9, also in 1980. The greatest aggregate score was 60 when the Korean women's team beat Czechoslovakia 33–27 in 1988, and the comparable men's figure was 62 when FRG beat Korea 37–25 in 1984. The record score by an individual in one game was 17 by Jasna Kolar-Merdan for the Yugoslavian women when they beat USA 33–20 in 1984. The male record is 13 by Istvan Varga (HUN) against the United States in 1972.

A member of the GDR winning team in 1980 was Hans-Georg Beyer, the brother of 1976 shot put champion Udo (who also won a bronze in

HANDBALL MEDALS

	Gold	Silver	Bronze
Men			
1936[1]	Germany	Austria	Switzerland
1972	Yugoslavia	Czechoslovakia	Romania
1976	Soviet Union	Romania	Poland
1980	GDR	Soviet Union	Romania
1984	Yugoslavia	FRG	Romania
1988	Soviet Union	Korea	Yugoslavia
1896–1932, 1948–1968 Event not held.			

[1]Field handball played outdoors.

	Gold	Silver	Bronze
Women			
1976	Soviet Union	GDR	Hungary
1980	Soviet Union	Yugoslavia	GDR
1984	Yugoslavia	Korea	China
1988	Korea	Norway	Soviet Union
1896–1972 Event not held			

HANDBALL MEDAL TOTALS

	MEN			WOMEN			
	G	S	B	G	S	B	Total
Soviet Union	2	1	–	2	–	1	6
Yugoslavia	2	–	1	1	1	–	5
Romania	–	1	3	–	–	–	4
GDR	1	–	–	–	1	1	3
Korea	–	1	–	1	1	–	3
Germany (FRG)	1	1	–	–	–	–	2
Austria	–	1	–	–	–	–	1
Czechoslovakia	–	1	–	–	–	–	1
Norway	–	–	–	–	1	–	1
China	–	–	–	–	–	1	1
Hungary	–	–	–	–	–	1	1
Poland	–	–	1	–	–	–	1
Switzerland	–	–	1	–	–	–	1
	6	6	6	4	4	4	30

1980). To complete an outstanding family trio their sister Gisela narrowly missed a bronze medal in the women's discus in Moscow. Another East German, Roswitha Krause, a member of the silver medal handball team of 1976 and the bronze medal side of 1980, had been a silver medallist in the 4 x 100m freestyle swimming quartet in 1968.

HOCKEY

The first Olympic hockey game was won by Scotland who beat Germany 4–0 in 1908, with the first goal scored by Ian Laing only two minutes after the start. In those Games, the British Isles provided four of the six teams competing, representing England, Ireland, Scotland and Wales. Since 1928 Olympic hockey has been dominated by teams from the Indian sub-continent, with India winning eight times and Pakistan three,

though it should be noted that Great Britain, probably the world's strongest team at the time, did not participate in 1932 and 1936.

The long-awaited meeting between Britain, the masters, and India, the pupils, came in the 1948 final which India won 4–0. In 1988, for the first time for 60 years, no team from the sub-continent won a medal. Interestingly, after years of decline, the Great Britain team – a last-minute replacement for the boycotting Soviet Union – won the bronze in 1984, their first medal for 32 years. Then in 1988 the British team won the gold medal again, after 68 years.

Several members of Indian teams have won a record three gold medals: Dhyan Chand (1928–36), Randhir Singh (1948–56), Balbir Singh (1948–56), Leslie Claudius (1948–56), Ranganandhan Francis (1948–56), and Udham Singh (1952, 1956 and 1964). Of these, Claudius and Udham Singh also won a silver each in 1960.

The oldest gold medallist whose age can be verified was Abdul Rashid (PAK), aged 38yr 100 days in 1960. Stanley Shoveller (GBR) was also over 38 in 1920, while Dharam Singh (IND) was reputed to be 45 years old in 1964. The youngest winner was Russell Garcia (GBR) in 1988, aged 18yr 103 days; Arlene Boxhall was also under 19 as a member of the 1980 Zimbabwe women's squad but she did not actually play in the tournament. The oldest female gold medallist was the Zimbabwe coach/player Anthea Stewart, aged 35yr 253 days.

The highest score ever achieved in international hockey was when India beat the United States 24–1 in 1932. The highest score in a final was also in 1932 when India beat Japan 11–1. Roop Singh (IND), the brother of the team captain Dhyan

The long awaited match between 'pupils' and 'teachers' resulted in India beating Britain 4–0 in the 1948 hockey final.

The England team which won the 1908 hockey tournament against three other home teams representing Ireland, Scotland and Wales.

HOCKEY MEDALS

	Gold	Silver	Bronze
Men			
1908[1]	England	Ireland	Scotland[2] Wales[2]
1920	England[3]	Denmark	Belgium
1928	India	Netherlands	Germany
1932	India	Japan	United States
1936	India	Germany	Netherlands
1948	India	Great Britain	Netherlands
1952	India	Netherlands	Great Britain
1956	India	Pakistan	Germany
1960	Pakistan	India	Spain
1964	India	Pakistan	Australia
1968	Pakistan	Australia	India
1972	FRG	Pakistan	India
1976	New Zealand	Australia	Pakistan
1980	India	Spain	Soviet Union
1984	Pakistan	FRG	Great Britain
1988	Great Britain	FRG	Netherlands

1896–1906, 1912, 1924 Event not held.

[1]*Great Britain had four teams entered.*
[2]*Tie for third place.*
[3]*Great Britain represented by England team.*

Women
1980	Zimbabwe	Czechoslovakia	Soviet Union
1984	Netherlands	FRG	United States

1896–1976 Event not held.

HOCKEY MEDAL TOTALS

	MEN			WOMEN			
Country	G	S	B	G	S	B	Total
India	8	1	2	–	–	–	11
Great Britain	3	2	4	–	–	–	9
Pakistan	3	3	1	–	–	–	7
Germany (FRG)	1	3	2	–	1	–	7
Netherlands	–	2	3	1	–	1	7
Australia	–	2	1	1	–	–	4
Spain	–	1	1	–	–	–	2
Soviet Union	–	–	1	–	–	1	2
United States	–	–	1	–	–	1	2
New Zealand	1	–	–	–	–	–	1
Zimbabwe	–	–	–	1	–	–	1
Czechoslovakia	–	–	–	–	1	–	1
Denmark	–	1	–	–	–	–	1
Japan	–	1	–	–	–	–	1
Korea	–	–	–	–	1	–	1
Belgium	–	–	1	–	–	–	1
	16	16	17[1]	3	3	3	58

[1]*Two bronzes in 1908.*

Chand, scored a record 12 goals in the aforementioned match against the United States in 1932. The Indian goalkeepers did not concede a single goal during the 1928 tournament (five games), and lost only three goals in 1932 (two games) and 1936 (five games) Over that period the Indians themselves scored a total of 102 goals. The longest game in Olympic hockey lasted 2hr 25 min (into the sixth period of extra time) when the Netherlands beat Spain 1–0 in Mexico on 25 October 1968.

The 1988 competitions were particularly noteworthy for family achievements. Sisters Lee and Michelle Capes won gold medals in the Australian women's team, and the Dutch siblings Marc and Carina Benninga gained bronze medals in their country's respective third-placed teams.

JUDO

This sport was introduced in 1964 and appropriately the first gold medal was won by Japan, Takehide Nakatani winning the lightweight class. However, one of the greatest upsets to a nation's sporting pride occurred at the same Games in Tokyo's Nippon Budokan Hall when the giant Dutchman Anton Geesink (1.98m) beat the Japanese favourite for the Open category title in front of 15 000 home supporters.

Another Dutchman, Willem Ruska, is the only man to win two gold medals at a single Games, with the Over 93kg and Open classes in 1972. Hiroshi Saito (JPN) and Peter Seisenbacher (AUT) are the only men to successfully defend their titles, both in 1984 and 1988. Angelo Parisi won a record four medals, with a bronze in 1972

Holland's Willem Ruska wins the Open title in 1972.

representing Great Britain and then gold and two silvers in 1980 and 1984 representing France. This winning of medals for two different countries at the Olympic Games is very rare, but not unique. Parisi was born in Italy, went to Britain as a child and became a British citizen, then married a French girl in 1973 and changed his nationality again.

The oldest gold medallist was Ruska when he won the 1972 Open class aged 32yr 11 days, and the youngest was Isao Okano (JPN) in the 1964 middleweight division, aged 20yr 275 days. The fastest throw in Olympic competition came after 4 sec, by Akio Kaminaga (JPN) against Thomas Ong (PHI) in 1964. The biggest of many big men in Olympic judo was Jong Gil Pak (PRK) who was 2.13m tall and weighed 163kg in the 1976 Games. In 1972 the Mongolian lightweight silver medallist, Bakhaavaa Buidaa, became the first competitor ever to be disqualified for failing a drug test in any international judo competition. An amusing sidelight was provided by the 1976 lightweight gold medal winner, Hector Rodriguez (CUB), who said that he took up the sport when young in order to defend himself against his six older brothers!

The 1988 Games witnessed another astonishing upset for Japanese judo, as they took only one gold and three bronze medals. Women's events were contested as a demonstration sport in Seoul. Of the seven events, two titles went to Great Britain, and one each to Australia, Belgium, China, Japan and the Netherlands. Women's judo has now been added to the official programme in 1992.

JUDO MEDAL TOTALS

Country	G	S	B	Total
Soviet Union	5	5	13	23
Japan	14	2	6	22
Korea	4	4	5	13
France	3	2	8	13
Great Britain	–	4	7	11
Germany (FRG)	1	5	4	10
GDR	1	2	6	9
United States	–	2	4	6
Netherlands	3	–	2	5
Poland	1	2	2	5
Brazil	1	1	3	5
Cuba	1	3	–	4
Austria	2	–	1	3
Italy	1	1	1	3
Switzerland	1	1	1	3
Hungary	–	–	3	3
Belgium	1	–	1	2
Bulgaria	–	1	1	2
Canada	–	1	1	2
Mongolia	–	1	1	2
Romania	–	–	2	2
Yugoslavia	–	–	2	2
Egypt	–	1	–	1
Australia	–	–	1	1
Czechoslovakia	–	–	1	1
Iceland	–	–	1	1
North Korea (PRK)	–	–	1	1
	39	38[1]	78	155

[1] *1972 silver withheld due to disqualification.*

JUDO MEDALS

	Gold	Silver	Bronze
Open Category, No Weight Limit			
1964	Antonius Geesink (HOL)	Akio Kaminaga (JPN)	Theodore Boronovskis (AUS)
			Klaus Glahn (GER)
1972	Willem Ruska (HOL)	Vitaliy Kuznetsov (URS)	Jean-Claude Brondani (FRA)
			Angelo Parisi (GBR)
1976	Haruki Uemura (JPN)	Keith Remfry (GBR)	Shota Chochoshvili (URS)
			Jeaki Cho (KOR)
1980	Dietmar Lorenz (GDR)	Angelo Parisi (FRA)	András Ozsvar (HUN)
			Arthur Mapp (GBR)
1984	Yasuhiro Yamashita (JPN)	Mohamed Rashwan (EGY)	Mihai Cioc (ROM)
			Arthur Schnabel (FRG)

1968 and 1988 Event not held.

Over 95kg			
1980	Angelo Parisi (FRA)	Dimitar Zaprianov (BUL)	Vladimir Kocman (TCH)
			Radomir Kovacevic (YUG)
1984	Hitoshi Saito (JPN)	Angelo Parisi (FRA)	Cho Yong-Chul (KOR)
			Mark Berger (CAN)
1988	Hitoshi Saito (JPN)	Henry Stöhr (GDR)	Cho Yong-Chul (KOR)
			Grigori Veritchev (URS)

Up to 95kg			
1980	Robert Van de Walle (BEL)	Tengiz Khubuluri (URS)	Dietmar Lorenz (GDR)
			Henk Numan (HOL)
1984	Ha Hyoung-Zoo (KOR)	Douglas Vieira (BRA)	Bjarni Fridriksson (ISL)
			Gunther Neureuther (FRG)
1988	Aurelio Miguel (BRA)	Marc Meiling (FRG)	Robert Van De Walle (BEL)
			Dennis Stewart (GBR)

Up to 86kg			
1980	Jürg Röthlisberger (SUI)	Isaac Azcuy Oliva (CUB)	Detlef Ultsch (GDR)
			Aleksandr Yatskevich (URS)
1984	Peter Seisenbacher (AUT)	Robert Berland (USA	Seiki Nose (JPN)
			Walter Carmona (BRA)
1988	Peter Seisenbacher (AUT)	Vladimir Chestakov (URS)	Ben Spijkers (HOL)
			Akinobu Osako (JPN)

Up to 78kg			
1980	Shota Khabaleri (URS)	Juan Ferrer La Hera (CUB)	Harald Heinke (GDR)
			Bernard Tchoullouyan (FRA)
1984	Frank Wieneke (FRG)	Neil Adams (GBR)	Michel Nowak (FRA)
			Mirces Fratica (ROM)
1988	Waldemar Legien (POL)	Frank Wieneke (FRG)	Torsten Brechot (GDR)
			Bachir Varayev (URS)

Up to 71kg			
1980	Ezio Gamba (ITA)	Neil Adams (GBR)	Karl-Heinz Lehmann (GDR)
			Ravdan Davaadalai (MGL)
1984	Ahn Byeong-Keun (KOR)	Ezio Gamba (ITA)	Luis Onmura (BRA)
			Kerrith Brown
1988	Marc Alexandre (FRA)	Sven Loll (GDR)	Michael Swain (USA)
			Guergui Tenadze (URS)

Up to 65kg			
1980	Nikolai Solodukhin (URS)	Tsendying Damdin (MGL)	Ilian Nedkov (BUL)
			Janusz Pawlowski (POL)
1984	Yoshiyuki Matsuoka (JPN)	Hwang Jung-Oh (KOR)	Josef Reiter (AUT)
			Marc Alexandre (FRA)
1988	Lee Kyung-Keun (KOR	Janusz Pawlowski (POL)	Bruno Carabetta (FRA)
			Yosuke Yamamoto (JPN)

Up to 60kg			
1980	Thierry Rey (FRA)	Rafael Carbonell (CUB)	Tibor Kincses (HUN)
			Aramby Emizh (URS)
1984	Shinji Hosokawa (JPN)	Kim Jae-Yup (KOR)	Edward Liddie (USA)
			Neil Eckersley (GBR)
1988	Kim Jae-Yup (KOR)	Kevin Asano (USA)	Shinji Hosokawa (JPN)
			Amiran Totikachvili (URS)

PREVIOUS WINNERS

Categories changed in 1980

Gold	Silver	Bronze
Over 93kg		
1964 Isao Inokuma (JPN)	AH Douglas Rogers (CAN)	Parnaoz Chikviladze (URS)
		Anzor Kiknadze (URS)
1972 Wilhelm Ruska (HOL)	Klaus Glahn (FRG)	Givi Onashvili (URS)
		Motoki Nishimura (JPN)
1976 Sergey Novikov (URS)	Gunther Neureuther (FRG)	Sumio Endo (JPN)
		Allen Coage (USA)
1968 Event not held.		
80kg to 93kg		
1972 Shota Chochoshvili (URS)	David Starbrook (GBR)	Chiaki Ishii (BRA)
		Paul Barth (FRG)
1976 Kazuhiro Ninomiya (JPN)	Ramaz Harshiladze (URS)	David Starbrook (GBR)
		Jürg Röthlisberger (SUI)
1964–1968 Event not held.		
70kg to 80kg		
1964 Isao Okano (JPN)	Wolfgang Hofmann (GER)	James Bergman (USA)
		Eui Tae Kim (KOR)
1972 Shinobu Sekine (JPN)	Oh Seung-Lip (KOR)	Brian Jacks (GBR)
		Jean-Paul Coche (FRA)
1976 Isamu Sonoda (JPN)	Valeriy Dvoinikov (URS)	Slavko Obadov (YUG)
		Park Youngchul (KOR)
1968 Event not held.		
63kg to 70kg		
1972 Toyojazu Nomura (JPN)	Anton Zajkowski (POL)	Dietmar Hötger (GDR)
		Anatoliy Novikov (URS)
1976 Vladimir Nevzorov (URS)	Koji Kuramoto (JPN)	Patrick Vial (FRA)
		Marian Talaj (POL)
1964–1968 Event not held.		
Up to 63kg		
1964 Takehide Nakatani (JPN)	Eric Haenni (SUI)	Oleg Stepanov (URS)
		Aron Bogulubov (URS)
1972 Takao Kawaguchi (JPN)	–[1]	Kim Yong Ik (PRK)
		Jean-Jacques Mounier (FRA)
1976 Hector Rodriguez (CUB)	Chang Eunkyung (KOR)	Felice Mariani (ITA)
		Jozsef Tuncsik (HUN)
1968 Event not held.		

[1]Bakhaavaa Buidaa (MGL) disqualified after positive drug test.

MODERN PENTATHLON

The five events constituting the modern pentathlon are: riding (Over an 800m course); fencing (with épée); swimming (300m freestyle); shooting (pistol at 25m); cross-country running (4000m). The order of events has differed over the years, as has the points system. Prior to 1956, competitors were given points according to their placings in each event, ie one point for first place, two points for second etc. Since 1956, however, points have been allocated according to an international scoring table.

It is therefore difficult to compare performers under the two systems, but it is generally accepted that the margin of victory by Willie Grut (SWE) in 1948 was the greatest ever. In that competition Grut, later the Secretary-General of the sport's governing body (UIPMB), finished first in the riding, fencing and swimming, fifth in the shooting and eighth in the running. The most gold medals have been won by András Balczó (HUN) with three, in 1960 (team), 1968 (team) and 1972 (individual). Only Lars Hall (SWE) has won two individual gold medals, in 1952 and 1956. Pavel Lednev (URS) won a record seven medals (two gold, two silver, three bronze) from 1968 to 1980. He was also the oldest gold medallist, in 1980 aged 37yr 121 days, while the

George Patton (USA), later the famous World War II general, was fifth in 1912 with results that indicated he was not very good at shooting. Three men have scored maximums of 200 hits in shooting: Charles Leonard (USA) in 1936, Daniele Massala (ITA) in 1976 and George Horvath (SWE)in 1980. The fastest time ever recorded in the 300m swimming event was 3min 10.58sec by Christophe Ruer (FRA) in 1988. It is noteworthy that the fastest time recorded for the 4000m cross-country run was 12min 9sec by Adrian Parker (GBR) in 1976. The other three disciplines are either not measurable or comparable.

In 1984 the competition was held, experimentally, over four days, but returned to the traditional five in 1988. One of the biggest scandals in Olympic history occurred in the fencing segment of the 1976 competition when Boris Onischenko (URS), previous winner of a gold and two silver medals, was disqualified for using an illegal weapon. It transpired that he had tampered with his épée so that it registered a hit even when contact with an opponent had not taken place. The incident caused speculation about whether he had used the implement in the 1972 Games, where his fencing victory over Jim Fox cost the Briton the individual bronze medal. By chance, Onischenko was fencing against Fox when the Montreal incident came to light.

MODERN PENTATHLON MEDAL TOTALS

Country	G	S	B	Total
Sweden	9	7	5	21
Hungary	8	6	3	17
Soviet Union	5	5	5	15
United States	–	5	3	8
Italy	2	2	2	6
Finland	–	1	4	5
Germany (FRG)	1	–	1	2
Great Britain	1	–	1	2
Czechoslovakia	–	1	1	2
France	–	–	2	2
Poland	1	–	–	1
	27	27	27	81

youngest was Aladár Kovácsi (HUN) in 1952 aged 19yr 227 days.

Gustaf Dyrssen (SWE), who won the gold medal in 1920 and a silver in 1924, and Sven Thofelt (SWE), who won the gold in 1928, both won silver medals as members of the 1936 Swedish épée fencing team. Thofelt also won a bronze in the Swedish fencing team in 1948, while his son competed in the 1960 modern pentathlon. Dyrssen later became Sweden's IOC representative, and Thofelt became president of the UIPMB.

MODERN PENTATHLON MEDALS

	Gold	Silver	Bronze
Individual			
1912	Gösta Lilliehöpök (SWE) 27	Gösta Asbrink (SWE) 28	Georg de Laval (SWE)
1920	Gustaf Dyrssen (SWE) 18	Erik de Laval (SWE) 23	Gösta Rüno (SWE) 27
1924	Bo Lindman (SWE) 18	Gustaf Dyrssen (SWE) 39.5	Bertil Uggla (SWE) 45
1928	Sven Thofelt (SWE) 47	Bo Lindman (SWE) 50	Helmuth Kahl (GER) 52
1932	Johan Gabriel Oxenstierna (SWE) 32	Bo Lindman (SWE) 35.5	Richard Mayo (USA) 38.5
1936	Gotthard Handrick (GER) 31.5	Charles Leonard (USA) 39.5	Silvano Abba (ITA) 45.5
1948	Willie Grut (SWE) 16	George Moore (USA) 47	Gösta Gärdin (SWE) 49
1952	Lars Hall (SWE) 32	Gábor Benedek (HUN) 39	István Szondi (HUN) 41
1956	Lars Hall (SWE) 4843	Olavi Nannonen (FIN) 4774.5	Väinö Korhonen (FIN) 4750
1960	Ferenc Németh (HUN) 5024	Imre Nagy (HUN) 4988	Robert Beck (USA) 4981
1964	Ferenc Török (HUN) 5024	Igor Novikov (URS) 5067	Albert Mokeyev (URS)
1968	Björn Ferm (SWE) 4964	András Balczó (HUN) 4953	Pavel Lednev (URS) 4795
1972	András Balczó (HUN) 5412	Boris Onischenko (URS) 5335	Pavel Lednev (URS) 5328
1976	Janusz Pyciak-Peciak (POL) 5520	Pavel Lednev (URS) 5485	Jan Bartu (TCH) 5466
1980	Anatoliy Starostin (URS) 5568	Tamás Szombathelyi (HUN) 5502	Pavel Lednev (URS) 5282
1984	Daniel Massala (ITA) 5469	Svante Rasmuson (SWE) 5456	Carlo Massullo (ITA) 5406
1988	Janos Martinek (HUN) 5404	Carlo Massullo (ITA) 5379	Vakhtang Iagorachvili (URS) 5367

1896–1908 Event not held.

Team			
1952	Hungary 116	Sweden 182	Finland 213
1956	Soviet Union 13 690.5	United States 13 482	Finland 13 185.5
1960	Hungary 14 863	Soviet Union 14 309	United States 14 192
1964	Soviet Union 14 961	United States 14 189	Hungary 14 173
1968	Hungary 14 325	Soviet Union 14 248	France 13 289[1]
1972	Soviet Union 15 968	Hungary 15 348	Finland 14 812
1976	Great Britain 15 559	Czechoslovakia 15 451	Hungary 15 395
1980	Soviet Union 16 126	Hungary 15 912	Sweden 15 845
1984	Italy 16 060	United States 15 568	France 15 565
1988	Hungary 15 886	Italy 15 571	Great Britain 15 276

1896–1948 Event not held.

[1] Sweden finished third in 1968 but were disqualified when a drug test indicated that a member of the team had an excessive level of alcohol.

ROWING

Rowing for men was first held in the 1900 Games over a 1750m course on the River Seine in Paris. In 1904 the course measured 2 miles (3219m), in 1908 it was 1.5 miles (2414m), and in 1948 1 mile 300 yards (1883m). Women's rowing was introduced in 1976 over a 1000m course, but since 1988 both men and women race over a standard 2000m course.

Even though recent Games rowing has been held on still water, as opposed to flowing rivers as in the past, water and weather conditions vary too much to allow official Olympic records. However, it is worthy of note that the fastest average speed achieved by a men's eight over the full course was 21.67kph when the GDR crew clocked 5min 32.17sec in 1976. In 1988 the United States crew averaged 22.55kph for the first 500m in a repechage. The 1988 GDR women's eight averaged 19.70kph, clocking 6min 05.50 sec in a repechage over the new 2000m distance and averaging 20.65kph for the first 500 metres. The narrowest winning margin in an Olympic final was 0.1sec in the 1924 pairs, although the 1932 coxed fours may actually have been closer.

One of the first winning crews in the Games, the 1900 German four, contained three brothers – Oskar, Gustav and Carl Gossler, the latter as coxswain. This was the beginning of a tradition of sibling participation and success which reached a landmark at Moscow in 1980 when the Landvoigt twins (GDR) beat the Pimenov twins (URS) in the coxless pairs final – and caused problems at the medal ceremony.

Fathers and sons have also had great success in the sport, but usually independently of each other. The most famous are: the Beresfords (GBR), Julius with a silver in 1912 and Jack with five medals (see below) in the next five Games; the Costellos (USA), Paul winning three golds in the 1920s and son Bernard a silver in 1956; the Kellys (USA), John Sr winning three gold medals (see below) and John Jr a bronze in 1956; and the Nickalls (GBR), with Guy Sr winning a gold in the 1908 eight and Guy Jr gaining two silvers in the 1920 and 1928

A close finish at Long Beach in the 1932 eights, with the USA winning from Italy, Canada and Great Britain.

crews. However, the Burnells (GBR), Charles (1908) and Richard (1948), are the only father and son in Olympic rowing to both win gold medals.

Six oarsmen have won a record three gold medals: John Kelly (USA), 1920–1924; his cousin Paul Costello (USA), 1920–1928; Jack Beresford (GBR), 1924, 1932–1936; Vyacheslav Ivanov (URS), 1956–1964; Siegfried Brietzke (GDR), 1972–1980; and Pertti Karppinen (FIN), 1976–1984. Jack Beresford also won two silvers to be the most successful Olympic rower of all time. Ivanov and Karppinen are the only men to win three individual golds, while Jack Beresford, again, is the only oarsman to win medals at five Games, from 1920–1936.

ROWING MEDAL TOTALS

Country	MEN			WOMEN			Total
	G	S	B	G	S	B	
United States	27	18	14	1	4	1	65
GDR	20	4	7	13	3	1	48
Soviet Union	11	14	7	1	6	4	43
Germany (FRG)	17	12	11	–	–	2	42
Great Britain	16	15	6	–	–	–	37
Italy	12	10	8	–	–	–	30
France	4	13	9	–	–	–	26
Canada	3	6	9	–	2	1	21
Romania	1	3	1	7	3	5	20
Switzerland	4	7	9	–	–	–	20
Netherlands	4	4	5	–	1	1	15
Denmark	3	3	6	–	–	1	13
Australia	3	4	4	–	–	1	12
New Zealand	3	2	5	–	–	1	11
Bulgaria	–	–	1	2	3	4	10
Czechoslovakia	2	1	7	–	–	–	10
Norway	1	3	6	–	–	–	10
Poland	–	1	7	–	1	–	9
Belgium	–	6	1	–	–	1	8
Finland	3	–	3	–	–	–	6
Yugoslavia	1	1	3	–	–	–	5
Greece	1	2	1	–	–	–	4
Argentina	1	1	2	–	–	–	4
Austria	–	2	2	–	–	–	4
Uruguay	–	1	3	–	–	–	4
Hungary	–	1	2	–	–	–	3
Sweden	–	2	–	–	–	–	2
China	–	–	–	–	1	1	2
Spain	–	1'	–	–	–	–	1
	137	137	139	24	24	24	485

Ivanov had an unfortunate experience after his first title win in Melbourne. He excitedly threw his medal into the air and lost it in the waters of Lake Wendouree. It was never recovered and later the IOC gave him a replacement.

The oldest gold medallist was Robert Zimonyi who coxed the United States eight in 1964 aged 46yr 180 days. In 1948 he had won a bronze, coxing a pair from his native Hungary. The oldest actual oarsman to win a gold medal was Guy Nickalls

(GBR) in the 1908 eight, aged 41yr 262 days. His compatriot Julius Beresford won his silver medal aged 44yr 20 days.

The youngest gold medallist was the unknown French boy who coxed the winning Dutch pair in 1900. Believed to have been between 7 and 10 years of age, he was recruited at the last moment out of the spectators to replace Hermanus Brockmann, their cox in the heats, who was considered to be too heavy. Incidentally, Brockmann coxed the Dutch fours to a silver medal

and the eight to a bronze.

Of the many other young winning coxes over the years, the youngest known for certain was another French boy, Noël Vandernotte, in the 1936 pairs and fours, aged 12yr 232 days. The latter crew included his father and uncle. The US oarsman Conn Findlay, winner of two golds and a bronze in coxed pairs (1956–64), also won a yachting bronze medal in 1976 in the Tempest class.

ROWING MEDALS – MEN

	Gold	Silver	Bronze
Single Sculls			
1900	Henri Barrelet (FRA) 7:35.6	André Gaudin (FRA) 7:41.6	St George Ashe (GBR) 8:15.6
1904	Frank Greer (USA) 10:08.5	James Juvenal (USA) 2 lengths	Constance Titus (USA) 1 length
1906	Gaston Delaplane (FRA) 5:53.4	Joseph Larran (FRA) 6:07.2	–
1908	Harry Blackstaffe (GBR) 9:26.0	Alexander McCulloch (GBR) 1 length	Bernhard von Gaza (GER) d.n.a.
			Károly Levitzky (HUN) d.n.a.
1912	William Kinnear (GBR) 7:47.6	Potydore Veirman (BEL) 1 length	Everard Butter (CAN) d.n.a.
			Mikhail Kusik (URS) d.n.a.
1920	John Kelly (USA) 7:35.0	Jack Beresford (GBR) 7:36.0	Clarence Hadfield d'Arcy (NZL) 7:48.0
1924	Jack Beresford (GBR) 7:49.2	William Garrett-Gilmore (USA) 7:54.0	Josef Schneider (SUI) 8:01.1
1928	Henry Pearce (AUS) 7:11.0	Kenneth Myers (USA) 7:20.8	David Collett (GBR) 7:19.8
1932	Henry Pearce (AUS) 7:44.4	William Miller (USA) 7:45.2	Guillermo Douglas (URU) 8:13.6
1936	Gustav Schäfer (GER) 8:21.5	Josef Hasenöhri (AUT) 8:25.8	Daniel Barrow (USA) 8:28.0
1948	Mervyn Wood (AUS) 7:24.4	Eduardo Risso (URU) 7:38.2	Romolo Catasta (ITA) 7:51.4
1952	Yuriy Tyukalov (URS) 8:12.8	Mervyn Wood (AUS) 8:14.5	Teodor Kocerka (POL) 8:19.4
1956	Vyacheslav Ivanov (URS) 8:02.5	Stuart Mackenzie (AUS) 8:07.0	John Kelly (USA) 8:11.8
1960	Vyacheslav Ivanov (URS) 7:13.96	Achim Hill (GER) 7:20.21	Teodor Kocerka (POL) 7:21.26
1964	Vyacheslav Ivanov (URS) 8:22.51	Achim Hill (GER) 8:26.34	Gottfried Kottmann (SUI) 8:29.68
1968	Henri Jan Wienese (HOL) 7.47.80	Jochen Meissner (FRG) 7:52.00	Alberto Demiddi (ARG) 7:57.19
1972	Yuriy Malishev (URS) 7:10.12	Alberto Demiddi (ARG) 7:11.53	Wolfgang Gueldenpfennig (GDR) 7:14.45
1976	Pertti Karppinen (FIN) 7:29.03	Peter Kolbe (FRG) 7:31.67	Joachim Dreifke (GDR) 7:38.03
1980	Pertti Karppinen (FIN) 7:09.61	Vasiliy Yakusha (URS) 7:11.66	Peter Kersten (GDR) 7:14.88
1984	Pertti Karppinen (FIN) 7:00.24	Peter Kolbe (FRG) 7:02.19	Robert Mills (CAN) 7:10.38
1988	Thomas Lange (GDR) 6:49.86	Peter Kolbe (FRG) 6:54.77	Eric Verdonk (NZL) 6:58.86

1896 Event not held.

Double Sculls			
1904	United States 10:03.2	United States d.n.a	United States d.n.a.
1920	United States 7:09.0	Italy 7:19.0	France 7:21.0
1924	United States 7:45.0	France 7:54.8	Switzerland d.n.a.
1928	United States 6:41.4	Canada 6:51.0	Austria 6:48.8
1932	United States 7:17.4	Germany 7:22.8	Canada 7:27.6
1936	Great Britain 7:20.8	Germany 7:26.2	Poland 7:36.2
1948	Great Britain 6:51.3	Denmark 6:55.3	Uruguay 7:12.4
1952	Argentina 7:32.2	Soviet Union 7:38.3	Uruguay 7:43.7
1956	Soviet Union 7:24.0	United States 7:32.2	Australia 7:37.4
1960	Czechoslovakia 6:47.50	Soviet Union 6:50.49	Switzerland 6:50.59
1964	Soviet Union 7:10.66	United States 7:13.16	Czechoslovakia 7:14.23
1968	Soviet Union 6:51.82	Netherlands 6:52.80	United States 6:54.21
1972	Soviet Union 7:01.77	Norway 7:02.58	GDR 7:05.55
1976	Norway 7:13.20	Great Britain 7:15.26	GDR 7:17.45
1980	GDR 6:24.33	Yugoslavia 6:26.34	Czechoslovakia 6:29.07
1984	United States 6:36.87	Belgium 6:38.19	Yugoslavia 6:39.59
1988	Netherlands 6:21.13	Switzerland 6:22.59	Soviet Union 6:22.87

1896–1900, 1906–1912 Event not held.

	Gold	Silver	Bronze
Coxless Quadruple Sculls			
1976	GDR 6:18.65	Soviet Union 6:19.89	Czechoslovakia 6:21.77
1980	GDR 5:49.81	Soviet Union 5:51.47	Bulgaria 5:52.38
1984	FRG 5:57.55	Australia 5:57.98	Canada 5:59.07
1988	Italy 5:53.37	Norway 5:55.08	GDR 5:56.13

1896–1972 Event not held.

Coxless Pairs			
1908	Great Britain 9:43.0	Great Britain 2½ lengths	Canada
			Germany
1924	Netherlands 8:19.4	France 8:21.6	–
1928	Germany 7:06.4	Great Britain 7:08.08	United States 7:20.4
1932	Great Britain 8:00.0	New Zealand 8:02.4	Poland 8:08.2
1936	Germany 8:16.1	Denmark 8:19.2	Argentina 8:23.0
1948	Great Britain 7:21.1	Switzerland 7:23.9	Italy 7:31.5
1952	United States 8:20.7	Belgium 8:23.5	Switzerland 8:32.7
1956	United States 7:55.4	Soviet Union 8:03.9	Austria 8:11.8
1960	Soviet Union 7:02.01	Austria 7:03.69	Finland 7:03.80
1964	Canada 7:32.94	Netherlands 7:33.40	Germany 7:38.63
1968	GDR 7:26.56	United States 7:26.71	Denmark 7:31.84
1972	GDR 6:53.16	Switzerland 6:57.06	Netherlands 6:58.70
1976	GDR 7:23.31	United States 7:26.73	FRG 7:30.03
1980	GDR 6:48.01	Soviet Union 6:50.50	Great Britain 6:51.47
1984	Romania 6:45.39	Spain 6:48.47	Norway 6:51.81
1988	Great Britain 6:36.84	Romania 6:38.06	Yugoslavia 6:41.01

1896–1906, 1912–1920 Event not held.

Coxed Pairs			
1900	Netherlands 7:34.2	France I 7:34.4	France II 7:57.2
1906[1]	Italy I 4:23.0	Italy II 4:30.0	France d.n.a.
1906[2]	Italy 7:32.4	Belgium 8:03.0	France 8:08.6
1920	Italy 7:56.0	France 7:57.0	Switzerland d.n.a.
1924	Switzerland 8:39.0	Italy 8:39.1	United States 3m
1928	Switzerland 7:42.6	France 7:48.4	Belgium 7:59.4
1932	United States 8:25.8	Poland 8:31.2	France 8:41.2
1936	Germany 8:363.9	Italy 8:49.7	France 8:54.0
1948	Denmark 8:00.5	Italy 8:12.2	Hungary 8:25.2
1952	France 8:28.6	Germany 8:32.1	Denmark 8:34.9
1956	United States 8:26.1	Germany 8:29.2	Soviet Union 8:2.0
1960	Germany 7:29.14	Soviet Union 7:30.17	United States 7:34.58
1964	United States 8:21.23	France 8:23.15	Netherlands 8:23.42
1968	Italy 8:04.81	Netherlands 8:06.80	Denmark 8:08.07
1972	GDR 7:17.25	Czechoslovakia 7:19.57	Romania 7:21.36
1976	GDR 7:58.99	Soviet Union 8:01.82	Czechoslovakia 8:03.28
1980	GDR 7:02.54	Soviet Union 7:03.35	Yugoslavia 7:04.92
1984	Italy 7:05.99	Romania 7:11.21	United States 7:12.81
1988	Italy 6:58.79	GDR 7:00.63	Great Britain 7:01.95

1896, 1904, 1908–1912 Event not held.

[1]*Over 1000m.* [2]*Over 1600m.*

Coxless Fours			
1904	United States 9:53.8	United States d.n.a.	–
1908	Great Britain 8:34.0	Great Britain 1½ lengths	Netherlands
			Canada
1924	Great Britain 7:08.6	Canada 7:18.0	Switzerland 2 lengths
1928	Great Britain 6:36.0	United States 6:37.0	Italy 6:31.6
1932	Great Britain 6:58.2	Germany 7:03.0	Italy 7:04.0
1936	Germany 7:01.8	Great Britain 7:06.5	Switzerland 7:10.6
1948	Italy 6:39.0	Denmark 6:43.5	United States 6:47.7
1952	Yugoslavia 7:16.0	France 7:18.9	Finland 7:23.3
1956	Canada 7:08.8	United States 7:18.4	France 7:20.9
1960	United States 6:26.26	Italy 6:28.78	Soviet Union 6:29.62
1964	Denmark 6:59.30	Great Britain 7:00.47	United States 7:01.37
1968	GDR 6:39.18	Hungary 6:41.64	Italy 6:44.01
1972	GDR 6:24.27	New Zealand 6:25.64	FRG 6:28.41
1976	GDR 6:37.42	Norway 6:41.22	Soviet Union 6:42.52
1980	GDR 6:08.17	Soviet Union 6:11.81	Great Britain 6:16.58
1984	New Zealand 6.03.48	United States 6:06.10	Denmark 6:07.72
1988	GDR 6:03.11	United States 6:05.53	FRG 6:06.22

1896–1900, 1906, 1912–1920 Event not held.

	Gold	Silver	Bronze
Coxed Fours			
1900[1]	Germany 5:59.0	Netherlands 6:33.0	Germany 6:35.0
1900[1]	France 7:11.0	France 7.18.0	Germany 7:18.2
1906	Italy 8:13.0	France d.n.a.	France d.n.a.
1912	Germany 6:59.4	Great Britain 2 lengths	Norway d.n.a.
			Denmark d.n.a.
1920	Switzerland 6:54.0	United States 6:58.0	Norway 7:02.0
1924	Switzerland 7:18.4	France 7:21.6	United States 1 length
1928	Italy 6:47.8	Switzerland 7:03.4	Poland 7:12.8
1932	Germany 7:19.0	Italy 7:19.2	Poland 7:26.8
1936	Germany 7:16.2	Switzerland 7:24.3	France 7:33.3
1948	United States 6:50.3	Switzerland 6:53.3	Denmark 6:58.6
1952	Csechoslovakia 7:33.4	Switzerland 7:36.5	United States 7:37.0
1956	Italy 7:19.4	Sweden 7:22.4	Finland 7:30.9
1960	Germany 6:39.12	France 6:411.62	Italy 6:43.72
1964	Germany 7:00.44	Italy 7:022.84	Netherlands 7:06.46
1968	New Zealand 6:45.62	GDR 6:48.20	Switzerland 6:49.04
1972	FRG 6:31.85	GDR 6:33.30	Czechoslovakia 6:35.64
1976	Soviet Union 6:40.22	GDR 6:42.70	FRG 6:46.96
1980	GDR 6:14.51	Soviet Union 6:19.05	Poland 6:22.52
1984	Great Britain 6:18.64	United States 6:20.28	New Zealand 6:23.68
1988	GDR 6:10.74	Romania 6:13.58	New Zealand 6:15.78

1896, 1904, 1908 Event not held.

[1] *Two separate finals were held in 1900.*

	Gold	Silver	Bronze
Eights			
1900	United States 6:09.8	Belgium 6:13.8	Netherlands 6:23.0
1904	United States 7:50.0	Canada d.n.a.	–
1908	Great Britain I 7:52.0	Belgium 2 lengths	Great Britain
			Canada
1912	Great Britain I 6:15.0	Great Britain II 6:19.0	Germany d.n.a.
1920	United States 6:02.6	Great Britain 6:05.0	Norway 6:36.0
1924	United States 6:33.4	Canada 6:49.0	Italy ¾ length
1928	United States 6:03.2	Great Britain 6:05.6	Canada 6:03.8
1932	United States 6:37.6	Italy 6:37.8	Canada 6:40.4
1936	United States 6:25.4	Italy 6:26.0	Germany 6:26.4
1948	United States 5:56.7	Great Britain 6:06.9	Norway 6:10.3
1952	United States 6:25.9	Soviet Union 6:31.2	Australia 6:33.1
1965	United States 6:35.2	Canada 6:37.1	Australia 6:39.2
1960	Germany 5:57.18	Canada 6:01.52	Czechoslovakia 6:04.84
1964	United States 6:18.23	Germany 6:23.29	Czechoslovakia 6:25.11
1968	FRG 6:07.00	Australia 6:07.98	Soviet Union 6:09.11
1972	New Zealand 6:08.94	United States 6:11.61	GDR 6:11.67
1976	GDR 5:58.29	Great Britain 6:00.82	New Zealand 6.03.51
1980	GDR 5:49.05	Great Britain 5:51.92	Soviet Union 5:52.66
1984	Canada 5:41.32	United States 5:41.74	Australia 5:42.40
1988	FRG 5:46.05	Soviet Union 5:48.01	United States 5:48.26

1896, 1906 Event not held.

DISCONTINUED EVENTS

	Gold	Silver	Bronze
Naval Rowing Boats (200m)			
1906	Italy 10:45.0	Greece d.n.a.	Greece d.n.a.
16-Man Naval Rowing Boats (3000m)			
1906	Greece 16:35.0	Greece 17:09.5	Italy d.n.a.
Coxed Fours (Inriggers)			
1912	Denmark 7:47.0	Sweden 1 length	Norway d.n.a.

ROWING MEDALS – WOMEN

Women's rowing was introduced in 1976 over a course of 1000 metres. From 1988 it was over 2000m.

	Gold	Silver	Bronze
Single Sculls			
1976	Christine Scheiblich (GDR) 4:05.56	Joan Lind (USA) 4:06.21	Elena Antonova (URS) 4:10.24
1980	Sandra Toma (ROM) 3:40.69	Antonina Makhina (URS) 3:41.65	Martina Schröter (GDR) 3:43.54
1984	Valeria Racila (ROM) 3:40.68	Charlotte Geer (USA) 3:43.89	Ann Haesebrouck (BEL) 3:45.72
1988	Jutta Behrednt (GDR) 7:47.19	Anne Marden (USA) 7:50.28	Magdalene Gueorguieva (BUL) 7:53.65
Double Sculls			
1976	Bulgaria 3:44.36	GDR 3:47.86	Soviet Union 3:49.93
1980	Soviet Union 3:16.27	GDR 3:17.63	Romania 3:18.91
1984	Romania 3:26.75	Netherlands 3:29.13	Canada 3:29.82
1988	GDR 7:00.48	Romania 7:04.36	Bulgaria 7:06.03
Coxed Quadruple Sculls			
1976	GDR 3:29.99	Soviet Union 3:32.49	Romania 3:32.76
1980	GDR 3:15.32	Soviet Union 3:15.73	Bulgaria 3:16.10
1984	Romania 3:14.11	United States 3:15.57	Denmark 3:16.02
1988*	GDR 6:21.06	Soviet Union 6:23.47	Romania 6:23.81

*Not coxed.

Coxless Pairs			
1976	Bulgaria 4:01.22	GDR 4:01.64	FRG 4:02.35
1980	GDR 3:30.49	Poland 3:30.95	Bulgaria 3:32.39
1984	Romania 3:32.60	Canada 3:36.06	FRG 3:40.50
1988	Romania 7:28.13	Bulgaria 7:31.95	New Zealand 7:35.68
Coxed Fours			
1976	GDR 3:45.08	Bulgaria 3:38.24	Soviet Union 3:49.38
1980	GDR 3:19.27	Bulgaria 3:20.75	Soviet Union 3:20.92
1984	Romania 3:19.30	Canada 3:21.55	Australia 3:23.29
1988	GDR 6:56.00	China 6:58.78	Romania 7:01.13
Eights			
1976	GDR 3:33.32	Soviet Union 3:36.17	United States 3:38.68
1980	GDR 3:03.32	Soviet Union 3:04.29	Romania 3:05.63
1984	United States 2:59.80	Romania 3:00.87	Netherlands 3:02.92
1988	GDR 6:15.17	Romania 6:17.44	China 6:21.83

SHOOTING

Baron de Coubertin, the founder of the modern Olympic Games, was a pistol shot of note in his youth, and this undoubtedly led to the sport being included in the first modern Games. The first champion was Pantelis Karasevdas (GRE) who won the free rifle event over 200m on 9 April 1896.

The number of events has varied considerably, especially in the early celebrations of the Games, from 21 in 1920 to only two in 1932. There were none at all in 1928. Since 1952 there has been some standardisation. In 1984 three events for women were introduced, with another added in 1988.

New regulations were introduced in 1988 in accordance with ISU rules. The leading eight competitors, in rifle and pistol shooting, at the end of the designated number of rounds, take part in a final shoot-out round with the target subdivided into tenths of a point. For trap and skeet, each of the leading competitors has 25 extra shots.

The most successful competitor has been Carl Osburn (USA), who won a record 11 medals (five gold, four silver, two bronze) from 1912 to 1924. Six other men have won five

gold medals: Konrad Stäheli (SUI), 1900–06; Louis Richardet (SUI), 1900–06; Alfred Lane (USA), 1912–20; Ole Lilloe-Olsen (NOR), 1920–24; Morris Fisher (USA), 1920–24; and Willis Lee (USA) all in 1920, a record for the sport. However, the only man to win three individual gold medals at one Games was Gudbrand Skatteboe (NOR) in 1906. Lloyd Spooner (USA) competed in 12 events at the 1920 Games, a record in any sport in Olympic history. Lars Madsen (DEN) won gold medals over a record 20 year span, 1900–1920.

Women first competed – in men's events – in 1968 when three countries, Poland, Peru and Mexico, entered one woman competitor each. Eulalia Rolinska (POL) and Gladys de Seminario (PER) were the first to compete, finishing 22nd and 31st respectively in the small-bore rifle (prone) event. The first woman to win a medal was Margaret Murdock (USA) in the 1976 small-bore rifle (three positions). Initially she was listed as the winner, but then it was discovered that an error had been made and she was equal with her team-mate, Lanny Bassham. Then on the count-back rule relating to the last ten shots she was placed second, much to the embarrassment of Bassham, who pulled her up to the top of the victory rostrum at the medal ceremony.

The oldest gold medallist in Olympic history, in any sport, was the remarkable Oskar Swahn (SWE) in the 1912 running deer team, aged 64yr 258 days (his son Alfred was also in the team). At Antwerp in 1920 he became the oldest medallist and indeed the oldest competitor at any sport in the Olympics ever, when he was again a member of the Swedish running deer silver medal team. He qualified for the 1924 Games in his 77th year, but illness prevented him from competing. He died three years later.

The youngest winner of a gold medal was George Généreux (CAN) in the 1952 trap shooting event, aged 17yr 147 days. The oldest female champion was Linda Thom (CAN), aged 40yr 212 days when winning the sport pistol in 1984. The youngest woman to win a gold was Pat Spurgin (USA) in the 1984 air rifle, aged 18yr 356 days. The youngest medallist was Marcus Dinwiddie (USA), silver in the 1924 small-bore rifle (prone) event aged 16yr 304 days. The youngest female medallist, Ulrike Holmer (FRG) with a silver in the 1984 standard rifle, was one day older.

John and Sumner Paine (USA) in 1896 were the first brothers to win gold medals at the Olympic Games, while the first twins to do so were Vilhelm and Eric Carlberg (SWE) in 1912. Károly Takács (HUN) was a European pistol champion in the 1930s using his right hand – then in 1938, while he was on army training, a grenade blew up in his hand destroying his right arm. After the war he won the rapid fire pistol event with his left hand at the 1948 and 1952 Games, one of only five shooters who have successfully defended an Olympic title.

The 1960 rapid fire pistol champion, William McMillan (USA), competed in his record sixth Games in 1976. Walter Winans (USA), who had won a gold medal in the 1908 running deer event, became the only man to win medals in both sporting and artistic events at the same Games in 1912 when he gained a silver in shooting and a gold at sculpture. Winans was born in Russia to Dutch-American parents and lived most of his life in England – he never set foot in America.

SHOOTING MEDALS TOTALS

Country	MEN			WOMEN[1]			Total
	G	S	B	G	S	B	
United States	42	23	17	1	1	1	85
Sweden	13	23	18	–	–	–	54
Soviet Union[2]	15	15	16	2	1	3	52
Great Britain	13	14	19	–	–	–	46
France	12	15	12	–	–	–	39
Norway	16	7	10	–	–	–	33
Switzerland	11	9	10	–	–	–	30
Germany (FRG)	5	6	5	1	2	–	19
Greece	5	7	6	–	–	–	18
Denmark	3	8	6	–	–	–	17
Finland	3	5	9	–	–	–	17
Italy	6	3	6	–	1	–	16
GDR	3	8	5	–	–	–	16
Hungary	6	3	6	–	–	–	15
Romania	5	4	3	–	–	–	12
Canada	3	3	2	1	–	–	9
China	2	1	3	1	–	2	8
Czechoslovakia	3	3	1	–	–	–	7
Belgium	2	3	2	–	–	–	7
Poland	2	1	3	–	–	–	6
Austria	1	1	3	–	–	–	5
Bulgaria	1	1	1	–	1	–	4
Japan	1	–	2	–	1	–	4
Yugoslavia	1	–	–	1	–	1	3
Brazil	1	1	1	–	–	–	3
Peru	1	1	–	–	–	–	2
Colombia	–	2	–	–	–	–	2
Netherlands	–	1	1	–	–	–	2
Spain	–	1	1	–	–	–	2
Australia	–	–	1	–	–	1	2
North Korea (PRK)	1	–	–	–	–	–	1
Argentina	–	1	–	–	–	–	1
Chile	–	1	–	–	–	–	1
Korea	–	1	–	–	–	–	1
Mexico	–	1	–	–	–	–	1
Portugal	–	1	–	–	–	–	1
South Africa	–	1	–	–	–	–	1
Cuba	–	–	1	–	–	–	1
Haiti	–	–	1	–	–	–	1
New Zealand	–	–	1	–	–	–	1
Venezuela	–	–	1	–	–	–	1
	177	175	173	7	7	7	546

[1]Excluding female medallists prior to 1984
[2]Including a silver and bronze for Russia in 1912

Gerald Ouellette (CAN) won the 1956 small-bore (prone) gold medal with a world record maximum possible score of 600, but it was not accepted as such as the range was found to be 1.5 metres short of the regulation 50m distance. When Li Ho Jun (PRK) won the same event in 1972 with a score of 599

he was asked how he concentrated so well. He answered that he pretended that he was 'aiming at a capitalist'. Francois La Fortuno Jr (BEL) competed in a record seven Games (1952–76), while his father, Francois Sr, competed over a 36 year span (1924–60).

One of the oddest occur-

rences in Olympic shooting was in the 1976 trap shooting event when 65-year-old Paul Cerutti of Monaco was disqualified for using drugs, even though he had finished 43rd out of 44 competitors – he is the oldest competitor ever so penalised.

SHOOTING MEDALS – MEN

	Gold	Silver	Bronze
Free Pistol (50 metres)			
1896	Sumner Paine (USA) 442	Viggo Jensen (DEN) 285	Holger Nielsen (DEN) d.n.a.
1900	Karl Röderer (SUI) 503	Achille Paroche (FRA) 466	Konrad Stäheli (SUI) 453
1906	Georgios Orphanidis (GRE) 221	Jean Fouconnier (FRA) 219	Aristides Rangavis (GRE) 218
1912	Alfred Lane (USA) 499	Peter Dolfen (USA) 474	Charles Stewart (GBR) 470
1920	Karl Frederick (USA) 496	Afranio da Costa (BRA) 489	Alfred Lane (USA) 481
1936	Torsten Ullmann (SWE) 559	Erich Krempel (GER) 544	Charles des Jammonières (FRA) 540
1948	Edwin Vazquez Cam (PER) 545	Rudolf Schnyder (SUI) 539	Torsten Ullmann (SWE) 539
1952	Huelet Benner (US) 553	Angel Léon de Gozalo (ESP) 550	Ambrus Balogh (HUN) 549
1956	Pentti Linnosvuo (FIN) 556	Makhmud Oumarov (URS) 556	Offutt Pinion (USA) 551
1960	Aleksey Gushchin (URS) 560	Makhmud Oumarov (URS) 552	Yoshihisa Yoshikawa (JPN) 552
1964	Väinö Markkanen (FIN) 560	Franklin Green (USA) 557	Yoshihisa Yoshikawa (JPN) 554
1968	Grigory Kossykh (URS) 562	Heinz Mertel (FRG) 562	Harald Vollmar (GDR) 560
1972	Ragnar Skanakar (SWE) 567	Dan Iuga (ROM) 562	Rudolf Dollinger (AUT) 560
1976	Uwe Potteck (GDR) 573	Harald Vollmar (GDR) 567	Rudolf Dollinger (AUT) 560
1980	Aleksandr Melentyev (URS) 581	Harald Vollmar (GDR) 568	Lubcho Diakov (URS) 565
1984	Xu Haifeng (CHN) 566	Ragnar Skanaker (SWE) 565	Wang Yifu (CHN) 564
1988	Sorin Babii (ROM) (566+94) 660	Ragnar Skanaker (SWE) (564+93) 657	Igor Bassinski (URS) (570+87) 657

1904, 1908, 1924–1932 Event not held.

	Gold	Silver	Bronze
Rapid-Fire Pistol			
1896	Jean Phrangoudis (GRE) 344	Georgios Orphanidis (GRE) 249	Holger Nielsen (DEN) d.n.a.
1900	Maurice Larrouy (FRA) 58	Léon Moreaux (FRA) 57	Eugene Balme (FRA) 57
1906	Maurice Lecoq (FRA) 250	Léon Moreaux (FRA) 249	Aristides Rangavis (GRE) 245
1908	Paul van Asbroeck (BEL) 490	Réginald Storms (BEL) 487	James Gorman (USA) 485
1912	Alfred Lane (USA) 287	Paul Palén (SWE) 286	Johan von Holst (SWE) 283
1920	Guilherme Paraense (BRA) 274	Raymond Bracken (USA) 272	Fritz Zulauf (SUI) 269
1924	Paul Bailey (USA) 18	Vilhelm Carlberg (SWE) 18	Lennart Hannelius (FIN) 18
1932	Renzo Morigi (ITA) 36	Heinz Hax (GER) 36	Domenico Matteucci (ITA) 36
1936	Cornelius van Oyen (GER) 36	Heinz Hax (GER) 35	Torsten Ullmann (SWE) 34
1948	Károly Takács (HUN) 580	Carlos Diaz Sáenz Valiente (ARG) 571	Sven Lundqvist (SWE) 569
1952	Károly Takács (HUN) 579	Szilárd Kun (HUN) 578	Gheorghe Lichiardopol (ROM) 578
1956	Stefan Petrescu (ROM) 587	Evgeniy Shcherkasov (URS) 585	Gheorghe Lichiardopol (ROM) 581
1960	William McMillan (USA) 587	Penttii Linnosvuo (FIN) 587	Aleksandr Zabelin (URS) 587
1964	Penttii Linnosvuo (FIN) 592	Ion Tripsa (ROM) 591	Lubomir Nacovsky (TCH) 590
1968	Jozef Zapedzki (POL) 593	Marcel Rosca (ROM) 591	Renart Suleimanov (URS) 591
1972	Jozef Zapedzki (POL) 593	Ladislav Faita (TCH) 594	Victor Torshin (URS) 593
1976	Norbert Klaar (GDR) 597	Jurgen Wiefel (GDR) 596	Roberto Ferraris (ITA) 595
1980	Corneliu Ion (ROM) 596	Jurgen Wiefel (GDR) 596	Gerhard Petrisch (AUT) 596
1984	Takeo Kamachi (JPN) 595	Corneliu Ion (ROM) 593	Rauno Bies (FIN) 591
1988	Afanasi Kouzmine (URS) (598+100) 698	Ralf Schumann (GDR) (597+99) 696	Zoltan Kovacs (HUN) (594+99) 693

1904, 1928 Event not held.

	Gold	Silver	Bronze
Small-Bore Rifle (Prone)[1]			
1908	AA Carnell (GBR) 387	Harry Humby (GBR) 386	George Barnes (GBR) 385
1912	Frederick Hird (USA) 194	William Milne (GBR) 193	Harry Burt (GBR) 192
1920	Lawrence Nuesslein (USA) 391	Arthur Rothrock (USA) 386	Dennis Fenton (USA) 385
1924	Pierre Coquelin de Lisle (FRA) 398	Marcus Dinwiddie (USA) 396	Josias Hartmann (SUI) 394
1932	Bertil Rönmark (SWE) 294	Gustavo Huet (MEX) 294	Zoltán Hradetsky-Soos (HUN) 293
1936	Willy Rögeberg (NOR) 300	Ralph Berzsenyi (HUN) 296	Wladyslaw Karás (POL) 296
1948	Arthur Cook (USA) 599	Walter Tomsen (USA) 599	Jonas Jonsson (SWE) 597
1952	Josif Sarbu (ROM) 400	Boris Andreyev (URS) 400	Arthur Jackson (USA) 399

	Gold	**Silver**	**Bronze**
1956	Gerald Ouellette (CAN) 600²	Vasiliy Borissov (URS) 599	Gilmour Boa (CAN) 598
1960	Peter Kohnke (GER) 590	James Hill (USA) 589	Enrico Pelliccione (VEN) 587
1964	László Hammerl (HUN) 597	Lones Wigger (USA) 597	Tommy Pool (USA) 596
1968	Jan Kurka (TCH) 598	László Hammerl (HUN) 598	Ian Ballinger (NZL) 597
1972	Li Ho Jun (PRK) 599	Victor Auer (USA) 598	Nicolae Rotaru (ROM) 595
1976	Karlheinz Smieszek (FRG) 599	Ulrich Lind (FRG) 597	Gennadiy Lushchikov (URS) 595
1980	Karoly Varga (HUN) 599	Hellfried Heilfort (GDR) 599	Petar Zapianov (BUL) 598
1984	Edward Etzel (USA) 599	Michel Bury (FRA) 596	Michael Sullivan (GBR) 596
1988	Miroslav Varga (TCH) (600+103.9) 703.9	Cha Young-Chul (KOR) (598 104.8) 702.8	Attila Zahonyi (HUN) (597+104.9) 701.9

[1]In 1908 and 1912 any position allowed; in 1920 it was a standing position.   *[2]Range found to be marginally short – record not allowed.*
1896–1906, 1928 Event not held.

Small-Bore Rifle – Three Positions (Prone, Kneeling, Standing)

1952	Erling Kongshaug (NOR) 1164	Viho Ylönen (FIN) 1164	Boris Andreyev (URS) 1163
1956	Anatoliy Bogdanov (URS) 1172	Otakar Horinek (TCH) 1172	Nils Sundberg (SWE) 1167
1960	Viktor Shamburkin (URS) 1149	Marat Niyasov (URS) 1145	Klaus Zähringer (GER) 1139
1964	Lones Wigger (USA) 1164	Velitchko Khristov (BUL) 1152	László Hammerl (HUN) 1151
1968	Bernd Klingner (FRG) 1157	John Writer (USA) 1156	Vitaly Parkhimovich (URS) 1154
1972	John Writer (USA) 1166	Lanny Bassham (USA) 1157	Werner Lippoldt (GDR) 1153
1976	Lanny Bassham (USA) 1162	Margaret Murdock (USA) 1162	Werner Seibold (FRG) 1160
1980	Viktor Vlasov (URS) 1173	Bernd Hartstein (GDR) 1166	Sven Johansson (SWE) 1165
1984	Malcolm Cooper (GBR) 1173	Daniel Kipkow (SUI) 1163	Alister Allan (GBR) 1162
1988	Malcolm Cooper (GBR) (1180+99.3) 1279.3	Alister Allan (GBR) (1181+94.6) 1275.6	Kirill Ivanov (URS) (1173+102) 1275.0

1896–1948 Event not held.

Running Game Target

1900	Louis Debray (FRA) 20	P Nivet (FRA) 20	Comte de Lambert (FRA) 19
1972	Lakov Zhelezniak (URS) 569	Hanspeter Bellingrodt (COL) 565	John Kynoch (GBR) 562
1976	Aleksandr Gazov (URS) 579	Aleksandr Kedyarov (URS) 576	Jerzy Greszkiewicz (POL) 571
1980	Igor Sokolov (URS) 589	Thomas Pfeffer (GDR) 589	Aleksandr Gasov (URS) 587
1984	Li Yuwei (CHN) 587	Helmut Bellingrodt (COL) 584	Shiping Huang (CHN) 581
1988	Tor Heiestad (NOR) (591+98) 689	Huang Shiping (CHN) (589+98) 686	Gennadiy Avramenko (URS) (591+95) 685

1896, 1904–1968 Event not held.

Olympic Trap Shooting

1900	Roger de Barbarin (FRA) 17	René Guyot (FRA) 17	Justinien de Clary (FRA) 17
1906[1]	Gerald Merlin (GBR) 24	Ioannis Peridis (GRE) 23	Sidney Merlin (GBR) 21
1906[2]	Sidney Merlin (GBR) 15	Anastasios Metaxas (GRE) 13	Gerald Merlin (GBR) 12
1908	Walter Ewing (CAN) 72	George Beattie (CAN) 60	Alexander Maunder (GBR) 57
			Anastasios Metaxas (GRE) 57
1912	James Graham (USA) 96	Alfred Goeldel-Bronikowen (GER) 94	Harry Blau (URS) 91
1920	Marke Arie (USA) 95	Frank Troeh (USA) 93	Frank Wright (USA) 87
1924	Gyula Halasy (HUN) 98	Konrad Huber (FIN) 98	Frank Hughes (USA) 97
1952	George Généreux (CAN) 192	Knut Holmquist (SWE) 191	Hans Liljedahl (SWE) 191
1956	Galliano Rossini (ITA) 195	Adam Smelczynski (POL) 190	Alessandro Ciceri (ITA) 188
1960	Ion Dumitrescu (ROM) 192	Galliano Rossini (ITA) 191	Sergey Kalinin (URS) 190
1964	Ennio Mattarelli (ITA) 198	Pavel Senichev (URS) 194	William Morris (USA) 194
1968	Robert Braithwaite (GBR) 198	Thomas Garrigus (USA) 196	Kurt Czekalla (GDR) 196
1972	Angelo Scalzone (ITA) 199	Michel Carrega (FRA) 198	Silvano Basagni (ITA) 195
1976	Don Haldeman (USA) 190	Armando Marques (POR) 189	Ubaldesco Baldi (ITA) 189
1980	Luciano Giovanetti (ITA) 198	Rustam Yambulatov (URS) 196	Jorg Damme (GDR) 196
1984	Luciano Giovanetti (ITA) 192	Francisco Boza (PER) 192	Daniel Carlisle (USA) 192
1988	Dmitriy Monakov (URS) (197+25) 222	Miloslav Bednarik (TCH) (197+25) 222	Frans Peeters (BEL) (195+24) 219

[1]Single shot.   [2]Double shot.
1896, 1904, 1928–1948 Event not held.

Skeet Shooting

1968	Evgeny Petrov (URS) 198	Romano Garagnani (ITA) 198	Konrad Wirnhier (FRG) 198
1972	Konrad Wirnhier (FRG) 195	Evgeny Petrov (URS) 195	Michael Buchheim (GDR) 195
1976	Josef Panacek (TCH) 198	Eric Swinkels (HOL) 198	Wieslaw Gawlikowski (POL) 196
1980	Hans Kjeld Rasmussen (DEN) 196	Lars-Goran Carlsson (SWE) 196	Roberto Garcia (CUB) 196
1984	Matthew Dryke (USA) 198	Ole Rasmussen (DEN) 196	Luca Scribani Rossi (ITA) 196
1988	Axel Wegner (GDR) (198+24) 222	Alfonso de Iruarrizaga (CHI) (198+23) 221	Jorge Guardiola (ESP) (196+24) 220

1896–1964 Event not held.

Air Pistol

1988	Taniou Kiriakov (BUL) (585+102.9) 687.9	Erich Buljung (USA) (590+97.9) 687.9	Xu Haifeng (CHN) (584+100.5) 684.5

1896–1964 Event not held.

	Gold		Bronze

Air Rifle

| 1984 | Philippe Herberle (FRA) 589 | Andreas Kronthaler (AUT) 587 | Barry Dagger (GBR) 587 |
| 1988 | Goran Maksimovic (YUG) (594+101.6) 695.6 | Nicolas Berthelot (FRA) (593+101.2) 694.2 | Johann Riederer (FRG) (592+102) 694.0 |

1896–1980 Event not held.

SHOOTING MEDALS – WOMEN   *Introduced in 1984*

	Gold	Silver	Bronze

Sport Pistol

| 1984 | Linda Thom (CAN) 585 | Ruby Fox (USA) 585 | Patricia Dench (AUS) 583 |
| 1988 | Nino Saloukvadze (URS) (591+99) 690 | Tomoko Hasegawa (JPN) (587+99) 686 | Jasna Sekaric (YUG) (591+95) 686 |

Standard Rifle

| 1984 | Wu Xiaoxuan (CHN) 581 | Ulrike Holmer (FRG) 578 | Wanda Jewell (USA) 578 |
| 1988 | Silvia Sperber (FRG) (590+95.6) 685.6 | Vessela Letcheva (BUL) (583.100.2) 683.2 | Valentina Tcherkassova (URS) (586+95.4) 681.4 |

Air Pistol

| 1988 | Jasna Sekaric (YUG) (389+100.5) 489.5 | Nino Saloukvadze (URS) (390+97.9) 487.9 | Marina Dobrantcheva (URS) (385+100.2) 485.2 |

1984 Event not held.

Air Rifle

| 1984 | Pat Spurgin (USA) 393 | Edith Gufler (ITA) 391 | Wu Xiaoxuan (CHN) 389 |
| 1988 | Irina Chilova (URS) (395+103.5) 498.5 | Silvia Sperber (FRG) (393+104.5) 497.5 | Anna Maloukhina (URS) (394+101.8) 495.8 |

The GDR's third and last shooting gold medal was won by Axel Wegner in the skeet event at Seoul. Henceforth the two Germanys will be combined in a single team.

DISCONTINUED EVENTS

	Gold	Silver	Bronze
Free Rifle (3 positions)			
1896	Georgios Orphanidis (GRE) 1583	Jean Phrangoudis (GRE) 1312	Viggo Jensen (DEN) 1305
1906	Gudbrand Skatteboe (NOR) 977	Konrad Stäheli (SUI) 943	Jean Reich (SUI) 933
1908	Albert Helgerud (NOR) 909	Harry Simon (USA) 887	Ole Saether (NOR) 883
1912	Paul Colas (FRA) 987	Lars Madsen (DEN) 981	Niels Larsen (DEN) 962
1920	Morris Fisher (USA) 997	Niels Larsen (DEN) 985	Östen Östensen (NOR) 980
1924	Morris Fisher (USA) 95	Carl Osrubn (USA) 95	Niels Larsen (DEN) 93
1948	Emil Grunig (SUI) 1120	Pauli Janhonen (FIN) 1114	Willy Rögeberg (NOR) 1112
1952	Anatoliy Bogdanov (URS) 1123	Robert Bürchler (SUI) 1120	Lev Vainschtein (URS) 1109
1956	Vasiliy Borissov (URS) 1138	Allan Erdman (URS) 1137	Vilho Ylönen (FIN) 1128
1960	Hubert Hammerer (AUT) 1129	Hans Spillmann (SUI) 1127	Vasiliy Borissov (URS) 1127
1964	Gary Anderson (USA) 1153	Shota Kveliashvili (URS) 1144	Martin Gunnarsson (USA) 1136
1968	Gary Anderson (USA) 1157	Vladimir Kornev (URS) 1151	Kurt Müller (SUI) 1148
1972	Lones Wigger (USA) 1155	Boris Melnik (URS) 1155	Lajos Papp (HUN) 1149

1900-1904, 1928-1936 Event not held.

	Gold	Silver	Bronze
Free Rifle			
1896[1]	Pantelis Karasevdas (GRE) 2320	Paulas Pavlidis (GRE) 1978	Nicolaos Tricoupes (GRE) 1718
1906[2]	Marcel de Stadelhofen (SUI) 243	Konrad Stäheli (SUI) 238	Léon Moreaux (FRA) 234
1906[3]	Gudbrand Skatteboe (NOR)	–	–
1906[4]	Konrad Stäheli (SUI)	–	–
1906[5]	Gudbrand Skatteboe (NOR)	–	–
1908[6]	Jerry Millner (GBR) 98	Kellogg Casey (USA) 93	Maurice Blood (GBR) 92

[1]*Over 200m.* [2]*Any position (300m).* [3]*Prone (300m).* [4]*Kneeling (300m).* [5]*Standing (300m).* [6]*Over 1000 yards.*
1900-1904 Event not held.

	Gold	Silver	Bronze
Free Rifle (Team)			
1906	Switzerland 4596	Norway 4534	France 4511
1908	Norway 5055	Sweden 4711	France 4652
1912	Sweden 5655	Norway 5605	Denmark 5529
1920	United States 4876	Norway 4741	Switzerland 4698
1924	United States 676	France 646	Haiti 646

1896-1904 Event not held.

	Gold	Silver	Bronze
Military Rifle			
1900[1]	Emil Kellenberger (SUI) 930	Anders Nielsen (DEN) 921	Ole Östmo (NOR) 917
1900[2]	Lars Madsen (DEN) 305	Ole Östmo (NOR) 299	Charles du Verger (BEL) 298
1900[3]	Konrad Stäheli (SUI) 324	Emil Kellenberger (SUI) 314	–
		Anders Nielsen (DEN) 314	
1900[4]	Achille Paroche (FRA) 332	Anders Nielsen (DEN) 330	Ole Östmo (NOR) 329
1906[5]	Léon Moreaux (FRA) 187	Louis Richardet (SUI) 187	Jean Reich (SUI) 183
1906[6]	Louis Richardet (SUI) 238	Jean Reich (SUI) 234	Raoul de Boigne (FRA) 232
1912[1]	Sándor Prokopp (HUN) 97	Carl Osburn (USA) 96	Embret Skogen (NOR) 95
1912[7]	Paul Colas (FRA) 94	Carl Osburn (USA) 94	Joseph Jackson (USA) 93
1920[4]	Otto Olsen (NOR) 60	Léon Johnson (FRA) 59	Fritz Kuchen (SUI) 59
1920[2]	Carl Osburn (USA) 56	Lars Madsen (DEN) 55	Lawrence Nuesslein (USA) 54
1920[8]	Hugo Johansson (SWE) 58	Mauritz Eriksson (SWE) 56	Lloyd Spooner (USA) 56

1908 Event not held.

	Gold	Silver	Bronze
Military Rifle (Team)			
1900	Switzerland 4399	Norway 4290	France 4278
1908	United States 2531	Great Britain 2497	Canada 2439
1912	United States 1687	Great Britain 1602	Sweden 1570
1920[2]	Denmark 266	United States 255	Sweden 255
1920[4]	United States 289	France 283	Finland 281
1920[8]	United States 287	South Africa 287	Sweden 287
1920[9]	United States 573	Norway 565	Switzerland 563

[1]*Three positions (300m).* [2]*Standing (300m).* [3]*Kneeling (300m).* [4]*Prone (300m).* [5]*Standing or kneeling (200m).*
[6]*Standing or kneeling (300m).* [7]*Any position (600m).* [8]*Prone (600m).* [9]*Prone (300m and 600m).*
1896, 1904 Event not held.

Gold	Silver	Bronze

Small Bore Rifle

	Gold	Silver	Bronze
1908[1]	AF Fleming (GBR) 24	MK Matthews (GBR) 24	WB Marsden (GBR) 24
1908[2]	William Styles (GBR) 45	HI Hawkins (GBR) 45	Edward Amoore (GBR) 45
1912[2]	Wilhelm Carlberg (SWE) 242	Johan von Holst (SWE) 233	Gustaf Ericsson (SWE) 231

[1]*Moving target.*   [2]*Disappearing target.*

Small Bore Rifle (Team)

	Gold	Silver	Bronze
1908	Great Britain 771	Sweden 737	France 710
1912[1]	Sweden 925	Great Britain 917	United States 881
1912[2]	Great Britain 762	Sweden 748	United States 744
1920	United States 1899	Sweden 1873	Norway 1866

[1]*Over 25m.*   [2]*Over 50m.*

Live Pigeon Shooting

	Gold	Silver	Bronze
1900	Léon de Lunden (BEL) 21	Maurice Faure (FRA) 20	Donald MacIntosh (AUS) 18
			Crittenden Robinson (GBR) 18

Clay Pigeons (Team)

	Gold	Silver	Bronze
1908	Great Britain 407	Canada 405	Great Britain 372
1912	United States 532	Great Britain 511	Germany 510
1920	United States 547	Belgium 503	Sweden 500
1924	United States 363	Canada 360	Finland 360

Running Deer Shooting

	Gold	Silver	Bronze
1908[1]	Oscar Swahn (SWE) 25	Ted Ranken (GBR) 24	Alexander Rogers (GBR) 24
1908[2]	Walter Winans (USA) 46	Ted Ranken (GBR) 46	Oscar Swahn (SWE) 38
1912[1]	Alfred Swahn (SWE) 41	Ake Lundeberg (SWE) 41	Nestori Toivonen (FIN) 41
1912[2]	Ake Lundeberg (SWE) 79	Edvard Benedicks (SWE) 74	Oscar Swahn (SWE) 72
1920[1]	Otto Olsen (NOR) 43	Alfred Swahn (SWE) 41	Harald Natwig (NOR) 41
1920[2]	Ole Lilloe-Olsen (NOR) 82	Fredrik Landelius (SWE) 77	Einar Liberg (NOR) 71
1924[1]	John Boles (USA) 40	Cyril Mackworth-Praed (GBR) 39	Otto Olsen (NOR) 39
1924[2]	Ole Lilloe-Olsen (NOR) 76	Cyril Mackworth-Praed (GBR) 72	Alfred Swahn (SWE) 72

[1]*Single shot.*   [2]*Double shot.*

Running Deer Shooting (Team)

	Gold	Silver	Bronze
1908	Sweden 86	Great Britain 85	–
1912	Sweden 151	United States 132	Finland 123
1920[1]	Norway 178	Finland 159	United States 158
1920[2]	Norway 343	Sweden 336	Finland 284
1924[1]	Norway 160	Sweden 154	United States 158
1924[2]	Great Britain 263	Norway 262	Sweden 250

[1]*Single shot.*   [2]*Double shot.*

Running Deer Shooting (Single & Double Shot)

	Gold	Silver	Bronze
1952	John Larsen (NOR) 413	Per Olof Sköldberg (SWE) 409	Tauno Mäki (FIN) 407
1956	Vitaliy Romanenko (URS) 441	Per Olof Sköldberg (SWE) 432	Vladimir Sevrugin (URS) 429

Military Revolver

	Gold	Silver	Bronze
1896	John Paine (USA) 442	Sumner Paine (USA) 380	Nikolaos Morakis (GRE) 205
1906	Louis Richardet (SUI) 253	Alexandros Theophilakis (GRE) 250	Georgios Skotadis (GRE) 240
1906[1]	Jean Fouconnier (FRA) 219	Raoul de Boigne (FRA) 219	Hermann Martin (FRA) 215

[1]*Model 1873.*   1900–1904 Event not held.

Duelling Pistol

	Gold	Silver	Bronze
1906[1]	Léon Moreaux (FRA) 242	Cesare Liverziani (ITA) 233	Maurice Lecoq (FRA) 231
1906[2]	Konstantinos Skarlatos (GRE) 133	Johann von Holst (SWE) 115	Wilhelm Carlberg (SWE) 115

[1]*Over 20m.*   [2]*Over 25m.*   1896–1904 Event not held.

Team Event

	Gold	Silver	Bronze
1900	Switzerland 2271	France 2203	Netherlands 1876
1908	United States 1914	Belgium 1863	Great Britain 1817
1912[1]	United States 1916	Sweden 1849	Great Britain 1804
1912[2]	Sweden 1145	Russia d.n.a.	Great Britain d.n.a.
1920[1]	United States 2372	Sweden 2289	Brazil 2264
1920[2]	United States 1310	Greece 1285	Switzerland 1270

[1]*Over 50m.*   [2]*Over 30m.*   1904–1906 Event not held.

SOCCER

There were two unofficial matches at Athens in the first Games of 1896 when after two Greek towns had played an eliminator, the winners, Smyrna, were defeated by a Danish side 15–0. Although sometimes considered unofficial as well, the tournaments of 1900, 1904 and 1906 are usually counted in medal tables. Therefore soccer was the first team game to be included in the Olympics.

The first goal was scored by Great Britain (represented by Upton Park FC) in a 4–0 win over France in 1900. The 1904 tournament only had three entries, one Canadian and two American teams, while in 1906 a Danish team again beat Smyrna (this time representing Greece). In that latter team were five Britons named Whittal, who, if they were brothers as seems likely, set some sort of Olympic record for siblings.

With the founding of FIFA in 1904, Olympic soccer came under their control and from 1908 the competition grew in stature. In 1920 Egypt became the first non-European country – excepting the North Americans of 1904 – to enter, and by 1924 there were 22 countries competing. That tournament and the next were won by Uruguay, who surprisingly never took part in Olympic soccer again. Two years after their Amsterdam victory Uruguay won the inaugural World Cup of 1930 with nine of their Olympic team playing. Only three other players, all Italian, have played in both Olympic (1936) and World Cup (1938) winning sides.

There has been considerable disillusionment with the interpretation of the term 'amateur' as applied to soccer at the Games, similar to the troubles in ice hockey. These arguments about pseudo-amateurs were exacerbated with the entry of the Eastern European powers into the game after 1948. Great Britain, after three gold medals in the early days, did not enter in 1924 and 1928 due to disagreements between the national Football Association (FA) and FIFA about broken time payments to amateurs. In 1984 professionals were allowed to take part, but only those who had not yet participated in World Cup competition were eligible. Currently the only restriction on players is that they must be under 23 years of age. In 1952, as entries increased, qualifying rounds were introduced to decide the final 16 teams for the Olympic tournament.

The highest team score in Olympic soccer was the 17–1 defeat of France by Denmark in 1908, during which the Danish

A Danish shot at the British goal in the 1912 soccer final. Great Britain won 4–0, the Danes playing much of the game with only ten men.

centre-forward Sophus Nielsen scored a record 10 goals. This mark was equalled by Gottfried Fuchs for Germany when they beat Russia 16–0 in 1912. The most goals scored by an individual in one tournament is 12 by Ferenc Bene (HUN) in 1964. The most scored in Olympic competition is 13 by Sophus Nielsen (DEN), 1908–1912, and by Antal Dunai (HUN), 1968–1972.

The highest score in a final since the institution of 'proper' tournaments in 1908 has been the 4–2 defeat of Denmark by Great Britain in 1912. France's victory in 1984 was the first win by a Western European side since the outstanding Swedish team of 1948, and the first medal place since the Swedish bronze of four years later. The 1968 final ended with only 18 players on the field as three Bulgarians and a Hungarian had been sent off.

There has only been one draw in an Olympic final, 1–1 in 1928 between Uruguay and Argentina. The replay was won by the defending champions Uruguay, 2–1. Hungary is the only country to win on three occasions. Their team which won in Helsinki in 1952 was virtually the same team that 16 months later inflicted the first home defeat on England's professionals at Wembley stadium.

The most successful player has been Dezso Nowak (HUN) who added gold medals in 1964 and 1968 to the bronze he won in 1960. Of the nine other players to win two gold medals only Arthur Berry and Vivian Woodward (both GBR) were not Uruguayans. Two of those latter, Antonio and Santos Urdinaran, became the first brothers to win soccer gold medals in 1924. This feat was surpassed by the Swedish Nordahl brothers, Bertil, Knut and Gunnar, in 1948. In 1960 another trio, Hans, Flemming

and Harald Nielsen (DEN) gained silver medals. In 1908 two other Danish brothers had gained silver medals in a team which included Harald Bohr, the brother of the famous atomic physicist Niels.

The oldest gold medallist was Vivian Woodward (GBR), who had just helped his club Chelsea get back into the English First Division, aged 33yr 32 days in the 1912 final. The youngest was Pedro Petrone (URU), the highest scoring player of the 1924 tournament, who was just two days short of his 19th birthday in the final match.

One of the most remarkable goals in international football involved the Swedish centre-forward Gunnar Nordahl in the 1948 semi-final against Denmark. Unexpectedly caught offside by a quick reversal of play, Nordahl realised that his team were attacking again. With lightning presence of mind he leapt into the back of the Danish goal,

SOCCER MEDALS

	Gold	Silver	Bronze
1900	Great Britain	France	Belgium
1904	Canada	United States	United States
1906	Denmark	Greece	Greece
1908	Great Britain	Denmark	Netherlands
1912	Great Britain	Denmark	Netherlands
1920	Belgium	Spain	Netherlands
1924	Uruguay	Switzerland	Sweden
1928	Uruguay	Argentina	Italy
1936	Italy	Austria	Norway
1948	Sweden	Yugoslavia	Denmark
1952	Hungary	Yugoslavia	Sweden
1956	Soviet Union	Yugoslavia	Bulgaria
1960	Yugoslavia	Denmark	Hungary
1964	Hungary	Czechoslovakia	Germany
1968	Hungary	Bulgaria	Japan
1972	Poland	Hungary	GDR[1]
			Soviet Union[1]
1976	GDR	Poland	Soviet Union
1980	Czechoslovakia	GDR	Soviet Union
1984	France	Brazil	Yugoslavia
1988	Soviet Union	Brazil	FRG

[1]*Tie declared after extra time played.*
1896, 1932 Event not held.

SOCCER MEDAL TOTALS

Country	G	S	B	Total
Hungary	3	1	1	5
Soviet Union	2	–	3	5
Denmark	1	3	1	5
Yugoslavia	1	3	1	5
Great Britain	3	–	–	3
GDR	1	1	1	3
Sweden	1	–	2	3
Netherlands	–	–	3	3
Uruguay	2	–	–	2
Czechoslovakia	1	1	–	2
France	1	1	–	2
Poland	1	1	–	2
Belgium	1	–	1	2
Italy	1	–	1	2
Brazil	–	2	–	2
Bulgaria	–	1	1	2
Greece	–	1	1	2
United States	–	1	1	2
Germany (FRG)	–	–	2	2
Canada	1	–	–	1
Argentina	–	1	–	1
Austria	–	1	–	1
Spain	–	1	–	1
Switzerland	–	1	–	1
Japan	–	–	1	1
Norway	–	–	1	1
	20	20	21[1]	61

[1]*Third place tie in 1972.*

taking himself off the field of play, and duly caught the goal-scoring header from his team-mate Henry Carlsson with the goalkeeper on the ground five metres away.

In the 1920 final between Belgium and Czechoslovakia, the Czechs walked off the field in protest against the referee before half-time when they were 2–0 down. The match was abandoned and Czechoslovakia disqualified. The 1936 tournament resulted in many incidents, not least the withdrawal of the Peruvian team when its win over Austria in the second round was ordered to be re-played. Austria went on to reach the final.

HIGHEST SCORERS IN OLYMPIC TOURNAMENTS

1908	11	Sophus Nielsen (DEN)	1960	7	Milan Galic (YUG) & Borivoje Kostic (YUG)
1912	10	Gottfried Fuchs (FRG)			
1920	7	Herbert Carlsson (SWE)	1964	12	Ferenc Bene (HUN)
1924	8	Pedro Petrone (URU)	1968	7	Kunishige Kamamoto (JPN)
1928	7	Domingo Tarasconi (ARG)	1972	9	Kazimiercz Deyna (POL)
1936	7	Annibale Frossi (ITA)	1976	6	Andrzej Szarmach (POL)
1948	7	Gunnar Nordahl (SWE) & Karl Aage Hansen (DEN)	1980	5	Sergey Andreyev (URS)
			1984	5	Borislav Cvetkovic (YUG), Stjepan Deveric (YUG) & Daniel Xuereb (FRA)
1952	7	Branko Zebec (YUG) & Rajko Mitic (YUG)			
1956	4	Dimiter Milanov (BUL) & Neville d'Souza (IND)	1988	7	Romario Farias (BRA)

After many years in the doldrums, Olympic soccer experienced a revival in 1980 when the 56 games of the tournament, played in Moscow, Leningrad, Minsk and Kiev, attracted nearly two million spectators – over a third of all spectators for the 1980 Games. This revival was reinforced, somewhat surprisingly, in Los Angeles in 1984, when nearly 1½ million watched the matches, including a record 101 799 audience for the final.

A spectacular leap by the Peruvian goalkeeper against Austria in the 1936 tournament, in a match won by Peru but ordered to be replayed. Peru refused – and Austria went on to take the silver medal, behind Italy.

SWIMMING

The sport has been an integral part of the Games since 1896 when the swimming was held in the Bay of Zea near Piraeus. The first champion was Alfred Hajós (ne Guttmann) of Hungary who won the 100m freestyle in freezing water. The first female champion (women's events were introduced in 1912) was Australia's Fanny Durack, also in the 100m freestyle. The first Olympic competition in a pool was in 1908, in a 100m long tank constructed inside the track at the White City Stadium, London. The first 50m pool was in 1924 (outdoors) and the first one indoors was at Wembley, London in 1948. Emil Rausch (GER) in 1904 was the last to win an Olympic title using the side-stroke technique.

The most successful swimmer was Mark Spitz (USA) with nine gold medals plus a silver and a bronze in 1968 and 1972. His seven golds at one Games (1972) is unmatched in any sport. The most individual event golds won is four by Charles Daniels (USA), 1904–1908, Roland Matthes (GDR) 1968–1972, Spitz 1972, and Kristin Otto (GDR) in 1988. Otto's final tally of six golds at Seoul set female records for most overall and most at a single Games.

Otto is also the only swimmer to win Olympic titles in three different strokes – freestyle, backstroke and butterfly. Dawn Fraser (AUS) is the only swimmer, male or female, to win the same event (100m freestyle) three times. Three women have won a record eight medals: Fraser (1956–64) and East German Kornelia Ender (1972–76), both with four golds and four silvers, and Shirley Babashoff (USA) with two gold and uniquely six silver medals in 1972 and 1976. Both Spitz and

Babashoff set an endurance record of sorts in 1972 and 1976 respectively by taking part in 13 races within eight days.

The first swimmer successfully to defend an Olympic swimming title was Charles Daniels (USA) when he retained the 100m freestyle title in 1908. The first woman to do so was Martha Norelius (USA) in 1928 with the 400m freestyle. She was born in Sweden and her father Charles had been a member of the 1906 Swedish Olympic swimming team, while an uncle, Bengt, had won gold in the 1912 gymnastics. Later she married the 1928 Canadian silver medallist oarsman Joseph Wright.

The oldest gold medallist was Italian-born Louis Handley (USA) in the 1904 relay team, aged 30yr 206 days. He later coached the aforementioned Norelius. The oldest female champion was Ursula Happe (GER) in the 1956 200m breaststroke, aged 30yr 41 days. The oldest medallist was William Henry (GBR), a last minute replacement in the 1906 relay, aged 46yr 301 days.

The youngest gold medallist was Lillian 'Pokey' Watson (USA) in the 4 × 100m freestyle in 1964, aged 14yr 96 days. The youngest male champion was Kusuo Kitamura (JPN) in the 1500m in 1932 aged 14yr 309 days, while the youngest known medallist in any sport at the Games was Inge Sörensen (DEN), aged 12yr 24 days when winning a bronze in the 200m breaststroke of 1936. The youngest known competitor in any Summer Games sport was swimmer Liana Vicens of Puerto Rico in 1968, aged 11yr 328 days.

The first dead heat in Games swimming came in the 1984 women's 100m freestyle final

when Carrie Steinsteifer and Nancy Hogshead (both USA) gained a gold medal each. Also in those Games there was a strange situation when the winner of the 400m freestyle 'B' final, Thomas Fahrner (FRG), set an Olympic record faster than the winner of the 'A' final. The closest to a dead heat in the men's events was in the 1972 400m medley when Gunnar Larsson (SWE) was given the decision over Tim McKee (USA). The margin was two-thousandths of a second or about 3 millimetres (estimated to be the length grown by a fingernail in 3 weeks). Happily, timings and placings are now decided to hundredths only, and the above would now be given as a dead heat. Another controversial decision occurred in the 1960 100m freestyle when Lance Larson (USA) was timed (manually) at one-tenth faster than John Devitt (AUS), but the judges placed the Australian first – and that is how the result remained despite protests.

In the 1912 100m competition, the three best American swimmers missed the semi-finals because they had been told that there would not be any. Following protests, it was agreed that if they were timed in a special race at faster than the slowest qualifier from those semis, then they would go forward to the final. The outstanding Hawaiian swimmer Duke Kahanamoku was so incensed that he broke the world record, and then won the final.

At the next Games in 1920, the final was re-swum after the Australian William Herald complained that he was impeded by Norman Ross (USA) – this was before lane dividers were used. The original winner, Duke Kahanamoku (USA), won again – in a slower time than before, but his first time of 60.4sec was recognised as a world record.

The three medallists in the Berlin high diving. From left: Kathe Köhler (GER) bronze, Velma Dunn (USA) silver, and Dorothy Poynton-Hill (USA) gold. The latter retained her 1932 title.

Kahanamoku, the first of the great Hawaiian swimmers, was born into the Hawaiian Royal Family and was named 'Duke' after the Duke of Edinburgh, Queen Victoria's second son, who was visiting the Palace at the time. He was a pioneer of surfing, made many movies in Hollywood, and was the oldest individual event champion in 1920 when 5 days past his 30th birthday.

Hollywood has attracted a number of Olympian swimmers. Romanian-born Johnny Weissmuller (USA) won five gold medals (1924–1928) and then became the most famous 'Tarzan' of them all. Clarence 'Buster' Crabbe (USA), the 1932 backstroke champion, became 'Flash Gordon' and 'Buck Rogers' in children's serials. Aileen Riggin (USA), the 1920 diving champion and Eleanor Holm (USA), the 1932 backstroke champion, both took their good looks into movies. Holm was also in a Tarzan movie in 1938 – she was Jane to the hero played by 1936 decathlon champion Glenn Morris.

Gertrude Ederle (USA) and Greta Andersen (DEN), gold medallists in 1924 and 1948 respectively, both later set English Channel swimming records.

DIVING

Men's diving was introduced into the Games in 1904, and women's in 1912. The most successful diver has been Greg Louganis (USA) with four golds (a double 'double') from 1984–1988 and a silver in 1976. Austrian-born Klaus Dibiasi (ITA) won three gold and two silver medals from 1964 to 1976, uniquely winning the same event three times and gaining medals in four Games.

Pat McCormick (USA) set a female record of four golds in 1952 and 1956. Her daughter

Kelly won a silver in 1984 and a bronze in 1988. Dorothy Poynton-Hill (USA) from 1928–1936 and Paula Myers-Pope (USA) from 1952–1960 have won medals in three separate Games, while Juno Stover-Irwin (USA) competed in four Games with fifth, third, second and fourth places respectively from 1948 to 1960.

The oldest gold medallist was Hjalmar Johansson (SWE), aged 34yr 186 days in the plain diving at London in 1908, and also the oldest ever medallist four years later in Stockholm with a silver aged 38yr 173 days. The youngest champion, and the youngest individual Olympic champion at any sport, was Marjorie Gestring (USA) who won the 1936 springboard title aged 13yr 267 days. The youngest male diving champion was Albert Zürner (GER) in 1908,

aged 18yr 170 days. Dorothy Poynton-Hill (USA) was the youngest medallist in 1928 aged 13yr 23 days, while the youngest male medallist was Nils Skoglund (SWE), aged 14yr 10 days, also in 1920. Greg Louganis (USA) won both diving titles in 1984 by the biggest margins ever recorded at the Games.

Four divers, three women and a man, have won medals at swimming as well as diving. The most successful was Aileen Riggin (USA) with gold and silver diving medals in 1920 and 1924 respectively, and a bronze in the backstroke at Paris. Georg Hoffmann (GER) won silvers in 1904 at diving and the 100m backstroke; Katherine Rawls (USA) won a silver in the 1936 springboard and a bronze in the relay; and Hjördis Töpel (SWE) won bronzes at diving and the

OLYMPIC SWIMMING RECORDS

Men

50m free	22.14s	Matt Biondi (USA)	1988
100m free	48.63s	Matt Biondi (USA)	1988
200m free	1m 47.25s	Duncan Armstrong (AUS)	1988
400m free	3m 46.95s	Uwe Dassler (GDR)	1988
1500m free	14m 58.27s	Vladimir Salnikov (URS)	1980
4 x 100m free	3m 16.53s	USA	1988
4 x 200m free	7m 12.51s	USA	1988
100m breast	1m 01.65s	Steve Lundquist (USA)	1984
200m breast	2m 13.34s	Victor Davis (CAN)	1984
100m back	54.512*	David Berkoff (USA)	1988
200m back	1m 58.99s*	Richard Carey (USA)	1984
100m butterfly	53.00s	Anthony Nesty (SUR)	1988
200m butterfly	1m 56.94s	Michael Gross (FRG)	1988
200m medley	2m 00.17s	Tamas Darnyi (HUN)	1988
400m medley	4m 14.75s	Tamas Darnyi (HUN)	1988
4 x 100m medley	3m 36.93s	USA	1988

Women

50m free	25.49s	Kristin Otto (GDR)	1988
100m free	54.79s	Barbara Krause (GDR)	1980
200m free	1m 57.65s	Heike Friedrich (GDR)	1988
400m free	4m 03.85s	Janet Evans (USA)	1988
800m free	8m 20.20s	Janet Evans (USA)	1988
4 x 100m free	3m 40.63s	GDR	1988
100m breast	1m 07.95s	Tania Dangalakova (URS)	1988
200m breast	2m 26.71s	Silke Hörner (GDR)	1988
100m back	1m 00.86s	Rica Reinisch (GDR)	1980
200m back	2m 09.29s	Krisztina Egerszegi (HUN)	1988
100m butterfly	59.00s	Kristin Otto (GDR)	1988
200m butterfly	2m 06.90s	Mary Meagher (USA)	1984
200m medley	2m 12.59s	Daniela Hunger (GDR)	1988
400m medley	4m 36.29s	Petra Schneider (GDR)	1980
4 x 100m medley	4m 03.74s	GDR	1988

*In preliminary round

London 1948, and the Hungarian water polo team practises in the Empire Pool, Wembley.

relay in 1924.

The most successful husband and wife team were the Americans Clarence and Elizabeth (née Becker) Pinkston, who between them won three golds, two silvers and two bronzes from 1920 to 1928. Elizabeth won her second gold medal, in 1928, on the second birthday of her twin children.

SYNCHRONIZED SWIMMING

Introduced into the Games in 1984, there are solo and duet events. The most successful women have been Tracie Ruiz-Conforto (USA) and Carolyn Waldo (CAN), both with two golds and one silver in 1984-88. The youngest gold medallist was Candy Costie (USA) in the 1984 duet, aged 21yr 150 days, while the oldest was Michelle Cameron (CAN) in the 1988 duet, aged 25yr 278 days. Sarah and Karen Josephson (USA) are among the most successful twins ever in Olympic swimming with their silver medal placing in 1988.

WATER POLO

The first Olympic contest was won by the Osborne Swimming Club, Manchester, representing Great Britain in 1900. Five players have won three gold medals each: George Wilkinson (GBR) in 1900, 1908 and 1912; Paul Radmilovic and Charles Smith (both GBR) from 1908-1920; and Dezsö Gyarmati and György Kárpáti (HUN) in 1952, 1956 and 1964. Of these, Radmilovic, Welsh-born of a Greek father and Irish mother, also won a gold in the 4 × 200m team in 1908, and competed in a record six Olympic tournaments from 1906-1928.

Gyarmati was the most successful player, adding a silver in 1948 and a bronze in 1960, and is one of the few Olympians in any sport to win medals in five Games. He also heads a fine Olympic family, as his wife Éva Székely won a gold (1952) and a silver (1956) in the 200m breaststroke, and their daughter Andrea won silver and bronze medals in the 1972 backstroke and butterfly events respec-

tively. She then added to the family total of medals by marrying Mihaly Hesz (HUN), a canoeist who won a gold (1968 K1) and a silver (1964 K1).

The oldest gold medallist was Charles Smith (GBR), aged 41yr 217 days in 1920, while the youngest was György Kárpáti (HUN) in 1952, aged 17yr 40 days. The first brothers to win gold medals in the same team were Ferenc and Alajos Keserü (HUN) in 1932, and they were matched by Tulio and Franco Pandolfini (ITA) in 1948. Georgi Mshvenieradze (URS) won a gold medal in 1980, going one better than his father Piotr who had gained a silver (1960) and a bronze (1956).

A number of men have won medals at both swimming and water polo, the most notable being Johnny Weissmuller (USA) who gained a bronze in 1924 on the same day that he won two freestyle golds. Tim Shaw (USA), who won a silver medal in the 1976 400m freestyle, won another in the 1984 water polo competition.

SWIMMING MEDALS – MEN

	Gold	Silver	Bronze

50 Metres Freestyle

	Gold	Silver	Bronze
1988	Matt Biondi (USA) 22.14*	Thomas Jager (USA) 22.36	Gennadiy Prigoda (URS) 22.71

1896–1984 Event not held.   *Olympic record

100 Metres Freestyle

	Gold	Silver	Bronze
1896	Alfred Hajos (HUN 1:22.2	Efstathios Choraphas (GRE) 1:23.0	Otto Herschmann (AUT) d.n.a.
1904¹	Zóltán Halmay (HUN) 1:02.8	Charles Daniels (USA) d.n.a.	Scott Leary (USA) d.n.a.
1906	Charles Daniels (USA) 1:13.4	Zóltán Halmay (HUN) 1:14.2	Cecil Healy (AUS) d.n.a.
1908	Charles Daniels (USA) 1:05.6	Zóltán Halmay (HUN) 1:06.2	Harald Julin (SWE) 1:08.0
1912	Duke Kahanamoku (USA) 1:03.4	Cecil Healy (AUS) 1:04.6	Kenneth Huszagh (USA) 1:05.6
1920	Duke Kahanamoku (USA) 1:01.4	Pua Kealoha (USA) 1:02.2	William Harris (USA) 1:03.0
1924	Johnny Weissmuller (USA) 59.0	Duke Kahanamoku (USA) 1:01.4	Sam Kahanamoku (USA) 1:01.8
1928	Johnny Weissmuller (USA) 58.6	István Bárány (HUN) 59.8	Katsuo Takaishi (JPN) 1:00.0
1932	Yasuji Miyazaki (JPN) 58.2	Tatsugo Kawaishi (JPN) 58.6	Albert Schwartz (USA) 58.8
1936	Ferenc Csik (HUN) 57.6	Masanori Yusa (JPN) 57.9	Shigeo Arai (JPN) 58.0
1948	Walter Ris (USA) 57.3	Alan Ford (USA) 57.8	Géza Kádas (HUN) 58.1
1952	Clarke Scholes (USA) 57.4	Hiroshi Suzuki (JPN) 57.4	Göran Larsson (SWE) 58.2
1956	Jon Henricks (AUS) 55.4	John Devitt (AUS) 55.8	Gary Chapman (AUS) 56.7
1960	John Devitt (AUS) 55.2	Lance Larson (USA) 55.2	Manuel dos Santos (BRA) 55.4
1964	Don Schollander (USA) 53.4	Bobbie McGregor (GBR) 53.5	Hans-Joachim Klein (GER) 54.0
1968	Mike Wenden (AUS) 52.2	Ken Walsh (USA) 52.8	Mark Spitz (USA) 53.0
1972	Mark Spitz (USA) 51.22	Jerry Heidenreich (USA) 51.65	Vladimir Bure (URS) 51.77
1976	Jim Montgomery (USA) 49.99	Jack Babashoff (USA) 50.81	Peter Nocke (FRG) 51.31
1980	Jörg Woithe (GDR) 50.40	Per Holmertz (SWE) 50.91	Per Johansson (SWE) 51.29
1984	Ambrose Gaines (USA) 49.80	Mark Stockwell (AUS) 50.24	Per Johansson (SWE) 50.31
1988	Matt Biondi (USA) 48.63*	Chris Jacobs (USA) 49.08	Stephan Caron (FRA) 49.62

¹100 yards.   *Olympic record.   1900 Event not held.

200 Metres Freestyle

	Gold	Silver	Bronze
1900	Frederick Lane (AUS) 2:25.2	Zóltán Halmay (HUN) 2:31.4	Karl Ruberl (AUT) 2:32.0
1904¹	Charles Daniels (USA) 2:44.2	Francis Gailey (USA) 2:46.0	Emil Raush (GER) 2:56.0
1968	Mike Wenden (AUS) 1:55.2	Don Schollander (USA) 1:55.8	John Nelson (USA) 1:58.1
1972	Mark Spitz (USA) 1:52.78	Steven Genter (USA) 1:53.73	Werner Lampe (FRG) 1:53.99
1976	Bruce Furniss (USA) 1:50.29	John Naber (USA) 1:50.50	Jim Montgomery (USA) 1:50.58
1980	Sergey Kopliakov (URS) 1:49.81	Andrej Krylov (URS) 1:50.76	Graeme Brewer (AUS) 1:51.60
1984	Michael Gross (FRG) 1:47.44	Michael Heath (USA) 1:49.10	Thomas Fahrner (FRG) 1:49.69
1988	Duncan Armstrong (AUS) 1:47.25*	Anders Holmertz (SWE) 1:47.89	Matt Biondi (USA) 1:47.99

¹220 yards.   *Olympic record.   1896, 1906–1964 Event not held.

400 Metres Freestyle

	Gold	Silver	Bronze
1896¹	Paul Neuman (AUT) 8:12.6	Antonios Pepanos (GRE) 30m	Efstathios Choraphas (GRE) d.n.a.
1904²	Charles Daniels (USA) 6:16.2	Francis Gailey (USA) 6:22.0	Otto Wahle (AUT) 6:39.0
1906	Otto Scheff (AUT) 6:23.8	Henry Taylor (GBR) 6:24.4	John Jarvis (GBR) 6:27.2
1908	Henry Taylor (GBR) 5:36.8	Frank Beaurepaire (AUS) 5:44.2	Otto Scheff (AUT) 5:46.0
1912	George Hodgson (CAN) 5:24.4	John Hatfield (GBR) 5:25.8	Harold Hardwick (AUS) 5:31.2
1920	Norman Ross (USA) 5:26.8	Ludy Langer (USA) 5:29.2	George Vernot (CAN) 5:29.8
1924	Johnny Weissmuller (USA) 5:04.2	Arne Borg (SWE) 5:05.6	Andrew Charlton (AUS) 5:06.6
1928	Alberto Zorilla (ARG) 5:01.6	Andrew Charlton (AUS) 5:03.6	Arne Borg (SWE) 5:04.6
1932	Buster Crabbe (USA) 4:48.4	Jean Taris (FRA) 4:48.5	Tautomu Oyokota (JPN) 4:52.3
1936	Jack Medica (USA) 4:44.5	Shumpei Uto (JPN) 4:45.6	Shozo Makino (JPN) 4:28.1
1948	William Smith (USA) 4:41.0	James McLane (USA) 4:43.4	John Marshall (AUS) 4:47.7
1952	Jean Boiteux (USA) 4:30.7	Ford Konno (USA) 4:31.3	Per-Olof Ostrand (SWE) 4:35.2
1956	Murray Rose (AUS) 4:27.3	Tsuyoshi Yamanaka (JPN) 4:30.4	George Breen (USA) 4:32.5
1960	Murray Rose (AUS) 4:18.3	Tsuyoshi Yamanaka (JPN) 4:21.4	John Konrads (AUS) 4:21.8
1964	Don Schollander (USA) 4:12.2	Frank Wiegand (GER) 4:14.9	Allan Wood (AUS) 4:15.1
1968	Mike Burton (USA) 4:09.0	Ralph Hutton (CAN) 4:11.7	Alain Mosconi (FRA) 4:13.3
1972	Brad Cooper (AUS) 4:00.27	Steven Genter (USA) 4:01.94	Tom McBeen (USA) 4:02.64
1976	Brian Goodell (USA) 3:51.93	Tim Shaw (USA) 3:52.54	Vladimir Raskatov (URS) 3:55.76
1980	Vladimir Salnikov (URS) 3:51.31	Andrej Krylov (URS) 3:53.24	Ivar Stukolkin (URS) 3:53.95
1984	George DiCarlo (USA) 3:51.23	John Mykkanen (USA) 3:51.49	Justin Lemberg (AUS) 3:51.79
1988	Uwe Dassler (GDR) 3:46.95*	Duncan Armstrong (AUS) 3:47.15	Artur Wojdat (POL) 3:47.34

¹500m.   ²440 yards.   *Olympic record.   1900 Event not held.

	Gold	Silver	Bronze

1500 Metres Freestyle

	Gold	Silver	Bronze
1896[1]	Alfred Hajós (HUN) 18;22.2	Jean Andreou (GRE) 21:03.4	Efstathios Choraphas (GRE) d.n.a.
1900[2]	John Jarvis (GBR) 13:40.2	Otto Wahle (AUT) 14:53.6	Zóltán Halmay (HUN) 15:16.4
1904[3]	Emil Rausch (GER) 27:18.2	Géza Kiss (HUN) 28:28.2	Francis Gailey (USA) 28:54.0
1906[3]	Henry Taylor (GBR) 28:28.0	John Jarvis (GBR) 30:13.0	Otto Scheff (AUT) 30:59.0
1908	Henry Taylor (GBR) 22:48.4	Sydney Battersby (GBR) 22:51.2	Frank Beaurepaire (AUS) 22:56.2
1912	George Hodgson (CAN) 22:00.0	John Hatfield (GBR) 22:39.0	Harold Hardwick (AUS) 23:15.4
1920	Norman Ross (USA) 22:23.2	George Vernot (CAN) 22:36.4	Frank Beaurepaire (AUS) 23:04.0
1924	Andrew Charlton (AUS) 20:06.6	Arne Borg (SWE) 20:41.4	Frank Beaurepaire (AUS) 21:48.4
1928	Arne Borg (SWE) 19:51.8	Andrew Charlton (AUS) 20:02.6	Buster Crabbe (USA) 20:28.8
1932	Kusuo Kitamura (JPN) 19:12.4	Shozo Makino (JPN) 19:14.1	James Christy (USA) 19:39.5
1936	Noboru Terada (JPN) 19:13.7	Jack Medica (USA) 19:34.0	Shumpei Uto (JPN) 19:34.5
1948	James McLane (USA) 19:18.5	John Marshall (AUS) 19:31.3	György Mitro (HUN) 19:43.2
1952	Ford Konno (USA) 18:30.0	Shiro Hashizune (JPN) 18:41.4	Tetsuo Okamoto (BRA) 18:51.3
1956	Murray Rose (AUS) 17:58.9	Tsuyoshi Yamanaka (JPN) 18:00.3	George Breen (USA) 18:08.2
1960	John Konrads (AUS) 17:19.6	Murray Rose (AUS) 17:21.7	George Breen (USA) 17:30.6
1964	Bob Windle (USA) 17:01.7	John Nelson (USA) 17:03.0	Allan Wood (AUS) 17:07.7
1968	Mike Burton (USA) 16:38.9	John Kinsella (USA) 16:57.3	Greg Brough (AUS) 17:04.7
1972	Mike Burton (USA) 15:52.58	Graham Windeatt (AUS) 15:58.48	Doug Northway (USA) 16:09.25
1976	Brian Goodell (USA) 15:02.40	Bobby Hackett (USA) 15:03.91	Steve Holland (AUS) 15:04.66
1980	Vladimir Salnikov (URS) 14:58.27*	Aleksandr Chaev (URS) 15:14.30	Max Metzker (AUS) 15:14.49
1984	Michael O'Brien (USA) 15:05.20	George DiCarlo (USA) 15:10.59	Stefan Pfeiffer (FRG) 15:12.11
1988	Vladimir Salnikov (URS) 15:00.40	Stevan Pfeiffer (FRG) 15:02.69	Uwe Dassler (GDR) 15:06.15

[1] 1200m. [2] 1000m. [3] 1 mile. *Olympic record.

100 Metres Breaststroke

	Gold	Silver	Bronze
1968	Don McKenzie (USA) 1:07.7	Vladimir Kossinsky (URS) 1:08.0	Nikolai Pankin (URS) 1:08.0
1972	Nobutaka Taguchi (JPN) 1:04.94	Tom Bruce (USA) 1:05.43	John Hencken (USA) 1:05.61
1976	John Hencken (USA) 1:03.11	David Wilkie (GBR) 1:03.43	Arvidas Iuozaytis (URS) 1:04.23
1980	Duncan Goodhew (GBR) 1:03.34	Arsen Miskarov (URS) 1:03.92	Peter Evans (AUS) 1:03.96
1984	Steve Lundquist (USA) 1:01.65*	Victor Davis (CAN) 1:01.99	Peter Evans (AUS) 1:02.97
1988	Adrian Moorhouse (GBR) 1:02.04	Karoly Guttler (HUN) 1:02.05	Dmitry Volkov (URS) 1:02.20

*Olympic record. 1896–1964 Event not held.

200 Metres Breaststroke

	Gold	Silver	Bronze
1908	Frederick Holman (GBR) 3:09.2	William Robinson (GBR) 3:12.8	Pontus Hansson (SWE) 3:14.6
1912	Walter Bathe (GER) 3:01.8	Wilhelm Lützow (GER) 3:05.2	Kurt Malisch (GER) 3:08.0
1920	Häken Malmroth (SWE) 3:04.4	Thor Henning (SWE) 3:09.2	Arvo Aaltonen (FIN) 3:12.2
1924	Robert Skelton (USA) 2:56.5	Joseph de Combe (BEL) 2:59.2	William Kirschbaum (USA) 3:01.0
1928	Yoshiyuki Tsuruta (JPN) 2:48.8	Erich Rademacher (GER) 2:50.6	Teofilo Ylidefonzo (PHI) 2:56.4
1932	Yoshiyuki Tsuruta (JPN) 2:45.4	Reizo Koike (JPN) 2:46.4	Teofilo Ylidefonzo (PHI) 2:47.1
1936	Tetsuo Hamuro (JPN) 2:42.5	Erwin Sietas (GER) 2:42.9	Reizo Koike (JPN) 2:44.2
1948	Joseph Verdeur[1] (USA) 2:39.3	Keith Carter (USA) 2:40.2	Robert Sohl (USA) 2:43.9
1952	John Davies[1] (AUS) 2:34.4	Bowen Stassforth (USA) 2:34.7	Herbert Klein (GER) 2:35.9
1956	Masaru Furukawa[2] (JPN) 2:34.7	Masahiro Yoshimura (JPN) 2:36.7	Charis Yunitschev (URS) 2:36.8
1960	William Mulliken (USA) 2:37.4	Yoshihiko Osaki (JPN) 2:38.0	Wieger Mensonides (HOL) 2:39.7
1964	Ian O'Brien (AUS) 2:27.8	Georgy Prokopenko (URS) 2:28.2	Chester Jastremski (USA) 2:29.6
1968	Felipe Munoz (MEX) 2:28.7	Vladimir Kossinsky (URS) 2:29.2	Brian Job (USA) 2:29.9
1972	John Hencken (USA) 2:21.55	David Wilkie (GBR) 2:23.67	Nobutaka Taguchi (JPN) 2:23.88
1976	David Wilkie (GBR) 2:15.11	John Hencken (USA) 2:17.26	Rick Colella (USA) 2:19.20
1980	Robertas Shulpa (URS) 2:15.85	Alban Vermes (HUN) 2:16.93	Arsen Miskarov (URS) 2:17.28
1984	Victor Davis (CAN) 2:13.34*	Glenn Beringen (AUS) 2:15.79	Etienne Dagon (SUI) 2:17.41
1988	Jozsef Szabo (HUN) 2:13.52	Nick Gillingham (GBR) 2:14.12	Sergio Lopez (ESP) 2:15.21

[1] Used then permissible butterfly stroke. [2] Used then permissible underwater technique. *Olympic record.
1896–1906 Event not held.

100 Metres Backstroke

	Gold	Silver	Bronze
1904[1]	Walter Brack (GER) 1:16.8	Georg Hoffmann (GER) 1:18.0	Georg Zacharias (GER) 1:19.6
1908	Arno Bieberstein (GER) 1:24.6	Ludvig Dam (DEN) 1:26.6	Herbert Haresnape (GBR) 1:27.0
1912	Harry Hebner (USA) 1:21.2	Otto Fahr (GER) 1:22.4	Paul Kellner (GER) 1:24.0
1920	Warren Kealoha (USA) 1:15.2	Ray Kegeris (USA) 1:16.2	Gérard Blitz (BEL) 1:19.0
1924	Warren Kealoha (USA) 1:13.2	Paul Wyatt (USA) 1:15.4	Károly Bartha (HUN) 1:17.8
1928	George Kojac (USA) 1:08.2	Walter Laufer (USA) 1:10.0	Paul Wyatt (USA) 1:12.0
1932	Masaji Kiyokawa (JPN) 1:08.6	Toshio Irie (JPN) 1:09.8	Kentaro Kawatsu (JPN) 1:10.0
1936	Adolf Kiefer (USA) 1:05.9	Albert Van de Weghe (USA) 1:07.7	Masaji Kiyokawa (JPN) 1:08.4
1948	Allen Stack (USA) 1:06.4	Robert Cowell (USA) 1:06.5	Georges Vallerey (FRA) 1:07.8
1952	Yoshinobu Oyakawa (USA) 1:05.4	Gilbert Bozon (FRA) 1:06.2	Jack Taylor (USA) 1:06.4

	Gold	Silver	Bronze
1956	David Theile (AUS) 1:02.2	John Monckton (AUS) 1:03.2	Frank McKinney (USA) 1:04.5
1960	David Theile (AUS) 1:01.9	Frank McKinney (USA) 1:02.1	Robert Bennett (USA) 1:02.3
1968	Roland Matthes (GDR) 58.7	Charles Hickcox (USA) 1:00.2	Ronnie Mills (USA) 1:00.5
1972	Roland Matthes (GDR) 56.58	Mike Stamm (USA) 57.70	John Murphy (USA) 58.35
1976	John Naber (USA) 55.49	Peter Rocca (USA) 45.34	Roland Matthes (GDR) 57.22
1980	Bengt Baron (SWE) 56.53	Viktor Kuznetsov (URS) 56.99	Vladimir Dolgov (URS) 57.63
1984	Richard Carey (USA) 55.79	David Wilson (USA) 56.35	Mike West (CAN) 56.49
1988	Daichi Suzuki (JPN) 55.05*	David Berkoff (USA) 55.18	Igor Polianski (URS) 55.20

¹ *100 yards.   *Olympic record of 54.51 in heats by Berkoff.*   1896–1900, 1906, 1964 Event not held.

200 Metres Backstroke

1900	Ernst Hoppenberg (GER) 2:47.0	Karl Ruberl (AUT) 2:56.0	Johannes Drost (HOL) 3:01.0
1964	Jed Graef (USA) 2:10.3	Gary Dilley (USA) 2:10.5	Robert Bennett (USA) 2:13.1
1968	Roland Matthes (GDR) 2:09.6	Mitchell Ivey (USA) 2:10.6	Jack Horsley (USA) 2:10.9
1972	Roland Matthes (GDR) 2:02.82	Mike Stamm (USA) 2:04.09	Mitchell Ivey (USA) 2:04.33
1976	John Naber (USA) 1:59.19	Peter Rocca (USA) 2:00.55	Don Harrigan (USA) 2:01.35
1980	Sandor Wladar (HUN) 2:01.93	Zóltán Verraszto (HUN) 2:02.40	Mark Kerry (AUS) 2:03.14
1984	Richard Carey (USA) 2:00.23*	Frederic Delcourt (FRA) 2:01.75	Cameron Henning (CAN) 2:02.37
1988	Igor Polianski (URS) 1:59.37	Frank Baltrusch (GDR) 1:59.50	Paul Kingsman (NZL) 2;00.48

Olympic record 1:58.99 in heats.   1896, 1904–1960 Event not held.

100 Metres Butterfly

1968	Doug Russell (USA) 55.9	Mark Spitz (USA) 56.4	Ross Wales (USA) 57.2
1972	Mark Spitz (USA) 54.27	Bruce Robertson (CAN) 55.56	Jerry Heidenreich (USA) 55.74
1976	Matt Vogel (USA) 54.35	Joe Bottom (USA) 54.50	Gary Hall (USA) 54.65
1980	Pär Arvidsson (SWE) 54.92	Roger Pyttel (GDR) 54.94	David Lopez (ESP) 55.13
1984	Michael Gross (FRG) 53.08	Pablo Morales (USA) 53.23	Glenn Buchanan (AUS) 53.85
1988	Anthony Nesty (SUR) 53.00*	Matt Biondi (USA) 53.01	Andy Jameson (GBR) 53.30

Olympic record.   1896–1964 Event not held.

200 Metres Butterfly

1956	William Yorzyk (USA) 2:19.3	Takashi Ishimoto (JPN) 2:23.8	György Tumpek (HUN) 2:23.9
1960	Mike Troy (USA) 2:12.8	Neville Hayes (AUS) 2:14.6	David Gillanders (USA) 2:15.3
1964	Kevin Berry (AUS) 2:06.6	Carl Robie (USA) 2:07.5	Fred Schmidt (USA) 2:09.3
1968	Carl Robie (USA) 2:08.7	Martyn Woodroffe (GBR) 2:09.0	John Ferris (USA) 2:09.3
1972	Mark Spitz (USA) 2:00.70	Gary Hall (USA) 2:02.86	Robin Backhaus (USA) 2:03.23
1976	Mike Bruner (USA) 1:59.23	Steven Gregg (USA) 1:59.54	William Forrester (USA) 1:59.96
1980	Sergey Fesenko (URS) 1:59.76	Phil Hubble (GBR) 2:01.20	Roger Pyttel (GDR) 2:01.39
1984	Jon Sieben (AUS) 1:57.04	Michael Gross (FRG) 1:57.40	Rafael Castro (VEN) 1:57.51
1988	Michael Gross (FRG) 1:56.94*	Benny Nielsen (DEN) 1:58.24	Anthony Mosse (NZL) 1:58.28

Olympic record.   1896–1952 Event not held.

200 Metres Individual Medley

1968	Charles Hickcox (USA) 2:12.0	Greg Buckingham (USA) 2:13.0	John Ferris (USA) 2:13.3
1972	Gunnar Larsson (SWE) 2:07.17	Tim McKee (USA) 2:08.37	Steve Furniss (USA) 2:08.45
1984	Alex Baumann (CAN) 2:01.42	Pablo Morales (USA) 2:03.05	Neil Cochran (GBR) 2:04.38
1988	Tamás Darnyi (HUN) 2:00.17*	Patrick Kühl (GDR) 2:01.61	Vadim Yarochtchouk (URS) 2:02.40

Olympic record.   1896–1964, 1976–1980 Event not held.

400 Metres Individual Medley

1964	Richard Roth (USA) 4:45.4	Roy Saari (USA) 4:47.1	Gerhard Hetz (GER) 4:51.0
1968	Charles Hickcox (USA) 4:48.4	Gary Hall (USA) 4:48.7	Michael Holthaus (FRG) 4:51.4
1972	Gunnar Larsson (SWE) 4:31.98	Tim McKee (USA) 4:31.98	András Hargitay (HUN) 4:32.70
1976	Rod Strachan (USA) 4:23.68	Tim McKee (USA) 4:24.62	Andrei Smirnov (URS) 4:26.90
1980	Aleksandr Sidorenko (URS) 4:22.89	Sergey Fesenko (URS) 4:23.43	Zóltán Verraszto (HUN) 4:24.24
1984	Alex Baumann (CAN) 4:17.41	Ricardo Prado (BRA) 4:18.45	Robert Woodhouse (AUS) 4:20.50
1988	Tamás Darnyi (HUN) 4:14.75*	David Wharton (USA) 4:17.36	Stefano Battistelli (ITA) 4:18.01

Olympic record.   1896–1960 Event not held.

4 x 100 Metres Freestyle Relay

1964	United States 3:33.2	Germany 3:37.2	Australia 3:39.1
1968	United States 3:31.7	Soviet Union 3:34.2	Australia 3:34.7
1972	United States 3:26.42	Soviet Union 3:29.72	GDR 3:32.42
1984	United States 3:19.03	Australia 3:19.68	Sweden 3:22.69
1988	United States 3:16.53*	Soviet Union 3:18.33	GDR 3:19.82

Olympic record.   1896–1960, 1976–1980 Event not held.

	Gold	Silver	Bronze
4 x 200 Metres Freestyle Relay			
1906[1]	Hungary 16:52.4	Germany 17:16.2	Great Britain n.t.a.
1908	Great Britain 10:55.6	Hungary 10:59.0	United States 11:02.8
1912	Australasia[2] 10:11.6	United States 10:20.2	Great Britain 10:28.2
1920	United States 10:04.4	Australia 10:25.4	Great Britain 10:37.2
1924	United States 9:53.4	Australia 10:02.2	Sweden 10:06.8
1928	United States 9:36.2	Japan 9:41.4	Canada 9:47.8
1932	Japan 8:58.4	United States 9:10.5	Hungary 9:31.4
1936	Japan 8:51.5	United States 9:03.0	Hungary 9:12.3
1948	United States 8:46.0	Hungary 8:48.4	France 9:08.0
1952	United States 8:31.1	Japan 8:33.5	France 8:45.9
1956	Australia 8:23.6	United States 8:31.5	Soviet Union 8:34.7
1960	United States 8:10.2	Japan 8:13.2	Australia 8:13.8
1964	United States 7:52.1	Germany 7:59.3	Japan 8:03.8
1968	United States 7:52.3	Australia 7:53.7	Soviet Union 8:01.6
1972	United States 7:35.78	FRG 7:41.69	Soviet Union 7:45.76
1976	United States 7:23.22	Soviet Union 7:27.97	Great Britain 7:32.11
1980	Soviet Union 7:23.50	GDR 7:28.60	Brazil 7:29.30
1984	United States 7:15.69	FRG 7:16.73	Great Britain 7:24.78
1988	United States 7:12.51*	GDR 7:13.68	FRG 7:14.35

[1] *4 x 250 metres.*   [2] *Composed of three Australians and a New Zealander.*   *Olympic record.*   1896–1904 Event not held.

	Gold	Silver	Bronze
4 x 100 Metres Medley Relay			
1960	United States 4:05.4	Australia 4:12.0	Japan 4:12.2
1964	United States 3:38.5	Germany 4:01.6	Australia 4:02.3
1968	United States 3:54.9	GDR 3:57.5	Soviet Union 4:00.7
1972	United States 3:48.16	GDR 3:52.12	Canada 3:52.26
1976	United States 3:42.22	Canada 3:45.94	FRG 3:47.29
1980	Australia 3:45.70	Soviet Union 3:45.92	Great Britain 3:47.71
1984	United States 3:39.30	Canada 3:43.23	Australia 3:43.25
1988	United States 3:36.93*	Canada 3:39.28	Soviet Union 3:3.39.96

Olympic record.   1896–1956 Event not held.

SWIMMING MEDALS – WOMEN

	Gold	Silver	Bronze
50 Metres Freestyle			
1988	Kristin Otto (GDR) 25.49*	Yang Wenyi (CHN) 25.64	Katrin Meissner (GDR) 25.71
			Jill Sterkel (USA) 25.71

Olympic record.   1896–1984 Event not held.

	Gold	Silver	Bronze
100 Metres Freestyle			
1912	Fanny Durack (AUS) 1:22.2	Wilhelmina Wylie (AUS) 1:25.4	Jennie Fletcher (GBR) 1:27.0
1920	Ethelda Bleibtrey (USA) 1:13.6	Irene Guest (USA) 1:17.0	Frances Schroth (USA) 1:17.2
1924	Ethel Lackie (USA) 1:12.4	Mariechen Wehselau (USA) 1:12.8	Gertrude Ederle (USA) 1:14.2
1928	Albina Osipowich (USA) 1:11.0	Eleanor Garatti (USA) 1:11.4	Joyce Cooper (GBR) 1:13.6
1932	Helene Madison (USA) 1:06.8	Willemijntje den Ouden (HOL) 1:07.8	Eleanor Garatti-Saville (USA) 1:08.2
1936	Henrika Mastenbroek (HOL) 1:05.9	Jeanette Campbell (ARG) 1:06.4	Gisela Arendt (GER) 1:06.6
1948	Greta Andersen (DEN) 1:06.3	Ann Curtis (USA) 1:06.5	Marie-Louise Vaessen (HOL) 1:07.6
1952	Katalin Szöke (HUN) 1:06.8	Johanna Termeulen (HOL) 1:07.0	Judit Temes (HUN) 1:07.1
1956	Dawn Fraser (AUS) 1:02.0	Lorraine Crapp (AUS) 1:02.3	Faith Leech (AUS) 1:05.1
1960	Dawn Fraser (AUS) 1:01.2	Chris von Saltza (USA) 1:02.8	Natalie Steward (GBR) 1:03.1
1964	Dawn Fraser (AUS) 59.5	Sharon Stouder (USA) 59.9	Kathleen Ellis (USA) 1:00.8
1968	Jan Henne (USA) 1:00.0	Susan Pedersen (USA) 1:00.3	Linda Gustavson (USA) 1:00.3
1972	Sandra Neilson (USA) 58.59	Shirley Babashoff (USA) 59.02	Shane Gould (AUS) 59.06
1976	Kornelia Ender (GDR) 55.65	Petra Priemer (GDR) 56.49	Enith Brigitha (HOL) 56.65
1980	Barbara Krause (GDR) 54.79*	Caren Metschuck (GDR) 55.16	Ines Diers (GDR) 55.65
1984	Carrie Steinseifer (USA) 55.92	–	Annemarie Verstappen (HOL) 56.08
	Nancy Hogshead (USA) 55.92		
1988	Kristin Otto (GDR) 54.93	Zhuang Yong (CHN) 55.47	Catherine Plewinski (FRA) 55.49

Olympic record.   1896–1908 Event not held.

Facing page *Dawn Fraser (right) being congratulated by Chris von Saltza (USA) in Rome, after winning the second of three consecutive 100m titles. Von Saltza later won the 400m freestyle.*

	Gold	Silver	Bronze

200 Metres Freestyle

	Gold	Silver	Bronze
1968	Debbie Meyer (USA) 2:10.5	Jan Henne (USA) 2:11.0	Jane Barkman (USA) 2:11.2
1972	Shane Gould (AUS) 2:03.56	Shirley Babashoff (USA) 2:04.33	Keena Rothhammer (USA) 2:04.92
1976	Kornelia Ender (GDR) 1:59.26	Shirley Babashoff (USA) 2:01.22	Enith Brigitha (HOL) 2:01.40
1980	Barbara Krause (GDR) 1:58.33	Ines Diers (GDR) 1:59.64	Carmela Schmidt (GDR) 2:01.44
1984	Mary Wayte (USA) 1:59.23	Cynthia Woodhead (USA) 1:59.50	Annemarie Verstappen (HOL) 1:59.69
1988	Heike Friedrich (GDR) 1:57.65*	Silvia Poll (CRC) 1:58.67	Manuela Stellmach (GDR) 1:59.01

Olympic record.   1896–1964 Event not held.

400 Metres Freestyle

	Gold	Silver	Bronze
1920[1]	Ethelda Bleibtrey (USA) 4:34.0	Margaret Woodbridge (USA) 4:42.8	Frances Schroth (USA) 4:52.0
1924	Martha Norelius (USA) 6:02.2	Helen Wainwright (USA) 6:03.8	Gertrude Ederle (USA) 6:04.8
1928	Martha Norelius (USA) 5:42.8	Marie Braun (HOL) 5:57.8	Josephine McKim (USA) 6:00.2
1932	Helene Madison (USA) 5:28.5	Lenore Kight (USA) 5:28.6	Jennie Maakal (SAF) 5:47.3
1936	Henrika Mastenbroek (HOL) 5:26.4	Ragnhild Hveger (DEN) 5:27.5	Lenore Kight-Wingard (USA) 5:29.0
1948	Ann Curtis (USA) 5:17.8	Karen Harup (DEN) 5:21.2	Cathy Gibson (GBR) 5:22.5
1952	Valeria Gyenge (HUN) 5:12.1	Eva Novak (HUN) 5:13.7	Evelyn Kawamoto (USA) 5:14.6
1956	Lorraine Crapp (USA) 4:54.6	Dawn Fraser (AUS) 5:02.5	Sylvia Ruuska (USA) 5:07.1
1960	Chris von Saltza (USA) 4:50.6	Jane Cederquist (SWE) 4:53.9	Catharina Lagerberg (HOL) 4:56.9
1964	Virginia Duenkel (USA) 4:43.3	Marilyn Ramenofsky (USA) 4:44.6	Terri Stickles (USA) 4:47.2
1968	Debbie Meyer (USA) 4:31.8	Linda Gustavson (USA) 4:35.5	Karen Moras (AUS) 4:37.0
1972	Shane Gould (AUS) 4:19.04	Novella Calligaris (ITA) 4:22.44	Gudrun Wegner (GDR) 4:23.11
1976	Petra Thuemer (GDR) 4:09.89	Shirley Babashoff (USA) 4:10.46	Shannon Smith (CAN) 4:14.60
1980	Ines Diers (GDR) 4:08.76	Petra Schneider (GDR) 4:09.16	Carmela Schmidt (GDR) 4:10.86
1984	Tiffany Cohen (USA) 4:07.10	Sarah Hardcastle (GBR) 4:10.27	June Croft (GBR) 4:11.49
1988	Janet Evans (USA) 4:03.85*	Heike Friedrich (GDR) 4:05.94	Anke Möhring (GDR) 4:06.62

[1]300 metres.   *Olympic record.*   1896–1912 Event not held.

	Gold	Silver	Bronze

800 Metres Freestyle

1968	Debbie Meyer (USA) 9:24.0	Pamela Kruse (USA) 9:35.7	Maria Ramirez (MEX) 9:38.5
1972	Keena Rothhammer (USA) 8:53.68	Shane Gould (AUS) 8:56.39	Novella Calligaris (ITA) 8:57.46
1976	Petra Thuemer (GDR) 8:37.14	Shirley Babashoff (USA) 8:37.59	Wendy Weinberg (USA) 8:42.60
1980	Michelle Ford (AUS) 8:28.9	Ines Diers (GDR) 8:32.55	Heike Dähne (GDR) 8:33.48
1984	Tiffany Cohen (USA) 8:24.95	Michele Richardson (USA) 8:30.73	Sarah Hardcastle (GBR) 8:32.60
1988	Janet Evans (USA) 8:20.20*	Astrid Strauss (GDR) 8:22.09	Julie McDonald (AUS) 8:22.93

Olympic record.   1896–1964 Event not held.

100 Metres Breaststroke

1968	Djurdjica Bjedov (YUG) 1:15.8	Galina Prozumenschchikova[1] (URS) 1:15.9	Sharon Wichman (USA) 1:16.1
1972	Catherine Carr (USA) 1:13.58	Galina Stepanova (URS) 1:14.99	Beverley Whitfield (AUS) 1:15.73
1976	Hannelore Anke (GDR) 1:11.16	Lubov Rusanova (URS) 1:13.04	Marina Kosheveya (URS) 1:13.30
1980	Ute Geweniger (GDR) 1:10.22	Elvira Vasilkova (URS) 1:10.41	Susanne Nielsson (DEN) 1:11.16
1984	Petra Van Staveren (HOL) 1:09.88	Anne Ottenbrite (CAN) 1:10.69	Catherine Poirot (FRA) 1:10.70
1988	Tania Dangalakova (URS) 1:07.95*	Antoaneta Frankeva (BUL) 1:08.74	Silke Hörner (GDR) 1:08.83

Olympic record.   [1]Later Stepanova.   1896–1964 Event not held.

200 Metres Breaststroke

1924	Lucy Morton (GBR) 3:33.2	Agnes Geraghty (USA) 3:34.0	Gladys Carson (GBR) 3:35.4
1928	Hilde Schrader (GER) 3:12.6	Mietje Baron (HOL) 3:15.2	Lotte Mühe (GER) 3:17.6
1932	Claire Dennis (AUS) 3:06.3	Hideko Maehata (JPN) 3:06.4	Else Jacobsen (DEN) 3:07.1
1936	Hideko Maehata (JPN) 3:03.6	Martha Genenger (GER) 3:04.2	Inge Sörensen (DEN) 3:07.8
1948	Petronella van Vliet (HOL) 2:57.2	Nancy Lyons (AUS) 2:57.7	Eva Novak (HUN) 3:00.2
1952	Eva Székely[1] (HUN) 2:51.7	Eva Novák (HUN) 2:54.4	Helen Gordon (GBR) 2:57.6
1956	Ursula Happe[2] (GER) 2:53.1	Eva Székely (HUN) 2:54.8	Eva-Maria ten Elsen (GER) 2:55.1
1960	Anita Lonsbrough (GBR) 2:49.5	Wiltrud Urselmann (GER) 2:50.0	Barbara Göbel (GER) 2:53.6
1964	Galina Prozumenshchikova (URS) 2:46.4	Claudia Kolb (USA) 2:47.6	Svetlana Babanina (URS) 2:48.6
1968	Sharon Wichman (USA) 2:44.4	Djurdjica Bjedov (YUG) 2:46.4	Galina Prozumenshchikova (URS) 2:47.0
1972	Beverly Whitfield (AUS) 2:41.7	Dana Schoenfield (USA) 2:42.05	Galina Stepanova (URS) 2:42.36
1976	Marina Kosheveya (URS) 2:33.35	Marina Yurchenia (URS) 2:36.08	Lubov Rusanova (URS) 2:36.22
1980	Lina Kachushite (URS) 2:29.54	Svetlana Varganova (URS) 2:29.61	Yulia Bogdanova (URS) 2:32.39
1984	Anne Ottenbrite (CAN) 2:30.38	Susan Rapp (USA) 2:31.15	Ingrid Lempereur (BEL) 2:31.40
1988	Silke Hörner (GDR) 2:26.71*	Huang Xiaomin (CHN) 2:27.49	Antoaneta Frankeva (BUL) 2:28.34

*[1]Used then permitted butterfly stroke.   [2]Used then permitted underwater technique.   *Olympic record.   1896–1920 Event not held.*

100 Metres Backstroke

1924	Sybil Bauer (USA) 1:23.2	Phyllis Harding (GBR) 1:27.4	Aileen Riggin (USA) 1:28.2
1928	Marie Braun (HOL) 1:22.0	Ellen King (GBR) 1:22.2	Joyce Cooper (GBR) 1:22.8
1932	Eleanor Holm (USA) 1:19.4	Philomena Mealing (AUS) 1:21.3	Valerie Davies (GBR) 1:22.5
1936	Dina Senff (HOL) 1:18.9	Hendrika Mastenbroek (HOL) 1:19.2	Alice Bridges (USA) 1:19.4
1948	Karen Harup (DEN) 1:14.4	Suzanne Zimmermann (USA) 1:16.0	Judy Davies (AUS) 1:16.7
1952	Joan Harrison (SAF) 1:14.3	Geertje Wielema (HOL) 1:14.5	Jean Stewart (NZL) 1:15.8
1956	Judy Grinham (GBR) 1:12.9	Carin Cone (USA) 1:12.9	Margaret Edwards (GBR) 1:13.1
1960	Lynn Burke (USA) 1:09.3	Natalie Steward (GBR) 1:10.8	Satoko Tanaka (JPN) 1:11.4
1964	Cathy Ferguson (USA) 1:07.7	Cristine Caron (FRA) 1:07.9	Virginia Duenkel (USA) 1:08.0
1968	Kaye Hall (USA) 1:06.2	Elaine Tanner (CAN) 1:06.7	Jane Swaggerty (USA) 1:08.1
1972	Melissa Belote (USA) 1:05.78	Andrea Gyarmati (HUN) 1:06.26	Susie Atwood (USA) 1:06.34
1976	Ulrike Richter (GDR) 1:01.83	Birgit Treiber (GDR) 1:03.41	Nancy Garapick (CAN) 1:03.71
1980	Rica Reinisch (GDR) 1:00.86*	Ina Kleber (GDR) 1:02.07	Petra Reidel (GDR) 1:02.64
1984	Theresa Andrews (USA) 1:02.55	Betsy Mitchell (USA) 1:02.63	Jolanda De Rover (HOL) 1:92.91
1988	Kristin Otto (GDR) 1:00.89	Krisztina Egerszegi (HUN) 1:01.56	Cornelia Sirch (GDR) 1:01.57

Olympic record.   1896–1920 Event not held.

200 Metres Backstroke

1968	Lillian Watson (USA) 2:24.8	Elaine Tanner (CAN) 2:27.4	Kaye Hall (USA) 2:28.9
1972	Melissa Belote (USA) 2:19.19	Susie Atwood (USA) 2:20.38	Donna Marie Gurr (CAN) 2:23.22
1976	Ulrike Richter (GDR) 2:13.43	Birgit Treiber (GDR) 2:14.97	Nancy Garapick (CAN) 2:15.60
1980	Rica Reinisch (GDR) 2:11.77	Cornelia Polit (GDR) 2:13.75	Birgit Treiber (GDR) 2:14.14
1984	Jolanda De Rover (HOL) 2:12.38	Amy White (USA) 2:13.04	Aneta Patrascoiu (ROM) 2:13.29
1988	Krisztina Egerszegi (HUN) 2:09.29*	Kathrin Zimmermann (GDR) 2:10.61	Cornelia Sirch (GDR) 2:11.45

Olympic record.   1896–1964 Event not held.

100 Metres Butterfly

1956	Shelley Mann (USA) 1:11.0	Nancy Ramey (USA) 1:11.9	Mary Sears (USA) 1:14.4
1960	Carolyn Schuler (USA) 1:09.5	Marianne Heemskerk (HOL) 1:10.4	Janice Andrew (AUS) 1:12.2
1964	Sharon Stouder (USA) 1:04.7	Ada Kok (HOL) 1:05.6	Kathleen Ellis (USA) 1:06.0

	Gold	Silver	Bronze
1968	Lynette McClements (AUS) 1:05.5	Ellie Daniel (USA) 1:05.8	Susan Shields (USA) 1:06.2
1972	Mayumi Aoki (JPN) 1:03.34	Roswitha Beier (GDR) 1:03.61	Andrea Gyarmati (HUN) 1:03.73
1976	Kornelia Ender (GDR) 1:00.13	Andrea Pollack (GDR) 1:00.98	Wendy Boglioli (USA) 1:01.17
1980	Caren Metschuck (GDR) 1:00.42	Andrea Pollack (GDR) 1:00.90	Christiane Knacke (GDR) 1:01.44
1984	Mary Meagher (USA) 59.26	Jenna Johnson (USA) 1:00.19	Karin Seick (FRG) 1:00.36
1988	Kristin Otto (GDR) 59.00*	Birte Weigang (GDR) 59.45	Qian Hong (CHN) 59.52

*Olympic record.   1896–1952 Event not held.

200 Metres Butterfly

1968	Ada Kok (HOL) 2:24.7	Helga Lindner (GDR) 2:24.8	Ellie Daniel (USA) 2:25.9
1972	Karen Moe (USA) 2:15.57	Lynn Colella (USA) 2:16.34	Ellie Daniel (USA) 2:26.74
1976	Andrea Pollack (GDR) 2:11.41	Ulrike Tauber (GDR) 2:12.50	Rosemarie Gabriel (GDR) 2:12.86
1980	Ines Geissler (GDR) 2:10.44	Sybille Schönrock (GDR) 2:10.45	Michelle Ford (AUS) 2:11.66
1984	Mary Meagher (USA) 2:06.90*	Karen Phillips (AUS) 2:10.56	Ina Beyermann (FRG) 2:11.91
1988	Kathleen Nord (GDR) 2:09.51	Birte Weigang (GDR) 2:09.91	Mary Meagher (USA) 2:10.80

*Olympic record.   1896–1964 Event not held.

200 Metres Individual Medley

1968	Claudia Kolb (USA) 2:24.7	Susan Pedersen (USA) 2:28.8	Jan Henne (USA) 2:31.4
1972	Shane Gould (AUS) 2:23.07	Kornelia Ender (GDR) 2:23.59	Lynn Vidali (USA) 2:24.06
1984	Tracy Caulkins (USA) 2:12.64	Nancy Hogshead (USA) 2:15.17	Michele Pearson (AUS) 2:15.92
1988	Daniela Hunger (GDR) 2:12.59*	Yelena Dendeberova (URS) 2:13.31	Noemi Ildiko Lung (ROM) 2:14.85

*Olympic record.   1896–1964, 1976–1980 Event not held.

400 Metres Individual Medley

1964	Donna De Varona (USA) 5:18.7	Sharon Finneran (USA) 5:24.1	Martha Randall (USA) 5:24.1
1968	Claudia Kolb (USA) 5:08.5	Lynn Vidali (USA) 5:22.2	Sabine Steinbach (GDR) 5:25.3
1972	Gail Neall (AUS) 5:02.97	Leslie Cliff (CAN) 5:03.57	Novella Calligaris (ITA) 5:03.99
1976	Ulrike Tauber (GDR) 4:42.77	Cheryl Gibson (CAN) 4:48.10	Becky Smith (CAN) 4:50.48
1980	Petra Schneider (GDR) 4:36.29*	Sharron Davies (GBR) 4:46.83	Agnieszka Czopek (POL) 4:48.17
1984	Tracy Caulkins (USA) 4:39.24	Suzanne Landells (AUS) 4:48.30	Petra Zindler (FRG) 4:48.57
1988	Janet Evans (USA) 4:37.76	Noemi Ildiko Lung (ROM) 4:39.46	Daniela Hunger (GDR) 4:39.76

*Olympic record.   1896–1960 Event not held.

4 x 100 Metres Freestyle Relay

1912	Great Britain 5:52.8	Germany 6:04.6	Austria 6:17.0
1920	United States 5:11.6	Great Britain 5:40.8	Sweden 5:43.6
1924	United States 4:58.8	Great Britain 5:17.0	Sweden 5:35.6
1928	United States 4:47.6	Great Britain 5:02.8	South Africa 5:13.4
1932	United States 4:38.0	Netherlands 4:47.5	Great Britain 4:52.4
1936	Netherlands 4:36.0	Germany 4:36.8	United States 4:40.2
1948	United States 4:29.2	Denmark 4:29.6	Netherlands 4:31.6
1952	Hungary 4:24.4	Netherlands 4:29.0	United States 4:30.1
1956	Australia 4:17.1	United States 4:19.2	South Africa 4:15.7
1960	United States 4:08.9	Australia 4:11.3	Germany 4:19.7
1964	United States 4:03.8	Australia 4:06.9	Netherlands 4:12.0
1968	United States 4:02.5	GDR 4:05.7	Canada 4:07.2
1972	United States 3:55.19	GDR 3:55.55	FRG 3:57.93
1976	United States 3:44.82	GDR 3:45.50	Canada 3:48.81
1980	GDR 3:42.71	Sweden 3:48.93	Netherlands 3:49.51
1984	United States 3:43.43	Netherlands 3:44.40	FRG 3:45.56
1988	GDR 3:40.63*	Netherlands 3:43.39	United States 3:44.25

*Olympic record.   1896–1908 Event not held.

4 x 100 Metres Medley Relay

1960	United States 4:41.1	Australia 4:45.9	Germany 4:47.6
1964	United States 4:33.9	Netherlands 4:37.0	Soviet Union 4:39.2
1968	United States 4:28.3	Australia 4:30.0	FRG 4:36.4
1972	United States 4:20.75	GDR 4:24.91	FRG 4:26.46
1976	GDR 4:07.95	United States 4:14.55	Canada 4:15.22
1980	GDR 4:06.67	Great Britain 4:12.24	Soviet Union 4:13.61
1984	United States 4:08.34	FRG 4:11.97	Canada 4:12.98
1988	GDR 4:03.74*	United States 4:07.90	Canada 4:10.49

*Olympic record.   1896–1956 Event not held.

DIVING MEDALS – MEN

	Gold	Silver	Bronze
Springboard Diving			
1908	Albert Zurner (GER) 85.5	Kurt Behrens (GER) 85.3	George Gaidzik (USA) 80.8
			Gottlob Walz (GER) 80.8
1912	Paul Günther (GER) 79.23	Hans Luber (GER) 76.78	Kurt Behrens (GER) 73.73
1920	Louis Kuehn (USA) 675.4	Clarence Pinkston (USA) 655.3	Louis Balbach (USA) 649.5
1924	Albert White (USA) 696.4	Pete Desjardins (USA) 693.2	Clarence Pinkston (USA) 653
1928	Pete Desjardins (USA) 185.04	Michael Galitzen (USA) 174.06	Farid Simaika (EGY) 172.46
1932	Michael Galitzen (USA) 161.38	Harold Smith (USA) 158.54	Richard Degener (USA) 151.82
1936	Richard Degener (USA) 163.57	Marshall Wayne (USA) 159.56	Al Greene (USA) 146.29
1948	Bruce Harlan (USA) 163.64	Miller Anderson (USA) 157.29	Samuel Lee (USA) 145.52
1952	David Browning (USA) 205.29	Miller Anderson (USA) 199.84	Robert Clotworthy (USA) 184.92
1956	Robert Clotworthy (USA) 159.56	Donald Harper (USA) 156.23	Joaquin Capilla Pérez (MEX) 150.69
1960	Gary Tobian (USA) 170.00	Samuel Hall (USA) 167.08	Juan Botella (MEX) 162.30
1964	Kenneth Sitzberger (USA) 159.90	Francis Gorman (USA) 157.63	Larry Andreasen (USA) 143.77
1968	Bernard Wrightson (USA) 170.15	Klaus Dibiasi (ITA) 159.74	James Henry (USA) 158.09
1972	Vladimir Vasin (URS) 594.09	F Giorgio Cagnotto (ITA) 591.63	Craig Lincoln (USA) 577.29
1976	Philip Boggs (USA) 619.05	F Giorgio Cagnotto (ITA) 570.48	Aleksandr Kosenkov (URS) 567.24
1980	Aleksandr Portnov (URS) 905.025	Carlos Giron (MEX) 892.140	F Giorgio Cagnotto (ITA) 871.500
1984	Greg Louganis (USA) 754.41	Tan Liangde (CHN) 662.31	Ronald Merriott (USA) 661.32
1988	Greg Louganis (USA) 730.80	Tan Liangde (CHN) 704.88	Li Deliang (CHN) 665.28

1896–1906 Event not held.

Highboard Diving			
1904[1]	George Sheldon (USA) 12.66	Georg Hoffmann (GER) 11.66	Frank Kehoe (USA) 11.33
			Alfred Braunschweiger (GER) 11.33
1906	Gottlob Walz (GER) 156.00	Georg Hoffmann (GER) 150.20	Otto Satzinger (AUT) 147.40
1908	Hjalmar Johansson (SWE) 83.75	Karl Malmström (SWE) 78.73	Arvid Spangberg (SWE) 74.00
1912	Erik Adlerz (SWE) 73.94	Albert Zürner (GER) 72.60	Gustaf Blomgren (SWE) 69.56
1920	Clarence Pinkston (USA) 100.67	Erik Adlerz (SWE) 99.08	Haig Prieste (USA) 93.73
1924	Albert White (USA) 97.46	David Fall (USA) 97.30	Clarence Pinkston (USA) 94.60
1928	Pete Desjardins (USA) 98.74	Farid Simaika (EGY) 99.58	Michael Galitzen (USA) 92.34
1932	Harold Smtih (USA) 124.80	Michael Galitzen (USA) 124.28	Frank Kurtz (USA) 121.98
1936	Marshall Wayne (USA) 113.58	Elbert Root (USA) 110.60	Hermann Stork (GER) 110.31
1948	Samuel Lee (USA) 130.05	Bruce Harlan (USA) 122.30	Joaquin Capilla Pérez (MEX) 113.52
1952	Samuel Lee (USA) 156.28	Joaquin Capilla Pérez (MEX) 145.21	Günther Haase (GER) 141.31
1956	Joaquin Capilla Pérez (MEX) 152.44	Gary Tobian (USA) 152.41	Richard Connor (USA) 149.79
1960	Robert Webster (USA) 165.56	Gary Tobian (USA) 165.25	Brian Phelps (GBR) 157.13
1964	Robert Webster (USA) 148.58	Klaus Dibiasi (ITA) 147.54	Thomas Gompf (USA) 146.57
1968	Klaus Dibiasi (ITA) 164.18	Alvaro Gaxiola (MEX) 154.49	Edwin Young (USA) 153.93
1972	Klaus Dibiasi (ITA) 504.12	Richard Rydze (USA) 480.75	F Giorgio Cagnotto (ITA) 475.83
1976	Klaus Dibiasi (ITA) 600.51	Greg Louganis (USA) 576.99	Vladimir Aleynik (URS) 548.61
1980	Falk Hoffmann (GDR) 835.650	Vladimir Aleynik (URS) 819.705	David Ambartsumyan (URS) 817.440
1984	Greg Louganis (USA) 710.91	Bruce Kimball (USA) 643.50	Li Kongzheng (CHN) 638.28
1988	Greg Louganis (USA) 638.61	Ni Xiong (CHN) 637.47	Jesus Mena (MEX) 594.39

[1]Combined springboard and highboard event. 1896–1900 Event not held.

DIVING MEDALS – WOMEN

Springboard Diving			
1920	Aileen Riggin (USA) 539.9	Helen Wainwright (USA) 534.8	Thelma Payne (USA) 534.1
1924	Elizabeth Becker (USA) 474.5	Aileen Riggin (USA) 460.4	Caroline Fletcher (USA) 434.4
1928	Helen Meany (USA) 78.62	Dorothy Poynton (USA) 75.62	Georgia Coleman (USA) 73.78
1932	Georgia Coleman (USA) 87.52	Katherine Rawls (USA) 82.56	Jane Fauntz (USA) 82.12
1936	Marjorie Gestring (USA) 89.27	Katherine Rawls (USA) 88.35	Dorothy Poynton-Hill (USA) 82.36
1948	Victoria Draves (USA) 108.74	Zoe Ann Olsen (USA) 108.23	Patricia Elsener (USA) 101.30
1952	Patricia McCormick (USA) 147.30	Madeleine Moreau (FRA) 139.34	Zoe Ann Jensen (USA) 127.57
1956	Patricia McCormick (USA) 142.36	Jeanne Stunyo (USA) 125.89	Irene Macdonald (CAN) 121.40
1960	Ingrid Krämer (GER) 155.81	Paula Myers-Pope (USA) 141.24	Elizabeth Ferris (GBR) 139.09
1964	Ingrid Krämer-Engel (GER) 145.00	Jeanne Collier (USA) 138.36	Mary Willard (USA) 138.18
1968	Sue Gossick (USA) 150.77	Tamara Pogozheva (URS) 145.30	Keala O'Sullivan (USA) 145.23
1972	Micki King (USA) 450.03	Ulrika Knape (SWE) 434.19	Marina Janicke (GDR) 430.92
1976	Jennifer Chandler (USA) 506.19	Christa Kohler (GDR) 469.41	Cynthia McIngvale (USA) 466.83
1980	Irina Kalinina (URS) 725.910	Martina Proeber (GDR) 698.895	Karin Guthke (GDR) 685.245
1984	Sylvie Bernier (CAN) 530.70	Kelly McCormick (USA) 527.46	Christina Seufert (USA) 517.62
1988	Gao Min (CHN) 580.23	Li Qing (CHN) 534.33	Kelly Anne McCormick (USA) 533.19

1896–1912 Event not held.

	Gold	Silver	Bronze
Highboard Diving			
1912	Greta Johansson (SWE) 39.9	Lisa Regnell (SWE) 36.0	Isabelle White (GBR) 34.0
1920	Stefani Fryland-Clausen (DEN) 34.6	Eileen Armstrong (GBR) 33.3	Eva Ollivier (SWE) 33.3
1924	Caroline Smith (USA) 10.5	Elizabeth Becker (USA) 11.0	Hjördis Töpel (SWE) 15.5
1928	Elizabeth Pinkston (USA) 31.6	Georgia Coleman (USA) 30.6	Lala Sjöqvist (SWE) 29.2
1932	Dorothy Poynton (USA) 40.26	Georgia Coleman (USA) 35.56	Marion Roper (USA) 35.22
1936	Dorothy Poynton-Hill (USA) 33.93	Velma Dunn (USA) 33.63	Käthe Köhler (GER) 33.43
1948	Victoria Draves (USA) 68.87	Patricia Elsener (USA) 66.28	Birte Christoffersen (DEN) 66.04
1952	Patricia McCormick (USA) 79.37	Paula Myers (USA) 71.63	Juno Irwin (USA) 70.49
1956	Patricia McCormick (USA) 84.85	Juno Irwin (USA) 81.64	Paula Myers (USA) 81.58
1960	Ingrid Krämer (GER) 91.28	Paula Myers-Pope (USA) 88.94	Ninel Krutova (URS) 86.99
1964	Lesley Bush (USA) 99.80	Ingrid Krämer-Engel (GER) 98.45	Galina Alekseyeva (URS) 97.60
1968	Milena Duchkova (TCH) 109.59	Natalia Lobanova (URS) 105.14	Ann Peterson (USA) 101.11
1972	Ulrika Knape (SWE) 390.00	Milena Duchkova (TCH) 370.92	Marina Janicke (GDR) 360.54
1976	Elena Vaytsekhovskaya (URS) 406.59	Ulrika Knape (SWE) 402.60	Deborah Wilson (USA) 401.07
1980	Martina Jäschke (GDR) 596.250	Servard Emirzyan (URS) 576.465	Liana Tsotadze (URS) 575.925
1984	Zhou Jihong (CHN) 435.51	Michele Mitchell (USA) 431.19	Wendy Wyland (USA) 422.07
1988	Xu Yanmei (CHN) 445.20	Michele Mitchell (USA) 436.95	Wendy Williams (USA) 400.44

1896–1908 Event not held.

SYNCHRONISED SWIMMING MEDALS

	Gold	Silver	Bronze
Solo			
1984	Tracie Ruiz (USA) 198.467	Carolyn Waldo (CAN) 195.300	Miwako Motoyoshi (JPN) 187.050
1988	Carolyn Waldo (CAN) 200.150	Tracie Ruiz-Conforto (USA) 197.633	Mikako Kotani (JPN) 191.850

1896–1980 Event not held.

Duet			
1984	United States 195.584	Canada 194.234	Japan 187.992
1988	Canada 197.717	United States 17.284	Japan 190.159

1896–1980 Event not held.

DISCONTINUED EVENTS

	Gold	Silver	Bronze
50 Yards Freestyle			
1904[1]	Zoltán Halmay (HUN) 28.0	Scott Leary (USA) 28.6	Charles Daniels (USA) n.t.a.

[1]Race reswum after judges disagreed on result of first race.

100 Metres Freestyle (Sailors)			
1896	Ioannis Malokinis (GRE) 2:20.4	S Chasapis (GRE) n.t.a.	Dimitrios Drivas (GRE) n.t.a.
200 Metres Obstacle Event			
1900	Frederick Lane (AUS) 2:38.4	Otto Wahle (AUT) 2:40.0	Peter Kemp (GBR) 2:47.4
400 Metres Breaststroke			
1904	Georg Zacharias (GER) 7:23.6	Walter Brack (GER) 20m	Jamison Handy (USA) d.n.a.
1912	Walter Bathe (GER) 6:29.6	Thor Henning (SWE) 6:35.6	Percy Courtman (GBR) 6:36.4
1920	Hakan Malmroth (SWE) 6:31.8	Thor Henning (SWE) 6:45.2	Arvo Aaltonen (FIN) 6:48.0
880 Yards Freestyle			
1904	Emil Rausch (GER) 13:11.4	Francis Gailey (USA) 13:23.4	Géza Kiss (HUN) n.t.a.
4000 Metres Freestyle			
1900	John Jarvis (GBR) 58:24.0	Zoltán Halmay (HUN) 1:08:55.4	Louis Martin (FRA) 1:13:08.4
Underwater Swimming			
1900	Charles de Vendeville (FRA) 188.4	A Six (FRA) 185.4	Peder Lykkeberg (DEN) 147.0
Plunge for Distance			
1904	Paul Dickey (USA) 19.05m	Edgar Adams (USA) 17.53m	Leo Goodwin (USA) 17.37m
200 Metres Team Swimming			
1900	Germany 32pts	France 51	France 61
4 x 50 Yards Relay			
1904	United States (New York AC) 2:04.6	United States (Chicago AC) n.t.a.	United States (Missouri AC) n.t.a.

	Gold	Silver	Bronze
Plain High Diving			
1912	Erik Adlerz (SWE) 40.0	Hjalmar Johansson (SWE) 39.3	John Jansson (SWE) 39.1
1920	Arvid Wallmann (SWE) 183.5	Nils Skoglund (SWE) 183.0	John Jansson (SWE) 175.0
1924	Richmond Eve (AUS) 160.0	John Jansson (SWE) 157.0	Harold Clarke (GBR) 158.0

SWIMMING MEDALS TOTALS
Excluding diving and synchronised

	MEN			WOMEN			
Country	G	S	B	G	S	B	Total
United States	91	69	48	63	41	36	368
Australia	23	18	27	14	12	9	103
GDR	6	7	5	32	25	17	92
Germany (FRG)	12	15	14	2	5	13	61
Soviet Union	9	14	18	4	7	8	60
Great Britain	10	12	12	4	9	12	59
Hungary	10	11	10	5	5	3	44
Japan	12	17	11	2	1	1	44
Netherlands	–	–	2	9	13	10	34
Canada	5	7	5	1	5	10	33
Sweden	7	7	9	–	2	2	27
France	2	5	7	–	1	2	17
Denmark	–	2	1	2	3	3	11
Austria	2	3	5	–	–	1	11
Greece	1	4	3	–	–	–	8
New Zealand	1	–	2	–	–	1	4
South Africa	–	–	–	1	–	3	4
China	–	–	–	–	3	1	4
Brazil	–	1	3	–	–	–	4
Italy	–	–	1	–	1	2	4
Belgium	–	1	1	–	–	1	3
Romania	–	–	–	–	1	2	3
Argentina	1	–	–	–	1	–	2
Yugoslavia	–	–	–	1	1	–	2
Mexico	1	–	–	–	–	1	2
Bulgaria	–	–	–	–	1	1	2
Finland	–	–	2	–	–	–	2
Philippines	–	–	2	–	–	–	2
Poland	–	–	1	–	–	1	2
Spain	–	–	2	–	–	–	2
Surinam	1	–	–	–	–	–	1
Costa Rica	–	–	–	–	1	–	1
Switzerland	–	–	1	–	–	–	1
Venezuela	–	–	1	–	–	–	1
	194[1]	193	193	140[2]	138	140[3]	998

[1]Double counting of Australia/New Zealand relay team in 1912
[2]Two golds in 1984 100m freestyle
[3]Two bronzes in 1988 50m freestyle

WATER POLO MEDALS TOTALS

Country	G	S	B	Total
Hungary	6	3	3	12
United States	1	3	4	8
Yugoslavia	3	4	–	7
Soviet Union	2	2	3	7
Belgium	–	4	2	6
Great Britain	4	–	–	4
Italy	2	1	1	4
Germany (FRG)	1	2	1	4
France	1	–	2	3
Sweden	–	1	2	3
Netherlands	–	–	2	2
	20	20	20	60

DIVING MEDALS TOTALS

	MEN			WOMEN			
Country	G	S	B	G	S	B	Total
United States	26	19	19	19	20	19	122
Sweden	4	5	4	2	3	3	21
Germany (FRG)	3	5	5	3	1	1	18
Soviet Union	2	1	3	2	3	3	14
China	–	3	2	3	1	–	9
Italy	3	4	2	–	–	–	9
Mexico	1	3	4	–	–	–	8
GDR	1	–	–	1	2	3	8
Great Britain	–	–	2	–	1	2	5
Czechoslovakia	–	–	–	1	1	–	2
Canada	–	–	–	1	–	1	2
Denmark	–	–	–	1	–	1	2
Egypt	–	1	1	–	–	–	2
Australia	1	–	–	–	–	–	1
France	–	–	–	–	1	–	1
Austria	–	–	1	–	–	–	1
	41	41	43[1]	33	33	33	224

[1]Two bronzes awarded in a 1904 and a 1908 event

SYNCHRONISED SWIMMING MEDAL TOTALS

Country	G	S	B	Total
Canada	2	2	–	4
United States	2	2	–	4
Japan	–	–	4	4
	4	4	4	12

WATER POLO MEDALS

	Gold	Silver	Bronze
1900[1]	Great Britain	Belgium	France
1904[1]	United States	United States	United States
1908	Great Britain	Belgium	Sweden
1912	Great Britain	Sweden	Belgium
1920	Great Britain	Belgium	Sweden
1924	France	Belgium	United States
1928	Germany	Hungary	France
1932	Hungary	Germany	United States
1936	Hungary	Germany	Belgium
1948	Italy	Hungary	Netherlands
1952	Hungary	Yugoslavia	Italy
1956	Hungary	Yugoslavia	Soviet Union
1960	Italy	Soviet Union	Hungary
1964	Hungary	Yugoslavia	Soviet Union
1968	Yugoslavia	Soviet Union	Hungary
1972	Soviet Union	Hungary	United States
1976	Hungary	Italy	Netherlands
1980	Soviet Union	Yugoslavia	Hungary
1984	Yugoslavia	United States	FRG
1988	Yugoslavia	United States	Soviet Union

[1]Entries were from clubs and not international teams.
1896, 1906 Event not held.

TABLE TENNIS

First recognised as an Olympic sport by the IOC in 1977, table tennis was first included in the Games in 1988. There were 64 men and 32 women, selected by an agreed international formula, competing in men's and women's singles and doubles events. The sport had never been included in the Olympics before, not even as a demonstration event.

The most successful player was Chen Jing (CHN) with a gold and a silver in the women's events at Seoul, while the most successful male was Yoo Nam-Kyu (KOR) with a gold and a bronze. The youngest gold medallist was Hyun Jung-Hwa (KOR) in the women's doubles, aged 18yr 360 days, while the youngest male champion was Yoo Nam-Kyu (KOR), winning the singles aged 20yr 119 days. The oldest gold medallist was Wei Qing-guang (CHN) in the men's doubles, aged 26yr 90 days, while the oldest female champion was Yang Young-Ja (KOR) in the women's doubles, aged 24yr 86 days. Jasna Fazlic (YUG) won a bronze in the women's doubles aged 17yr 285 days.

TABLE TENNIS MEDALS
Introduced in 1988

	Gold	Silver	Bronze
Men's Singles			
1988	Yoo Nam-Kyu (KOR)	Kim Ki-Taik (KOR)	Erik Lindh)SWE)
Men's Doubles			
1988	China	Yugoslavia	Korea
Women's Singles			
1988	Chen Jing (CHN)	Li Huifen (CHN)	Jiao Zhimin (CHN)
Women's Doubles			
1988	Korea	China	Yugoslavia

TABLE TENNIS MEDAL TOTAL

Country	G	S	B	Total
China	2	2	1	5
Korea	2	1	1	4
Yugoslavia	–	1	1	2
Sweden	–	–	1	1
	4	4	4	12

Chen Jing of China won the inaugural women's table tennis singles at Seoul, having celebrated her 20th birthday while in the Olympic village. She also gained silver in the doubles.

TENNIS

The inclusion of tennis in the Games was suspended from 1924 until 1988, although it was a demonstration sport in 1968 and 1984. The first gold medallist was Irish-born John Pius Boland (GBR) in the 1896 singles. He happened to be in Athens, visiting the famous German archaeologist Schliemann, and entered the Games at the last minute. The ladies' singles champion in 1900, Charlotte Cooper (GBR), became the first woman to win an Olympic title in any sport.

Over the years a number of medal-winning pairs were composed of players from two countries, thus Boland combined with a German to win the first mixed doubles title. The most successful player was Max Décugis (FRA) with a total of six medals comprising four golds, one silver and a bronze between 1900 and 1920. Britain's Kitty McKane won a record total for a woman of five (one gold, two silvers and two bronzes) in 1920

and 1924.

The oldest gold medallist was George Hillyard (GBR) in the 1908 men's doubles, aged 44yr 160 days. The oldest female champion was Winifred McNair (GBR), aged 43yr 14 days, in the women's doubles of 1920. She was also the oldest British female competitor to win a gold medal in any sport. The youngest gold medallist in tennis was Helen Wills (USA), winner of the 1924 singles aged 18yr 288 days, while the youngest male was Fritz Traun (GER), Boland's partner in 1896, aged 20yr 13 days.

The husband and wife team of Max and Marie Décugis (FRA) won the mixed title in 1906, while brothers Reggie and Laurie Doherty (GBR) added the 1900 Olympic title to the eight Wimbledon doubles championships they won. Steffi Graf (FRG), in 1988, is the only Grand Slam winner also to win an Olympic title.

Many of the greatest names in tennis have played in the Games and there have been 24 gold medal winners who also were

successful at Wimbledon. One of the most remarkable of these was Swiss-born Norris Williams (USA), who survived the sinking of the *Titanic* in 1912, swimming in icy water for over an hour, won the Croix de Guerre and the Legion d'Honneur in the First World War, a Wimbledon title in 1920, an Olympic gold medal in 1924, and died aged 77.

TENNIS MEDAL TOTALS

Country	G	S	B	Total
Great Britain	16	13	15	44
France	8	7	6	21
United States	9	5	6	20
Greece	1	5	2	8
Czechoslovakia	1	1	6	8
Germany (FRG)	3	2	2	7
Sweden	–	2	5	7
South Africa	3	1	–	4
Japan	–	2	–	2
Argentina	–	1	–	1
Austria	–	1	–	1
Denmark	–	1	–	1
Spain	–	1	–	1
Australia	–	–	1	1
Bulgaria	–	–	1	1
Italy	–	–	1	1
Netherlands	–	–	1	1
New Zealand	–	–	1	1
Norway	–	–	1	1
	41	42	48	131[1]

[1]*Two-country pairs counted as two medals.*

TENNIS MEDALS

	Gold	Silver	Bronze
Men's Singles			
1896	John Boland (GBR)	Demis Kasdaglis (GRE)	–
1900[1]	Hugh Doherty (GBR)	Harold Mahoney (GBR)	Reginald Doherty (GBR)
			AB Norris (GBR)
1904	Beals Wright (USA)	Robert LeRoy (USA)	–
1906	Max Décugis (FRA)	Maurice Germot (FRA)	Zdenek Zemla (BOH)
1908	Josiah Ritchie (GBR)	Otto Froitzheim (GER)	Wilberforce Eves (GBR)
1908[2]	Wentworth Gore (GBR)	George Caridia (GBR)	Josiah Ritchie (GBR)
1912	Charles Winslow (SAF)	Harold Kitson (SAF)	Oscar Kreuzer (GER)
1912[2]	André Gobert (FRA)	Charles Dixon (GBR)	Anthony Wilding (NZL)
1920	Louis Raymond (SAF)	Ichiya Kumagae (JPN)	Charles Winslow (GBR)
1924	Vincent Richards (USA)	Henri Cochet (FRA)	Umberto De Morpurgo (ITA)
1988[1]	Miloslav Mecir (TCH)	Tim Mayotte (USA)	Stefan Edberg (SWE)
			Brad Gilbert (USA)

[1]*Two bronze medals.*   [2]*Indoor tournaments.*

	Gold	Silver	Bronze
Men's Doubles			
1896	GBR/Germany	Greece	–[1]
1900[2]	Great Britain	USA/France	France
			Great Britain[2]
1904	United States	United States	United States
			United States[2]
1906	France	Greece	Bohemia
1908	Great Britain	Great Britain	Great Britain
1908[3]	Great Britain	Great Britain	Sweden

	Gold	Silver	Bronze
1912	South Africa	Austria	France
1912[3]	France	Sweden	Great Britain
1920	Great Britain	Japan	France
1924	United States	France	France
1988[2]	United States	Spain	Czechoslovakia
			Sweden

[1]No bronze medal.   [2]Two bronze medals.   [3]Indoor tournaments.

Mixed Doubles

1900[1]	Great Britain	France/GBR	Bohemia/GBR
			United States/GBR
1906	France	Greece	Greece
1912	Germany	Sweden	France
1912[2]	Great Britain	Great Britain	Sweden
1920	France	Great Britain	Czechoslovakia
1924	United States	United States	Netherlands

[1]Two bronze medals in 1900.   [2]Indoor tournament.   1928–1988 Event not held.

Women's Singles

1900[1]	Charlotte Cooper (GBR)	Hélène Prévost (FRA)	Marion Jones (USA)
			Hedwiga Rosenbaumova (BOH)
1906	Esmee Simiriotou (GRE)	Sophia Marinou (GRE)	Euphrosine Paspati (GRE)
1908	Dorothea Chambers (GBR)	Dorothy Boothby (GBR)	Joan Winch (GBR)
1908[2]	Gwen Eastlake-Smith (GBR)	Angela Greene (GBR)	Märtha Adlerstrahle (SWE)
1912	Marguerite Broquedis (FRA)	Dora Köring (GER)	Molla Bjurstedt (NOR)
1912[2]	Ethel Hannam (GBR)	Thora Castenschiold (DEN)	Mabel Parton (GBR)
1920	Suzanne Lenglen (FRA)	Dorothy Holman (GBR)	Kitty McKane (GBR)
1924	Helen Wills (USA)	Julie Vlasto (FRA)	Kitty McKane (GBR)
1988[1]	Steffi Graf (FRG)	Gabriela Sabatini (ARG)	Zina Garrison (USA)
			Manuela Maleyeva (BUL)

[1]Two bronze medals.   [2]Indoor tournaments.   1928–1984 Event not held.

Women's Doubles

1920	Great Britain	Great Britain	France
1924	United States	Great Britain	Great Britain
1988	United States	Czechoslovakia	Australia
			FRG

1928–1984 Event not held.

TRACK & FIELD (ATHLETICS)

The track and field events have been the centre-piece of every Olympic Games since 1896. From 1920 until the International Amateur Athletics Federation (IAAF) inaugurated their first world title meeting in 1983, the Olympic events were also official world championships. The first champion in modern Olympic history was James Connolly (USA) who won the triple jump (then called the hop, step and jump) on 6 April 1896. He also won medals in the high and long jumps, and was later a novelist and war correspondent.

The first winner of an Olympic event was Francis Lane (USA) who had won the first heat of the 100m earlier the same day. Women's events were introduced in 1928, and the first female gold medallist was Halina Konopacka (POL) in the discus. Again the first winner of an Olympic women's event was Anni Holdmann (GER) who took the first heat of the 100m the day before.

A record ten gold medals were won by Ray Ewry (USA) in the standing jumps from 1900 to 1908. It is a feat unsurpassed in any sport, and achieved despite the fact that Ewry had contracted polio as a child. The Finnish distance runner Paavo Nurmi won a total of twelve medals from 1920 to 1928, comprising nine golds and three silvers. He won them in an unmatched seven different events, and his five golds in 1924 are a record for one Games. Incidentally, Ewry had uniquely won three of his titles on the same day in 1900.

The most individual titles at one Games is four by Alvin Kraenzlein (USA) in 1900. This total was equalled by Jesse Owens (USA) in 1936 and Carl Lewis (USA) in 1984, but they only gained three individual events – 100m, 200m and long jump – with the fourth gold medal in the relay. Nurmi's team-mate Ville Ritola won a record six medals in 1924, consisting of four golds and two silvers, incurring eight distance races in eight days. In 1912 the forerunner of all 'Flying Finns', Hannes Kolehmainen, had won six such races within nine days.

Four gold medals have been won by three women: Fanny Blankers-Koen (HOL), all in 1948 which is also a female record for one Games, as is the three individual titles included; Betty Cuthbert (AUS) in 1956 and 1964; and East Germany's Bärbel Wöckel (née Eckert) in 1976 and 1980. Shirley Strickland (later de la Hunty) of Australia won a record seven medals from 1948 to 1956, comprising three golds, one silver and three bronzes. This total was equalled by Irena Szewińska (née Kirszenstein) (POL) with three golds, two silvers and two bronzes from 1964 to 1976. Szewińska is the only woman to win medals at three successive Games, and also in five different events. It is worth noting that photo-finish evidence indicates that Strickland also came in third in the 200m of 1948, but no move has been made to change the result officially.

A unique track and field achievement, equalling that of yachting's Paul Elvström, was the four successive gold medals won in the discus by Al Oerter (USA) from 1956–1968. Almost as worthy were the three golds and one silver won by Viktor Saneyev (URS) in the triple jump, 1968–1980. Mildred Didrikson (USA) – who later achieved golf fame as Babe Zaharias – achieved a unique treble in 1932 when she won medals in a run (80m hurdles – gold), a jump (high jump silver) and a throw (javelin – gold).

Another unusual spread of medals went to Micheline Ostermeyer (FRA) in 1948, with golds

Micheline Ostermeyer of France, perhaps the only concert pianist to win Olympic glory, with shot and discus gold medals.

in the shot and discus and a bronze in the high jump. Perhaps even more unusual was the fact that she was a concert pianist. The best male equivalent was Robert Garrett (USA) with gold in the shot and discus, and silver in the high and long jumps, in 1896. Australian Stanley Rowley won bronze medals in the 60m, 100m and 200m in 1900 representing Australasia, and then was drafted into the British team for the 5000m team race and won a gold medal, although he did not finish the race.

The oldest gold medallist was Patrick 'Babe' McDonald (USA), winning the 56lb weight throw

in 1920 aged 42yr 23 days. The youngest gold medallist was Barbara Jones (USA) in the 1952 sprint relay, aged 15yr 123 days, while the youngest individual event champion was Ulrike Meyfarth (FRG) who won the high jump in 1972 aged exactly one year older than Jones. The youngest male champion was Robert Mathias (USA) who won the 1948 decathlon aged 17yr 263 days, and later (1966) became a US Congressman. The oldest female champion was Lia Manoliu (ROM) in the 1968 discus, aged 36yr 176 days.

Manoliu is also co-holder of another female record, that of attending six Games (1952–

1972). Her 20-year span of competition matched that of Dorothy Odam-Tyler (GBR), 1936–1956. At least eight men have attended five Games.

The oldest medallist was Tebbs Lloyd Johnson (GBR) in the 50km walk of 1952, aged 48yr 115 days, and the oldest female medallist was Dana Zatopkova (TCH) in the 1960 javelin, aged 37yr 248 days. Barbara Jones (see above) was also the youngest medallist, while the youngest male medallist was Pál Simon (HUN) in the 1908 medley relay, aged 17yr 206 days. The oldest competitor ever in Olympic athletics was John Deni (USA), aged 49yr 74 days when 15th in the 50km walk in 1952. The oldest female competitor was Joyce Smith (GBR), aged 46yr 282 days when finishing 11th in the 1984 marathon.

The first brothers to win medals were Patrick and Con Leahy, Irishmen representing Great Britain, in 1900 and 1906 respectively. The first to gain medals at the same Games were Platt and Ben Adams (USA), who came first and second in the 1912 standing high jump. The most successful siblings were the Press sisters (URS), Tamara with three golds and a silver, and Irina with two golds, in 1960 and 1964. The only twins to win medals were Patrick and Pascal Barré (FRA) in the bronze medal sprint relay of 1980.

Father and son gold medallists are represented by two families. Werner Järvinen (FIN) won the 1906 Greek style discus, his son Matti won the javelin in 1932, and another son, Akilles, gained silver medals in the 1928 and 1932 decathlons. In 1948 Imre Németh (HUN) won the hammer, and 28 years later his son Miklos won the javelin with a world record throw. The most successful mother/daugh-

ter combination was Elisabeta Bagriantseva (URS) with a silver in the 1952 discus and Irina Nazarova with a gold in the 4 × 400m relay of 1980.

One of the more poignant Olympic stories relates to Marie Dollinger, who was one of the girls involved in dropping the baton in the 1936 sprint relay when the German girls 'couldn't lose'. One imagines the thoughts of her daughter, Brunhilde Hendrix, running in the 1960 relay final – happily, she won a silver medal.

The first married couple to win gold medals were Emil and Dana Zatopek (TCH). Even more remarkable is the fact that Dana won her javelin title on the

same afternoon as one of Emil's in 1952 – both of them were also born on the same day. The only other couple to achieve this were Victor Bryzgin (URS), in the 4 × 100m in 1988, and his wife Olga, gold medallist in the 400m and 4 × 400m.

Frank Wykoff (USA) is the only sprinter to win gold medals in three Games, in relay teams from 1928 to 1936. The first Olympic athlete to be disqualified for contravening the drug regulations was Danuta Rosani (POL) in the 1976 discus. By far the biggest uproar occurred with the positive testing of Ben Johnson (CAN) after he had won the 1988 100m title in an apparently fabulous new world

Pat McDonald (USA) winning the 1912 shot. Success in the 56lb weight throw in 1920 makes him the oldest ever athletics champion.

Silver medallist in the standing long jump of 1912 was Platt Adams of the United States. His brother Ben took the bronze, and each went one better in the standing high jump event that year.

OLYMPIC RECORDS – MEN

100m	9.92s	Carl Lewis (USA)	1988
200m	19.75s	Joe DeLoach (USA)	1988
400m	43.86s	Lee Evans (USA)	1968
800m	1m 43.00s	Joaquim Cruz (BRA)	1984
1500m	3m 32.53s	Sebastian Coe (GBR)	1984
5000m	13m 05.59s	Saïd Aouita (MOR)	1984
10 000m	27m 21.46s	Brahim Boutayeb (MOR)	1988
Marathon	2h 09m 21s	Carlos Lopes (POR)	1984
110mH	12.98s	Roger Kingdom (USA)	1988
400mH	47.19s	Andre Phillips (USA)	1988
3000mSt	8m 05.51s	Julius Kariuki (KEN)	1988
20km W	1h 19m 57s	Jozef Pribilinec (TCH)	1988
50km W	3h 38m 29s	Vyacheslav Ivanenko (URS)	1988
4 x 100m	37.83s	USA	1984
4 x 400m	2m 56.16s	USA	1968
	2m 56.16s	USA	1988
High Jump	2.38m	Gennadiy Avdeyenko (URS)	1988
Pole Vault	5.90m	Sergey Bubka (URS)	1988
Long Jump	8.90m	Bob Beamon (USA)	1968
Triple Jump	17.61m	Khristo Markov (BUL)	1988
Shot	22.47m	Ulf Timmermann (GDR)	1988
Discus	68.82m	Jurgen Schult (GDR)	1988
Hammer	84.80m	Sergey Litvinov (URS)	1988
Javelin	85.90m*	Jan Zelezny (TCH)	1988
Decathlon	8847pts	Daley Thompson (GBR)	1984

In qualifying round.

OLYMPIC RECORDS – WOMEN

100m	10.62s*/10.54sw	Florence Griffith-Joyner (USA)	1988
200m	21.34s	Florence Griffith-Joyner (USA)	1988
400m	48.65s	Olga Bryzgina (USA)	1988
800m	1m 53.43s	Nadyezda Olizarenko (URS)	1980
1500m	3m 53.96s	Paula Ivan (ROM)	1988
3000m	8m 26.53s	Tatyana Samolenko (URS)	1988
10 000m	31m 05.21s	Olga Bondarenko (URS)	1988
Marathon	2h 24m 52s	Joan Benoit (USA)	1984
100mH	12.38s	Yordanka Donkova (BUL)	1988
400mH	53.17s	Debbie Flintoff-King (AUS)	1988
4 x 100m	41.60s	GDR	1980
4 x 400m	3m 15.17s	USSR	1988
10km W	–	Not previously held	
High Jump	2.03m	Louise Ritter (USA)	1988
Long Jump	7.40m	Jackie Joyner-Kersee (USA)	1988
Shot	22.41m	Ilona Slupianek (GDR)	1980
Discus	72.30m	Martina Hellmann (GDR)	1988
Javelin	74.68m	Petra Felke (GDR)	1988
Heptathlon	7291pts	Jackie Joyner-Kersee (USA)	1988

In preliminary round.   w wind assisted.

record time of 9.79sec. The repercussions on world attitudes to drug testing were immense.

The scrutiny of 'sex testing' of women was introduced into the Games in 1968, many years too late in the opinion of many. They had in mind the case of Dora Ratjen (GER), who placed fourth in the 1936 high jump and was later found to be a man posing as a woman. Less clear cut was the case of Stella Walasiewicz (later Walsh), Polish-born but later an American citizen, who won gold and silver medals in the 100m of 1932 and 1936 respectively, and was reported, after her violent death in 1980, to have 'primary male characteristics'.

The shortest time that an athlete has held an Olympic record was 0.4sec by Olga Ruka-vishnikova (URS) in the 1980 pentathlon. That is the difference between her second place 800m time of 2min 04.8sec in the final event of the five-event contest, and the time of third-placed Nadyezda Tkachenko (URS) whose overall points score exceeded her team-mate's by 146.

Only three athletes have actually 'lost' a title and then won it back. Nina Romashkova-Ponomareva (URS) won the discus in 1952, came third in 1956, then won again in 1960. Similarly Ulrike Meyfarth (FRG) won the high jump in 1972, did not make the final in 1976, but won again in 1984. The only man to do so was Vladimir Golubnichiy (URS) in the 20km walk, winning in 1960, finishing third in 1964 and then first again in 1968. (He also finished second in 1972). Meyfarth's 12 years between gold medals is matched only by Al Oerter and Irena Szewińska.

A number of Olympic athletics medallists have later made their mark in Hollywood films.

TUG OF WAR

	Gold	Silver	Bronze
1900	Sweden/Denmark	United States	France
1904	United States	United States	United States
1906	Germany	Greece	Sweden
1908	Great Britain	Great Britain	Great Britain
1912	Sweden	Great Britain	–
1920	Great Britain	Netherlands	Belgium

Great Britain beat the USA in the tug-of-war at Antwerp in 1920, the last time the event would be held after 20 years in the Games.

In particular, they have come from the ranks of the decathletes – Jim Thorpe, Glenn Morris, Bob Mathias, Rafer Johnson, CK Yang, Floyd Simmons and Bruce Jenner. The 1928 silver medallist in the shot, Herman Brix, changed his name to Bruce Bennett and had many 'serious' roles after an initial Tarzan appearance. Norman Pritchard (IND), a 1900 medallist, made many silent films, while more recent additions to the Hollywood scene have been 1952 sprint relay gold winner Dean Smith (USA) and 1968 pole vault champion Bob Seagren (USA).

The film industries of other countries have welcomed Tapio Rautavaara (FIN), the 1948 javelin champion, Giuseppe Tosi (ITA), 1948 discus silver medallist, Giuseppe Gentile (ITA), 1968 triple jump bronze, and Adhemar Ferreira da Silva (BRA), the 1952 and 1956 triple jump champion.

TUG OF WAR

This sport was part of the athletics programme from 1900–1920. Three men won a record two golds and one silver from 1908 to 1920: John Shepherd, Frederick Humphreys and Edwin Mills, all from Great Britain. The oldest gold medallist was Humphreys, aged 42yr 204 days in 1920, while the youngest was Karl Staaf (SWE) aged 19yr 101 days in 1900.

There were some strange team compositions in the early days. The winning 1900 team was composed of three Swedes and three Danes; the 1904 competition was between American clubs; and the 1908 tournament was between British Police Clubs with London City police beating their colleagues from Liverpool.

TRACK & FIELD MEDAL TOTALS *Including Tug-of-War*

Country	MEN			WOMEN			Total
	G	S	B	G	S	B	
United States[1]	244	186	151	32	21	11	645
Soviet Union	34	35	40	30	20	34	193
Great Britain	43	57	40	4	20	12	176
Germany (FRG)	11	29	34	12	18	15	119[2]
Finland	47	32	29	–	2	–	110
GDR	14	14	14	24	23	21	110
Sweden	19	24	42	–	–	3	88
Australia	6	9	11	11	8	11	56
France	7	20	19	3	1	3	53
Italy	13	7	18	3	4	2	47
Canada	9	9	16	2	5	6	47
Poland	9	7	4	6	8	7	41
Hungary	6	13	16	3	1	2	41
Kenya	10	8	6	–	–	–	24
Romania	–	–	1	9	8	6	24
Greece	3	9	12	–	–	–	24
Czechoslovakia	6	7	3	3	2	2	23
Jamaica[3]	4	9	4	–	1	3	21
New Zealand	7	1	7	1	–	1	17
South Africa	4	4	4	1	1	1	15
Netherlands	–	2	5	5	2	1	15
Japan	4	4	6	–	1	–	15
Bulgaria	1	–	1	2	6	4	14
Norway	3	2	7	–	1	–	13
Cuba	2	5	1	1	1	2	12
Belgium	2	6	3	–	–	–	11
Ethiopia	5	1	4	–	–	–	10
Brazil	3	2	5	–	–	–	10
Switzerland	–	6	2	–	–	–	8
Ireland	4	1	–	–	–	–	5
Mexico	3	2	–	–	–	–	5
Morocco	2	1	1	1	–	–	5
Argentina	2	2	–	–	1	–	5
Portugal	1	1	1	1	–	1	5
Austria	–	–	–	1	1	3	5
Tunisia	1	2	1	–	–	–	4
Denmark	1	1	1	–	–	1	4
Trinidad	1	1	2	–	–	–	4
Chile	–	1	–	–	1	–	2
India	–	2	–	–	–	–	2
Tanzania	–	2	–	–	–	–	2
Yugoslavia	–	2	–	–	–	–	2
Estonia	–	1	1	–	–	–	2
Latvia	–	1	1	–	–	–	2
Spain	–	1	1	–	–	–	2
Taipei	–	1	–	–	–	1	2
China	–	–	1	–	–	1	2
Panama	–	–	2	–	–	–	2
Philippines	–	–	2	–	–	–	2
Luxembourg	1	–	–	–	–	–	1
Uganda	1	–	–	–	–	–	1
Haiti	–	1	–	–	–	–	1
Iceland	–	1	–	–	–	–	1
Ivory Coast	–	1	–	–	–	–	1
Senegal	–	1	–	–	–	–	1
Sri Lanka	–	1	–	–	–	–	1
Barbados[3]	–	–	1	–	–	–	1
Djibouti	–	–	1	–	–	–	1
Nigeria	–	–	1	–	–	–	1
Turkey	–	–	1	–	–	–	1
Venezuela	–	–	1	–	–	–	1
	533	535	524	155	157	154	2058

[1]Includes 2 additional golds awarded when Jim Thorpe reinstated to 1912 decathlon/pentathlon titles.
[2]Includes 1 gold, 11 silvers and 3 bronzes won by GDR athletes in combined German teams 1956–1964.
[3]Two bronzes counted for joint British West Indies 4 x 400m relay team in 1960.

I.A.A.F. TIMING RULES (Fully-automatic timing)

Automatic timing has a surprisingly long history (dating back to the 1920s), but rules governing its use were not formulated until the 1960s. In 1955, Rule 119 was adjusted to include the clause 'electrical timing may be used', but with no precise instructions; by inference, rounding off followed the rules for manual timing. Subsequent changes may be summarised as follows:

(A) Events up to 400m/440y

pre-1965 No formal rule. 1964 Olympic Games times were issued rounded off to the nearest tenth (but see note below).

1965–72 The above method was formally adopted into Rule 119.

1973–76 Rule unchanged, but in practice times were issued in hundredths (following the example of the 1972 Olympic Games).

1977– All times issued in hundredths.

(B) Events above 400m/440y

pre-1965 No formal rule. 1964 Olympic

Games times were rounded off according to the manual timing rule (and see also note below) (e.g. 0.05 to 0.14=0.1 for events up to 1 mile; 0.05 to 0.14=0.2 for events above 1 mile; 0.15 to 0.24=0.2 for all events).

1965–76 The above method was formally adopted into Rule 119.

1977–78 Rounding off to the nearest tenth for all events (e.g. 0.05 to 0.14= 0.1; 0.15 to 0.24=0.2, etc)

1979–80 Rounding up to the complete tenth for all events (e.g. 0.1 to 0.10=0.1; 0.11 to 0.20=0.2, etc)

1981– Rule changed – times issued in hundredths throughout.

(Note: For the period 1964–1970, the timing mechanism in photo-finish cameras was adjusted to delay the start by 0.05sec. Only knowledge of the actual photo-finish readings can enable us to correct the times.)

Implications of the above, for middle/long distance events

The result of all these changes is that the same actual time might have been issued (in tenths) with any of three different values, depending upon the year it was recorded.

For example, third place in the 1972 steeplechase (8:24.66) was recorded as 8:24.8. In the 1980 Games, the same time would have been issued as 8:24.7, while in 1968 (taking into account the timing delay of 0.05) it would have been 8:24.6 (i.e. rounded down from 8:24.61).

Another case: the winning time for the women's 800m in the 1976 Olympic Games is shown officially as 1:54.9; in 1980, the same time was recorded for second place. For the former, however, the actual time was 1:54.94 (rounded down), while for the latter it was 1:54.81 (rounded up). Continuing to show both as identical (1:54.9) is surely a nonsense.

TRACK & FIELD – MEN

Prior to 1972 automatic timings in the shorter distances to one-hundredths of a second are shown additionally, where known.

	Gold	Silver	Bronze
100 Metres			
1896	Thomas Burke (USA) 12.0	Fritz Hofmann (GER) 12.2	Alajos Szokolyi (HUN) 12.6
1900	Frank Jarvis (USA) 11.0	Walter Tewksbury (USA) 11.1	Stanley Rowley (AUS) 11.2
1904	Archie Hahn (USA) 11.0	Nathaniel Cartmell (USA) 11.2	William Hogenson (USA) 11.2
1906	Archie Hahn (USA) 11.2	Fay Moulton (USA) 11.3	Nigel Barker (AUS) 11.3
1908	Reginald Walker (SAF) 10.8	James Rector (USA) 10.9	Robert Kerr (CAN) 11.0
1912	Ralph Craig (USA) 10.8	Alvah Meyer (USA) 10.9	Donald Lippincott (USA) 10.9
1920	Charles Paddock (USA) 10.8	Morris Kirksey (USA) 10.8	Harry Edward (GBR) 11.0
1924	Harold Abrahams (GBR) 10.6	Jackson Scholz (USA) 10.7	Arthur Porritt (NZL) 10.8
1928	Percy Williams (CAN) 10.8	Jack London (GBR) 10.9	Georg Lammers (GER) 10.9
1932	Eddie Tolan (USA) 10.3 (10.38)	Ralph Metcalfe (USA) 10.3 (10.38)	Arthur Jonath (GER) 10.4 (10.50)
1936	Jesse Owens (USA) 10.3	Ralph Metcalfe (USA) 10.4	Martinus Osendarp (HOL) 10.5
1948	Harrison Dillard (USA) 10.3	Norwood Ewell (USA) 10.4	Lloyd LaBeach (PAN) 10.4
1952	Lindy Remigino (USA) 10.4 (10.79)	Herb McKenley (JAM) 10.4 (10.70)	Emmanuel McD Bailey (GBR) 10.4 (10.83)
1956	Bobby Joe Morrow (USA) 10.5 (10.62	Thane Baker (USA) 10.5 (10.77)	Hector Hogan (AUS) 10.6 (10.77)
1960	Armin Hary (GER) 10.2 (10.32)	David Sime (USA) 10.2 (10.35)	Peter Radford (GBR) 10.3 (10.42)
1964	Bob Hayes (USA) 10.0 (10.06)[1]	Enrique Figuerola (CUB) 10.2 (10.25)	Harry Jerome (CAN) 10.2 (10.27)
1968	James Hines (USA) 9.9 (9.95)	Lennox Miller (JAM) 10.0 (10.04)	Charles Greene (USA) 10.0 (10.07)
1972	Valeriy Borzov (URS) 10.14	Robert Taylor (USA) 10.24	Lennox Miller (JAM) 10.33
1976	Hasely Crawford (TRI) 10.06	Don Quarrie (JAM) 10.08	Valeriy Borzov (URS) 10.14
1980	Allan Wells (GBR) 10.25	Silvio Leonard (CUB) 10.25	Petar Petrov (BUL) 10.39
1984	Carl Lewis (USA) 9.99	Sam Graddy (USA) 10.19	Ben Johnson (CAN) 10.22
1988	Carl Lewis (USA) 9.92*[2]	Linford Christie (GBR) 9.97	Calvin Smith (USA) 9.99

*Olympic record.   [1]Hayes ran a wind-assisted 9.91 in the semi-final.   [2]Ben Johnson (CAN) won in 9.79 but was later disqualified.

200 Metres			
1900	Walter Tewksbury (USA) 22.2	Norman Pritchard (IND) 22.8	Stanley Rowley (AUS) 22.9
1904[1]	Archie Hahn (USA) 21.6	Nathaniel Cartmell (USA) 21.9	William Hogenson (USA) d.n.a.
1908	Robert Kerr (CAN) 22.6	Robert Cloughen (USA) 22.6	Nathaniel Cartmell (USA) 22.7
1912	Ralph Craig (USA) 21.7	Donald Lippincott (USA) 21.8	Willie Applegarth (GBR) 22.0
1920	Allen Woodring (USA) 22.0	Charles Paddock (USA) 22.1	Harry Edward (GBR) 22.2
1924	Jackson Scholz (USA) 21.6	Charles Paddock (USA) 21.7	Eric Liddell (GBR) 21.9
1928	Percy Williams (CAN) 21.8	Walter Rangeley (GBR) 21.9	Helmut Körnig[2] (GER) 21.9
1932	Eddie Tolan (USA) 21.2 (21.12)	George Simpson (USA) 21.4	Ralph Metcalfe[3] (USA) 21.5
1936	Jesse Owens (USA) 20.7	Mack Robinson (USA) 21.1	Martinus Osendarp (HOL) 21.3
1948	Mel Patton (USA) 21.1	Norwood Ewell (USA) 21.1	Lloyd LaBeach (PAN) 21.2
1952	Andrew Stanfield (USA) 20.7 (20.81)	Thane Baker (USA) 20.8 (20.97)	James Gathers (USA) 20.8 (21.08)
1956	Bobby Joe Morrow (USA) 20.6 (20.75)	Andrew Stanfield (USA) 20.7 (20.97)	Thane Baker (USA) 20.9 (21.05)

	Gold	Silver	Bronze
1960	Livio Berruti (ITA) 20.5 (20.62)	Lester Carney (USA) 20.6 (20.69)	Abdoulaye Seye (FRA) 20.7 (20.83)
1964	Henry Carr (USA) 20.3 (20.36)	Paul Drayton (USA) 20.5 (20.58)	Edwin Roberts (TRI) 20.6 (20.63)
1968	Tommie Smith (USA) 19.8 (19.83)	Peter Norman (AUS) 20.0 (20.06)	John Carlos (USA) 20.0 (20.10)
1972	Valeriy Borzov (URS) 20.00	Larry Black (USA) 20.19	Pietro Mennea (ITA) 20.30
1976	Don Quarrie (JAM) 20.23	Millard Hampton (USA) 20.29	Dwayne Evans (USA) 20.43
1980	Pietro Mennea (ITA) 20.19	Allan Wells (GBR) 20.21	Don Quarrie (JAM) 20.29
1984	Carl Lewis (USA) 19.80	Kirk Baptiste (USA) 19.96	Thomas Jefferson (USA) 20.26
1988	Joe DeLoach (USA) 19.75*	Carl Lewis (USA) 19.79	Robson da Silva (BRA) 20.04

[1]*Race over straight course. Hahn's three opponents were all given 2yd handicaps for false starting.* [2]*Awarded bronze medal when Scholz (USA) refused to re-run after tie.* [3]*Metcalfe's lane was later found to be 1½m too long.* *Olympic record.*
1896, 1906 Event not held.

400 Metres

1896	Thomas Burke (USA) 54.2	Herbert Jamison (USA) 55.2	Fritz Hofmann (GER) 55.6
1900	Maxwell Long (USA) 49.4	William Holland (USA) 49.6	Ernst Schultz (DEN) 15m
1904	Harry Hillman (USA) 49.2	Frank Waller (USA) 49.9	Herman Groman (USA) 50.0
1906	Paul Pilgrim (USA) 53.2	Wyndham Halswelle (GBR) 53.8	Nigel Barker (AUS) 54.1
1908[1]	Wyndham Halswelle (GBR) 50.0	–	–
1912	Charles Reidpath (USA) 48.2	Hanns Braun (GER) 48.3	Edward Lindberg (USA) 48.4
1920	Bevil Rudd (SAF) 49.6	Guy Butler (GBR) 49.9	Nils Engdahl (SWE) 50.0
1924	Eric Liddell (GBR) 47.6	Horatio Fitch (USA) 48.4	Guy Butler (GBR) 48.6
1928	Ray Barbuti (USA) 47.8	James Ball (CAN) 48.0	Joachim Büchner (GER) 48.2
1932	William Carr (USA) 46.2 (46.28)	Ben Eastman (USA) 46.4 (46.50)	Alexander Wilson (CAN) 47.4
1936	Archie Williams (USA) 46.5 (46.66)	Godfrey Brown (GBR) 46.7 (46.68)	James LuValle (USA) 46.8 (46.84)
1948	Arthur Wint (JAM) 46.2	Herb McKenley (JAM) 46.4	Mal Whitfield (USA) 46.6
1952	George Rhoden (JAM) 45.9 (46.09)	Herb McKenley (JAM) 45.9 (46.20)	Ollie Matson (USA) 46.8 (46.94)
1956	Charles Jenkins (USA) 46.7 (46.85)	Karl-Friedrich Haas (GER) 46.8 (47.12)	Voitto Hellsten (FIN) 47.0 (47.15) Ardalion Ignatyev (URS) 47.0 (47.15)
1960	Otis Davis (USA) 44.9 (45.07)	Carl Kaufmann (GER) 44.9 (45.08)	Mal Spence (SAF) 45.5 (45.60)
1964	Mike Larrabee (USA) 45.1 (45.15)	Wendell Mottley (TRI) 45.2 (45.24)	Andrzej Badenski (POL) 45.6 (45.64)
1968	Lee Evans (USA) 43.8 (43.86)*	Lawrence James (USA) 43.9 (43.97)	Ron Freeman (USA) 44.4 (44.41)
1972	Vince Matthews (USA) 44.66	Wayne Collett (USA) 44.80	Julius Sang (KEN) 44.92
1976	Alberto Juantorena (CUB) 44.26	Fred Newhouse (USA) 44.40	Herman Frazier (USA) 44.95
1980	Viktor Markin (URS) 44.60	Rick Mitchell (AUS) 44.84	Frank Schaffer (GDR) 44.87
1984	Alonzo Babers (USA) 44.27	Gabriel Tiacoh (CIV) 44.54	Antonio McKay (USA) 44.71
1988	Steve Lewis (USA) 43.87	Harry Reynolds (USA) 43.93	Danny Everett (USA) 44.09

[1]*Re-run ordered after John Carpenter (USA) disqualified in first final. Only Halswelle showed up and 'walked over' for the title.* *Olympic record.*

800 Metres

1896	Edwin Flack (AUS) 2:11.0	Nandor Dáni (HUN) 2:11.8	Dimitrios Golemis (GRE) 2:28.0
1900	Alfred Tysoe (GBR) 2:01.2	John Cregan (USA) 2:03.0	David Hall (USA) d.n.a.
1904	James Lightbody (USA) 1:56.0	Howard Valentine (USA) 1:56.3	Emil Breitkreutz (USA) 1:56.4
1906	Paul Pilgrim (USA) 2:01.5	James Lightbody (USA) 2:01.6	Wyndham Halswelle (GBR) 2:03.0
1908	Mel Sheppard (USA) 1:52.8	Emilio Lunghi (ITA) 1:54.2	Hanns Braun (GER) 1:55.2
1912	James Meredith (USA) 1:51.9	Mel Sheppard (USA) 1:52.0	Ira Davenport (USA) 1:52.0
1920	Albert Hill (GBR) 1:53.4	Earl Eby (USA) 1:53.6	Bevil Rudd (SAF) 1:54.0
1924	Douglas Lowe (GBR) 1:52.4	Paul Martin (SUI) 1:52.6	Schuyler Enck (USA) 1:53.0
1928	Douglas Lowe (GBR) 1:51.8	Erik Bylehn (SWE) 1:52.8	Hermann Engelhardt (GER) 1:53.2
1932	Thomas Hampson (GBR) 1:49.7	Alexander Wilson (CAN) 1:49.9	Phil Edwards (CAN) 1:51.5
1936	John Woodruff (USA) 1:52.9	Mario Lanzi (ITA) 1:53.3	Phil Edwards (CAN) 1:53.6
1948	Mal Whitfield (USA) 1:49.2	Arthur Wint (JAM) 1:49.5	Marcle Hansenne (FRA) 1:49.8
1952	Mal Whitfield (USA) 1:49.2	Arthur Wint (JAM) 1:49.4	Heinz Ulzheimer (GER) 1:49.7
1956	Tom Courtney (USA) 1:47.7	Derek Johnson (GBR) 1:47.8	Audun Boysen (NOR) 1:48.1
1960	Peter Snell (NZL) 1:46.3	Roger Moens (BEL) 1:46.5	George Kerr[1] (BWI) 1:47.1
1964	Peter Snell (NZL) 1:45.1	Bill Crothers (CAN) 1:45.6	Wilson Kiprugut (KEN) 1:45.9
1968	Ralph Doubell (AUS) 1:44.3	Wilson Kiprugut (KEN) 1:44.5	Tom Farrell (USA) 1:45.4
1972	Dave Wottle (USA) 1:45.9	Yevgeniy Arzhanov (URS) 1:45.9	Mike Boit (KEN) 1:46.0
1976	Alberto Juantorena (CUB) 1:43.5	Ivo Van Damme (BEL) 1:34.9	Richard Wohlhuter (USA) 1:44.1
1980	Steve Ovett (GBR) 1:45.4	Sebastian Coe (GBR) 1:45.9	Nikolai Kirov (URS) 1:46.0
1984	Joaquim Cruz (BRA) 1:43.00*	Sebastian Coe (GBR) 1:43.64	Earl Jones (USA) 1:43.83
1988	Paul Ereng (KEN) 1:43.45	Joaquim Cruz (BRA) 1:43.90	Saïd Aouita (MAR) 1:44.06

[1]*Kerr was a Jamaican in the combined British West Indies team.* *Olympic record.*

	Gold	Silver	Bronze

1500 Metres

Year	Gold	Silver	Bronze
1896	Edwin Flack (AUS) 4:33.2	Arthur Blake (USA) 4:34.0	Albin Lermusiaux (FRA) 4:36.0
1900	Charles Bennett (GBR) 4:06.2	Henri Deloge (FRA) 4:06.6	John Bray (USA) 4:07.2
1904	James Lightbody (USA) 4:05.4	William Verner (USA) 4:06.8	Lacey Hearn (USA) d.n.a.
1906	James Lightbody (USA) 4:12.0	John McGough (GBR) 4:12.6	Kristian Hellström (SWE) 4:13.4
1908	Mel Sheppard (USA) 4:03.4	Harold Wilson (GBR) 4:03.6	Norman Hallows (GBR) 4:04.0
1912[1]	Arnold Jackson (GBR) 3:56.8	Abel Kiviat (USA) 3:56.9	Norman Taber (USA) 3:56.9
1920	Albert Hill (GBR) 4:01.8	Philip Baker[1] (GBR) 4:02.4	Lawrence Shields (USA) 4:03.1
1924	Paavo Nurmi (FIN) 3:53.6	Willy Schärer (SUI) 3:55.0	Henry Stallard (GBR) 3:55.6
1928	Harri Larva (FIN) 3:53.2	Jules Ladoumègue (FRA) 3:53.8	Eino Purje (FIN) 3:56.4
1932	Luigi Beccali (ITA) 3:51.2	John Cornes (GBR) 3:52.6	Phil Edwards (CAN) 3:52.8
1936	Jack Lovelock (NZL) 3:47.8	Glenn Cunningham (USA) 3:48.4	Luigi Beccali (ITA) 3:49.2
1948	Henry Eriksson (SWE) 3:49.8	Lennart Strand (SWE) 3:50.4	Willem Slijkhuis (HOL) 3:50.4
1952	Josef Barthel (LUX) 3:45.1	Bob McMillen (USA) 3:45.2	Werner Lueg (GER) 3:45.4
1956	Ron Delany (IRL) 3:41.2	Klaus Richtzenhain (GER) 3:42.0	John Landy (AUS) 3:42.0
1960	Herb Elliott (AUS) 3:35.6	Michel Jazy (FRA) 3:38.4	István Rózsavölgyi (HUN) 3:39.2
1964	Peter Snell (NZL) 3:38.1	Josef Odlozil (TCH) 3:39.6	John Davies (NZL) 3:39.6
1968	Kipchoge Keino (KEN) 3:34.9	Jim Ryun (USA) 3:37.8	Bodo Tümmler (FRG) 3:39.0
1972	Pekka Vasala (FIN) 3:36.3	Kipchoge Keino (KEN) 3:36.8	Rod Dixon (NZL) 3:37.5
1976	John Walker (NZL) 3:39.2	Ivo Van Damme (BEL) 3:39.3	Paul-Heinz Wellmann (FRG) 3:39.3
1980	Sebastian Coe (GBR) 3:38.4	Jürgen Straub (GDR) 3:38.8	Steve Ovett (GBR) 3:39.0
1984	Sebastian Coe (GBR) 3:32.53*	Steve Cram (GBR) 3:33.40	Jose Abascal (ESP) 3:34.30
1988	Peter Rono (KEN) 3:35.96	Peter Elliott (GBR) 3:36.15	Jens-Peter Herold (GDR) 3:36.21

[1]*Jackson later changed name to Strode-Jackson and Baker changed to Noel-Baker.*   *Olympic record.*

5000 Metres

Year	Gold	Silver	Bronze
1912	Hannes Kolehmainen (FIN) 14:36.6	Jean Bouin (FRA) 14:36.7	George Hutson (GBR) 15:07.6
1920	Joseph Guillemot (FRA) 14:55.6	Paavo Nurmi (FIN) 15:00.0	Erik Backman (SWE) 15:13.0
1924[1]	Paavo Nurmi (FIN) 14:31.2	Ville Ritola (FIN) 14:31.4	Edvin Wide (SWE) 15:01.8
1928	Ville Ritola (FIN) 14:38.0	Paavo Nurmi (FIN) 14:40.0	Edvin Wide (SWE) 14:41.2
1932	Lauri Lehtinen (FIN) 14:30.0	Ralph Hill (USA) 14:30.0	Lauri Virtanen (FIN) 14:44.0
1936	Gunnar Höckert (FIN) 14:22.2	Lauri Lehtinen (FIN) 14:25.8	Henry Jonsson[2] (SWE) 14:29.0
1948	Gaston Reiff (BEL) 14:17.6	Emil Zatopek (TCH) 14:17.8	Willem Slijkhuis (HOL) 14:26.8
1952	Emil Zatopek (TCH) 14:06.6	Alain Mimoun (FRA) 14:07.4	Herbert Schade (GER) 14:08.6
1956	Vladimir Kuts (URS) 13:39.6	Gordon Pirie (GBR) 13:50.6	Derek Ibbotson (GBR) 13:54.4
1960	Murray Halberg (NZL) 13:43.4	Hans Grodotzki (GER) 13:44.6	Kazimierz Zimny (POL) 13:44.8
1964	Bob Schul (USA) 13:48.8	Harald Norpoth (GER) 13:49.6	Bill Dellinger (USA) 13:49.8
1968	Mohamed Gammoudi (TUN) 14:05.0	Kipchoge Keino (KEN) 14:05.2	Naftali Temu (KEN) 14:06.4
1972	Lasse Viren (FIN) 13:26.4	Mohamed Gammoudi (TUN) 13:27.4	Ian Stewart (GBR) 13:27.6
1976	Lasse Viren (FIN) 13:24.8	Dick Quax (NZL) 13:25.2	Klaus-Peter Hildenbrand (FRG) 13:25.4
1980	Miruts Yifter (ETH) 13:21.0	Suleiman Nyambui (TAN) 13:21.6	Kaarlo Maaninka (FIN) 13:22.0
1984	Saïd Aouita (MAR) 13:05.59*	Markus Ryffel (SUI) 13:07.54	Antonio Leitao (POR) 13:09.20
1988	John Ngugi (KEN) 13:11.70	Dieter Baumann (FRG) 13:15.52	Hansjörg Kunze (GDR) 13:15.73

[1]*Nurmi won 5000m only 1½ hours after winning the 1500m.*   [2]*Jonsson later changed name to Kälarne.*   *Olympic record.*
1896–1908 Event not held.

10 000 Metres

Year	Gold	Silver	Bronze
1906[1]	Henry Hawtrey (GBR) 26:11.8	John Svanberg (SWE) 26:19.4	Edward Dahl (SWE) 26:26.2
1908[1]	Emil Voigt (GBR) 25:11.2	Edward Owen (GBR) 25:24.0	John Svanberg (SWE) 25:37.2
1912	Hannes Kolehmainen (FIN) 31;20.8	Louis Tewanima (USA) 32:06.6	Albin Stenroos (FIN) 32:21.8
1920	Paavo Nurmi (FIN) 31:45.8	Joseph Guillemot (FRA) 31:47.2	James Wilson (GBR) 31:50.8
1924	Ville Ritola (FIN) 30:23.2	Edvin Wide (SWE) 30:55.2	Eero Berg (FIN) 31:43.0
1928	Paavo Nurmi (FIN) 30:18.8	Ville Ritola (FIN) 30:19.4	Edwin Wide (SWE) 31:00.8
1932	Janusz Kusocinski (POL) 30:11.4	Volmari Iso-Hollo (FIN) 30:12.6	Lauri Virtanen (FIN) 30:35.0
1936	Ilmari Salminen (FIN) 30:15.4	Arvo Askola (FIN) 30:15.6	Volmari Iso-Hollo (FIN) 30:20.2
1948	Emil Zatopek (TCH) 29:59.6	Alain Mimoun (FRA) 30:47.4	Bertil Albertsson (SWE) 30:53.6
1952	Emil Zatopek (TCH) 29:17.0	Alain Mimoun (FRA) 29:32.8	Aleksandr Anufriyev (URS) 29:48.2
1956	Vladimir Kuts (URS) 28:45.6	József Kovács (HUN) 28:52.4	Allan Lawrence (AUS) 28:53.6
1960	Pyotr Bolotnikov (URS) 28:32.2	Hans Grodotzki (GER) 28:37.0	David Power (AUS) 28:38.2[2]
1964	Billy Mills (USA) 28:24.4	Mohamed Gammoudi (TUN) 28:24.8	Ron Clarke (AUS) 28:25.8
1968	Naftali Temu (KEN) 29:27.4	Mamo Wolde (ETH) 29:28.0	Mohamed Gammoudi (TUN) 29:34.2
1972	Lasse Viren (FIN) 27:38.4	Emiel Puttemans (BEL) 27:39.6	Miruts Yifter (ETH) 27:41.0
1976	Lasse Viren (FIN) 27:44.4	Carlos Lopes (POR) 27:45.2	Brendan Foster (GBR) 27:54.9
1980	Miruts Yifter (ETH) 27:42.7	Kaarlo Maaninka (FIN) 27:44.3	Mohammed Kedir (ETH) 27:44.7
1984	Alberto Cova (ITA) 27:47.54	Mike McLeod (GBR) 28:06.22[3]	Mike Musyoki (KEN) 28:06.46
1988	Brahim Boutayeb (MAR) 27:21.46*	Salvatore Antibo (ITA) 27:23.55	Kipkemboi Kimeli (KEN) 27:25.16

[1]*5 miles (8046m).*   [2]*Recent investigation suggests 28:37.7.*   [3]*Martti Vainio (FIN) finished second but failed a drugs test.*
Olympic record.   1896–1904 Event not held.

Gold	Silver	Bronze

Marathon

The length of the marathon was standardised at the 1908 distance of 26 miles 385 yards (42 195 metres) from 1924. Previously the distances had been: 1896 & 1904 – 40 000m, 1900 – 40 260m, 1906 – 41 860m, 1912 – 40 200m, 1920 – 42 750m.

Year	Gold	Silver	Bronze
1896	Spyridon Louis (GRE) 2h 58:50	Charilaos Vasilakos (GRE) 3h 06:03	Gyula Kellner (HUN) 3h 09:35
1900	Michel Theato (FRA) 2h 59:45	Emile Champion (FRA) 3h 04:17	Ernst Fast (SWE) 3h 36:14
1904	Thomas Hicks (USA) 3h 28:35	Albert Coray[1] (FRA) 3h 34:52	Arthur Newton (USA) 3h 47:33
1906	William Sherring (CAN) 2h 51:23.6	John Svanberg (SWE) 2h 58:20.8	William Frank (USA) 3h 00:46.8
1908[2]	John Hayes (USA) 2h 55:18.4	Charles Hefferon (SAF) 2h 56:06.0	Joseph Forshaw (USA) 2h 57:10.4
1912	Kenneth McArthur (SAF) 2h 36:54.8	Christian Gitsham (SAF) 2h 37:52.0	Gaston Strobino (USA) 2h 38:42.4
1920	Hannes Kolehmainen (FIN) 2h 32:35.8	Jüri Lossman (EST) 2h 32:48.6	Valerio Arri (ITA) 2h 36:32.8
1924	Albin Stenroos (FIN) 2h 41:22.6	Romeo Bertini (ITA) 2h 47:19.6	Clarence DeMar (USA) 2h 48:14.0
1928	Mohamed El Ouafi (FRA) 2h 32:57	Miguel Plaza (CHI) 2h 33:23	Martti Marttelin (FIN) 2h 35:02
1932	Juan Carlos Zabala (ARG) 2h 31:56	Sam Ferris (GBR) 2h 31:55	Armas Toivonen (FIN) 2h 32:12
1936	Sohn Kee-Chung[3] (JPN) 2h 29:19.2	Ernest Harper (GBR) 2h 31:23.2	Nam Seong-Yong[3] (JPN) 2h 31:42.0
1948	Delfo Cabrera (ARG) 2h 34:51.6	Tom Richards (GBR) 2h 35:07.6	Etienne Gailly (BEL) 2h 35:33.6
1952	Emil Zatopek (TCH) 2h 23:03.2	Reinaldo Gorno (ARG) 2h 25:35.0	Gustaf Jansson (SWE) 2h 26:07.0
1956	Alain Mimoun (FRA) 2h 25:00	Franjo Mihalic (YUG) 2h 26:32	Veikko Karvonen (FIN) 2h 27:47
1960	Abebe Bikila (ETH) 2h 15:16.2	Rhadi Ben Abdesselem (MAR) 2h 15:41.6	Barry Magee (NZL) 2j 17:18.2
1964	Abebe Bikila (ETH) 2h 12:11.2	Basil Heatley (GBR) 2h 16:19.2	Kokichi Tsuburaya (JPN) 2h 16:22.8
1968	Mamo Wolde (ETH) 2h 20:26.4	Kenji Kimihara (JPN) 2h 23:31.0	Michael Ryan (NZL) 2h 23:45.0
1972	Frank Shorter (USA) 2h 12:19.8	Karel Lismont (BEL) 2h 14:31.8	Mamo Wolde (ETH) 2h 15:08.4
1976	Waldemar Cierpinski (GDR) 2h 09:55.0	Frank Shorter (USA) 2h 10:45.8	Karel Lismont (BEL) 2h 11:12.6
1980	Waldemar Cierpinski (GDR) 2h 11:03	Gerard Nijboer (HOL) 2h 11:20	Satymkul Dzhumanazarov (URS) 2h 11:35
1984	Carlos Lopes (POR) 2h 09:21*	John Treacy (IRL) 2h 09:56	Charles Spedding (GBR) 2h 09:58
1988	Gelindo Bordin (ITA) 2h 10:32	Douglas Wakiihuri (KEN) 2h 10:47	Ahmed Saleh (DJI) 2h 10:59

[1]*Usually shown as an American incorrectly.* [2]*Dorando Pietri (ITA) finished first but was disqualified due to assistance by officials on last lap of the track.* [3]*Then known as Kitei Son and Shoryu Nan – both from Korea.* *Olympic record.*

3000 Metres Steeplechase

Year	Gold	Silver	Bronze
1900[1]	George Orton (CAN) 7:34.4	Sidney Robinson (GBR) 7:38.0	Jacques Chastanié (FRA) d.n.a.
1900[2]	John Rimmer (GBR) 12:58.4	Charles Bennett (GBR) 12:58.6	Sidney Robinson (GBR) 12:58.8
1904[3]	James Lightbody (USA) 7:39.6	John Daly (GBR) 7:40.6	Arthur Newton (USA) 25m
1908[4]	Arthur Russell (GBR) 10:47.8	Archie Robertson (GBR) 10:48.4	John Eisele (USA) 20m
1920	Percy Hodge (GBR) 10:00.4	Patrick Flynn (USA) 100m	Ernesto Ambrosini (ITA) 30m
1924	Ville Ritola (FIN) 9:33.6	Elias Katz (FIN) 9:44.0	Paul Bontemps (FRA) 9:45.2
1928	Toivo Loukola (FIN) 9:21.8	Paavo Nurmi (FIN) 9:31.2	Ove Andersen (FIN) 9:35.6
1932[5]	Volmari Iso-Hollo (FIN) 10:33.4	Tom Evenson (GBR) 10:46.0	Joseph McCluskey (USA) 10:46.2
1936	Volmari Iso-Hollo (FIN) 9:03.8	Kaarlo Tuominen (FIN) 9:06.8	Alfred Dompert (GER) 9:07.2
1948	Tore Sjöstrand (SWE) 9:04.6	Erik Elmsäter (SWE) 9:08.2	Göte Hagström (SWE) 9:11.8
1952	Horace Ashenfelter (USA) 8:45.4	Vladimir Kazantsev (URS) 8:51.6	John Disley (GBR) 8:51.8
1956	Chris Brasher (GBR) 8:41.2	Sándor Rozsnyói (HUN) 8:43.6	Ernst Larsen (NOR) 8:44.0
1960	Zdzslaw Krzyszkowiak (POL) 8:34.2	Nikolai Sokolov (URS) 8:36.4	Semyon Rzhischin (URS) 8:42.2
1964	Gaston Roelants (BEL) 8:30.8	Maurice Herriott (GBR) 8:32.4	Ivan Belyayev (URS) 8:33.8
1968	Amos Biwott (KEN) 8:51.0	Benjamin Kogo (KEN) 8:51.6	George Young (USA) 8:51.8
1972	Kipchoge Keino (KEN) 8:23.6	Benjamin Jipcho (KEN) 8:24.6	Tapio Kantanen (FIN) 8:24.8
1976	Anders Garderud (SWE) 8:08.0	Bronislaw Malinowski (POL) 8:09.1	Frank Baumgartl (GDR) 8:10.4
1980	Bronislaw Malinowski (POL) 8:09.7	Filbert Bayi (TAN) 8:12.5	Eshetu Tura (ETH) 8:13.6
1984	Julius Korir (KEN) 8:11.80	Joseph Mahmoud (FRA) 8:13.31	Brian Diemer (USA) 8:14.06
1988	Julius Kariuki (KEN) 8:05.51*	Peter Koech (KEN) 8:06.79	Mark Rowland (GBR) 8:07.96

[1]*2500m.* [2]*4000m.* [3]*2590m.* [4]*3200m.* [5]*3460m in final due to lap scoring error. Iso-Hollo clocked 9:14.6 in a heat.*
Olympic record (8:08.02). 1896, 1906, 1912 Event not held.

110 Metres Hurdles

Year	Gold	Silver	Bronze
1896[1]	Thomas Curtis (USA) 17.6	Grantley Goulding (GBR) 18.0	–
1900	Alvin Kraenslein (USA) 15.4	John McLean (USA) 15.5	Fred Moloney (USA) 15.6
1904	Frederick Schule (USA) 16.0	Thadeus Shideler (USA) 16.3	Lesley Ashburner (USA) 16.4
1906	Robert Leavitt (USA) 16.2	Alfred Healey (GBR) 16.3	Vincent Duncker (SAF) 16.3
1908	Forrest Smithson (CAN) 15.0	John Carrels (USA) 15.7	Arthur Shaw (USA) 15.8
1912	Frederick Kelly (USA) 15.1	James Wendell (USA) 15.2	Martin Hawkins (USA) 15.3
1920	Earl Thomson (CAN) 14.8	Harold Barron (USA) 15.1	Frederick Murray (USA) 15.2
1924	Daniel Kinsey (USA) 15.0	Sydney Atkinson (SAF) 15.0	Sten Pettersson (SWE) 15.4
1928	Sydney Atkinson (SAF) 14.8	Stephen Anderson (USA) 14.8	John Collier (USA) 15.0
1932	George Saling (USA) 14.6 (14.57)	Percy Beard (USA) 14.7	Don Finlay (GBR) 14.8
1936	Forrest Towns (USA) 14.2	Don Finlay (GBR) 14.4	Fred Pollard (USA) 14.4
1948	William Porter (USA) 13.9	Clyde Scott (USA) 14.1	Craig Dixon (USA) 14.1
1952	Harrison Dillard (USA) 13.7 (13.91)	Jack Davis (USA) 13.7 (14.00)	Art Barnard (USA) 14.1 (14.40)
1956	Lee Calhoun (USA) 13.5 (13.70)	Jack Davis (USA) 13.5 (13.73)	Joel Shankle (USA) 14.1 (14.25)
1960	Lee Calhoun (USA) 13.8 (13.98)	Willie May (USA) 13.8 (13.99)	Hayes Jones (USA) 14.0 (14.17)

	Gold	Silver	Bronze
1964	Hayes Jones (USA) 13.6 (13.67)	Blaine Lindgren (USA) 13.7 (13.74)	Anatoliy Mikhailov (URS) 13.7 (13.78)
1968	Willie Davenport (USA) 13.3 (13.33)	Ervin Hall (USA) 13.4 (13.42)	Eddy Ottoz (ITA) 13.4 (13.46)
1972	Rod Milburn (USA) 13.24	Guy Drut (FRA) 13.34	Tom Hill (USA) 13.48
1976	Guy Drut (FRA) 13.30	Alejandro Casanas (CUB) 13.33	Willie Davenport (USA) 13.38
1980	Thomas Munkelt (GDR) 13.39	Alejandro Casanas (CUB) 13.40	Aleksandr Puchkov (URS) 13.44
1984	Roger Kingdom (USA) 13.20	Greg Foster (USA) 13.23	Arto Bryggare (FIN) 13.40
1988	Roger Kingdom (USA) 12.98*	Colin Jackson (GBR) 13.28	Tonie Campbell (USA) 13.38

[1]Only two finalists.   *Olympic record.

400 Metres Hurdles

1900	Walter Tewksbury (USA) 57.6	Henri Tauzin (FRA) 58.3	George Orton (CAN) d.n.a.
1904[1]	Harry Hillman (USA) 53.0	Frank Waller (USA) 53.2	George Poage (USA) 30m
1908	Charles Bacon (USA) 55.0	Harry Hillman (USA) 55.3	Leonard Tremeer (GBR) 57.0
1920	Frank Loomis (USA) 54.0	John Norton (USA) 54.3	August Desch (USA) 54.5
1924	Morgan Taylor (USA) 52.6[2]	Erik Vilen (FIN) 53.8	Ivan Riley (USA) 54.2
1928	Lord Burghley (GBR) 53.4	Frank Cuhel (USA) 53.6	Morgan Taylor (USA) 53.6
1932	Bob Tisdall (IRL) 51.7[2] (51.67)	Glenn Hardin (USA) 51.9 (51.85)	Morgan Taylor (USA) 52.0 (51.96)
1936	Glenn Hardin (USA) 52.4	John Loaring (CAN) 52.7	Miguel White (PHI) 52.8
1948	Roy Cochran (USA) 51.1	Duncan White (SRI) 51.8	Rune Larsson (SWE) 52.2
1952	Charlie Moore (USA) 50.8 (51.06)	Yuriy Lituyev (URS) 51.3 (51.51)	John Holland (NZL) 52.2 (52.26)
1956	Glenn Davis (USA) 50.1 (50.29)	Eddie Southern (USA) 50.8 (50.94)	Josh Culbreath (USA) 51.6 (51.74)
1960	Glenn Davis (USA) 49.3 (49.51)	Cliff Cushman (USA) 49.6 (49.77)	Dick Howard (USA) 49.7 (49.90)
1964	Rex Cawley (USA) 49.6	John Cooper (GBR) 50.1	Salvatore Morale (ITA) 50.1
1968	David Hemery (GBR) 48.1 (48.12)	Gerhard Hennige (FRG) 49.0 (49.02)	John Sherwood (GBR) 49.0 (49.03)
1972	John Akii-Bua (UGA) 47.82	Ralph Mann (USA) 48.51	David Hemery (GBR) 48.52
1976	Edwin Moses (USA) 47.64	Mike Shine (USA) 48.69	Yevgeniy Gavrilenko (URS) 49.45
1980	Volker Beck (GDR) 48.70	Vasiliy Arkhipenko (URS) 48.86	Gary Oakes (GBR) 49.11
1984	Edwin Moses (USA) 47.75	Danny Harris (USA) 48.13	Harald Schmid (FRG) 48.19
1988	Andre Phillips (USA) 47.19*	Amadou Dia Ba (SEN) 47.23	Edwin Moses (USA) 47.56

[1]Hurdles only 2ft 6in (76.2cm) high instead of usual 3ft (91.4cm).   [2]Record not allowed because hurdle knocked down.   *Olympic record.
1896, 1906, 1912 Event not held.

4 x 100 Metres Relay

1912[1]	Great Britain 42.4	Sweden 42.6	–
1920	United States 42.2	France 42.6	Sweden 42.9
1924	United States 41.0	Great Britain 41.2	Netherlands 41.8
1928	United States 41.0	Germany 41.2	Great Britain 41.8
1932	United States 40.0 (40.10)	Germany 40.9	Italy 41.2
1936	United States 39.8	Italy 41.1	Germany 41.2
1948[2]	United States 40.6	Great Britain 41.3	Italy 41.5
1952	United States 40.1 (40.26)	Soviet Union 40.3 (40.58)	Hungary 40.5 (40.83)
1956	United States 39.5 (39.60)	Soviet Union 39.8 (39.92)	Germany 40.3 (40.34)
1960[3]	Germany 39.5 (39.66)	Soviet Union 40.1 (40.24)	Great Britain 40.2 (40.32)
1964	United States 39.0 (39.06)	Poland 39.3 (39.36)	France 39.3 (39.36)
1968	United States 38.2 (38.24)	Cuba 38.3 (38.40)	France 38.4 (38.43)
1972	United States 38.19	Soviet Union 38.50	FRG 38.79
1976	United States 38.33	GDR 38.66	Soviet Union 38.78
1980	Soviet Union 38.26	Poland 38.33	France 38.53
1984	United States 37.83*	Jamaica 38.62	Canada 38.70
1988	Soviet Union 38.19	Great Britain 38.28	France 38.40

[1]German team finished second but was disqualified.   [2]United States disqualified but later reinstated.   [3]United States finished first (39.60)
but disqualified.   *Olympic record.   1896–1908 Event not held.

4 x 400 Metres Relay

1908[1]	United States 3:29.4	Germany 3:32.4	Hungary 3:32.5
1912	United States 3:16.6	France 3:20.7	Great Britain 3:23.2
1920	Great Britain 3:22.2	South Africa 3:24.2	France 3:24.8
1924	United States 3:16.0	Sweden 3:17.0	Great Britain 3:17.4
1928	United States 3:14.2	Germany 3:14.8	Canada 3:15.4
1932	United States 3:08.2 (3:08.14)	Great Britain 3:11.2	Canada 3:12.8
1936	Great Britain 3:09.0	United States 3:11.0	Germany 3:11.8
1948	United States 3:10.4	France 3:14.8	Sweden 3:16.3
1952	Jamaica 3:03.9 (3.04.04)	United States 3:04.0 (3:04.21)	Germany 3:06.6 (3:06.78)
1956	United States 3:04.8	Australia 3:06.2 (3:06.19)	Great Britain 3:07.2 (3:07.19)
1960	United States 3:02.2 (3:02.37)	Germany 3:02.7 (3:02.84)	British West Indies[2] 3:04.0 (3:04.13)
1964	United States 3:00.7	Great Britain 3:01.6	Trinidad 3:01.7
1968	United States 3:56.1 (2:56.16)*	Kenya 2:59.6 (2:59.64)	FRG 3:00.5 (3:00.57)

		Gold	Silver	Bronze
1972		Kenya 2:59.83	Great Britain 3:00.46	France 3:00.65
1976		United States 2:58.65	Poland 3:01.43	FRG 3:01.98
1980		Soviet Union 3:01.08	GDR 3:01.26	Italy 3:04.3
1984		United States 2:57.91	Great Britain 2:59.13	Nigeria 2:59.32
1988		United States 2:56.16*	Jamaica 3:00.30	FRG 3:00.56

[1]*Medley relay – 200m, 200m, 400m, 800m.* [2]*Three from Jamaica, one from Barbados.* *Olympic record.* 1896–1906 Event not held.

20 000 Metres Road Walk

1956	Leonid Spirin (URS) 1h 31:27.4	Antonas Mikenas (URS) 1h 32:03.0	Bruno Junk (URS) 1h 32:12.0
1960	Vladimir Golubnichiy (URS) 1h 34:07.2	Noel Freeman (AUS) 1h 34:16.4	Stan Vickers (GBR) 1h 34:56.4
1964	Ken Matthews (GBR) 1h 29:34.0	Dieter Lindner (GER) 1h 31:13.2	Vladimir Golubnichiy (URS) 1h 31:59.4
1968	Vladimir Golubnichiy (URS) 1h 33:58.4	José Pedraza (MEX) 1h 34:00.0	Nikolai Smaga (URS) 1h 34:03.4
1972	Peter Frenkel (GDR) 1h 26:42.4	Vladimir Golubnichiy (URS) 1h 26:55.2	Hans Reimann (GDR) 1h 27:16.6
1976	Daniel Bautista (MEX) 1h 24:40.6	Hans Reimann (GDR) 1h 25:13.8	Peter Frenkel (GDR) 1h 25:29.4
1980	Maurizio Damilano (ITA) 1h 23:35.5	Pyotr Pochenchuk (URS) 1h 24:45.4	Roland Wieser (GDR) 1h 25:58.2
1984	Ernesto Canto (MEX) 1h 23:13	Raul Gonzalez (MEX) 1h 23:20	Maurizio Damilano (ITA) 1h 23:26
1988	Jozef Pribilinec (TCH) 1h 19:57*	Ronald Weigel (GDR) 1h 20:00	Maurizio Damilano (ITA) 1h 20:14

Olympic record. 1896–1952 Event not held.

50 000 Metres Road Walk

1932	Thomas Green (GBR) 4h 50:10	Janis Dalinsh (LAT) 4h 47:20	Ugo Frigerio (ITA) 4h 59:06
1936	Harold Whitlock (GBR) 4h 30:41.1	Arthur Schwab (SUI) 4h 32:09.2	Adalberts Bubenko (LAT) 4h 32:42.2
1948	John Ljunggren (SWE) 4h 41:52	Gaston Godel (SUI) 4h 48:17	Tebbs Lloyd Johnson (GBR) 4h 48:31
1952	Giuseppe Dordoni (ITA) 4h 28:07.8	Josef Dolezal (TCH) 4h 30:17.8	Antal Tóka (HUN) 4h 31:P27.2
1956	Norman Read (NZL) 4h 30:42.8	Yevgeniy Maskinov (URS) 4h 32:57.0	John Ljunggren (SWE) 4h 35:02.0
1960	Don Thompson (GBR) 4h 25:30.0	John Ljunggren (SWE) 4h 25:47.0	Abdon Pamich (ITA) 4h 27:55.4
1964	Abdon Pamich (ITA) 4h 11:12.4	Paul Nihill (GBR) 4h 11:31.2	Ingvar Pettersson (SWE) 4h 14:17.4
1968	Christoph Höhne (GDR) 4h 20:13.6	Antal Kiss (HUN) 4h 30:17.0	Larry Young (USA) 4h 31:55.4
1972	Bernd Kannenberg (FRG) 3h 56:11.6	Venjamin Soldatenko (URS) 3h 58:24.0	Larry Young (USA) 4h 00:46.0
1980	Hartwig Gauder (GDR) 3h 49:24	Jorge Llopart (ESP) 3h 51:25	Yevgeniy Ivchenko (URS) 3h 56:32
1984	Raul Gonzalez (MEX) 3h 47:26	Bo Gustafsson (SWE) 3h 53.19	Sandro Bellucci (ITA) 3h 53:45
1988	Vyacheslav Ivanenko (URS) 3h 38:29*	Ronald Weigel (GDR) 3h 38:56	Hartwig Gauder (GDR) 3h 39:45

Olympics record. 1896–1928, 1976 Event not held.

High Jump

1896	Ellery Clark (USA) 1.81m	James Connolly (USA) 1.65m Robert Garrett (USA) 1.65m	–
1900	Irving Baxter (USA) 1.90m	Patrick Leahy (GBR) 1.78m	Lajos Gönczy (HUN) 1.75m
1904	Samuel Jones (USA) 1.80m	Garrett Serviss (USA) 1.77m	Paul Weinstein (GER) 1.77m
1906	Con Leahy (GBR) 1.77m	Lajos Gönczy (HUN) 1.75m	Herbert Kerrigan (USA) 1.72m Themistoklis Diakidis (GRE) 1.72m
1908	Harry Porter (USA) 1.905m	Con Leahy (GBR) 1.88m István Somodi (HUN) 1.88m Georges André (FRA) 1.88m	–
1912	Alma Richards (USA) 1.93m	Hans Liesche (GER) 1.91m	George Horine (USA) 1.89m
1920	Richmond Landon (USA) 1.94m	Harold Muller (USA) 1.90m	Bo Ekelund (SWE) 1.90m
1924	Harold Osborn (USA) 1.98m	Leroy Brown (USA) 1.95m	Pierre Lewden (FRA) 1.92m
1928	Robert King (USA) 1.94m	Ben Hedges (USA) 1.91m	Claude Ménard (FRA) 1.91m
1932	Duncan McNaughton (CAN) 1.97m	Robert Van Osdel (USA) 1.97m	Simeon Toribio (PHI) 1.97m
1936	Cornelius Johnson (USA) 2.03m	David Albritton (USA) 2.00m	Delos Thurber (USA) 2.00m
1948	John Winter (AUS) 1.98m	Björn Paulsen (NOR) 1.95m	George Stanich (USA) 1.95m
1952	Walt Davis (USA) 2.04m	Ken Wiesner (USA) 2.01m	Jose Telles da Conceicao (BRA) 1.98m
1956	Charlie Dumas (USA) 2.12m	Chilla Porter (AUS) 2.10m	Igor Kashkarov (URS) 2.08m
1960	Robert Shavlakadze (URS) 2.16m	Valeriy Brumel (URS) 2.16m	John Thomas (USA) 2.14m
1964	Valeriy Brumel (URS) 2.18m	John Thomas (USA) 2.18m	John Rambo (USA) 2.16m
1968	Dick Fosbury (USA) 2.24m	Ed Caruthers (USA) 2.22m	Valentin Gavrilov (URS) 2.20m
1972	Yuriy Tarmak (URS) 2.23m	Stefan Junge (GDR) 2.21m	Dwight Stones (USA) 2.21m
1976	Jacek Wszola (POL) 2.25m	Greg Joy (CAN) 2.23m	Dwight Stones (USA) 2.21m
1980	Gerd Wessig (GDR) 2.36m	Jacek Wszola (POL) 2.31m	Jörg Freimuth (GDR) 2.31m
1984	Dietmar Mögenburg (FRG) 2.35m	Patrik Sjöberg (SWE) 2.33m	Zhu Jianhua (CHN) 2.31m
1988	Gennadiy Avdeyenko (URS) 2.38m*	Hollis Conway (USA) 2.36m	Rudolf Povarnitsin (URS) 2.36m Patrik Sjöberg (SWE) 2.36m

Olympic record.

	Gold	Silver	Bronze

Pole Vault

	Gold	Silver	Bronze
1896	William Hoyt (USA) 3.30m	Albert Tyler (USA) 3.25m	Evangelos Damaskos (GRE) 2.85m
1900	Irving Baxter (USA) 3.30m	Meredith Colkett (USA) 3.25m	Carl-Albert Andersen (NOR) 3.20m
1904	Charles Dvorak (USA) 3.50m	LeRoy Samse (USA) 3.43m	Louis Wilkins (USA) 3.43m
1906	Fernand Gonder (FRA) 3.40m	Bruno Söderstrom (SWE) 3.40m	Ernest Glover (USA) 3.35m
1908	Edward Cooke (USA) 3.70m	–	Edward Archibald (CAN) 3.58m
	Alfred Gilbert (USA) 3.70m		Charles Jacobs (USA) 3.58m
1912	Harry Babcock (USA) 3.95m	Frank Nelson (USA) 3.85m	–
		Marcus Wright (USA) 3.85m	
1920	Frank Foss (USA) 4.09m	Henry Petersen (DEN) 3.70m	Edwin Meyers (USA) 3.60m
1924	Lee Barnes (USA) 3.95m	Glenn Graham (USA) 3.95m	James Brooker (USA) 3.90m
1928	Sabin Carr (USA) 4.20m	William Droegemuller (USA) 4.10m	Charles McGinnis (USA) 3.95m
1932	William Miller (USA) 4.31m	Shuhei Nishida (JPN) 4.26m	George Jefferson (USA) 4.19m
1936	Earle Meadows (USA) 4.35m	Shuhei Nishida (JPN) 4.25m	Sueo Oe (JPN) 4.25m
1948	Guinn Smith (USA) 4.30m	Erkki Kataja (FIN) 4.20m	Bob Richards (USA) 4.20m
1952	Bob Richards (USA) 4.55m	Don Laz (USA) 4.50m	Ragnar Lundberg (SWE) 4.40m
1956	Bob Richards (USA) 4.56m	Bob Gutowski (USA) 4.53m	Georgios Roubanis (GRE) 4.50m
1960	Don Bragg (USA) 4.70m	Ron Morris (USA) 4.60m	Eeles Landstrom (FIN) 4.55m
1964	Fred Hansen (USA) 5.10m	Wolfgang Reinhardt (GER) 5.05m	Klaus Lehnertz (GER) 5.00m
1968	Bob Seagren (USA) 5.40m	Claus Schiprowski (FRG) 5.40m	Wolfgang Nordwig (GDR) 5.40m
1972	Wolfgang Nordwig (GDR) 5.50m	Bob Seagren (USA) 5.40m	Jan Johnson (USA) 5.35m
1976	Tadeusz Slusarski (POL) 5.50m	Antti Kalliomaki (FIN) 5.50m	David Roberts (USA) 5.50m
1980	Wladislaw Kozakiewicz (POL) 5.78m	Tadeusz Slusarski (POL) 5.65m	–
		Konstantin Volkov (URS) 5.65m	
1984	Pierre Quinon (FRA) 5.75m	Mike Tully (USA) 5.65m	Earl Bell (USA) 5.60m
			Thierry Vigneron (FRA) 5.60m
1988	Sergey Bubka (URA) 5.90m*	Rodion Gataullin (URS) 5.85m	Grigory Yegorov (URS) 5.80m

Olympic record.

Long Jump

	Gold	Silver	Bronze
1896	Ellery Clark (USA) 6.35m	Robert Garrett (USA) 6.18m	James Connolly (USA) 6.11m
1900	Alvin Kraenslein (USA) 7.18m	Myer Prinstein (USA) 7.17m	Patrick Leahy (GBR) 6.95m
1904	Myer Prinstein (USA) 7.34m	Daniel Frank (USA) 6.89m	Robert Stangland (USA) 6.88m
1906	Myer Prinstein (USA) 7.20m	Peter O'Connor (GBR) 7.02m	Hugo Friend (USA) 6.96m
1908	Francis Irons (USA) 7.48m	Daniel Kelly (USA) 7.09m	Calvin Bricker (CAN) 7.08m
1912	Albert Gutterson (USA) 7.60m	Calvin Bricker (CAN) 7.21m	Georg Aberg (SWE) 7.18m
1920	William Pettersson (SWE) 7.15m	Carl Johnson (USA) 7.09m	Erik Abrahamsson (SWE) 7.08m
1924	William DeHart Hubbard (USA) 7.44m	Ed Gourdin (USA) 7.27m	Sverre Hansen (NOR) 7.26m
1928	Edward Hamm (USA) 7.73m	Silvio Cator (HAI) 7.58m	Alfred Bates (USA) 7.40m
1932	Ed Gordon (USA) 7.63m	Lambert Redd (USA) 7.60m	Chuhei Nambu (JPN) 7.44m
1936	Jesse Owens (USA) 8.06m	Luz Long (GER) 7.87m	Naoto Tajima (JPN) 7.74m
1948	Willie Steele (USA) 7.82m	Thomas Bruce (AUS) 7.55m	Herbert Douglas (USA) 7.54m
1952	Jerome Biffle (USA) 7.57m	Meredith Gourdine (USA) 7.53m	Odön Földessy (HUN) 7.30m
1956	Greg Bell (USA) 7.83m	John Bennett (USA) 7.68m	Jorma Valkama (FIN) 7.48m
1960	Ralph Boston (USA) 8.12m	Irvin Roberson (USA) 8.11m	Igor Ter-Ovanesyan (URS) 8.04m
1964	Lynn Davies (GBR) 8.07m	Ralph Boston (USA) 8.03m	Igor Ter-Ovanesyan (URS) 7.99m
1968	Bob Beamon (USA) 8.90m*	Klaus Beer (GDR) 8.19m	Ralph Boston (USA) 8.16m
1972	Randy Williams (USA) 8.24m	Hans Baumgartner (FRG) 8.18m	Arnie Robinson (USA) 8.03m
1976	Arnie Robinson (USA) 8.35m	Randy Williams (USA) 8.11m	Frank Wartenberg (GDR) 8.02m
1980	Lutz Dombrowski (GDR) 8.54m	Frank Paschek (GDR) 8.21m	Valeriy Podluzhny (URS) 8.18m
1984	Carl Lewis (USA) 8.54m	Gary Honey (AUS) 8.24m	Giovanni Evangelisti (ITA) 8.24m
1988	Carl Lewis (USA) 8.72m	Mike Powell (USA) 8.49m	Larry Myricks (USA) 8.27m

Olympic record.

Triple Jump
(Formerly known as the Hop, step and jump)

	Gold	Silver	Bronze
1896[1]	James Connolly (USA) 13.71m	Alexandre Tuffere (FRA) 12.70m	Ioannis Persakis (GRE) 12.52m
1900	Myer Prinstein (USA) 14.47m	James Connolly (USA) 13.97m	Lewis Sheldon (USA) 13.64m
1904	Myer Prinstein (USA) 14.35m	Frederick Englehardt (USA) 13.90m	Robert Stangland (USA) 13.36m
1906	Peter O'Connor (GBR) 14.07m	Con Leahy (GBR) 13.98m	Thomas Cronan (USA) 13.70m
1908	Tim Ahearne (GBR) 14.91m	Garfield McDonald (CAN) 14.76m	Edvard Larsen (NOR) 14.39m
1912	Gustaf Lindblom (SWE) 14.76m	Georg Aberg (SWE) 14.51m	Erik Almlöf (SWE) 14.17m
1920	Vilho Tuulos (FIN) 14.50m	Folke Jansson (SWE) 14.48m	Erik Almlöf (SWE) 14.27m
1924	Anthony Winter (AUS) 15.52m	Luis Brunetto (ARG) 15.42m	Vilho Tuulos (FIN) 15.37m
1928	Miklo Oda (JPN) 15.21m	Levi Casey (USA) 15.17m	Vilho Tuulos (FIN) 15.11m
1932	Chuhei Nambu (JPN) 15.72m	Erik Svensson (SWE) 15.32m	Kenkichi Oshima (JPN0 15.12m
1936	Naoto Tajima (JPN) 16.00m	Masao Harada (JPN) 15.66m	John Metcalfe (AUS) 15.50m
1948	Arne Ahman (SWE) 15.40m	George Avery (AUS) 15.36m	Ruhi Sarialp (TUR) 15.02m

	Gold	Silver	Bronze
1952	Adhemar Ferreira da Silva (BRA) 16.22m	Leonid Shcherbakov (URS) 15.98m	Arnoldo Devonish (VEN) 15.52m
1956	Adhemar Ferreira da Silva (BRA) 16.35m	Vilhjalmur Einarsson (ISL) 16.26m	Vitold Kreyer (URS) 16.02m
1960	Jozef Schmidt (POL) 16.81m	Vladimir Goryayev (URS) 16.63m	Vitold Kreyer (URS) 16.43m
1964	Jozef Schmidt (POL) 16.85m	Oleg Fedoseyev (URS) 16.58m	Viktor Kravchenko (URS) 16.57m
1968	Viktor Saneyev (URS) 17.39m	Nelson Prudencio (BRA) 17.27m	Giuseppe Gentile (ITA) 17.22m
1972	Viktor Saneyev (URS) 17.35m	Jörg Drehmel (GDR) 17.31m	Nelson Prudencio (BRA) 17.05m
1976	Viktor Saneyev (URS) 17.29m	James Butts (USA) 17.18m	Joao de Oliveira (BRA) 16.90m
1980	Jaak Uudmae (URS) 17.35m	Viktor Saneyev (URS) 17.24m	Joao de Oliveira (BRA) 17.22m
1984	Al Joyner (USA) 17.26m	Mike Conley (USA) 17.18m	Keith Connor (GBR) 16.87m
1988	Khristo Markov (BUL) 17.61m*	Igor Lapshin (URS) 17.52m	Alexandr Kovalenko (URS) 17.42m

[1]*Winner took two hops with his right foot, contrary to present rules.*   *Olympic record.*

Shot Put

	Gold	Silver	Bronze
1896[1]	Robert Garrett (USA) 11.22m	Miltiades Gouskos (GRE) 11.15m	Georgios Papasideris (GRE) 10.36m
1900[1]	Richard Sheldon (USA) 14.10m	Josiah McCracken (USA) 12.85m	Robert Garrett (USA) 12.37m
1904[1]	Ralph Rose (USA) 14.80m	Wesley Coe (USA) 14.40m	Leon Feuerbach (USA) 13.37m
1906	Martin Sheridan (USA) 12.32m	Mihály Dávid (HUN) 11.83m	Erik Lemming (SWE) 11.26m
1908	Ralph Rose (USA) 14.21m	Dennis Horgan (GBR) 13.61m	John Garrels (USA) 13.18m
1912	Patrick McDonald (USA) 15.34m	Ralph Rose (USA) 15.25m	Lawrence Whitney (USA) 14.15m
1920	Ville Pörhölä (FIN) 14.81m	Elmer Niklander (FIN) 14.155m	Harry Liversedge (USA) 14.15m
1924	Clarence Houser (USA) 14.99m	Glenn Hartranft (USA) 14.98m	Ralph Hills (USA) 14.64m
1928	John Kuck (USA) 15.87m	Herman Brix (USA) 15.75m	Emil Hirschfeld (GER) 15.72m
1932	Leo Sexton (USA) 16.00m	Harlow Rothert (USA) 15.67m	Frantisek Douda (TCH) 15.60m
1936	Hans Woellke (GER) 16.20m	Sulo Bärlund (FIN) 16.12m	Gerhard Stöck (GER) 15.66m
1948	Wilbur Thompson (USA) 17.12m	Jim Delaney (USA) 16.68m	Jim Fuchs (USA) 16.42m
1952	Parry O'Brien (USA) 17.41m	Darrow Hooper (USA) 17.39m	Jim Fuchs (USA) 17.06m
1956	Parry O'Brien (USA) 18.57m	Bill Nieder (USA) 18.18m	Jiri Skobla (TCH) 17.65m
1960	Bill Nieder (USA) 19.68m	Parry O'Brien (USA) 19.11m	Dallas Long (USA) 19.01m
1964	Dallas Long (USA) 20.33m	Randy Matson (USA) 20.20m	Vilmos Varju (HUN) 19.39m
1968	Randy Matson (USA) 20.54m	George Woods (USA) 20.12m	Eduard Gushchin (URS) 20.09m
1972	Wladyslaw Komar (POL) 21.18m	George Woods (USA) 21.17m	Hartmut Briesenick (GDR) 21.14m
1976	Udo Beyer (GDR) 21.05m	Yevgeniy Mironov (URS) 21.03m	Aleksandr Baryshnikov (URS) 21.00m
1980	Volodimir Kiselyev (URS) 21.35m	Aleksandr Baryshnikov (URS) 21.08m	Udo Beyer (GDR) 21.06m
1984	Alessandro Andrei (ITA) 21.26m	Michael Carter (USA) 21.09m	Dave Laut (USA) 20.97m
1988	Ulf Timmermann (GDR) 22.47m*	Randy Barnes (USA) 22.39m	Werner Günthör (SUI) 21.99m

[1]*From a 7ft (2.13m) square.*   *Olympic record.*

Discus

	Gold	Silver	Bronze
1896[1]	Robert Garrett (USA) 29.15m	Panoyotis Paraskevopoulos (GRE) 28.95m	Sotirios Versis (GRE) 28.78m
1900	Rudolf Bauer (HUN) 36.04m	Frantisek Janda-Suk (BOH) 35.25m	Richard Sheldon (USA) 34.60m
1904[2]	Martin Sheridan (USA) 39.28m	Ralph Rose (USA) 39.28m	Nicolaos Georgantas (GRE) 37.68m
1906	Martin Sheridan (USA) 41.46m	Nicolaos Georgantas (GRE) 38.06m	Werner Jarvinen (FIN) 36.82m
1908	Martin Sheridan (USA) 40.89m	Merritt Giffin (USA) 40.70m	Marquis Horr (USA) 39.44m
1912	Armas Taipale (FIN) 45.21m	Richard Byrd (USA) 42.32m	James Duncan (USA) 42.28m
1920	Elmer Niklander (FIN) 44.68m	Armas Taipale (FIN) 44.19m	Augustus Pope (USA) 42.13m
1924	Clarence Houser (USA) 46.15m	Vilho Niittymaa (FIN) 4.95m	Thomas Lieb (USA) 44.83m
1928	Clarence Houser (USA) 47.23m	Antero Kivi (FIN) 47.10m	James Corson (USA) 47.10m
1932	John Anderson (USA) 49.49m	Henri Laborde (USA) 48.47m	Paul Winter (FRA) 47.85m
1936	Ken Carpenter (USA) 50.48m	Gordon Dunn (USA) 49.36m	Giorgio Oberweger (ITA) 49.23m
1948	Adolfo Consolini (ITA) 52.78m	Giuseppe Tosi (ITA) 51.78m	Fortune Gordien (USA) 50.77m
1952	Sim Iness (USA) 55.03m	Adolfo Consolini (ITA) 53.78m	James Dillion (USA) 52.38m
1956	Al Oerter (USA) 56.36m	Fortune Gordien (USA) 54.81m	Des Koch (USA) 54.40m
1960	Al Oerter (USA) 59.18m	Rink Babka (USA) 58.02m	Dick Cochran (USA) 57.16m
1964	Al Oerter (USA) 61.00m	Ludvik Danek (TCH) 60.52m	Dave Weill (USA) 59.49m
1968	Al Oerter (USA) 64.78m	Lothar Milde (GDR) 63.08m	Ludvik Danek (TCH) 62.92m
1972	Ludvik Danek (TCH) 64.40m	Jay Silvester (USA) 63.50m	Ricky Bruch (SWE) 63.40m
1976	Mac Wilkins (USA) 67.50m	Wolfgang Schmidt (GDR) 66.22m	John Powell (USA) 65.70m
1980	Viktor Rashchupkin (URS) 66.64m	Imrich Bugár (TCH) 66.38m	Luis Delis (CUB) 66.32m
1984	Rolf Danneberg (FRG) 66.60m	Mac Wilkins (USA) 66.30m	John Powell (USA) 65.46m
1988	Jürgen Schult (GDR) 68.82m*	Romas Ubartas (URS) 67.48m	Rolf Danneberg (FRG) 67.38m

[1]*From 2.50m square.*   [2]*First place decided by a throw-off.*   *Olympic record.*

Hammer

	Gold	Silver	Bronze
1900[1]	John Flanagan (USA) 49.73m	Truxton Hare (USA) 49.13m	Josiah McCracken (USA) 42.46m
1904	John Flanagan (USA) 51.23m	John De Witt (USA) 50.26m	Ralph Rose (USA) 45.73m
1908	John Flanagan (USA) 51.92m	Matt McGrath (USA) 51.18m	Con Walsh (CAN) 48.50m
1912	Matt McGrath (USA) 54.74m	Duncan Gillis (CAN) 48.39m	Clarence Childs (USA) 48.17m
1920	Patrick Ryan (USA) 52.87m	Carl Lind (SWE) 48.43m	Basil Bennett (USA) 48.25m

	Gold	Silver	Bronze
1924	Fred Tootell (USA) 53.29m	Matt McGrath (USA) 50.84m	Malcolm Nokes (GBR) 48.87m
1928	Patrick O'Callaghan (IRL) 51.39m	Ossian Skjöld (SWE) 51.29m	Edmund Black (USA) 49.03m
1932	Patrick O'Callaghan (IRL) 53.92m	Ville Pörhölä (FIN) 52.27m	Peter Zaremba (USA) 50.33m
1936	Kerl Hein (GER) 56.49m	Erwin Blask (GER) 55.04m	Fred Warngard (SWE) 54.83
1948	Imre Németh (HUN) 56.07m	Ivan Gubijan (YUG) 54.27m	Bob Bennett (USA) 53.73m
1952	József Csermák (HUN) 60.34m	Karl Storch (GER) 58.86m	Imre Németh (HUN) 57.74m
1956	Harold Connolly (USA) 63.19m	Mikhail Krivonosov (URS) 63.03m	Anatoliy Samotsvetov (URS) 62.56m
1960	Vasiliy Rudenkov (URS) 67.10m	Gyula Zsivótzky (HUN) 65.79m	Tadeusz Rut (POL) 65.64m
1964	Romuald Klim (URS) 69.74m	Gyula Zsivótzky (HUN) 69.09m	Uwe Beyer (GER) 68.09m
1968	Gyula Zsivótzky (HUN) 73.36m	Romuald Klim (URS) 73.28m	Lázár Lovász (HUN) 69.78m
1972	Anatoliy Bondarchuk (URS) 75.50m	Jochen Sachse (GDR) 74.96m	Vasiliy Khmelevski (URS) 74.04m
1976	Yuriy Sedykʰ (URS) 77.52m	Aleksey Spiridonov (URS) 76.08m	Anatoliy Bondarchuk (URS) 75.48m
1980	Yuriy Sedykh (URS) 81.80m	Sergey Litvinov (URS) 80.64m	Juriy Tamm (URS) 78.96m
1984	Juha Tiainen (FIN) 78.08m	Karl-Hans Riehm (FRG) 77.98m	Klaus Ploghaus (FRG) 76.68m
1988	Sergey Litvinov (URS) 84.80m*	Yuriy Sedykh (URS) 83.76m	Juriy Tamm (URS) 81.16m

[1]From a 9ft (2.74m) circle.   *Olympic record.   1896, 1906 Event not held.

Javelin

1906	Erik Lemming (SWE) 53.90m	Knut Lindberg (SWE) 45.17m	Bruno Söderström (SWE) 44.92m
1908	Erik Lemming (SWE) 54.82m	Arne Halse (NOR) 50.57m	Otto Nilsson (SWE) 47.09m
1912	Erik Lemming (SWE) 60.64m	Juho Saaristo (FIN) 58.66m	Mór Kóczán (HUN) 55.50m
1920	Jonni Myyrä (FIN) 65.78m	Urho Peltonen (FIN) 63.50m	Pekka Johansson (FIN) 63.09m
1924	Jonni Myyrä (FIN) 62.96m	Gunnar Lindström (SWE) 60.92m	Eugene Oberst (USA) 58.35m
1928	Erik Lundkvist (SWE) 66.60m	Béla Szepes (HUN) 65.26m	Olva Sunde (NOR) 63.97m
1932	Matti Järvinen (FIN) 72.71m	Matti Sippala (FIN) 69.79m	Eino Penttila (FIN) 68.69m
1936	Gerhard Stöck (GER) 71.84m	Yrjö Nikkanen (FIN) 70.77m	Kalervo Toivonen (FIN) 70.72m
1948	Tapio Rautavaara (FIN) 69.77m	Steve Seymour (USA) 67.56m	Joszef Várszegi (HUN) 67.03m
1952	Cyrus Young (USA) 73.78m	Bill Miller (USA) 72.46m	Toivo Hyytiainen (FIN) 71.89m
1956	Egil Danielsen (NOR) 85.71m	Janusz Sidlo (POL) 79.98	Viktor Tsibulenko (URS) 79.50m
1960	Viktor Tsibulenko (URS) 84.64m	Walter Krüger (GER) 79.36m	Gergely Kulcsár (HUN) 78.57m
1964	Pauli Nevala (FIN) 82.66m	Gergely Kulcsár (HUN) 82.32m	Janis Lusis (URS) 80.57m
1968	Janis Lusis (URS) 90.10m	Jorma Kinnunen (FIN) 88.58m	Gergely Kulcsár (HUN) 87.06m
1972	Klaus Wolfermann (FRG) 90.48m	Janis Lusis (URS) 90.46m	Bill Schmidt (USA) 84.42m
1976	Miklos Németh (HUN) 94.58m	Hannu Siitonen (FIN) 87.92m	Gheorghe Megelea (ROM) 87.16m
1980	Dainis Kula (URS) 91.20m	Aleksandr Makarov (URS) 89.64m	Wolfgang Hanisch (GDR) 86.72m
1984	Arto Härkonen (FIN) 86.76m	David Ottley (GBR) 85.74m	Kenth Eldebrink (SWE) 83.72m
1988[1]	Tapio Korjus (FIN) 84.28m*	Jan Zelezny (TCH) 84.12m	Seppo Räty (FIN) 83.26m

[1]New javelin introduced.   *Olympic record 85.90m by Zelezny (TCH) in qualifying round.   1896–1904 Event not held.

Decathlon[1,2]

1904[3]	Thomas Kiely (GBR) 6036pts	Adam Gunn (USA) 5907pts	Truxton Hare (USA) 5813pts
1912[4]	Hugo Wieslander (SWE) 5965pts	Charles Lomberg (SWE) 5721pts	Gösta Holmér (SWE) 5768pts
1920	Helge Lövland (NOR) 5803pts	Brutus Hamilton (USA) 5739pts	Bertil Ohlsson (SWE) 5639pts
1924	Harold Osborn (USA) 6476pts	Emerson Norton (USA) 6117pts	Alexander Klumberg (EST) 6056pts
1928	Paavo Yrjölä (FIN) 6587pts	Akilles Järvinen (FIN) 6645pts	Ken Doherty (USA) 6428pts
1932	Jim Bausch (USA) 6735pts	Akilles Järvinen (FIN) 6879pts	Wolrad Eberle (GER) 6661pts
1936	Glenn Morris (USA) 7254pts	Robert Clark (USA) 7063pts	Jack Parker (USA) 6760pts
1948	Bob Mathias (USA) 6628pts	Ignace Heinrich (FRA) 6559pts	Floyd Simmons (USA) 6531pts
1952	Bob Mathias (USA) 7592pts	Milt Campbell (USA) 6995pts	Floyd Simmons (USA) 6945pts
1956	Milt Campbell (USA) 7614pts	Rafer Johnson (USA) 7457pts	Vasiliy Kuznetsov (URS) 7337pts
1960	Rafer Johnson (USA) 7926pts	Yang Chuan-Kwang (TPE) 7839pts	Vasiliy Kuznetsov (URS) 7557pts
1964	Willi Holdorf (GER) 7794pts	Rein Aun (URS) 7744pts	Hans-Joachim Walde (GER) 7735pts
1968	Bill Toomey (USA) 8144pts	Hans-Joachim Walde (FRG) 8094pts	Kurt Bendlin (FRG) 8071pts
1972	Nikolai Avilov (URS) 8466pts	Leonid Litvinenko (URS) 7970pts	Ryszard Katus (POL) 7936pts
1976	Bruce Jenner (USA) 8634pts	Guido Kratschmer (FRG) 8407pts	Nikolai Avilov (URS) 8378pts
1980	Daley Thompson (GBR) 8522pts	Yuri Kutsenko (URS) 8369pts	Sergei Zhelanov (URS) 8135pts
1984	Daley Thompson (GBR) 8847pts*	Jürgen Hingsen (FRG) 8695pts	Siegfried Wentz (FRG) 8416pts
1988	Christian Schenk (GDR) 8488pts	Torsten Voss (GDR) 8399pts	Dave Steen (CAN) 8328pts

[1]The decathlon consists of 100m, long jump, shot put, high jump, 400m, 110m hurdles, discus, pole vault, javelin and 1500m. The competition occupies two days, although in 1912 it took three days.
[2]The scores since 1912 given above have been recalculated on the current, 1984, scoring tables for purposes of comparison. (Note that in 1912, 1928, 1932 and 1948 the original medal order would have been different if these tables had been in force.
[3]Consisted of 100yd, 1 mile, 120yd hurdles, 880yd walk, high jump, long jump, pole vault, shot put, hammer and 56lb weight.
[4]Jim Thorpe (USA) finished first with 6564pts but was later disqualified for a breach of the then amateur rules. He was reinstated posthumously by the IOC in 1982, but only as joint first.   *Olympic record.
1896–1900, 1906–1908 Event not held.

TRACK & FIELD MEDALS – WOMEN

	Gold	Silver	Bronze

100 Metres

	Gold	Silver	Bronze
1928	Elizabeth Robinson (USA) 12.2	Fanny Rosenfeld (CAN) 12.3	Ethel Smith (CAN) 12.3
1932	Stanislawa Walasiewicz (POL) 11.9	Hilda Strike (CAN) 11.9	Wilhelmina von Bremen (USA) 12.0
1936	Helen Stephens (USA) 11.5	Stanislawa Walasiewicz (POL) 11.7	Kathe Krauss (GER) 11.9
1948	Fanny Blankers-Koen (HOL) 11.9	Dorothy Manley (GBR) 12.2	Shirley Strickland (AUS) 12.2
1952	Marjorie Jackson (AUS) 11.5 (11.67)	Daphne Hasenjager (SAF) 11.8 (12.05)	Shirley Strickland (AUS) 11.9 (12.12)
1956	Betty Cuthbert (AUS) 11.5 (11.82)	Christa Stubnick (GER) 11.7 (11.92)	Marlene Matthews (AUS) 11.7 (11.94)
1960	Wilma Rudolph (USA) 11.0 (11.18)	Dorothy Hyman (GBR) 11.3 (11.43)	Giuseppina Leone (ITA) 11.3 (11.48)
1964	Wyomia Tyus (USA) 11.4 (11.49)	Edith Maguire (USA) 11.6 (11.62)	Ewa Klobukowska (POL) 11.6 (11.64)
1968	Wyomia Tyus (USA) 11.0 (11.08)	Barbara Ferrell (USA) 11.1 (11.5)	Irena Szewińska (POL) 11.1 (11.19)
1972	Renate Stecher (GDR) 11.07	Raelene Boyle (AUS) 11.23	Silvia Chivas (CUB) 11.24
1976	Annegret Richter (FRG) 1.08	Renate Stecher (GDR) 11.13	Inge Helten (FRG) 11.17
1980	Ludmila Kondratyeva (URS) 11.06	Marlies Göhr (GDR) 11.07	Ingrid Auerswald (GDR) 11.14
1984	Evelyn Ashford (USA) 10.97	Alice Brown (USA) 11.13	Merlene Ottey-Page (JAM) 11.16
1988	Florence Griffith-Joyner (USA) 10.54*	Evelyn Ashford (USA) 10.83	Heike Drechsler (GDR) 10.85

Olympic record. Final was wind-assisted; 10.62 in preliminary round.

200 Metres

	Gold	Silver	Bronze
1948	Fanny Blankers-Koen (HOL) 24.4	Audrey Williamson (GBR) 25.1	Audrey Patterson[1] (USA) 25.2
1952	Marjorie Jackson (AUS) 23.7 (23.89)	Bertha Brouwer (HOL) 24.2 (24.25)	Nadyezda Khnykina (URS) 24.2 (24.37)
1956	Betty Cuthbert (AUS) 23.4 (23.55)	Christa Stubnick (GER) 23.7 (23.89)	Marlene Matthews (AUS) 23.8 (24.10)
1960	Wilma Rudolph (USA) 24.0 (24.13)	Jutta Heine (GER) 24.4 (24.58)	Dorothy Hyman (GBR) 24.7 (24.82)
1964	Edith Maquire (USA) 23.0 (23.05)	Irena Kirszenstein (POL) 23.1 (23.13)	Marilyn Black (AUS) 23.1 (23.18)
1968	Irena Szewińska (POL) 22.5 (22.58)	Raelene Boyle (AUS) 22.7 (22.74)	Jennifer Lamy (AUS) 22.8 (22.88)
1972	Renate Stecher (GDR) 22.40	Raelene Boyle (AUS) 22.45	Irena Szewińska (POL) 22.74
1976	Bärbel Eckert (GDR) 22.37	Annegret Richter (FRG) 22.39	Renate Stecher (GDR) 22.47
1980	Bärbel Wöckel (GDR) 22.03	Natalya Bochina (URS) 22.19	Merlene Ottey (JAM) 22.20
1984	Valerie Brisco-Hooks (USA) 21.81	Florence Griffith (USA) 22.04	Merlene Ottey-Page (JAM) 22.09
1988	Florence Griffith-Joyner (USA) 21.34*	Grace Jackson (JAM) 21.72	Heike Drechsler (GDR) 21.95

[1]*A recently discovered photo-finish picture indicates that Shirley Strickland (AUS) was third. *Olympic record.*
1928–1936 Event not held.

400 Metres

	Gold	Silver	Bronze
1964	Betty Cuthbert (AUS) 52.0 (52.01)	Ann Packer (GBR) 52.2 (52.20)	Judith Amoore (AUS) 53.4
1968	Colette Besson (FRA) 52.0 (52.03)	Lillian Board (GBR) 52.1 (52.12)	Natalya Burda (URS) 52.2 (52.25)
1972	Monika Zehrt (GDR) 51.08	Rita Wilden (FRG) 51.21	Kathy Hammond (USA) 51.64
1976	Irena Szewińska (POL) 49.29	Christina Brehmer (GDR) 50.51	Ellen Streidt (GDR) 50.55
1980	Marita Koch (GDR) 48.88	Jarmila Kratochvilova (TCH) 49.46	Christina Lathan (GDR) 49.66
1984	Valerie Brisco-Hooks (USA) 48.83	Chandra Cheeseborough (USA) 49.05	Kathy Cook (GBR) 49.43
1988	Olga Brzygina (URS) 48.65*	Petra Muller (GDR) 49.45	Olga Nazarova (URS) 49.90

Olympic record.   1928–1960 Event not held.

800 Metres

	Gold	Silver	Bronze
1928	Lina Radke (GER) 2:16.8	Kinuye Hitomi (JPN) 2:17.6	Inga Gentzel (SWE) 2:17.8
1960	Lyudmila Shevtsova (URS) 2:04.3	Brenda Jones (AUS) 2:04.4	Ursula Donath (GER) 2:05.6
1964	Ann Packer (GBR) 2:01.1	Maryvonne Dupureur (FRA) 2:01.9	Marise Chamberlain (NZL) 2:02.8
1968	Madeline Manning (USA) 2:00.9	Ilona Silai (ROM) 2:02.5	Maria Gommers (HOL) 2:02.6
1972	Hildegard Falck (FRG) 1:58.6	Niole Sabaite (URS) 1:58.7	Gunhild Hoffmeister (GDR) 1:59.2
1976	Tatyana Kazankina (URS) 1:54.9	Nikolina Shtereva (BUL) 1:55.4	Elfi Zinn (GDR) 1:55.6
1980	Nadyezda Olizarenko (URS) 1:53.5*	Olga Mineyeva (URS) 1:54.9	Tatyana Providokhina (URS) 1:55.5
1984	Doina Melinte (ROM) 1:57.60	Kim Gallagher (USA) 1:58.63	Fita Lovin (ROM) 1:58.83
1988	Sigrun Wodars (GDR) 1:56.10	Christine Wachtel (GDR) 1:56.64	Kim Gallagher (USA) 1:56.91

Olympic record (1:53.43).   1932–1956 Event not held.

1500 Metres

	Gold	Silver	Bronze
1972	Lyudmila Brágina (URS) 4:01.4	Gunhild Hoffmeister (GDR) 4:02.8	Paola Cacchi-Pigni (ITA) 4:02.9
1976	Tatyana Kazankina (URS) 4:05.5	Gunhild Hoffmeister (GDR) 4:06.0	Ulrike Klapezynski (GDR) 4:06.1
1980	Tatyana Kazankina (URS) 3:56.6	Christiane Wartenberg (GDR) 3:57.8	Nadyezda Olizarenko (URS) 3:59.6
1984	Gabriella Dorio (ITA) 4:03.25	Doina Melinte (ROM) 4:03.76	Maricica Puica (ROM) 4:04.15
1988	Paula Ivan (ROM) 3:53.96*	Laima Baikauskaite (URS) 4:00.24	Tatyana Samolenko (URS) 4:00.30

Olympic record.   1928–1968 Event not held.

3000 Metres

	Gold	Silver	Bronze
1984	Maricica Puica (ROM) 8:35.96	Wendy Sly (GBR) 8:39.47	Lynn Williams (CAN) 8:42.14
1988	Tatyana Samolenko (URS) 8:26.53*	Paula Ivan (ROM) 8:27.15	Yvonne Murray (GBR) 8:29.02

Olympic record.   1928–1980 Event not held.

	Gold	Silver	Bronze

10 000 Metres
| 1988 | Olga Bondarenko (URS) 31:05.21* | Liz McColgan (GBR) 31:08.44 | Yelena Zhupiyeva (URS) 31:19.82 |

Olympic record. 1928–1984 Event not held.

Marathon
| 1984 | Joan Benoit (USA) 2h 24:52* | Grete Waitz (NOR) 2h 26:18 | Rosa Mota (POR) 2h 26:57 |
| 1988 | Rosa Mota (POR) 2h 25:40 | Lisa Martin (AUS) 2h 25:53 | Kathrin Dörre (GDR) 2h 26:21 |

Olympic record. 1928–1980 Event not held.

100 Metres Hurdles
(Over 80m hurdles 1932–1968)

1932	Mildred Didrikson (USA) 11.7	Evelyne Hall (USA) 11.7	Marjorie Clark (SAF) 11.8
1936	Trebisonda Valla (ITA) 11.7 (11.75)	Anny Steuer (GER) 11.7 (11.81)	Elizabeth Taylor (CAN) 11.7 (11.81)
1948	Fanny Blankers-Koen (HOL) 11.2	Maureen Gardner (GBR) 11.2	Shirley Strickland (AUS) 11.4
1952	Shirley de la Hunty (AUS) 10.8 (11.01)	Maria Golubnichaya (URS) 11.1 (11.24)	Maria Sander (GER) 11.1 (11.38)
1956	Shirley de la Hunty (AUS) 10.7 (10.96)	Gisela Köhler (GER) 10.9 (11.12)	Norma Thrower (AUS) 11.0 (11.25)
1960	Irina Press (URS) 10.8 (10.93)	Carol Quinton (GBR) 10.9 (10.99)	Gisela Birkemeyer (GER) 11.0 (11.13)
1964	Karin Balzer (GER) 10.5 (10.54)	Teresa Ciepla (POL) 10.5 (10.55)	Pam Kilborn (AUS) 10.5 (10.56)
1968	Maureen Caird (AUS) 10.3 (10.39)	Pam Kilborn (AUS) 10.4 (10.46)	Chi Cheng (TIE) 10.4 (10.51)
1972	Annelie Ehrhardt (GDR) 12.59	Valeria Bufanu (ROM) 12.84	Karin Balzer (GDR) 12.90
1976	Johanna Schaller (GDR) 12.77	Tatyana Anisimova (URS) 12.78	Natalya Lebedeva (URS) 12.80
1980	Vera Komisova (URS) 12.56	Johanna Klier (GDR) 12.63	Lucyna Langer (POL) 12.65
1984	Benita Fitzgerald-Brown (USA) 12.84	Shirley Strong (GDR) 12.88	Kim Turner (USA) 13.06
			Michele Chardonnet (FRA) 13.06
1988	Yordanka Donkova (BUL) 12.38*	Gloria Siebert (GDR) 12.61	Claudia Zaczkiewicz (FRG) 12.75

Olympic record. 1928 Event not held.

400 Metres Hurdles
| 1984 | Nawal El Moutawakel (MAR) 54.61 | Judi Brown (USA) 55.20 | Cristina Cojocaru (ROM) 55.41 |
| 1988 | Debbie Flintoff-King (AUS) 53.17* | Tatyana Ledovskaya (URS) 53.18 | Ellen Fiedler (GDR) 53.63 |

Olympic record. 1928–1980 Event not held.

4 x 100 Metres Relay
1928	Canada 48.4	United States 48.8	Germany 49.2
1932	United States 47.0 (46.86)	Canada 47.0	Great Britain 47.6
1936	United States 46.9	Great Britain 47.6	Canada 47.8
1948	Netherlands 47.5	Australia 47.6	Canada 47.8
1952	United States 45.9 (46.14)	Germany 45.9 (46.18)	Great Britain 46.2 (46.41)
1956	Australia 44.5 (44.65)	Great Britain 44.7 (44.70)	United States 44.9 (45.04)
1960	United States 44.5 (44.72)	Germany 44.8 (45.00)	Poland 45.0 (45.19)
1964	Poland 43.6 (43.69)	United States 43.9 (43.92)	Great Britain 44.0 (44.09)
1968	United States 42.8 (42.88)	Cuba 43.3 (43.36)	Soviet Union 43.4 (43.41)
1972	FRG 42.81	GDR 42.95	Cuba 43.36
1976	GDR 42.55	FRG 42.59	Soviet Union 43.09
1980	GDR 41.60*	Soviet Union 41.20	Great Britain 42.43
1984	United States 41.65	Canada 42.77	Great Britain 43.11
1988	United States 41.98	GDR 42.09	Soviet Union 42.75

Olympic record.

4 x 400 Metres Relay
1972	GDR 3:22.95	United States 3:35.15	FRG 3:26.51
1976	GDR 3:19.23	United States 3:22.81	Soviet Union 3:24.24
1980	Soviet Union 3:20.12	GDR 3:20.35	Great Britain 3:27.5
1984	United States 3:18.29	Canada 3:21.21	FRG 3:22.98
1988	Soviet Union 3:15.17*	United States 3:15.51	GDR 3:18.29

Olympic record. 1928–1968 Event not held.

High Jump
1928	Ethel Catherwood (CAN) 1.59m	Carolina Gisolf (HOL) 1.56m	Mildred Wiley (USA) 1.56m
1932	Jean Shiley (USA) 1.657m[1]	Mildred Didrikson (USA) 1.657m[1]	Eva Dawes (CAN) 1.60m
1936	Ibolya Csák (HUN) 1.60m	Dorothy Odam (GBR) 1.60m	Elfriede Kaun (GER(1.60m
1948	Alice Coachman (USA) 1.68m	Dorothy Tyler (GBR) 1.68m	Micheline Ostermeyer (FRA) 1.61m
1952	Esther Brand (SAF) 1.67m	Sheila Lerwill (GBR) 1.65m	Aleksandra Chudina (URS) 1.63m
1956	Mildred McDaniel (USA) 1.76m	Thelma Hopkins (GBR) 1.67m	–
		Maria Pisaryeva (URS) 1.67m	

	Gold	Silver	Bronze
1960	Iolanda Balas (ROM) 1.85m	Jaroslawa Jozwiakowska (POL) 1.71m	–
		Dorothy Shirley (GBR) 1.71m	
1964	Iolanda Balas (ROM) 1.90m	Michelle Brown (AUS) 1.80m	Tasia Chenchik (URS) 1.78m
1968	Miloslava Rezkova (TCH) 1.82m	Antonina Okorokova (URS) 1.80m	Valentina Kozyr (URS) 1.80m
1972	Ulrike Meyfarth (FRG) 1.92m	Yordanka Blagoyeva (BUL) 1.88m	Ilona Gusenbauer (AUT) 1.88m
1976	Rosemarie Ackermann (GDR) 1.93m	Sara Simeoni (ITA) 1.91m	Yordanka Blagoyeva (BUL) 1.91m
1980	Sara Simeoni (ITA) 1.97m	Urszula Kielan (POL) 1.94m	Jutta Kirst (GDR) 1.94m
1984	Ulrike Meyfarth (FRG) 2.02m	Sara Simeoni (ITA) 2.00m	Joni Huntley (USA) 1.97m
1988	Louise Ritter (USA) 2.03m*	Stefka Kostadinova (BUL) 2.01m	Tamara Bykova (URS) 1.99m

[1]Some sources suggest 1.66m.   *Olympic record.

Long Jump

1948	Olga Gyarmati (HUN) 5.69m	Noemi Simonetto de Portela (ARG) 5.60m	Ann-Britt Leyman (SWE) 5.57m
1952	Yvette Williams (NZL) 6.24m	Aleksandra Chudina (URS) 6.14m	Shirley Cawley (GDR) 5.92m
1956	Elzbieta Krzesinska (POL) 6.35m	Willye White (USA) 6.09m	Nadyezda Dvalishvili (URS) 6.07m
1960	Vera Krepkina (URS) 6.37m	Elzbieta Krzesinska (POL) 6.27m	Hildrun Claus (GER) 6.21m
1964	Mary Rand (GBR) 6.76m	Irena Kirszenstein (POL) 6.60m	Tatyana Schelkanova (URS) 6.42m
1968	Viorica Viscopoleanu (ROM) 6.82m	Sheila Sherwood (GBR) 6.68m	Tatyana Talysheva (URS) 6.66m
1972	Heidemarie Rosendahl (FRG) 6.78m	Diana Yorgova (BUL) 6.77m	Eva Suranova (TCH) 6.67m
1976	Angela Voigt (GDR) 6.72m	Kathy McMillan (USA) 6.66m	Lidia Alfeyeva (URS) 6.60m
1980	Tatyana Kolpakova (URS) 7.06m	Brigitte Wujak (GDR) 7.04m	Tatyana Skatchko (URS) 7.01m
1984	Anisoara Stanciu (ROM) 6.96m	Vali Ionescu (ROM) 6.81m	Susan Hearnshaw (GBR) 6.80m
1988	Jackie Joyner-Kersee (USA) 7.40m*	Heike Drechsler (GDR) 7.22m	Galina Chistiakova (URS) 7.11m

*Olympic record.   1928–1936 Event not held.

Shot Put

1948	Micheline Ostermeyer (FRA) 13.75m	Amelia Piccinini (ITA) 13.09m	Ina Schäffer (AUT) 13.08m
1952	Galina Sybina (URS) 15.28m	Marianne Werner (GER) 14.57m	Klavdia Tochonova (URS) 14.50m
1956	Tamara Tyshkevich (URS) 16.59m	Galina Zybina (URS) 16.53m	Marianne Werner (GER) 15.61m
1960	Tamara Press (URS) 17.32m	Johanna Lüttge (GER) 16.61m	Earlene Brown (USA) 16.42m
1964	Tamara Press (URS) 18.14m	Renate Garisch (GDR) 17.61m	Galina Zybina (URS) 16.42m
1968	Margitta Gummel (GDR) 19.61m	Marita Lange (GDR) 18.78m	Nadyezda Chizhova (URS) 18.19m
1972	Nadyezda Chizhova (URS) 21.03m	Margitta Gummel (GDR) 20.22m	Ivanka Khristova (BUL) 19.35m
1976	Ivanka Khristova (BUL) 21.16m	Nadyezda Chizhova (URS) 20.96m	Helena Fibingerova (TCH) 20.67m
1980	Ilona Slupianek (GDR) 22.41m*	Svetlana Krachevskaya (URS) 21.42m	Margitta Pufe (GDR) 21.20m
1984	Claudia Losch (FRG) 20.48m	Mihaela Loghin (ROM) 20.47m	Gael Martin (AUS) 19.19m
1988	Natalya Lisovskaya (URS) 22.24m	Kathrin Neimke (GDR) 21.07m	Li Meisu (CHN) 21.06m

*Olympic record.   1928–1936 Event not held.

Discus

1928	Helena Konopacka (POL) 39.62m	Lilian Copeland (USA) 37.08m	Ruth Svedberg (SWE) 35.92m
1932	Lilian Copeland (USA) 40.58m	Ruth Osburn (USA) 40.11m	Jadwiga Wajsacowna (POL) 38.73m
1936	Gisela Mauermayer (GER) 47.63m	Jadwiga Wajsówna (POL) 46.22m	Paula Mollenhauer (GER) 39.80m
1948	Micheline Ostermeyer (FRA) 41.92m	Edera Gentile (ITA) 41.17m	Jacqueline Mazeas (FRA) 40.47m
1952	Nina Romashkova (URS) 51.42	Elizaveta Bagryantseva (URS) 47.08m	Nina Dumbadze (URS) 46.29m
1956	Olga Fikotova (TCH) 53.69m	Irina Begiyakova (URS) 52.54m	Nina Ponomaryeva (URS) 52.02m[1]
1960	Nina Ponomaryeva (URS) 55.10m	Tamara Press (URS) 52.59m	Lia Manoliu (ROM) 52.36m
1964	Tamara Press (URS) 57.25m	Ingrid Lotz (GER) 57.21m	Lia Manoliu (ROM) 56.97m
1968	Lia Manoliu (ROM) 58.28m	Liesel Westermann (FRG) 57.76m	Jolán Kleiber (HUN) 54.90m
1972	Faina Melnik (URS) 66.62m	Argentina Menis (ROM) 65.06m	Vasilka Stoyeva (BUL) 64.34m
1976	Evelin Schlaak (GDR) 69.00m	Maria Vergova (BUL) 67.30m	Gabriele Hinzmann (GDR) 66.84m
1980	Evelin Jahl (GDR) 69.96m	Maria Petkova (BUL) 67.90m[2]	Tatyana Lesovaya (URS) 67.40m
1984	Ria Stalman (HOL) 65.36m	Leslie Deniz (USA) 64.86m	Florenta Craciunescu (ROM) 63.64m
1988	Martina Hellmann (GDR) 72.30m*	Diana Gansky (GDR) 71.88m	Tsvetanka Khristova (BUL) 69.74m

[1]Formerly Romashkova.   [2]Formerly Vergova.   *Olympic record.

Javelin

1932	Mildred Didrikson (USA) 43.68m	Ellen Braumüller (GER) 43.49m	Tilly Fleischer (GER) 43.40m
1936	Tilly Fleischer (GER) 45.18m	Luise Krüger (GER) 43.29m	Marja Kwasniewska (POL) 41.80m
1948	Herma Bauma (AUT) 45.57m	Kaisa Parviainen (FIN) 43.79m	Lily Carlstedt (DEN) 42.08m
1952	Dana Zatopková (TCH) 50.47m	Aleksandra Chudina (URS) 50.01m	Yelena Gorchakova (URS) 49.76m
1956	Inese Jaunzeme (URS) 53.86m	Marlene Ahrens (CHI) 50.38m	Nadyezda Konyeyeva (URS) 50.28m
1960	Elvira Ozolina (URS) 55.98m	Dana Zatopková (TCH) 53.78m	Birute Kalediene (URS) 53.45m
1964	Mihaela Penes (ROM) 60.64m	Marta Rudas (HUN) 58.27m	Yelena Gorchakova (URS) 57.07m
1968	Angela Németh (HUN) 60.36m	Mihaela Penes (ROM) 59.92m	Eva Janko (AUT) 58.04m
1972	Ruth Fuchs (GDR) 63.88m	Jacqueline Todten (GDR) 62.54m	Kathy Schmidt (USA) 59.94m
1976	Ruth Fuchs (GDR) 65.94m	Marion Becker (FRG) 64.70m	Kathy Schmidt (USA) 63.96m

	Gold	Silver	Bronze
1980	Maria Colon (CUB) 68.40m	Saida Gunba (URS) 67.76m	Ute Hommola (GDR) 66.56m
1984	Tessa Sanderson (GBR) 69.56m	Tiina Lillak (FIN) 69.00m	Fatima Whitbread (GBR) 67.14m
1988	Petra Felke (GDR) 74.68m*	Fatima Whitbread (GBR) 70.32m	Beate Koch (GDR) 67.30m

*Olympic record.   1928 Event not held.

Pentathlon[1]

	Gold	Silver	Bronze
1964	Irina Press (URS) 5246pts	Mary Rand (GBR) 5035pts	Galina Bystrova (URS) 4956
1968	Ingrid Becker (FRG) 5098pts	Liese Prokop (AUT) 4966pts	Annamaria Tóth (HUN) 4959pts
1972[2]	Mary Peters (GBR) 4801pts	Heidemarie Rosendahl (FRG) 4791pts	Burglinde Pollak (GDR) 4768pts
1976[3]	Siegrun Siegl (GDR) 4745pts	Christine Laser (GDR) 4745pts	Burglinde Pollak (GDR) 4740pts
1980	Nadyezda Tkachenko (URS) 5083pts	Olga Rukivichnikova (URS) 4937pts	Olga Kuragina (URS) 4875pts

[1]The pentathlon consisted of 100m hurdles, shot put, high jump, long jump and 200m from 1964 to 1976. In 1980 the 200m was replaced by 800m. [2]New scoring tables were introduced in May 1971. [3]Siegl finished ahead of Laser in three events.   1928–1960 Event not held.

Heptathlon[4]
(Replaced Pentathlon in 1984)

	Gold	Silver	Bronze
1984	Glynis Nunn (AUS) 6387pts[5]	Jackie Joyner (USA) 6363pts	Sabine Everts (FRG) 6388pts
1988	Jackie Joyner-Kersee (US) 7291pts*	Sabine John (GDR) 6897pts	Anke Behmer (GDR) 6858pts

[4]The Heptathlon consists of 100m hurdles, high jump, shot, 200m on the first day; long jump, javelin and 800m on the second day.
[5]Re-calculated on 1984 tables.   *Olympic record.

WOMEN WHO HAVE WON MEDALS UNDER BOTH THEIR MAIDEN AND MARRIED NAMES:

Becker – Mickler (FRG)	Kirszenstein – Szewińska (POL)	Schaller – Klier (GDR)
Brehmer – Lathan (GDR)	Köhler – Birkemeyer (GDR)	Schlaak – Jahl (GDR)
Eckert – Wöckel (GDR)	Manning – Jackson (USA)	Vergova – Petkova (BUL)
Foulds – Paul (GBR)	Odam – Tyler (GBR)	Wieczorek – Ciepla (POL)
Kersee – Joyner (USA)	Richter – Górecka (POL)	Zharkova – Maslakova (URS)
Khnykina – Dvalishvili (URS)	Romashkova – Ponomaryeva (URS)	

DISCONTINUED EVENTS

	Gold	Silver	Bronze
60 Metres			
1900	Alvin Kraenzlein (USA) 7.0	Walter Tewksbury (USA) 7.1	Stanley Rowley (AUS) 7.2
1904	Archie Hahn (USA) 7.0	William Hogenson (USA) 7.2	Fay Moulton (USA) 7.2
3000 Team Race			
1912	United States 9pts	Sweden 13pts	Great Britain 23pts
1920	United States 10pts	Great Britain 20pts	Sweden 24pts
1924	Finland 8pts	Great Britain 14pts	·United States 25pts
3 Miles Team Race			
1908	Great Britain 6pts	United States 19pts	France 32pts
5000 Metres Team Race			
1900	Great Britain 26pts	France 29 pts	–
Individual Cross-Country			
1912[1]	Hannes Kolehmainen (FIN) 45:11.6	Hjalmar Andersson (SWE) 45:44.8	John Eke (SWE) 46:37.6
1920[2]	Paavo Nurmi (FIN) 27:15.0	Erick Backman (SWE) 27:17.6	Heikki Liimatainen (FIN) 27:37.4
1924[3]	Paavo Nurmi (FIN) 32:54.8	Ville Ritola (FIN) 34:19.4	Earl Johnson (USA) 35:21.0

[1]12 000 metres. [2]8000 metres. [3]10 000 metres.

	Gold	Silver	Bronze
Team Cross-Country			
1904	United States (New York AC)	United States (Chicago AA)	–
1912	Sweden 10pts	Finland 11pts	Great Britain 49pts
1920	Finland 10pts	Great Britain 21pts	Sweden 23pts
1924	Finland 11pts	United States 14pts	France 20pts
200 Metres Hurdles			
1900	Alvin Kraenzlein (USA) 25.4	Norman Pritchard (IND) 26.6	Walter Tewksbury (USA) n.t.a.
1904	Harry Hillman (USA) 24.6	Frank Castleman (USA) 24.9	George Poage (USA) n.t.a.
1500 Metres Walk			
1906	George Bonhag (USA) 7:12.6	Donald Linden (CAN) 7:19.8	Konstantin Spetsiotis (GRE) 7:22.0

	Gold	Silver	Bronze

3000 Metres Walk

| 1906 | György Sztantics (HUN) 15:13.2 | Hermann Müller (GER) 15:20.0 | Georgios Saridakis (GRE) 15:33.0 |
| 1920 | Ugo Frigerio (ITA) 13:14.2 | George Parker (AUS) n.t.a. | Richard Remer (USA) n.t.a. |

3500 Metres Walk

| 1908 | George Larner (GBR) 14:55.0 | Ernest Webb (GBR) 15:07.4 | Harry Kerr (NZL) 15:43.4 |

10 000 Metres Walk

1912	George Goulding (CAN) 46:28.4	Ernest Webb (GBR) 46:50.4	Fernando Altimani (ITA) 47:37.6
1920	Ugo Frigerio (ITA) 48:06.2	Joseph Pearman (USA) n.t.a.	Charles Gunn (GBR) n.t.a.
1924	Ugo Frigerio (ITA) 47:49.0	Gordon Goodwin (GBR) 200m	Cecil McMaster (SAF) 300m
1948	John Mikaelsson (SWE) 45:13.2	Ingemar Johansson (SWE) 45:43.8	Fritz Schwab (SUI) 46:00.2
1952	John Mikaelsson (SWE) 45:02.8	Fritz Schwab (SUI) 45:41.0	Bruno Junk (URS) 45:41.2

1928–1936 Event not held.

10 Miles Walk

| 1908 | George Larner (GBR) 1h 15:57.4 | Ernest Webb (GBR) 1h 17:31.0 | Edward Spencer (GBR) 1h 21:20.2 |

Pentathlon

1906[1]	Hjalmar Mellander (SWE) 24pts	Istvan Mudin (HUN) 25pts	Erik Lemming (SWE) 29pts
1912[2,3]	Ferdinand Bie (NOR) 16pts	James Donahue (USA) 24pts	Frank Lukeman (CAN) 24pts
1920[2]	Eero Lehtonen (FIN) 14pts	Everett Bradley (USA) 24pts	Hugo Lahtinen (FIN) 26pts
1924[2]	Eero Lehtonen (FIN) 14pts	Elemér Somfay (HUN) 16pts	Robert LeGendre (USA) 18pts

[1]*Consisted of standing long jump, discus (Greek style), javelin, one-lap race (192m), Greco-Roman wrestling.* [2]*Consisted of long jump, javelin, 200n, discus, 1500m.* [3]*Jim Thorpe (USA) finished first with 7 points but was subsequently disqualified. He was reinstated posthumously in 1982, but as joint first.*

Standing High Jump

1900	Ray Ewry (USA) 1.655m	Irving Baxter (USA) 1.525m	Lewis Sheldon (USA) 1.50m
1904	Ray Ewry (USA) 1.50m	James Stadler (USA) 1.45m	Lawson Robertson (USA) 1.45m
1906	Ray Ewry (USA) 1.565m	Martin Sheridan (USA) 1.50m	–
		Léon Dupont (BEL) 1.40m	
		Lawson Robertson (USA) 1.40m	
1908	Ray Ewry (USA) 1.575m	Konstantin Tsiklitiras (GRE) 1.55m	–
		John Biller (USA) 1.55m	
1912	Platt Adams (USA) 1.63m	Benjamin Adams (USA) 1.60m	Konstantin Tsiklitiras (GRE) 1.55m

Standing Long Jump

1900	Ray Ewry (USA) 3.21m	Irving Baxter (USA) 3.135m	Emile Torcheboeuf (FRA) 3.03m
1904	Ray Ewry (USA) 3.476m	Charles King (USA) 3.28m	John Biller (USA) 3.26m
1906	Ray Ewry (USA) 3.30m	Martin Sheridan (USA) 3.095m	Lawson Robertson (USA) 3.05m
1908	Ray Ewry (USA) 3.335m	Konstantin Tsiklitiras (GRE) 3.23m	Martin Sheridan (USA) 3.225m
1912	Konstantin Tsiklitiras (GRE) 3.37m	Platt Adams (USA) 3.36m	Benjamin Adams (USA) 3.28m

Standing Triple Jump

| 1900 | Ray Ewry (USA) 10.58m | Irving Baxter (USA) 9.95m | Robert Garrett (USA) 9.50m |
| 1904 | Ray Ewry (USA) 10.55m | Charles King (USA) 10.16m | James Stadler (USA) 9.53m |

Stone (6.40kg) Put

| 1906 | Nicolaos Georgantas (GRE) 19.925m | Martin Sheridan (USA) 19.053m | Michel Dorizas (GRE) 18.585m |

Shot (Both Hands) *Aggregate of throws with right and left hands.*

| 1912 | Ralph Rose (USA) 27.70m | Patrick McDonald (USA) 27.53m | Elmer Niklander (FIN) 27.14m |

Discus (Both Hands) *Aggregate of throws with right and left hands.*

| 1912 | Armas Taipale (FIN) 82.86m | Elmer Niklander (FIN) 77.96m | Emil Magnusson (SWE) 77.37m |

Discus (Greek Style)

| 1906 | Werner Järvinen (FIN) 35.17m | Nicolaos Georgantas (GRE) 32.80m | Istvan Mudin (HUN) 31.91m |
| 1908 | Martin Sheridan (USA) 38.00m | Marquis Horr (USA) 37.325m | Werner Järvinen (FIN) 36.48m |

Javelin (Both Hands) *Aggregate of throws with right and left hands.*

| 1912 | Julius Saaristo (FIN) 109.42m | Väinö Siikaniemi (FIN) 101.13m | Urho Peltonen (FIN) 100.24m |

Javelin (Free Style)

| 1908 | Erik Lemming (SWE) 54.445m | Michel Dorizas (GRE) 51.36m | Arne Halse (NOR) 49.73m |

56-Pound (25.4kg) Weight Throw

| 1904 | Etienne Desmarteau (CAN) 10.465m | John Flanagan (USA) 10.16m | James Mitchel (USA) 10.135m |
| 1920 | Patrick McDonald (USA) 11.265m | Patrick Ryan (USA) 10.965m | Carl Lind (SWE) 10.25m |

VOLLEYBALL

Introduced into the Games in 1964 for men and women, volleyball has been dominated by Soviet teams. Their men's teams played 39 matches losing only four from 1964 to 1980, and their women played 28 matches losing only two in the same period. The most successful player was Inna Ryskal (URS) with two gold and two silver medals (1964–1976). The best by a male player was two golds and a silver by Yuriy Poyarkov (URS) from 1964–1972. Ryskal has competed in a record four Games in the women's sport, which is matched by Katsutoshi Nekoda (JPN) and Antonio Moreno (BRA) in the men's.

The oldest gold medallist was Georgi Mondsolevski (URS), aged 34yr 274 days in 1968, and the oldest female winner was Ludmila Buldakova (URS), aged 34yr 105 days in 1972. The youngest gold medallist was Ludmila Borozna (URS) in 1972, aged 18yr 249 days, and the youngest male was Lech Lasko (POL), aged 20yr 58 days in 1976. The oldest medallist was Bohumil Golian (TCH), winning a bronze in 1968 aged 37yr 215 days, while the youngest was Heike Lehmann (GDR) with a silver in 1980 aged 18yr 123 days.

Three Brazilians jump to spike a return from the Bulgarians during the 1964 Games in Tokyo, the first to feature a volleyball tournament.

VOLLEYBALL MEDALS – MEN

	Gold	Silver	Bronze
1964	Soviet Union	Czechoslovakia	Japan
1968	Soviet Union	Japan	Czechoslovakia
1972	Japan	GDR	Soviet Union
1976	Poland	Soviet Union	Cuba
1980	Soviet Union	Bulgaria	Romania
1984	United States	Brazil	Italy
1988	United States	Soviet Union	Argentina

1896–1960 Event not held.

VOLLEYBALL MEDALS – WOMEN

	Gold	Silver	Bronze
1964	Japan	Soviet Union	Poland
1968	Soviet Union	Japan	Poland
1972	Soviet Union	Japan	North Korea
1976	Japan	Soviet Union	South Korea
1980	Soviet Union	GDR	Bulgaria
1984	China	United States	Japan
1988	Soviet Union	Peru	China

1896–1960 Event not held.

VOLLEYBALL MEDALS TOTALS

Country	MEN			WOMEN			Total
	G	S	B	G	S	B	
Soviet Union	3	2	1	4	2	–	12
Japan	1	1	1	2	2	1	8
United States	2	–	–	–	1	–	3
Poland	1	–	–	–	–	2	3
China	–	–	–	1	–	1	2
GDR	–	1	–	–	1	–	2
Bulgaria	–	1	–	–	–	1	2
Czechoslovakia	–	1	1	–	–	–	2
Brazil	–	1	–	–	–	–	1
Peru	–	–	–	–	1	–	1
Argentina	–	–	1	–	–	–	1
Cuba	–	–	1	–	–	–	1
Italy	–	–	1	–	–	–	1
Korea	–	–	–	–	–	1	1
North Korea (PRK)	–	–	–	–	–	1	1
Romania	–	–	1	–	–	–	1
	7	7	7	7	7	7	42

WEIGHTLIFTING

Two events were held in 1896, consisting of one-arm and two-arm lifts. The first Olympic weightlifting champion was Viggo Jensen (DEN) who won the two-arm competition from Launceston Eliot (GBR); both had lifted the same weight but the Briton had moved one of his feet. The positions were reversed in the other event. An amusing incident occurred when an attendant was having great trouble moving one of the weights. Prince George of Greece, a member of the organising committee and an immensely big and strong man, bent down and easily lifted it aside. Jensen was one of the first great all-rounders, as he won silver and bronze medals at pistol and rifle shooting, and took fourth place in the rope climb.

The sport was not included in the Games of 1900, 1908 or 1912. In 1920 the contests were decided on the aggregate of a one-hand snatch, a one-hand jerk, and a two-hands jerk. In 1924 an additional two lifts were included, two-hands press and snatch. From 1928 to 1972 the result depended on the aggregate of three two-handed lifts: the press, the snatch and the clean and jerk. By 1976 the press was eliminated, owing to difficulty in judging it correctly, and the total now is for the snatch and the clean and jerk. At the suggestion of the IOC, the forerunner of the International Weightlifting Federation was formed in 1920 to control the sport.

Of the ten men to win two gold medals, only Tommy Kono (USA) and Norair Nurikyan (BUL) have won them in different categories. Kono won the 67.5kg (1952) and the 82.5kg (1956), while more unusually

Nurikyan moved down from the 60kg (1972) to the 56kg (1976). Norbert Schemansky (USA) has won the most medals with one gold, one silver and two bronze medals from 1948 to 1964.

The oldest gold medallsit was Rudolf Plukfelder (URS) in the 82.5kg class of 1964, aged 36yr 40 days, while Schemansky in 1964 was the oldest medallist, aged 40yr 141 days. The youngest gold medallist was Zeng Guoqiang (CHN) who won the 52kg class in 1984 aged 19yr 133 days, and the youngest ever medallist was Andrei Socaci (ROM) who won a 1984 silver in the 67.5kg category aged 17yr 330 days. The oldest known competitor was 56-year-old Teunist Jonck (SAF) in 1952, and the youngest known was 13-year-old M Djemal (TUR) in 1924.

The only brothers to win medals in the same event at the same Games were Yoshinobu and Yoshiyuki Miyake (JPN), who won gold and bronze medals respectively in the 60kg in 1968. Yoshinobu also won another gold and a silver, but Peter and James George (USA) hold the family record for medals with one gold, three silvers and a bronze from 1948 to 1960.

The silver medallist in the 82.5kg class in 1948, Harold Sakata (USA), later gained fame portraying 'Oddjob' in the James Bond film *Goldfinger*. Incidentally, the margin of victory, 37.5kg, of the winner in this event, Stanley Stanczyk (USA), was a record for Olympic competition. In the 1988 featherweight class (up to 60kg) Naim Suleymanoglu (TUR) – for whose emigration the Turkish government is reported to have paid $1 million to Bulgaria – set an Olympic record equalling that for the next weight class.

Disqualification due to use of drugs has affected this sport more than most with the first cases, gold medallist Zbigniew Kaczmarek (POL) and silver medallist Blagoi Blagoyev (BUL), being disqualified in 1976.

WEIGHTLIFTING MEDAL TOTALS

Country	G	S	B	Total
Soviet Union	39	21	3	63
United States	15	16	10	41
Bulgaria	9	11	3	23
Poland	4	2	16	22
Germany (FRG)	5	4	10	19
Hungary	2	7	8	17
France	9	2	4	15
Italy	5	5	5	15
Austria	5	5	2	12
Japan	2	2	8	12
GDR	1	5	6	12
China	4	3	4	11
Egypt	5	2	2	9
Romania	2	6	1	9
Iran	1	3	5	9
Czechoslovakia	3	2	3	8
Estonia	1	3	3	7
Great Britain	1	3	3	7
Korea	–	1	4	5
Greece	2	–	2	4
Belgium	1	2	1	4
Switzerland	–	2	2	4
Sweden	–	–	4	4
Denmark	1	2	–	3
Australia	1	1	1	3
Finland	1	–	2	3
Trinidad	–	1	2	3
Netherlands	–	–	3	3
Cuba	1	–	1	2
Canada	–	2	–	2
Argentina	–	1	1	2
North Korea (PRK)	–	1	1	2
Norway	1	–	–	1
Turkey	1	–	–	1
Lebanon	–	1	–	1
Luxembourg	–	1	–	1
Singapore	–	1	–	1
Iraq	–	–	1	1
Taipei	–	–	1	1
	122[1]	118	122[2]	362

[1]*Tie for gold in 1928 and 1936 lightweight class.*
[2]*Triple tie for bronze in 1906 heavyweight class.*

WEIGHTLIFTING MEDALS

	Gold	Silver	Bronze

Flyweight
(Up to 52kg)

	Gold	Silver	Bronze
1972	Zygmunt Smalcerz (POL) 337.5kg	Lajos Szuecs (HUN) 330kg	Sandor Holczreiter (HUN) 327.5kg
1976	Aleksandr Voronin (URS) 242.5kg	Gyorgy Koszegi (HUN) 237.5kg	Mohammad Nassiri (IRN) 235kg
1980	Kanybek Osmonoliev (URS) 245kg	Bong Chol Ho (PRK) 245kg	Gyond Si Han (PRK) 245kg
1984	Zeng Guoqiang (CHN) 235kg	Zhou Peishujn (CHN) 235kg	Kazushito Manabe (JPN) 232.5kg
1988	Sevdalin Marinov (BUL) 270kg*	Chun Byung-Kwan (KOR) 260kg	He Zhuogiang (CHN) 257.5kg

Olympic record. 1896–1968 Event not held.

Bantamweight
(Up to 56kg)

	Gold	Silver	Bronze
1948	Joseph de Pietro (USA) 307.5kg	Julian Creus (GBR) 297.5kg	Richard Tom (USA) 295kg
1952	Ivan Udodov (URS) 315kg	Mahmoud Namdjou (IRN) 307.5kg	Ali Mirzai (IRN) 300kg
1956	Charles Vinci (USA) 342.5kg	Vladimir Stogov (URS) 337.5kg	Mahmoud Namdjou (IRN) 332.5kg
1960	Charles Vinci (USA) 345kg	Yoshinobu Miyake (JPN) 337.5kg	Esmail Khan (IRN) 330kg
1964	Aleksey Vakhonin (URS) 357.5kg	Imre Földi (HUN) 355kg	Shiro Ichinoseki (JPN) 347.5kg
1968	Mohammad Nassiri (IRN) 367.5kg	Imre Földi (HUN) 367.5kg	Henryk Trebicki (POL) 357.5kg
1972	Imre Földi (HUN) 377.5kg	Mohammad Nassiri (IRN) 370kg	Gennadiy Chetin (URS) 367.5kg
1976	Norair Nurikyan (BUL) 262.5kg	Grzegorz Cziura (POL) 252.5kg	Kenkichi Ando (JPN) 250kg
1980	Daniel Nunez (CUB) 275kg	Yurik Sarkisian (URS) 270kg	Tadeusz Dembonczyk (POL) 265kg
1984	Wu Shude (CHN) 267.5kg	Lai Runming (CHN) 265kg	Masahiro Kotaka (JPN) 252.5kg
1988	Oxen Mirzoyan (URS) 292.5kg*[1]	He Yingqiang (CHN) 287.5kg	Liu Shoubin (CHN) 267.5kg

[1]*Mitko Grablev (BUL) finished in first place with 297.5kg, but was subsequently disqualified.* *Olympic record.* 1896–1936 Event not held.

Featherweight
(Up to 60kg)

	Gold	Silver	Bronze
1920	Frans de Haes (BEL) 220kg	Alfred Schmidt (EST) 212.5kg	Eugène Ryther (SUI) 210kg
1924[1]	Pierino Gabetti (ITA) 402.5kg	Andreas Stadler (AUT) 385kg	Arthur Reinmann (SUI) 382.5kg
1928	Franz Andrysek (AUT) 287.5kg	Pierino Gabetti (ITA) 282.5kg	Hans Wölpert (GER) 282.5kg
1932	Raymond Suvigny (FRA) 287.5kg	Hans Wölpert (GER) 282.5kg	Anthony Terlazzo (USA) 280kg
1936	Anthony Terlazzo (USA) 312.5kg	Saleh Mohammed Soliman (EGY) 305kg	Ibrahim Shams (EGY) 300kg
1948	Mahmoud Fayad (EGY) 332.5kg	Rodney Wilkes (TRI) 317.5kg	Jaffar Salmassi (IRN) 312.5kg
1952	Rafael Chimishkyan (URS) 337.5kg	Nikolai Saksonov (URS) 332.5kg	Rodney Wilkes (TRI) 332.5kg
1956	Isaac Berger (USA) 352.5kg	Yevgeniy Minayev (URS) 342.5kg	Marian Zielinski (POL) 335kg
1960	Yevgeniy Minayev (URS) 372.5kg	Isaac Berger (USA) 362.5kg	Sebastiano Mannironi (IT) 352.5kg
1964	Yoshinobu Miyake (JPN) 397.5kg	Isaac Berger (USA) 382.5kg	Mieczyslaw Nowak (POL) 377.5kg
1968	Yoshinobu Miyake (JPN) 392.5kg	Dito Shanidze (URS) 387.5kg	Yoshiyuki Miyake (JPN) 385kg
1972	Norair Nurikyan (BUL) 402.5kg	Dito Shanidze (URS) 400kg	Janos Benedek (HUN) 390kg
1976	Nikolai Kolesnikov (URS) 285kg	Georgi Todorov (BUL) 280kg	Kuzumasa Hirai (JPN) 275kg
1980	Viktor Mazin (URS) 290kg	Stefan Dimitrov (BUL) 287.5kg	Marek Seweryn (POL) 282.5kg
1984	Chen Weiqiang (CHN) 282.5kg	Gelu Radu (ROM) 280kg	Tsai Wen-Yee (TPE) 272.5kg
1988	Naim Suleymanoglu (TUR) 342.5kg*	Stefan Topourov (BUL) 312.5kg	Ye Huanming (CHN) 287.5kg

[1]*Aggregate of five lifts.* *Olympic record.* 1896–1912 Event not held.

Lightweight
(Up to 67.5kg)

	Gold	Silver	Bronze
1920	Alfred Neuland (EST) 257.5kg	Louis Williquet (BEL) 240kg	Florimond Rooms (BEL) 230kg
1924[1]	Edmond Decottignies (FRA) 440kg	Anton Zwerina (AUT) 427.5kg	Bohumil Durdis (TCH) 425kg
1928[2]	Kurt Helbig (GER) 322.5kg	–	Fernand Arnout (FRA) 302.5kg
	Hans Haas (AUT) 322.5kg		
1932	René Duverger (FRA) 325kg	Hans Haas (AUT) 307.5kg	Gastone Pierini (ITA) 302.5kg
1936[2]	Anwar Mohammed Mesbah (EGY) 342.5kg	–	Karl Jansen (GER) 327.5kg
	Robert Fein (AUT) 342.5kg		
1948	Ibrahim Shams (EGY) 360kg	Attia Hamouda (EGY) 360kg	James Halliday (GBR) 340kg
1952	Tommy Kono (USA) 362.5kg	Yevgeniy Lopatin (URS) 350kg	Verne Barberis (AUS) 350kg
1956	Igor Rybak (URS) 380kg	Ravil Khabutdinov (URS) 372.5kg	Chang-Hee Kim (KOR) 370kg
1960	Viktor Bushuyev (URS) 397.5kg	Howe-Liang Tan (SIN) 380kg	Abdul Wahid Aziz (IRQ) 380kg
1964	Waldemar Baszanowski (POL) 432.5kg	Vladimir Kaplunov (URS) 432.5kg	Marian Zielinski (POL) 420kg
1968	Waldemar Baszanowski (POL) 437.5kg	Parviz Jalayer (IRN) 422.5kg	Marian Zielinski (POL) 420kg
1972	Mukharbi Kirzhinov (URS) 460kg	Mladen Koutchev (BUL) 450kg	Zbigniev Kaczmarek (POL) 437.5kg
1976[3]	Pyotr Korol (URS) 305kg	Daniel Senet (300kg	Kazimierz Czarnecki (POL) 295kg
1980	Yanko Rusev (BUL) 342.5kg*	Joachin Kunz (GDR) 335kg	Mintcho Pachov (BUL) 325kg
1984	Yao Jingyuan (CHN) 320kg	Andrei Socaci (ROM) 312.5kg	Jouni Gronman (FIN) 312.5kg
1988	Joachim Kunz (GDR) 340kg	Israil Militossian (URS) 337.5kg	Li Jinhe (CHN) 325kg

[1]*Aggregate of five lifts.* [2]*Tie-breaker rule relating to bodyweight not yet introduced.* [3]*Zbigniev Kaczmarek (POL) finished in first place with 307.5kg but was subsequently disqualified.* *Olympic record.* 1896–1912 Event not held.

	Gold	Silver	Bronze

Middleweight
(Up to 75kg)

1920	Henri Gance (FRA) 245kg	Pietro Bianchi[1] (ITA) 237.5kg	Albert Pettersson (SWE) 237.5kg
1924[2]	Carlo Galimberti (ITA) 492.5kg	Alfred Neuland (EST) 455kg	Jaan Kikas (EST) 450kg
1928	Roger Francois (FRA) 335kg	Carlo Galimberti (ITA) 332.5kg	August Scheffer (HOL) 327.5kg
1932	Rudolf Ismayr (GER) 345kg	Carlo Galimberti (ITA) 340kg	Karl Hipfinger (AUT) 337.5kg
1936	Khadr El Thouni (EGY) 387.5kg	Rudolf Ismayr (GER) 352.5kg	Adolf Wagner (GER) 352.5kg
1948	Frank Spellman (USA) 390kg	Peter George (USA) 382.5kg	Sung-Jip Kim (KOR) 380kg
1952	Peter George (USA) 400kg	Gerard Gratton (CAN) 390kg	Sung-Jip Kim (KOR) 382.5kg
1956	Fyodor Bogdanovski (URS) 420kg	Peter George (USA) 412.5kg	Ermanno Pignatti (ITA) 382.5kg
1960	Aleksandr Kurinov (URS) 437.5kg	Tommy Kono (USA) 427.5kg	Gyözö Veres (HUN) 405kg
1964	Hans Zdrazila (TCH) 445kg	Viktor Kurentsov (URS) 440kg	Masashi Ouchi (JPN) 437.5kg
1968	Viktor Kurentsov (URS) 475kg	Masashi Ouchi (JPN) 455kg	Károly Bakos (HUN) 440kg
1972	Yordan Bikov (BUL) 485kg	Mohamed Trabulsi (LIB) 472.5kg	Anselmo Silvino (ITA) 470kg
1976	Yordan Mitkov (BUL) 335kg	Vartan Militosyan (URS) 330kg	Peter Wenzel (GDR) 327.5kg
1980	Asen Zlatev (BUL) 360kg	Aleksandr Pervy (URS) 357.5kg	Nedeltcho Kolev (BUL) 345kg
1984	Karl-Heinz Radschinsky (FRG) 340kg	Jacques Demers (CAN) 335kg	Dragomir Cioroslan (ROM) 332.5kg
1988	Borislav Guidikov (BUL) 375kg*	Ingo Steinhöfel (GDR) 360kg	Alexandr Varbanov (URS) 357.5kg

[1]Bianchi and Pettersson drew lots for the silver medal.   [2]Aggregate of five lifts.   *Olympic record.   1896–1912 Event not held.

Light-Heavyweight
(Up to 82.5kg)

1920	Ernest Cadine (FRA) 290kg	Fritz Hünenberger (SUI) 275kg	Erik Pettersson (SWE) 272.5kg
1924[1]	Charles Rigoulot (FRA) 502.5kg	Fritz Hünenberger (SUI) 490kg	Leopold Friedrich (AUT) 490kg
1928	Said Nosseir (EGY) 355kg	Louis Hostin (FRA) 352.5kg	Johannes Verheijen (HOL) 337.5kg
1932	Louis Hostin (FRA) 372.5kg	Svend Olsen (DEN) 360kg	Henry Duey (USA) 330kg
1936	Louis Hostin (FRA) 372.5kg	Eugen Deutsch (GER) 365kg	Ibrahim Wasif (EGY) 360kg
1948	Stanley Stanczyk (USA) 417.5kg	Harold Sakata (USA) 380kg	Gösta Magnussen (SWE) 375kg
1952	Trofim Lomakin (URS) 417.5kg	Stanley Stanczyk (USA) 415kg	Arkadiy Vorobyev (URS) 407.5kg
1956	Tommy Kono (USA) 447.5kg	Vassily Stepanov (URS) 427.5kg	James George (USA) 417.5kg
1960	Ireneusz Palinski (POL) 442.5kg	James George (USA) 430kg	Jan Bochenek (POL) 420kg
1964	Rudolf Plukfelder (URS) 475kg	Géza Toth (HUN) 467.5kg	Gyözö Veres (HUN) 467.5kg
1968	Boris Selitsky (URS) 485kg	Vladimir Belyayev (URS) 485kg	Norbert Ozimek (POL) 472.5kg
1972	Leif Jenssen (NOR) 507.5kg	Norbert Ozimek (POL) 497.5kg	György Horvath (HUN) 495kg
1976[2]	Valeriy Shary (URS) 365kg	Trendachil Stoichev (BUL) 360kg	Peter Baczako (HUN) 345kg
1980	Yurik Vardanyan (URS) 400kg*	Blagoi Blagoyev (BUL) 372.5kg	Dusan Poliacik (TCH) 367.5kg
1984	Petre Becheru (ROM) 355kg	Robert Kabbas (AUS) 342.5kg	Ryoji Isaoka (JPN) 340kg
1988	Israil Arsamakov (URS) 377.5kg	Istvan Messzi (HUN) 370kg	Lee Hyung-Kun (KOR) 367.5kg

[1]Aggregate of five lifts.   [2]Blagoi Blagoyev (BUL) finished in second place with 362.5kg but was subsequently disqualified.   *Olympic record.
1896–1912 Event not held.

Middle-Heavyweight
(Up to 90kg)

1952	Norbert Schemansky (USA) 445kg	Grigoriy Nowak (URS) 410kg	Lennox Kilgour (TRI) 402.5kg
1956	Arkadiy Vorobyev (URS) 462.5kg	David Sheppard (USA) 442.5kg	Jean Debuf (FRA) 425kg
1960	Arkadiy Vorobyev (URS) 472.5kg	Trofim Lomakin (URS) 457.5kg	Louis Martin (GBR) 445kg
1964	Vladimir Golovanov (URS) 487.5kg	Louis Martin (GBR) 475kg	Ireneusz Palinski (POL) 467.5kg
1968	Kaarlo Kangasniemi (FIN) 517.5kg	Jan Talts (URS) 507.5kg	Marek Golab (POL) 495kg
1972	Andon Nikolov (BUL) 525kg	Atanas Chopov (BUL) 517.5kg	Hans Bettembourg (SWE) 512.5kg
1976	David Rigert (URS) 382.5kg	Lee James (USA) 362.5kg	Atanas Chopov (BUL) 360kg
1980	Peter Baczako (HUN) 377.5kg	Rumen Alexandrov (BUL) 375kg	Frank Mantek (GDR) 375kg
1984	Nicu Vlad (ROM) 392.5kg	Dumitru Petre (ROM) 360kg	David Mercer (GBR) 352.5kg
1988	Anatoly Khrapatiy (URS) 412.5kg*	Nail Moukhamediarov (URS) 400kg	Slawomir Zawada (POL) 400kg

*Olympic record.   1896–1948 Event not held.

Up to 100kg

1980	Ota Zaremba (TCH) 395kg	Igor Nikitin (URS) 392.5kg	Alberto Blanco (CUB) 385kg
1984	Rolf Milser (FRG) 385kg	Vasile Gropa (ROM) 382.5kg	Pekka Niemi (FIN) 367.5kg
1988	Pavel Kuznetsov (URS) 425kg*	Nicu Vlad (ROM)[1] 402.5kg	Peter Immesberger (FRG) 395kg

[1]Andor Szanyi (HUN) finished second with 407.5kg, but was subsequently disqualified.   *Olympic record.   1896–1976 Event not held.

Heavyweight
(From 1920 to 1948 class was over 82.5kg. From 1952 to 1968 class was over 90kg. Since 1972 weight limit has been up to 110kg)

1896[1]	Launceston Eliot (GBR) 71kg	Viggo Jensen (DEN) 57.2kg	Alexandros Nikolopoulos (GRE) 57.2kg
1896[2]	Viggo Jensen (DEN) 111.5kg	Launceston Eliot (GBR) 111.5kg	Sotirios Versis (GRE) 100kg
1904[3]	Oscar Osthoff (USA) 48pts	Frederick Winters (USA) 45pts	Frank Kungler (USA) 10pts
1904[2]	Perikles Kakousis (GRE) 111.58kg	Oscar Osthoff (USA) 84.36kg	Frank Kungler (USA) 79.83kg
1906[1]	Josef Steinbach (AUT) 76.55kg	Tullio Camilotti (ITA) 73.75kg	Heinrich Schneidereit (GER) 70.75kg

	Gold	Silver	Bronze
1906[2]	Dimitrios Tofalos (GRE) 142.5kg	Josef Steinbach (AUT) 136.5kg	Alexandre Maspoli (FRA) 129.5kg
			Heinrich Rondl (GER) 129.5kg
			Heinrich Schneidereit (GER) 129.5kg
1920	Filippo Bottino (ITA) 270kg	Joseph Alzin (LUX) 225kg	Louis Bernot (FRA) 250kg
1924[4]	Giuseppe Tonani (ITA) 517.5kg	Franz Aigner (AUT) 515kg	Harald Tammer (EST) 497.5kg
1928	Josef Strassberger (GER) 372.5kg	Arnold Luhaäär (EST) 360kg	Jaroslav Skobla (TCH) 357.5kg
1932	Jaroslav Skobla (TCH) 380kg	Václav Psenicka (TCH) 377.5kg	Josef Strassberger (GER) 377.5kg
1936	Josef Manger (AUT) 410kg	Václav Psenicka (TCH) 402.5kg	Arnold Luhaäär (EST) 400kg
1948	John Davis (USA) 452.2kg	Norbert Schemansky (USA) 425kg	Abraham Charité (HOL) 412.5kg
1952	John Davis (USA) 460kg	James Bradford (USA) 437.5kg	Humberto Selvetti (ARG) 432.5kg
1956	Paul Anderson (USA) 500kg	Humberto Selvetti (ARG) 500kg	Alberto Pigaiani (ITA) 452.5kg
1960	Yuriy Vlasov (URS) 537.5kg	James Bradford (USA) 512.5kg	Norbert Schemansky (USA) 500kg
1964	Leonid Zhabotinsky (URS) 572.5kg	Yuriy Vlasov (URS) 570kg	Norbert Schemansky (USA) 537.5kg
1968	Leonid Zhabotinsky (URS) 572.5kg	Serge Reding (BEL) 555kg	Joseph Dube (USA) 555kg
1972	Jan Talts (URS) 580kg	Alexandre Kraitchev (BUL) 562.5kg	Stefan Grützner (GDR) 555kg
1976[5]	Yuriy Zaitsev (URS) 385kg	Krastio Semerdiev (BUL) 385kg	Tadeusz Rutkowski (POL) 377.5kg
1980	Leonid Taranenko (URS) 422.5kg	Valentin Christov (BUL) 405kg	György Szalai (HUN) 390kg
1984	Norberto Oberburger (ITA) 390kg	Stefan Tasnadi (ROM) 380kg	Guy Carlton (USA) 377.5kg
1988	Yuriy Zakharevich (URS) 455kg*	Jozsef Jacso (HUN) 427.5kg	Ronny Weller (GDR) 425kg

[1]One-hand lift. [2]Two-hand lift. [3]Dumbell lift. [4]Aggregate of five lifts. [5]Valentin Christov (BUL) finished in first palce with 400kg but was subsequently disqualified. *Olympic record.. 1900, 1908–1912 Event not held.

Super-Heavyweight
(Over 110kg)

1972	Vasiliy Alexeyev (URS) 640kg	Rudolf Mang (GDR) 610kg	Gerd Bonk (GDR) 572.5kg
1976	Vasiliy Alexeyev (URS) 440kg	Gerd Bonk (GDR) 405kg	Helmut Losch (GDR) 387.5kg
1980	Sultan Rakhmanov (URS) 440kg	Jürgen Heuser (GDR) 410kg	Tadeusz Rutkowski (POL) 407.5kg
1984	Dinko Lukin (AUS) 412.5kg	Mario Martinez (USA) 410kg	Manfred Nerlinger (FRG) 397.5kg
1988	Alexandr Kurlovich (URS) 462.5kg*	Manfred Nerlinger (FRG) 430kg	Martin Zawieja (FRG) 415kg

*Olympic record. 1896–1968 Event not held.

WRESTLING

Wrestling was the most popular sport in the ancient Games with victors recorded from 708 BC. The most famous was Milon of Kroton, a five-time winner. Greco-Roman wrestling was included in the 1896 Games and freestyle in 1904. There was no bodyweight limit in Athens and it was won, surprisingly, by gymnastics triple gold medallist Carl Schuhmann (GER), who was only 1.63m (5ft 4in) tall, and who defeated Games weightlifting champion Launceston Eliot (GBR) in the preliminaries.

Until a time limit was set in 1924, bouts often lasted for remarkable lengths of time. The most extreme was when Martin Klein, an Estonian representing Russia, and Alfred 'Alpo' Asikáinen (FIN) wrestled for 11 hours 40 minutes in the 1912 Greco-Roman middleweight class. Klein won, but was too exhausted to challenge for the gold medal! In the light-heavyweight final that year, Anders Ahlgren (SWE) and Ivar Böhling (FIN) were declared equal second after nine hours without a decision, and no gold medal was awarded.

Three men have won three gold medals: Carl Westergren (SWE), Ivar Johansson (SWE) and Aleksandr Medved (URS). Johansson and Kristjan Palusalu (FIN) are the only men to win titles in both styles at the same Games. Wilfried Dietrich (GER/FRG) won most medals with one gold, two silvers and two bronzes at both styles from 1956 to 1968. Dietrich and George Mackenzie (GBR) competed at a record five Games, 1956–1972 and 1908–1928 respectively, while Mackenzie also competed over a record span of 20 years.

The most successful brothers have been Kustaa and Hermanni Pihlajamäki (FIN) with three golds, one silver and a bronze between 1924 and 1936. The only twins to win gold medals were Anatoliy and Sergey Beloglazov (URS) in 1980, and Ed and Lou Banach (USA) in 1984. The first black champion was Kenny Monday (USA) in the 1988 freestyle welterweight division. The only Greek to win a gold medal in Greco-Roman wrestling was Stilianos Migiakis in 1980.

Although a number of brothers have each won gold medals, uniquely two pairs of brothers, Ed and Lou Banach and Dave and Mark Schultz, all from the United States, won titles in 1984. The only father and son to become champions were Kaarlo (1928 freestyle) and Rauno (1956 Greco-Roman) Mäkinen (FIN). The oldest gold medallist was Anatoliy Roschin (URS) in 1972, aged 40yr 184 days, while

Greco-Roman wrestling champions in 1932. From left: Westergren, Svensson, Johansson and Malmberg (SWE), Gozzi (ITA) and Brendel (GER).

the youngest was Saban Trstena (YUG) in 1984, aged 19yr 222 days. The heaviest competitor ever in any Olympic event was the 1972 super-heavyweight bronze medallist Chris Taylor (USA), who weighed between 182kg (401lb) and 190kg (419lb). When Osamu Watanabe (JPN) won the 1964 freestyle feather-weight title it was his 186th successive victory in the sport.

WRESTLING MEDAL TOTALS

Country	FREESTYLE			GRECO-ROMAN			Total
	G	S	B	G	S	B	
Soviet Union	28	15	13	34	19	10	119
United States	38	30	20	2	1	2	93
Finland	8	7	10	19	19	18	81
Sweden	8	10	8	19	15	17	77
Bulgaria	6	14	8	8	14	7	57
Hungary	3	4	7	13	9	11	47
Turkey	15	10	5	8	3	2	43
Japan	16	9	6	4	4	2	41
Germany (FRG)	1	3	5	4	14	8	35
Romania	1	–	4	6	8	12	31
Iran	3	7	9	–	1	1	21
Korea	3	3	6	2	1	4	19
Italy	1	–	–	5	3	9	18
Great Britain	3	4	10	–	–	–	17
Yugoslavia	1	1	2	3	5	4	16
Poland	–	1	3	2	5	5	16
Czechoslovakia	–	1	3	1	6	4	15
Switzerland	4	4	5	–	–	1	14
France	2	2	3	1	1	2	11
Denmark	–	–	–	1	3	7	11
Estonia	2	1	–	3	–	4	10
Greece	–	–	1	1	3	4	9
Mongolia	–	4	4	–	–	–	8
Canada	–	3	5	–	–	–	8
GDR	–	2	1	2	1	1	7
Austria	–	–	1	1	2	1	5
Egypt (UAR)	–	–	–	1	2	2	5
Norway	–	1	–	1	1	1	4
Belgium	–	3	–	–	–	1	4
North Korea (PRK)	–	2	1	–	–	–	3
Australia	–	1	2	–	–	–	3
Lebanon	–	–	–	–	1	2	3
Latvia	–	–	–	–	1	–	1
Mexico	–	–	–	–	1	–	1
Syria	–	1	–	–	–	–	1
India	–	–	1	–	–	–	1
Pakistan	–	–	1	–	–	–	1
	143	143	144[1]	141[2]	143	142	856

[1]*Two bronzes in 1920 heavyweight class.*
[2]*No gold in 1912 light-heavyweight class.*

WRESTLING MEDALS

The contemporary descriptions of some bodyweight classes have varied during the history of the Games. Current descriptions are used in the lists below.

Gold	Silver	Bronze

Free-Style – Light Flyweight
(Weight up to 48kg)

	Gold	Silver	Bronze
1904	Robert Curry (USA)	John Heim (USA)	Gustav Thiefenthaler (USA)
1972	Roman Dmitriev (URS)	Ognian Nikolov (BUL)	Ebrahim Javadpour (IRN)
1976	Khassan Issaev (BUL)	Roman Dmitriev (URS)	Akira Kudo (JPN)
1980	Claudio Pollio (ITA)	Se Hong Jang (PRK)	Sergey Kornilayev (URS)
1984	Robert Weaver (USA)	Takashi Irie (JPN)	Son Gab-Do (KOR)
1988	Takashi Kobayashi (JPN)	Ivan Tzonov (BUL)	Sergey Karamtchakov (URS)

1896–1900, 1906–1968 Event not held.

Free-Style – Flyweight
Note: 1904 weight up to 115lb (52.16kg). From 1948 weight up to 52kg.

	Gold	Silver	Bronze
1904	George Mehnert (USA)	Gustave Bauer (USA)	William Nelson (USA)
1948	Lennart Viitala (FIN)	Halit Balamir (TUR)	Thure Johansson (SWE)
1952	Hasan Gemici (TUR)	Yushu Kitano (JPN)	Mahmoud Mollaghassemi (IRN)
1956	Mirian Tsalkalamanidze (URS)	Mohamad-Ali Khojastenpour (IRN)	Hüseyin Akbas (TUR)
1960	Ahmet Bilek (TUR)	Masayuki Matsubara (JPN)	Mohamad Saifpour Saidabadi (IRN)
1964	Yoshikatsu Yoshida (JPN)	Chang-sun Chang (KOR)	Said Aliaakbar Haydari (IRN)
1968	Shigeo Nakata (JPN)	Richard Sanders (USA)	Surenjav Sukhbaatar (MGL)
1972	Kiyomi Kato (JPN)	Arsen Alakhverdiev (URS)	Hyong Kim Gwong (PRK)
1976	Yuji Takada (JPN)	Aleksandr Ivanov (URS)	Jeon Hae-Sup (KOR)
1980	Anatoliy Beloglazov (URS)	Wladyslaw Stecyk (POL)	Nermedin Selimov (BUL)
1984	Saban Trstena (YUG)	Kim Jong-Kyu (KOR)	Yuji Takada (JPN)
1988	Mitsuru Sato (JPN)	Saban Trstena (YUG)	Vladimir Togouzov (URS)

1896–1900, 1906–1936 Event not held.

Free-Style – Bantamweight
Note: The weight limit for this event has been: 1904, 125lb (56.70kg); 1908, 119lb (54kg); 1924–1936, 56kg and from 1948, 57kg.

	Gold	Silver	Bronze
1904	Isidor Niflot (USA)	August Wester (USA)	ZB Strebler (USA)
1908	George Mehnert (USA)	William Press (GBR)	Aubert Côté (CAN)
1924	Kustaa Pihlajamaki (FIN)	Kaarlo Mäkinen (FIN)	Bryant Hines (USA)
1928	Kaarlo Mäkinen (FIN)	Edmond Spapen (BEL)	James Trifunov (CAN)
1932	Robert Pearce (USA)	Odön Zombori (HUN)	Aatos Jaskari (FIN)
1936	Odön Zombori (HUN)	Ross Flood (USA)	Johannes Herbert (GER)
1948	Nasuk Akar (TUR)	Gerald Leeman (USA)	Charles Kouyov (FRA)
1952	Shohachi Ishii (JPN)	Rashid Mamedbekov (URS)	Kha-Shaba Jadav (IND)
1956	Mustafa Dagistanli (TUR)	Mohamad Yaghoubi (IRN)	Mikhail Chakhov (URS)
1960	Terrence McCann (USA)	Nejdet Zalev (BUL)	Tadeusz Trojanowski (POL)
1964	Yojiro Uetake (JPN)	Hüseyin Akbas (TUR)	Aidyn Ibragimov (URS)
1968	Yojiro Uetake (JPN)	Donald Behm (USA)	Abutaleb Gorgori (IRN)
1972	Hideaki Yanagide (JPN)	Richard Sanders (USA)	László Klinga (HUN)
1976	Vladimir Yumin (URS)	Hans-Dieter Brüchert (GDR)	Masao Arai (JPN)
1980	Sergey Beloglazov (URS)	Li Ho Pyong (PRK)	Dugarsuren Ouinbold (MGL)
1984	Hideyaki Tomiyama (JPN)	Barry Davis (USA)	Kim Eui-Kon (KOR)
1988	Sergey Beloglazov (URS)	Askari Mohammadian (IRN)	Noh Kyung-Sun (KOR)

1896–1900, 1906, 1912–1920 Event not held.

Free-Style – Featherweight
Note: The weight limit for this event has been: 1904, 135lb (61.24kg); 1908, 133lb (60.30kg); 1920, 60kg; 1924–1936, 61kg; 1948–1960, and 1972 62kg; 1964–1968, 63kg; 1984, 62kg.

	Gold	Silver	Bronze
1904	Benjamin Bradshaw (USA)	Theodore McLear (USA)	Charles Clapper (USA)
1908	George Dole (USA)	James Slim (GBR)	William McKie (GBR)
1920	Charles Ackerly (USA)	Samuel Gerson (USA)	PW Bernard (GBR)
1924	Robin Reed (USA)	Chester Newton (USA)	Katsutoshi Naito (JPN)
1928	Allie Morrison (USA)	Kustaa Pihlajamaki (FIN)	Hans Minder (SUI)
1932	Hermanni Pihlajamaki (FIN)	Edgar Nemir (USA)	Einar Karlsson (SWE)
1936	Kustaa Pihlajamaki (FIN)	Francis Millard (USA)	Gösta Jönsson (SWE)
1948	Gazanfer Bilge (TUR)	Ivar Sjölin (SWE)	Adolf Müller (SUI)
1952	Bayram Sit (TUR)	Nasser Guivehtchi (IRN)	Josiah Henson (USA)
1956	Shozo Sasahara (JPN)	Joseph Mewis (BEL)	Erkki Penttilä (FIN)
1960	Mustafa Dagistanli (TUR)	Stantcho Ivanov (BUL)	Vladimir Rubashbili (URS)
1964	Osamu Watanabe (JPN)	Stantcho Ivanov (BUL)	Nodar Khokhashvili (URS)

	Gold	Silver	Bronze
1968	Masaaki Kaneko (JPN)	Enyu Todorov (BUL)	Shamseddin Seyed-Abbassi (IRN)
1972	Zagalav Abdulbekov (URS)	Vehbi Akdag (TUR)	Ivan Krastev (BUL)
1976	Yang Jung-Mo (KOR)	Zeveg Oidov (MGL)	Gene Davis (USA)
1980	Magomedgasan Abushev (URS)	Mikho Doukov (BUL)	Georges Hadjiioannidis (GRE)
1984	Randy Lewis (USA)	Kosei Akaishi (JPN)	Lee Jung-Keun (KOR)
1988	John Smith (USA)	Stepan Sarkissian (URS)	Simeon Chterev (BUL)

1896–1900, 1906, 1912 Event not held.

Free-Style – Lightweight

Note: The weight limit for this event has been: 1904, 145lb (65.77kg); 1908, 146¾lb (66.60kg); 1920 67.5kg; 1924 to 1936, 66kg; 1948 to 1960, 67kg; 1964 and 1968, 70kg and from 1972, 68kg.

1904	Otton Roehm (USA)	Rudolph Tesing (USA)	Albert Zirkel (USA)
1908	George de Relwyskow (GBR)	William Wood (GDR)	Albert Gingell (GBR)
1920	Kalle Anttila (FIN)	Gottfrid Svensson (SWE)	Peter Wright (GBR)
1924	Russell Vis (USA)	Volmart Wickström (FIN)	Arvo Haavisto (FIN)
1928	Osvald Käpp (EST)	Charles Pacôme (FRA)	Eino Leino (FIN)
1932	Charles Pacôme (FRA)	Károly Kárpáti (HUN)	Gustaf Klarén (SWE)
1936	Károly Kárpáti (HUN)	Wolfgang Ehrl (GER)	Hermanni Pihlajamaki (FIN)
1948	Celál Atik (TUR)	Gösta Frandfors (SWE)	Hermann Baumann (SUI)
1952	Olle Anderberg (SWE)	Thomas Evans (USA)	Djahanbakte Tovfighe (IRN)
1956	Emamali Habibi (IRN)	Shigeru Kasahara (JPN)	Alimberg Bestayev (URS)
1960	Shelby Wilson (USA)	Viktor Sinyavskiy (URS)	Enyu Dimov (BUL)
1964	Enyu Valtschev[1] (BUL)	Klaus-Jürgen Rost (GER)	Iwao Horiuchi (JPN)
1968	Abdollah Movahed Ardabili (IRN)	Enyu Valtschev[1] (BUL)	Sereeter Danzandarjaa (MGL)
1972	Dan Gable (USA)	Kikuo Wada (JPN)	Ruslan Ashuraliev (URS)
1976	Pavel Pinigin (URS)	Lloyd Keaser (USA)	Yasaburo Sagawara (JPN)
1980	Saipulla Absaidov (URS)	Ivan Yankov (BUL)	Saban Sejdi (YUG)
1984	You In-Tak (KOR)	Andrew Rein (USA)	Jukka Rauhala (FIN)
1988	Arsen Fadzayev (URS)	Park Jang-Soon (KOR)	Nate Carr (USA)

[1]*Valtschev competed as Dimov in 1960.*   1896–1900, 1906, 1912 Event not held.

Free-Style – Welterweight

Note: The weight limit for this event has been: 1904, 158lb (71.67kg); 1924 to 1936, 72kg; 1948 to 1960, 73kg; from 1972, 74kg.

1904	Charles Erikson (USA)	William Beckmann (USA)	Jerry Winholtz (USA)
1924	Hermann Gehri (SUI)	Eino Leino (FIN)	Otto Müller (SUI)
1928	Arvo Haavisto (FIN)	Lloyd Appleton (USA)	Maurice Letchford (CAN)
1932	Jack van Bebber (USA)	Daniel MacDonald (CAN)	Eino Leino (FIN)
1936	Frank Lewis (USA)	Ture Andersson (SWE)	Joseph Schleimer (CAN)
1948	Yasar Dogu (TUR)	Richard Garrard (AUS)	Leland Merrill (USA)
1952	William Smith (USA)	Per Berlin (SWE)	Abdullah Modjtabavi (IRN)
1956	Mitsuo Ikeda (JPN)	Ibrahim Zengin (TUR)	Vakhtang Balavadze (URS)
1960	Douglas Blubaugh (USA)	Ismail Ogan (TUR)	Mohammed Bashir (PAK)
1964	Ismail Ogan (TUR)	Guliko Sagaradze (URS)	Mohamad-Ali Sanatkaran (IRN)
1968	Mahmut Atalay (TUR)	Daniel Robin (FRA)	Dagvasuren Purev (MGL)
1972	Wayne Wells (USA)	Jan Karlsson (SWE)	Adolf Seger (FRG)
1976	Jiichiro Date (JPN)	Mansour Barzegar (IRN)	Stanley Dziedzic (USA)
1980	Valentin Raitchev (BUL)	Jamtsying Davaajav (MGL)	Dan Karabin (TCH)
1984	David Schultz (USA)	Martin Knosp (FRG)	Saban Sejdi (YUG)
1988	Kenneth Monday (USA)	Adlan Varayev (URS)	Rakhmad Sofiadi (BUL)

1896–1900, 1906–1920 Event not held.

Freestyle – Middleweight

Note: The weight limit for this event has been: 1908, 161lb (73kg); 1920, 165¼lb (75kg); 1924 to 1960, 79kg; 1964 and 1968, 87kg; from 1972, 82kg.

1908	Stanley Bacon (GBR)	George de Relwyskow (GBR)	Frederick Beck (GBR)
1920	Eino Leino (FIN)	Väinö Penttala (FIN)	Charles Johnson (USA)
1924	Fritz Hagmann (SUI)	Pierre Ollivier (BEL)	Vilho Pekkala (FIN)
1928	Ernst Kyburz (SUI)	Donald Stockton (CAN)	Samuel Rabin (GBR)
1932	Ivar Johansson (SWE)	Kyösti Luukko (FIN)	József Tunyogi (HUN)
1936	Emile Poilvé (FRA)	Richard Voliva (USA)	Ahmet Kireiççi (TUR)
1948	Glen Brand (USA)	Adil Candemir (TUR)	Erik Lindén (SWE)
1952	David Tsimakuridze (URS)	Gholamheza Takhti (IRN)	György Gurics (HUN)
1956	Nikola Stantschev (BUL)	Daniel Hodge (USA)	Georgiy Skhirtladze (URS)
1960	Hasan Güngör (TUR)	Georgiy Skhirtladze (URS)	Hans Antonsson (SWE)
1964	Prodan Gardschev (BUL)	Hasan Güngör (TUR)	Daniel Brand (USA)
1968	Boris Gurevitch (URS)	Munkbat Jigjid (MGL)	Prodan Gardschev (BUL)
1972	Leven Tediashvili (URS)	John Peterson (USA)	Vasile Jorga (ROM)

Wrestler Alexandr Medved (URS) wins the 1972 freestyle super-heavyweight title, beating the Bulgarian Osman Duralyev. It was Medved's record-equalling third consecutive gold medal, having won the light-heavyweight class in 1964 and the heavyweight crown in 1968.

	Gold	Silver	Bronze
1976	John Peterson (USA)	Viktor Novoshilev (URS)	Adolf Seger (FRG)
1980	Ismail Abilov (BUL)	Magomedhan Aratsilov (URS)	Istvan Kovacs (HUN)
1984	Mark Schultz (USA)	Hideyuki Nagashima (JPN)	Chris Rinke (CAN)
1988	Han Myung-Woo (KOR)	Necmi Gencalp (TUR)	Josef Lohyna (TCH)

1896–1906, 1912 Event not held.

Free-Style – Light-Heavyweight
Note: The weight limit for this event has been: 1920, 82.5kg; 1924 to 1960, 87kg; 1964 and 1968, 97kg; from 1972. 90kg.

1920	Anders Larsson (SWE)	Charles Courant (SUI)	Walter Maurer (USA)
1924	John Spellman (USA)	Rudolf Svensson (SWE)	Charles Courant (SUI)
1928	Thure Sjöstedt (SWE)	Anton Bögli (SUI)	Henri Lefèbre (FRA)
1932	Peter Mehringer (USA)	Thure Sjöstedt (SWE)	Eddie Scarf (AUS)
1936	Knut Fridell (SWE)	August Neo (EST)	Erich Siebert (GER)
1948	Henry Wittenberg (USA)	Fritz Stöckli (SUI)	Bengt Fahlkvist (SWE)
1952	Wiking Palm (SWE)	Henry Wittenberg (USA)	Adil Atan (TUR)
1956	Gholam Reza Tahkti (IRN)	Boris Kulayev (URS)	Peter Blair (USA)
1960	Ismet Atli (TUR)	Cholam Reza Tahkti (IRN)	Anatoliy Albul (URS)
1964	Aleksandr Medved (URS)	Ahmet Ayik (TUR)	Said Mustafafov (BUL)
1968	Ahmet Ayik (TUR)	Shota Lomidze (URS)	József Csatári (HUN)
1972	Ben Peterson (USA)	Gennadiy Strakhov (URS)	Karoly Bajko (HUN)
1976	Levan Tediashvili (URS)	Ben Peterson (USA)	Stelica Morcov (ROM)
1980	Sanasar Oganesyan (URS)	Uwe Neupert (GDR)	Aleksandr Cichon (POL)
1984	Ed Banach (USA)	Akira Ota (JPN)	Noel Loban (GBR)
1988	Makharbek Khadartsev (URS)	Akira Ota (JPN)	Kim Tae-Woo (KOR)

1896–1912 Event not held.

Free-Style – Heavyweight
Note: The weight limit for this event has been: 1904, over 158lb (71.6kg); 1908, over 73kg; 1920, over 82.5kg' 1924 to 1960, over 87kg; 1964 and 1968, over 97kg; from 1972, up to 100kg.

1904	Bernhuff Hansen (USA)	Frank Kungler (USA)	Fred Warmbold (USA)
1908	George O'Kelly (GBR)	Jacob Gundersen (NOR)	Edmond Barrett (GBR)
1920	Robert Roth (SUI)	Nathan Pendleton (USA)	Ernst Nilsson (SWE)
			Frederick Meyer (USA)
1924	Harry Steele (USA)	Henry Wernli (SUI)	Andrew McDonald (GBR)
1928	Johan Richthoff (SWE)	Aukusti Sihovla (FIN)	Edmond Dame (FRA)
1932	Johan Richthoff (SWE)	John Riley (USA)	Nikolaus Hirschl (AUT)
1936	Kristjan Palusalu (EST)	Josef Klapuch (TCH)	Hjalmar Nyström (FIN)
1948	Gyula Bóbis (HUN)	Bertil Antonsson (SWE)	Joseph Armstrong (AUS)
1952	Arsen Mekokishvili (URS)	Bertil Antonsson (SWE)	Kenneth Richmond (GBR)
1956	Hamit Kaplan (TUR)	Hussein Mekhmedov (BUL)	Taisto Kangasniemi (FIN)
1960	Wilfried Dietrich (GER)	Hamit Kaplan (TUR)	Savkus Dzarassov (URS)
1964	Aleksandr Ivanitsky (URS)	Liutvi Djiber (BUL)	Hamit Kaplan (TUR)
1968	Aleksandr Medved (URS)	Osman Duraliev (BUL)	Wilfried Dietrich (FRG)
1972	Ivan Yaragin (URS)	Khorloo Baianmunkh (MGL)	József Csatári (HUN)
1976	Ivan Yaragin (URS)	Russell Hellickson (USA)	Dimo Kostov (BUL)
1980	Ilya Mate (URS)	Slavtcho Tchervenkov (BUL)	Julius Strnisko (TCH)
1984	Lou Banach (USA)	Joseph Atiyeh (SYR)	Vasile Pascasu (ROM)
1988	Vasile Puscasu (ROM)	Leriy Khabelov (URS)	William Scherr (USA)

[1]*Tie for third place.*   1896–1900, 1906, 1912 Event not held.

Free-Style – Super-Heavyweight
(Weight over 100kg)

1972	Aleksandr Medved (URS)	Osman Duraliev (BUL)	Chris Taylor (USA)
1976	Sosian Andiev (URS)	Jozsef Balla (HUN)	Ladislau Simon (ROM)
1980	Sosian Andiev (URS)	Jozsef Balla (HUN)	Adam Sandurski (POL)
1984	Bruce Baumgartner (USA)	Bob Molle (CAN)	Ayhan Taskin (TUR)
1988	David Gobedjichvili (URS)	Bruce Baumgartner (USA)	Andreas Schröder (GDR)

1896–1968 Event not held.

	Gold	Silver	Bronze

Greco-Roman – Light-Flyweight
(Weight up to 48kg)

1972	Gheorghe Berceanu (ROM)	Rahim Ahabadi (IRN)	Stefan Anghelov (BUL)
1976	Aleksey Shumakov (URS)	Gheorghe Berceanu (ROM)	Stefan Anghelov (BUL)
1980	Zaksylik Ushkempirov (URS)	Constantin Alexandru (ROM)	Ferenc Seres (HUN)
1984	Vincenzo Mzenza (ITA)	Markus Scherer (FRG)	Ikuzo Saito (JPN)
1988	Vincenzo Maenza (ITA)	Andrzej Glab (POL)	Bratan Tzenov (BUL)

1896–1968 Event not held.

Greco-Roman – Flyweight
(Weight up to 52kg)

1948	Pietro Lombardi (ITA)	Kenan Olcay (TUR)	Reino Kangasmäki (FIN)
1952	Boris Gurevich (URS)	Ignazio Fabra (ITA)	Leo Honkala (FIN)
1956	Nikolai Solovyov (URS)	Ignazio Fabra (ITA)	Durum Ali Egribas (TUR)
1960	Dumitru Pirvulescu (ROM)	Osman Sayed (UAR)	Mohamad Paziraye (IRN)
1964	Tsutomu Hanahara (JPN)	Angel Kerezov (BUL)	Dumitru Pirvulescu (ROM)
1968	Petar Kirov (BUL)	Vladimir Bakulin (URS)	Miroslav Zeman (TCH)
1972	Petar Kirov (BUL)	Koichiro Hirayama (JPN)	Giuseppe Bognanni (ITA)
1976	Vitaliy Konstantinov (URS)	Nicu Ginga (ROM)	Koichiro Kirayama (JPN)
1980	Vakhtang Blagidze (URS)	Lajos Racz (HUN)	Mladen Mladenov (BUL)
1984	Atsuji Miyahara (JPN)	Daniel Aceves (MEX)	Bang Dae-Du (KOR)
1988	Jon Ronningen (NOR)	Atsuji Miyahara (JPN)	Lee Jae-Suk (KOR)

1896–1936 Event not held.

Greco-Roman – Bantamweight
Note: The weight limit for this event has been: 1924 to 1928, 58kg; 1932 to 1936, 56kg; since 1948, 57kg.

1924	Eduard Pütsep (EST)	Anselm Ahlfors (FIN)	Väinö Ikonen (FIN)
1928	Kurt Leucht (GER)	Jindrich Maudr (TCH)	Giovanni Gozzi (ITA)
1932	Jakob Brendel (GER)	Marcello Nizzola (ITA)	Louis François (FRA)
1936	Márton Lörincz (HUN)	Egon Svensson (SWE)	Jakob Brendel (GER)
1948	Kurt Pettersén (SWE)	Aly Mahmoud Hassan (EGY)	Habil Kaya (TUR)
1952	Imre Hódos (HUN)	Zakaria Chihab (LIB)	Artem Teryan (URS)
1956	Konstantin Vyrupayev (URS)	Evdin Vesterby (SWE)	Francisco Horvat (ROM)
1960	Oleg Karavayev (URS)	Ion Cernea (ROM)	Petrov Dinko (BUL)
1964	Masamitsu Ichiguchi (JPN)	Vladlen Trostiansky (URS)	Ion Cernea (ROM)
1968	János Varga (HUN)	Ion Baciu (ROM)	Ivan Kochergin (URS)
1972	Rustem Kazakov (URS)	Hans-Jürgen Veil (FRG)	Risto Björlin (FIN)
1976	Pertti Ukkola (FIN)	Iván Frgic (YUG)	Farhat Mustafin (URS)
1980	Shamil Serikov (URS)	Jozef Lipien (POL)	Benni Ljungbeck (SWE)
1984	Pasquale Passarelli (FRG)	Masaki Eto (JPN)	Haralambos Holidis (GRE)
1988	Andras Sike (HUN)	Stoyan Balov (BUL)	Haralambos Holidis (GRE)

1896–1920 Event not held.

Greco-Roman – Featherweight
Note: The weight limit for this event has been: 1912 to 1920, 60kg; 1924 to 1928, 1948 59 1960 and since 1972, 62kg; 1932 to 1936, 61kg; 1964 to 1968, 63kg.

1912	Kaarlo Koskelo (FIN)	Georg Gerstacker (GER)	Otto Lasanen (FIN)
1920	Oskari Friman (FIN)	Hekki Kähkönen (FIN)	Fridtjof Svensson (SWE)
1924	Kalle Antila (FIN)	Aleksanteri Toivola (FIN)	Erik Malmberg (SWE)
1928	Voldemar Väli (EST)	Erik Malmberg (SWE)	Giacomo Quaglia (ITA)
1932	Giovanni Gozzi (ITA)	Wolfgang Ehrl (GER)	Lauri Koskela (FIN)
1936	Yasar Erkan (TUR)	Aarne Reini (FIN)	Einar Karlsson (SWE)
1948	Mehmet Oktav (TUR)	Olle Anderberg (SWE)	Ferenc Tóth (HUN)
1952	Yakov Punkin (URS)	Imre Polyák (HUN)	Abdel Rashed (EGY)
1956	Rauno Mäkinen (FIN)	Imre Polyák (HUN)	Roman Dzneladze (URS)
1960	Muzahir Sille (TUR)	Imre Pllyák (HUN)	Konstantin Vyrupayev (URS)
1964	Imre Polyak (HUN)	Roman Rurua (URS)	Branko Martinovic (YUG)
1968	Roman Rurua (URS)	Hideo Fujimoto (JPN)	Simeon Popescu (ROM)
1972	Gheorghi Markov (BUL)	Heinz-Helmut Wehling (GDR)	Kazimierz Lipien (POL)
1976	Kazimierz Lipien (POL)	Nelson Davidian (URS)	Laszlo Reczi (HUN)
1980	Stilianos Migiakis (GRE)	Istvan Toth (HUN)	Boris Kramorenko (URS)
1984	Kim Weon-Kee (KOR)	Kentolle Johansson (SWE)	Hugo Dietsche (SUI)
1988	Kamandar Madjidov (URS)	Jivko Vanguelov (BUL)	An Dae-Hyun (KOR)

1896–1908 Event not held.

	Gold	Silver	Bronze

Greco-Roman – Lightweight

Note: The weight limit for this event has been: 1906, 75kg; 1908, 66.6kg; 1912 to 1928, 67.5kg; 1932 to 1936, 66kg; 1948 59 1960, 67kg; 1964 to 1968, 70kg; since 1972, 68kg.

Year	Gold	Silver	Bronze
1906	Rudolf Watzl (AUT)	Karl Karlsen (DEN)	Ferenc Holuban (HUN)
1908	Enrico Porro (ITA)	Nikolav Orlov (URS)	Avid Lindén-Linko (FIN)
1912	Eemil Wäre (FIN)	Gustaf Malmström (SWE)	Edvin Matiasson (SWE)
1920	Eemil Wäre (FIN)	Taavi Tamminen (FIN)	Fritjof Andersen (NOR)
1924	Oskari Friman (FIN)	Lajos Keresztes (HUN)	Kalle Westerlund (FIN)
1928	Lajos Keresztes (HUN)	Eduard Sperling (GER)	Eduard Westerlund (FIN)
1932	Erik Malmberg (SWE)	Abraham Kurland (DEN)	Eduard Sperling (GER)
1936	Lauri Koskela (FIN)	Josef Herda (TCH)	Voldemar Väli (EST)
1948	Gustaf Freij (SWE)	Aage Eriksen (NOR)	Károly Ferencz (HUN)
1952	Shazam Safin (URS)	Gustaf Freij (SWE)	Mikulás Athanasov (TCH)
1956	Kyösti Lentonen (FIN)	Riza Dogan (TUR)	Gyula Tóth (HUN)
1960	Avtandil Koridza (URS)	Branislav Martinovic (YUG)	Gustaf Freij (SWE)
1964	Kazim Avvaz (TUR)	Valeriu Bularca (ROM)	David Gvantseladze (URS)
1968	Munji Mumemura (JPN)	Stevan Horvat (YUG)	Petros Galaktopoulos (GRE)
1972	Shamil Khisamutdinov (URS)	Stoyan Apostolov (BUL)	Gian Matteo Ranzi (ITA)
1976	Suren Nalbandyan (URS)	Stefan Rusu (ROM)	Heinz-Helmut Wehling (GDR)
1980	Stefan Rusu (ROM)	Andrzej Supron (POL)	Lars-Erik Skiold (SWE)
1984	Vlado Lisjak (YUG)	Tapio Sipila (FIN)	James Martinez (USA)
1988	Levon Djoulfalakian (URS)	Kim Sung-Moon (KOR)	Tapio Sipila (FIN)

1896–1904 Event not held.

Greco-Roman – Welterweight

Note: The weight limit for this event has been: 1932 to 1936, 72kg; 1948 to 1960, 73kg; 1964 to 1968, 78kg; since 19762, 74kg.

Year	Gold	Silver	Bronze
1932	Ivar Johansson (SWE)	Väinö Kajander (FIN)	Ercole Gallegatti (ITA)
1936	Rudolf Svedberg (SWE)	Fritz Schäfer (GER)	Eino Virtanen (FIN)
1948	Gösta Andersson (SWE)	Miklós Szilvási (HUN)	Henrik Hansen (DEN)
1952	Miklós Szilvási (HUN)	Gösta Andersson (SWE)	Khalil Taha (LIB)
1956	Mithat Bayrak (TUR)	Vladimir Maneyev (URS)	Per Berlin (SWE)
1960	Mithat Bayrak (TUR)	Günther Maritschnigg (GER)	René Schiermeyer (FRA)
1964	Anatoliy Kolesov (URS)	Cyril Todorov (BUL)	Bertil Nyström (SWE)
1968	Rudolf Vesper (GDR)	Daniel Robin (FRA)	Károly Bajkó (HUN)
1972	Vitezslav Macha (TCH)	Petros Galaktopoulos (GRE)	Jan Karlsson (SWE)
1976	Anatoliy Bykov (URS)	Vitezslav Macha (TCH)	Karlheinz Helbing (FRG)
1980	Ferenc Kocsis (HUN)	Anatoliy Bykov (URS)	Mikko Huhtala (FIN)
1984	Jonko Salomaki (FIN)	Roger Tallroth (SWE)	Stefan Rusu (ROM)
1988	Kim Young-Nam (KOR)	Daoulet Tourlykhanov (URS)	Jozef Tracz (POL)

1896–1928 Event not held.

Greco-Roman – Middleweight

Note: The weight limit for this event has been: 1906, 85kg; 1908, 73kg; 1912 to 1928, 75kg; 1932 to 1960, 79kg; 1964 to 1968, 87kg; since 1972, 82kg.

Year	Gold	Silver	Bronze
1906	Verner Weckman (FIN)	Rudolf Lindmayer (AUT)	Robert Bebrens (DEN)
1908	Frithiof Märtensson (SWE)	Mauritz Andersson (SWE)	Anders Andersen (DEN)
1912	Claes Johansson (SWE)	Martin Klein (URS)	Alfred Asikainen (FIN)
1920	Carl Westergren (SWE)	Artur Lindfors (FIN)	Matti Perttila (FIN)
1924	Eduard Westerlund (FIN)	Artur Lindfors (FIN)	Roman Steinberg (EST)
1928	Väinö Kokkinen (FIN)	László Papp (HUN)	Albert Kusnetz (EST)
1932	Väinö Kokkinen (FIN)	Jean Földeák (GER)	Axel Cadier (SWE)
1936	Ivar Johansson (SWE)	Ludwig Schweikert (GER)	József Palotás (HUN)
1948	Axel Grönberg (SWE)	Muhlis Tayfur (TUR)	Ercole Gallegatti (ITA)
1952	Axel Grönberg (SWE)	Kalervo Rauhala (FIN)	Nikolai Belov (URS)
1956	Givi Kartiziya (URS)	Dimiter Dobrev (BUL)	Rune Jansson (SWE)
1960	Dimiter Dobrev (BUL)	Lothar Metz (GER)	Ion Taranu (ROM)
1964	Branislav Simič (YUG)	Jiri Kormanik (TCH)	Lothar Metz (GER)
1968	Lothar Metz (GDR)	Valentin Olenik (URS)	Branislav Simič (YUG)
1972	Csaba Hegedus (HUN)	Anatoliy Nazarenko (URS)	Milan Nenadic (YUG)
1976	Momir Petkovic (YUG)	Vladimir Cheboksarov (URS)	Ivan Kolev (BUL)
1980	Gennadiy Korban (URS)	Jan Polgowicz (POL)	Pavel Pavlov (BUL)
1984	Ion Draica (ROM)	Dimitrios Thanapoulos (GRE)	Soren Claeson (SWE)
1988	Mikhail Mamiachvili (URS)	Tibor Komaromi (HUN)	Kim Sang-Kyu (KOR)

1896'1904 Event not held.

	Gold	Silver	Bronze

Greco-Roman – Light-Heavyweight

Note: The weight limit in this event has been: 1908, 93kg; 1912 to 1928, 82.5kg; 1932 to 1960, 87kg; 1964 to 1968, 97kg; since 1972, 90kg.

Year	Gold	Silver	Bronze
1908	Verner Weckman (FIN)	Yrjö Saarela (FIN)	Carl Jensen (DEN)
1912	–¹	Anders Ahlgren (SWE)	Béla Varga (HUN)
		Ivor Böhling (FIN)	
1920	Claes Johansson (SWE)	Edil Rosenqvist (FIN)	Johannes Eriksen (DEN)
1924	Carl Westergren (SWE)	Rudolf Svensson (SWE)	Onni Pellinen (FIN)
1928	Ibrahim Moustafa (EGY)	Adolf Rieger (GER)	Onni Pellinen (FIN)
1932	Rudolf Svensson (SWE)	Onni Pellinen (FIN)	Mario Gruppioni (ITA)
1936	Axel Cadier (SWE)	Edwins Bietags (LAT)	August Néo (EST)
1948	Karl-Erik Nilsson (SWE)	Kaelpo Gröndahl (FIN)	Ibrahim Orabi (EGY)
1952	Kaelpo Gröndahl (FIN)	Shalva Shikhladze (URS)	Karl-Erik Nilsson (SWE)
1956	Valentin Nikolayev (URS)	Petko Sirakov (BUL)	Karl-Erik Nilsson (SWE)
1960	Tevfik Kis (TUR)	Krali Bimbalov (BUL)	Givi Kartoziya (URS)
1964	Boyan Radev (BUL)	Per Svensson (SWE)	Heinz Kiehl (GER)
1968	Boyan Radev (BUL)	Nikolai Yakovenko (URS)	Nicolae Martinescu (ROM)
1972	Valeriy Rezantsev (URS)	Josip Corak (YUG)	Czeslaw Kwiecinski (POL)
1976	Valeriy Rezantsev (URS)	Stoyan Ivanov (BUL)	Czeslaw Kwiecinski (POL)
1980	Norbert Nottny (HUN)	Igor Kanygin (URS)	Petre Disu (ROM)
1984	Steven Fraser (USA)	Ilie Matei (ROM)	Frank Andersson (SWE)
1988	Atanas Komchev (BUL)	Harri Koskela (FIN)	Vladimir Popov (URS)

¹*Ahlgren and Böhling declared equal second after 9 hours of wrestling.*   1896–1906 Event not held.

Greco-Roman – Heavyweight

Note: The weight limit for this event has been: 1896, open; 1906, over 85kg; 1908, over 93kg; 1912 to 1928, over 82.5kg; 1932 to 1960, over 81kg; 1964 to 1968, over 91kg; since 1972, up to 100kg.

Year	Gold	Silver	Bronze
1896	Carl Schuhmann (GER)	Georgios Tsitas (GRE)	Stephanos Christopoulos (GRE)
1906	Sören Jensen (DEN)	Henri Baur (AUT)	Marcel Dubois (BEL)
1908	Richard Weisz (HUN)	Aleksandr Petrov (URS)	Sören Jensen (DEN)
1912	Yrjö Saarela (FIN)	Johan Olin (FIN)	Sören Jensen (DEN)
1920	Adolf Lindfors (FIN)	Poul Hansen (DEN)	Martti Nieminen (FIN)
1924	Henri Deglane (FRA)	Edil Rosenqvist (FIN)	Raymund Badó (HUN)
1928	Rudolf Svensson (SWE)	Hjalmar Nyström (FIN)	Georg Gehring (GER)
1932	Carl Westergren (SWE)	Josef Urban (TCH)	Nikolaus Hirschl (AUT)
1936	Kristjan Palusalu (EST)	John Nyman (SWE)	Kurt Hornfischer (GER)
1948	Ahmet Kireçci (TUR)	Tor Nilsson (SWE)	Guido Fantoni (ITA)
1952	Johannes Kotkas (URS)	Josef Ružička (TCH)	Tauno Kovanen (FIN)
1956	Anatoliy Parfenov (URS)	Wilfried Dietrich (GER)	Adelmo Bulgarelli (ITA)
1960	Ivan Bogdan (URS)	Wilfried Dietrich (GER)	Bohumil Kubat (TCH)
1964	István Kozma (HUN)	Anatoliy Roschin (URS)	Wilfried Dietrich (GER)
1968	István Kozma (HUN)	Anatoliy Roschin (URS)	Petr Kment (TCH)
1972	Nicolae Martinescu (ROM)	Nikolai Yakovenko (URS)	Ferenc Kiss (HUN)
1976	Nikolai Bolboshin (URS)	Kamen Goranov (BUL)	Andrzej Skrzylewski (POL)
1980	Gheorghi Raikov (BUL)	Roman Bierla (POL)	Vasile Andrei (ROM)
1984	Vasile Andrei (ROM)	Greg Gibson (USA)	Jozef Tertelje (YUG)
1988	Andrzej Wronski (POL)	Gerhard Himmel (FRG)	Dennis Koslowski (USA)

1900–1904 Event not held.

Greco-Roman – Super-Heavyweight
(Weight over 100kg)

Year	Gold	Silver	Bronze
1972	Anatoliy Roschin (URS)	Alexandre Tomov (BUL)	Victor Dolipschi (ROM)
1976	Aleksandr Kolchinsky (URS)	Alexandre Tomov (BUL)	Roman Codreanu (ROM)
1980	Aleksandr Kolchinsky (URS)	Alexandre Tomov (BUL)	Hassan Bchara (LIB)
1984	Jeffrey Blatnick (USA)	Refik Memisevic (YUG)	Victor Dolipschi (ROM)
1988	Aleksandr Kareline (URS)	Ranguel Guerovski (BUL)	Tomas Johansson (SWE)

1896–1968 Event not held.

YACHTING

The first Olympic regatta should have been on the Bay of Salamis, but it was cancelled due to bad weather. Since 1900 the classes were changed regularly until very recently when some measure of standardisation was imposed. The current classes are as follows: Finn, 470, Tornado, Star, Flying Dutchman, Soling, and Board Sailing.

In each class there are seven races over a prescribed course in which the fastest time wins. Yachts count their six best results. The only event which has been a permanent fixture is the Olympic monotype, ie one-man dinghy, albeit represented by different classes of boat prior to 1952 (now the Finn).

The most successful yachtsman is Paul Elvström (DEN) who won four successive Olympic monotype titles from 1948–1960 – the first man to achieve such a run in any sport. He competed again in the 1968 Star (fourth), 1972 Soling (13th), 1984 Tornado (fourth), and 1988 Tornado (15th) – in the last two partnering his daughter Trine. Frances Clytie Rivett-Carnac (GBR) was the first female gold medallist in the 7m class of 1908 with her husband, and she was the first woman to win in an event not restricted to women or mixed pairs in any sport. She and her husband were the first married couple to win gold medals in the Olympic Games.

The oldest gold medallist was Everard Endt (USA) in the 1952 6m class, aged 59yr 112 days, while the oldest in a single-handed event was Leon Huybrechts (BEL), aged 47yr 215 days, in 1924. The oldest female winner was Virginie Hériot (FRA) in the 1928 8m class, aged 38yr 16 days. The youngest gold medallist was Franciscus Hin

(HOL), aged 14yr 163 days, in the 1920 12-foot dinghy event with his brother Johannes. The oldest medallist was Louis Noverraz (SUI) in the 5.5m category in 1968, aged 66yr 143 days.

Olympic yachting has witnessed some outstanding family achievements. In 1920 four Norwegian brothers, Henrik, Jan, Ole and Kristian Östervold, won gold medals in the 12m (1907 rating) class. The full crew of the winning 5.5m in 1968 were brothers Ulf, Jörgen and Peter Sundelin (SWE), and the winning 6m in 1912 was crewed by Amédée, Gaston and Jacques Thubé (FRA). The only twins to win gold were Sumner and Edgar White (USA) in the 5.5m of 1952.

The first father and son to win together were Emile and Florimond Cornellie (BEL) in the 6m (1907 rating) in 1920. However, the greatest Olympic yachting family must be the Lunde clan from Norway. Eugen won a gold in the 1924 6m class; his son Peder and daughter-in-law Vibeke, along with Vibeke's brother, won a silver in the 5.5m in 1952; and grandson Peder Jr won a gold in the 1960 Flying Dutchman contest.

Rodney Pattisson and Iain Macdonald-Smith (GBR) scored the lowest number of penalty points (three) ever achieved in Olympic yachting when they won the 1968 Flying Dutchman class with five wins, a second place and a disqualification (finished first) in their seven starts. Their boat *Superdocius* is now in the National Maritime Museum, Greenwich. The only boat to win two gold medals in the same Games was *Scotia*, crewed by Lorne Currie and John Gretton for Great Britain,

in the 0.5–1 ton and Open classes in 1900. The United States yacht *Llanoria* won the 6m class in 1948 and 1952, skippered both times by Herman Whiton.

In 1948 Magnus Konow (NOR) equalled the longest span of Olympic competition when he took part in the 6m event 40 years after his debut in the 8m class of 1908. He won two golds and a silver in 1912, 1920 and 1936, the only other Games he attended. Durward Knowles competed in a record eight Games, all in the Star class, from 1948 when he competed for Great Britain. He represented the Bahamas in the next six celebrations, and then in 1988 aged 71, probably the oldest Olympic yachtsman ever.

YACHTING MEDAL TOTALS

Country	G	S	B	Total
United States	15	13	11	39
Great Britain	15	8	7	30
Sweden	9	11	9	29
Norway	14	11	1	26
France	9	8	8	25
Denmark	8	8	3	19
Germany (FRG)	4	5	6	15
Soviet Union	4	5	4	13
Netherlands	4	3	5	12
New Zealand	5	1	2	8
Australia	3	1	4	8
Brazil	2	1	5	8
Italy	2	1	5	8
Finland	1	1	6	8
Belgium	2	3	2	7
GDR	2	2	2	6
Canada	–	2	4	6
Spain	3	1	1	5
Greece	1	1	1	3
Switzerland[1]	1	1	1	3
Austria[1]	–	3	–	3
Portugal	–	2	1	3
Bahamas	1	–	1	2
Argentina	–	2	–	2
Cuba	–	1	–	1
Ireland	–	1	–	1
Netherlands Antilles	–	1	–	1
Virgin Islands	–	1	–	1
Estonia	–	–	1	1
Hungary[1]	–	–	1	1
	105	98[2]	91[2]	294

[1]Note: Austria, Hungary and Switzerland have no direct access to the sea.
[2]Some events in the early Games had no silver and/or bronze medals.

The record of eight Games was matched by Paul Elvström, also in 1988, and they both equalled the 40-year span record. Tore Holm (SWE) won medals over a record span of 28 years (1920–48) and, more unusual, Hans Fogh won medals 24 years apart (1960–84), firstly for Denmark and then for Canada.

The helmsman of the third-placed *Tempest* in 1976 was Dennis Conner (USA), who won the America's Cup for the United States in 1980 and then lost it in 1983. His Montreal partner Conn Findlay had won rowing golds in 1956 and 1964. In the 1984 Games, all 13 members of the United States team won either gold or silver med-als, a unique team achievement. The greatest number of boats in an Olympic regatta was the 159 (plus 45 sailboards) at Pusan in 1988. The 1960 regatta had 138 boats in only five categories. The greatest entry in just one yacht class was 36 in the 1968 Finn competition.

An attempt has been made to bring some method of compari-son to the Olympic results, made particularly difficult due to the wide variety of classes and types of boat used over the years. Where boats have been superseded by those of similar type, they have been listed in the same table. Purists may be unhappy but the general reader will find it easier to follow.

OLYMPIC YACHTING VENUE

1900	River Seine at Meulan (10–20 tonners at Le Havre)
1908	Cowes, Isle of Wight, and the Clyde
1912	Nyhashamn
1920	Ostend
1924	River Seine at Meulan (6m and 8m at Le Havre)
1928	Zuider-Zee
1932	San Pedro Bay
1936	Kiel
1948	Torbay, Devon
1952	Harmaja
1956	Port Phillip Bay
1960	Bay of Naples
1964	Sagami Bay
1968	Acapulco Bay
1972	Kiel
1976	Kingston, Lake Ontario
1980	Tallinn
1984	Long Beach
1988	Pusan

YACHTING MEDALS – MEN

	Gold	Silver	Bronze
Olympic Monotype			
1920[1]	Netherlands	Netherlands	–
	Franciscus Hin	Arnoud van der Biesen	
	Joahannes Hin	Petrus Beikers	
1920[2]	Great Britain	–	–
	FA Richards		
	T Hedberg		
1924[3]	Léon Huybrechts (BEL)	Henrik Robert (NOR)	Hans Dittmar (FIN)
1928[4]	Sven Thorell (SWE)	Henrik Robert (NOR)	Bertil Broman (FIN)
1932[5]	Jacques Lebrun (FRA)	Adriaan Maas (HOL)	Santiago Cansino (ESP)
1936[6]	Daniel Kagchelland (HOL)	Werner Krogmann (GER)	Peter Scott (GBR)
1948[7]	Paul Elvström (DEN)	Ralph Evans (USA)	Jacobus de Jong (HOL)
1952[8]	Paul Elvström (DEN)	Charles Currey (GBR)	Rickard Sarby (SWE)
1956	Paul Elvström (DEN)	André Nelis (BEL)	John Marvin (USA)
1960	Paul Elvström (DEN)	Aleksandr Chuchelov (URS)	André Nelis (BEL)
1964	Willi Kuhweide (GER)	Peter Barrett (USA)	Henning Wind (DEN)
1968	Valentin Mankin (URS)	Hubert Raudaschl (AUT)	Fabio Albarelli (ITA)
1972	Serge Maury (FRA)	Ilias Hatzipavlis (GRE)	Viktor Potapov (URS)
1976	Jochen Schümann (GDR)	Andrei Balashov (URS)	John Bertrand (AUS)
1980	Esko Rechardt (FIN)	Wolfgang Mayrhofer (AUT)	Andrei Balashov (URS)
1984	Russell Coutts (NZL)	John Bertrand (USA)	Terry Neilson (CAN)
1988	Jose Luis Doreste (ESP)	Peter Holmberg (ISV)	John Cutler (NZL)

[1]*12-foot dinghy (note two-handed), no bronze medal.* [2]*18-foot dinghy (note two-handed), no silver and bronze medals.* [3]*Meulan class, 12-foot dinghy.* [4]*International 12-foot class.* [5]*Snowbird class.* [6]*International Olympia class.* [7]*Firefly class.* [8]*Since 1952 Finn class.* 1896–1912 Event not held.

Windglider Class

	Gold	Silver	Bronze
1984	Steve Van Den Berg (HOL)	Randall Steele (USA)	Bruce Kendall (NZL)
1988	Bruce Kendall (NZL)	Jan Boersma (AHO)	Michael Gebhardt (USA)

1896–1980 Event not held.

International Soling

	Gold	Silver	Bronze
1972	United States	Sweden	Canada
1976	Denmark	United States	GDR
1980	Denmark	Soviet Union	Greece
1984	United States	Brazil	Canada
1988	GDR	United States	Denmark

1896–1968 Event not held.

	Gold	Silver	Bronze
International 470			
1976	FRG	Spain	Australia
1980	Brazil	GDR	Finland
1984	Spain	United States	France
1988	France	Soviet Union	United States

1896–1972 Event not held.

	Gold	Silver	Bronze
International Tornado			
1976	Great Britain	United States	FRG
1980	Brazil	Denmark	Sweden
1984	New Zealand	United States	Australia
1988	France	New Zealand	Brazil

1896–1972 Event not held.

	Gold	Silver	Bronze
International Star			
1932	United States	Great Britain	Sweden
1936	Germany	Sweden	Netherlands
1948	United States	Cuba	Netherlands
1952	Italy	United States	Portugal
1956	United States	Italy	Bahamas
1960	Soviet Union	Portugal	United States
1964	Bahamas	United States	Sweden
1968	United States	Norway	Italy
1972	Australia	Sweden	FRG
1980	Soviet Union	Austria	Italy
1984	United States	FRG	Italy
1988	Great Britain	United States	Brazil

1896–1928, 1976 Event not held.

	Gold	Silver	Bronze
Flying Dutchman			
1956[1]	New Zealand	Australia	Great Britain
1960	Norway	Denmark	Germany
1964	New Zealand	Great Britain	United States
1968	Great Britain	FRG	Brazil
1972	Great Britain	France	FRG
1976	FRG	Great Britain	Brazil
1980	Spain	Ireland	Hungary
1984	United States	Canada	Great Britain
1988	Denmark	Norway	Canada

[1]Sharpie class.   1896–1952 Event not held.

YACHTING MEDALS – WOMEN

	Gold	Silver	Bronze
International 470			
1988	United States	Sweden	Soviet Union

1896–1984 Event not held.

DISCONTINUED EVENTS

	Gold	Silver	Bronze		Gold	Silver	Bronze
Swallow				**6 Metres (1907 Rating)**			
1948	Great Britain	Portugal	United States	1920	Belgium	Norway	Norway
International Tempest				**6.5 Metres**			
1972	Soviet Union	Great Britain	United States	1920	Netherlands	France	–
1976	Sweden	Soviet Union	United States				
				7 Metres			
Dragon				1908	Great Britain	–	–
1948	Norway	Sweden	Denmark	1920	Great Britain	–	–
1952	Norway	Sweden	Germany	1912 Event not held.			
1956	Sweden	Denmark	Great Britain				
1960	Greece	Argentina	Italy	**30 Square Metres**			
1964	Denmark	Germany	United States	1920	Sweden	–	–
1968	United States	Denmark	GDR				
1972	Australia	GDR	United States				

	Gold	Silver	Bronze
40 Square Metres			
1920	Sweden	Sweden	–
5.5 Metres			
1952	United States	Norway	Sweden
1956	Sweden	Great Britain	Australia
1960	United States	Denmark	Switzerland
1964	Australia	Sweden	United States
1968	Sweden	Switzerland	Great Britain
6 Metres			
1908	Great Britain	Belgium	France
1912	France	Denmark	Sweden
1920	Norway	Belgium	–
1924	Norway	Denmark	Netherlands
1928	Norway	Denmark	Estonia
1932	Sweden	United States	Canada
1936	Great Britain	Norway	Sweden
1948	United States	Argentina	Sweden
1952	United States	Norway	Finland
8 Metres			
1908	Great Britain	Sweden	Great Britain
1912	Norway	Sweden	Finland
1920	Norway	Norway	Belgium
1924	Norway	Great Britain	France
1928	France	Netherlands	Sweden
1932	United States	Canada	–
1936	Italy	Norway	Germany
8 Metres (1907 Rating)			
1920	Norway	Norway	–
10 Metres			
1912	Sweden	Finland	Russia

	Gold	Silver	Bronze
10 Metres (1907 Rating)			
1920	Norway	–	–
12 Metres			
1908	Great Britain	Great Britain	–
1912	Norway	Sweden	Finland
12 Metres (1907 Rating)			
1920	Norway	–	–
12 Metres (1919 Rating)			
1920	Norway	–	–
½ Ton Class			
1900	France	France	France
½–1 Ton Class			
1900	Great Britain	France	France
1–2 Ton Class			
1900	Switzerland	France	France
2–3 Ton Class			
1900	Great Britain	France	France
3–10 Ton Class			
1900	France	France	Netherlands
10–20 Ton Class			
1900	France	France	Great Britain
Open Class			
1900	Great Britain	Germany	France

DISCONTINUED SPORTS

In the early celebrations of the Games there were a number of sports included which were often of a purely local interest to the host country. The last of these was polo which had its final outing in 1936. Below are listed all the medallists in these sports.

CRICKET

On the only occasion that cricket was played at the Games, in 1900, Great Britain, represented by the Devon Wanderers CC, beat a French team consisting of mainly expatriate Britons in a 12-a-side match, scoring 117 and 145 for five declared, against the French score of 73 and 26.

CROQUET

It was only contested in 1900 when all the competitors were French. Only gold medals were awarded in the singles (*simple à la boule*), won by Aumoitte, and the doubles, won by Aumoitte and Johin. In the singles (*simple à deux boules*) the medals went respectively to Waydelick, Vignerot and Sautereau.

GOLF

George Lyon (CAN) was 46yr 59days when he won the 1904 title, while the most medals were won by Chandler Egan (USA) with a team gold and individual silver in 1904.

GOLF MEDALS

	Gold	Silver	Bronze
Men's Singles			
1900	Charles Sands (USA)	Walter Rutherford (GBR)	David Robertson (GBR)
1904	George Lyon (CAN)	Chandler Egan (USA)	Burt McKinnie (USA)
Men's Team			
1904	United States	United States	–
Women's Singles			
1904	Margaret Abbott (USA)	Polly Whittier (USA)	Daria Pratt (USA)

DISCONTINUED SPORTS

JEU DE PAUME
Held only once, in 1908, it was a demonstration sport in 1928. The medals in 1908 were won by Jay Gould (USA), Eustace Miles (GBR) and Neville Lytton (GBR).

LACROSSE
Held in 1904 and 1908, it was won both times by Canada, with the silvers going to the United States and Great Britain respectively. Only two teams competed each time. The highest score was when Canada beat Great Britain 14–10 in 1908. Demonstrations were held in 1928, 1932 and 1948.

MOTORBOATING
Held only in 1908, when just one boat finished in each of the three classes. The Open class was won by France, the 60-foot and the 8-metre classes went to Great Britain.

POLO
Only Sir John Wodehouse (GBR), the 3rd Earl of Kimberley, won a silver (1908) to add to a gold (1920). The oldest gold medallist was Manuel Andrada (ARG) in 1936, aged 46yr 211 days, and the youngest was his team-mate Roberto Cavanagh, aged 21yr 269 days. The biggest winning margin was 16–2 by Argentina v Spain and Great Britain v France, both in 1924, and by Mexico v Hungary in 1936. A number of Americans played for Great Britain in 1900.

ROQUE
Held only in 1904, with all competitors from the United States. The medals were won by Charles Jacobus, Smith Streeter and Charles Brown respectively.

RACKETS
Held only in 1908, the singles went to Evan Noel (GBR) from Henry Leaf (GBR) and John Jacob Astor (GBR), with Great Britain gaining all three medals in the team event.

RUGBY UNION
Only six countries competed in the four tournaments held – Australia, France, Germany, Great Britain, Romania and the United States. The 1908 title was won by Australia while the Wallabies were on the first tour of Britain. The team they beat in the final was Cornwall, the English County champions.

Four American players won two gold medals in 1920 and 1924: Charles Doe, John O'Neil, John Patrick and Rudolph Scholz. Additionally, Daniel Carroll won his second gold with the 1920 US team, having been on the 1908 Australian squad when only 16yr 149 days old. This makes him the youngest player ever to represent his country at the sport, although 'purists' have never considered the Olympic matches to be 'full' internationals. In 1920, sprint relay gold medallist Morris Kirksey, also runner-up in the 100m, won another gold in the winning US rugby team. The highest score was when France beat Romania 61–3 in 1924.

It always comes as a shock to enthusiasts to realise that the United States is the reigning Olympic champion at rugby. Incidentally, after their Paris victory, they played in Britain and were beaten by the Harlequins and Blackheath club teams. It was probably because Baron de Coubertin was such a keen follower that the game was an Olympic sport originally; he actually refereed France's first international match, against New Zealand, in 1906.

POLO MEDALS

	Gold	Silver	Bronze
1900	Great Britain	Great Britain	France
1908	Great Britain	Great Britain	Great Britain
1920	Great Britain	Spain	United States
1924	Argentina	United States	Great Britain
1936	Argentina	Great Britain	Mexico

RUGBY UNION MEDALS

	Gold	Silver	Bronze
1900	France	Germany	Great Britain
1908	Australia	Great Britain	–
1920	United States	France	–
1924	United States	France	Romania

THE WINTER OLYMPIC SPORTS

ALPINE SKIING

Separate Alpine skiing events were first introduced into the Games in 1948, but this style had appeared in 1936 as an Alpine combination event, consisting of an aggregate of points scored in a downhill and a slalom race. Toni Sailer (AUT) in 1956 and Jean-Claude Killy (FRA) in 1968 both won a record three gold medals. Five women have won two golds each but only German-born Hanni Wenzel (LIE) also won a silver and a bronze to make her the only Alpine skier, male or female, to win four medals.

Uniquely for Alpine skiers, Trude Jochum-Beiser (AUT) and Marielle Goitschel (FRA) gained gold medals in two Games, 1948–1952 and 1964–1968 respectively.

The oldest gold medallist was Zeno Colo (ITA) who won the 1952 downhill aged 31yr 231 days, while the youngest was Michela Figini (SUI), aged 17yr 314 days when winning the 1984 downhill. The youngest male winner was Toni Sailer, aged 20yr 73 days in the 1956 slalom, and the oldest female champion was Ossi Reichert (GER) in the 1956 giant slalom, aged 30yr 33 days.

Heinrich Messner (AUT) was the oldest medallist with the downhill bronze in 1972 aged 32yr 159 days, and the youngest medallist was Gertraud 'Traudl' Hecher (AUT), aged 16yr 145 days, with the bronze in the 1960 downhill race. The youngest male medallist was Alfred Matt (AUT) with the 1968 slalom bronze aged 19yr 281 days, and the oldest female medallist was Dorothea Hochleitner (AUT), aged 30yr 201 days when she won the 1956 giant slalom bronze.

The highest average speed attained in an Olympic down-

The brash American Bill Johnson may even have surprised himself by winning his country's first ever downhill skiing title at a record average speed of over 104kph.

hill race was 104.532kph/64.953 mph by Bill Johnson (USA) in 1984. The highest in the women's event was 99.598kph/61.887mph by Annemarie Moser-Pröll (AUT) in 1980. Appended below is a table of average speeds in Olympic downhill races since 1936:

The greatest margin of victory in downhill was 4.7sec by Madeleine Berthod (SUI) in 1956, while the best in the male race was 4.1sec by Henri Oreiller (FRA) in 1948. The smallest margin was 0.05sec in the 1984 women's race, while that for the men was 0.08sec in 1968.

The greatest margin in slalom was 11.3sec by Christl Cranz (GER) in the 1936 combination event, when that in the men's equivalent was 5.9sec by Franz Pfnur (GER). Since then, Toni Sailer (AUT) won by 4.0sec in 1956 and Anne Heggtveit

(CAN) the 1960 women's race by 3.3sec. The smallest margin was 0.02sec in the 1972 women's event, with a 0.06sec margin in the 1988 men's race.

In the giant slalom the biggest margin was 6.2sec by Sailer in 1956, while that for women was 2.64 sec by Nancy Greene (CAN) in 1968. The smallest margin was 0.1sec (before electronic timing) by Yvonne Rüegg (SUI) in 1960, and 0.12sec by Kathy Kreiner (CAN) in 1976. The smallest for men was 0.20 sec by Heini Hemmi (SUI) in 1976.

Freestyle skiing for men and women was a demonstration sport in 1988 comprising ballet, aerials and mogul events. The mogul events were won by competitors from Sweden (men) and FRG (women). Mogul events will become an Olympic medal sport in 1992.

AVERAGE SPEED – MEN

Year	kph	Winner
1936	47.599	Ruud (NOR)
1948	66.034	Oreiller (FRA)
1952	57.629	Colo (ITA)
1956	72.356	Sailer (AUT)
1960	88.429	Vuarnet (FRA)
1964	81.297	Zimmermann (AUT)
1968	86.808	Killy (FRA)
1972	85.291	Russi (SUI)
1976	102.828	Klammer (AUT)
1980	102.677	Stock (AUT)
1984	104.532	Johnson (USA)
1988	94.702	Zurbriggen (SUI)

AVERAGE SPEED – WOMEN

Year	kph	Winner
1936	39.031	Schou-Nilsen (NOR)
1948	43.695	Schlunegger (SUI)
1952	50.420	Jochum-Beiser (AUT)
1956	55.484	Berthod (SUI)
1960	67.426	Biebl (GER)
1964	74.496	Haas (AUT)
1968	77.080	Pall (AUT)
1972	78.568	Nadig (SUI)
1976	85.286	Mittermaier (FRG)
1980	99.598	Moser-Pröll (AUT)
1984	96.428	Figini (SUI)
1988	93.836	Kiehl (FRG)

Left *Annemarie Moser-Pröll, Austria's only female gold medallist at Lake Placid in 1980, winning the downhill race in record speed. She had taken the bronze in the same event at Sapporo in 1972.*

ALPINE SKIING MEDAL TOTALS

Country	MEN			WOMEN			Total
	G	S	B	G	S	B	
Austria	10	12	11	7	8	8	56
Switzerland	6	9	7	9	6	5	42
France	8	3	7	3	6	5	32
Germany (FRG)	1	3	1	6	7	4	22
United States	2	3	1	5	5	4	20
Italy	5	2	2	1	1	2	13
Liechtenstein	–	1	3	2	1	2	9
Canada	–	–	1	3	1	3	8
Sweden	2	–	3	–	–	–	5
Norway	1	1	1	–	–	1	4
Yugoslavia	–	1	–	–	1	–	2
Spain	1	–	–	–	–	–	1
Japan	–	1	–	–	–	–	1
Czechoslovakia	–	–	–	–	–	1	1
Soviet Union	–	–	–	–	–	1	1
	36	36	37[1]	36	36	36	217

[1]*Two bronzes in 1948 downhill.*

ALPINE SKIING MEDALS – MEN

	Gold	Silver	Bronze
Downhill			
1948	Henri Oreiller (FRA) 2:55.0	Franz Gabl (AUT) 2:59.1	Karl Molitor (SUI) 3:00.3
			Rolf Olinger (SUI) 3:00.3
1952	Zeno Colo (ITA) 2:30.8	Othmar Schneider (AUT) 2:32.0	Christian Pravda (AUT) 2:32.4
1956	Anton Sailer (AUT) 2:52.2	Raymond Fellay (SUI) 2:55.7	Andreas Molterer (AUT) 2:56.2
1960	Jean Vuarnet (FRA) 2:06.0	Hans-Peter Lanig (GER) 2:06.5	Guy Perillat (FRA) 2:06.9
1964	Egon Zimmermann (AUT) 2:18.16	Leo Lacroix (FRA) 2:18.90	Wolfgang Bartels (GER) 2:19.48
1968	Jean-Claude Killy (FRA) 1:59.85	Guy Périllat (FRA) 1:59.93	Jean-Daniel Dätwyler (SUI) 2:00.32
1972	Bernhard Russi (SUI) 1:51.43	Roland Collombin (SUI) 1:52.07	Heinrich Messner (AUT) 1:52.40
1976	Franz Klammer (AUT) 1:45.73	Bernhard Russi (SUI) 1:46.06	Herbert Plank (ITA) 1:46.59
1980	Leonhard Stock (AUT) 1:45.50	Peter Wirnsberger (AUT) 1:46.12	Steve Podborski (CAN) 1:46.62
1984	Bill Johnson (USA) 1:45.59	Peter Müller (SUI) 1:45.86	Anton Steiner (AUT) 1:45.95
1988	Pirmin Zurbriggen (SUI) 1:59.63	Peter Müller (SUI) 2:00.14	Franck Piccard (FRA) 2:01.24

1908–1936 Event not held.

	Gold	Silver	Bronze
Slalom			
1948	Edi Reinalter (SUI) 2:10.3	James Couttet (FRA) 2:10.8	Henri Oreiller (FRA) 2:12.8
1952	Othmar Schneider (AUT) 2:00.0	Stein Eriksen (NOR) 2:01.2	Guttorm Berge (NOR) 2:01.7
1956	Anton Sailer (AUT) 3:14.7	Chiharu Igaya (JPN) 3:18.7	Stig Sollander (SWE) 3:20.2
1960	Ernst Hinterseer (AUT) 2:08.9	Matthias Leitner (AUT) 2:10.3	Charles Bozon (FRA) 2:10.4
1964	Josef Stiegler (AUT) 2:21.13	William Kidd (USA) 2:21.27	James Hengu (USA) 2:21.52
1968	Jean-Claude Killy (FRA) 1:39.73	Herbert Huber (AUT) 1:39.82	Alfred Matt (AUT) 1:40.09
1972	Francisco Fernandez Ochoa (ESP) 1:49.27	Gustavo Thoeni (ITA) 1:50.28	Rolando Thoeni (ITA) 1:50.30
1976	Piero Gros (ITA) 2:03.29	Gustavo Thoeni (ITA) 2:03.73	Willy Frommelt (LIE) 2:04.28
1980	Ingemar Stenmark (SWE) 1:44.26	Phil Mahre (USA) 1:44.76	Jacques Lüthy (SUI) 1:45.06
1984	Phil Mahre (USA) 1:39.21	Steve Mahre (USA) 1:39.62	Didier Bouvet (FRA) 1:40.20
1988	Alberto Tomba (ITA) 1:39.47	Frank Wörndl (FRG) 1:39.53	Paul Frommelt (LIE) 1:39.84

1908–1936 Event not held.

	Gold	Silver	Bronze
Giant Slalom			
1952	Stein Eriksen (NOR) 2:25.0	Christian Pravda (AUT) 2:26.9	Toni Spiss (AUT) 2:28.8
1956	Anton Sailer (AUT) 3:00.1	Andreas Molterer (AUT) 3:06.3	Walter Schuster (AUT) 3:07.2
1960	Roger Staub (SUI) 1:48.3	Josef Stiegler (AUT) 1:48.7	Ernst Hinterseer (AUT) 1:49.1
1964	François Bonlieu (FRA) 1:46.71	Karl Schranz (AUT) 1:47.09	Josef Stiegler (AUT) 1:48.05
1968	Jean-Claude Killy (FRA) 3:29.28	Willy Favre (SUI) 3:31.50	Heinrich Messner (AUT) 3:31.83
1972	Gustavo Thoeni (ITA) 3:09.62	Edmund Bruggmann (SUI) 3:10.75	Werner Mattle (SUI) 3:10.99
1976	Heini Hemmi (SUI) 3:26.97	Ernst Good (SUI) 3:27.17	Ingemar Stenmark (SWE) 3:27.41
1980	Ingemar Stenmark (SWE) 2:40.74	Andreas Wenzel (LIE) 2:41.49	Hans Enn (AUT) 2:42.51
1984	Max Julen (SUI) 2:41.18	Juriy Franko (YUG) 2:41.41	Andreas Wenzel (LIE)
1988	Alberto Tomba (ITA) 2:06.37	Hubert Strolz (AUT) 2:07.41	Pirmin Zurbriggen (SUI) 2:08.39

1908–1948 Event not held.

	Gold	Silver	Bronze
Super Giant Slalom			
1988	Franck Piccard (FRA) 1:39.66	Helmut Mayer (AUT) 1:40.96	Lars-Börje Eriksson (SWE) 1:41.08
Alpine Combination (Downhill and Slalom)			
1936	Franz Pfnür (GER) 99.25pts	Gustav Lantschner (GER) 96.26pts	Emile Allais (FRA) 94.69pts
1948	Henri Oreiller (FRA) 3.27pts	Karl Molitor (SUI) 6.44pts	James Couttet (FRA) 6.95pts
1988	Hubert Strolz (AUT) 36.55pts	Bernhard Gstrein (AUT) 43.45pts	Paul Accola (SUI) 48.24pts

1952–1984 Event not held.

ALPINE SKIING – WOMEN

	Gold	Silver	Bronze
Downhill			
1948	Hedy Schlunegger (SUI) 2:28.3	Trude Beiser (AUT) 2:29.1	Resi Hammerer (AUT) 2:30.2
1952	Trude Jochum-Beiser (AUT) 1:47.1	Annemarie Buchner (GER) 1:48.0	Giuliana Minuzzo (ITA) 1:49.0
1956	Madeleine Berthod (SUI) 1:40.7	Freida Dänzer (SUI) 1:45.4	Lucile Wheeler (CAN) 1:45.9
1960	Heidi Biebl (GER) 1:37.6	Penelope Pitou (USA) 1:38.6	Traudl Hecher (AUT) 1:38.9
1964	Christl Haas (AUT) 1:55.39	Edith Zimmerman (AUT) 1:56.42	Traudl Hecher (AUT) 1:56.66
1968	Olga Pall (AUT) 1:40.87	Isabelle Mir (FRA) 1:41.33	Christl Haas (AUT) 1:41.41
1972	Marie-Thérèse Nadig (SUI) 1:36.68	Annemarie Pröll (AUT) 1:37.00	Susan Corrock (USA) 1:37.68
1976	Rosi Mittermaier (FRG) 1:46.16	Brigitte Totschnig (AUT) 1:46.68	Cindy Nelson (USA) 1:47.50
1980	Annemarie Moser-Pröll (AUT) 1:37.52	Hanni Wenzel (LIE) 1:38.22	Marie-Thérèse Nadig (SUI) 1:38.36
1984	Michela Figini (SUI) 1:13.36	Maria Walliser (SUI) 1:13.41	Olga Chartova (TCH) 1:13.53
1988	Marina Kiehl (FRG) 1:25.86	Brigitte Oertli (SUI) 1:26.61	Karen Percy (CAN) 1:26.62

1908–1936 Event not held.

	Gold	Silver	Bronze
Slalom			
1948	Gretchen Fraser (USA) 1:57.2	Antoinette Meyer (SUI) 1:57.7	Erika Mahringer (AUT) 1:58.0
1952	Andrea Mead-Lawrence (USA) 2:10.6	Ossi Reichert (GER) 2:11.4	Annemarie Buchner (GER) 2:13.3
1956	Renée Colliard (SUI) 1:52.3	Regina Schöpf (AUT) 1:55.4	Jevginija Sidorova (URS) 1:56.7
1960	Anne Heggtveit (CAN) 1:49.6	Betsy Snite (USA) 1:52.9	Barbi Henneberger (GER) 1:56.6
1964	Christine Goitschel (FRA) 1:29.86	Marielle Goitschel (FRA) 1:30.77	Jean Saubert (USA) 1:31.36
1968	Marielle Goitschel (FRA) 1:25.86	Nancy Greene (CAN) 1:26.15	Annie Famose (FRA) 1:27.89
1972	Barbara Cochran (USA) 1:31.24	Danielle Debernard (FRA) 1:31.26	Florence Steurer (FRA) 1:32.69
1976	Rosi Mittermaier (FRG) 1:30.54	Claudia Giordani (ITA) 1:30.87	Hanni Wenzel (LIE) 1:32.20
1980	Henni Wenzel (LIE) 1:25.09	Christa Kinshofer (FRG) 1:26.50	Erika Hess (SUI) 1:27.89
1984	Paolette Magoni (ITA) 1:36.47	Perrine Pelen (FRA) 1:37.38	Ursula Konsett (LIE) 1:37.50
1988	Vreni Schneider (SUI) 1:36.69	Mateja Svet (YUG) 1:38.37	Christa Kinshofer-Gütlein (FRG) 1:38.40

1908–1936 Event not held.

	Gold	Silver	Bronze
Giant Slalom			
1952	Andrea Mead-Lawrence (USA) 2:06.8	Dagmar Rom (AUT) 2:09.0	Annemarie Buchner (GER) 2:10.0
1956	Ossi Reichert (GER) 1:56.5	Josefine Frandl (AUT) 1:57.8	Dorothea Hochleitner (AUT) 1:58.2
1960	Yvonne Rüegg (SUI) 1:39.9	Penelope Pitou (USA) 1:40.0	Giuliana Chenal-Minuzzo (ITA) 1:40.2
1964	Marielle Goitschel (FRA) 1:52.24	Christine Goitschel (FRA) 1:53.11	Jean Saubert (USA) 1:53.11
1968	Nancy Greene (CAN) 1:51.97	Annie Famose (FRA) 1:54.61	Fernande Bochatay (SUI) 1:54.74
1972	Marie-Thérèse Nadig (SUI) 1:29.90	Annemarie Pröll (AUT) 1:30.75	Wiltrud Drexel (AUT) 1:32.35
1976	Kathy Kreiner (CAN) 1:29.13	Rosi Mittermaier (FRG) 1:29.25	Danielle Debernard (FRA) 1:29.95
1980	Hanni Wenzel (LIE) 2:41.66	Irene Epple (FRG) 2:42.12	Perrine Pelen (FRA) 2:42.41
1984	Debbie Armstrong (USA) 2:20.98	Christin Cooper (USA) 2:21.38	Perrine Pelen (FRA) 2:21.40
1988	Vreni Schneider (SUI) 2:06.49	Christa Kinshofer-Gütlein (FRG) 2:07.42	Maria Walliser (SUI) 2:07.72

1908–1948 Event not held.

	Gold	Silver	Bronze
Super Giant Slalom			
1988	Sigrid Wolf (AUT) 1:19.03	Michela Figini (SUI) 1:20.03	Karen Percy (CAN) 1:20.29

1908–1984 Event not held.

	Gold	Silver	Bronze
Alpine Combination (Downhill and Slalom)			
1936	Christel Cranz (GER) 97.06pts	Käthe Grasegger (GER) 95.26pts	Laila Schou Nilsen (NOR) 93.48pts
1948	Trude Beiser (AUT) 6.58pts	Gretchen Fraser (USA) 6.95pts	Erika Mahringer (AUT) 7.04pts
1988	Anita Wachter (AUT) 29.25pts	Brigitte Oertli (SUI) 29.48pts	Maria Walliser (SUI) 51.28pts

BOBSLEDDING

A bob competition for 4-man sleds was first held in 1924. The rules allowed for 4- or 5-man teams in 1924 and 1928. The 2-man event was introduced in 1932. Both competitions have been held ever since, except for 1960 when the Squaw Valley Organising Committee refused to build a run.

In 1952 a situation arose which led to changes in the rules governing the overall weight of teams and bobs. The Germans combined their heaviest men from their two vehicles into one 4-man sled averaging over 118kg per man, and won easily. Resulting complaints led to rules stipulating that the maximum weight of the bobs, with crews, must not exceed 375kg (2-man) and 630kg (4-man), but that extra weights may be added within those limits. Speeds of up to 150kph are now attained.

The most gold medals won by an individual is three by Bernhard Germeshausen (GDR) and Meinhard Nehmer (GDR), both 1976–1980, and Bogdan Musiol (GDR) from 1980–1988. The most medals won is six by Eugenio Monti (ITA), 2 gold, 2 silver and 2 bronze from 1956–1968, and Bogdan Musiol (GDR), 3 gold, 2 silver and 1 bronze from 1980–1988.

The oldest gold medallist, and indeed medallist, was Jay O'Brien (USA) in the 4-man in 1932, aged 48yr 359 days, which also makes him the oldest gold medallist in Winter Games history. The youngest champion was William Fiske (USA) who piloted the winning 5-man bob in 1928, aged 16yr 260 days, which makes him the youngest male Winter Games gold medallist ever. The youngest medallist was Thomas Doe Jr (USA), aged 15yr 127 days in the 1928 silver medal bob.

That 1932 American 4-man team had eventful lives outside bobsledding. Fiske had the distinction of being the first American to join the RAF in the Second World War – he was killed in the Battle of Britain. O'Brien married silent film star Mae Murray. Clifford 'Tippy' Gray was a songwriter who composed *If You Were the Only Girl in the World*, while Eddie Eagan was

BOBSLEDDING MEDAL TOTALS

Country	G	S	B	Total
Switzerland	7	6	7	20
Untied States	5	4	5	14
GDR	5	5	3	13
Germany (FRG)	3	3	4	10
Italy	3	4	2	9
Great Britain	1	1	1	3
Soviet Union	1	–	2	3
Austria	–	2	–	2
Belgium	–	1	1	2
Canada	1	–	–	1
Romania	–	–	1	1
	26	26	26	78

BOBSLEDDING MEDALS

	Gold	Silver	Bronze		Gold	Silver	Bronze
2-Man Bob				**4-Man Bob**			
1932	United States I 8:14.14	Switzerland II 8:16.28	United States II 8:29.15	1924	Switzerland I 5:45.54	Great Britain II 5:48.63	Belgium I 6:02.29
1936	United States I 5:29.29	Switzerland II 5:30.64	United States II 5:33.96	1928[1]	United States II 3:20.5	United States I 3:21.0	Germany II 3:21.9
1948	Switzerland II 5:29.2	Switzerland I 5:30.4	United States II 5:35.3	1932	United States I 7:53.68	United States II 7:55.70	Germany I 8:00.04
1952	Geremany I 5:24.54	United States I 5:26.89	Switzerland I 5:27.71	1936	Switzerland II 5:19.85	Switzerland I 5:22.73	Great Britain I 5:23.41
1956	Italy I 5:39.14	Italy II 5:31.45	Switzerland I 5:37.46	1952	Germany 5:07.84	United States I 5:10.48	Switzerland I 5:11.70
1964	Great Britain I 4:21.90	Italy II 4:22.02	Italy I 4:22.63	1956	Switzerland I 5:10.44	Italy II 5:12.10	United States I 5:12.39
1968	Italy I 4:41.54	FRG I 4:41.54	Romania 4:44.46	1964	Canada 4:14.46	Austria 4:15.48	Italy II 4:15.60
1972	FRG II 4:47.07	FRG I 4:58.84	Switzerland I 4:59.33	1968[2]	Italy I 2:17.39	Austria I 2:17.48	Switzerland I 2:18.04
1976	GDR II 3:44.42	FRG I 3:44.99	Switzerland I 3:45.70	1972	Switzerland 4:43.07	Italy I 4:43.83	FRG I 4:43.92
1980	Switzerland II 4:09.36	GDR II 4:10.93	GDR I 4:11.08	1976	GDR I 3:40.43	Switzerland II 3:40.89	FRG I 3:41.37
1984	GDR II 3:28.56	GDR I 3:26.04	Soviet Union II 3:26.16	1980	GDR I 3:59.92	Switzerland I 4:00.87	GDR II 4:00.97
1988	Soviet Union I 3:53.48	GDR I 3:54.19	GDR II 3:54.64	1984	GDR I 3:20.22	GDR II 3:20.78	Switzerland I 3:21.39
				1988	Switzerland I 3:47.51	GDR I 3:47.58	Soviet Union II 3:48.26

1908–1928, 1960 Event not held.

[1]*Five-man team in 1928; aggregate of two runs.* [2]*Aggregate of two runs.* 1908–1920, 1960 Event not held.

the only man to win medals in Summer and Winter Games. The tallest gold medallist was Edy Hubacher (SUI) in the 1972 4-man bob at 2.01m/6ft 7in. He also competed in the 1968 Summer Games shot event. Carl-Erik Eriksson (SWE) was the first Olympic competitor to compete in six Winter Games, 1964–84.

The first brothers to win gold medals were Alfred and Heinrich Schläppi (SUI) in the 4-man bob of 1924, while the inaugural 2-man event of 1932 was won by Hubert and Curtis Stevens (USA). The closest finish in Olympic bobsledding occurred in the 2-man of 1968 when Italy I and FRG I had identical aggregate times after the four runs. The title went to Italy, driven by the 40-year-old Monti, as they had the fastest single run. The smallest margin in 4-man was 0.07sec after four runs in 1988.

FIGURE SKATING

The first Olympic title at a Winter Games event was won by Ulrich Salchow (SWE) in 1908 at the Prince's Rink, London. Salchow gave his name to one of the most popular jumps. In those 1908 Games there was also a special figures event which was won by a Russian (Czarist variety), Nikolai Panin, who had been too ill to compete in the main event. The first women's title went to Madge Syers (GBR), who six years previously had entered the World Championships, ostensibly for men only, and had placed second to Salchow.

The most gold medals won by a figure skater is three by Gillis Grafström (SWE) 1920–1928, Sonja Henie (NOR) 1928–1936, and Irina Rodnina (URS) in the pairs, 1972–1980. Of these only Grafström also won a silver, in 1932, and thus is the only skater to win medals in four Games. No skater has doubled completely successfully in singles and pairs at the Games. The best have been Ernst Baier (GER) with the pairs gold and a singles silver in 1936, and Madge Syers (GBR) with a singles gold and a pairs bronze in 1908.

The oldest gold medallist was Walter Jakobsson (FIN) who won the 1920 pairs with his German-born wife Ludowika, aged 38yr 80 days. Ludowika became the oldest ever female winner, aged 35yr 276 days. The youngest was Maxi Herber (GER), aged 15yr 128 days in the 1936 pairs with Baier, whom she later married.

The youngest male champion was Richard Button (USA), aged 18yr 202 days, winning the 1948 singles. Sonja Henie (NOR) was remarkably 50 days short of her 16th birthday when she won her first title in 1928, after some last minute coaching by Britain's Alex Adams. She had been eighth and last in 1924 when still under 12 years of age. However, the youngest ever Winter Games competitor was her rival of 1936, Cecilia Colledge (GBR), who had been 11yr 73 days old at the 1932 Games. The youngest male competitor was Jan Hoffman (GDR), aged 12yr 110 days in 1968. Twelve years later he gained the silver medal.

The youngest medallist was Scott Allen (USA), 2 days short of his 15th birthday when taking the 1964 singles bronze, while the youngest female medallist was Manuela Gross (GDR), just ten days past her 15th birthday in the 1972 bronze-winning pair. The oldest medallist was Martin Stixrud (NOR), with the 1920 singles bronze aged 44yr 78 days, while the oldest female medallist was Ludowika Jacobsson (FIN), with a pairs silver in 1924 aged 39yr 189 days.

Sonja Henie won three Olympic, six European and ten World titles before turning professional and making an estimated $47 million in ice shows and films. The film world has attracted a number of other Olympic skaters. Down the field (16th) in 1936 was Gladys Jepson-Turner (GBR), who had a Hollywood career as Belita, and Vera Hruba (TCH), one place behind the British girl, who married the head of Republic Pictures and starred in many films as Vera Hruba Ralston.

Sonja Henie is usually credited with introducing jumps into the women's event, but in 1920 Theresa Weld (USA), the bronze medal winner, included a salchow in her programme, which brought a reprimand from the judges and a threat that she would be penalised if she continued with such 'unfeminine behaviour'.

A change of marking in the sport was brought about by Trixie Schuba (AUT) winning the 1972 title primarily on the

FIGURE SKATING MEDAL TOTALS

Country	G	S	B	Total
United States	10	10	14	34
Soviet Union	11	9	5	25
Austria	7	9	4	20
Great Britain	5	3	6	14
Canada	2	6	6	14
Sweden	5	3	2	10
GDR	3	3	4	10
Germany (FRG)	4	3	2	9
France	2	1	4	7
Norway	3	2	1	6
Hungary	–	2	4	6
Czechoslovakia	1	1	2	4
Netherlands	1	2	–	3
Finland	1	1	–	2
Belgium	1	–	1	2
Switzerland	–	1	1	2
	56	56	56	168

basis of her excellent set figures (she was only placed seventh in free skating). At that time the marks were divided 50–50 between sections, but they were then changed to give greater emphasis to free skating. Set figures were skated for the last time in Calgary in 1988, and will no longer be included in Olympic competition. On the subject of marks, Jayne Torvill and Christopher Dean (GBR) were awarded a maximum nine sixes for their artistic impression in the 1984 ice dancing event, as well as another three sixes for technical merit – unsurpassed marking at the Games.

In 1972, although Irina Rodnina and Aleksey Ulanov (URS) won the pairs, it was the latter's dalliance with Ludmila Smirnova, silver medallist with Andrey Suraikin, which caught the media interest. The result was a break-up of the top Soviet pair. Rodnina then teamed with Alexandr Zaitsev, while Ulanov and Smirnova got married. In the World Championships the Rodnina/Zaitsev partnership beat the other pair and, getting married themselves in 1975, they went on to win two Olympic titles, the second less than a year after the birth of a son.

In 1976 John Curry won what was only Great Britain's second skating gold medal since 1908, and its first male individual title ever. He was coached by Carlo and Christa Fassi, who also trained the women's champion that year, Dorothy Hamill (USA), and then Curry's successor Robin Cousins.

FIGURE SKATING MEDALS

	Gold	Silver	Bronze
Men			
1908[1]	Nikolai Panin (URS) 219pts	Arthur Cumming (GBR) 164pts	George Hall-Say (GBR) 104pts
1908	Ulrich Salchow (SWE) 1886.5pts	Richard Johansson (SWE) 1826.0pts	Per Thorén (SWE) 1787.0pts
1920	Gillis Gräfström (SWE) 2838.5pts	Andreas Krogh (NOR) 2634pts	Martin Stixrud (NOR) 2561.5pts
1924	Gillis Gräfström (SWE) 2757.2pts	Willy Böckl (AUT) 2518.75pts	Georges Gautschi (SUI) 2233.5pts
1928	Gillis Gräfström (SWE) 2698.5pts	Willy Böckl (AUT) 2682.50pts	Robert v. Zeebroeck (BEL) 2578.75pts
1932	Karl Schäfer (AUT) 2602.0pts	Gillis Gräfström (SWE) 2514.5pts	Montgomery Wilson (CAN) 2448.3pts
1936	Karl Schäfer (AUT) 2959.0pts	Ernst Baier (GER) 2805.3pts	Felix Kaspar (AUT) 2801.0pts
1948	Richard Button (USA) 1720.6pts	Hans Gerschwiler (SUI) 1630.1pts	Edi Rada (AUT) 1603.2pts
1952	Richard Button (USA) 1730.3pts	Helmut Seibt (AUT) 1621.3pts	James Grogan (USA) 1627.4pts
1956	Hayes Alan Jenkins (USA) 1497.95pts	Ronald Robertson (USA) 1492.15pts	David Jenkins (USA) 1465.41pts
1960	David Jenkins (USA) 1440.2pts	Karol Divin (TCH) 1414.3pts	Donald Jackson (CAN) 1401.0pts
1964	Manfred Schnelldorfer (GER) 1916.9pts	Alain Calmat (FRA) 1876.5pts	Scott Allen (USA) 1873.6pts
1968	Wolfgang Schwarz (AUT) 1894.1pts	Tim Woods (USA) 1891.6pts	Patrick Péra (FRA) 1864.5pts
1972	Ondrej Nepela (TCH) 2739.1pts	Sergey Tchetveroukhin (URS) 2762.4pts	Patrick Péra (FRA) 2653.1pts
1976	John Curry (GBR) 192.74pts	Vladimir Kovalev (URS) 187.64pts	Toller Cranston (CAN) 187.38pts
1980	Robin Cousins (GBR) 189.48pts[2]	Jan Hoffmann (GDR) 189.72pts[2]	Charles Tickner (USA) 187.06pts
1984	Scott Hamilton (USA) 3.4pl	Brian Orser (CAN) 5.6pl	Jozef Sabovtchik (TCH) 7.4pl
1988	Brian Boitano (USA) 3.0pl	Brian Orser (CAN) 4.2pl	Viktor Petrenko (URS) 7.8pl

[1]*Special Figures competition.* [2]*The majority of judges were in favour of Cousins. Since then, all medals have been decided by judges' placements.* 1912 Event not held.

	Gold	Silver	Bronze
Women			
1908	Madge Syers (GBR) 1262.5pts	Elsa Rendschmidt (GER) 1055.0pts	Dorothy Greenhough-Smith (GBR) 960.5pts
1920	Magda Mauroy-Julin (SWE) 913.5pts	Svea Norén (Swe) 887.75pts	Theresa Weld (USA) 898.0pts
1924	Herma Planck-Szabo (AUT) 2094.25pts	Beatrix Loughran (USA) 1959.0pts	Ethel Muckelt (GBR) 1750.50pts
1928	Sonja Henie (NOR) 2452.25pts	Fritzi Burger (AUT) 2248.50pts	Beatrix Loughran (USA) 2254.50pts
1932	Sonja Henie (NOR) 2302.5pts	Fritzi Burger (AUT) 2167.1pts	Maribel Vinson (USA) 2158.5pts
1936	Sonja Henie (NOR) 2971.4pts	Cecilia Colledge (GBR) 2926.8pts	Vivi-Anne Hultén (SWE) 2763.2pts
1948	Barbara Scott (CAN) 1467.7pts	Eva Pawlik (AUT) 1418.3pts	Jeanette Altwegg (GBR) 1405.5pts
1952	Jeanette Altwegg (GBR) 1455.8pts	Tenley Albright (USA) 1432.2pts	Jacqueline du Bief (FRA) 1422.0pts
1956	Tenley Albright (USA) 1866.39pts	Carol Heiss (USA) 1848.24pts	Ingrid Wendl (AUT) 1753.91pts
1960	Carol Heiss (USA) 1490.1pts	Sjoukje Dijkstra (HOL) 1424.8pts	Barbara Roles (USA) 1414.8
1964	Sjoukje Dijkstra (HOL) 2018.5pts	Regine Heitzer (AUT) 1945.5pts	Petra Burka (CAN) 1940.0pts
1968	Peggy Fleming (USA) 1970.5pts	Gabrielle Seyfert (GDR) 1882.3pts	Hana Maskova (TCH) 1828.8pts
1972	Beatrix Schuba (AUT) 2751.5pts	Karen Magnussen (CAN) 2763.2pts	Janet Lynn (USA) 2663.1pts
1976	Dorothy Hamill (USA) 193.80pts	Dianne De Leeuw (HOL) 190.24pts	Christine Errath (GDR) 188.16pts
1980	Annet Pötzsch (GDR) 189.00pts	Linda Fratianne (USA) 188.30pts	Dagmar Lurz (FRG) 183.04pts
1984	Katarina Witt (GDR) 3.2pl	Rosalyn Sumners (USA) 4.6pl	Kira Ivanova (URS) 9.2pl
1988	Katarina Witt (GDR) 4.2pl	Elizabeth Manley (CAN) 4.6pl	Debra Thomas (USA) 6.0pl

1912 Event not held.

	Gold	Silver	Bronze
Pairs			
1908	Germany 56.0pts	Great Britain 51.5pts	Great Britain 48.0pts
1920	Finland 80.75pts	Norway 72.75pts	Great Britain 66.25pts
1924	Austria 74.50pts	Finland 71.75pts	France 69.25pts
1928	France 100.50pts	Austria 99.25pts	Austria 93.25pts
1932	France 76.7pts	United States 77.5pts	Hungary 76.4pts
1936	Germany 103.3pts	Austria 102.7pts	Hungary 97.6pts
1948	Belgium 123.5pts	Hungary 122.2pts	Canada 121.0pts
1952	Germany 102.6pts	United States 100.6pts	Hungary 97.4pts
1956	Austria 101.8pts	Canada 101.9pts	Hungary 99.3pts
1960	Canada 80.4pts	Germany 76.8pts	United States 76.2pts
1964[1]	Soviet Union 104.4pts	Canada 98.5pts	United States 98.2pts
1968	Soviet Union 315.2pts	Soviet Union 312.3pts	FRG 304.4pts
1972	Soviet Union 420.4pts	Soviet Union 419.4pts	GDR 411.8pts
1976	Soviet Union 140.54pts	GDR 136.35pts	GDR 134.57pts
1980	Soviet Union 147.26pts	Soviet Union 143.80pts	GDR 140.52pts
1984	Soviet Union 1.4pl	United States 2.8pl	Soviet Union 3.8pl
1988	Soviet Union 1.4pl	Soviet Union 2.8pl	United States 4.2pl

[1]*Marika Kilius and Hansjürgen Bäumler (GER) finished second but were subsequently disqualified.* 1912 Event not held.

	Gold	Silver	Bronze
Ice Dance			
1976	Soviet Union 209.92pts	Soviet Union 204.88pts	United States 202.64pts
1980	Soviet Union 205.48pts	Hungary 204.52pts	Soviet Union 201.86pts
1984	Great Britain 2.0pl	Soviet Union 4.0pl	Soviet Union 7.0pl
1988	Soviet Union 2.0pl	Soviet Union 4.0pl	Canada 6.0pl

1908–1972 Event not held.

ICE HOCKEY

The game was introduced in 1920 as part of the Summer Games. The tournament was won by Canada, the first of a run of six victories interrupted only by Great Britain's win in 1936. However, the record number of wins is seven by the Soviet Union between 1956 and 1988. In the early days the Canadians were always represented by a club rather than a national side, so that the first Olympic champions were actually the Winnipeg Falcons.

Since 1948 the tournament has been decided on a championship format and not, as previously, on a knock-out basis – thus there is no Olympic final as such. The game has been the centre of much bitter argument about amateur/professional status, and in 1972 Canada withdrew in protest against alleged 'professionalism' of the Eastern European teams in particular. Happily, they returned in 1980.

In 1948 there was a strange situation when two teams turned up to represent the United States, one from the Amateur Hockey Association (AHA) and the other picked by the US Olympic Committee. The AHA, while not affiliated to the USOC, was a member of the International Hockey Federation (IHF), the governing body of most of the other teams present in St Moritz. The IHF threatened to withdraw all the other teams if the AHA team did not play, while the USOC threatened to withdraw the whole Olympic team if the AHA team did play. Initially the IOC barred both teams, but then agreed to allow the AHA team to compete. They eventually finished fourth, but a year later they were disqualified for non-affiliation to the Olympic movement. Strangely, the USOC hockey team members marched in the opening ceremony.

Five Soviet players have won a record three gold medals, but only goalminder Vladislaw Tretyak (1972-1984) also won a silver. Richard 'Bibi' Torriani (SUI) won a bronze in 1928 and another in 1948, for a record 20-year span.

The oldest gold medallist was Carl Erhardt (GBR) in 1936 on the day after his 39th birthday. The youngest was Alexandr Moguilny (URS) in 1988, aged 19yr 9 days, while the youngest medallist was Richard Torriani (SUI) at 16yr 141 days in 1928. The oldest medallist was also Erhardt in 1936.

The first brothers to win gold were Herbert, Hugh and Roger Plaxton along with Frank and Joseph Sullivan in the 1928

The Soviet ice hockey team beat the Canadians 5–0 in 1988 and also surpassed them by winning a record seventh title; they have never missed out on a medal since their debut in 1956.

ICE HOCKEY MEDAL TOTALS

Country	G	S	B	Total
Canada	6	2	2	10
Soviet Union	7	1	1	9
United States	2	6	1	9
Czechoslovakia	–	4	3	7
Sweden	–	2	4	6
Great Britain	1	–	1	2
Germany (FRG)	–	–	2	2
Switzerland	–	–	2	2
Finland	–	1	–	1
	16	16	16	48

ICE HOCKEY MEDALS

	Gold	Silver	Bronze
1920	Canada	United States	Czechoslovakia
1924	Canada	United States	Great Britain
1928	Canada	Sweden	Switzerland
1932	Canada	United States	Germany
1936	Great Britain	Canada	United States
1948	Canada	Czechoslovakia	Switzerland
1952	Canada	United States	Sweden
1956	Soviet Union	United States	Canada
1960	United States	Canada	Soviet Union
1964	Soviet Union	Sweden	Czechoslovakia
1968	Soviet Union	Czechloslovakia	Canada
1972	Soviet Union	United States	Czechoslovakia
1976	Soviet Union	Czechoslovakia	FRG[1]
1980	United States	Soviet Union	Sweden
1984	Soviet Union	Czechoslovakia	Sweden
1988	Soviet Union	Finland	Sweden

[1] Three-way tie for bronze with the United States and Finland decided on goal average.

Canadian team. The only twins to do so were Boris and Yevgeniy Maiorov (URS) in 1964. The only known father and son gold medallists were Bill and David Christian (USA) who won in 1960 and 1980 respectively. Another distinction for Bill is that he and his brother Roger were one of two sets of brothers – the other was Bill and Bob Cleary – who helped the USA to win its first ice hockey gold in 1960.

The highest score and aggregate in Olympic ice hockey was the 33–0 victory by Canada over Switzerland in 1924. In that tournament the Canadians totalled 110 goals in five matches, with only three against. When the Czechs won the 1948 silver medal, a member of the team was 1954 Wimbledon tennis champion Jaroslav Drobny.

NORDIC SKIING

CROSS-COUNTRY SKIING
This was the first form of skiing in the Olympics. The most successful competitor was Sixten Jernberg (SWE) with four gold, three silver and two bronze medals, for a record total of nine medals from 1956 to 1964. The best by a woman was three gold, five silver and one bronze – equalling that record total of nine – by Raisa Smetanina (URS) from 1976 to 1988. However, her compatriot Galina Kulakova won four golds from 1968 to 1980. Only Jernberg has won individual titles in three successive Games. Marja-Liisa Hämäläinen (FIN) won a record three individual gold medals at one Games in 1984.

The oldest gold medallist was Veikko Hakulinen (FIN), aged 35yr 52 days in the 1960 relay, and the youngest was Gunde Swan (SWE) who won the 15km race in 1984 aged 22yr 32 days. The oldest male medallist was Olaf Ökern (NOR) in the 1948 relay, aged 36yr 235 days, and the youngest was Ivar Formo (NOR) in the 1972 relay, aged 20yr 234 days.

The oldest female gold medallist was Galina Kulakova (URS) in the 1976 relay, aged 33yr 289 days, and the youngest was Carola Anding (GDR), aged 19yr 54 days in the 1980 relay. Kulakova was also the oldest medallist, male or female, aged 37yr 298 days in the 1980 relay, and the youngest female medallist was Marjo Matikainen (FIN) in the 1984 relay, aged 19yr 12 days.

The 1928 50km race was won by Per Erik Hedlund (SWE) with a remarkable margin of 13min 27sec over the second man. Currently the men's 50km and 4 × 10km relay, and women's 20km and 4 × 5km relay, are designated as freestyle events, ie the 'skating' technique may be used. Otherwise only the classical 'stride and glide' is allowed. The shock silver medal won by Bill Koch (USA) in the 1976 50km was credited to his development of the former style.

NORDIC COMBINATION
The event was the 'blue riband' of Nordic skiing in the early Games. The all-round title, comprising a cross-country race and a jump, was won three successive times by Ulrich Wehling (GDR) from 1972–1980. The oldest medallist was Simon Slattvik (NOR), who won the title in 1952 aged 34yr 209 days, and the youngest was Wehling in 1972, aged 19yr 212 days. Up until 1952 the cross-country segment was held first, but at Oslo the order of events was reversed, and has remained so.

Sixten Jernberg won a record 4 gold, 3 silver and 2 bronze medals in Nordic skiing at three Olympic Games.

BIATHLON

This combination of skiing and shooting was introduced in 1960. Aleksandr Tikhonov (URS) set a Winter Games record by winning a gold medal in the relay on four successive occasions (1968–1980). The oldest gold medallist was Magnar Solberg (NOR), uniquely defending his title in 1972, aged 35yr 5 days. The youngest winner was Yuriy Kachkarov (URS) in the 1984 relay, aged 20yr 75 days,

while Frank Peter Rötsch (GDR) won a silver in the 20km event in 1984 aged only 19yr 298 days. In 1992 there will be women's events in this discipline.

SKI JUMPING

The most successful jumper since the sport's Olympic debut in 1924 has been Matti Nykänen (FIN) with 4 golds and one silver medal in 1984 and 1988, including three golds at one Games. However, his successes include

the team competition, introduced in 1988. Prior to him the most successful had been Birger Ruud (NOR) with two golds and a silver medal from 1932 to 1948, the only other man to win at two Games. He also came fourth in the Alpine Combination event of 1936, winning the downhill segment. His brother Sigmund won a silver in 1928, while a third brother, Asbjörn, was seventh in 1948.

The longest jump achieved

in Olympic competition was 118.5m by Matti Nykänen (FIN) in 1988 on the 90m hill. The oldest gold medallist was Yukio Kasaya (JPN), aged 28yr 173 days in 1972, while the youngest was Wojciech Fortuna (POL) also in 1972, aged 19yr 189 days. The oldest medallist was Birger Ruud in 1948, aged 36yr 168 days, and the youngest Toni Innauer (AUT) in 1976, aged 17yr 320 days. Anders Haugen (USA), the story of whose extraordinary 50-year wait for his bronze medal is told elsewhere, was also over 36 years old. Sepp Bradl (AUT) – the first man ever to jump over 100m – competed over a period of 20 years, from 1936–1956, but never won a medal.

Thomas Sandberg of Norway won the Nordic Combination event at Sarajevo in 1984, surprisingly his country's first medal in the discipline for 20 years.

NORDIC SKIING MEDAL TOTALS
Including Nordic Combination, Biathlon & Ski Jumping

Country	MEN			WOMEN			Total
	G	S	B	G	S	B	
Soviet Union	21	14	20	14	14	9	92
Norway	29	30	23	2	3	5	92
Finland	18	25	17	7	8	8	83
Sweden	19	14	15	3	2	2	55
GDR	8	8	10	2	–	1	29
Germany (FRG)	5	3	4	–	–	–	12
Czechoslovakia	1	2	4	–	1	3	11
Austria	2	4	4	–	–	–	10
Switzerland	1	3	3	–	–	–	7
Japan	1	2	1	–	–	–	4
Italy	1	1	2	–	–	–	4
Poland	1	–	1	–	–	–	2
United States	–	1	1	–	–	–	2
Yugoslavia	–	1	1	–	–	–	2
	107	108[1]	106	28	28	28	405

NORDIC SKIING MEDALS – MEN

	Gold	Silver	Bronze
15 000 Metres			
1924[1]	Thorleif Haug (NOR) 1h 14:31.0	Johan Gröttumsbraaten (NOR) 1h 15:51.0	Tipani Niku (FIN) 1h 26:26.0
1928[2]	Johan Gröttumsbraaten (NOR) 1h 37:01.0	Ole Hegge (NOR) 1h 39:01.0	Reidar Odegaard (NOR) 1h 40:11.0
1932[3]	Sven Utterström (SWE) 1h 23:07.0	Axel Wikström (SWE) 1h 25:07.0	Veli Saarinen (FIN) 1h 25:24.0
1936[1]	Erik-August Larsson (SWE) 1h 14:38.0	Oddbjörn Hagen (NOR) 1h 15:33.0	Pekka Niemi (FIN) 1h 16:59.0
1948[1]	Martin Lundström (SWE) 1h 13:50.0	Nils Ostensson (SWE) 1h 14:22.0	Gunnar Eriksson (SWE) 1h 16:06.6
1952[1]	Hallgeir Brenden (NOR) 1h 1:34.0	Tapio Mäkelä (FIN) 1h 2:09.0	Paavo Lonkila (FIN) 1h 2:20.0
1956	Hallgeir Brenden (NOR) 49:39.0	Sixten Jernberg (SWE) 50:14.0	Pavel Koltschin (URS) 50:17.0
1960	Haakon Brusveen (NOR) 51:55.5	Sixten Jernberg (SWE) 51:58.6	Veikko Hakulinen (FIN) 52:03.0
1964	Eero Mäntyranta (FIN) 50:54.1	Harald Grönningen (NOR) 51:34.8	Sixten Jernberg (SWE) 51:42.2
1968	Harald Grönningen (NOR) 47:54.2	Eero Mäntyranta (FIN) 47:56.1	Gunnar Larsson (SWE) 48:33.7
1972	Sven-Ake Lundback (SWE) 45:28.24	Fedor Simaschov (URS) 46:00.84	Ivar Formo (NOR) 46:02.86
1976	Nikolai Bajukov (URS) 43:58.47	Yevgeniy Beliayev (URS) 44:01.10	Arto Koivisto (FIN) 44:19.25
1980	Thomas Wassberg (SWE) 41:57.63	Juha Mieto (FIN) 41:57.64	Ove Aunli (NOR) 42:28.62
1984	Gunde Swan (SWE) 41:25.6	Aki Karvonen (FIN) 41:34.9	Harri Kirvesniemi (FIN) 41:45.6
1988	Michael Deviatyarov (URS) 41:18.9	Pal Mikkelsplass (NOR) 41:33.4	Vladimir Smirnov (URS) 41:48.5

[1]*The distance was 18km.*   [2]*The distance was 19.7km.*   [3]*The distance was 18.2km.*   1908–1920 Event not held.

	Gold	Silver	Bronze
30 000 Metres			
1956	Veikko Hakulinen (FIN) 1h 44:06.0	Sixten Jernberg (SWE) 1h 44:30.0	Pavel Koltschin (URS) 1h 45:45.0
1960	Sixten Jernberg (SWE) 1h 51:03.9	Rolf Rämgard (SWE) 1h 51:16.9	Nikolai Anikin (URS) 1h 52:28.2
1964	Eero Mäntyranta (FIN) 1h 30:50.7	Harald Grönningen (NOR) 1h 32:02.3	Igor Voronchikin (URS) 1h 32:15.8
1968	Franco Nones (ITA) 1h 35:29.2	Odd Martinsen (NOR) 1h 36:28.9	Eero Mäntyranta (FIN) 1h 36:55.3
1972	Vyacheslav Vedenine (URS) 1h 36:31.2	Paal Tyldum (NOR) 1h 37:25.3	Johs Harviken (NOR) 1h 36:32.4
1976	Sergey Savelyev (URS) 1h 30:29.38	William Koch (USA) 1h 30:57.84	Ivan Garanin (URS) 1h 31:09.29
1980	Nikolai Simyatov (URS) 1h 27:02.80	Vasiliy Rochev (URS) 1h 27:34.22	Ivan Lebanov (BUL) 1h 28:03.87
1984	Nikolai Simyatov (URS) 1h 28:56.3	Alexandre Zavialov (URS) 1h 29:23.3	Gunde Swan (SWE) 1h 29:35.7
1988	Alexey Prokororov (URS) 1h 24:26.3	Vladimir Smirnov (URS) 1h 24:35.1	Vegard Ulvang (NOR) 1h 25:11.6

1908–1952 Event not held.

	Gold	Silver	Bronze
50 000 Metres			
1924	Thorleif Haug (NOR) 3h 44:32.0	Thoralf Strömstad (NOR) 3h 46:23.0	Johan Gröttumsbraaten (NOR) 3h 47:46.0
1928	Per Erik Hedlund (SWE) 4h 52:03.0	Gustaf Jonsson (SWE) 5h 05:30.0	Volger Andersson (SWE) 5h 05:46.0
1932	Veli Saarinen (FIN) 4h 28:00.0	Väinö Likkanen (FIN) 4h 28:20.0	Arne Rustadstuen (NOR) 4h 31:53.0
1936	Elis Wiklung (SWE) 3h 30:11.0	Axel Wikström (SWE) 3h 33:20.0	Nils-Joel Englund (SWE) 3h 34:10.0
1948	Nils Karlsson (SWE) 3h 47:48.0	Harald Eriksson (SWE) 3h 52:20.0	Benjamin Vanninen (SWE) 3h 57:28.0
1952	Veikko Hakulinen (FIN) 3h 33:33.0	Eero Kolehmainen (FIN) 3h 38:11.0	Magnar Estenstad (NOR) 3h 38:28.0
1956	Sixten Jernberg (SWE) 2h 50:27.0	Veikko Hakulinen (FIN) 2h 51:45.0	Fedor Terentyev (URS) 2h 53:32.0
1960	Kalevi Hämäläinen (FIN) 2h 59:06.3	Veikko Hakulinen (FIN) 2h 59:26.7	Rolf Rämgard (SWE) 3h 02:46.7
1964	Sixten Jernberg (SWE) 2h 43:52.6	Assar Rönnlund (SWE) 2h 44:58.2	Arto Tiainen (FIN) 2h 45:30.4
1968	Olle Ellefsaeter (NOR) 2h 28:45.8	Vyacheslav Vedenine (URS) 2h 29:02.5	Josef Haas (SUI) 2h 29:14.8
1972	Paal Tyldrum (NOR) 2h 43:14.75	Magne Myrmo (NOR) 2h 43:29.45	Vyacheslav Vedenine (URS) 2h 44:00.19
1976	Ivar Formo (NOR) 2h 37:30.50	Gert-Dietmar Klause (GDR) 2h 38:13.21	Benny Södergren (SWE) 2h 39:39.21
1980	Nikolai Simyatov (URS) 2h 27:24.60	Juha Mieto (FIN) 2h 30:20.52	Aleksandr Savyalov (URS) 2h 30:51.52
1984	Thomas Wassberg (SWE) 2h 15:55.8	Gunde Swan (SWE) 2h 16:00.7	Aki Karvonen (FIN) 2h 17:04.7
1988	Gunde Svan (SWE) 2h 04:30.9	Maurilio De Zolt (ITA) 2h 05:36.4	Andy Grünenfelder (SUI) 2h 06.01.9

1908–1920 Event not held.

	Gold	Silver	Bronze
4 x 10 000 Metres Relay			
1936	Finland 2h 41:33.0	Norway 2h 41:39.0	Sweden 2h 43:03.0
1948	Sweden 2h 32:08.0	Finland 2h 41:06.0	Norway 2h 44:33.0
1952	Finland 2h 20:16.0	Norway 2h 23:13.0	Sweden 2h 24:13.0
1956	Soviet Union 2h 15:30.0	Finland 2h 16:31.0	Sweden 2h 17:42.0
1960	Finland 2h 18:45.6	Norway 2h 18:46.4	Soviet Union 2h 21:21.6
1964	Sweden 2h 18:34.6	Finland 2h 18:42.4	Soviet Union 2h 18:46.9
1968	Norway 2h 08:33.5	Sweden 2h 10:13.2	Finland 2h 10:56.7
1972	Soviet Union 2h 04:47.94	Norway 2h 04:57.6	Switzerland 2h 07:00.06
1976	Finland 2h 07:59.72	Norway 2h 09:58.36	Soviet Union 2h 10:51.46
1980	Soviet Union 1h 57:03.6	Norway 1h 58:45.77	Finland 2h 00:00.18
1984	Sweden 1h 55:06.3	Soviet Union 1h 55:16.5	Finland 1h 56:31.4
1988	Sweden 1h 43:58.6	Soviet Union 1h 44:11.3	Czechoslovakia 1h 45:22.7

1908–1932 Event not held.

NORDIC SKIING MEDALS – WOMEN

	Gold	Silver	Bronze
5000 Metres			
1964	Klaudia Boyarskikh (URS) 17:50.5	Mirja Lehtonen (FIN) 17:52.9	Alevtina Koltschina (URS) 18:08.4
1968	Toini Gustafsson (SWE) 16:45.2	Galina Kulakova (URS) 16:48.4	Alevtina Koltschina (URS) 16:51.6
1972	Galina Kulakova (URS) 17:00.50	Marjatta Kajosmaa (FIN) 17:05.50	Helena Sikolova (TCH) 17:07.32
1976	Helena Takalo (FIN) 15:48.69	Raisa Smetanina (URS) 15:49.73	Nina Baldycheva[1] (URS) 16:12.82
1980	Raisa Semtanina (URS) 15:06.92	Hikka Riihivuori (FIN) 15:11.96	Kvetoslava Jeriova (TCH) (TCH) 15:23.44
1984	Marja-Liisa Hämäläinen (FIN) 17:04.0	Berit Aunli (NOR) 17:14.1	Kvetoslava Jeriova (TCH) 17:18.3
1988	Marjo Matikainen (FIN) 15:04.0	Tamara Tikhonova (URS) 15:05.3	Vida Ventsene (URS) 15:11.1

[1]*Galina Kulakova (URS) finished third but was disqualifed.*   1908–1960 Event not held.

	Gold	Silver	Bronze
10 000 Metres			
1952	Lydia Wideman (FIN) 41:40.0	Mirja Hietamies (FIN) 42:39.0	Siiri Rantanen (FIN) 42:50.0
1956	Lubov Kozyryeva (URS) 38:11.0	Radya Yeroschina (URS) 38:16.0	Sonja Edström (SWE) 38:23.0
1960	Maria Gusakova (URS) 39:46.6	Lubov Baranova-Kozyryeva (URS) 40:04.2	Radya Yeroschina (URS) 40:06.0
1964	Klaudia Boyarskikh (URS) 40:24.3	Yevdokia Mekshilo (URS) 40:26.6	Maria Gusakova (URS) 40:46.6
1968	Toini Gustafsson (SWE) 36:46.5	Berit Mördre (NOR) 37:54.6	Inger Aufles (NOR) 37:59.9
1972	Galina Kulakova (URS) 34:17.8	Alevtina Olunina (URS) 34:54.1	Marjatta Kajosmaa (FIN) 34:56.5
1976	Raisa Smetanina (URS) 30:13.41	Helena Takalo (FIN) 30:14.28	Galina Kulakova (URS) 30:38.61
1980	Barbara Petzold (GDR) 30:31.54	Hilkka Riihivuori (FIN) 30:35.05	Helena Takalo (FIN) 30:45.25
1984	Marja-Liisa Hämäläinen (FIN) 31:44.2	Raisa Smetanina (URS) 32:02.9	Brit Pettersen (NOR) 32:12.7
1988	Vida Ventsene (URS) 30:08.3	Raisa Smetanina (URS) 30:17.0	Marjo Matikainen (FIN) 30:20.5

1908–1948 Event not held.

	Gold	Silver	Bronze
20 000 Metres			
1984	Marja-Liisa Hämäläinen (FIN) 1h 01:45.0	Raisa Smetanina (URS) 1h 02:26.7	Anne Jahren (NOR) 1h 03:13.06
1988	Tamara Tikhonova (URS) 55:53.6	Anfissa Reztsova (URS) 56:12.8	Raisa Smetanina (URS) 57:22.1

1908–1980 Event not held.

	Gold	Silver	Bronze
4[1] x 5000 Metres Relay			
1956	Finland 1h 09:01.0	Soviet Union 1h 09:28.0	Sweden 1h 09:48.0
1960	Sweden 1h 04:21.4	Soviet Union 1h 05:02.6	Finland 1h 06:27.5
1964	Soviet Union 59:20.2	Sweden 1h 01:27.0	Finland 1h 02:45.1
1968	Norway 57:30.0	Sweden 57:51.0	Soviet Union 58:13.6
1972	Soviet Union 48:46.15	Finland 49:19.37	Norway 49:51.49
1976	Soviet Union 1h 07:49.75	Finland 1h 08:36.57	GDR 1h 09:57.95
1980	GDR 1h 02:11.10	Soviet Union 1h 03:18.30	Norway 1h 04:13.50
1984	Norway 1h 06:49.7	Czechoslovakia 1h 07:34.7	Finland 1h 07:36.7
1988	Soviet Union 59:51.1	Norway 1h 01:33.0	Finland 1h 01:53.8

[1]*Over three stages prior to 1976.*   1908–1952 Event not held.

BIATHLON MEDALS

	Gold	Silver	Bronze
10 000 Metres			
1980	Frank Ullrich (GDR) 32:10.69	Vladimir Alikin (URS) 32:53.10	Anatoliy Alyabiev (URS) 33:09.16
1984	Eirik Kvalfoss (NOR) 30:53.8	Peter Angerer (FRG) 31:02.4	Matthias Jacob (GDR) 31:10.5
1988	Frank-Peter Rötsch (GDR) 25:08.1	Valeri Medvedtsev (URS) 25:23.7	Sergei Tchepikov (URS) 25:29.4

1908–1976 Event not held.

	Gold	Silver	Bronze
20 000 Metres			
1960	Klas Lestander (SWE) 1h 33:21.6	Antii Tyrväinen (FIN) 1h 33:57.7	Aleksandr Privalov (URS) 1h 34:54.2
1964	Vladimir Melyanin (URS) 1h 20:26.8	Aleksandr Privalov (URS) 1h 23:42.5	Olav Jordet (NOR) 1h 24:38.8
1968	Magnar Solberg (NOR) 1h 13:45.9	Aleksandr Tikhonov (URS) 1h 14:40.4	Vladimir Gundartsev (URS) 1h 18:27.4
1972	Magnar Solberg (NOR) 1h 15:55.5	Hans-Jürg Knauthe (GDR) 1h 16:07.6	Lars Arvidsson (SWE) 1h 16:27.03
1976	Nikolai Kruglov (URS) 1h 14:12.26	Heikki Ikola (FIN) 1h 15:54.10	Aleksandr Elizarov (URS) 1h 16:05.57
1980	Anatoliy Alyabiev (URS) 1h 08:16.31	Frank Ullrich (GDR) 1h 08:27.79	Eberhard Rösch (GDR) 1h 11:11.73
1984	Peter Angerer (FRG) 1h 11:52.7	Frank-Peter Rötsch (GDR) 1h 13:21.4	Eirik Kvalfoss (NOR) 1h 14:02.4
1988	Frank-Peter Rötsch (GDR) 56:33.3	Valeri Medvedtsev (URS) 56:54.6	Johann Pasler (ITA) 57:10.1

1908–1956 Event not held.

	Gold	Silver	Bronze
Biatholon Relay (4 x 7 500 Metres)			
1968	Soviet Union 2h 13:02.4	Norway 2h 14:50.2	Sweden 2h 17:26.3
1972	Soviet Union 1h 51:44.92	Finland 1h 54:37.22	GDR 1h 54:57.67
1976	Soviet Union 1h 57:55.64	Finland 2h 01:45.58	GDR 2h 04:08.61
1980	Soviet Union 1h 34:03.27	GDR 1h 34:56.99	FRG 1h 37:30.26
1984	Soviet Union 1h 38:51.7	Norway 1h 39:03.9	FRG 1h 39:05.1
1988	Soviet Union 1h 22:30.0	FRG 1h 23:37.4	Italy 1h 23:51.5

1908–1964 Event not held.

The Finnish team which won the inaugural 90m team jumping: Ari Nikkola, Matti Nykänen, Jari Puikkonen and Tuomo Ylipulli. Nykänen also won both individual events at Calgary in 1988.

NORDIC COMBINED MEDALS

	Gold	Silver	Bronze
Individual			
1924[2]	Thorleif Haug (NOR)	Thoralf Strömstad (NOR)	Johan Gröttumsbraaten (NOR)
1928[2]	Johan Gröttumsbraaten (NOR)	Hans Vinjarengen (NOR)	John Snersrud (NOR)
1932	Johan Gröttumsbraaten (NOR) 446.0pts	Ole Stenen (NOR) 436.05pts	Hans Vinjarengen (NOR) 434.60pts
1936	Oddbjörn Hagen (NOR) 430.30pts	Olaf Hoffsbakken (NOR) 419.80pts	Sverre Brodahl (NOR) 408.10pts
1948	Heikki Hasu (FIN) 448.80pts	Martti Huhtala (FIN) 433.65pts	Sven Israelsson (SWE) 433.40pts
1952	Simon Slåttvik (NOR) 451.621pts	Heikki Hasu (FIN) 447.50pts	Sverre Stenersen (NOR) 436.335pts
1956	Sverre Stenersen (NOR) 455.0pts	Bengt Eriksson (SWE) 437.4pts	Franciszek Gron-Gasienica (POL) 436.8pts
1960	Georg Thoma (GER) 457.952pts	Tormod Knutsen (NOR) 453.000pts	Nikolai Gusakow (URS) 452.000pts
1964	Tormod Knutson (NOR) 469.28pts	Nikolai Kiselyev (URS) 453.04pts	Georg Thoma (GER) 452.88pts
1968	Frantz Keller (FRG) 449.04pts	Alois Kälin (SUI) 447.94pts	Andreas Kunz (GDR) 444.10pts
1972	Ulrich Wehling (GDR) 413.34pts	Rauno Miettinen (FIN) 405.55pts	Karl-Heinz Luck (GDR) 398.80pts
1976	Ulrich Wehling (GDR) 423.39pts	Urban Hettich (FRG) 418.90pts	Konrad Winkler (GDR) 417.47pts
1980	Ulrich Wehling (GDR) 432.20pts	Jouko Karjalainen (FIN) 429.50pts	Konrad Winkler (GDR) 425.32pts
1984	Tom Sandberg (NOR) 422.595pts	Jouko Karjalainen (FIN) 416.900pts	Jukka Ylipulli (FIN) 410.825pts
1988	Hippolyt Kempt (SUI)	Klaus Sulzenbacher (AUT)	Allar Levandi (URS)

[1]*From 1924–1952 distance was 18km.*   [2]*In 1924 and 1928, the scoring was decided upon a different basis from that used from 1932 onwards.*
1908–1920 Event not held.

Team

1988	FRG	Switzerland	Austria

1908–1984 Event not held.

SKI JUMPING MEDALS

	Gold	Silver	Bronze
70 Metre Hill			
1924[1]	Jacob Tullin Thams (NOR) 18 960pts	Narve Bonna (NOR) 18 689pts	Anders Haugen (USA) 17 916pts
1928	Alf Andersen (NOR) 19 208pts	Sigmund Ruud (NOR) 18 542pts	Rudolf Burkert (TCH) 17 937pts
1932	Birger Ruud (NOR) 228.1pts	Hans Beck (NOR) 227.0pts	Kaare Wahlberg (NOR) 219.5pts
1936	Birger Ruud (NOR) 232.0pts	Sven Eriksson (SWE) 230.5pts	Reidar Andersen (NOR) 228.9pts
1948	Petter Hugsted (NOR) 228.1pts	Birger Ruud (NOR) 226.6pts	Thorleif Schjeldrup (NOR) 225.1pts
1952	Arnfinn Bergmann (NOR) 226.0pts	Torbjörn Falkanger (NOR) 221.5pts	Karl Holmström (SWE) 219.5pts
1956	Antti Hyvärinen (FIN) 227.0pts	Aulis Kallakorpi (FIN) 225.0pts	Harry Glass (GER) 224.5pts
1960	Helmut Recknagel (GER) 227.2pts	Niilo Halonen (FIN) 222.6pts	Otto Leodolter (AUT) 219.4pts
1964	Veikko Kankkonen (FIN) 229.9pts	Toralf Engan (NOR) 226.3pts	Torgeir Brandtzaeg (NOR) 222.9pts
1968	Jiri Raska (TCH) 216.5pts	Reinhold Bachler (AUT) 214.2pts	Baldur Preiml (AUT) 212.6pts
1972	Yukio Kasaya (JPN) 224.2pts	Akitsugu Konno (JPN) 234.8pts	Seiji Aochi (JPN) 229.5pts
1976	Hans-Georg Aschenbach (GDR) 252.0pts	Jochen Danneberg (GDR) 246.2pts	Karl Schnabl (AUT) 242.0pts
1980	Toni Innauer (AUT) 266.3pts	Manfred Deckert (GDR) 249.2pts Hirokazu Yagi (JPN) 249.2pts	–
1984	Jens Weissflog (GDR) 215.2pts	Matti Nykänen (FIN) 214.0pts	Jari Puikkonen (FIN) 212.8pts
1988	Matti Nykänen (FIN) 229.1pts	Pavel Ploc (TCH) 212.1pts	Jiri Malec (TCH) 211.8pts

[1]*Originally Thorleif Haug (NOR) placed third due to incorrect calculations at time. Error discovered and corrected in 1974.*
1908–1920 Event not held.

90 Metre Hill

1964	Toralf Engan (NOR) 230.7pts	Veikko Kankkonen (FIN) 228.9pts	Torgeir Brandtzaeg (NOR) 227.2pts
1968	Vladimir Belousov (URS) 231.3pts	Jiri Raska (TCH) 229.4pts	Lars Grini (NOR) 214.3pts
1972	Wojciech Fortuna (POL) 219.9pts	Walter Steiner (SUI) 219.8pts	Rainer Schmidt (GDR) 219.3pts
1976	Karl Schnabl (AUT) 234.8pts	Toni Innauer (AUT) 232.9pts	Henry Glass (GDR) 221.7pts
1980	Jouko Törmänen (FIN) 271.0pts	Hubert Neuper (AUT) 262.4pts	Jari Puikkonen (FIN) 248.5pts
1984	Matti Nykänen (FIN) 232.2pts	Jens Weissflog (GDR) 213.7pts	Pavel Ploc (TCH) 202.9pts
1988	Matti Nykänen (FIN) 224.0pts	Erik Johnsen (NOR) 207.9pts	Matjaz Debelak (YUG) 207.7pts

1908–1960 Event not held.

90 Metre – Team

1988	Finland 634.4pts	Yugoslavia 625.5pts	Norway 596.1pts

1908–1984 Event not held.

SPEED SKATING

The sport was introduced into the Olympics in 1924, with the first official events for women in 1960. There have been two major controversies over the years. In 1928 the 10km event was cancelled by the Norwegian referee due to bad weather, causing much ill-feeling in the American camp because at the time Irving Jaffee (USA) was the surprise leader, and with all the best skaters having competed, the medal positions seemed assured. Despite vigorous protests by all nationalities, no medals were awarded. The other occasion was in 1932 when the American 'mass start' system was used, for the only time in Olympic competition. This undoubtedly gave the Americans and Canadians a tremendous advantage as the Europeans were completely unfamiliar with the tactics involved – only two medals were won by European skaters.

Lydia Skoblikova (URS) won a record six gold medals in 1960 and 1964, which is a record for any sport in the Winter Games for either a male or female competitor. The most by a man is five by Clas Thunberg (FIN) in 1924 and 1928, and by Eric Heiden (USA) with all five in 1980. There have only been five events for men since 1976, while a fifth event was added for women in 1988.

The most medals won is eight by Karin Enke-Kania (GDR) with three golds, four silvers and a bronze from 1980 to 1988. The most by a male skater is seven by Thunberg, who added a silver and a bronze to

his golds, and by Ivar Ballangrud (NOR) who won four golds, two silvers and a bronze from 1928 to 1936. Skoblikova won her four golds on four successive days.

The oldest gold medallist was Thunberg, aged 35yr 315 days in the 1928 1500m. The youngest winner was Anne Henning (USA) in the 500m in 1952, aged 16yr 157 days. The youngest male champion was Igor Malkov (URS), winning the 10km in 1984 aged 19yr 9 days, while the oldest woman was Christina Baas-Kaiser (HOL), who won the 3000m title in 1972 aged 33yr 268 days. The youngest ever medallist was Andrea Mitscherlich (GDR),

who won the 3000 m silver in 1976 when only 15yr 69 days old.

Frank Stack (CAN) competed over a 20-year period from 1932 to 1952 (by which time he was 46), winning a bronze in 1932, while Colin Coates (AUS) also competed for 20 years (1968–1988) but his best placing was sixth in the 10km in 1976.

A number of speed skaters have found a happy affinity with cycle racing. One of the most successful at both roles has been Sheila Young (USA), who won the 500m Olympics skating title in 1976 and the world amateur sprint cycle championship in 1973 and 1976. However, Christa Rothenburger-Luding (GDR) possibly surpassed that in 1988. Having won the 1984 Olympic 500m gold and the

Lydia Skoblikova of the Soviet Union wins the first of her record four gold medals in 1964, in the 500m event.

world cycling sprint title in 1986, she then won the skating 1000m at Calgary and gained a cycling silver in Seoul, to become the first competitor to win medals at Summer and Winter games in the same year.

In 1988 Short-Track speed skating was a demonstration sport, comprising five events each for men and women. Of these, two each went to Korea, Great Britain and the Netherlands and one each to Canada, China, Italy and Japan. In 1992 this form of speed skating becomes a medal sport.

SPEED SKATING MEDAL TOTALS

Country	MEN			WOMEN			Total
	G	S	B	G	S	B	
Norway	18	24	22	1	–	1	66
Soviet Union	12	10	9	12	7	10	60
United States	13	7	3	4	8	6	41
Netherlands	5	11	8	7	4	4	39
GDR	2	1	2	6	11	7	29
Finland	6	6	7	1	2	2	24
Sweden	7	4	5	–	–	–	16
Canada	2	2	6	–	1	–	11
Germany (FRG)	2	–	–	2	1	–	5
Austria	–	1	2	–	–	–	3
Japan	–	1	1	–	–	–	2
Poland	–	–	–	–	1	1	2
North Korea (PRK)	–	–	–	–	1	–	1
	67	67	65	33	36	31	299

SPEED SKATING – MEN

	Gold	Silver	Bronze
500 Metres			
1924	Charles Jewtraw (USA) 44.0	Oskar Olsen (NOR) 44.2	Roald Larsen (NOR) 44.8
			Clas Thunberg (FIN) 44.8
1928	Clas Thunberg (FIN) 43.4	–	John Farrell (USA) 43.6
	Bernt Evensen (NOR) 43.4		Roald Larsen (NOR) 43.6
			Jaako Friman (FIN) 43.6
1932	John Shea (USA) 43.4	Bernt Evensen (NOR) 5m	Alexander Hurd (CAN) 8m
1936	Ivar Ballangrud (NOR) 32.4	Georg Krog (NOR) 43.5	Leo Freisinger (USA) 44.0
1948	Finn Helgesen (NOR) 43.1	Kenneth Bartholomew (USA) 43.2	–
		Thomas Byberg (NOR) 43.2	
		Robert Fitzgerald (USA) 43.2	
1952	Kenneth Henry (USA) 43.2	Donald McDermott (USA) 43.9	Arne Johansen (NOR) 44.0
			Gordon Audley (CAN) 44.0
1956	Yevgeniy Grischin (URS) 40.2	Rafael Gratsch (URS) 40.8	Alv Gjestvang (NOR) 41.0
1960	Yevgeniy Grischin (URS) 40.2	William Disney (USA) 40.3	Rafael Gratsch (URS) 40.4
1964	Richard McDermott (USA) 40.1	Yevgeniy Grischin (URS) 40.6	–
		Vladimir Orlov (URS) 40.6	
		Alv Gjestvang (NOR) 40.6	
1968	Erhard Keller (FRG) 40.3	Richard McDermott (USA) 40.5	–
		Magne Thomassen (NOR) 40.5	
1972	Erhard Keller (FRG) 39.44	Hasse Borjes (SWE) 39.69	Valeriy Muratov (URS) 39.80
1976	Yevgeniy Kulikov (URS) 39.17	Valeriy Muratov (URS) 39.25	Daniel Immerfall (USA) 39.54
1980	Eric Heiden (USA) 38.03	Yevgeniy Kulikov (URS) 38.37	Lieuwe de Boer (HOL) 38.48
1984	Sergey Fokitchev (URS) 38.19	Yoshihiro Kitazawa (JPN) 38.30	Gaetan Boucher (CAN) 38.39
1988	Jens-Uwe Mey (GDR) 36.45*	Jan Ykema (HOL) 36.76	Akira Kuroiwa (JPN) 36.77

Olympic record. 1908–1920 Event not held.

	Gold	Silver	Bronze
1000 Metres			
1976	Peter Mueller (USA) 1:19.32	Jorn Didriksen (NOR) 1:20.45	Valeriy Muratov (URS) 1:20.57
1980	Eric Heiden (USA) 1:15.18	Gaetan Boucher (CAN) 1:16.68	Frode Rönning (NOR) 1:16.91
			Vladimir Lobanov (URS) 1:16.91
1984	Gaetan Boucher (CAN) 1:15.80	Sergey Khlebnikov (URS) 1:16.63	Kai Arne Engelstad (NOR) 1:16.75
1988	Nikolay Gouliayev (URS) 1:13.03*	Jens-Uwe Mey (GDR) 1:13.11	Igor Gelezovsky (URS) 1:13.19

Olympic record. 1908–1972 Event not held.

	Gold	Silver	Bronze
1500 Metres			
1924	Clas Thunberg (FIN) 2:20.8	Roald Larsen (NOR) 2:22.0	Sigurd Moen (NOR) 2:25.6
1928	Clas Thunberg (FIN) 2:21.1	Bernt Evensen (NOR) 2:21.9	Ivar Ballangrud (NOR) 2:22.6
1932	John Shea (USA) 2:57.5	Alexander Hurd (CAN) 5m	William Logan (CAN) 6m
1936	Charles Mathiesen (NOR) 2:19.2	Ivar Ballangrud (NOR) 2:20.2	Birger Wasenius (FIN) 2:20.9
1948	Sverre Farstad (NOR) 2:17.6	Ake Seyffarth (SWE) 2:18.1	Odd Lundberg (NOR) 2:18.9
1952	Hjalmar Andersen (NOR) 2:20.4	Willem van der Voort (HOL) 2:20.6	Roald Aas (NOR) 2:21.6
1956	Yevgeniy Grischin (URS) 2:08.6	–	Tiovo Salonen (FIN) 2:09.4
	Yuriy Michailov (URS) 2:08.6		

Taking the 10 000m title, Ard Schenk (HOL) wins his third gold medal at Sapporo in 1972.

	Gold	Silver	Bronze
1960	Roald Aas (NOR) 2:10.4	–	Boris Stenin (URS) 2:11.5
	Yevgeniy Grischin (URS) 2:10.4		
1964	Ants Antson (URS) 2:10.3	Cornelis Verkerk (HOL) 2:10.6	Villy Haugen (NOR) 2:11.25
1968	Cornelis Verkerk (HOL) 2:03.4	Ard Schenk (HOL) 2:05.0	–
		Ivar Eriksen (NOR) 2:05.0	
1972	Ard Schenk (HOL) 2:02.96	Roar Gronvold (NOR) 2:04.26	Goran Clässon (SWE) 2:05.89
1976	Jan Egil Storholt (NOR) 1:59.38	Yuriy Kondakov (URS) 1:59.97	Hans Van Helden (HOL) 2:00.87
1980	Eric Heiden (USA) 1:55.44	Kai Stenshjemmet (NOR) 1:56.81	Jerje Andersen (NOR) 1:56.92
1984	Gaetan Boucher (CAN) 1:58.36	Sergey Khlebnikov (URS) 1:58.83	Oleg Bogiev (URS) 1:58.89
1988	Andre Hoffmann (GDR) 1:52.06*	Eric Flaim (USA) 1:52.12	Michael Hadschieff (AUT) 1:52.31

Olympic record.   1908–1920 Event not held.

	Gold	Silver	Bronze

5000 Metres

Year	Gold	Silver	Bronze
1924	Clas Thunberg (FIN) 8:39.0	Julius Skutnabb (FIN) 8:48.4	Roald Larsen (NOR) 8:50.2
1928	Ivar Ballangrud (NOR) 8:50.5	Julius Skutnabb (FIN) 8:59.1	Bernt Evensen (NOR) 9:01.1
1932	Irving Jaffee (USA) 9:40.8	Edward Murphy (USA) 2m	William Logan (CAN) 4m
1936	Ivar Ballangrud (NOR) 8:19.6	Birger Wasenius (FIN) 8:23.3	Antero Ojala (FIN) 8:30.1
1948	Reidar Liaklev (NOR) 8:29.4	Odd Lundberg (NOR) 8:32.7	Göthe Hedlund (SWE) 8:34.8
1952	Hjalmar Andersen (NOR) 8:10.6	Kees Broekman (HOL) 8:21.6	Sverre Haugli (NOR) 8:22.4
1956	Boris Schilkov (URS) 7:48.7	Sigvard Ericsson (SWE) 7:56.7	Oleg Gontscharenko (URS) 7:57.5
1960	Viktor Kositschkin (URS) 7:51.3	Knut Johannesen (NOR) 8:00.8	Jan Pesman (HOL) 8:05.1
1964	Knut Johannesen (NOR) 7:38.4	Per Moe (NOR) 7:38.6	Anton Maier (NOR) 7:42.0
1968	Anton Maier (NOR) 7:22.4	Cornelis Verkerk (HOL) 7:23.2	Petrus Nottet (HOL) 7:25.5
1972	Ard Schenk (HOL) 7:23.6	Roar Gronvold (NOR) 7:28.18	Sten Stensen (NOR) 7:33.39
1976	Sten Stensen (NOR) 7:24.48	Piet Kleine (HOL) 7:26.47	Hans Van Helden (HOL) 7:26.54
1980	Eric Heiden (USA) 7:02.29	Kai Stenshjemmet (NOR) 7:03.28	Tom Oxholm (NOR) 7:05.59
1984	Tomas Gustafson (SWE) 7:12.28	Igor Malkov (URS) 7:12.30	Rene Schoefisch (GDR) 7:17.49
1988	Tomas Gustafson (SWE) 6:44.63*	Leendert Visser (HOL) 6:44.98	Gerard Kemkers (HOL) 6:45.92

Olympic record.   1908–1920 Event not held.

10 000 Metres

Year	Gold	Silver	Bronze
1924	Julius Skutnabb (FIN) 18:04.8	Clas Thunberg (FIN) 18:97.8	Roald Larsen (NOR) 18:12.2
1932	Irving Jaffee (USA) 19:13.6	Ivar Ballangrud (NOR) 5m	Frank Stack (CAN) 6m
1936	Ivar Ballangrud (NOR) 17:24.3	Birger Wasenius (FIN) 17:28.2	Max Stiepl (AUT) 17:30.0
1948	Ake Seyffarth (SWE) 17:26.3	Lauri Parkkinen (FIN) 17:36.0	Pentti Lammio (FIN) 17:42.7
1952	Hjalmar Andersen (NORT) 16:45.8	Kees Broekman (HOL) 17:10.6	Carl-Erik Asplund (SWE) 17:16.6
1956	Sigvard Ericsson (SWE) 16:35.9	Knut Johannesen (NOR) 16:36.9	Oleg Gontscharenko (URS) 16:42.3
1960	Knut Johannesen (NOR) 15:46.6	Viktor Kositschkin (URS) 15:49.2	Kjell Bäckman (SWE) 16:14.2
1964	Jonny Nilsson (SWE) 15:50.1	Anton Maier (NOR) 16:06.0	Knut Johannesen (NOR) 16:06.3
1968	Johnny Höglin (SWE) 15:23.6	Anton Maier (NOR) 15:23.9	Orjan Sandler (SWE) 15:31.8
1972	Ard Schenk (HOL) 15:01.35	Cornelis Verkerk (HOL) 15:04.70	Sten Stensen (NOR) 15:07.08
1976	Piet Kleine (HOL) 14:50.59	Sten Stensen (NOR) 14:53.30	Hans Van Helden (HOL) 15:02.02
1980	Eric Heiden (USA) 14:28.13	Piet Kleine (HOL) 14:36.03	Tom Oxholm (NOR) 14:36.60
1984	Igor Malkov (URS) 14:39.90	Tomas Gustafson (SWE) 14:39.95	Rene Schoefisch (GDR) 14:46.91
1988	Tomas Gustafson (SWE) 13:48.20*	Michael Hadschieff (AUT) 13:56.11	Leendert Visser (HOL) 14:00.55

Olympic record.   1908–1920 Event notheld. 1928 Event abandoned.

DISCONTINUED EVENT

All-Round Championship
(Aggregate of placings in 500m, 1500m, 5km and 10km)

1924	Clas Thunberg (FIN) 5.5pts	Roald Larsen (NOR) 9.5pts	Julius Skutnabb (FIN) 11pts

SPEED SKATING MEDALS – WOMEN

	Gold	Silver	Bronze

500 Metres

Year	Gold	Silver	Bronze
1960	Helga Haase (GER) 45.9	Natalya Dontschenko (URS) 46.0	Jeanne Ashworth (USA) 46.1
1964	Lydia Skoblikova (URS) 45.0	Irina Yegorova (URS) 45.4	Tatyana Sidorova (URS) 45.5
1968	Ludmila Titova (URS) 46.1	Mary Meyers (USA) 46.3 Dianne Holum (USA) 46.3 Jennifer Fish (USA) 46.3	–
1972	Anne Henning (USA) 43.33	Vera Krasnova (URS) 44.01	Ludmila Titova (URS) 44.45
1976	Sheila Young (USA) 42.76	Catherine Priestner (CAN) 43.12	Tatyana Averina (URS) 43.17
1980	Karin Enke (GDR) 41.78	Leah Poulos-Mueller (USA) 42.26	Natalya Petruseva (URS) 42.42
1984	Christa Rothenburger (GDR) 41.02	Karin Enke (GDR) 41.28	Natalya Chive (URS) 41.50
1988	Bonnie Blair (USA) 39.10*	Christa Rothenburger (GDR) 39.12	Karin Enke-Kania (GDR) 39.24

Olympic record.

1000 Metres

Year	Gold	Silver	Bronze
1960	Klara Guseva (URS) 1:34.1	Helga Haase (GER) 1:34.3	Tamara Rylova (URS) 1:34.8
1964	Lydia Skoblikova (URS) 1:33.2	Irina Yegorova (URS) 1:34.3	Kaija Mustonen (FIN) 1:34.8
1968	Carolina Geijssen (HOL) 1:32.6	Ludmila Titova (URS) 1:32.9	Dianne Holum (USA) 1:33.4
1972	Monika Pflug (FRG) 1:31.40	Atje Keulen-Deelstra (HOL) 1:31.61	Anne Henning (USA) 1:31.62
1976	Tatyana Averina (URS) 1:28.43	Leah Poulos (USA) 1:28.57	Shjeila Young (USA) 1:29.14
1980	Natalya Petruseva (URS) 1:24.10	Leah Poulos-Mueller (USA) 1:25.41	Sylvia Albrecht (GDR) 1:26.46
1984	Karin Enke (GDR) 1:21.61	Andrea Schöne (GDR) 1:22.83	Natalya Petruseva (URS) 1:23.21
1988	Christa Rothenburger (GDR) 1:17.65*	Karin Enke-Kania (GDR) 1:17.70	Bonnie Blair (USA) 1:18.31

Olympic record.

Gold	Silver	Bronze

1500 Metres

	Gold	Silver	Bronze
1960	Lydia Skoblikova (URS) 2:25.2	Elvira Seroczynska (POL) 2:25.7	Helena Pilejeyk (POL) 2:27.1
1964	Lydia Skoblikova (URS) 2:22.6	Kaija Mustonen (FIN) 2:25.5	Berta Kolokoltseva (URS) 2:27.1
1968	Kaija Mustonen (FIN) 2:22.4	Carolina Geijssen (HOL) 2:22.7	Christina Kaiser (HOL) 2:24.5
1972	Dianne Holum (USA) 2:20.85	Christina Baas-Kaiser (HOL) 2:21.05	Atje Keulen-Deelstra (HOL) 2:22.05
1976	Galina Stepanskaya (URS) 2:16.58	Sheila Young (USA) 2:17.06	Tatyana Averina (URS) 2:17.96
1980	Annie Borckink (HOL) 2:10.95	Ria Visser (HOL) 2:12.35	Sabine Becker (GDR) 2:12.38
1984	Karin Enke (GDR) 2:03.42	Andrea Schöne (GDR) 2:05.29	Natalya Petruseva (URS) 2:05.78
1988	Yvonne Van Gennip (HOL) 2:00.68*	Karin Enke-Kania (GDR) 2:00.82	Andrea Schöne-Ehrig (GDR) 2:01.49

Olympic record.

3000 Metres

	Gold	Silver	Bronze
1960	Lydia Skoblikova (URS) 5:14.3	Valentina Stenina (URS) 5:16.9	Eevi Huttunen (FIN) 5:21.0
1964	Lydia Skoblikova (URS) 5:14.9	Valentina Stenina (URS) 5:18.5	–
		Pil-Hwa Han (PRK) 5:18.5	
1968	Johanna Schut (HOL) 4:56.2	Kaija Mustonen (FIN) 5:01.0	Christina Kaiser (HOL) 5:01.3
1972	Christina Baas-Kaiser (HOL) 4:52.14	Dianne Holum (USA) 4:58.67	Atje Keulen-Deelstra (HOL) 4:59.91
1976	Tatyana Averina (URS) 4:45.19	Andrea Mitscherlich (GDR) 4:45.23	Lisbeth Korsmo (NOR) 4:45.24
1980	Björg Eva Jensen (NOR) 4:32.13	Sabine Becker (GDR) 4:32.79	Beth Heiden (USA) 4:33.77
1984	Andrea Schöne (GDR) 4:24.79	Karin Enke (GDR) 4:26.33	Gabi Schönbrunn (GDR) 4:33.13
1988	Yvonne Van Gennip (H(OL) 4:11.94*	Andrea Schöne-Ehrig (GDR) 4:12.09	Gabi Schönbrunn-Zange (GDR) 4:16.92

Olympic record.

5000 Metres

	Gold	Silver	Bronze
1988	Yvonne Van Gennip (HOL) 7:14.13*	Andrea Schöne-Ehrig (GDR) 7:17.2	Gabi Schönbrunn-Zange (GDR) 7:21.61

1960–1984 Event not held.

TOBOGGANING (LUGEING)

In 1928 and 1948 there were one-man skeleton sled races held on the famous Cresta Run at St Moritz. In those events the contestants laid face down. Luge racing, in which contestants sit up or lie back, was introduced in 1964. The most successful luger was Thomas Köhler (GDR) with two gold medals and a silver in 1964 and 1968. Hans Rinn (GDR) won the 2-man event twice, with Norbert Hahn in 1976–1980, and gained a bronze in the 1976 singles. The most successful woman was Steffi Martin-Walter (GDR) with two golds in 1984 and 1988.

The oldest gold medallist was Paul Hildgartner (ITA), aged 31yr 249 days in the 1984 singles, while the youngest was Manfred Stengl (AUT) in the 2-man in 1964, aged 17yr 310 days. The youngest female winner was Ortrun Enderlein (GER), aged 20yr 65 days in 1964, and the oldest was Vera Sosulya (URS) in 1980, aged 24yr 35 days. The youngest medallist has been Ute Rührold (GDR), aged 17yr 60 days, gaining the silver in 1972. Probably the heaviest winner of a luge title was Hans Stanggassinger (FRG) in the 2-man of 1984 at a weight of 111kg/244lb.

The Heaton brothers (USA) starred on the skeleton sleds as well as in bobs. Jennison won the 1928 skeleton event and a silver in the 5-man bob that year. Brother John was second in the 1928 skeleton, won a bronze in the 1932 2-man bob and then returned in 1948, in his 40th year, to win another skeleton silver. Also in that 1948 competition was James Coats (GBR), at 53yr 297 days, the oldest ever competitor in the Winter Olympic Games.

In 1968 a scandal shook the Games when the first, second and fourth-placed women from the GDR were all disqualified for illegally heating the runners of their sleds. The leading girl, Ortrun Enderlein, would have been the only female luger to retain her title, to that time.

LUGEING – MEDAL TOTALS
Including Skeleton Sled

Country	MEN			WOMEN			Total
	G	S	B	G	S	B	
GDR	9	3	5	4	5	3	29
Germany (FRG)	2	4	4	1	2	2	15
Italy	3	2	1	1	–	–	7
Austria	2	2	2	–	–	1	7
Soviet Union	–	2	2	1	–	1	6
United States	1	2	–	–	–	–	3
Great Britain	–	–	2	–	–	–	2
	17[1]	15	16	7	7	7	69

[1] *Two golds in 1972 2-man event.*

LUGEING MEDALS – MEN

	Gold	Silver	Bronze
Singles			
1964	Thomas Köhler (GER) 3:26.77	Klaus Bonsack (GER) 3:27.04	Hans Plenk (GER) 3:30.15
1968	Manfred Schmid (AUT) 2:52.48	Thomas Köhler (GDR) 2:52.66	Klaus Bonsack (GDR) 2:55.33
1972	Wolfgang Scheidel (GDR) 3:27.58	Harald Ehrig (GDR) 3:28.39	Wolfram Fiedler (GDR) 3:28.73
1976	Detlef Günther (GDR) 3:27.688	Josef Fendt (FRG) 3:28.196	Hans Rinn (GDR) 3:28.574
1980	Bernhard Glass (GDR) 2:54.796	Paul Hildgartner (ITA) 2:55.372	Anton Winkler (FRG) 2:56.545
1984	Paul Hildgartner (ITA) 3:04.258	Sergey Danilin (URS) 3:04.962	Valeriy Dudin (URS) 3:05.012
1988	Jens Müller (GDR) 3:05.548	Georg Hackl (FRG) 3:05.916	Yuriy Khartchenko (URS) 3:06.274

1908–1960 Event not held.

	Gold	Silver	Bronze
2-Man			
1964	Austria 1:41.62	Austria 1:41.91	Italy 1:42.87
1968	GDR 1:35.85	Austria 1:36.34	FRG 1:37.29
1972	Italy 1:28.35	–	GDR 1:29.16
	GDR 1:28.35		
1976	GDR 1:25.604	FRG 1:25.889	Austria 1:25.919
1980	GDR 1:19.331	Italy 1:19.606	Austria 1:19.795
1984	FRG 1:23.620	Soviet UNion 1:23.660	GDR 1:23.887
1988	GDR 1:31.940	GDR 1:32.039	FRG 1:32.274

1908–1960 Event not held.

LUGEING MEDALS – WOMEN

	Gold	Silver	Bronze
Singles			
1964	Ortrun Enderlein (GER) 3:24.67	Ilse Geisler (GER) 3:27.42	Helene Thurrier (AUT) 3:29.06
1968	Erica Lechner (ITA) 2:28.66	Christa Schmuck (FRG) 2:29.37	Angelika Dünhaupt (FRG) 2:29.56
1972	Anna-Maria Müller (GDR) 2:59.18	Ute Rührold (GDR) 2:59.49	Margit Schumann (GDR) 2:59.54
1976	Margit Schumann (GDR) 2:50.621	Ute Rührold (GDR) 2:50.846	Elisabeth Demleitner (FRG) 2:51.056
1980	Vera Sosulya (URS) 2:36.537	Melitta Sollmann (GDR) 2:37.657	Ingrida Amantova (URS) 2:37.817
1984	Steffi Martin (GDR) 2:46.570	Bettine Schmidt (GDR) 2:46.873	Ute Weiss (GDR) 2:47.248
1988	Steffi Martin-Walter (GDR) 3:03.973	Ute Weiss-Oberhoffner (GDR) 3:04.105	Cerstin Schmidt (GDR) 3:04.181

1908–1960 Event not held.

DISCONTINUED EVENT

Tobogganing – Skeleton Sled

	Gold	Silver	Bronze
1928[1]	Jennison Heaton (USA) 3:01.8	John Heaton (USA) 3:02.8	Earl of Northesk (GBR) 3:05.1
1948[2]	Nino Bibbia (ITA) 5:23.2	John Heaton (USA) 5:24.6	John Crammond (GBR) 5:25.1

[1]Aggregate of three runs.   [2]Aggregate of six runs.

DEMONSTRATION SPORTS

Since 1904 there have been a variety of demonstration sports held as part of the Games but not as official events eligible for medals. Some of them have later become official sports and are mentioned elsewhere. Other than those, there have been the following:

AMERICAN FOOTBALL
In 1932 two teams representing the East and West of America played an exhibition which the West won 7–6.

AUSTRALIAN RULES FOOTBALL
Two amateur Australian teams played an exhibition in 1956 which resulted in a 250–135 score.

BANDY
A tournament was included in the 1952 Winter Games. Final placings were decided on goal average, with Sweden winning from Norway and Finland.

BUDO
Exhibitions of Japanese archery, wrestling and fencing were given in 1964.

CURLING
A three-country contest was held in 1924, won by Great Britain from Sweden and France. In 1932 there were four Canadian Provincial and four American club teams. The Canadians took the first four places with the title won by Manitoba.

In 1936 eight teams from Austria (3), Germany (3) and Czechoslovakia (2) competed in a specialised version of the game, German curling, with the Austrian number one team from the Tyrol winning. The Austrians demonstrated the game in 1964 at Innsbruck, and it was a demonstration sport again in 1988 at Calgary, Canada.

DOG SLED RACING
A race for 12 sled teams, seven dogs to a sled, was held in 1932. There were actually two races of approximately 25 miles/40km each, with the aggregate times added together. The Canadian Emile St Goddard won easily, finishing first both times in a combined 4hr 23min 12.5sec, nearly eight minutes ahead of Lennard Seppala (USA).

GLIDING
Fourteen countries took part in an exhibition in 1936, but the main demonstrations were by German gliders.

MILITARY PATROL
Held at four Winter Games, it is considered to be the forerunner of the official biathlon contests introduced in 1960. Switzerland won in 1924 and 1948, Norway in 1928, and Italy took the 1936 title.

PELOTA BASQUE
Demonstrated in 1924 by teams from Spain and France, and again in 1968 when the same countries were joined by Mexico, Argentina and Uruguay. It will be seen again in 1992.

ROLLER HOCKEY
This will be demonstrated for the first time in 1992.

TAEKWONDO
This was demonstrated in 1988 and will again be on show in 1992.

WATER SKIING
Held in Kiel in 1972 with 36 competitors from 20 countries, including many of the best skiers in the world. Events were won by Roby Zucchi (ITA), Ricky McCormick (USA), Willy Stähle (HOL), Liz Allan-Shetter (USA) and Sylvie Maurial (FRA).

WINTER PENTATHLON
Held in 1948 and comprising a 10km cross-country skiing race, a pistol shoot, fencing, downhill skiing and horse-riding over a distance of 3500m. Gustaf Lindh (SWE) came first, with his team-mate Willie Grut second. Grut won the modern pentathlon in the Summer Games that year by a record margin. In sixth place was Derek Allhusen (GBR) who 20 years later, in his 55th year, won an equestrian gold medal at Mexico City.

INDEX

Date of birth–death given in brackets, where known. Page numbers in italics refer to illustrations; *1–16c* indicates illustration in 16-page colour section.

Abbagnale, Agostino (25 Aug 1966) 92
Abbagnale, Carmine (5 Jan 1962) 86, 92
Abbagnale, Giuseppe (24 Jul 1959) 86, 92
Abrahams, Harold (1899–1978) 27
Absent 130
Adams, Alex 230
Adams, Ben (1890–1961) 189
Adams, Platt (1885–1961) 189, *190*
Aethlius, King of Elis 9
Ahlerich 93, 132
Ahlgren, Anders (1888–1976) 211
Akron 34
Albert, King of Belgium (1875–1934) 23, 96
Albert, Prince of Monaco (14 Mar 1958) 89
Albertville
    Winter Games 1992 93
Albright, Tenley (18 Jul 1935) 46, 50
Alexandra, Queen (1844–1925) 20
Ali Baba 131
Allan-Shetter, Liz (b. 1950) 247
Allen, Richard (4 Jun 1902) 32
Allen, Scott (8 Feb 1949) 58, 106, 230
Allhusen, Derek (9 Jan 1914) 132, 247
Altwegg, Jeannette (8 Sep 1930) 46, 47
Amateur Athletic Association 18
Amateur Swimming Association 18
Amsterdam
    Summer Games 1928 30–32
Andersen, Greta (1 May 1927) 44, 173
Andersen, Hjalmar (12 Mar 1923) 45
Andersson, Agneta (25 Apr 1961) 120
Anding, Carola (29 Dec 1960) 234
Andrada, Manuel (9 Jan 1890) 224
André, Georges (1889–1943) 27, 96
Andreyev, Sergey (16 May 1956) 170
Andrianov, Nikolai (14 Oct 1952) 74, 77, 96, 104, *105*, 140
Anker, Johann (1871–1940) 32
Anquetil, Jacques (8 Jan 1934) 125
Antwerp
    Summer Games 1920 23–25
Arrachion of Phigalia 112
Ashenfelter, Horace (23 Jan 1923) 48
Asikáinen, Alfred (1888–1942) 21, 211
Aste, Paul 57, 96
Astor, John Jacob (1886–1971) 224
Athens
    Summer Games 1896 12–13
    Summer Games 1906 16–17
Atlanta
    Summer Games 1996 94
Aumoitte 223
Averina, Tatyana (25 Jun 1950) 71, 104
Averoff (Avykeris), Georgios 12
Ayat, Albert (1876–1935) 135

Baas-Kaiser, Christina (20 May 1938) 66, 241
Babashoff, Shirley (31 Jan 1957) 171
Babinov, Sergey (11 Jul 1955) 72
Bagriantseva, Elisabeta (27 Aug 1929) 189
Baier, Ernst (27 Sep 1905) 38, 230
Baillet-Latour, Count Henri de (1876–1942) 23, 36, 39, 98
Baker (Noel-Baker), Philip (1889–1982) 24
Baker, Reg 'Snowy' (1886–1953) 113
Balck, General Victor (1844–1929) *11*
Balczó, András (16 Aug 1938) 70, 153, *155*
Balk, Klaas (27 Dec 1949) *126*
Ball, Rudi (27 Mar 1910) 38
Ballangrud, Ivar (1904–69) 38, 241
Banach, Ed (6 Feb 1960) 86, 211
Banach, Lou (6 Feb 1960) 86, 211
Barcelona
    Summer Games 1992 94
Barker, Val 114
Barré, Pascal (12 Apr 1959) 189
Barré, Patrick (12 Apr 1959) 189
Barthel, Josy (24 Apr 1927) 48
Basilio, Enriqueta (15 Jul 1948) 62, 98
Bassham, Lanny (2 Jan 1947) 75, 162
Baumann, Dieter (9 Feb 1965) *5c*
Baumler, Hansjürgen (28 Jan 1942) 58
Baxter, Irving (1876–1957) 14, *14*
Beamon, Bob (29 Aug 1946) 62
Behrendt, Wolfgang (14 Jul 1936) 54
Belistike of Macedonia 10
Belita 38, 230
Beloglazov, Anatoliy (16 Sep 1956) 81, 211
Beloglazov, Sergey (16 Sep 1956) 81, 211
Belousova (Protopopov), Ludmila (22 Nov 1935) *57*, 58, 61
Belov, Aleksandr (1951–78) 110
Belov, Sergey (23 Jan 1944) 98, 110
Bene, Ferenc (17 Dec 1944) 169, 170
Benninga, Carina (18 Aug 1962) 151
Benninga, Marc (15 Feb 1961) 151
Benter, Uwe (1 Dec 1955) 70
Benvenuti, Giovanni 'Nino' (26 Apr 1938) 114
Beresford, Jack (1899–1977) 156
Beresford, Julius (1868–1959) 156, 157, 158
Berger, Samuel (1884–1925) 113
Berlin
    Summer Games 1936 38–41
Berry, Arthur (4 Jan 1888) 169
Berthod, Madeleine (1 Feb 1931) 50, 226
Beyer, Gisela (16 Jul 1960) 149

Beyer, Hans-Georg (3 Sep 1956) 148
Beyer, Udo (14 Apr 1945) 148
Bibbia, Nino (9 Sep 1924) 42
Bickford, James 105
Bie, Ferdinand (1888–1961) 22
Biebl, Heidi (17 Feb 1941) 54
Bikila, Abebe (1932–73) 55, 59, 64
Biondi, Matt (8 Oct 1965) 92
Blagoyev, Blagoi (4 Dec 1956) 208
Blanchonnet, Armand (1903–68) 28
Blankers-Koen, Fanny (26 Apr 1918) 43, 188
Bleibtrey, Ethelda (1902–78) 24
Blixen-Finecke jr, Hans von (20 Jul 1916) 130
Blixen-Finecke sr, Hans von (1886–1917) 130
Böhling, Ivar (1889–1921) 211
Bogen, Albert (1882–1961) 135
Bogen, Erna (31 Dec 1906) 135
Bogner, Wilhelm 37, 96
Bohr, Harald (1887–1951) 169
Bohr, Niels (1885–1962) 169
Boin, Victor (1886–1974) 23, 96
Boisvert, Serge 89
Boiteux, Jean (20 Jun 1933) 48
Boland, John Pius (1870–1958) 13, 186
Boldt, Harry (23 Feb 1930) 75
Boltenstern, Gustav-Adolf (15 May 1904) 130, 131
Bonhag, George (1882–1960) 16
Borozna, Ludmila (2 Jan 1954) 207
Borzov, Valeriy (20 Oct 1949) 68
Bouin, Jean (1888–1914) 20
Boúrquin, Hans (b. 1914) 32
Boutovsky, A de *11*
Boxhall, Neroli (9 Oct 1961) 149
Boyarskikh, Klaudia (11 Nov 1939) 58
Bradl, Sepp (1918–84) 105, 236
Bradley, Bill (28 Jul 1943) 60
Branko, Jure (28 Mar 1962) 82
Bréal, Michel 13
Breland, Mark (11 May 1963) 114
Brendel, Jakob (1907–64) *212*
Brenden, Hallgeir (10 Feb 1929) 46, 50
Brezhnev, Leonid (1906–82) 77, 96
Brietzke, Siegfried (12 Jun 1952) 157
Brisco-Hooks, Valerie (6 Jul 1960) *84*, 85
Brockmann, Hermanus (b. 1871) 158
Brookes, Dr William Penny (1809–95) 11
Brookins, Charles (17 Sep 1899) 27
Broome, David (1 Mar 1940) 93
Brown, Charles (1867–1937) 224
Brix, Herman (Bruce Bennett) (1906–78) *192*
Brumel, Valeriy (14 Apr 1942) 131
Brundage, Avery (1887–1975) 22, 38, 50, 98, 110

Brunet (Joly), Andrée (16 Sep 1901) 34
Brunet, Pierre (28 Jun 1902) 34
Bryzgin, Viktor (22 Aug 1962) 92, 189
Bryzgina, Olga (30 Jun 1963) 92, 189
Buchan, William (9 May 1935) 86
Buchan jr, William (23 Dec 1956) 86
Bukic, Perica (20 Nov 1966) 86
Buldakova, Ludmila (25 May 1938) 207
Buidaa, Bakhaavaa (20 May 1946) 70, 151
Bures, Otomar 132
Burghley, Lord (1905–81) 30, 36, 43
Burleson, Tommy (14 Feb 1952) 70, 112
Burnell, Charles (1876–1969) 157
Burnell, Richard (26 Jul 1917) 157
Burtsev, Mikhail (21 Jun 1956) 136
Button, Dick (18 Jul 1929) *41*, 42, 46, 230

Calgary
  Winter Games 1988 86–9
Calmat, Alain (31 Aug 1940) 60
Calnan, George (1900–33) 34, 96
Cameron, Michelle (28 Dec 1962) 174
Campbell-Grey, Ian (14 Jul 1901) *138*
Capes, Lee (3 Oct 1961) 151
Capes, Michelle (3 Oct 1966) 151
Caroli, Guido 50
Carlos, John (5 Jun 1945) 63
Carlberg, Eric (1880–1963) 21, 162
Carlberg, Vilhelm (1880–1970) 21, 162
Carlsson, Henry (29 Oct 1917) 170
Carlsson, Herbert (1896–1952) 170
Carpenter, John C 19
Carpenter-Phinney, Connie (20 Feb 1957) 125
Carroll, Daniel (1892–1956) 24, 224
Cáslavská, Vera (3 May 1942) *62*, 64, 140
Castro, Domingos (22 Nov 1963) *5c*
Catherwood, Ethel (2 May 1910)
Cavanagh, Roberto (12 Nov 1914) 224
Celio, President Enrico (1889–1980) 42, 96
Cerutti, Paul (30 Nov 1910) 163
Cesana, Giorgio (14 Apr 1892) 17
Chambers, Dorothea (1878–1960) 20
Chamonix
  Winter Games 1924 25–26
Chand, Dhyand (1907–79) 149
Charisma 132, *9c*
Charpentier, Robert (1916–66) 40, 124
Chataway, Chris (31 Jan 1931) 48
Chenal-Minuzzo, Giuliana (26 Nov 1931) 50, 96
Chionis of Sparta 10
Choe, Myong Hui (13 Jun 1966) 81
Chouchounova, Yelena (23 May 1969) 141
Christian, Bill (29 Jan 1938) 234
Christian, Dave (12 May 1959) 234
Christian, Roger (1 Dec 1935) 234
Christie, Linford (4 Apr 1960) *5c*
Chukarin, Viktor (1921–84) 49
Chun-Ae, Lim (1 Jul 1969) 90
Cierpinski, Waldemar (3 Aug 1950) 79
Clarke, Ron (21 Feb 1937) 51, 59, 62, 98
Claudius, Leslie (25 Mar 1927) 149
Clay, Cassius (Muhammad Ali) (17 Jan 1942) *56*, 57, 114

Cleary, Bill (19 Aug 1934) 234
Cleary, Bob (21 Apr 1936) 234
Clement, Elspeth (19 Jun 1956) 93
Coakes, Marion (6 Jun 1947) 131
Coates, Colin (4 Apr 1946) 105, 241
Coats, James (1894–1966) 106, 245
Cochran, Barbara (4 Jan 1951) 65
Cochran, Bob 65
Cochran, Marilyn 65
Codrean, Roman (17 Nov 1952) 81
Coe, Sebastian (29 Sep 1956) 79, *79*, *11c*
Coffin, Edmund (9 May 1955) 130
Colledge, Cecilia (28 Nov 1920) 34, 106, 230
Colo, Zeno (30 Jun 1920) 225
Comaneci, Nadia (12 Nov 1961) 72, *73*, 75, 77, 141
Conner, Dennis (16 Sep 1942) 221
Connolly, Harold (1 Aug 1931) 54
Connolly, James Brendan (1865–1957) 13, 187
Consolini, Adolfo (1917–69) 58, 96
Constantine, Crown Prince (1866–1923) 12, 13
Constantine, Crown Prince (later King) (2 Jun 1940) 56
Conti, Giacomo (24 Jun 1908) 50
Cook, Gary (10 Jan 1958) 86
Cook, Kathy (3 May 1960) 86
Cooper, Charlotte (1870–1966) 14, 186
Cooper, Cynthia (14 Apr 1963) *6c*
Copeland, Lillian (1904–64) 36
Corbett, 'Gentleman Jim' (1866–1933) 113
Cornellie, Emile (1869–1945) 220
Cornellie, Florimond (1 May 1894) 220
Coroibis of Elis 9
Corsiglia, Robin (12 Aug 1962) 75
Cortina d'Ampezzo
  Winter Games 1956 50
Costello, Bernard (12 Mar 1929) 156
Costello, Paul (1899–1986) 156, 157
Costie, Candy (12 Mar 1963) 174
Cotswold Olympic Games 11
Coubertin, Pierre de Fredi, Baron de (1863–1937) 11, *11*, 12, 13, 15, 20, 23, 30, 36, 43, 94, 98, 161, 224
Cousins, Robin (17 Mar 1957) 46, 77
Crabbe, Clarence 'Buster' (1910–83) 173
Craig, Ralph (1889–1972) 20, 44
Cram, Steve (14 Oct 1960) *11c*
Cranz, Christl (1 Jul 1914) 38, 54, 226
Cripps, Winsome (9 Feb 1931) *49*
Cruz, Nadia (12 Jul 1975) 93
Cruz, Teofilo (1 Aug 1942) 110
Cuelenaere, Philippe (2 Sep 1971) 86
Cunningham, Glenn (1909–88) 40
Currie, Lorne (1871–1926) 220
Curry, John (9 Sep 1949) 46, 72, *231*
Curtis, Charles (1860–1936) 34, 96
Curtius, Ernst (1814–96) 11
Cushing, Alexander 54
Cuthbert, Betty (20 Apr 1938) 51, 188
Cvetkovic, Borislav (30 Sep 1962) 170

Daly, John (b. 1880) 15
Daniels, Charles (1885–1973) 15, 19, 171
Da Silva, Robson (4 Sep 1964) *5c*
Davenport, Willie (8 Jun 1943) 77

Davis, Howard (14 Feb 1956) 114
Davis, Walt (5 Jan 1931) 48
Day, Jim (7 Jul 1946) 131
Dean, Christopher (27 Jul 1958) 82, 231, *13c*
Deardurff, Deena (8 May 1957) 70
Décugis, Marie (1884–1969) 186
Décugis, Max (1882–1978) 186
De Gaulle, General Charles (1890–1970) 60, 96
Delaney, Ronnie (6 Mar 1935) 51
Delle-Barth, Werner 70, 96
DeLoach, Joe (5 Jun 1967) *5c*
DeMont, Rick (21 Apr 1956) 68, 70
Dench, Patricia (8 Mar 1932) 86
Deni, John 189
Denis, Harris (1896–1971) 96
Dennis, Claire (1916–71) 36
Derbyshire, John (1878–1938) 106
Desborough, Lord (1855–1945) 18
Desjardins, Pete (10 Apr 1907) 31
Desmarteau, Etienne (1873–1905) 15
Deveric, Stjepan (20 Aug 1961) 170
Devitt, John (4 Feb 1937) 56, 171
Deyna, Kazimiercz (23 Oct 1947) 170
Dibiasi, Klaus (6 Oct 1947) 74, 173
Dickson, Robert (22 Apr 1931) 46
Didon, Father Henri (1840–1900) 26
Didrikson, Mildred 'Babe' (1914–56) *35*, 36, 188
Diem, Carl (1882–1962) 38
Diers, Ines (2 Nov 1963) 79
Diesch, Eckhardt (1 May 1954) 75
Diesch, Jörg (29 Sep 1951) 75
Diessner, Ullrich (27 Dec 1954) 75, 81
Diessner, Walter (27 Dec 1954) 75, 81
Dietrich, Wilfried (19 Oct 1933) 211
Dijkstra, Sjoukje (28 Jan 1942) 58
Dillard, Harrison (8 Jul 1923) 44, 48
Dinwiddie, Marcus (1907–51) 162
Disney, Walt (1901–66) 54
Dityatin, Aleksandr (7 Aug 1957) 77, *78*, 104, 140, 141
Dixon, Robin (21 Apr 1935) *58*, 58
Djemal, M (b. 1911) 208
Dod, Charlotte 'Lottie' (1871–1960) 107
Dod, William (1867–1954) 107
Doe, Charles (4 Sep 1898) 224
Doe jr, Thomas (1912–69) 229
Doherty, Laurie (1875–1919) 186
Doherty, Reggie (1872–1910) 186
Dollinger, Marie (28 Oct 1910) 189
Donovan, Anne (1 Nov 1961) 112
Douglas, John (1882–1930) 112
Doumergue, Pres. Gaston (1863–1937) 26, 96
Downing, Burton (1885–1929) 124
Doyle, Sir Arthur Conan (1859–1930) 20
Drapeau, Jean (b. 1916) 72
Draves, Vicki (31 Dec 1924) 44
Drobny, Jaroslav (12 Oct 1921) 234
Dubravcic, Sanda (24 Aug 1964) 81
Ducret, Roger (1888–1962) 28, 135
Dunai, Antal (21 Mar 1943) 169
Dunn, Velma (9 Oct 1918) *172*
Dupont, Helena (6 Jul 1939) 132
Duquesne, Lucien 30
Durack, Fanny (1893–1956) *171*
Duralyev, Osman (15 Jan 1939) *215*

Duvall, Samuel Harding (1836–1908) 16, 109
Dyrssen, Gustaf (1891–1981) 154

Eagan, Eddie (1897–1967) 34, 106, 229
Ederle, Gertrude (23 Oct 1906) 28, 173
Edinburgh, Prince Philip, Duke of (10 Jun 1921) 51, 96
Edström, Sigfrid (1870–1964) 22, 47, 98
Edward VII, King (1841–1910) 18, 96
Edwards, Eddie (5 Dec 1963) 87
Edwards, Teresa (19 Jul 1964) 112
Egan, Chandler (1884–1936) 223
Eidenbenz, Hans 28, 96
Ekhardt, Carl (1897–1988) 233
Elek, Ilona (1907–88) 39, 40, 44, 45, 49, 136
Elek, Margit 44
Eliot, Launceston (1873–1930) 208, 211
Eliot 131
Elizabeth II, Queen (21 Apr 1926) 72, 96
Elliott, Herb (25 Feb 1938) 55, *55*
Elvström, Paul (25 Feb 1928) 56, 93, 105, 188, 220, 221
Elvström, Trine (6 Mar 1962) 93, 220
Emirzyan, Zirvard (5 Jun 1966) 81
Ender, Kornelia (25 Oct 1958) 74, 171
Enderlein, Ortrun (1 Dec 1943) 245
Endt, Everard (7 Apr 1893) 49, 220
Enke (Kania), Karin (20 Jun 1961) 77, *88*, 89, 104, 241
Erhardt, Carl (1897–1988) 38, 233
Eriksen, Harald (3 Jul 1888) 141
Eriksen, Stein (11 Dec 1927) *45* 45
Eriksson, Carl Erik (20 May 1930) 72, 83, 105, 229
Ewing, Patrick (5 Aug 1962) 110
Ewry, Ray (1873–1937) *14*, 14, 15, 16, 19, 104, 187
Eyser, George (b. 1871) 141

Fahrner, Thomas (2 Jul 1963) 171
Fairhall, Neroli (26 Aug 1944) 109
Falkanger, Torbjörn (8 Oct 1927) 45, 96
Fanshawe, Capt Richard (22 Jun 1906) 40, 132
Farias, Romario (29 Jan 1966) 170
Fasser, Ekkehard (3 Sep 1952) 89
Fassi, Carlo 46, 72, 231
Fassi, Christa 231
Fazlic, Jasna (20 Dec 1970) 185
Fedotkin, Aleksandr (3 Nov 1955) *80*
Feistmantl, Josef (23 Feb 1939) 70
Ferguson, Ian (20 Jul 1952) 120
Fernandez-Ochoa, Francisco (25 Feb 1950) 65
Fields (Finkelstein), Jackie (1908–87) 28, 113, 114
Figini, Michela (7 Apr 1966) 82, 83, 225, *14c*
Figuerola, Enrique (25 Jul 1938) *59*
Fikotova, Olga (13 Nov 1932) 54
Filatov, Sergey (25 Sep 1926) 130
Findlay, Conn (24 Apr 1930) 158, 221
Finland 20
Finlay, Donald (1909–70) 96
Fischer, Birgit (25 Feb 1962) 120
Fisher, Morris (1890–1968) 161
Fiske, William (1911–40) 30, 106, 229
Flameng, Léon (1877–1917) 124

Flanagan, John (1873–1938) 19
Fleming, Peggy (27 Jul 1948) 46, 61
Fogh, Hans (8 Mar 1938) 221
Fonst, Ramón (1883–1959) 135, 136
Foreman, George (10 Jan 1949) 114
Formo, Ivar (24 Jun 1951) 234
Fortuna, Wojciech (6 Aug 1952) 66, 236
Fosbury, Dick (6 Mar 1947) *63*, 63
Foster, William (1890–1963) 20
Fox, Francine (16 Mar 1949) 121
Fox, Jim (19 Sep 1941) 154
Francis, David 96
Francis, Ranganandhan (15 Mar 1920) 149
Frederika, Queen 56
Fredriksson, Gert (21 Nov 1919) 120
Fried, Edgar (b. 1894) 70
Fraser, Dawn (4 Sep 1937) 60, 171, *179*
Fraser, Gretchen (11 Feb 1919) 47
Frazier, Joe (12 Jan 1944) 114
Frossi, Annibale (6 Aug 1911) 170
Fuchs, Gottfried (1889–1972) 169, 170
Fuchs, Jenö (1882–1955) 136

Gailly, Etienne (1922–71) 44
Galic, Milan (8 Mar 1938) 170
Garcia, Russell (20 Jun 1970) 149
Garmisch-Partenkirchen
   Winter Games 1936 37–8
Garrett, Robert (1875–1961) 13, *14*, 188
Garrido, Pablo (22 Jun 1938) 96
Gebhardt, Dr Willibald (1861–1921) *11*
Gedovari, Imre (1 Jul 1951) *7c*
Geesink, Anton (6 Apr 1934) 60, 151
Genaro, Frankie (1901–66) 114
Généreux, George (1 Mar 1935) 162
Gentiule, Giuseppe (4 Sep 1943) 192
George, James (1 Jun 1935) 208
George, Peter (29 Jun 1929) 208
George, King of Greece (1845–1913) 12, 96
George VI, King (1895–1952) 43, 45, 96
George, Prince of Greece 13, *17*, 208
Georgiadis, Jean (1874–1960) 136
Gerevich, Aladár (16 Mar 1910) 56, 135, 136
Gerevich, Pal (10 Aug 1948) 135
Gerhard, Friedrich (1884–1950) 40
Germeshausen, Bernhard (21 Aug 1951) 229
Gestring, Marjorie (18 Nov 1922) 40, 106, 173
Gil-Pak, Jong (14 Jan 1951) 151
Giorgetti, Franco (13 Oct 1902) 125
Glass, Harry (11 Oct 1930) 56
Goebbels, Josef (1897–1945) 38
Götze, Bruno (1882–1913) 124
Götze, Max (1880–1944) 124
Gogoladze, Vladimir (13 Aug 1966) 141
Goitschel, Christine (9 Jun 1944) 58
Goitschel, Marielle (28 Sep 1948) 58, 61, 225
Golian, Bohumil (25 Mar 1931) 207
Golubnichiy, Vladimir (2 Jun 1936) 191
Gonzalez, Raul (18 Apr 1964) 114
Goodell, Brian (2 Apr 1959) 75
Gordiyeva, Ekaterina (28 May 1971) 89
Gordon-Watson, Mary (3 Apr 1948) 132
Gorokhovskaya, Maria (17 Oct 1921) 49, 104
Gossler, Carl (1885–1914) 156

Gossler, Gustav (1879–1940) 156
Gossler, Oskar (1875–1953) 156
Gould, Jay (1888–1935) 224
Gould, Shane (23 Nov 1956) 68
Gozzi, Giovanni (18 Oct 1902) *212*
Graf, Steffi (14 Jul 1969) 186, *7c*
Grafström, Gilles (1893–1938) 26, 30, 33, 230
Gravelotte, Emile (1876–1939) 135
Gray, Clifford (29 Jan 1892) 229
Greene, Nancy (11 May 1943) 226
Grenoble
   Winter Games 1968 60–2
Gretton, John (1867–1947) 220
Griffith-Joyner, Florence (21 Dec 1959) 92, *4c*
Grishin, Yevgeniy (23 Nov 1931) 50, 54
Gronchi, Pres. Giovanni (1887–1978) 50, 55, 96
Gross, Manuela (29 Jan 1957) 66, 106, 230
Grut, Torben 20
Grut, Willie (17 Sep 1914) 42, 44, 153, *154*, 247
Guerrero, Ruben (1 Nov 1954) 64
Guillemot, Joseph (1899–1975) 24
Gunn, Richard (1871–1961) 113
Guoqiang, Zeng (18 Mar 1965) 208
Gushiken, Koji (12 Nov 1956) 141
Guss, Sam (10 Jun 1965) 82
Gustafsson, Toini (17 Jan 1938) 61
Gustafsson, Tomas (28 Dec 1959) 82
Gustav V, King of Sweden (1858–1950) 20, 21, 96
Guth-Jarkovsky, Jiri *11*
Guts Muth, Johann (1759–1839) 11
Gyarmati, Andrea (15 May 1954) 174
Gyarmati, Dezsö (23 Oct 1927) 48, 60, 174

Haakon, King of Norway (1872–1957) 45
Haas, Christl (19 Sep 1943) 70
Haase, Helga (9 Jun 1934) 54
Haegeman, Aimé 130
Hahn, Archie (1880–1955) 15, 63
Hahn, Norbert (6 Jan 1954) 245
Haifeng, Xu (10 Aug 1957) 85
Hajós, Alfred (1878–1955) 13, 171
Hakulinen, Veikko (4 Jan 1925) 54, 234
Halberg, Murray (7 Jul 1933) 55
Halderson, Burdette (12 Jan 1934) 110
Hall, Lars (30 Apr 1927) 153
Halla 131
Halmay, Zoltan von (1881–1956) 19
Halswelle, Wyndham (1882–1915) 19
Hämäläinen, Marja-Liisa (10 Sep 1955) 82, 83, 104, 234
Hamill, Dorothy (26 Jul 1956) 46, 72
Hamrin, Sten (30 Mar 1941) 124
Handley, Louis (1874–1956) 171
Hansen, Alf (13 Jul 1948) 75
Hansen, Frank (4 Aug 1945) 75
Hansen, Karl Aage (4 Jul 1921) 170
Happe, Ursula (20 Oct 1926) 171
Harald, Prince of Norway (21 Feb 1937) 31
Hardin, Glenn (1910–75) 36
Hartel, Lis (14 Mar 1921) 130, 131
Hartono, Rudy 110
Harvey, Pierre (24 Mar 1957) 87, 96

Haug, Thorleif (1894–1934) 26
Haugen, Anders (1888–1984) 26, 236
Hayes, Bob (20 Dec 1942) 59, 59
Hayes, Johnny (1886–1965) 20
Haywood, Spencer (22 Apr 1949) 110, 112
Heaton, Jennison (1903–71) 30, 245
Heaton, John (9 Sep 1908) 30, 42, 105, 245
Hecher, Gertraud (28 Sep 1943) 55, 225
Hedlund, Per Erik (1897–1975) 234
Hegg, Steve (3 Dec 1963) 10c
Heggtveit, Anne (11 Jan 1939) 54, 226
Heida, Anton (b. 1878) 15
Heiden, Beth (27 Sep 1959) 76
Heiden, Eric (14 Jun 1958) 76, 96, 104, 241
Heineman, Pres. Gustav (1899–1976) 67, 96
Heiss, Carol (20 Jan 1940) 54, 96
Helsinki
    Summer Games 1952 46–50
Hemmi, Heini (17 Jan 1949) 226
Hemphill, Gina 83
Hencken, John (29 May 1954) 74
Henderson, Sandra (b. 1961) 72, 98
Hendrik, Prince of the Netherlands 30, 96
Hendrix, Brunhilde (2 Aug 1938) 189
Henie, Sonja (1912–69) 26, 29, 30, 33, 34, 38, 230
Henning, Anne (6 Sep 1955) 66, 241
Henry, Bill 36
Henry, Ken (7 Jan 1929) 54
Henry, William (28 Jun 1859) 171
Herald, William (13 Mar 1897) 171
Herber, Maxi (8 Oct 1920) 38, 106, 230
Hériot, Virginie (1890–1932) 32, 220
Herodes Atticus (101–177) 12
Hesz, Mihaly (15 Dec 1943)174
Hickcox, Charles (6 Feb 1947) 64
Hicks, Thomas (1875–1963) 16
Hildgartner, Paul (8 Jun 1952) 245
Hill, Albert (1889–1969) 23, 24
Hill, Ralph (26 Dec 1908) 36
Hillman, Harry (1881–1945) 15
Hillyard, George (1864–1943) 186
Himmler, Heinrich (1900–45) 38
Hin, Franciscus (29 Jan 1906) 220
Hin, Johannes (3 Jan 1898) 220
Hindenburg 38
Hirohito, Emperor of Japan (1901–89) 59, 65, 96
Hitler, Adolf (1889–1945) 37, 38, 96
Hochleitner, Dorothea (10 Jul 1925) 225
Hoffmann, Georg 173
Hoffmann, Jan (26 Oct 1955) 61, 106, 230
Hofmann, Fritz (1871–1927) 13
Hofschmid, Willy (9 Oct 1918) 148
Hogshead, Nancy (17 Apr 1962) 171
Ho Jun, Li (1 Dec 1946) 163
Holdmann, Anni (28 Jan 1900) 30, 187
Holgate (Leng), Virginia (1 Feb 1955) 131, 131
Holm, Eleanor (6 Dec 1913) 173
Holm, Tore (1896–1977) 221
Holmer, Ulrike (6 Oct 1967) 162
Holzner-Pflug, Monika (1 Mar 1954) 89, 105

Hook, Harvey (b. 1936) 89
Hoover, Herbert (1874–1964) 34
Hörnlein, Horst (31 May 1945) 89
Horvath, George (14 Mar 1960) 154
Hoskyns, Bill (19 Mar 1931) 135
Houben, Max (1898–1949) 42, 105, 106
Hougland, Bill (20 Jun 1930) 110
Howell, Lida (1859–1939) 16
Hruba-Ralston, Vera (b. 1921) 230
Hubacher, Edy (15 Apr 1940) 230
Hubbard, William DeHart (1903–76) 26
Huber, Herbert (1944–70) 61
Huelamo, Jaime (17 Nov 1948) 70
Humphreys, Frederick (1878–1954) 192
Hunter, George (22 Jul 1927) 44, 114
Hunty, Shirley de la see Strickland
Hurley, Marcus (1885–1941) 124, 151
Huybrechts, Leon (1876–1956) 220
Hyang-Soo, Seo (8 Jul 1967) 109

Igaya, Chiharu (20 May 1931) 50
Innauer, Toni (1 Apr 1958) 72, 236
Innis, Hubert van (1866–1961) 24, 107, 109
Innsbruck
    Winter Games 1964 57–8
    Winter Games 1976 70–2
Inoue, Kikuko (3 Dec 1924) 93
International Olympic Committee
    Inauguration 12
    Presidents 98
International Ski Federation 26
Inzeo, Raimondo d' (8 Feb 1925) 75, 105, 130
Iphitus, King of Elis 9
Ismayr, Rudolf (14 Oct 1908) 96
Iso-Hollo, Volmari (1907–69) 40
Ivanov, Vyacheslav (30 Jul 1938) 53, 60, 157, 158

Jackson, Grace (14 Jun 1961) 84
Jackson, Marjorie (13 Sep 1931) 46, 49
Jacobus, Charles (1859–1929) 224
Jae, Hur (28 Sep 1965) 90, 96
Järvinen, Akilles (1905–43) 189
Järvinen, Matti (1909–85) 189
Järvinen, Werner (1870–1941) 189
Jaffe, Irving (1906–81) 28, 241
Jakobsson, Ludowika (1884–1968) 25, 26, 30, 106, 230
Jakobsson, Walter (1882–1957) 25, 26, 30, 230
Jenkins, David (29 Jun 1936) 50, 54
Jenkins, Hayes (23 Nov 1933) 50, 54
Jenner, Bruce (28 Oct 1949) 83, 192
Jensen, Knut (d. 1960) 57, 124)
Jensen, Viggo (1874–1930) 106, 208
Jepson-Turner, Gladys (b. 1924) 38, 230
Jernberg, Sixten (6 Feb 1929) 50, 58, 104, 234, 235
Jerome, Harry (1940–82) 59
Jewtraw, Charles (5 May 1900) 26
Jing, Chen (20 Sep 1968) 185, 185
Jobier, Henri (b. 1879) 135
Jochum-Beiser, Trude (2 Sep 1927) 225
Johannesen, Knut (6 Nov 1933) 54
Johansson, Greta (1895–1978) 22
Johansson, Hjalmar (1874–1957) 173
Johansson, Ingemar (22 Sep 1932) 49, 113
Johansson, Ivar (1903–79) 40, 211, 212

Johin 223
Johnson, Ben (30 Dec 1961) 92, 92, 189
Johnson, Bill (30 Mar 1960) 82, 225, 226
Johnson, Cornelius (1913–46) 40
Johnson, Marvin (12 Apr 1954) 114
Johnson, Rafer (18 Aug 1934) 56, 83, 98, 192
Johnson, Roy 21
Johnson, Tebbs Lloyd (1900–84) 189
Johnstone, Lorna (1902–90) 64, 70, 106, 132
Jokiel, Anita (2 Dec 1966) 81
Jonck, Teunist (b. 1896) 208
Jones, Barbara (26 Mar 1937) 46, 50, 188, 189
Jones, KC (25 May 1932) 110
Jones, Roy (16 Jan 1969) 93, 114, 6c
Jones, Dr William 110
Jong-Il, Byun (16 Nov 1968) 93
Jordan, Michael (17 Feb 1963) 110
Josephson, Karen (10 Jan 1964) 174
Josephson, Sarah (10 Jan 1964) 174
Jousseaume, André (1894–1960) 49
Joyner, Al (19 Jan 1960) 86
Joyner-Kersee, Jackie (3 Mar 1962) 86, 92
Juantorena, Alberto (21 Nov 1950) 75
Juhász-Nagy, Katalin (24 Nov 1932) 60
Jung-Hwa, Hyun (6 Oct 1969) 185

Kachkarov, Yuriy (4 Dec 1963) 235
Kaczmarek, Zbigniew (21 Jul 1946) 208
Kahanemoku, Duke (1890–1968) 21, 24, 171, 173
Kajosmaa, Marjatta (3 Feb 1938) 72
Kalama, Thelma (24 Mar 1931) 44
Kalita, Ivan (14 Jan 1927) 130
Kamamoto, Kunishige (15 Apr 1944) 170
Kaminaga, Akio (22 Dec 1936) 151
Karasevdas, Pantelis (1877–1946) 161
Karlova, Larissa (7 Aug 1958) 148
Kárpáti, György (23 Jun 1935) 174
Kárpáti, Rudolf (17 Jul 1920) 136
Karppinen, Pertti (17 Feb 1953) 157
Kasaya, Yukio (17 Aug 1943) 236
Katseli, Aleka 39
Keino, Kipchoge (17 Jan 1940) 69, 70
Keleti, Agnes (9 Jan 1921) 53, 141
Kelly, Grace, Princess of Monaco (1928–82) 24
Kelly Jr, John (1927–85) 24, 53, 89, 156
Kelly Sr, John (1890–1960) 24, 89, 156, 157
Kemény, François 11
Kemser, Franz (11 Nov 1910) 46
Kent-Hughes, WS 54
Kerr, Dr Charles 76
Keserü, Alajos (1905–65) 174
Keserü, Ferenc (1903–68) 174
Kharikov, Sergey (17 Nov 1970) 93
Kiefer, Adolph (27 Jun 1918) 40
Kiely, Thomas (1869–1951) 15
Kilius, Marika (24 Mar 1943) 58
Killanin, Lord, Michael Morris, (30 Jul 1914) 98
Killy, Jean-Claude (30 Aug 1943) 60, 61, 71, 93, 225
Kim, Nelli (29 Jul 1957) 74, 141
Kirchschläger, Dr Rudolf (20 Mar 1915) 70, 96

Kirk, Oliver (20 Apr 1884) 113
Kirksey, Morris (1895–1982) 106, 224
Kitamura, Kusuo (9 Oct 1917) 36, 171
Klammer, Franz (3 Dec 1953) *71*, 71
Klein, Martin (1884–1947) 21
Klimke, Reiner (14 Jan 1936) 86, 93,
  130, 132
Klimov, Yuriy (22 Jul 1940) 148
Knowles, Durward (2 Nov 1917) 44, 93,
  105, 220
Koch, Bill (7 Jun 1955) 71, 234
Kochergina, Tatyana (26 Mar 1956) 148
Köhler, Kathe (10 Nov 1913) *172*
Köhler, Thomas (25 Jun 1940) 245
Kolar-Merdan, Jasna (19 Oct 1956) 148
Kolehmainen, Hannes (1889–1966) 20,
  22, 46, 98, 188
Koltschina, Alevtina (11 Feb 1930) 58,
  61
Kondylis 39
Kono, Tommy (27 Jun 1930) 208
Konopacka, Halina (1900–89) 187
Konow, Magnus (1887–1972) 20, 105,
  220
Kopylov, Sergey (29 Jul 1960) 125
Korbut, Olga (16 May 1955) 68, 72, 140
Kostic, Borivoje (14 Jun 1930) 170
Kovács, Pal (17 Jul 1912) 136
Kovácsi, Aladár (11 Dec 1932) 154
Kraenzlein, Alvin (1876–1929) 14, *14*,
  187
Krause, Roswitha (3 Nov 1949) 106, 149
Kreiner, Kathy (4 May 1957) 72, 226
Krizaj, Bojan (3 Jan 1957) 81, 96
Krovopouskov, Viktor (29 Sep 1948) 136
Kruyff, Gerard de (1890–1968) 132
Kulakova, Galina (29 Apr 1942) 65, *66*,
  71, 72, 76, 234
Kungler, Frank 16, 106
Kunze, Hansjörg (28 Dec 1959) *5c*
Kurland, Bob (23 Dec 1942) 110
Kuts, Vladimir (1927–75) 51

La Barba, Fidel (1905–81) 114
Lachtchenova, Natalya (16 Sep 1973) 93
Lacroix, Leo (26 Nov 1937) 60, 96
La Fortuno Jr, François 163
La Fortuno Sr, François 163
Lake Placid
  Winter Games 1932 32–4
  Winter Games 1980 75–7
Lamour, Jean François (2 Feb 1956) 136
Landon, Dick (1898–1971) 25
Landvoigt, Bernd (23 Nov 1951) 75, 81,
  156
Landvoigt, Jörg (23 Nov 1951) 75, 81,
  156
Landy, John (12 Apr 1930) 96
Lane, Alfred (26 Sep 1891) 161
Lane, Francis (1875–1927) 13, 187
Lapébie, Guy (28 Nov 1916) 124
Larking, Gunhild (13 Jan 1936) 53
Larsen, Roald (1898–1959) 104
Larson, Lance (3 Jul 1940) 56, 171
Larsson, Gunnar (12 May 1951) 68, 171
Lasko, Lech (2 Jun 1956) 207
Latynina, Larissa (27 Dec 1934) 60, 79,
  104, 140
Lauria, Louis (19 Nov 1919) 114
Lazzaro, Francisco (d. 1912) 22
Leaf, Henry (1862–1931) 224

Leahy, Con (1876–1921) 189
Leahy, Patrick (1877–1926) 189
Leconey, Alfred (1901–59) 34
Lecoq, Maurice (26 Mar 1854) 17
Lednev, Pavel (25 Mar 1943) 153
Lee, Norvel (22 Sep 1924) 114
Lee, Sammy (1 Aug 1920) 49
Lee, Willis (1889–1945) 24, 161
LeGendre, Robert (1898–1931) 26
Lehmann, Heike (29 Mar 1962) 207
Lehtinen, Lauri (1908–73) 35
Lekarski, Kroum 130
Lemming, Erik (1880–1930) 16
Lenglen, Suzanne (1899–1938) 24, *25*
Lentauw 16
Leonard, Charles (23 Feb 1913) 154
Leonard, Ray (17 May 1956) 154
Leonard, Silvio (20 Sep 1954) 79
Leonidas of Rhodes 10
Lesage, Xavier (1885–1969) 36
Lestander, Klas (18 Apr 1931) 54
Lewis, Carl (1 Jul 1961) 85, 92, 187, *5c*
Lewis, Rudolph (1888–1933) 21
Liddell, Eric (1902–45) 27
Lindh, Gustaf 247
Lindner, Ernst (1868–1943) 130
Lightbody, James (1882–1953) 15, 70
Lillehammer
  Winter Games 1994 94
Lilloe-Olsen, Ole (1883–1940) 161
Linsenhoff, Ann-Kathrin (1 Aug 1960)
  93, 130, 132
Linsenhoff, Liselott (27 Aug 1927) 64,
  70, 130, 131
Llanoria 220
Lobatch, Marina (26 Jun 1970) 141
London
  Summer Games 1908 17–20
  Summer Games 1948 42–5
Lonsbrough, Anita (10 Aug 1941) 56
Lord, Alice 28
Lorz, Fred (b. 1880) 16
Los Angeles
  Summer Games 1932 34–6
  Summer Games 1984 83–6
Louganis, Greg (29 Jan 1960) 92, 173, *2c*
Loundras, Dimitrios (1885–1971) 141
Louis, Spyridon (1873–1940) *12*, 13, 39
Lovelock, Jack (1910–49) *40*, 40
Lowe, Douglas (1902–81) 31
Lucas, Jerry (30 Mar 1940) 110
Lunde, Eugen (1887–1963) 220
Lunde, Peder (25 May 1918) 220
Lunde Jr, Peder (9 Feb 1942) 56, 220
Lunde, Vibeke (1921–62) 220
Lundström, Åge (1890–1975) 130
Lycurgus (390–*c*324 BC) 12
Lyon, George (1858–1938) 223
Lytton, Neville (1879–1951) 224

Madigan, Tony (4 Feb 1936) *56*
Madörin, Albert (17 Mar 1905) 46
Madsen, Lars (1871–1925) 161
Mahre, Phil (10 May 1957) 82, *82*
Mahre, Steve (10 May 1957) 82, *82*
Maiorov, Boris (11 Feb 1938) 234
Maiorov, Yevgeniy (11 Feb 1938) 234
Mäkinen, Kaarlo (1892–1980) 211
Mäkinen, Rauno (22 Jan 1931) 211
Malivoire, Bernard (20 Mar 1938) 46, 50
Malkov, Igor (9 Feb 1965) 82, 83, 241

Mallin, Harry (1892–1969) 113
Malmberg, Erik (1897–1964) *212*
Mandrillon, Camille 25
Mangiarotti, Dario (18 Dec 1915) 135
Mangiarotti, Edoardo (7 Apr 1919) 56,
  135, 136
Mankin, Valentin (19 Aug 1938) 81
Manoliu, Lia (25 Apr 1932) 70, 188
March, Werner, (1894–1976) 38
Marcroix 132
Marini, Fiorenzo (14 Mar 1914) 136
Mark, John 98
Martin (Walter), Steffi (17 Sep 1962) 89,
  245
Marusarz, Stanislaw 105
Mary, Princess (1867–1953) 20
Massala, Daniel (12 Feb 1955) 154
Maslakova, Ludmila (26 Jul 1952) 79
Masson, Paul (1874–1945) 13, 124
Mastenbroek, Hendrika (26 Feb 1919)
  40
Mathias, Bob (17 Nov 1930) 43, 44, 188
Matikainen, Marjo (3 Feb 1965) 234
Matt, Alfred (11 May 1948) *61*, 225
Matthes, Roland (17 Nov 1950) 74, 171
Maurial, Sylvie 247
Mauroy-Julin, Magda (24 Jul 1894) 25
Mayer, Helene (1910–53) 38, 136
MacArthur, Douglas (1880–1964) 31
McCormick, Kelly (13 Feb 1960) 173
McCormick, Pat (12 May 1930) 53, 173
McCormick, Ricky 247
McDonald, Patrick (1878–1954) 188,
  189
MacDonald-Smith, Iain (3 Jul 1945) 220
McKane, Kitty (7 May 1897) 186
McKee, Tim (14 Mar 1953) 68, 171
McKenley, Herb (10 Jul 1922) *43*
Mackenzie, George (1888–1957) 211
McMillan, William (29 Jan 1929) 162
McNair, Winifred (1877–1954) 24, 186
McTaggart, Dick (15 Oct 1935) 114
Mead-Lawrence, Andrea (19 Apr 1932)
  46
Medved, Aleksandr (16 Sep 1937) 70,
  211, *215*
Melbourne
  Summer Games 1956 50–4
Mellander, Hjalmar (1880–1919) 16
Merckx, Eddy (17 Jun 1945) 125
Meredith, Ted (1891–1957) 20
Merkens, Toni (1912–44) 40
Messner, Heinrich (1 Sep 1939) 225
Metcalfe, Ralph (1910–78) 36, *39*
Metschuck, Caren (27 Sep 1963) 79
Mexico City
  Summer Games 1968 62–4
Meyer, Debbie (14 Aug 1952) 64
Meyfarth, Ulrike (4 May 1956) 68, 188,
  191
Mi-Chung, Sohn 90, 98
Mieto, Juha (20 Nov 1949) 76
Milanov, Dimiter (b. 1927) 170
Miles, Eustace (1868–1948) 224
Millner, Joshua (*c*1848–1931) 20
Mills, Billy (30 Jun 1938) 59
Mills, Edwin (1878–1946) 192
Milon of Kroton 10, 211
Mimoun, Alain (1 Jan 1921) *48*, 53
Minicus, Lucius 94
Misevich, Vera (10 Apr 1945) 81

Mitic, Rajko (6 Nov 1922) 170
Mitscherlich, Andrea (1 Dec 1960) 241
Mittermaier, Rosi (5 Aug 1950) 71
Miyake, Yoshinobu (24 Nov 1939) 208
Miyake, Yoshiyuki (30 Sep 1945) 208
Moguilny, Aleksandr (18 Feb 1969) 233
Mondale, Walter (5 Jan 1928) 76, 96
Monday, Kenny (25 Nov 1961) 93, 211
Mondsolevski, Georgi (26 Jan 1934) 207
Monti, Eugenio (23 Jan 1928) 58, 61,
    229, 230
Montigny, Fernand de (1885–1974) 106
Montreal
    Summer Games 1976 72–5
Moore, Isabella (1894–1975) 22
Morelon, Daniel (28 Jul 1944) 70, 124,
    125, 126
Moreno, Antonio (11 Jun 1948) 207
Morgan, Sandra (6 Jun 1942) 53
Morris, Glenn (1912–74) 40, 173, 192
Morrow, Bobby-Joe (15 Oct 1935) 51
Mortanges, Charles Pahud de (1896–
    1971) 132
Moscow
    Summer Games 1980 77–81
Moser Proll, Annemarie (27 Mar 1953)
    226, 226
Moses, Edwin (31 Aug 1955) 83, 96
Moustafa, Ibrahim (1904–68) 37
Mshvenieradze, Georgi (12 Aug 1960)
    174
Mshvenieradze, Piotr (24 Mar 1929)
    174
Much Wenlock Olympic Society 11
Müller, Anna-Maria (23 Feb 1949) 65
Müller, Jutta 82
Müller-Preis, Ellen (6 May 1912) 44,
    105, 136, 136
Mueller, Peter (27 Jul 1954) 76
Munich
    Summer Games 1972 67–70
Muñoz, Felipe (3 Feb 1951) 64
Murdock, Margaret (25 Aug 1942) 75,
    162
Murray, Mae (1889–1965) 229
Musiol, Bogdan (25 Jul 1957) 89, 229
Mussabini, Sam 27
Myers-Pope, Paula (11 Nov 1934) 173
Mygiakis, Stylianos (5 May 1952) 211

Naber, John (20 Jan 1956) 74
Nadi, Aldo (1899–1965) 24, 135
Nadi, Nedo (1894–1940) 22, 24, 135
Naismith, Dr James (1861–1939) 41,
    110
Nakatani, Takehide (9 Jul 1941) 151
Nam-Kyu, Yoo (24 Jun 1968) 185
Nansen, Eigil 45
Nansen, Fridtjof (1861–1930) 45
Nash, Tony (18 Mar 1936) 58, 58
Nazarova, Irina (31 Jul 1957) 189
Neckarmann, Josef (5 Jun 1912) 64,
    130, 131
Nehmer, Meinhard (13 Jan 1941) 72,
    77, 229
Nekoda, Katsutoshi (1 Feb 1944) 207
Nemeth, Imre (1917–89) 189
Nemeth, Miklos (23 Oct 1946) 75, 189
Nenenene, Aldona (13 Oct 1949) 148
Nero, Emperor (37–68) 10
Nesty, Anthony (25 Nov 1967) 93, 3c

Newall, Queenie (1854–1929) 106, 107,
    109
Ngugi, John (5 Oct 1962) 5c
Ni Xiong (24 Jan 1974) 93
Nickalls Jr, Guy (1899–1974) 156
Nickalls Sr, Guy (1866–1935) 156, 158
Nielsen, Flemming (24 Feb 1934) 169
Nielsen, Hans (10 May 1928) 169
Nielsen, Harald (26 Oct 1941) 169
Nielsen, Sophus (1888–1963) 169, 170
Nilsen, Laila Schou (18 Mar 1919) 38
Nikkola, Ari Pekka (16 May 1969) 89,
    239
Ning, Li (8 Sep 1963) 86
Nixon, Richard (19 Jan 1913) 54, 96
Noel, Evan (1879–1928) 224
Nones, Franco (1 Feb 1941) 61
Nordahl, Bertil (26 Jul 1917) 169
Nordahl, Gunnar (19 Oct 1921) 44, 169,
    170
Nordahl, Knut (1920–84) 169
Nordheim, Sondre 45
Norelius, Bengt (1886–1974) 171
Norelius, Charles (14 Mar 1882) 171
Norelius, Martha (1908–55) 28, 171
Norling, Daniel (1888–1958) 106
Northam, William (28 Sep 1905) 60
Noverraz, Louis (1902–72) 64, 220
Novikova-Belova, Elena (28 Jul 1947)
    75, 136
Nowak, Dezsö (3 Feb 1939) 169
Nurikyan, Norair (26 Jul 1948) 208
Nurmi, Paavo (1897–1973) 24, 27, 30,
    35, 46, 47, 98, 187
Nurmi 40
Nykänen, Matti (17 Jul 1963) 83, 89,
    235, 26, 239, 16c

O'Brien, Jay (1883–1940) 34, 106, 229
Oda, Mikio (30 Mar 1905) 30, 59
Oddjob 208
Odinkova, Lubov (24 Jul 1955) 148
Odlozil, Josef (11 Nov 1938) 64
Oerter, Al (19 Sep 1936) 52, 63, 188,
    191
Ökern, Olaf (3 Jun 1911) 234
Östervold, Henrik (1878–1957) 220
Östervold, Jan (1876–1945) 220
Östervold, Kristian (1885–1960) 220
Östervold, Ole (1872–1936) 220
Okano, Isao (20 Jan 1944) 151
Olav, Crown Prince (later King) (1903–
    91) 31, 32
Oliva, Patrizio (28 Jan 1959) 114
Olympic Games
    ancient 9–10
    celebrations of 95–6
    demonstration sports 247
    discontinued sports 223–4
    flame 98
    mascots 98
    medal table by nations 103–4
    official openings 96
    oath 96
    participating countries 100–2
    sports doubles 106
    table of superlatives 104–6
    1896 Summer 12–13, 95
    1900 Summer 13–15, 95
    1904 Summer 15–16, 95
    1906 Summer 16–17, 95

1908 Summer 17–20, 95
1912 Summer 20–2, 95
1920 Summer 23–5, 95
1924 Winter 25–6, 95
1924 Summer 26–8, 95
1928 Winter 28–30, 95
1928 Summer 30–2, 95
1932 Winter 32–4, 95
1932 Summer 34–6, 95
1936 Winter 37–8, 95
1936 Summer 38–41, 95
1948 Winter 41–2, 95
1948 Summer 42–5, 95
1952 Winter 45–6, 95
1952 Summer 46–50, 95
1956 Winter 50, 95
1956 Summer 50–4, 95
1960 Winter 54–5, 95
1960 Summer 55–7, 95
1964 Winter 57–8, 95
1964 Summer 59–60, 95
1968 Winter 60–2, 95
1968 Summer 62–4, 95
1972 Winter 64–6, 95
1972 Summer 67–70, 95
1976 Winter 70–2, 95
1976 Summer 72–5, 95
1980 Winter 75–7, 95
1980 Summer 77–81, 95
1984 Winter 81–3, 95
1984 Summer 83–6, 95
1988 Winter 86–9, 95
1988 Summer 90–3, 95
1992 Winter 93, 96
1992 Summer 94, 95
1994 Winter 94, 96
1996 Summer 94, 95
1998 Winter 94
2000 Summer 94
Olympische Spiele 41
O'Neil, John (1897–1950) 224
Ong, Thomas 151
Onischenko, Boris (19 Sep 1937) 75,
    154
Ono, Takaschi (26 Jul 1931) 96
Onomastos of Smyrna 112
Ordaz, Pres. Gustavo Diaz (12 Mar
    1911) 62, 96
Oreiller, Henri (1925–62) 42, 226
Oriola, Christian d' (3 Oct 1928) 135
Oriola, Pierre Jonquéres d' (1 Feb 1920)
    130, 131
Orphanidis, Georgios (b. 1859) 13
Ortmann, Günther (30 Nov 1916) 148
Orton, George (1873–1958) 15
Osborn, Harold (1899–1975) 27, 27
Osburn, Carl (1884–1966) 28, 161
Osendarp, Marthinus (21 May 1916) 39
Osiier, Ivan (1888–1965) 20, 105, 135
Osiier, Ellen (1890–1962) 135
Oslo
    Winter Games 1952 45–6
Ostermeyer, Micheline (23 Dec 1922)
    188, 188
Otsuka, Miyako 112
Otto, Kristin (7 Feb 1966) 92, 171, 3c
Ouafi, Mohamed El (1899–1959) 31
Ouellette, Gerald (1934–75) 53, 163
Ovett, Nick (4 Jan 1967) 89
Ovett, Steve (9 Oct 1955) 79, 79, 89, 11c
Owens, Jesse (1913–80) 39, 39, 83, 187

Paasikivi, Pres. Juho (1870–1956) 46, 96
Packer, Ann (18 Mar 1942) 59
Paddock, Charley (1900–43) 24
Paine, John (1870–1951) 13, 162
Paine, Sumner (1868–1904) 13, 162
Palm, Kerstin (5 Feb 1946) 105, 136
Palusalu, Kristjan (10 Mar 1908) 40, 211
Pandolfini, Franco (16 Sep 1920) 174
Pandolfini, Tulio (6 Aug 1914) 174
Panin (Kolemkin), Nikolai (1874–1956) 19, 230
Papp, László (25 Mar 1926) 53, 81, *113*, 113
Paraense, Guilherme (1885–1968) 24
Parfenovich, Vladimir (2 Dec 1958) 79, 120
Paris
    Summer Games 1900 13–15
    Summer Games 1924 26–8
Parisi, Angelo (3 Jan 1953) 151
Parker, Adrian (2 Mar 1951) 154
Parker, Bridget (5 Jan 1939) 132
Parker, Denise (12 Dec 1973) 109
Parlov, Mate (16 Nov 1948) 114
Patrick, John (1898–1959) 224
Patterson, Floyd (4 Jan 1935) 49, 113, 114
Pattisson, Rodney (5 Aug 1943) 220
Patton, George S (1885–1945) 20, 154
Patzaichin, Ivan (26 Nov 1949) 121
Pauca, Simona (19 Sep 1969) 86
Pausin, Erik (18 Apr 1920) 38
Pausin, Ilse (7 Feb 1919) 38
Pedersen, Susan (16 Oct 1953) 64
Peeters, Maurice (1882–1957) 125
Pelen, Perrine (3 Jul 1960) 82
Perez, Pascual (1926–77) 114
Peris, Giancarlo 98
Perry, Charles 20, 23
Perry, Robyn (b. 1965) 87
Persson, Gehnäll (1910–76) 44, 131
Peters, Mary (6 Jul 1939) 70
Petrone, Pedro (1905–64) 169, 170
Pettersson, Erik (4 Apr 1944) 124
Pettersson, Gösta (23 Nov 1940) 124
Pettersson, Sture (30 Sep 1942) 124
Pettersson, Tomas (15 May 1947) 124
Petushkova, Yelena (17 Nov 1940) 131
Pfnür, Franz (21 Nov 1908) 38, 226
Phanas of Pellene 10
Pheidippides 13
Pherenice of Rhodes 10
Phillips, Molliue (20 Jun 1907) 33
Phinney, Davis (10 Jul 1959) 125
Pietri, Dorando (1885–1942) *19*, 20
Pietrzykowski, Zbigniew (4 Oct 1934) *56*
Pihlajamäki, Hermanni (1903–82) 211
Pihlajamäki, Kustaa (1902–44) 211
Pilgrim, Paul (1883–1958) 16, 75
Pimenov, Nikolay (29 Mar 1958) 81, 156
Pimenov, Yuriy (29 Mar 1958) 81, 156
Pinayeva (Khvedosyuk), Ludmila (4 Jan 1936) 120
Pinkston, Clarence (1900–61) 174
Pinkston (née Becker), Elizabeth (6 Mar 1903) 174
Pisidores 10
Pitou, Penny (8 Oct 1938) 54
Plaxton, Herbert 233
Plaxton, Hugh (16 May 1904) 233
Plaxton, Roger 233

Plukfelder, Rudolf (6 Sep 1928) 208
Plumb, Mickey (28 Mar 1940) 132
Poage, George (1880–1962) 15
Pötsch, Annet (3 Sep 1960) 82
Polyák, Imre (16 Apr 1932) 60
Pongracz, General Arthur von (1864–1942) 131
Ponomareva (Romashkova), Nina (27 Apr 1929) 48, 57, 191
Popentschenko, Valeriy (1937–75) 114
Poradnik, Ludmila (11 Jan 1946) 148
Porritt, Arthur (10 Aug 1900) 27
Post, Albertson Van Zo (1866–1938) 135
Poulos-Mueller, Leah (5 Oct 1951) 76
Pourtales, Hermann, Comte de (1847–1904) 14
Poyarkov, Yuriy (10 Feb 1937) 207
Poynton-Hill, Dorothy (17 Jul 1915) 31, 32, *172*, 173
Pratsika, Koula 39
Préfontaine, Stéphane (b. 1961) 72, 98
Press, Irina (10 Mar 1939) 56, 189
Press, Tamara (10 May 1937) 56, 189
Preussler, Babette (28 Sep 1968) 83
Priestner, Cathy (27 May 1956) 87
Prinstein, Myer (1880–1925) 14, 15
Pritchard, Norman 14, 192
Protopopov, Oleg (6 Jul 1932) *57*, 58, 61
Protopopov, Ludmila *see* Belousova
Prozumenschikova (née Stepanova), Galina (26 Nov 1948) 59
Puikkonen, Jari (25 Jun 1959) *239*
Pyrgos, Léon 135

Quartey, Clement 'Ike' (12 Apr 1938) 56
Qing-guang, Wei (2 Jul 1962) 185

Radke, Lina (1903–83) 30
Radmilovic, Paul (1886–1968) 106, 174
Ragnhild, Princess of Norway 45, 96
Ramsey, Mike (3 Dec 1960) 77
Rand, Mary (10 Feb 1940) 59
Randolph, Leo (27 Feb 1958) 114
Ransehousen (Newberry), Jessica (14 Oct 1938) 130
Rantanen, Siiri (14 Dec 1924) 50
Rasch, Bent Peder (31 May 1934) 120
Rashid, Abdul (1 Jun 1922) 149
Ratjen, Dora (20 Nov 1918) 191
Rausch, Emil (1883–1954) 171
Rautavaara, Tapio (1915–79) 192
Rawls, Katharine (1918–82) 36, 173
Read, Ken (6 Nov 1955) 87
Read, Norman (13 Aug 1931) 53
Reagan, Pres. Ronald (6 Feb 1911) 83, 96
Real, Antonia (14 Sep 1963) 75
Rechardt, Esko (9 May 1958) 79
Reichert, Ossi (25 Dec 1925) 225
Reinisch, Rica (6 Apr 1965) 79, 81
Renaud, Philippe (23 Nov 1962) 121
Retton, Mary Lou (24 Jan 1968) 141
Riccardi, Franco (1905–68) *138*
Richardet, Louis (1864–1923) 161
Richardson, Henry (1889–1963) 109
Rieder, Joseph 57
Riefenstahl, Leni (22 Aug 1902) 41
Riggin, Aileen (2 May 1906) 24, 173
Rinn, Hans (19 Mar 1953) 245
Ritola, Ville (1896–1982) 27, 188

Rivett-Carnac, Francis Clytie (1875–1962) 220
Robertson, Oscar (24 Nov 1938) 110
Robinson, Elizabeth (23 Aug 1911) 32, *32*
Robinson, Jackie (1919–72) 39
Robinson, Mack (18 Jul 1914) 39
Rodnina, Irina (12 Sep 1949) 66, 71, 77, 230, 231
Rodriguez, Hector (12 Aug 1951) 151
Rötsch, Frank-Peter (19 Apr 1964) 89, 235
Rolinska, Eulalia (6 Jan 1946) 162
Romary, Janice (6 Aug 1928) 64
Romashkova (Ponomareva), Nina (27 Apr 1929) 48, 57, 191
Rome
    Summer Games 1960 55–7
Roosevelt, Eleanor (1884–1962) 32
Roosevelt, Franklin D (1882–1945) 32, 96
Roosevelt, Theodore (1858–1919) 15
Roschin, Anatoliy (10 Mar 1932) 211
Rose, Murray (6 Jan 1939) *53*, 53
Rose, Ralph (1885–1913) 16, 18
Rosendahl, Heidi (14 Feb 1947) 70
Rosenfeld, Fanny (1905–69) *32*
Ross, Norman (1896–1953) 24, 171
Roth, Richard (26 Sep 1947) 60
Rothenburger (Luding), Christa (4 Dec 1959) 89, 93, 106, 241, *10c*
Rowley, Stanley (b. 1877) 188
Roycroft, William (17 Mar 1915) 132
Roycroft, Wayne (23 Jun 1940) 132
Rudolph, Wilma (23 Jun 1940) 56
Rüegg, Yvonne (2 Aug 1938) 226
Rührold, Ute (9 Dec 1954) 245
Ruer, Christophe (3 Jul 1965) 154
Ruiz-Conforto, Tracie (4 Feb 1963) 174
Rukavishnikova, Olga (13 Mar 1955) 79, 191
Rusani, Danuta (30 Apr 1951) 189
Ruska, Willem (29 Aug 1940) 151, *151*
Russell, Bill (12 Feb 1934) 110
Ruthström, Sonja (13 Nov 1930) 55
Ruud, Asbjörn 42, 235
Ruud, Birger (23 Aug 1911) 34, *37*, 38, 42, 235, 236
Ruud, Sigmund (30 Dec 1907) 42, 235
Ryskal, Inna (15 Jun 1944) 207
Ryun, Jim (29 Apr 1947) 68

Sabonis, Arvidas (19 Dec 1964) 93, 112
Sagi-Retjö, Ildikó (18 May 1937) 75, 136
Sailer, Toni (17 Nov 1935) 50, 60, *61*, 71, 225, 226
Saimo, Sylvi (12 Nov 1914) 50, 120
St Cyr, Henri (1902–79) 53, 131
St Goddard, Emile 33, 247
St Jean, Pierre (28 Mar 1947) 96
St Louis
    Summer Games 1904 15–16
St Moritz
    Winter Games 1928 28–30
    Winter Games 1948 41–2
Saito, Hiroshi (2 Jan 1961) 151
Sakai, Yoshinori 98
Sakata, Harold (1920–82) 208
Sakharova, Nadyezda (9 Feb 1945) 112
Salchow, Ulrich (1877–1949) 230

Salnikov, Vladimir (21 May 1960) 92
Saloukvadze, Nino (1 Feb 1969) 7c
Saltza, Christine von (3 Jan 1944) 56, 179
Samaranch, Juan Antonio (17 Jul 1920) 94, 98
Sandberg, Thomas (6 Aug 1955) 236
Saneyev, Viktor (3 Oct 1945) 79, 188
Sapporo
    Winter Games 1972 64–6
Sarajevo
    Winter Games 1984 81–3
Saraudi, Giulio (3 Jul 1938) 56
Sautereau 223
Sauvé, Jeanne (26 Apr 1922) 87, 96
Savage, Joseph (b. 1879) 34
Savolainen, Heikki (28 Sep 1907) 44, 49, 96, 141
Schade, Herbert (26 May 1922) 48
Schärer, Erich (1 Sep 1946) 89
Schärf, Dr Adolf (1890–1965) 57, 96
Schemansky, Norbert (30 May 1924) 60, 208
Schenk, Ard (16 Sep 1944) 65, 243
Schilgen, Fritz 39, 98
Schläppi, Alfred (30 Jan 1898) 230
Schläppi, Heinrich (30 Apr 1905) 26, 230
Schliemann, Heinrich (1822–90) 186
Schmid, Franz (17 Jan 1905) 36
Schmid, Toni (1909–32) 36
Schmidt, Birgit (25 Feb 1962) 120
Schmidt, Oscar (16 Feb 1958) 112
Schneider, Vreni (26 Nov 1964) 87 89
Schockemöhle, Alwin (29 May 1937) 75, 131
Schollander, Don (30 Aug 1946) 60
Scholz, Rudolph (1896–1981) 224
Schranz, Karl (18 Nov 1938) 60, 61, 65
Schuba, Trixie (13 Apr 1951) 66, 230
Schuhmann, Carl (1869–1946) 13, 106, 140, 211
Schüller, Heidi (15 Jun 1950) 67, 96
Schulthess, Edmund (1868–1944) 28, 96
Schultz, Dave (6 Jun 1959) 86, 211
Schultz, Mark (26 Oct 1960) 86, 211
Schumacher, Sandra (25 Dec 1966) 125
Schwarz, Elisabeth (19 May 1936) 50
Schwarz, Wolfgang (14 Sep 1947) 61
Scotia 220
Scott, Barbara-Ann (9 May 1928) 42
Scott, Peter (1909–89) 41
Seagren, Bob (17 Oct 1946) 192
Seisenbacher, Peter (25 Mar 1960) 151
Semenova, Iuliana (9 Mar 1952) 75, 112
Seminario, Gladys de (18 Sep 1937) 162
Seoul
    Summer Games 1988 90–3
Seppala, Lennard 247
Sercu, Patrick (27 Jun 1944) 124, 125
Seyfert, Gabriele (23 Nov 1948) 82
Seyffarth, Ake (15 Dec 1919) 42
Shakhlin, Boris (27 Jan 1932) 56, 60, 140, 140
Shaw, Tim (8 Nov 1957) 174
Shea, Jack (7 Sep 1910) 32, 96
Sheen, Gillian (21 Aug 1928) 136
Shepherd, John (1884–1954) 192
Sheppard, Mel (1883–1942) 18, 19
Sheridan, Martin (1881–1918) 16
Sherring, William (1878–1964) 17, 17

Shevtsova, Ludmila (26 Nov 1934) 56
Shiley, Jean (20 Nov 1911) 36
Shorter, Frank (31 Oct 1947) 70
Shoveller, Stanley (1881–1959) 149
Si-Hun, Park (16 Dec 1965) 93, 6c
Silivas, Daniela (9 May 1971) 141
Silva, Adhemar Ferreira da (29 Sep 1927) 192
Silver Piece 132
Simaika, Farid (b. 1907) 31
Simmons, Floyd (10 Apr 1923) 192
Simon, Pál (1891–1922) 189
Simyatov, Nikolay (28 Jun 1955) 76
Singh, Balbir (9 Oct 1924) 149
Singh, Dharam (19 Jan 1919) 149
Singh, Randhir (1922–81) 149
Singh, Roop (1910–77) 36, 149
Singh, Udham (4 Aug 1928) 149
Skanaker, Ragnar (8 Jun 1934) 93
Skatteboe, Gudbrand (1875–1965) 161
Skoblikova, Lydia (8 Mar 1939) 57, 104, 241, 241
Skoglund, Nils (1906–80) 24, 173
Skutnabb, Julius (1889–1965) 26
Small, Irving (1881–1925) 26
Smart, Hilary (29 Jul 1925) 44
Smart, Paul (1892–1979) 44
Smetanina, Raisa (29 Feb 1952) 71, 89, 104, 234
Smirnova, Ludmila (21 Jul 1949) 66, 231
Smith, Charles (1879–1951) 174
Smith, Dean (15 Jan 1932) 192
Smith, Ethel (5 Jul 1907) 32
Smith, Joyce (26 Oct 1937) 189
Smith, Tommie (5 Jun 1944) 63
Smith, Willie (5 Aug 1905) 114
Smithson, Forrest (1881–1963) 19
Smythe, Pat (22 Nov 1928) 51, 130
Socaci, Andrei (6 Sep 1966) 208
Solberg, Magnar (4 Feb 1937) 235
Son, Kitei (Sohn Kee-Chung) (29 Aug 1912) 90, 91
Sörensen, Inge (18 Jul 1924) 106, 171
Sosulya, Vera (15 Jan 1956) 245
Soundy, Roberto (4 Mar 1900) 64
Souza, Neville d' 170
Spencer, Rev Galen (1840–1904) 16, 109
Spiljak, Mika (28 Nov 1916) 81, 96
Spinks, Leon (11 Jul 1953) 114
Spinks, Michael (22 Jul 1956) 114
Spitz, Mark (10 Feb 1950) 64, 67, 92, 104, 171
Spock, Benjamin (2 May 1903) 28
Spooner, Lloyd (6 Oct 1884) 24, 161
Spurgin, Pat (10 Aug 1965) 162
Squaw Valley
    Winter Games 1960 54–5
Staaf, Karl (1881–1953) 192
Stack, Frank (1 Jan 1906) 105, 241
Stadler, Joseph 15
Stäheli, Konrad (1866–1931) 161
Stähle, Willy 247
Stanczyk, Stanley (10 May 1925) 208
Stanggassinger, Hans (5 Jan 1960) 83, 245
Stecca, Maurizio (9 Mar 1963) 114
Steinkraus, Bill (12 Oct 1925) 131
Steinsteifer, Carrie (12 Feb 1968) 171
Stengl, Manfred (1 Apr 1946) 58, 245

Stenmark, Ingemar (18 Mar 1956) 76, 81, 14c
Stephens, Helen (3 Feb 1918) 40
Stevens, Curtis (1898–1979) 34, 230
Stevens, Hubert (1890–1950) 34, 230
Stevens, Paul (1889–1949) 34
Stevenson, Teofilo (29 Mar 1952) 79, 113, 114
Stewart, Anthea (20 Nov 1944) 149
Stives, Karen (3 Nov 1950) 131 132
Stixrup, Martin (9 Feb 1876) 230
Stockholm
    Summer Games 1912 20–2
    Summer Games (Equestrian) 1956 50–1
Stokken, Martin (16 Jan 1923) 46
Stouder, Sharon (9 Nov 1948) 60
Stover-Irwin, Juno (22 Nov 1928) 173
Straub, Jürgen (3 Nov 1953) 79
Strauss, Richard (1864–1949) 39
Streeter, Smith (1861–1931) 224
Strickland, Shirley (18 Jul 1925) 53, 188
Stubbendorf, Ludwig (1906–41) 40
Suleymanoglu, Naim (23 Jan 1967) 208, 9c
Sullivan, Frank 233
Sullivan, Joseph 233
Sundelin, Jörgen (15 Mar 1945) 62, 220
Sundelin, Peter (13 Jan 1947) 64, 220
Sundelin, Ulf (26 Aug 1943) 64, 220
Sung-Soo, Park (19 May 1970) 109
Sun-Man, Ching 90, 98
Superdocious 220
Suraikin, Andrey (20 Oct 1948) 66, 231
Suzuki, Keichi 65, 96
Svensson, Rudolf (1899–1978) 212
Swahn, Alfred (1879–1931) 19, 28, 162
Swahn, Oscar (1847–1927) 19, 20, 22, 24, 28, 106, 162
Swan, Gunde (12 Jan 1962) 234
Syers, Madge (1881–1917) 46, 230
Szabo, Ecaterina (22 Jan 1968) 85
Szarmach, Andrzej (3 Oct 1950) 170
Székely, Éva (3 Apr 1927) 48, 174
Szewinska (Kirszenstein), Irena (24 May 1946) 75, 188, 191
Szivós, István (24 Apr 1948) 74

Tae-Woo, Pres. Roh (4 Dec 1932) 90, 96
Takács, Károly (1910–76) 49, 162
Takada, Hideki 65
Takemoto, Masao (29 Sep 1919) 141
Talbot, Bishop Ethelbert 36
Tarasconi, Domingo (20 Dec 1903) 170
Tarzan 28, 40, 173, 192
Tauskey, Mary (3 Dec 1955) 130, 132
Taylor, Chris (1950–79) 70, 212
Taylor, Frank Morgan (1903–75) 27, 36
Taylor, Henry (1885–1951) 19
Taylor, John (1882–1908) 19
Taylor, Meldrick (19 Oct 1966) 114
Tcherkasova, Marina (17 Nov 1964) 77
Tewksbury, John (1878–1968) 14
Thams, Jacob Tullin (1898–1954) 30, 106
Theagenes of Thassos 10
Théato, Michel (1878–1919) 15
Theodosius I, Emperor (347–395) 10, 55
Thoeni, Gustavo (28 Feb 1951) 65, 65
Thoeni, Roland (17 Jan 1951) 65

Thofelt, Sven (19 May 1904) 154
Thom, Linda (30 Dec 1943) 86, 162
Thomas, Debi (25 Mar 1967) 89
Thoma, George (20 Aug 1937) 54
Thompson, Francis 'Daley' (30 Jul 1958) *85*
Thorpe, Bill 83
Thorpe, Jim (1888–1953) 21, 22, *22*, 83, 192
Thubé, Amédée (1884–1941) 21, 220
Thubé, Gaston (1876–1974) 21, 220
Thubé, Jacques (1882–1969) 21, 220
Thunberg, Clas (1893–1973) 26, 28, 30, 33, 104, 241
Tiersch, Günther (30 Apr 1954) 64
Tikhonov, Aleksandr (2 Jan 1947) 76, 235
Tillman, Henry (1 Aug 1960) 83
Tisdall, Robert (16 May 1907) 36
Titanic 28, 186
Tkachenko, Nadyezda (19 Sep 1948) 191
Tkachenko, Vladimir (20 Sep 1957) 81
Todd, Mark (1 Mar 1956) *131*, 132, *9c*
Töpel, Hjördis (1904–87) 173
Tokyo
  Summer Games 1964 59–60
Tomba, Alberto (19 Dec 1966) 89, *15c*
Törmänen, Juoko (10 Apr 1954) 76
Torriani, Richard 'Bibi' (1 Oct 1911) 42, 96, 105, 233
Torvill, Jayne (7 Oct 1957) 82, 231, *13c*
Tosi, Giuseppe (1916–81) 192
Tourchina, Zinaida (17 May 1946) 75, 148
Touristcheva, Ludmila (7 Oct 1952) 68, 140, *146*
Traun, Fritz (1876–1908) 186
Trentin, Pierre (15 May 1964) 125
Tretyak, Vladyslav (24 Apr 1952) 83, 233
Trstena, Saban (1 Jan 1965) 212
Tucker, Nion (1885–1950) 30
Tyler (Odam), Dorothy (14 Mar 1920) 43, 189
Tyler, Francis (1904–56) 42
Tyus, Wyomia (29 Aug 1945) 63

Ueberroth, Peter (2 Sep 1937) 86
Ulanov, Alexey (4 Nov 1947) 66, 231
Uphoff, Nicole (25 Jan 1967) 132
Urdinaran, Antonio (b. 1898) 169
Urdinaran, Santos (b. 1900) 169

Vaage, Jacob 26
Vainio, Martti (30 Dec 1950) 86
Vandernotte, Noël (25 Dec 1923) 158
Van Gennip, Yvonne (1 May 1964) 89, *12c*

Van Rosen, Maud (24 Dec 1925) 70
Varazdetes (Varastedes) 112
Varga, Istvan (7 Sep 1943) 148
Ventura, Frantisek (1895–1969) 131
Verri, Francesco (1885–1945) 124
Vidal, Gaston 25, 96
Vicens, Liana (25 Nov 1956) 64, 106, 171
Vidmar, Pete (3 Jun 1961) 141
Vignerot 223
Vikelas, Demetrius (1835–1908) *11*, 12, 98
Vilén, Erik (1898–1982) 27
Villanueva, Anthony (18 Mar 1945) 114
Villanueva, Jose 113
Viren, Lasse (22 Jul 1949) 70, 75
Voderzova, Yelena (21 May 1963) 72
Volnov, Gennadiy (29 Nov 1939) 110
Voronin, Mikhail (26 Mar 1945) 64
Voronin, Sinaida (10 Dec 1947) 64

Walasiewicz (Walsh), Stella (1911–80) 191
Waldo, Carolyn (11 Dec 1964) 174
Walker, Reggie (1889–1914) 27
Wangila, Robert (3 Sep 1967) 113
Waruinge, Philip (3 Feb 1945) 114
Warwick Rex 131
Wassberg, Thomas (27 Mar 1956) 76
Watanabe, Osamu (21 Oct 1940) 212
Watson, Lillian 'Pokey' (11 Jul 1950) 60, 171
Waydelick 223
Webster, Bob (25 Oct 1938) 49
Wegner, Axel (3 Jun 1963) *165*
Wehling, Ulrich (8 Jul 1952) 76, 234
Weingärtner, Hermann (1864–1919) 13
Weissmuller, Johnny (1904–84) 28, 30, 173, 174
Weld, Theresa (1893–1978) 230
Wells, Allan (3 May 1952) 79
Wendl, Ingrid (17 May 1940) 50
Wenzel, Andreas (18 Mar 1958) 76
Wenzel, Hanni (14 Dec 1956) 76, 81, 225, *15c*
Wenzel, Petra (20 Nov 1961) 76
West, Jerry (28 May 1938) 110
Westergren, Carl (1895–1958) 211, *212*
Whitaker, Pernell (2 Jan 1964) 114
White, Duncan (1 Mar 1928) 44
White, Edgar (17 Nov 1929) 220
White, Herman (1904–67) 220
White, Sumner (17 Nov 1929) 220
Whitfield, Mal (11 Oct 1924) *43*
Whittal, Albert 168
Whittal, Donald 168
Whittal, Edward 168
Whittal, Godfrey 168
Whittal, Herbert 168

Whitty, Allen 1866–1949) 28
Wicki, Jean (18 Jun 1933) 66
Wideman, Lydia (17 May 1920) 46
Wieslander, Hugo (1889–1976) 22
Wightman, Hazel (1886–1974) 28
Wilhelmina, Queen (1880–1962) 30
Wilkie, David (8 Mar 1954) *74*, 74
Wilkinson, George (1879–1946) 174
Williams, Nõrris (1891–1968) 28, 186
Williams, Percy (1908–82) 30, *31*
Williams, Thomas (7 Aug 1940) 55
Wills-Moody, Helen (6 Oct 1905) 186, *C*
Wils, Jan (22 Feb 1891) 30
Wilson, Harold (1885–1916) *18*
Winans, Walter (1852–1920) 162
Wing, John 54
Winkler, Hans-Günter (24 Jul 1926) 70, 86, 130, 131
Wint, Arthur (25 May 1920) *43*
Witt, Axel 82
Witt, Katarina (3 Dec 1965) 82, 89, *13c*
Wladar, Sandor (19 Jul 1963) 81
Wöckel, Bärbel (21 Mar 1955) 79, 188
Wodehouse, Sir John (1883–1941) 224
Wolde, Mamo (12 Jun 1932) 64
Wolper, David (b. 1928) 83
Won-Tuk, Kim 90, 98
Wood, Carolyn (18 Dec 1945) 57
Woodward, Vivian (1897–1954) 169
Wottle, Dave (7 Aug 1950) 68
Wright, Joseph (28 Mar 1906) 171
Wykoff, Frank (1909–80) 189

Xuereb, Daniel (22 Jun 1959) 170

Yamashita, Yasuhiro (1 Jun 1957) 86
Yang, Chuan-Kwang (10 Jul 1933) 55, 192
Yang, Young-Ja (6 Jul 1964) 185
Yifter, Miruts (15 May 1944) 79, *80*
Ylipulli, Tuomo *239*
Young, Sheila (14 Oct 1950) 71, 241

Zaharias, 'Babe' (see Didrikson)
Zahn, Gunter 98
Zaitsev, Aleksandr (16 Jun 1952) 72, 77, 231
Zappas, Major Evangelis 11
Zatopek, Emil (19 Sep 1922) 44, 46, *48*, 53, 54, 75, 189
Zatopkova, Dana (19 Sep 1922) 46, 189
Zebec, Brank (17 May 1929) 170
Zerta, Klaus (25 Nov 1945) 57
Zijp, Adolph van der Voort van (1892–1978) 132
Ziller 12
Zimonyi, Robert (18 Apr 1918) 60, 158
Zucchi, Roby 247
Zürner, Albert (1890–1920) 173